TOUR G
TO THE
OLD WEST

TOUR GUIDE TO THE OLD WEST

ALICE CROMIE

Times BOOKS

Published by TIMES BOOKS, a division of
Quadrangle/The New York Times Book Co., Inc.
Three Park Avenue, New York, N.Y. 10016

Published simultaneously in Canada by
Fitzhenry & Whiteside, Ltd., Toronto

Library of Congress Cataloging in Publication Data

Cromie, Alice Hamilton.
Tour guide to the Old West.

1. The West—Description and travel—1860-1880.
I. Title.
F595.2C76 1976 917.8'04'3 76-9695
ISBN 0-8129-0641-1 (hardcover)
ISBN 0-8129-6323-7 (paper)

Designed by Beth Tondreau

Manufactured in the United States of America

10 9 8 7 6 5 4 3 2 1

For Bob and Mike and Rick and Barb and Jamie with love

CONTENTS

Maps by Bill O'Brien

ACKNOWLEDGMENTS

My everlasting thanks to my husband, Bob Cromie, who despite a schedule that included hosting his television shows, Book Beat, and The Cromie Circle, and National Public Radio's American Issues Forum which required his being "live," as they say, in Washington, D.C., once a month, his cross-country lecturing, and writing a book of his own, managed to copyread most of this guide and to catch many errors; more importantly, he learned how to defrost a dinner. (My thanks also go to Stouffers, Sara Lee, Swansons, Birds-Eye and other purveyors of reasonably edible frozen foods.) A very special thank you to S. Omar Barker and the Western Writers of America, to Don Russell and The Westerners, to the Society of American Travel Writers, the National Council for Historic Preservation, the Council on Abandoned Military Camps, the National Park Service, the historical societies and chambers of commerce and tourist bureaus of 19 states. One loud hurrah for Paul Kelvyn, Jane Janson, Eleanore Devine, Al Saunders, Eugene Powers, Carol Spelius, and countless others who helped all along the way. And one very heartfelt thanks to my editors, Emanuel Geltman and Edward McLeroy, who were mere boys when this book began.

The author is grateful to the following publishers for their permission to quote copyrighted materials:

Illinois State Historical Library. *An Illinois Gold Hunter in the Black Hills.* Introduction and Notes by Clyde C. Walton (Springfield, Ill.: Illinois State Historical Society, 1960), Pamphlet Series No.2.

Alfred A. Knopf, Inc. *New Mexico* by Erna Fergusson, Second Edition, 1964.

Harper & Row Publishers, Inc. *The Uncrowned Queen* by Ishbel Ross, 1972.

University of Oklahoma Press. *Fort Smith: Little Gibraltar on the Arkansas* by Ed Bearss and Orrell M. Gibson, 1969. *On the Western Tour with Washington Irving: The Journal and Letters of Count de Pourtalès,* edited by George F. Spaulding, 1967. *The Life and Adventures of a Quaker Among the Indians* by Thomas C. Battey, 1968. *The Road to Virginia City: The Diary of James Knox Polk Miller,* edited by Andrew F. Rolle, 1960.

University of Texas Press. *The Golden Frontier* by Nunis, 1962. *The Texas Rangers* by Walter Prescott Webb.

Swallow Press. *Battle Drums and Geysers* by Orrin & Lorraine Bonney, 1970.

Rand McNally & Co. *High West* by Bill Ballantine, 1969.

T.Y. Crowell, Inc. *Paintbox on the Frontier* by Alberta Wilson Constant, 1974.

Yale University Press. *The Truth About Geronimo* by Britton Davis. *Twenty Years on the Pacific Slope,* edited by W. Turrentine Jackson.

Hastings House Publishers, Inc. *Washington, Arizona,* and *Arkansas* Guide Books.

INTRODUCTION

The entertaining part of preparing a guide lies wholly in the reading, clipping and going to see the sites. I managed to stretch out this kind of research (rambling and stalling) for nearly a decade before I settled down to collating, sorting and discarding, and inevitably to writing the book. Then I spent more than four months wandering no farther than our rural delivery mailbox, except for three brief (less than a day) sorties which worked as little to insure happiness in confinement as that one drink does to improve an alcoholic.

Friends and relatives who hadn't been warned against it and reached me when the phone wasn't turned off usually complained that I sounded "far away." To which I invariably snapped something like, "Well, I *am* in The Dalles today," or Yuma, Pocatello, Tuba City or wherever. I once phoned a much-traveled but easily rattled friend and announced without preamble, "Hey, I'm just coming into Billings and I want to know if they've still got that Range Rider of the Yellowstone standing near the airport?" After a pause, she asked cautiously, "You mean you're calling from the plane?"

A fellow journalist with whom I went to Northeast High School in Kansas City (Mo.) and who recently moved into my area code got tired of having me recheck once familiar haunts with her more up-to-date memory and finally declared, "I think I'll move out of town until you get past Westport Landing."

There were days when I was convinced that every son of a sodbuster or daughter of a trailblazer who had managed to lay hands on two tomahawks or an arrowhead and a wagon wheel had opened an End of the Trail Museum. There were times when it seemed that the most interesting National Historic Landmarks were those "not open to the public at this time." (But there is a reason for this, and the situation frequently changes. Often the site is unsafe for visitors in its present condition, sometimes excavations are still in progress, and some areas are still in private ownership, even in use as part of a working ranch or farm.)

Some days it seemed as if CAMP, the excellent and active Council on Abandoned Military Posts, was determined to do itself out of existence by salvaging and stabilizing every condemned or long-lost piece of onetime military property I had already checked off as inundated, inaccessible or gone to grass. There were also moments of author's paranoia: When an earthquake shook the Pacific Northwest some years ago, every decent human being was worrying about the possible loss of life and personal property while I was fretting that Grant's house as a quartermaster at Fort Vancouver might have toppled into dust and wondering what hardship the Gods had in mind for me next.

One of the delights of a guidebook is that it provides countless serendipitous discoveries and meanderings along unexpected byways whether the reader travels by armchair, jeep, motorcar, burro-back or on foot. Americans are insatiably curious which is why a lot of us got here in the first place. Our forefathers, to put it grandly, always had to know what lay just beyond the next obstacle, be it river, mesa, arroyo, mountain, or staked plain. Before I began this latest venture into the Old West, I had only a vague, disinterested schoolgirl remembrance of Lewis and Clark from geography and history books long left behind in grammar school. But by the time I had remade acquaintance with their surprisingly youthful and divergent selves (the introverted Meriwether Lewis was 29; the gregarious William Clark was 33) and had followed them to the Pacific and back to a joyous welcome in St. Louis, I couldn't bear not to know what happened next and kept on going in my own reading, though this guidebook necessarily stops at the west bank of the Mississippi River.

Briefly, for those equally curious, their homecoming was not unlike that of astronauts in our day. As the authors of *Lewis and Clark,* a volume issued by the National Park Service, so aptly put it: "These strangers to roofs and beds, with a far-off look in their eyes, the first U.S. citizens to cross the continent, were a special breed. Until the day they died, no matter what fate might inflict or where it might scatter them, they would always stand apart from other men —united in memory with their old comrades of the 7,000 mile trip to the Pacific that no one else could ever share."

Meriwether Lewis was to die all too soon, and probably by his own hand, during a journey in Tennessee in 1809. William Clark lived happily and usefully until September 1, 1838, when he died at the home of his eldest son, Meriwether Lewis Clark, in St. Louis. Sacajawea, whose name was put down in Lewis's journal for May 20, 1805, as "Sah-ca-gee Me-ah or bird woman," corrected later to Sah-ca-gar-wea, and spelled variously ever since in print and bronze and granite, probably died in December, 1812, at Fort Manuel in the Dakota territory; Charbonneau outlived her by 28 years. Their son, Jean Baptiste, whom Clark nicknamed "Little Pomp" and for whom he called a landmark "Pompy's Tower," after education abroad, returned to become a mountain man, guide and interpreter. In 1846 he guided Philip St. George Cooke and his Mormon Battalion to California, and so it goes. Trails cross and recross. The Old West is still here, just turn the page.

TOUR GUIDE
TO THE
OLD WEST

ARIZONA

—The natives had still greater leaders—Victorio, Mangas Coloradas, Cochise, Juh, Nana, Chato—men so outstanding that not even their enemies could forget them. And what we know of them, for the most part, was written by their enemies.

Dan L. Thrapp *Al Sieber; Chief of Scouts* (University of Oklahoma Press, 1964)

They'll go in the hall with spurs on their heel,
They'll get them a partner to dance the next reel,
Saying, "How do I look in my new brown suit,
With my pants stuffed down in the top of my boot?"

"The Arizona Boys and Girls," from *Cowboy Songs,* collected by John Lomax (Macmillan, 1925)

The Indian is a peculiar institution. . . . you cannot tell by their looks whether there is honey or vinegar inside. . . . But all this time he is reading you as if you were an open book. He can almost tell from your expression what you had for breakfast! I have known one of these Apaches to go 60 miles out of his way to ask a man the same question he had asked a month before, and see if he would get the same answer. . . . You can't bull-doze these fellows, either, when they are loose in a wilderness as big as Europe.

Gen. George Crook, *Army and Navy Journal,* May 22, 1886

ARIZONA FACTS: Territory acquired by the Treaty of Guadalupe Hidalgo, 1848, and the Gadsden Purchase, 1853. Territory of Arizona statute signed by

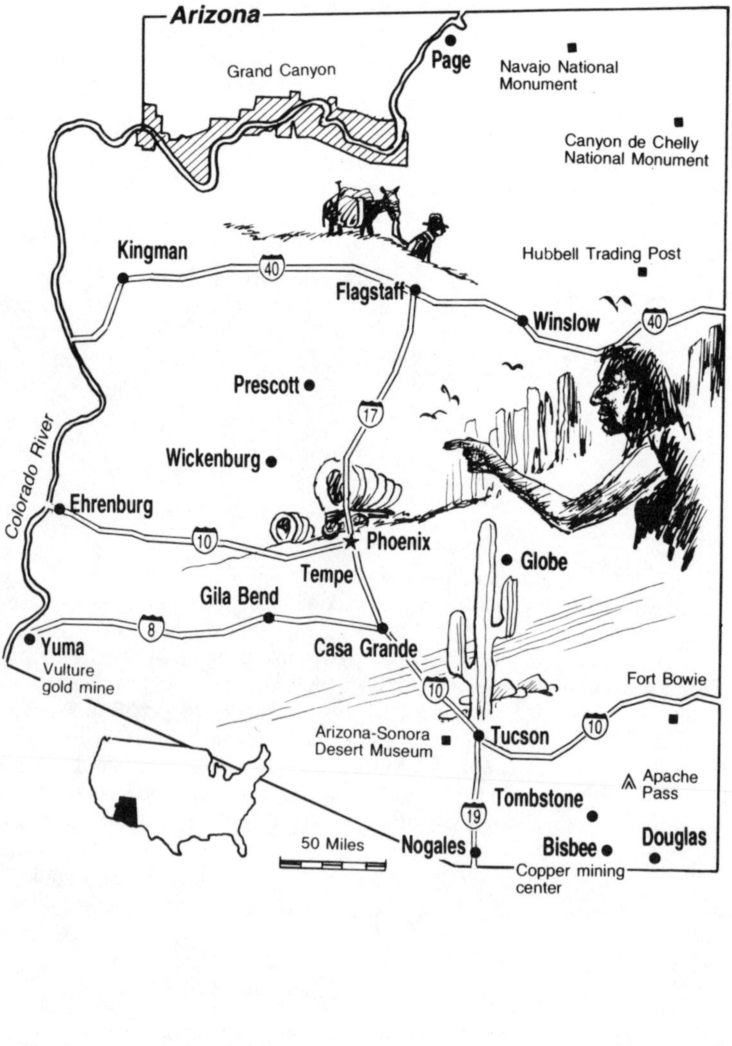

Arizona
Grand Canyon
Page
Navajo National Monument
Canyon de Chelly National Monument
Kingman
40
Hubbell Trading Post
Flagstaff
Winslow
40
Prescott
17
Wickenburg
Colorado River
Ehrenburg
10
Phoenix
Globe
Tempe
Gila Bend
8
Yuma
Casa Grande
Vulture gold mine
10
Fort Bowie
10
Arizona-Sonora Desert Museum
Tucson
Apache Pass
Tombstone
19
50 Miles
Nogales
Bisbee
Douglas
Copper mining center

President Lincoln, February 24, 1863. Admitted to Union February 14, 1912, the 48th state.

Arizona. The word is from the Papago *ali* (small) and *shonak* (place of the spring) was translated by Spaniards as *Arizonac,* later reduced. Nickname: The Grand Canyon State. Capital: Phoenix. First capital: Prescott. Arizona has two national parks, seven national forests, 16 national monuments, two national recreation areas, two national historic sites, and 19 Indian Reservations.

Chief Tribes. Apache, Chemehuevi, Cocopah, Havasupai, Hopi, Hualpai, Maricopa, Mohave, Navajo, Papago, Paiute, Pima and Yaqui.

Early Routes. Beale's Wagon Road, Butterfield Overland Mail, Cooke's Road, El Camino del Diablo (Devil's Highway), Gila Trail, Mormon Road, San Antonio & San Diego Stage Company Line, Texas & California Stage Company, The Colorado River Navigation Company, Atlantic & Pacific Railroad (later the Atchison, Topeka & Santa Fe), Southern Pacific Railroad.

AJO, Pima County. State 85,86. Ajo (Ah-ho), Spanish for garlic, is not a comment on the community; the Papago word for the red ore, used for pigment, sounded rather like *au-auho.* The Spaniards found copper here in the 1750s. Mexicans were working the area when the Gadsden Purchase of 1854 brought the region into U.S. possession. Mines have been worked continuously ever since.

Arizona's first incorporated mining company was orgainzed in 1854. Ajo ore was shipped down the Colorado River, and around Cape Horn, to Swansea, Wales, for smelting.

New Cornelia Copper Pit. 1 mi. S. The 485-acre, 800-ft. deep open pit is 1½ miles wide from lookout point.

ALAMO CROSSING, Mohave County. On Bill Williams River, 60 miles NW. of Wickenburg, US 89, 93.

The mining community established late in 1899 has the ruins of a five-stamp mill where gold and silver ore was crushed by falling steel hammers. Earlier stamping mills were water-powered, with wood stampers covered with iron. Multiple stampers took much less time and produced greater quantity. The Alamo Crossing operation was used mostly by itinerant prospectors.

ALAMO LAKE STATE PARK, Yuma County. 38 miles N. of Wenden (US 60) on Bill Williams River. The park comprises 4,900 acres in the Buckskin Mountains. The Santa Maria and Big Sandy Rivers form the Bill Williams, named for the mountain man and trapper. It empties into the Colorado near Parker Dam (state 95) and was discovered by the Spaniards in the 17th century. It became a favorite route for beaver trappers in Arizona territory.

ALPINE, Apache County. US 66, 180, on the Coronado Trail.

Alpine Cemetery has the grave of Jacob V. Hamblin, 1819–1886, Mormon missionary and trail-blazer, who built the Mormon Road from Utah to Arizona. He was ordained "Apostle to the Lamanites" by Brigham Young in 1876.

Hamblin, a friend of Hopi and Navajo Indians, opened the Grand Wash Trail to connect with Beale's Wagon Road across Arizona; he also led the first party of colonists to settlements on the Little Colorado. He was a ploygamist on the run from prosecution in his later years but returned from Mexico to die of malaria at Pleasanton, New Mexico. His remains were moved here in 1888.

Early map readers note that the town was first called Bush Valley for pioneer settler Anderson Bush. When colonized by the Mormons in 1879 it was first Frisco for the nearby San Francisco River and finally Alpine for its resemblance to a mountain range few of its citizens ever saw.

APACHE JUNCTION, Pinal County. US 60, 80, 89, E. of Phoenix. The western end of the Apache Trail

Apacheland Movie Ranch, 7 miles east and 4 miles north of US 60, 80, 89, is a popular movie and television background. A replica of a frontier town.

APACHE NATIONAL FOREST, Greenlee and Apache Counties, also in New Mexico. An outstandingly scenic area of more than 1,800,000 acres.

Coronado Trail. US 666 from Clifton, Greenlee County, to Alpine, Apache County, follows part of the vast trail taken by Don Francisco de Coronado and his adventurers in the 16th century as they searched for the fabled Seven Cities of Cibola. A twisting road reaches heights of 8,550 ft. at Rose Peak where the U.S. Forest Service maintians a lookout tower. Northward, from the foot of the Mogollon Rim, the road again rises, to 9,200 ft. at K.P. Cienaga.

Coronado's expedition was mounted in Mexico City early in 1540 when an Italian-born Franciscan in the service of Spain, Fray Marcos de Niza, brought back what seemed to be confirmation that earlier rumors of cities whose streets were lined with gold and precious gems were indeed true. The Zuni villages of New Mexico looked golden in the sunset from afar which is how the discreet De Niza viewed them after a Moor, Estevan, sent ahead to investigate the area was killed by Zunis. Coronado with some 300 horsemen, 800 Indian footmen, and herds of sheep and cattle, headed north. Ultimately the expedition found the Grand Canyon and even reached Kansas, but the gold they sought was too far underfoot to be detected by the *conquistadores.*

APACHE PASS, Cochise County, Interstate 8, is a twisting, rocky difile between the foothills of the Dos Cabesas and Chiricahua mountains and was the most dangerous point along the southern Overland Mail route, which ran from Tipton, Mo., to San Francisco. In 1857 the San Antonio–San Diego Mail passed here. In 1858 the Butterfield Overland Mail built a stage relay station and corral just west of the spring. Stone foundations remain. The only organized Indian attack on the Butterfield Stage took place here in 1861. (See Fort Bowie)

APACHE TRAIL, Pinal and Gila counties, State 88, begins at Apache Junction ca. 33 miles east of Phoenix, and ends in Globe. It is rich in siteseeing as it passes north of the Superstition Mountains and Tonto National Monument, with the Salt river's dam-formed lakes, Saguaro, Canyon, Apache and Roosevelt, to the north of the route.

Apache Lake Recreation Area is about 10 miles east of Torilla Flat.

ARIVACA, Pima County. Road goes SW. from Arivaca Junction, just above Amado, State 93. Ca. 22 miles SW. of turn-off.

Heintzleman Mine attracted investors in 1856. It was also known as the Cerro Colorado (red peak) for the nearby mountain. Samuel Peter Heintzleman, later a Union general wounded at First Manassas (Bull Run), was an army officer stationed at Fort Yuma when he became interested in mining and served as president of the Sonora Exploring and Mining Company. Samuel Colt, the arms manufacturer, was also an investor. In 1857 a train of twelve wagons, each pulled by twelve horses, hauled ore from Arivaca to Kansas City for 12.5 cents per pound. The handpicked ore ran to $1500 per ton in silver.

ARIZOLA, Pinal County. IS 8. 10. State 84.

Established 1892 as a desert station on the Southern Pacific line, the town became known as headquarters for a colorful scoundrel who called himself the Baron of the Colorados. James Addison Reavis, a former horse-car conductor and newspaper subscription salesman, claimed no less than twelve and one-half million acres of central Arizona and western New Mexico, including Phoenix, Florence, Globe, Safford and Silver City, as the Peralta Grant, given to his wife's family by King Philip V of Spain.

In a brick house at Arizola he and his family lived up to his notion of baronial spendor with footman, coachman, house servants, and his two children dressed in royal purple velvet, their Russion caps embellished with monogram coronets. Reavis had falsified church records in Spain and Mexico and sold quit-claim deeds to those legally entitled to the land. The Southern Pacific reputedly paid $50,000 for right of way across the barony. A sharp-eyed printed in Florence, who took the time to look over old documents filed in Phoenix, observed that one of the ancient claim papers had been printed in type invented only a few years earlier and another bore the water-mark of a Wisconsin mill that had been in business no more than a dozen years.

In 1895 Reavis was sentenced to six years in the Santa Fe penitentiary, served less than two, and was often seen on the streets of Phoenix looking weary but hopeful about recouping his lost fortune.

ARIZONA-SONORA DESERT MUSEUM, Pima County. 16 miles W. of Tucson. State 86 to Kinney Rd. in Tucson Mountain Park.

As part of the Carnegie Institution of Washington, the Desert Laboratory initiated the study of the ecology of arid regions. The excellent museum now features exhibits of desert botany, zoology, geology and anthropology. Nature trails through well-labeled botanical gardens, areas with more than 750 living animals to be viewed, an aviary, and a lighted tunnel show desert existence on, above and below ground.

AWATOBI RUINS, Navajo County. 8 miles S. of Keams Canyon, State 264, on Hopi Indian Reservation (also spelled Awatovi).

In the summer of 1540 Coronado

sent Pedro de Továr to investigate the Indian villages in a province called Tusayan by the Spanish. This was the first European visit to a Hopi queblo. There were a number of converts to Christianity from 1628 until the Pueblo Rebellion of 1680, with Awatobi showing the highest number and thereby being destroyed in 1700 by neighboring pueblos whose residents had kept the Indian faith. Excavations have uncovered three churches among the ruins, along with aboriginal material and some Spanish fragments.

Mining experts have determined that the Hopis were burning the black rock they found as early as 1300, using it to bake pottery. In 1697, Fray Agustin de Vetancourt wrote about the Awatobi Mission Hopis having "stones which served for coal but the smoke is noxious in its strength." (Note that "b's" and "v's" are almost interchangeable in early Spanish-Indian names, depending possible on the ear of the recorder or the choice of the translator.)

BENSON,Cochise County, IS 10, was a stop on the Butterfield Stage line in the 1860s. In 1880 the town was founded as a railroad center for the Tombstone mines. Two years later it was part of the Atchison railroad on what was hailed as the longest rail route in the world under one management, from Kansas City to Guaymas, Sonora. A silver spike in a mahogany tie symbolized the completion of the project at Nogales in October of 1882 but the Mexican part of the railroad proved a financial disaster.

Council Rocks, at Dragoon Springs, ca. 4 miles off State 86. A peace treaty made by Apache chief Cochise and Gen. O. O. Howard was ratified here in 1872, ending years of warfare, and honored for the remainder of Cochise's lifetime. Large boulders mark the treaty site, but no one now alive knows where the great Apache is buried in the Dragoon Mountains, his stronghold for many years.

BERNARDINO, Cochise County. Just N. of US 80.

San Bernardino Ranch, on international boundary, was located on a Mexican land grant dating from 1822 and was a favorite stopping place for travelers, including the Mormon Battalion in 1846, and thousands of gold-seekers in 1849. On March 22, 1822, Ignacio Perez had paid $90 for a grant of 73,240 acres. When the boundary was surveyed in 1850, 8,-688 acres of the property were found to be in the U.S. The abundant springs were sought by all who passed by whether they were on military expeditions, stock drives, or emigrating. Because of Apache raids the ranch was twice abandoned. John Slaughter purchased the place in 1884. The present Headquarters Complex, still in use, dates from this time. It is now a national historic landmark, not accessible to the public.

BISBEE, Cochise County, US 80, has long taken pride in being too perpendicular for home mail delivery service. It boomed into existence in the 1880s following the discovery of the Copper Queen Lode. From Mule Pass Gulch, now US 80, the town grew up the sides of surrounding mountains. Its history, as well as local names (Quality Hill, Tombstone Canyon, Brewery Gulch, O.K. Street, etc.), might have been invented by a Hollywood script writer:

A prospector looking for silver in

1875 went on by in some disgust, having found only what he called "copper stains." Two years later three army scouts camped here: U.S. Cavalryman John Dunn found ore samples and took them with him, later sending George Warren to grubstake in his behalf. Warren posted the proper claims and named the area the Warren Mining District.

Two early companies merged for the Copper Queen Consolidated Mining Co. which attracted prospectors from all over the world. The town is named for Judge DeWitt Bisbee, a shareholder in the Copper Queen. Warren fell on self-induced hard times; he had a thirst and he also bet one of his million-dollar claims on a horse race in which he was the losing jockey—or so the stories go. In any case he was found insame in 1881, and a guardian was appointed who had him jailed for his own safety. On release he went to Mexico but wandered back to die a pauper in 1892 in the heart of one of the world's richest copper fields.

Mining and Historical Museum and Civic Center, Copper Queen Plaza, intersection of Main St. and Brewery Gulch. The brick building erected in 1890 as offices for the mining company has dioramas depiction early techniques, mineral displays, and local memorabilia.

Lavender Pit, US 80, has lookout stop for viewing the 296 acre open-pit copper mine owned by the Phelps-Dodge Corporation.

Mule Pass Tunnel, US 80, is Arizona's longest: 6042 ft. high, 1400 ft. long.

Chamber of Commerce, 21 Main St.

Cochise County Courthouse, Quality Hill on US 80, has plaster panels depicting the city's history and a relief map of particular interest on the staircase wall leading to second floor.

Miners' Monument, at the foot of Quality Hill, US 80, is mounted on granite used for miners' drilling contests in the 1890s.

Observation Point, School Hill, via Clawson St. and High Rd. A paved area for a fine view of the up-and-down town.

Evergreen Cemetery, US 80 SE. of town near Warren-Bisbee cut-off. In 1914 Prospector George Warren's grave was found under a rotting wooden headboard; three years later it was moved and properly marked with monument.

Southwest Trail Dust Zoo, About 6 miles E. off US 80 on Double Adobe Rd. Reptiles and animals of this area as well as some from Central and South America.

Lehner-Mammoth Kill Site, 10 miles W. of Bisbee, is an outstanding site and national historic landmark, privately owned at present. Radiocarbon dates for artifacts found here serve in analysis of pollen chronology. Stone butchering tools with Clovis fluted spear points were discovered here, adding much to present knowledge of nomadic hunters.

BONITA, Graham County. State 266, in Aravaipa Valley.

Sierra Bonita Ranch, 10 miles SW of town, is a national historic landmark, privately owned at present. It was founded in 1872 by Col. Henry C. Hooker who was the first American to establish a continuously successful cattle-ranch and to introduce graded stock. He built wisely against Apache attack, maintaining large buildings with thick adobe walls and gunports in the parapets. These were on the site of a Spanish hacienda abandoned early in the century because of Apache depredations. Five water springs aided Hooker in maintaining a range of nearly 30 square miles. At 4,000-feet elevation, it provided ideal breeding temperatures. When Hooker died in 1907 he was still cattle king of Arizona.

CALABASAS, Santa Cruz County. State 93. About 10 miles N. of Nogales on the Santa Cruz River. Now a ghost town, this was a Papago Indian village visited by Jesuit missionaries in the 1700s; mined by the Spanish, who also built Arizona's first Christian church at nearby Guevavi; Calabasas became a military outpost, then a large ranch. After the Gadsden Purchase, U.S. Dragoons established Camp Calabasas. (Also called Calabazas and Fort Mason during the Civil War when the California Volunteers camped here.) The town was named Calabasas in 1865 when it became the headquarters for a mining company. Its busiest time was in the 1880s as a construction camp on the railroad being built from Benson to Sonora, Mexico.

CAMERON, Coconino County. US 89. Originally Tanner's Crossing, renamed to honor Ralph Cameron, one of Arizona's first senators who had been a pioneer in developing trails and copper mines and a territorial delegate. Seth Tanner was a Mormon pioneer. The Mormon Trail crossed the treacherous Little Colorado here at one of the few rock-bottom passages in an area of quicksand.

Cameron Indian Trading Post has a variety of Indian handiwork.

Some of the results of Arizona's famous "Shootout at O.K. Corral"
(Arizona Office of Tourism)

CAMP DATE CREEK, Yavapai County. State 93, near the forks of Date Creek W. of highway, between Congress Junction and Hillside. 3 or 4 miles S. of Date Creek railroad station. Established as Camp McPherson in late 1860s, the camp became the Date Creek agency in 1871; Mohave Indians were given food rations. In 1872 when Lt. Col. George Crook tracked renegade Yavapais to the Date Creek Reservation, he narrowly escaped being killed by their treachery at a so-called Peace Conference. They fled to hideouts in the canyons of the Santa Maria. Crook pursued, capturing and killing as many as possible. This led to the Battle of Skull Cave in the Salt River Canyon, Dec. 28, 1872. (See Salt River Canyon Battlefield.)

CAMPS, Early. Various sites.

Camp Beale's Springs, 1871–1874, NE of Kingman, below the Music Mountains, near present US 66.

Camp Bear Springs, 1863–1864, NW of Flagstaff, N. of present US 66, 89.

Camp Colorado, 1868–1871, on Colorado river below junction with Bill Williams river, near present State 95.

Camp El Dorado, 1867, in present Hoover Dam area.

Camp Lewis, 1865–1870, SE of Fort Verde, on the Verde river, below the Mogollon Rim.

Camp Price, 1881–1883, SE of Fort Bowie, near the New Mexico state line, in the Coronado National Forest.

Camp Rawlins, 1870–1871, SE of Camp Hualpai, SW of Fort Whipple No. 1, in Prescott National Forest.

Camp Rigg, 1864–1870, N. of Safford, a few miles SE of Fort Thomas.

Camp Rucker, 1878, NE of Bisbee, just SW of Camp Price.

Camp Reventon, 1862–1864, NW of Tubac and old Camp Tubac, on Santa Cruz river.

Camp Willow Grove, 1867–1869, SE of Kingman, near Wikeup.

CAMP PINAL, Gila County, near US 60 between Miami and Claypool.

Weaver's Needle, a peak seen on the west, was named for Paulino Weaver, early scout.

Pinal Mountain and Pioneer Pass Recreation Areas are south of Globe, just west of State 77.

In 1870 Camp Pinal was garrisoned with 400 cavalrymen. An old wagon road heading south from US 60 led to the Irions Ranch, now Pinal Ranch, once a haven for travelers beset by Apaches. In the early years the area was a nearly impregnable Apache stronghold. Later the great leader Eskiminzin raised corn and melons and very little fuss even though his family had been massacred, he had been imprisoned, and had repeatedly lost land to encroaching whites.

CAMP RENO, Gila County. On Reno Creek on the east slopes of Mazatzal Mountains, near Tonto Basin on road between Roosevelt Dam and Payson. From 1866 to 1868, an outpost of Fort McDowell, the camp was a departure point for the military expeditions against the Tonto and Pinal Apache Indians. Located a few miles above the confluence of Reno and Tonto Creeks, the garrison enjoyed a sweeping view of the valley from the Mogollon Rim to the Pinal Mountains, had plenty of water, a rarity at many posts, and was cooler than many. Troops often bivouacked here after the post was abandoned. In 1882 it was the meeting site for the 14 troops of cavalry led by Captain A. R. Chaffee against the Coyotero Apaches in the Battle of Big Dry Wash. (See General Springs).

CAMP VERDE, Yavapai County. I-17, State 79. Originally the post was located on the west bank of the Rio Verde, to protect settlers for the newly opened Prescott mining district, in 1864. Named for the president, it was Camp Lincoln until 1868 when the name was changed to avoid confusion with Camp Lincoln, Dakota Territory. Occupied by regular troops in 1866; moved four miles south and a mile west of the river, half a mile below the mouth of Beaver Creek, where it was hoped the air would be more healthful. Designated Fort Verde, 1879; abandoned 1890.

Fort Verde State Historic Park, 2 miles off State 79, is located on the site of the original fort, restored buildings, museum with artifacts. In 1872–1873, the fort served as a base for General George Crook's campaign against the Apaches.

CAMP WHIPPLE, Yavapai County. US 89. Marker on highway at road leading to Del Rio Ranch in Little Chino Valley. A camp was established here late in 1863 which served as Arizona's first capital. From January to May, 1864, the territorial government maintained "offices" in tents and log cabins at this site before moving to Prescott, the first permanent capital. Amiel Weeks Whipple was a cartographer and army officer who had explored the area in the 1850s. The Massachusetts-born soldier was fatally wounded at Chancellorsville in May, 1863. He was promoted to Major General on May 5, 1863, and died the following day. The camp was designated Fort Whipple in 1870. (Which see.) Del Rio Springs also was known as Postle's Ranch and Banghart's Ranch. (See Navajo.)

CANYON DE CHELLY NATIONAL MONUMENT, Apache County (CAN-yun duh SHAY). From Ganado 33 miles N. on Navajo 8 to headquarters and Visitor Center at Chinle (Chin-LEE). The name comes from the Navajo *tseyi,* meaning "among the cliffs" or "rocky." The Spanish spelled it in their fashion, and Americans gave it a French pronunciation. George R. Stewart, author of "American Place Names," aptly calls it a "museum piece of a name!" The canyon was first occupied by Anasazi Indians, ancestors of the Pueblo Indians, who moved out about 1300. The Navajo came long after the original apartment builders had abandoned their settlement. In 1864 Kit Carson's men drove most of the Navajo out of the area, on the Long March to Bosque Redondo, New Mexico. The Navajo resettled here in 1868.

Visitor Center houses a museum, offices and a reception hall. A 15-mile rim drive offers a view of the more than 100 major ruins. A self-guiding tour leads to the canyon floor, and to *White House* ruin. *Antelope House,* protected by an undercut cliff, and *Mummy Cave* are of particular interest.

CANYON DIABLO, Coconino County, US 66, 180. Ca. 26 miles W. of Winslow. In 1857, Edward F. Beale, surveying for a wagon road from Ft. Defiance, New Mexico, to the Colorado River, passed here with his camels, and found the name was indeed appropriate for the deep gorge in Kaibab sandstone with nearly perpendicular walls. The desert pack column of dromedaries from Mediterranean countries was an experiment cut short by the Civil War. The animals could travel for long periods without water and seemed less gun-shy than horses but cowboys never quite got the hang of camel-busting. They weren't tossed by their steeds but they frequently complained of a nausea akin to seasickness from the swaying ride. In March, 1889, an Atlantic & Pacific train stopped at the Canyon Diablo station and was robbed by four bandits who were then chased by Sheriff William "Bucky" O'Neill and three deputies over 300 miles in two weeks before a successful capture in Utah. The recovered loot: $1000. When Lewis Kingman and others surveyed the area for a railroad route in 1880, they used notes made by Lt. Amiel Whipple and his party of 1853–1854. Kingman hired Apache, Navajo and Mojave Indians who proved to be excellent workers in the difficult job of bridging the canyon. At the July 1882 grand opening the iron bridge soared 222½ feet above the canyon floor. It was 250 ft. long and had cost some $250,000.

CASA GRANDE RUINS NATIONAL MONUMENT, Pinal County. 1 mile N. of Coolidge on State 87. As early as 300 to 400 B.C. the Hohokam Indians developed an extensive irrigation system with canals that enabled them to farm the arid lands of the Gila and Salt River Valleys. Casa Grande, built in the 14th century, was a four-story structure with packed earthen walls; it served as astronomical observatory as well as apartment house. Father Eusebio Francisco Kino discovered and named the ruins in 1694, nearly two and one-half centuries after it had been abandoned. Today the monument comprises more than 472 acres, with a museum and archaeological exhibits. The site lies by the edge of the Pima Indian Reservation.

CHARLESTON, Cochise County. 9 miles SW of Tombstone on the banks of the San Pedro River. This ghost town has a few adobes, the ruins of a silver mill, and some interesting old grave markers, in a quiet atmosphere that once was thick with milling and general excitement. Undesirable citizens or transients, booted from Tombstone, landed here. Jim Burnett, justice of the peace, assessed large fines, kept plenty for himself, and wore a well-oiled gun while offering to shoot anyone who complained that he'd been overcharged. Among temporary residents: Johnny Ringo (John Ringgold), the Clanton boys, the McLaurys (sometimes spelled McLowerys), and Curly Bill Brocius whose surname has come down the years variously as Borcius and Brockus. A Law and Order League, of 50 armed men, frequently rode out from Tombstone to try to tame the outlaws of Charleston and nearby Galeyville, but Ringo and others remained at large, to come to grief elsewhere. Charleston was the "Red Dog" of Alfred Henry Lewis's stories, as Tombstone was his "Wolfville."

CHIRICAHUA NATIONAL MONUMENT, Cochise County. 37 miles SE of Willcox on State 186. A stronghold of the Chiricahua (Cheeree-CAH-wah) Apache Indians under such leaders as Cochise, Geronimo, Massai and others now has a Visitor Center, near entrance, with a variety of exhibits, including botanical and zoological displays as well as historical. Cochise Head is a notable rock profile in the Chiricahua Mountains. At Massai Point Overlook geological displays explain the origin of the monument. There are a number of overlooks on the road up Bonita Canyon leading to the monument headquarters.

CHLORIDE, Mojave County. US 93, State 62. The partial ghost town is NW of Kingman, about 4 miles E. of Grasshopper Junction. There is still much rose quartz in this area which was once a silver-mining center. Tiffany & Co. of New York has mined turquoise here. About 5 miles away, along the Sacramento Wash, is a remarkable forest of Joshua trees (Yucca palms); many are 25 to 30 feet high.

CHRISTMAS, Gila County. State 77, 9 miles N. of Winkleman. In 1878 and 1882, two separate copper claims were made in the Dripping Springs Mountains, but the land lay within the San Carlos Apache Indian Reservation. Shortly after the turn of the century when boundaries were resurveyed, prospectors who knew of the earlier claims hastened to the site and staked their land early on Christmas morning of 1902. There are ruins of a mill where more than $9,000,000 in copper was processed. The town has long been a popular seasonal mail address.

CIBECUE CREEK BATTLEFIELD, Navajo County. W. of US 60 on Fort Apache Indian Reservation, 2½ miles S. of Cibecue. (Cibecue, Apache for "reddish bottom-land.") In 1881 a medicine man, Nakaidoklini, was preaching a new religion to his followers and also stirring them up to increased resentment of white settlers. The local Indian agent appealed to Fort Apache for assistance in controlling the group. In a series of wrong moves both sides of the controversy brought on a pitched battle in August. Col. E. A. Carr, commanding 85 men from the fort and 23 Apache scouts, arrested Nakaidoklini at his camp on Cibecue Creek. At their encampment that night the Americans were attacked by one hundred of the medicine man's followers. Nakaidoklini was killed by his guard during the fighting. Carr and his men retreated to Fort Apache and were attacked there on September 1 by White Mountain Apaches under Na-ti-o-ish. Hostilities were kept up, and the Battle of Big Dry Wash was fought on East Clear Creek, July 17, 1882, ending with the death of 22 Apaches and the surrender of the others. It was the last real battle between soldiers and the Indians on Arizona land but the war was not over until Geronimo's surrender in 1886. The last of the warfare took place in northern Mexico.

CLIFTON, Greenlee County. US 666, State 75. The Coronado Trail begins here, just south of the Apache National Forest, and runs north to Alpine along US 666.

The Copper Head, a 20-inch narrow-gauge railroad locomotive, is on display in front of the old jail in the heart of town. Copper ore was hauled from Metcalf to the smelter here, drawn by The Copper Head, which itself arrived from La Junta, Colorado, towed by oxen for some 600 miles.

Chase Creek, one of the main streets, was once a narrow-gauge thoroughfare also, with board walks, saloons and plenty of gunplay.

Clifton Cliff Jail, blasted from rock in the spot where an ancient Indian cave existed, held many ruffians in the town's boom days. A Mexican laborer who set off the blast apparently used his pay to take on a load of liquid dynamite and was the jail's first customer.

Henry Clifton and other prospectors from Silver City, N.M., uncovered copper ore in the area, as well as turquoise, agate and azurite. The first claims were staked in 1872.

COCHISE, Cochise County. US 666. In 1887 the town was established as a station on the Southern Pacific Railroad. Stage and train robberies were almost an every-week occurrence, causing little stir, but the theft in September, 1899, turned heads and made tongues wag because the men who took more than $10,000 from the Southern Pacific were supposed to be operating on the right side of the law. Burt Alvord, who planned the affair with the help of a cattleman, William Downing, was the constable of Willcox. W.N. Stiles, deputy-constable of Pearce, and Matt Burts, a cowboy, actually did the work. Both officers tried to lead investigators down the wrong path to the criminals. Stiles finally confessed and agreed to be a witness for the prosecution, but before the trial could get underway he shot and wounded the Tombstone jailer and freed Alvord. Later Stiles and Burts surrendered and served time at Yuma. In an up and down, or rather in and out, existence, Alvord surrendered in Mexico, served little or no time at Tombstone because he had helped capture a Mexican desperado. The second time the Alvord-Stiles combination landed in Tombstone they dug their way to freedom. Alvord went to Panama; Stiles was killed in Nevada.

COCHISE STRONGHOLD, Cochise County. 10½ miles from US 666 in the Dragoon Mountains. In a canyon on the western slopes of the mountains, Cochise met with General O. O. Howard in 1872 for talks that brought a peace which lasted for the duration of the Apache chieftain's life. Arrangements for the conference were made by Tom Jeffords, a New York-born but Western-wise supervisor of the Overland Mail depot at Tucson, who had made friends with the great Apache and became a "blood brother" by exchanging a few drops in the ritualistic way. Jeffords was with Cochise on the night before his death, had left to bring a doctor, but returned too late. Cochise's men rode their horses back and forth over the chief's grave to obliterate any traces for white men to discover.

The Cochise Stronghold Recreation Area is in the Coronado Forest.

COCONINO NATIONAL FOREST, Coconino County. US 89. The forest comprises about 1,999,000 acres, with the San Francisco peaks rising to 12,680 feet, highest in Arizona and other areas reaching deep into canyons. The Mogollon Rim and Oak Creek Canyon are particularly noteworthy.

Winona Site, 5 miles NE of Winona on US 66, is a national historic landmark. Winona was one of the Indian villages that developed just after the eruption of Sunset Crater. The site, which has yielded valuable information on the culture in the area up to 1130, shows how three groups merged to form a new pattern of life in the Southwest.

C. Hart Merriam Base Camp Site, 20 miles NW of Flagstaff, is a national historic landmark, privately owned at present. Dr. Hart formulated the Life Zone concept, basic in the development of the science of ecology. His investigations were made from this base camp.

COLOSSAL CAVE, Pima County. 28 miles SW of Tucson off I-10, US 80. About 5 miles east of Vail. In the 1880s masked bandits robbed the Southern Pacific train of $62,000 and hid out here, while a sheriff's posse waited after setting brush fires at the cave's entrance to smoke out the thieves. The besieged men found another exit, but later were caught in Willcox where three died in a gun battle. A fourth was captured and sentenced to serve 28 years. On his release in 1912, he showed up briefly in Tucson, then vanished. A Wells-Fargo agent trailing the released convict found only empty money sacks in Colossal Cave. The loot and the fourth robber were gone forever.

CONTENTION CITY, Cochise County. On banks of the San Pedro River. A dirt road leads NW of Fairbank (State 82) to site. Adobe walls of the former railroad station still stand along with other adobe ruins, a small cemetery and the remains of a mill. For nearly a decade from 1879, the town thrived as three mills reduced ore from the Tombstone mines.

COOLIDGE DAM, Gila County. US 70. The Apache tribal burying grounds and Geronimo's onetime camp are deep under water. The Apaches claimed in vain that the dam violated their treaty rights. They would not let their dead be moved and an $11,000 concrete slab covers the principal burying ground.

CORONADO NATIONAL FOREST, Cochise, Pima and Graham Counties. Southeast corner of state. The forest has 12 widely scattered sections in Arizona and New Mexico and covers some 1,800,000 acres. Among scenic drives, US 80 and Rucker Canyon Road, Hitchcock Highway to Mount Lemmon, Mount Graham Road, Onion Saddle Road. District headquarters are in Douglas, Nogales, Patagonia, Safford, Tucson and Willcox. Cochise Stronghold in the Dragoon Mountains is noteworthy. Among spectacular mountain ranges within the forest are the Santa Teresa, Galiuro, Pinaleno, Dragoon, Chiricahua, Huachuca, Santa Catalina, Las Guijas, Santa Rita, Rincon and Whetstone Mountains.

CORONADO NATIONAL MEMORIAL, Cochise County. Secondary Road leading west from State 92. When Hernando De Soto was making history in Florida, another Spanish gallant, Francisco Vasquez de Coronado, with a large force and plenty of supplies set out from Compostela, Mexico, to see for himself if the rumors of Seven Cities of Cibola, with gold and other treasures to be had for the taking, were indeed true. Here his expedition entered what is now U.S. territory. From Coronado Peak visitors can look out across the Sonoran desert, the route of the Conquistadors. A footpath from the parking area at Montezuma Pass leads to this high point; exhibits along the way pertain to natural features of the terrain and to the expedition. A wilderness trail leads from Montezuma Pass area, along Smuggler's Ridge and through Joe's Canyon. A Living History program with park attendants in period costume is presented on weekends. The Memorial, which is a national historic landmark, comprises 2,834 acres.

DEWEY, Yavapai County. State 69.

Old Orchard Ranch, 3 miles W. on highway. The homestead and ranch established in 1882 where Miss Sharlot Hall wrote poetry which became very popular in Arizona. The Sharlot Hall Museum is in Prescott. Miss Hall also was a territorial historian.

Woolsey's Ranch, 1 mile N. of Humboldt on the road to Cherry Creek and Dewey. The first Anglo-American ranch in northern Arizona was the irrigated farm established in 1863 by King S. Woolsey, a miller, guide, merchant, miner, trailblazer, Indian fighter and legislator. Woolsey built the original Black Canyon Road which connected Yavapai County to settlements further south and was the first public road approved and financed by the Territorial government. Ranch ruins are visible slightly to the east of a marker on State 69.

DOS CABEZAS, Cochise County. 14 miles SE of Willcox on State 186. Spanish adventurers of the Coronado expedition named the area for the two headlike mountain peaks. The first settlers were Chiricahua Apaches. Gold was discovered and a small mining camp was set up with the town having three stamp mills, a brewery, brickyard, and barber shop as well as a general store and a district school by the 1880s. The town also was a stop on the stage lines and has an interesting connection with the Confederate general, Richard Stoddert "Dick" Ewell. During the Gadsden Purchase negotiations, Capt. Ewell, a West Pointer who had fought in the Mexican War and stayed on to fight Indians, camped with his men on the mesa near the Dos Cabezas spring, where he conceived the idea of setting up a stage route along an early Indian trail, which also had been used by the '49ers. He established a station near each waterhole on the route. The one here was renamed Ewell's Springs. Later other lines used the trail. Adobe ruins and a cemetery at site.

DOUGLAS, Cochise County. US 80.

Double Adobe Site, 12 miles NW on the west bank of Whitewater Creek. A national historic landmark not accessible to the public at this time. The site, preserved in its natural state, was discovered in 1926; it contains the remains of tribes who lived by gathering wild plants, nuts and seeds as well as by hunting.

Tenth Street Park, 10th St., has a visitors' clubhouse. Douglas is a company town, named for Dr. Joseph Douglas, former president of the Phelps Dodge copper company. In early days the deep street dust rose above boot tops, planks were laid down at corner crossings, and the first cafe was made of railroad ties. It opened on 10th Street.

DRAGOON, Cochise County. Just E. of I-10.

Dragoon Springs, just S. of town, was a stop on the Overland Stage. (Until the 1860s, U.S. mounted troops were known as Dragoons.) The original stops on the Overland in Arizona territory were: Stein's Peak, Apache Pass, Dragoon Springs, Cienaga, Tucson, Point-of-Mountain, Picacho Pass, Sacaton, Maricopa Wells, Gila Ranch, Murderer's Grave, Flap-Jack Ranch, Peterman's Filibuster Camp, Snively's Ranch and Yuma. This particular watering hole was discovered by the Dragoons in 1856.

Amerind Foundation Museum is private, open by appointment. It has a superb collection of prehistoric material from the area which was once known as Pimeria Atta. Write Amerind Foundation, Inc., Dragoon, AZ 85609 for appointment.

EHRENBERG, Yuma County. US 60, 95, I-10. Herman Ehrenberg, who platted the site, slightly north of the present town, on the Colorado River, never got to see the settlement named for him. He was murdered in Dos Palmas, California, before the village became a principal shipping port in the 1870s. The California and Arizona Stage Co. had offices here and the road leading east was aptly known as the Trail of Graves. Martha Summerhayes, a New England bride who followed her army lieutenant husband to his far western posts, wrote a wholly fascinating account of her 1870s life in "Vanished Arizona" in 1908. Her memories of Ehrenberg are vivid. Visitors who arrived by steamer on the Colorado were never prepared for the sight of the Summerhayes butler, Charley, a Cocopah Indian, who waited table wearing "nothing but his loin-cloth, with about a yard of calico floating out behind."

Boothill Cemetery, E. end of town, has a remarkable monument erected by highway department employees: the cement base is studded with guns, burro shoes, branding irons, miners' candles, picks, and other gear of early workers.

FAIRBANK, Cochise County. On San Pedro River, 10 miles W. of Tombstone on State 82. The town named for N. K. Fairbank, a Chicago merchant who organized the Grand Central Mining Co. in Tombstone, was a supply point on the railroad line and a stage terminal. In the 1700s it had been an Indian village, Santa Cruz.

Quiburi, north of town, is a pre-Columbian site which has been surveyed by the Historic American Buildings Department of the National Park Service but is privately owned at present. The earliest structures unearthed date from 1200. The Sobaipuri Indians lived here since prehistoric times. The presidio of Santa Cruz de Terrenate was established in the 1770s to guard Sonora from Apache attacks. A few old walls remain.

FLAGSTAFF, Coconino County. I-40, 17. On the 4th of July, 1876, a group of scouts stripped a tall pine of its branches, tied an American flag to it with rawhide strings, and gave the town its name. The Atlantic & Pacific Railroad (now the Santa Fe) arrived in 1882.

Museum of Northern Arizona, 3 miles NW on US 180, has excellent archaeological exhibits, geology, natural science and an Indian arts and crafts shop. Of particular interest are the first oil landscapes painted by Frederic Dellenbaugh and Elbert Burr, who strapped their easels to the backs of mules and explored the trails of the Grand Canyon in the 1870s, stopping to paint when they felt like it. Also not to be missed are the dioramas of Anasazi villages and the ceremonial dance. There is a full-scale reproduction of a Hopi underground ceremonial chamber (or Kiva) decorated with original murals from Awatovi, ancient village on Hopi Indian reservation.

Northern Arizona Pioneers' Historical Museum, 2 miles NW on Fort Valley Rd., US 180. Exhibits pertain to the history of the area.

Northern Arizona University, SW part of town, on US 66, has an unusual history. In 1893, the territorial legislature set aside $500,000 for a boys' reformatory, but there were no misguided boys to be found; in 1897, more funds were appropriated for an insane asylum. Cell block construction was begun but no Flagstaffians were mentally off-balance. By 1899 the legislators under pressure to use the funds voted to establish an ordinary school. By the end of the century there were only a few students but the institution grew into today's university which now has a 357-acre campus.

Lowell Observatory, 1 mile W. on Mars Hill Rd., was established by Percival Lowell in 1894. From here the planet Pluto was discovered. The 24-inch refracting telescope installed in 1896 still is in operation in its original housing.

Buffalo Park, N. of US 66 on Cedar Road, has 217 acres devoted to a wildlife refuge and gives the modern visitor some idea of how the terrain looked in the Old West.

City Park, W. end of Cherry Ave., is the scene for an annual Indian Powwow (Nahohi). Thousands of Indians from as many as 20 tribes usually attend, early in July. The Chamber of Commerce, Santa Fe & Beaver, has tickets.

Leroux Springs, ca. 7 miles NW on Fort Valley Road near the Museum of Northern Arizona, a water supply for early travelers, named for Antoine Leroux, French-born guide and trapper. He led the Mormon Battalion in 1846 and other important expeditions including Edward Beale's camel corps in 1854.

FLORENCE, Pinal County. US 80, 89.

Adamsville Ruin, ca. 3½ miles SW. on State 287. In the 40 acres of the national historic landmark mounds mark a prehistoric village; a ballcourt has been partially excavated. There are also ancient irrigation ditches.

Pinal County Historical Museum, 2201 Main St. Exhibits of local history.

Home of Pauline Cushman, W. 6th St. The peripatetic actress and sometime spy of the Civil War lived here when she was married to Pinal County sheriff, Jere Fryer (1879). She was a suicide in California in 1893 and is buried at the Presidio near San Francisco with full honors on her tombstone.

Ruggles House, W. end of 5th St., was the home of Levi Ruggles, first white settler in 1866. The town was a trading center for miners and a stage stop. Other old adobe houses along 5th St. are of interest. The Pinal County Hospital building at the NW corner of Main and 5th was the courthouse from 1879 till 1887.

FORT APACHE, Navajo County. State 73. The fort was established in the spring of 1870, to control the Apache Indians in the area, particularly those of the White Mountain Reservation. Originally known as Camp Ord, then Camp Mogollon, Camp Thomas, Camp Apache, and designated Fort Apache in 1879. In 1871 General George Crook organized his Indian scouts, a tactical innovation that was successful, though never approved by General Nelson Miles who succeeded Crook in the area. The fort has a long history of turmoil, bad living conditions, friction with civil and military authorities and Indians, and corruption by Indian agents. Today the Fort Apache Indian Reservation comprises 2,600 square miles, with headquarters at Whiteriver. Many buildings remain. Lt. Corydon Cooley, chief of scouts under Gen. Crook and responsible for naming Show Low, is buried in the old military cemetery at the post.

Fort Apache Cultural Center has Indian, pioneer and military relics.

FORT BOWIE NATIONAL HISTORIC SITE, Cochise County. On secondary road from I-10 ca. 13 miles S. of Bowie. The fort, in the Chiricahua Mountains near the eastern entrance of Apache Pass, is one of the most colorful in Arizona's history. It was the red hot center for military actions against the Chiricahua Indians who were masters of guerrilla tactics and of defense. Indians, Spanish and other early travelers had used Apache Pass for centuries before the San Antonio-San Diego mail route arrived here in 1857. The next year the Butterfield Overland Mail built a relay station west of the spring near the future site of the fort.

In February of 1861, Lt. George Bascom tried to arrest Cochise in a misunderstanding that had violent consequences and became known as "The Bascom Affair" in the history of the Old West. It began when John Ward, a rancher in the Sonoita Valley who had a stepson named Mickey Free, beat the boy so badly that Free ran away. Ward, though a drunkard, convinced authorities that Cochise had stolen the boy and some cattle. Lt. Bascom with 54 soldiers set out to retrieve Ward's losses. A fight ensued when Cochise was confronted and denied any knowledge of the matter. Though the chief escaped, several Apaches were seized and Cochise wasted little time in retaliation. He attacked the wagon train entering Apache Pass that evening, and on the following morning with both Chiricahua and Coyotero Apaches behind him, attacked the Butterfield station. Both sides had hostages which were the luckless victims of the battle and did not live to be exchanged or freed. (But Mickey Free became a scout for Gen. George Crook). Because of this unfortunate affair, Cochise began a long and expensive war with Arizona Americans. The Civil War was just beginning; troops were being withdrawn and settlers were in great peril. When Confederate forces arrived in the summer of 1861, they soon learned that Cochise's men would just as soon attack a gray uniform as a blue one.

It took Gen. James H. Carleton's California Volunteers to drive the Confederates from Arizona territory, but the Apache menace remained. In July 1862, some 500 Chiricahua and Gila Indians, under Cochise and Mangas Coloradas, ambushed a detachment of the California soldiers in the pass. The troops used the first artillery the Indians had seen. There was some justification for the complaint Cochise later made in reminiscing with one of the victors, Lt. Albert Fountain: "You never would have whipped us if you had not shot wagons at us."

Stabilized adobe walls mark the Fort site. The National Park Service has done extensive restoration and set up an interpretive program for the Fort's history which continued active throughout the Indian Wars.

FORT BRECKINRIDGE, Old Camp Grant, Pinal County. E. of State 77, ca. 10 miles N. of Mammoth. A confusion of names applies to this post which was probably established in May, 1860, though some sources claim an earlier date. It has been known variously as Fort Aravaipa, Fort Stanford, and Camp Grant (also Old Camp Grant). Situated on the north side of Aravaipa Creek at junction with the San Pedro River, the fort was set up to protect the emigrant route across southern Arizona from the ever-present Apache threat. Mosquitoes were an almost equal menace, bringing malaria to such an extent the post was abandoned early in the 1870s.

A horrendous raid, known as the Camp Grant Massacre, took place in 1871 when a group of Tucson citizens with a number of Papago Indians slaughtered about 100 Aravaipa Apaches near the camp. Their stated excuse was that the Apaches had raided cattle ranches near Tucson. Women, children and elderly men comprised the majority of casualties, and those children who survived were taken as slaves. A marker on State 77 is adjacent to camp ruins.

FORT BUCHANAN, Santa Cruz County. Just W. of State 82, about 1 mi. W. of Sonoita. The first military post established by the U.S. in territory acquired by the Gadsden Purchase. Located on the Sonoita River, it was intended to control Apaches and protect travelers. Originally called Camp Moore, designated Fort Buchanan in 1857 for the president, it was in an unhealthful spot and was poorly constructed. It was burned in midsummer, 1861, as Confederate forces invaded Arizona. When Brig. Gen. James Carleton retook the site which had been occupied briefly by the southerners, he raised the U.S. flag but did not regarrison the post. In 1868 Camp Crittenden was established nearby. As a footnote to its lacklustre history, the expedition Lt. George Bascom led against Cochise at Apache Pass to touch off the Apache Wars was organized here.

FORT DEFIANCE, Apache County. State 7. 5 miles N. of Window Rock, in the Navajo Indian Reservation. The first military post established in present Arizona (1851) was named by the soldiers sent to build the post "in defiance of and to the Navajo." Several treaties with the Indians had failed. In April of 1860 1,000 Navajos attacked the fort but were driven off. In 1868 the fort became the Navajo Indian Agency. Window Rock today is the Navajo Area Office. The site is at the mouth of Canyon Bonito, where sheer walls rise some 400 feet high. A Navajo school and hospital occupy the original grounds but fort outlines still are visible.

FORT GRANT, Graham County. State 366. New Camp Grant was established on the route taken by Apaches fleeing into Mexico from the San Carlos Reservation. Photographs of the First Infantry band in 1882 and of officers and wives on the ample porch of a Victorian manse-style quarters in 1885 show that it was largely a peacetime post. The garrison was withdrawn in 1898 to participate in the Spanish-American War. Modern construction has destroyed a large part of the old site. A swimming pool takes up much of the onetime parade ground.

FORT HUACHUCA, Cochise County. State 90. Entrance to fort at the town of Sierra Vista. Founded by the U.S. cavalry on Lincoln's birthday in 1877, Huachuca was one of the last important military posts established to protect the settlers against Apache attack. It saw little activity after Geronimo's surrender. The military reservation comprises 113,000 acres, and is now the headquarters of the U.S. Army Communications Command.

Museum, Bldg. 41401, Boyd and Grierson Aves., just W. of Sierra Vista, or at N. gate in Huachuca City.

FORT LOWELL, Pima County. Craycroft Rd. 7 miles NE of downtown Tucson. The fort was originally located in the city where it was moved several times. The Santa Rita Hotel in recent years has occupied the original site. It was established May 20, 1862, by Lt. Col. Joseph R. West, 1st California Infantry, and was a supply depot for southern Arizona. Later it was a base for operations against the Apaches. In 1873 it was the base for General Nelson Miles' final campaign against Geronimo. The post was named for Brig. Gen. Charles R. Lowell, wounded fatally at Cedar Creek, Va., in October, 1864. Extensive remaining walls have been stabilized; buildings have been reconstructed.

FORT McDOWELL, Maricopa County. 4 miles N. of State 87. Founded by California Volunteers in 1865 on the Verde River above its junction with the Salt River, the fort was an isolated post, but a base in General George Crook's Tonto Basin campaign. Originally Camp Verde, it was designated Fort McDowell in 1879, honoring Maj. Gen. Irvin McDowell, commanding the department. McDowell at one point during the Civil War had almost as much trouble with the government as Gen. Crook had after Geronimo reneged on his first surrender and fled back to Sonora. McDowell was severely criticized for his performance at 2nd Bull Run and relieved of command, but he was exonerated by the court of inquiry he demanded be held.

The fort became the agency for the Yavapai and some of the Pimas in 1890. Wassaja, a famous Mojave Apache who became a successful doctor in the east, is buried here. Wassaja was captured by the Pimas when he was six. An itinerant photographer, Charles Gentile, paid $30 for him, but when Gentile returned home to Chicago he found himself out of business because of the Great Fire. He left Wassaja with friends in New York and promised to return for him. When the money Gentile had left ran out, the Indian boy was put in an orphanage. Eventually he was taken into the home of a Chicago minister, enrolled in Illinois University at 14, was graduated at 17, and had a wealthy practice until he became ill. He then returned to Fort McDowell and lived in a brush hut, refusing all medical aid until his death. He was buried with Masonic services. His gravestone reads: WASSAJA CARLOS MONTEZUMA M.D. MOHAVE APACHE INDIAN.

FORT MASON, Santa Cruz County. State 93. N. of Nogales, at Calabasas on the Santa Cruz River. 13 miles S. of Tubac. This Fort was an important post, replacing the one at Tubac, on the main route to Guaymas and other Mexican settlements. Established August 21, 1865, never officially designated a fort, it became Camp McKee on September 6, 1866 but was soon shifted to Tubac.

FORT THOMAS, Graham County. US 70. Established in August, 1876, just south of the Gila River on the site of present town of Geronimo, the post was moved two years later to the site of present town of Fort Thomas. It was set up in connection with the removal of the Chiricahua Apaches to the San Carlos Reservation and to replace Camp Goodwin. Designated a fort in 1881, it was named for Brig. Gen. Lorenzo Thomas, who had fought in the Seminole, Mexican and Civil Wars.

FORT WHIPPLE, Yavapai County. US 89, State 69, E. of Prescott. The central location made this post important in the Apache Wars. It served as headquarters for department commanders Crook and Stoneman. As Camp Whipple, the post was originally established about 24 miles N. of Prescott at Del Rio Springs. Relocated on the bank of Granite Creek in 1864, it served as protection for the newly opened gold-mining district. It has been variously known as Camp Clark, Camp and Fort Whipple, Whipple Depot, Prescott Barracks and Whipple Barracks, as parts of the post were combined or relocated. It is now a Veterans' Administration Hospital. Site of the original stockade is marked.

GANADO, Apache County. State 264. Originally known as Pueblo Colorado, the town was renamed for an Indian chief called Ganado Mucho. Ganado is Spanish for herds.

Hubbell Trading Post National Historic Site, 1 mile W. on State 264, is still active. It was established in the 1870s, although the present post was built in 1885. John Lorenzo Hubbell is a true Western hero (as Wyatt Earp and others are not). Called the "King of Northern Arizona," he was the son of a Connecticut Yankee who had married into a New Mexican family of Spanish descent. Hubbell was born in Pajarito, N.M., in 1853. In his travels he learned the ways and language of the Navajo and became their teacher and friend. He eventually owned 14 trading posts, a wholesale house in Winslow, Ariz., and a stage and freight line. But he remained a genuine help to the Navajo all of his life, translating their letters, settling disputes, and trying to explain the ever-changing, often baffling and unfair government policy. He is buried on Hubbell Hill, overlooking the trading post, in a small cemetery that also has the graves of his family and his close friend, Many Horses, a Navajo. The stone post appears much as it did in Hubbell's day. Guided tours available.

GENERAL SPRINGS, Coconino County. On Mogollon Rim Rd. in Coconino National Forest. Here in July 1882, Capt. Adna R. Chaffee with men of the 6th Cavalry from Fort Whipple fought White Mountain Apaches under Nantiatish. The Indians, still aroused by the killing of their medicine man Nakaidoklini in the Battle of Cibecue Creek the previous year, had raided the San Carlos Agency and settlements in the Tonto Basin, and had evaded 14 cavalry troops from various forts until this confrontation. A stone monument at the southern edge of the canyon gives details of the battle. There is an explanatory marker also at General Springs.

GERONIMO, Graham County. US 70. Camp Goodwin, the first army post in the upper Gila Valley, was established in 1864 2 miles E. of the present site of Geronimo on Goodwin Wash near the Gila River in Tularosa Valley. Though located on a crossroads of military and wagon roads, it was abandoned in 1871 because malaria was rampant as mosquitoes bred in the nearby marshes. The Apache chief for whom the town was named lived a few miles west of here for a number of years as a reluctant but peaceful farmer.

GILA BEND, Maricopa County. US 80, I-8.

Painted Rocks State Historic Park, 8 miles W. on I-8, then 12 miles N. on Painted Rocks road. Self-guiding tour for Indian petroglyph writings.

Gila Bend Indian Reservation Museum has fine silver among craftsmanship displays.

Fortaleza, on Reservation, is an excavated pre-Columbian ruin consisting of a village of about 50 stone houses. It was constructed about the 14th century, occupied by Hohokam Indians. The Fortaleza is located on one of six bluffs; starting from the south, the fifth escarpment sloping toward the west in a line perpendicular to the Gila River.

Gatlin Site, 3 miles N. of town, a national historic landmark which was a ceremonial platform of the Hohokams. The mound, cremation area and ball court are visible.

GLEN CANYON NATIONAL RECREATION AREA, Coconino County. US 89. The area extends into Utah and surrounds Lake Powell. The second largest dam in the U. S. impounds the 186 mile-long lake. A Visitor Center, adjacent to US 89 and Glen Canyon Bridge, has exhibits which include several pertaining to the history of the area. Self-guiding tour.

GLOBE, Gila County. US 60. Legend is that the town was named for a globe-shaped piece of almost pure silver with surface markings that resembled continents. Besh-ba-Gowah, the Apache name for the area, means Place of Metal. Silver brought the first settlers, but copper sustained them. The Old Dominion copper mine is no longer in operation; others still are working, however.

The silver discovery first brought pioneers onto the San Carlos Reservation, which the soldiers of the area called Hell's Forty Acres. Typically, white Americans took back the 12-mile strip which contained silver, although the land had been set aside for the Apaches. Globe is the eastern end of the Apache Trail.

Besh-ba-Gowah Ruin, 1½ mi. S. on S. Broad St., was inhabited by Salado Indians ca. 1225–1400. Partially excavated.

Gila County Archaeological Museum, N. Broad St., has artifacts from the Besh-ba-Gowah ruins.

Old Dominion Mine and Smelter Ruins, 1 mile N. on US 60, 70.

Gila County Courthouse, S. Broad St. between W. Cedar and W. Oak. The banisters of stairways are sheeted with copper from the Old Dominion.

Hunt House, 548 East St., was the home of George W. P. Hunt, a governor for 7 terms. He arrived in Globe driving a burro and worked in a Chinese restaurant as well as a mine to get started.

Globe Cemetery, S. end of Hackney Ave., has a memorial shaft at the grave of Al Sieber, chief of scouts at the San Carlos Reservation, an invaluable aid to Generals Crook and Miles. Lt. Britton Davis, who served in the Apache Wars, wrote of Sieber: "He was in constant danger of assassination, as many of the Indians had personal grudges against him; but he went about his work as though all the world were his friends. Apache Kid shot him and caused him the loss of a leg. . . ." Sieber survived the Apache campaigns and the Apache Kid to die in an odd accident. He was killed by a falling boulder while supervising Indian labor in the building of Roosevelt Dam in 1907. The Arizona legislature provided the monument at his grave; another, at the site of his death, was erected by his fellow-employees at the dam. A biographer, Dan L. Thrapp, footnotes the possi-

An ancient Hopi village in northeastern Arizona
(Arizona Office of Tourism)

bility that the Indians had the last move in their long war with Sieber: "I have been told, by a border adventurer, that the Apaches *pushed* the rock down on Sieber. The informant said he was told this by the Indians themselves during a drinking bout at a later date." Thrapp found no supportive evidence.

El Capitan Pass, S. on State 77. The pass was used by Kearny's Army of the West in their march to California in 1846. Kit Carson led them around the canyon on the Gila River where Coolidge Dam is today. Lt. Emory, of the expedition, called it "Carson's Old Trail," which led to "Disappointment Creek" (no grass and very little water). This now is Dripping Springs Creek, also aptly named.

Coolidge Dam, SW. of Globe on State 170. The dam did not exist, of course, in the Old West but John V. Young recalling its dedication in *The New York Times* in 1965, wrote in true Western fashion: ". . . If the usually silent Mr. Coolidge (who was on hand) said anything, nobody remembers what it was. But the master of ceremonies was Will Rogers. . . . He looked out over the sea of grass that waved where San Carlos Lake was supposed to be filling up, and remarked: 'If that was my lake, I'd mow it.' "

GRAND CANYON NATIONAL PARK, Coconino County. US 180, State 64. People of the Desert Culture moved into the canyon more than 3,000 years ago. By the time of the Spanish explorations, the Havasupai occupied the area. Garcia Lopez de Cardenas, a member of the 1540 Coronado expedition, was selected to lead a party from Cibola to find a river the Hopis had talked of and thereby became the first white man to see the Grand Canyon of the Colorado River. Hernando de Alarcon had discovered the river itself, some months earlier at a point lower down its course. Cardenas and others who followed thought it was a useless piece of real estate. Lt. Joseph Ives, in 1857, called it a "profitless locality." Not so today; visitors will find spring and fall seasons are slightly less crowded than summer, when there are frequent traffic jams and filled campgrounds. The North Rim is open from mid-May to mid-October. The Visitor Center, on South Rim, eastern area of Grand Canyon Village, has information, maps and a museum.

HARRISBURG, Yuma County. 5 miles SE of Salome (US 60). Founded in 1886 by Capt. Charles Harris, a Civil War veteran, and Arizona's Territorial Governor Frederick A. Tritle, a Pennsylvanian. The old cemetery has a monument in memory of pioneers massacred enroute to the California Gold Rush. The memorial is a white quartz rock pile with a silhouette of a covered wagon. Harrisburg is now a ghost town.

HOLBROOK, Navajo County. I-40, State 77. Named for H. R. Holbrook, first engineer of the Atlantic & Pacific Railroad (now Santa Fe). The once tough cowtown is now headquarters for the Sitgreaves National Forest. (See Show Low.)

The Aztec Land and Cattle Co., known as the Hashknife Posse, drove cattle here from Texas, shot out town lights and cut up generally, but some Hashknifers were known to be killers. The old Apache Telephone Office has interesting framed documents including invitations to a hanging: "You are hereby cordially invited to attend the hanging of one George Smiley, Murderer. His soul will be swung into eternity on Dec. 8, 1899, at 2 o'clock P.M. sharp. Latest improved methods in the art of strangulation will be employed and everything possible will be done to make the proceedings cheerful and the execution a success." So read the first announcement, which was picked up by the Associated Press and reached the attention of no less than President McKinley who—spurred by the public outcry—ordered the sheriff to cut the comedy and delay the execution.

The sheriff then tacked up a second announcement: "The said George Smiley will be executed on Jan. 8, 1900 at 2 o'clock P.M. You are expected to deport yourself in a respectful manner and any 'flippant' or 'unseemly' language on your part will not be allowed."

A typical shoot-out occurred at the Blevins house on Central St. in September 1887 when Sheriff Commodore Owens, one of the fastest gunfighters in the West, with witnesses—though nobody he ever aimed at—to prove it, killed Andy Cooper who was resisting arrest at the home of his parents. Andy was a Blevins who had changed his name because he was wanted for murder in Texas. As Cooper he had led a gang that shot John Tewksbury and William Jacobs—as part of the Pleasant Valley War. (See Young.)

HOOVER DAM, Mohave County. US 95. The Exhibit Building at W. end of the dam has a topographical model of the entire river basin. The Colorado River was of vast importance in the Old West; parts of it still look much the same as in the 17th to 19th centuries. The dam, 726 feet high, is one of the highest in the world. Lake Mead, impounded by Hoover Dam, extends some 115 navigable miles through the Colorado River canyons.

JEROME HISTORICAL DISTRICT, Yavapai County. US 89A. The largest ghost town in Arizona is a lively tourist attraction. In the Verde Valley, its old buildings still cling to the slopes of Mingus Mountain. A sign at "city limits" reads: "POPULATION, 15,000, 10,000, 5,000, 1,000 and Ghost City" with all but the last crossed out.

Douglas Memorial Mining Museum, in Jerome State Historic Park, occupies the old mansion of James S. Douglas, an early mining executive and father of Lewis W. Douglas, former Ambassador to the Court of St. James. Douglas family memorabilia, and mining exhibits are featured. There are self-guiding tours of an old mining complex in the Park.

KINISHBA PUEBLO RUINS, Gila County. 15 miles W. of Whiteriver on State 73 and secondary road. The national historic landmark can be viewed through a barbed wire fence. One of the largest ruins in the southwest, it once housed up to 1,000 Indians, a mixture of the Mogollon and Anasazi. The fence is both for visitor safety and for protection of the ruins. There are plans for restoration and a museum. The partly restored pueblo was built ca. 1200–1350.

KINLICHEE TRIBAL PARK, Apache County. W. from Window Rock 22 miles on State 264 (Navajo 3) to Cross Canyon Trading Post, then 2½ miles N. on dirt road. The Anasazi Indians lived here for 500 years. Ruins are preserved by the Navajo. The oldest dwelling is a pit house believed to date from A.D. 800. A self-guided trail is provided. One ruin has been reconstructed.

KIRKLAND, Yavapai County. State 96, SW of Prescott. 4 miles NW of Kirkland Junction on US 89. William H. Kirkland arrived here in 1856. His marriage in Tucson in 1860 was claimed to be the first wedding of white Americans in the territory, but Charles Poston, sometimes known as the "Father of Arizona," officiated at a ceremony in Tubac in February (Valentine's Day, no less) 1858 which was probably the *official* first. No historians seem to dispute that the first paleface baby on record was a male born on the banks of the Gila River to a Mrs. Howard who was part of Charles E. Pancoasts's immigrant party. The date was October 12, 1849. The child's name: Gila Howard.

In Skull Valley, due north, a battle occurred in 1864 between soldiers and the Mohave and Tonto Apaches. The Americans left without burying the dead. Bones and skulls were found bleaching in the valley by emigrants, and a scouting party later gave these a proper burial.

KITT PEAK NATIONAL OBSERVATORY, Pima County. State 386, ca. 45 miles SW of Tucson. The curvesome road which climbs to the summit of the 6,875-foot peak gives an Indian's (or an eagle's) eyeview of what once was Apacheland. Papago Indians who held the mountain sacred had to agree to let scientists establish their observatory on Indian land.

LA PAZ, Yuma County. 6 miles N. of Ehrenberg. In the Colorado River Indian Tribe Reservation. This ghost town was once the county seat and had missed becoming the capital of Arizona Territory by only two votes. Pauline (Paulino) Weaver, noted scout, discovered placer gold near the Colorado River in 1862. La Paz became a boom town. Ca. $8 million was mined before the area was played out.

During its busiest days La Paz was partially a tent city, filled with scoundrels, schemers, and drifters who vaguely hoped to get rich with no work, and was an active port on the river. Because of Indian troubles gold was shipped to Mexico, a drain of resource that was quickly noticed in Washington and helped to hasten the creating of the Territory. Soldiers were dispatched to La Paz to guard gold shipments east. In 1870 the Colorado shifted course, leaving La Paz stranded two miles inland. Now a town of mounds where adobe houses and buildings once stood, the area is still of historical interest and is included in the National Register of Historic Places. The old well at the southern end of the reservation, is now protected from vandals.

McMILLENVILLE, Gila County. 18 miles NE of Globe on US 60, State 77. The Stonewall Jackson mine was discovered by accident either in 1874 or in 1876. The story is that Charles McMillen, after a night of drinking, picked a shady spot to sleep while his prospector companion, Dory Harris, stayed awake and drove a pick into nearby rock, breaking off a chunk that contained silver. They staked a claim and the news spread as usual bringing hundreds of silver-seekers. A shanty town was set up, followed by saloons, dance halls, casinos and killings. In the 1880s a five-stamp mill was replaced by a twenty-stamp. A few ruins remain.

Arizona historian Bert Fireman followed the sad story of the careless McMillen and his friend Harris. After taking out $60,000 in ore they sold the mine for $160,000. (It yielded ca. $2 million in silver.) In a few months McMillen had died from rich living and drink. Harris lost his money more slowly but just as irretrievably, became a dishwasher, joined the Salvation Army, and married one of the bonneted girls.

In 1882 a band of Coyotero-Apaches attacked McMillenville; soldiers from Fort McDowell gave chase, killed at least 25 Indians, and the uprising was over.

McNARY, Apache County. State 260. In the Fort Apache Indian Reservation.

White Mountain Scenic Railroad, E. on State 73. A 6-hour, 40-mile trip on a steam train through the reservation, with picnic lunch on Big Cienaga Mountain.

Cooley Mountain, State 73 near Indian Pine, was named for Corydon E. Cooley, guide, scout and Indian interpreter, who served in the U.S. army in the Apache wars but married an Apache girl and was the cofounder of Show Low. Cooley's Cienaga Ranch became the town of McNary. Cooley is buried at Fort Apache.

MARICOPA WELLS, Pinal County. N. of Maricopa on unmarked road in Maricopa Indian Reservation, on the Santa Cruz River. This was a watering place and crossroads for early traffic before the arrival of the railroad. It had the last available water for travelers going west until they reached the big bend of the Gila River. The stage station of the San Antonio to San Diego Line opened here in 1857. The company was known as the Jackass Line because part of the route had to be traversed by mule back.

An ad in the *San Francisco Herald* in the fall of 1858 read in part: "Passengers and Express matter forwarded in NEW COACHES, drawn by six mules over the entire length of our Line, excepting from San Diego to Fort Yuma, a distance of 180 miles, which we cross on mule back. Passengers are Ticketed from San Diego to:

Fort Yuma,	Maricopa Wells,
Tucson,	La Mesilla,
Fort Fillmore,	El Paso,
Fort Bliss,	Fort Davis
Fort Lawson,	Fort Lancaster
Fort Hudson	Fort Clark and

San Antonio, Texas.

"The Coaches of our Line leave Semi-monthly from each end, on the 9th and 24th of each month, at SIX O'CLOCK A.M.

"An ARMED ESCORT travels through the Indian Country with each mail train, for the protection of Mails and Passengers. . . . Each passenger is allowed thirty pounds of personal baggage, exclusive of blanket and arms."

MESA, Maricopa County. US 60, 70.

Mormon Temple, 525 E. Main St., has a Visitor Center just north of the Temple; history, films, guided tours. The town was settled by the Mormons. The Hohokam Canals were used until modern times.

METEOR CRATER, Coconino County. S. of US 66, 180. Ca. 12 miles W. of Winslow. It's safe to say the meteor hit Arizona territory thousands of years ago, although the exact number ranges in argument from 2,000 to 50,000. It probably displaced about 6 million tons of ground, left a hole 600 feet deep and nearly a mile wide.

MIAMI, Gila County. US 60, 70. From the highway the extensive works of copper mining can be seen. Mountains have been gouged out to smelt copper; new foothills have been piled up from the residue of mining. Bloody Tanks Wash runs through the town. The canal is now arched by bridges. Bloody Tanks was an Indian water hole that got its name from the 24 Apaches killed in January of 1864 when volunteers led by King S. Woolsey, a rancher from the Agua Fria River area, took reprisal for raids upon Yavapai County settlers.

Bert Fireman, Arizona newspaperman and historian, writes that the 28 volunteers were joined by a group of friendly Maricopa and Pima Indians led by the Maricopa chief, Juan Chivari. The Yavapai and Tonto Apaches who had been raiding local ranches were persuaded to hold a conference at a water tank now covered by the highway. The peace talk seemed to get nowhere and both sides had come to the meeting secretly armed in violation of agreements. At a signal from Woolsey, the volunteers attacked. Blood ran into the water tank as the battle progressed. One white man was killed. There have been many stories of white Americans feeding poison to the red men. One of them begins here. Fireman states: "The raid is sometimes called the Pinole Treaty, due to the story (denied by Woolsey and highly unlikely) that he tried to feed the Indians poisoned pinole (parched corn)."

MONTEZUMA CASTLE NATIONAL MONUMENT, Yavapai County. I-17. 40 miles S. of Flagstaff. 20 miles SE of Cottonwood, off State 79.

Visitor Center, E. of highway. The 5-story, 20-room structure was built by Indians more than 500 years ago. A self-guiding trail offers a good view of the monument and of other pueblo ruins. Dioramas with audio-tape on the footpaths to the Castle explain life here 600 years ago.

Montezuma Well, 7 miles NW, is a limestone sinkhole with a lake about 50 to 60 feet deep, 400 feet wide. It is fed by a spring which yields 1½ million gallons of water daily.

MONUMENT VALLEY NAVAJO TRIBAL PARK, Navajo County. US 163.

Visitor Center, 4 miles SE of highway. There are self-guiding tours to view the many monoliths of red sandstone, or jeep trips through the valley are available from Kayenta. Descendants of the early Indian inhabitants still dress colorfully and maintain many ancient tribal customs.

MOWRY, Santa Cruz County. E. of State 82. The Patagonia Mine was discovered by Mexicans in 1858, and was purchased by Lt. Sylvester Mowry two years later when he was stationed at Fort Crittenden. In 1862 Mowry was arrested on the charge of selling lead to the Confederates for ammunition. He was held in the Yuma Territorial Prison for 4 months. When released he went to England looking for financial backing to continue his operations at the mine he had renamed for himself. He died abroad. During the war years Apaches on raids drove out most of the settlers in the region and destroyed the smelter. Later new owners put the mine back in operation.

Mowry is now a ghost town with adobe ruins and a cemetery.

NAVAJO, Apache County. US 66. A marker on the south side of highway where the road turns off to Navajo Springs locates the site where the territorial officers took the oath of office, December 29, 1863. Gov. John N. Goodwin and others arrived from the East in a snowstorm, parked their wagons, raised a flag on an improvised flagpole, had champagne, speeches and prayers and were officially in office. They chose a temporary site safely in northern Arizona as the southern part had Confederate leanings. Their pay did not begin until they were within the territorial borders. Lt. Col. J. Francisco Chaves of the First New Mexico Cavalry had led them to Navajo Springs where there was water for the horses and 66 mules. (Also see Camp Whipple.)

NAVAJO AND HOPI INDIAN RESERVATIONS, Coconino and Navajo Counties. The Reservation occupies about 11,500,000 acres of the northeast corner of Arizona with 2,500,000 acres in New Mexico, 1,-500,000 acres in Utah. About 69,000 Navajos live in Arizona.

Kit Carson led the march of the Navajos to Bosque Redondo in New Mexico during the Civil War when it was hoped the geographical change and confinement would help to control their predatory ways. In 1868 they were returned to their native area. The Hopi Reservation is within the Navajo. The Hopi Indians are of pueblo Shoshone origin and were traditional enemies of the Navajo but the two get along peacefully today. Most roads are passable, some are excellent; in bad weather local inquiries should be made.

NAVAJO NATIONAL MONUMENT, Navajo County. From Tuba City, 56 miles NE on US 160, then 9 miles NW on paved road. Or 30 miles SW of Kayenta on State 64, N. on paved road. Three small, separate areas comprise 600 acres of the Monument which is on the Navajo Indian Reservation. A 13th-century pueblo ruin is in each site. The Visitor Center is near Betatakin. Slide program gives Anasazi history. Guided tours daily in summer. Betatakin also may be seen from the Sandal Trail overlook on a self-guiding trail. (Be-TAH-tah-kin means "ledge house" in Navajo.) It is a village of some 135 rooms built in a vast cave. *Keet Seel* ("broken pottery") can be reached by an 8-mile trip down canyon and along stream, a full day's journey. (Horseback trips must be arranged a day in advance.)

Inscription House, 30 miles W., has "1661" carved on a plastered wall. It is not always open to public.

NOGALES, Santa Cruz County. US 89.

Pena Blanca Lake and Recreation Area, 18 miles W. on US 89 and Ruby Rd., is in the Coronado Forest.

Pete Kitchen Museum, 5 miles N. on US 89. On the Santa Cruz River, rancher Pete Kitchen established his home in 1854. The ranchhouse served as a fort and refuge for travelers and settlers. The original adobe is still standing, as well as the greater house Kitchen built as he prospered. Now a museum.

OATMAN-GOLDROAD MINING DISTRICT, Mohave County. On old US 66 between Kingman and Topock, in the foothills of the Black Mountains. The mine here was not developed until the turn of the century but the town allegedly was named for Olive Oatman, the unfortunate tattooed girl who was born too soon for plastic surgery.

The Oatmans were part of a wagon train headed for California in January 1850 when they decided to push ahead of their fellow travelers who had stopped to camp at the Pima Villages. In mid-March, camped on the banks of the Gila, the Oatmans were attacked by Yavapai Indians who killed Oatman, his wife and three youngest children. Lorenzo was clubbed and thrown over a cliff. Olive, age twelve, and Mary, age eight, were taken captive. Lorenzo had not been killed but was picked up by a wagon train and eventually arrived in Los Angeles where he tried to get help in rescuing his sisters. The girls were traded to the Mohaves. Mary died but Olive survived the traditional Mohave tattooing of her chin and the slave labor. A carpenter at Fort Yuma in 1856 heard tales of the white captive and managed to trick the Indians into believing a large party of Americans was coming to rescue her and punish her captors. A Yuma Indian brought the girl to the fort. She was eventually reunited with Lorenzo and moved to Oregon.

ORAIBI, Navajo County. State 264. (Oh-RYE-bee). The oldest and once largest of the Hopi Indian pueblos has been inhabited continuously since 1300. The site consists of seven house rows with most houses three to four stories high. There are 13 kivas and a number of enclosed courts. The Hopi culture is the least changed of any North American tribe. Pedro de Tovar was here in 1540. In July 1776, when important matters were being resolved in the east, Father Francisco Tomas Garces, who replaced Father Kino at San Xavier del Bac, was visiting, and writing of his travels here to the Franciscans in New Mexico. A national historic landmark, privately maintained.

ORGAN PIPE CACTUS NATIONAL MONUMENT, Pima County. State 85. Arizona's largest national monument comprises 516 square miles of Sonoran desert area on the border of Mexico. The Ajo-Sonoyta-Rocky Point Rd. loops Ajo Mountain and covers 21 miles; the Puerto Blanco Dr. covers 51 miles. Shorter scenic drives lead into the desert.

Visitor Center, 17 mi. S. of north entrance to monument.

PAGE, Coconino County. US 89, State 98. The town is at the E. end of Glen Canyon Dam on the Colorado River. Lake Powell, formed by the dam, is 186 miles long. The lake is named for John Wesley Powell, a geologist and surveyor, who led one of the most important expeditions in the 19th century, down the Colorado.

John Wesley Powell Memorial Museum, 6 N. 7th St. Powell memorabilia, Indian artifacts, and a film.

PARKER, Yuma County. State 95.

Colorado River Indian Tribes Museum and Library, 2nd Ave. at Mohave Rd. Exhibits pertain to the history of the four Colorado River tribes. The Colorado River Indian Tribes Reservation comprises more than 268,000 acres, extending to California.

Buckskin Mountain State Park is 11 mi. N. on State 95.

PAYSON, Gila County. State 87, 260. The town was founded in 1886. It is a fine starting point for a scenic drive along the Mogollon Rim. It was a popular cowtown and was named for Louis Edwin Payson, a Representative from Illinois, who never saw it. The area had been platted by John H. Wise, Surveyor General, who named it for the man responsible for his appointment to office. During the Indian wars a fort was established here for protection against Apaches. The area has been used for Western movie backgrounds.

Zane Grey's Cabin, 17 miles NE off State 260, in the Tonto National Forest. Grey wrote *To the Last Man* here; it is the story of the Pleasant Valley War (which see).

Tonto Natural Bridge, 12 miles N. on State 87, in the Tonto National Forest, is 128 to 150 feet above the creek. The opening beneath the bridge is 150 feet wide and 400 feet long. Caves in canyon walls have traces of prehistoric life.

PETRIFIED FOREST NATIONAL PARK, Navajo and Apache Counties. N. entrance on US 66, I-40, S. entrance on US 180.

Orientation Building, at entrance from US 66, I-40. Information about the park which comprises 94,161 acres.

Museum, in Rainbow Forest Visitor Center, off US 180, has exhibits that show sections of petrified wood, fossils, crystals.

Note: no souvenirs may be taken. Nearby curio shops have wood found in areas outside the national park. Throughout the area will be found petroglyphs carved in sandstone by prehistoric Pueblo Indians. These are treasured. No modern visitors should carve anything.

PHOENIX, Maricopa County. I-17, I-10.

Chamber of Commerce, 805 N. 2nd St., has free literature pertaining to the history of and many recreational facilities in the city.

State Capitol, W. Washington St. & 17th Ave. Museum is on 3rd floor.

Arizona Museum, 1002 W. Van Buren St. at 10 Ave. Pioneer and Indian relics.

Heard Museum of Anthropology and Primitive Arts, 22 E. Monte Vista Rd. Indian exhibits feature Kachina dolls.

Pueblo Grande Museum, 4619 E. Washington, is at the site of a Hohokam ruin, a national historic landmark. The Pueblo Grande Ruin is a large house mound, with four prehistoric irrigation canals visible across the existing canal in the "Park of Four Waters." A ball court is also visible. Trails have explanatory signs. In the museum are materials recovered from the site. The city of Phoenix maintains both the museum and the archaeological site.

Arizona Mineral Museum, 1826 W. McDowell Rd., 2 miles NW on US 60, 89. Mining exhibits and mineral displays.

Arizona History Room, First National Bank Plaza, 1st Ave. & Washington St., has changing exhibits pertaining to local and state history.

Pioneer Arizona Museum, 24 miles N. off I-17 at Pioneer Rd. exit. The 550-acre area includes original and replica pioneer homes, shops, church, schoolhouse, miners' camp.

Desert Botanical Garden, in Papago Park, 8 miles E. on US 60, 80, 89. Entrances at 6400 E. McDowell and 5800 E. Van Buren. Self-guiding walks among plantings from the world's deserts. 150 acres.

Phoenix South Mountain Park, S. end of Central Ave., in the Salt River Mountains. Hieroglyph Canyon in park has ancient pictographs. Park comprises 15,000 acres.

PICACHO PEAK STATE PARK, Pinal County, I-10 at Picacho. Park is 3 miles S. of Friendly Corners. The only Confederate-Federal battle in Arizona occurred in mid-April, 1862, when Lt. Jack Swilling and his Texas troops were attacked by the California cavalry led by Lt. James Barrett. Barrett and two of his men were killed; three were captured. A monument ca. two miles north of the battlefield is dedicated to Captain Sherod Hunter's Arizona Volunteers who were based at Tucson at this time.

PICKET POST MOUNTAIN, Pinal County. S. of US 60, 70, ca. 3 miles W. of Superior. A landmark and lookout point during the Apache Wars. Camp Pinal, garrisoned with 400 cavalry at one point in the conflict, was set up at the head of Stoneman Grade to the east. Ruins of Pinal City are along the creek bank, NE of the mountain.

Pinal Ranch, US 60, 70, between Superior and Miami, the Apache farmers cultivated corn and melons here when they were at least temporarily subdued. In the 1870s the area became the eastern anchor of the Stoneman Grade, a military road built by Gen. George Stoneman to lead to Picket Post Butte in the heart of Apache country. When the Silver King mine was developed a few miles NE in the late 1870s, troops were again brought in to protect settlers on Queen Creek.

Boyce Thompson Southwestern Arboretum, at mountain base, US 60, 3 miles W. of Superior, has an outstanding collection of plants from arid sections of the world, as well as flora native to the high Sonoran Desert. A 20-acre garden.

PIPE SPRING NATIONAL MONUMENT, Mohave County. 14 miles W. of Fredonia on spur off State 389. Mormon pioneers were responsible for the exploration and settlement of the area. A well-preserved fort constructed in 1871 is in the monument area. Jacob Hamblin (see Alpine) led a party here in 1858; his favorable report brought cattlemen. The Mormons held the land until 1875. It is now administered by the National Park Service and comprises 40 acres. Guide services. Cattle-branding demonstrations. Legend has it that Hamblin, an expert rifleman, shot the bottom out of a pipe at 50 paces and thereby gave the place its name. Anson P. Winsor, an English-born Mormon bishop, constructed the Pipe Spring fort of sandstone and heavy logs, beside a fresh-water spring. It came to be known as Winsor's Castle. The fort which has been partially restored has the territory's first telegraph office, which was operated by Mrs. David King Udall in 1871. Her descendants, Stewart L. and Morris K., both served in Congress.

PRESCOTT, Yavapai County. US 89.

First Governor's Mansion and Sharlot Hall Museum. W. Gurley St. Was built for Gov. John Goodwin in 1864, restored in 1927 by Sharlot Hall, poet and historian. Indian and pioneer relics, mining equipment. Also on the grounds is John C. Fremont House, which the Fremonts occupied when he was Territorial Governor. Period furnishings. The ambitious Mrs. Fremont, daughter of Thomas Hart Benton, was miserable in the backwoods of Prescott, as she saw it. The first house in town was a two-room log cabin known as Ft. Misery; it served as courthouse and judge's residence. The grave of Pauline Weaver is also in Pioneer Square, NE corner.

Weaver was a hunter, trapper, scout and guide.

Bucky O'Neill Statue, Courthouse grounds on Gurley St. William O'-Neill was an editor, judge, sheriff, lawyer and fighter. He was killed leading his men up San Juan Hill.

Smoki Museum, Arizona Ave. between E. Willis and Gurley. Many Indian artifacts, arts and handicraft. There is a replica of a Hopi kiva and an outstanding collection of Kachina dolls.

QUARTZSITE, Yuma County. US 60, 70.

Tyson Wells on W. edge of town was an old stage station, a stop between Ehrenberg and Wickenburg. Charles Tyson fortified his adobe buildings and the station was sometimes known as Fort Tyson but was never designated a fort.

Quartzsite Cemetery, US 60 east part of town, has the Hi-Jolly Memorial, erected for Hadji Ali, an Arab camel driver who stayed on after the desert experiment was abandoned during the Civil War.

SACATON, Pinal County. Off State 187, SW of Olberg.

Gila River Indian Reservation in northern Pinal County has the first government school for Indians. It was established for Pimas and Maricopas in 1871. The reservation was the first in Arizona and was established on February 28, 1859. Ira Hayes, Pima Indian Marine, who took part in the flag-raising on Iwo Jima in World War II was born and died here. He is buried at Arlington National Cemetery but the Casa Blanca Indian school has a memorial plaque.

Gila River Arts and Crafts Center has a museum.

SAGUARO NATIONAL MONUMENT, Pima County. N. of US 80. (Sah-WAH-ro). Visitor Center in eastern section with museum. Self-guiding drive.

SALT RIVER CANYON BATTLEFIELD (Skeleton Cave), Maricopa County. In canyon near Horse Mesa Dam. The area is accessible only with guides, by boat from Canyon Lake, or on unimproved road from Horse Mesa.

The Battle of Skull Cave is sometimes called the greatest victory of the army in the Apache Wars. On December 28, 1872, troops under Maj. William H. Brown trapped more than 100 Yavapai Indians in a cave on the north wall of the canyon, in the angle of a sharp turn to the south. After the event, which was known as the Salt Creek Massacre locally, so many differing stories were told that arguments continue to the present. It is certain that the Indians had an excellent hideaway that could only be reached in single file across lava beds. They were probably betrayed by a young warrior who revealed their location to the army. How many Indians were killed has never been determined. To reach the site, hardy adventurers must climb a mountainside, cross a lava bed, and descend from the rim of a gorge by a trail which follows the face of a cliff. A misstep could mean a 1200 foot fall to the river. The cave's ceiling is scarred by carbine bullets and blackened by Indian smoke. I am taking someone else's word for it.

SAN CARLOS INDIAN AGENCY, Gila County. State 170. The original site of the agency was covered by water when Coolidge Dam was built. The tribe, which is governed by its own council, operates a vast cattle ranch these days but times were different when Lt. Britton Davis was stationed at the reservation in the 1880s. He writes extensively of army life under Gen. George Crook in *The Truth About Geronimo* (Yale, 1929) and his memories of San Carlos are both grim and entertaining by turn:

". . . there was an Indian trader's store in a building two hundred yards to the north of the Agency building. The trader was under the control of the Agent if he saw fit to exercise control; which he did not. . . . The trader fixed the prices on what he sold and the Indians could 'take it or leave it.' They were not allowed to leave the Reservation, and thus were at his mercy. . . .

"The Indians had complained to the General of the quality and quantity of beef issued to them. Crawford ordered me to investigate. . . . The beef herd was kept south of the Gila River. The slaughter pen was north of it. Deliveries were made about sunrise. To reach the pen, the beeves had to cross the river. Having had no water since some time the day before, they stopped and filled up just before being weighed. In that hot, dry climate they came on the scales looking like miniature Zeppelins. The Government was paying a pretty stiff price for half a barrel of Gila River water delivered with each beef."

SKELETON CANYON, Cochise County. Ca. 8 miles SE of Apache, on unimproved road, just off US 80. In this area, which was also known as Canon Bonita, Geronimo and Natchez surrendered to General Miles on September 3, 1886, bringing an end to the Apache Wars. Lt. Charles B. Gatewood, who had been a friend to Geronimo, and two Chiricahua Apache scouts met with Geronimo and Natchez, who as the son of Cochise was the hereditary chief of the tribe, in northern Mexico and persuaded them to meet with Miles in Skeleton Canyon. A cairn of rocks, 6-feet high marks the site. A large stone monument on US 80 at Apache also commemorates the occasion.

SUNSET CRATER NATIONAL MONUMENT, Coconino County. 15 miles N. of Flagstaff on US 89. In the 11th century volcanic eruptions built a cone of cinders and ash. Molten lava flowed from cracks in the earth. Homes of Indians were buried. The cone stands about 1,000 feet high. A self-guiding trail at base of crater. Visitor Center open daily except major holidays. Visitors are warned not to leave the roads; cinders are too soft for safety.

TONTO NATIONAL MONUMENT, Gila County. State 88. 3 miles SE of Roosevelt. Monument comprises 1,120 acres. Two of the most accessible cliff dwellings in the south-central area are preserved here. The ruins were occupied in the 14th century by Salado Indians. A foot trail is half a mile long and rises 350 ft. Visitor Center has a museum with artifacts and explanatory displays.

TUBA CITY, Coconino County. US 164, State 264. The town was settled by the Mormons in 1875. Blocks of stone from nearby prehistoric sites were used. Arizona's first woolen mill was located between Tuba City and Moenkapi, a Hopi village (also spelled Moencopi and Moen Copie). This was a stopping place on the road from Lee's Ferry at Paria Crossing and an important trading post. Dinosaur tracks, 3-toed imprints in sandstone are ca. 10 miles W.

TOMBSTONE HISTORIC DISTRICT, Cochise County. US 80.

Tombstone Courthouse State Historical Monument and Museum, Toughnut and 3rd St., on US 80, has much Wyatt Earp memorabilia and town history. The second floor courtroom saw many frontier trials. A reconstructed gallows in a rear courtyard shows how the decision often went.

Office of the Tombstone Epitaph, 5th St. near Allen. Not the first but the oldest continuously published newspaper in Arizona was established by John P. Clum, former Indian agent active in the Apache wars, who opened business in a tent-covered shack on May 1, 1880. Clum wrote: "Every Tombstone needs an epitaph."

Bird Cage Theatre, Allen and 6th St., has original furnishings and a museum.

Wyatt Earp Museum, Toughnut and 5th St. Wyatt Earp, like George Armstrong Custer, has fallen from high heroism in fable and song to more earthly size. Earp's fall is more justified than Custer's who was a fine cavalryman and tactician despite vanity and a fatal error of judgment in his last days. Earp and his brother Virgil were never the monuments of law and order dime novels and Police Gazettes made them out to be. But colorful they were.

O.K. Corral, Allen St. between 3rd and 4th. Restored stagecoach office and stables where the most famous private battle of the Old West took place. Life-size figures may or may not help the visitor to imagine how it must have been here on the afternoon of October 26, 1881, when the Earps and Doc Holliday shot it out with Ike and Bill Clanton, Frank and Tom McLaury (often spelled McLowery) and Billy Claiborne. The McLaurys and Billy Clanton were killed; Holliday and Virgil Earp were wounded. In the countless versions of what actually took place almost the only thing that stays the same is the spelling of Earp's name. The recreated gallery of pioneer photographer Camillas Fry is nearby with original photos of the Earp days and of Geronimo's surrender. Studio is on Fremont between 3rd and 4th.

Wells Fargo Museum and Tombstone General Store, 511 Allen. Life-size figures of the Earps, Geronimo and others, Old West relics.

Tombstone Historama, Schieffelin Hall, Fremont & 4th. Electronic story of Tombstone, in adobe hall which has been restored.

Crystal Palace Saloon, Allen and 5th, restored.

St. Paul's Episcopal Church, 3rd and Safford, is the oldest Protestant church in Arizona.

Rose Tree Inn Museum, Toughnut and 4th St. Very little in Tombstone's early history came up smelling like roses but this is the largest rose bush in the world and blooms in April. The 1880 home has a museum with original furniture, dioramas.

Boothill Graveyard, NW on US 80, has many graves with "reconstructed" markers, touched up since the fame of the burial ground spread. Of note is the grave of Ed Schieffelin, who staked the first claims here in perilous Apache country where scoffers said he would only find his tombstone.

TUBAC, Santa Cruz County. State 93, I-19.

Presidio of San Ignacio de Tubac, Broadway and River Rd. The oldest of three Spanish military outposts in

Arizona was established as a result of the Pima Indian rebellion of 1751. Low mounds mark the walls. Excellent museum, styled after original post. A national historic landmark.

Old Tubac Schoolhouse, a remodeled adobe, first built in 1885, used by community for a town center. A national historic landmark.

Historical marker in town plaza. The five-acre historical monument is rich in genuine displays which pertain to an exciting part of Arizona's history. 300-year-old church vestments, early Spanish weapons and furnishings are exhibited. Captain Juan Bautista de Anza was one of the outstanding early commanders of the fort. In 1774 he led a march to the Presidio of Monterey in California; the following year he helped to found San Francisco. In the 1850s Charles D. Poston, who has been called the "Father of Arizona," organized and led an expedition which developed the Heintzleman Mine, 30 miles away. The community prospered but was frequently attacked by Apaches. In 1859 Ed Cross, editor of the *Weekly Arizonian* fought a well-publicized duel with Sylvester Mowry. Although they chose Burnside rifles as their weapons, each missed several times before they adjourned to a saloon and, according to historian Odie B. Faulk, "broke open a forty-two-gallon barrel of whisky."

TUCSON, Pima County. I-10, I-19.

Arizona State Museum, on University of Arizona campus, at University Blvd. entrance. Extensive exhibits on the culture of the Southwest Indians and state history.

Arizona Historical Society, 949 E. 2nd St. at Park Ave. Exhibits from Spanish times to the present. Excellent library with Western history collections and manuscripts.

Mineralogy Museum, on campus. North Dr. in Geology Bldg., has exhibits of rocks, minerals, gem stones from early times to present.

Old Tucson, in Tucson Mountain Park, 12 miles W. State 86 to Kinney Rd. A replica of the 1860s village which was built as a movie and television background. Arizona-Sonora Desert Museum (which see) is also in the park.

Mission San Xavier Del Bac, 9 miles SW on Mission Rd. in the Papago Indian Reservation, called the "White Dove of the Desert," is probably the most photographed mission in the world and still worth more camera snapping. Father Eusebio Kino established a mission here in 1700. The church was abandoned twice because of Indian hostilities. The present structure was completed in 1797. A national historic landmark.

Charles O. Brown House (The Old Adobe Patio), 40 W. Broadway, is two houses connected by a row of rooms. The Jackson St. part is the older with some rooms probably dating from the 1850s. Brown, a pioneer settler, remodeled part of the structure in 1868.

John C. Fremont House (Casa de Gobernador), 151 S. Granada is a Territorial Government Museum. Period furnishings.

Edward Nye Fish House, 208 N. Main, was built in 1868 and was a social center of the city. Fish was a merchant and politician.

Chamber of Commerce, 420 W. Congress, has brochures on sight-seeing and current events.

TUMACACORI NATIONAL MONUMENT, Santa Cruz County. I-19. The mission of San Jose de Tumacacori (Pima for "carved peak") was founded by the Jesuits in the 17th century. The present church was built in the early 1800s by the Franciscans. It has been stabilized by the National Park Service. Museum with excellent dioramas.

TUZIGOOT NATIONAL MONUMENT, Yavapai County. US 89A. The pueblo was occupied ca. 1100 to 1450. A museum contains material excavated from the site. The monument comprises nearly 43 acres. An easy trail goes through the terraced ruin.

WALNUT CANYON NATIONAL MONUMENT, Coconino County. US 66. More than 300 prehistoric cliff dwellings are on the monument. They were occupied by the Sinagua Indians ca. 1120–1250. An observation building is at the canyon rim, also a fine museum with displays showing the culture of the Sinagua. Self-guiding path leads past a number of dwellings. A trail at rim level is also self-guiding.

WALPI, Navajo County. State 264, N. at directional sign. There is a short but steep and very narrow road to Sichomovi from where you can walk along a path to Walpi. In odd-numbered years the world-famous Snake Dance is held here. But Walpi is one of the most interesting of all Hopi villages with or without ceremonial dancing. It occupies the very end of a high mesa, and has been inhabited since the early 16th century.

WICKENBURG, Maricopa County. US 89, 60. The pioneer road between here and Ehrenberg was called the Trail of Graves.

The Jail Tree, Tegner and Center Sts. From 1863 to 1890 outlaws were chained to this tree for lack of a building to house them.

Frontier St. still has hitching rails.

Vulture Gold Mine, 16 miles SW, yielded more than $20 million during its best days. It was discovered in 1863 by Henry Wickenburg, born in Austria, who was headed for the Colorado River hoping to find a mine in the Harqua Hala Mountains when he happened upon the ore here. In 1866 Benjamin Phelps bought a majority share of the Vulture and erected a 20-stamp mill. (Wickenburg, broke in his old age, shot himself with a Colt revolver.) A descriptive marker is 2 miles W. of town at the Vulture Rd. turnoff.

Desert Caballeros Western Museum, 20 N. Frontier, is a reconstructed assayer's office, bank and saloon.

WINDOW ROCK, Apache County. State 264. The rock for which the town is named is a natural bridge formation N. on Navajo 7.

Navajo Arts and Crafts Guild, S. on State 264, has Navajo handicrafts.

Navajo Tribal Museum, State 264 on fairgrounds. Visitor Center, dioramas showing culture of prehistoric Anasazi Indians, research library, maps and brochures.

WUPATKI NATIONAL MONUMENT, Coconino County. US 89. (Woo-POT-key). Visitor Center is 14 miles E. of the Sunset Crater Loop Rd. entrance. Self-guiding trails to two ruins, with guidebooks available at starting points. The more than 800 ruins were occupied ca. 1100–1200. Wupatki had more than one hundred rooms and was about three stories high. The monument comprises 35,-232 acres.

YOUNG, Gila County. State 288, on Cherry Creek.

Site of the Pleasant Valley War: Having read numerous accounts of the Graham-Tewksbury feud which vary in detail if not in outcome, I decided to let Bert Fireman, Arizona historian who compiled information for the state's historical markers, tell it in his own words as printed in *Amazing Arizona,* an excellent two-volume story of state historical markers published by the Arizona Development Board. But lo and behold, as some old Westerners used to say, when I turned to the proper page in Vol. 1, I found Fireman had chosen to let the WPA guide say it: "*The Arizona Guide* gives this concise, plausible explanation," writes Mr. Fireman. So . . .

"All details of this war are controversial," begins the explanation. Briefly, the Tewksburys and the Grahams stole cattle from their employer James Stinson and fell to quarreling. Then a band of sheep was driven over the Mogollon Rim and nearly everyone got into a quarrel. Cattlemen wanted no part of sheep raising. A five-year bushwhacking feud began. At least 19 deaths were recorded. The law was ineffective to useless. Every settler in the area took part in the conflict before it was over. In 1892 Tom, last of the Grahams, was killed near Tempe. Before he died he'd managed to say that Ed Tewksbury and John Rhodes had ambushed him. There were other witnesses who testified the same, but the two, though tried for murder, were freed.

YUMA, Yuma County. I-8. Hernando de Alarcon who was supposed to connect with members of the Coronado expedition came this way in 1540. Father Kino was here in 1683, Father Francisco Garces in 1779 and 1781. Martha Summerhayes came with her soldier-husband in the 19th century and wrote a peerless account of her travels on the Colorado river and on land in *Vanished Arizona.*

Yuma Territorial Prison State Historic Park, E. of Main St. off US 80. Museum is in former mess hall. The 6-foot adobe walls with iron barred doorways housed some of the most notorious villains in the old west at various times. Pearl Hart, Buckskin Frank Leslie and many others were here. Some cubicles were hewn from solid rock.

Century House, 248 Madison Ave., was the home of an early merchant. It has Historical Territory rooms. (Also see Fort Yuma, California.)

YUMA CROSSING, Yuma County. Between US 80 and the old highway bridge over the Colorado River. The major crossing for wagon trains, railroads and latter-day transportation began as an Indian trail in prehistoric times. Many Spanish explorers used this route. The Yuma, Mohave, Apache and other Indians prevented the use of the crossing toward the end of the 18th century, but Gen. Stephen W. Kearny's Army of the West passed here in 1846 as did Lt. Col. Philip St. George Cooke's Mormon Battalion in 1847. The Gold Rush of 1848–49 made Yuma Crossing a crowded highway of prospectors and other emigrants. A short distance west of the crossing are some adobe and plaster buildings that were once part of the Yuma Quartermaster Depot.

ARKANSAS

The zigzag rail fences overgrown with honeysuckle, the clear smokeless air in the cities, the tumbling of the mountains eastward from Winslow, the smell of woodsmoke from a great stone chimney at the end of a cabin, the pungency of pine sawdust and the whine of the saw biting into a log, the clumps of mistletoe in leafless trees. You won't forget those things soon, even though they are not the important aspects of Arkansas, where the politeness of the South and the friendliness of the West are both responsible for that personal tone in "Y'awl hurry back."

Arkansas; A Guide to the State (New York, 1941)

Come and go,
Bring and fetch,
Ring and twist.
Catch your partner by the craw
And swing around old Arkansas.

Square dance song

Wright Daniel's FERRY,
Four Miles Below Little Rock

For a large wagon and team.	$1.00
Wagon with two horses	75
Wagon or cart, with one horse	50
Man and horse	12½
Footman or loose horses	6¼
Each head of cattle	6¼
Hogs and sheep, per load	50

Travelers can be supplied with CORN, at 50 cents per bushel, at the Ferry.

Advertisement in the *Arkansas Gazette* June, 1825

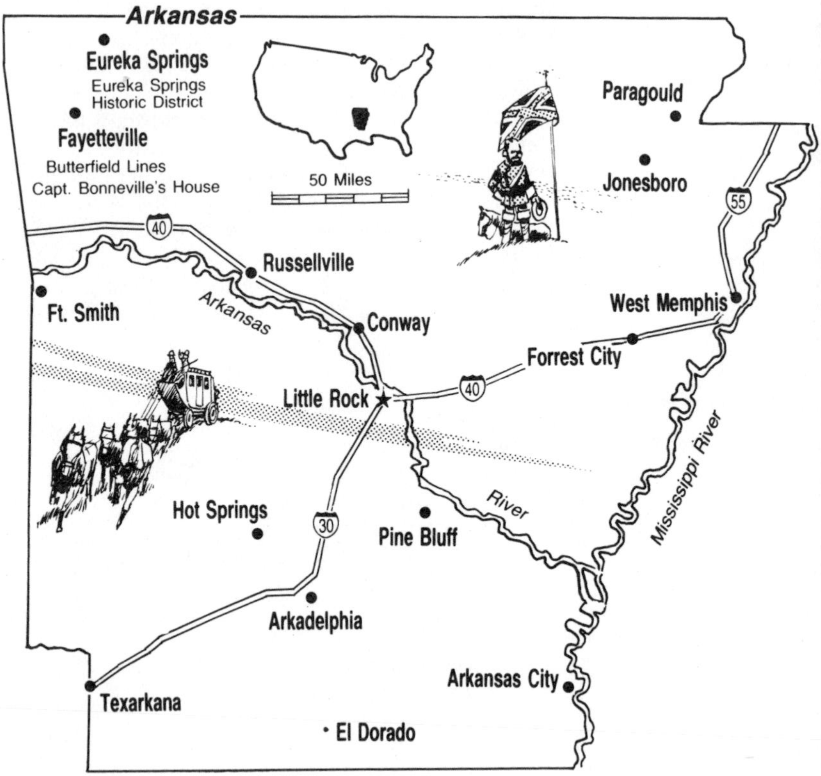
Arkansas
Eureka Springs
Eureka Springs
Historic District
Fayetteville
Butterfield Lines
Capt. Bonneville's House
50 Miles
Paragould
Jonesboro
55
40
Russellville
Ft. Smith
Arkansas
Conway
West Memphis
Forrest City
Little Rock
40
River
Mississippi River
Hot Springs
30
Pine Bluff
Arkadelphia
Arkansas City
Texarkana
El Dorado

ARKANSAS FACTS: Territory acquired by the Louisiana Purchase, 1803. In 1812 when Louisiana became a state the Arkansas District became part of the Territory of Missouri. Arkansas created a separate Territory by Congress in 1819. Entered Union June 15, 1836, the 25th state. *Arkansas:* A village and tribe, *Arkansea,* were recorded by the French as *Arkansa,* with s for plural, pronounced Arkansaw, which was the spelling used in the Act creating the territory, and remains the pronunciation. Nickname: Land of Opportunity. Capital: Little Rock. Territorial capital: Arkansas Post. Confederate capital: Washington. Arkansas has Arkansas Post National Memorial, Buffalo National River Park, Fort Smith National Historic Site, two national parks, and three national forests.

Chief Tribes. The Mound-Builders, Caddo, Cherokee, Tula, Quapaw, Chickasaw, and Chickasawba.

Early Routes. Butterfield Overland Mail, The Great River Road, The Old Wire Road, the Southwest Trail (also in part the Chihuahua Trail), the Trail of Tears.

Battles. Pea Ridge, Poison Spring, Marks' Mill, Jenkins Ferry, and Prairie Grove.

Names That Made News.

James Woodson Bates
The Butterfields
Hernando De Soto
Henri de Tonti
Bernard de la Harpe
John Law
William L. Lovely
Carrie Nation
Thomas Nuttall
Isaac Parker
Albert Pike
John Rogers
A.J. Smith
Belle Starr
Zachary Taylor
Tahlonteskee
Mark Twain
The Washburns
William E. Woodruff

ALBERT PIKE RECREATIONAL AREA, Montgomery County. State 27. Albert Pike, Confederate general, was also explorer, newspaperman, teacher, poet, and Indian Commissioner for the Confederacy. He had been forced to leave Harvard because of insufficient funds but by the time of the Civil War he was a wealthy journalist, a Mexican war veteran, and a lawyer who had won a suit in behalf of the Creek Indians. In the summer of 1861 he was sent by the Confederacy to try to win the Five Nations for the southern cause. He led a force of Indians in the battle of Pea Ridge (which see), but submitted his resignation in July 1862 because he resented the authority of Thomas Hindman, commanding the Trans-

Mississippi department. He probably spent the fall and winter of 1862 in this area. He was regarded with suspicion by both sides after his resignation and his movements are obscured by varying stories. According to old settlers he built a house in Montgomery County, began a history of Freemasonry, but was driven out of his home by guerrillas, and his possessions were destroyed. He was active in Washington after the war as a newspaperman, lawyer, and Freemason.

ALTUS, Franklin County. US 64. The town was so named because it was the highest point between Little Rock and Fort Smith when the railroad was built in the 1870s. *The Wiederkehr Wine Cellars,* N. of town on St. Mary's Mt., were not here when the pioneers were pushing westward but their tasting room would have been a popular stop. There is a 15-minute tour of cellars, a self-guiding tour of vineyards, and an observation tower.

ARKADELPHIA, Clark County. US 67. The town was once an important steamboat landing on the Ouachita River.

Ouachita Baptist University, overlooking the river, Ouachita Ave. at 5th St., was founded in 1886. Its ivy-covered Gothic Tower was erected that year.

Henderson State College, 11th St. and Henderson Ave., was founded in 1890. There are giant water oaks and wild roses on campus.

ARKANSAS CITY, Desha County. State 4. The town was founded when the Mississippi River flooded the onetime shipping center of Napoleon, a river town that was established by Frederick Notrebe, one of Napoleon Bonaparte's generals. Napoleon was a wide-open settlement filled with travelers, gamblers, and roustabouts. Mark Twain wrote of Arkansas City in *Life on the Mississippi:* "It was born of a railway; the Little Rock, Mississippi River and Texas Railroad touches the river there. We asked a passenger who belonged there what sort of a place it was. 'Well,' said he, after considering, and with the air of one who wishes to take time and be accurate, 'it's a h—l of a place.' A description which was photographic for exactness. There were several rows and clusters of shabby frame houses, and a supply of mud sufficient to insure the town against a famine in that article for a hundred years. . . ."

ARKANSAS POST NATIONAL MEMORIAL, Arkansas County. State 1, 54, 169. In 1686 Henri de Tonti descended the Mississippi River, planning to meet Sieur La Salle, but he failed to find him. (La Salle had been stranded in what is now Texas.) Tonti left a garrison here on his return trip. In 1717 a dreamer-exploiter with the curious name of John Law proposed a scheme for securing control of the monetary system of France, which included issuing a flock of notes to be paid off eventually with wealth expected to flow from the valleys of the Mississippi. Law recruited immigrants for the Louisiana territory, which included the present Arkansas. More Germans than French believed in Law's plans. Law had reserved land for himself near Arkansas Post and shipped slaves here in 1719. By 1720 Law's schemes had come to nothing. What was called the "Mississippi Bubble" burst. Most of the settlers moved farther south.

In 1722 Bénard de La Harpe found

47 persons living at the Post in 20 cabins, too crowded and underfed, with no communication or exchange with the Indians. The Chickasaw Indians attacked in 1783. Explorer and author Thomas Nuttall in the early 19th century found "one vast trackless wilderness of trees, a dead solemnity."

A post office was established in 1817; two years later William E. Woodruff brought a printing press upriver and founded the *Arkansas Gazette.* The town prospered until the Civil War when a three-day battle did such damage the town never quite recovered. The National Park Service maintains the memorial site which comprises 220.6 acres.

AUGUSTA, Woodruff County. Off US 64. The town is built on the east bank of the White River on the site of an Indian village which early settlers called Chickasaw Crossing. In 1848 Thomas Gough, a Maryland Quaker, established a trading post and four years later named the settlement for his niece. In the Civil War, Gen. Frederick Steele and his Federal forces occupied the town and camped on the courthouse lawn. In Reconstruction days martial law had to be declared as the Ku Klux Klan was active. Ten citizens were killed in 1868 by militiamen who were searching for Klansmen. A one-mile railroad was built in the 1880s to connect the town with the Iron Mountain Railway (now the Missouri Pacific). It was known locally as the "Little Dummy."

Woodruff County Courthouse, 3rd St., has a jail which had been the diningroom and kitchen for slaves of Thomas Hough.

Augusta Cemetery, end of 3rd St., has a grave said to be that of William Quantrill, guerrilla of the Civil War and an outlaw in Kansas and Missouri in mid-century. According to local legend, a Capt. L.J. Crocker, who moved to Augusta soon after the war, said just before his death in 1917 that he was Francis Quantrell and had escaped prison in a dress brought to him by his wife. Quantrill was called a lot of things but Francis wasn't one of them. (Charley Hart and Billy Quantrill were two of his aliases; his surname, however, was often spelled Quantrell by his contemporaries.) Among other points Crocker apparently didn't know when he told his story: Quantrill had a mistress, Kate King (often called Kate Clarke), not a wife; he was in the prison hospital in his last days, had been shot in the abdomen and was paralyzed, according to witnesses, so that escape would have been unlikely.

BATESVILLE, Independence County. US 167. About 1812 John Reed, a Missourian, built a house on Poke Bayou where he traded whisky and supplies for furs and hides. By 1818 a ferry was in use and the town was named for Territorial Judge James Woodson Bates. In 1831 the first steamboat to ascend the White River docked here; thereafter the town was a steamboat stop.

Arkansas College, Boswell and 8th St., was founded in 1836 as Batesville Academy. The building burned before the first class could meet. The rebuilt school was discontinued during the Civil War and reestablished in 1868 during the Reconstruction days of such extreme poverty that classes met in kitchens.

Garrott House (Case-Maxfield House), 561 E. Main St. The gabled house built in 1842 for George Case and later owned by Will Maxfield is a registered historic place.

Spring Mill, 6 miles N. on State 69. The oldest waterpowered mill in Arkansas.

BENTON, Saline County. US 67. In 1542 DeSoto called the area Provincia de la Sal (Province of Salt). The town was established in the 1820s. Salt was shipped to Tennessee, Louisiana, and Texas as well as to other parts of Arkansas. In 1887 when bauxite, the ore from which aluminum is extracted, was discovered in the foothills of the Ouachita Mountains, Benton became the "gateway" to these fields, which still produce more than 90 percent of all bauxite mined in the U.S.

BENTONVILLE, Benton County. US 71. The town and county were named for Thomas Hart Benton, first senator from Missouri and a champion of frontiersmen. He was the father of individualist Jessie Benton Fremont, wife of John C. Fremont—"The Little Pathfinder."

Cherokee Trail of Tears passed through Benton County. In 1838–39, 20,000 Cherokees were driven by the U.S. army from their Tennessee, North Carolina, and Georgia mountain homes, to Indian Territory. At least a third died on the way. The contract for moving them was let to individual bidders for the sum of $54 a head. The Indians were put into groups of 1,000 for the sad journey; they brought what possessions they could, though much already had been stolen from them, along with their homes. Some were lucky enough to ride in wagons, carriages, or on horseback but many had to walk. Arkansas historian Alvin Seamster writes that Judge Alfred Greenwood, who had started from Georgia with one of the Cherokee bands, surrendered his command in Tennessee and then brought his family to Bentonville. In March the following year the same troop he had been in charge of passed through town. Greenwood was later made Commissioner of the Five Civilized Tribes.

BERRYVILLE, Carroll County. State 21.

Saunders Museum, 314 E. Madison, on highway. An outstanding collection of guns used by outlaws and others, including sidearms carried by Jesse James, Wild Bill Hickok, Billy the Kid, Annie Oakley, Cole Younger, Sam Houston, Cherokee Bill, William Quantrill, Pancho Villa, and the like.

BLANCHARD SPRINGS RECREATION AREA, Stone County. State 14.

Visitor Center, at entrance to caverns, has an interpretive program. An elevator descends 216 feet to a cavern large enough to contain three football fields. Maintained by the National Forest Service, the Visitor Center has tours departing every twenty minutes with guides to lead along the well-developed trails. The Dripstone Trail is a tour that takes about 90 minutes.

BUFFALO NATIONAL RIVER PARK, Marion County. State 14. This first national river park preserves 132 miles of the Buffalo River in Buffalo Point area which comprises 2,020 acres.

Lost Valley, near Ponca, is part of the National Park development. The valley is formed by towering limestone cliffs. A hiking trail runs through a natural cave and past unusual rock formations and waterfalls.

BULL SHOALS, Marion County. State 178.

Mountain Village, ½ mile S. off highway. An authentic restoration of an early Ozark town with a general store, school, bank, church, blacksmith shop, and other buildings.

Penrod's Museum, 1 mile E. of Bull Shoals Dam in Lakeview. Antique glass, coins, stamps, dolls, old guns, and Indian relics.

CADDO GAP, Montgomery County. State 8. A bronze statue of a Tula Indian stands at the crossroads with an inscription saying that this is the farthest point west reached by Hernando (also Fernando) De Soto in his journey from Florida. He reached the Mississippi in 1541. The Caddoans were a very early tribal grouping scattered through the Southern Great Plains. The name Caddo is a shortened form of *Kadohadacho,* meaning "real chiefs." Most Caddoans lived in Texas and Oklahoma and have passed out of existence.

CALION, Union County. US 167. The town located at the S. end of the bridge spanning the Ouachita River is said to be the site where Hernando De Soto built a stockade in 1541 which became the village named Utiangue. The bluff later was a stopping place for packets and was known as El Dorado Landing.

CAMDEN, Ouachita County. US 79.

Chidester House, 926 Washington St., built in 1847, was once a stage stop, and has furnishings from the Civil War period. A registered historic building.

Confederate Cemetery, Adams Ave. and Pearl St., has more than 300 markers for unknown soldiers.

CLINTON, Van Buren County. State 16.

Natural Bridge, N. on US 65, is a large sandstone arch over an old log road. Though said to be millions of years old, it was used as a bridge in the 18th and early 19th centuries.

Watergate, 6 miles N. of town, turn SW on County Rd. A collection of Americana, including guns, on the old Patton farm.

CONWAY, Faulkner County. I-40. The town is named for a family which moved down to a Red River plantation from Missouri in pioneer days. Ann Conway was an early leader of the Methodist Church in Arkansas. Her oldest son (of seven), Henry Conway, became a Territorial Delegate to Congress; two others were Governor of the state. Opie Read (1852–1939) edited a newspaper here in the 1870s. He was a well-known humorist, one of many in Arkansas' history.

Hendrix College, Washington Ave. and Independence St., was founded in 1876 at Altus; it moved and changed its name in 1884.

Greathouse Home, Faulkner St. on courthouse grounds, is a restored farmhouse and inn with period furnishings. It dates from 1830.

CROWLEY'S RIDGE STATE PARK, Greene County. State 141. The 265-acre park is on the site of the original homestead of an early settler, Benjamin Crowley. His tomb is also here.

DARDANELLE, Yell County. State 22. A rocky point jutting into the Arkansas River made a landmark for explorers and other early travelers. Thomas Nuttall found a Cherokee trading post here in 1819. The town was platted in 1843. It changed hands a few times during the Civil War. The coming of the railroad in the 1870s created prosperity for a time.

Council Rock, on riverbank near Front St., was the meeting place in 1820 for Robert Crittenden, Secretary of Arkansas Territory, and Cherokee leaders. Chief Black Fox and the other Cherokee Indians present reluctantly agreed to give up more land to white settlers.

Dardanelle Rock is reached by a stiff climb up a footpath that begins at the N. end of Front St.

DEVIL'S DEN STATE PARK, Washington County. State 170. A heavily wooded, 1,765-acre area with deep fissure in sandstone and many caves which once served as refuge for Civil War renegades. Winding trail.

DE WITT, Arkansas County. State 30.

Arkansas County Courthouse is no older than four decades, but it holds records dating back to 1803, moved here when the county seat was changed from Arkansas Post in 1855. There are land titles in Spanish, French, and English.

Halliburton House, at N. end of town on Halliburton St., was built in 1854 by Col. W. H. Halliburton, who wrote a fine history of the county.

DOVER, Pope County. US 70. The town was the flourishing county seat in the 1840s. Supplies arrived from boat landings on the Arkansas and were distributed throughout the Ozark country from here. When the railroad reached Russellville after the Civil War, Dover's day was over.

Old Jail was built on a solid rock foundation with walls a foot thick and no door in the bottom story so that the only entrance or exit was by an opening in the ceiling. The last legal hanging in Pope County was that of Lee Barnes in 1885.

EDGEMONT, Cleburne County. State 16. Far up the side of a mountain which is just off the highway is a series of caves known as "Indian Rock Houses," with traces of Indian habitation in previous centuries.

EL DORADO, Union County. US 82, 167. The town was founded, according to local legend, when pioneer Matthew F. Rainey's wagon broke down and he offered all his goods for quick sale. The response was so great he changed his mind and decided to open a store. Rainey's settlement was selected for county seat in 1843. (In 1921 someone struck oil, creating a boom town, with 460 producing wells by Christmas.)

EUREKA SPRINGS HISTORIC DISTRICT, Carroll County. US 62. Dr. Alvah Jackson is credited with discovery of the spring water's medicinal qualities. County residents began building cabins during the summer of 1879. Invalids came in wagons and lived in tents, collected around Basin Spring. A building boom took place in 1881; soon there were 13 hotels. Today the buildings date almost exclusively from 1880 to 1900. Though only water flowed from the springs, it was here that Carrie Nation, the militant prohibitionist, gave her last speech. She probably had the stroke that ended her life five months later while she was still onstage. Her face twisted with pain and her words came with difficulty: "I—have—done—what—I—could."

Hatchet Hall, 31 Steel St., was Carrie Nation's residence in her last years, later was used as an academy to train saloon-busters, presumably, in the proper way to swing an axe or a beer bottle as did Carrie in her heyday.

Blue Spring, 7 miles W., off State 62. The water flows from a depth which has been sounded to 510 feet. The Cherokee Trail of Tears crossed just above the spring (or so goes the local claim). The Cherokees were said to camp here in 1839 on their long journey from Georgia to Indian Territory. Hieroglyphic Rock with early Indian writings is above the Blue Lagoon. Shawnee, Delaware, Osage, and Cherokee were here at various periods.

The Castle, at Inspiration Point, 5½ miles W. of Eureka Springs on State 62, shows family life just after the turn of the century. Horsedrawn farm equipment, blacksmith shop, country store, post office, period furnishings.

Pivot Rock and Natural Bridge, 1½ miles NW on US 62, then 2 miles N. on Pivot Rock Rd. A balanced boulder is 15 times as wide at the top as at the bottom. (Looks rather like this author standing on her head.)

Onyx Cave Park, 3 miles E. on US 62, N. on county rd. Onyx formations in cave which has an average temperature of 52° F.

Miles Mountain Musical Museum, 1½ miles NW on US 62. Many old instruments, Indian relics, assorted memorabilia.

The Rosalie, 282 Spring St., was built of handmade bricks in the 1880s. Period furnishings.

Eureka Springs Historical Museum, 95 S. Main St., has many interesting household items, including tools of the 19th century.

Church in the Wildwood Bible Museum, 3 miles E. on US 62. More than 10,000 Bibles in many languages are housed in a restored church. The Bible probably played a more important role in the conquering of the old West than was ever recorded. Women must have packed the family Bible first when planning What to Take on a Wagon Train.

FAYETTEVILLE, Washington County. US 71.

The Butterfield Overland Stage Line came through town with a station stop on a 5-acre plot bought from William McGarrah in July 1858. The company also operated a hotel on the property across the street N. of the present courthouse, and owned a 360-acre farm just W. of town. Charles Butterfield, son of John, operated the Fayetteville holdings. John Butterfield found this area a lovely retreat with beneficial air and often brought prominent Easterners to vacation with him. Alfred Hossman, one of Butterfield's drivers, lived in Lincoln, Ark., until his death in 1932 at the age of 95.

Fayetteville changed hands several times during the Civil War and two major battles were fought nearby. W. C. Roberts was a native, born May 12, 1850, who enlisted in the Union Army at the age of 13, which was not too unusual for the eager boys of the day, but Roberts' father and two older brothers were officers in the Confederate army. Roberts took part in a number of engagements, was slightly wounded and given an honorable discharge at age 15. He became a revenue officer in Madison County toward the end of the century and in 1906 became Fayetteville postmaster under President Teddy Roosevelt.

University of Arkansas was founded in 1871. Its main campus comprises 140 acres. Old Main on Arkansas Ave. is a historic landmark. The University

Museum, old Student Union on campus, has vastly interesting collections from the bluff shelters of the Ozark Mountains and from the Spiro Mound in Oklahoma.

Stone House, 207 Center St., is a registered historic house built in 1845. Stephen K. Stone purchased the house from Judge David Walker in 1850.

Headquarters House, 118 W. Dickson St., was the home of Jonas Tebbetts, a wealthy Union sympathizer. It was occupied by both forces during the Civil War. Period furnishings, Civil War relics.

Confederate Cemetery has the grave of Gen. W.Y. Slack, who was shot at Elkhorn Tavern during the Battle of Pea Ridge (which see).

Waxhaws, South College Ave., was built in the 1830s by Archibald Yell and named for his birthplace in North Carolina.

The Reed House, West Dickson St., was occupied in the 1850s by J.W. Washburn, son of missionary Cephas Washburn. J.W.'s wife was a Cherokee. (Elias Boudinot, lawyer and editor of the 19th century, was also a distinguished Cherokee of Fayetteville.) Edward Payson Washburn, another son of Cephas, painted the *Arkansas Traveler,* which is probably the best known of the state's paintings.

FORT SMITH, Sebastian County. I-40. Established by Major William Bradford and a company of the Rifles Regiment to keep peace between the Osage Indians upstream and the Cherokees downstream, the first log-stockade, at the confluence of the Poteau and Arkansas Rivers, was called Belle Point. It was renamed for Gen. Thomas A. Smith, commander of all military forces west of the Mississippi River in 1817. The fort was occupied and abandoned so often, it was tagged Belle Point Phoenix, the fort that "refused to die." It was reoccupied in the 1830s as a supply depot for the Choctaws in their mass migration, and it was an army base in the "White Lightnin' Wars," a struggle against bootleggers vending their wares to the Indians. The fort first served as supply center for the Confederate forces at Pea Ridge and Prairie Grove but became a Union base in 1863. In 1871 the fort was abandoned again, but before the buildings were disposed of, the Federal Court for the Western District of Arkansas took possession.

Captain John Rogers was the first settler of the town in 1821. When the California Gold Rush began, Fort Smith became a busy supply center and starting point for wagon trains. While it was a boom town with the usual assortment of riffraff that collected wherever the 19th century action was, this was nothing compared to the post-Civil War years. National Park historian Edwin C. Bearss and Prof. Arrell M. Gibson wrote a comprehensive history of the fort (*Fort Smith: Little Gibraltar on the Arkansas,* University of Oklahoma Press, 1969), which described Indian Territory conditions: ". . . a sanctuary for raiding banks, stagecoaches, trains, and businesses in adjacent states. . . . These desperadoes even robbed and killed ordinary citizens. . . . The reputation of Indian Territory spread far and wide as 'Robbers' Roost' and 'Land of the Six-gun' and was epitomized in the tag 'There is no Sunday west of St. Louis—and no God west of Fort Smith.' "

After President Grant appointed Isaac Parker judge of the Western District of Arkansas and Parker soon became "the hanging judge of Fort

Smith," the gallows became one of the most popular entertainments in town, for the audience. Bearss and Gibson write: "For years, the attraction that drew the largest crowds on the Southwestern frontier was the annual mass execution on the gallows at Fort Smith. In April, 1876, more than seven thousand gathered to watch the hanging of five Indian Territory criminals. By 1880, Parker, embarrassed by the carnival-like atmosphere these executions generated, decided to restrict attendance. For the September, 1881, execution, only about fifty newspapermen, attorneys, clergymen, and court officials were permitted to witness the hanging of five convicted murderers."

Fort Smith National Historic Site, Rogers Ave. between 2nd and 3rd Sts. Restored, but contains the foundation of the first fort. Judge Parker's courtroom and the gallows are reconstructed.

Old Fort Museum, 111 Rogers Ave., has displays in the only remaining building of the second fort. It was the commissary.

National Cemetery, Garland at S. end of 6th St. The old burial ground for fort soldiers was made national property in 1867. Judge Isaac Parker was buried here in 1896. Some of the oldest graves are those of War of 1812 veterans.

Chimney of Gen. Zachary Taylor's Home, located at the E. end of Garrison Ave. on grounds of the Convent of Mercy. The old fireplace and chimney of the home occupied by General Zachary Taylor have been converted to a shrine. Taylor was Commander of the Second Military Department from 1841–1844 when he lived in Fort Smith.

KFSA-TV Studios now occupy the onetime city library building at 318 N. 13th St., on the site of Judge Parker's house.

Free Ferry Road led, as the name indicates, to the free ferry, which gave wealthy Fort Smithians access to their large farm holdings. Many old homes here belonged to the town's aristocracy.

Bonneville House, 318 N. 7th St., has been restored. It was for many years the home of Mrs. Susan Neis Bonneville, widow of Gen. B.L.E. Bonneville, explorer, author, and veteran of the Mexican and Civil Wars. Washington Irving used his journal as the basis for "The Adventures of Captain Bonneville" (1843). A registered national historic house.

Fort Smith Art Center, 423 N. 6th St., is housed in one of the town's best 19th century homes.

Clayton House, 514 N. 6th St., is typical of Fort Smith residences toward the end of the century. William Henry Harrison Clayton came to town in 1874 when he was appointed U.S. District Attorney for the Western District, which then included Indian Country. He often appeared as prosecutor in Judge Parker's court. A national historic landmark, not open to the public at present.

FULTON, Hempstead County. I-30. The American part of the great Southwest Trail ended here. At Dooley's Ferry a few miles up the Red River were the crossings into Mexican territory in the early part of the 19th century. The town was founded in 1813 and was a frontier trading post and departure point for the Southwest. Side-wheelers brought supplies for this and other parts of Arkansas from New Orleans. Goods were transferred to freighters pulled by six-mule teams to other settlements. Riverboat gamblers and other adventurers liked to hang out here, but the frontier town quieted considerably when the railroad was built at Texarkana.

GALLA CREEK, now GALLA ROCK, Pope County. State 105. An Indian village established by the Western Cherokee Indians was here early in the 19th century. After the Osage had gone from the area, Chief Tahlonteskee led 300 of his tribe to settle in the valley of the Arkansas River. Major William L. Lovely came in 1813 as Indian agent. He bought a large piece of land known as "Lovely's Purchase" from the Osage, an area that is now partly northwestern Arkansas and northeastern Oklahoma. After Lovely died, his widow remained with the Cherokees; when a treaty was signed requiring all whites to vacate Cherokee territory she was the only exception. After the death of Tahlonteskee, his brother, John Jolly, became the leader and Galla Rock became a model village. Thomas Nuttall was here in 1819 on his trip upriver. He found the houses well furnished and the Indians wearing a combination of native and American dress, with a good deal of prosperity in the town. In 1829 when the Cherokees were pushed farther west into Oklahoma, Sam Houston went with them. He had abandoned a bride and the governorship of Tennessee to set up a trading post and a common law relationship with an Indian girl. He considered Tahlonteskee his foster father.

THE GREAT RIVER ROAD, parallels the Mississippi River from Blytheville to Helena. The region is bisected by a ridge of loess formation which forms the only hills in the river delta, Crowley's Ridge (which see).

GREENWOOD, Sebastian County. State 10.

Jail House was built in the 1800s when there were plenty of criminals from Indian Territory to be lodged in the two-story stone building, now a museum.

HARRISON, Boone County. US 65.

Hurricane River Cave, 16 miles SE on US 65, follows an underground river.

Rally Hill Museum & Heritage Center, 8 miles SE on US 65 to Valley Springs, then 3 miles E. Museum, housed in a barn and three log houses, has a doctor's office, chapel, school, general store, all furnished in pioneer life-style.

HELENA, Phillips County. US 49. Hernando De Soto visited the Indian village that was once here. Sylvanus Phillips was an early settler and the town was named for his daughter, ca. 1820. In *Life on the Mississippi,* Mark Twain wrote: "Helena occupies one of the prettiest situations on the Mississippi. Her perch is the last, the southernmost group of hills which one sees on that side of the river. In its normal condition it is a pretty town. . . ." At the time of Twain's visit a flood had just receded: "Stranded and discarded scows lay all about; plank sidewalks on stilts four feet high were still standing; the broad sidewalks on the ground level were loose and ruinous—a couple of men trotting along them could make a blind man think a cavalry charge was coming."

Phillips County Museum, 623 Pecan St., has Mound Builders artifacts. The Mound Builders who occupied the delta area seemed to have built high for protection against floods. The platform-like mounds were dwelling places, though used for ceremonies as well. The museum also has Civil War artifacts. Helena has the distinction of having been the home of seven Confederate generals, and the city was a strategic prize sought by both sides in the war. There are many fine antebellum homes in the vicinity.

HOT SPRINGS NATIONAL PARK, Garland County. State 7. The park comprises 3,140 acres. It is the nation's oldest national park, set aside in 1832. The springs were located in an area occupied by the Tunica Indians, a tribe of the Caddoes. The Quapaws also came down a north trail to the hot springs, probably arriving after they were forced from their Ohio Valley homes. De Soto was here in the fall of 1541; a plaque on Tufa Rock in Arlington Park describes his visit. The vaporous springs appear in many early journals and diaries. The park headquarters and Visitor Center have a museum with exhibits on the history of the area and a slide program. Self-guiding tours start here at Reserve and Central Aves.

JACKSONPORT STATE PARK, Jackson County. State 69.

Jacksonport Courthouse Museum, between Dillard and the White River, in the park, has been restored. It was a mustering point for the Confederate Army of Northern Arkansas.

The Mary Woods, a riverboat that once plied the White River, is permanently docked here. The park comprises 90 acres.

JENKINS FERRY BATTLEGROUND STATE PARK, Grant County. NE of Leola on State 46. Union Gen. Frederick Steele, leading his men in a retreat toward Little Rock, tried to stall their Confederate pursuers by erecting a breastwork on the right bank of the Saline River. A delaying action was fought on April 30, 1864. Casualties were high; the Union forces lost their ammunition and supply trains.

JONESBORO, Craighead County. US 63. The city was founded in 1859 atop Crowley's Ridge.

Arkansas State University, E. edge of town on State 1, has a fine museum with natural and state history displays. One exhibit features the Ballard Site, an early temple mound dating from 700. A cutaway shows various strata, artifacts associated with each one and tools used by archaeologists in excavating.

LESLIE, Searcy County. US 65. This little town has an interesting connection with the Mountain Meadows Massacre (see Utah). Twittie Baker, the youngest survivor, spent his last years here as a drayman. In 1857, when he was an infant, his parents joined a wagon train bound for the far West. They were unlucky enough to be in the group slaughtered at Mountain Meadows. Baker and two of his sisters were spared and returned to Arkansas. The records of how many died are confused but a letter in the National Archives, among the papers of the Office of Indian Affairs, Utah Superintendency, dated "Crooked Creek, Arkansas, April 27, 1860," gives the names of surviving children and a list of "those that was masacreed at the Mountain Meadows in September 1867. Capt. John T. Baker, George W. Baker, Wife & 1 child, and Abel Baker are on the list of the dead, as are 58 other Arkansans from Carroll, Marion, Johnson, and Benton Counties."

LITTLE ROCK, Pulaski County. I-40. French explorers were here in the 18th century. The town was staked out in 1819, and became the territorial capital in 1821, when the seat of government was moved from Arkansas Post.

State Capitol, W. end of Capitol Ave. The Geology Department has a mineral display.

Arkansas Territorial Capital Restoration, E. 3rd and Cumberland Sts. Entrance at 214 E. 3rd. A state-financed and excellently executed restoration of 13 buildings in the complex. Built in 1820, they occupy about a city block with landscaping in keeping with the early period. Guided tours.

Old Arkansas State House, 300 W. Markham, was built in 1833–1842, and served as the capital from 1836 until 1911. The Arkansas Archives are here. Six rooms are furnished with antiques.

Museum of Science and Natural History, in U.S. Arsenal Bldg., MacArthur Park, 500 E. 9th St. General Douglas MacArthur was born here. Now houses many archaeological and Indian collections. The arsenal was operative from 1838 until 1892.

Angelo Marre House, 1321 Scott St. Period furnishings in an 1881 Italianate Victorian house.

River Museum, 111 E. 3rd St., has a scale model steamboat and replica of Arkansas River Navigation.

The Little Rock, on S. bank of river at the foot of Rock St. The city is named for this rock formation, which also served as the starting point for most land surveys south of the river. The first known reference to the area was made by Bénard de La Harpe in 1722. It was used as a reference point for a survey of Indian lands in 1818. Not much of the original formation remains, but it still rises about 18 feet above the river and extends some 40 feet along the bank. A national historic landmark.

Mount Holly Cemetery, 12th St. and Broadway, was established in 1843. Ten former governors, three U.S. Senators, and five Confederate generals are interred here among other illustrious former citizens.

Ten Mile House (Stagecoach House), N. of Mabelvale on State 5. On the Old Southwest Trail, the house was popular with travelers who were friends of Archibald McHenry, the first occupant. A registered historic building, not accessible to the public at present.

Albert Pike House, 411 E. 7th, was built in 1840 for the volatile explorer, soldier, and author. The *Albert Pike Memorial Temple* is on Scott St. between 7th and 8th. He was an authority on Masonic law.

MALVERN, Hot Spring County. US 67. The town was a transfer point for railroad passengers who had to board Concord Stages for the ride to Hot Springs. Many wore jewels and carried enough money to entice bandits. The local legend is that Jesse James and his brother Frank, Jim and Cole Younger, Arthur McCoy and Belle Starr robbed the stage near here. A former member of Quantrill's guerrillas writing his memoirs in 1914 (Kit Dalton, *Under the Black Flag*) included an enthusiastic chapter about Belle Starr and her fatal beauty; he also said: "The history of Arkansas would be as incomplete without the name of Belle Star (sic) as it would without that of Jeff Davis of sacred memory." Historian Ramon F. Adams, in his incomparable *Burs Under the Saddle* (University of Oklahoma Press, 1964) in which he corrects innumerable errors of Western history, says: "I'm afraid Belle had little to do with the history of Arkansas other than her visits to the court of Judge Parker at Fort Smith."

MARKS' MILLS BATTLEFIELD PARK, Cleveland County. Junction of Ark. 8 and 97. Confederate raiders captured a 240-wagon train from Union troops led by Lt. Col. Francis M. Drake on the morning of April 25, 1864, and forced Major General Frederick Steele to retreat to Little Rock. Major General James Fagan led the Confederates.

MOUNTAIN HOME, Baxter County. US 62.

Wolf House, 14 miles SE on State 5 in Norfolk, is a restored and refurnished 1809 house. The two-story log structure served as first county courthouse. Pioneer artifacts.

MOUNTAIN VIEW, Stone County. State 9, 14.

Ozark Folk Center, 2 miles N. The 915-acre site has a Visitor Center with information on the complex designed as a living museum of mountain life and heritage.

Blanchard Springs Recreation Area (which see) is 14 miles NW in Ozark National Forest.

MOUNT IDA, Montgomery County. US 270. The town was settled in 1836 by Granville Whittington, who came from Massachusetts and opened a general store here. Many of the early settlers arrived by dugout on the Ouachita River. The town is now surrounded by the Ouachita National Forest.

MURFREESBORO, Pike County. State 27.

Crater of Diamonds State Park, 3 miles S. on State 301, sounds like the end of the rainbow for diamond fanciers. Visitors are allowed to search for and keep any rocks they find. A Dallas housewife found a rough stone which was appraised at over $80,000 and is now called "The Star of Arkansas." Museum has rocks and minerals and a short orientation in how to recognize diamonds that would have astounded the '49ers.

Ancient Burial Grounds, State 27, just W. of town turn N. following directional signs, is a privately owned and operated archaeological site. Excavations have uncovered a temple mound and some well-preserved skeletons. A museum displays artifacts.

OSCEOLA, Mississippi County. US 61. The town is named for Chief Osceola (1804–38) who never fought any wars here but led his people during the Seminole War in Florida. When William B. Edrington first arrived the site was occupied by an Indian village. The early settlers were canny enough to keep cheap firewood on the shore so that steamboat captains would be inclined to stop here. When the town was incorporated in 1838 it was known as Plum Point. J.W. DeWitt, the first postmaster, built a house of lumber picked up after steamboat explosions. Trappers on long hunts came here for the mail from home.

PARKIN, Cross County. US 64, State 75.

Parkin Indian Mound, north edge of town. The temple mound culture of northeast Arkansas can be studied from excavations here. Many burials were accompanied by pottery vessels and other artifacts. It is a national historic landmark.

Charm and potential destruction side-by-side at the Prairie Grove Battlefield
(Dept. of Parks & Tourism)

PEA RIDGE NATIONAL MILITARY PARK, Benton County. N. of Rogers on US 62. Visitor Center at Park headquarters has excellent displays and a fine interpretive program for the park which was the site of one of the most important battles of the Civil War in the Trans-Mississippi area. Elkhorn Tavern has been restored. The park comprises 4278.75 acres.

PETIT JEAN STATE PARK, 6 miles S. of Morrilton on State 9, then 15 miles W. on State 154. The oldest, largest, and best developed of Arkansas' nature parks comprises 3,484 acres. Cedar Falls is a feature.

PINE BLUFF, Jefferson County. US 79. The town was settled in 1819 as a trading post by Joseph Bonne, who got on well with the Quapaws because he was half Quapaw. Before the attack on Fort Sumter, a musket shot was fired on a Federal gunboat in the Arkansas River here. Gov. Rector seized the cargo for the Confederacy and Pine Bluffians ever since have claimed the first shot of the Civil War was fired here. Many antebellum homes embellish the old river town.

DuBocage, 1115 W. 4th St., was built for Joseph W. Bocage in 1866. He was a lawyer and planter who turned to the manufacture of lumber after the Civil War. The house is a registered historic home. It has been restored. Period furnishings.

Hudson-Grace-Borreson House, 716 W. Barraque, evolved from a 19th century one-story, two-room cabin. A registered historic house.

PLUMMERVILLE, Conway County. US 64.

Samuel Plummer settled here in 1825 and made saddles for the Cherokee. When the Little Rock–Fort Smith stage line was established, his house became a station.

POCAHONTAS, Randolph County. US 62.

Old Davidsonville State Park, 2 miles W. on US 62, then 9 miles S. on State 166. The first post office was established at this site, which is now a 28-acre park on the Black River. The year was 1817 and mail was brought from St. Louis once a month by a rider on horseback, who continued on to Arkansas Post and to Monroe, Louisiana. The town had a courthouse, a distillery and a smelter, general stores, a blacksmith shop, a land office, and seemed set for centuries, but it went out of business and no one seems to know exactly why. Some old settlers used to say that passengers coming upriver from New Orleans brought the threat of yellow fever, which scared townspeople into departing anywhere yonder.

Old Randolph County Courthouse, in the center of Pocahontas, was built in 1872. A meteorite fell on the lawn nearby in 1859.

POISON SPRING STATE PARK, Ouachita County. State 24, 18 miles NW of Camden. The site of a Civil War battle on April 18, 1864, between Confederates under Gen. John Marmaduke and Federals under Col. James Williams, is now part of a state park. A Federal wagon was returning to Camden with a load of corn when it was attacked and captured.

POTTSVILLE, Pope County. Old US 64.

Potts' Inn, Main and Center Sts., was built by Kirkbride Potts and became a stage stop on the Memphis to Fort Smith line, part of the Butterfield Overland stage line. Doors and windows were shipped up the Arkansas River; bricks for the chimneys were baked in a kiln on the property. The house also served as trading post, post office, and tavern. It is a registered historic place.

POWHATAN COURTHOUSE, Lawrence County. State 25. The town was founded in 1820 as a ferry landing on the Black River and flourished with the coming of the steamboats. In 1883 the route of the Springfield & Memphis Railroad was built a few miles away and caused the town's decline. The Courthouse, built in 1888, is a registered historic place. Its old records date back to 1815.

PRAIRIE GROVE BATTLEFIELD PARK, Washington County. US 62. The 62-acre site was the scene of a major Civil War conflict in the winter of 1862. Maj. Gen. Thomas Hindman's Confederates attacked forces commanded by Gen. Francis J. Herron. Gen. James Blunt (often spelled Blount) reinforced Herron. Both sides laid a tentative claim to victory. Battles lines are well marked. A museum has explanatory displays and relics. Several houses have been restored. The Battle Monument is a chimney from Rhea's Mill; 55 feet tall, weighing 200,000 pounds, it was moved here and re-erected.

ROGERS, Benton County. US 71. The first stop in Arkansas on the Butterfield Line was at Callahan's Tavern, which became the town of Rogers. Highway markers describe the route. The town has many associations with the Battle of Pea Ridge. The National Park is 10 miles N. Veterans of the Civil War are buried here and at War Eagle, 13 miles E. There is a Mill Museum at War Eagle with antiques and displays of 19th-century tools. Rogers' first mayor was a Pea Ridge veteran. The Rev. J. Wade Sikes was a minister, soldier, and civil servant. He lost his left arm in the Battle of Atlanta. In 1881 he was elected mayor; he was also a practicing lawyer and a Baptist minister. He was 100 years old when he died in January 1929.

The Wire Road, used by early travelers heading west, ran through Rogers, somewhere N. of Arkansas St. The exact route is not marked but it ran through Cross Hollows and Shiloh, now Springdale, and Fayetteville. The name was given the old wagon road in 1862 when Union army soldiers strung telegraph wires from Rolla, Missouri, to Fort Smith to enable the Federal government to check on the troops.

International Air Gun Museum, at Daisy Manufacturing Plant, US 71 S. Daisy B-B guns and early-day competitors make up one of the displays.

SPRINGDALE, Benton County. US 71.

Shiloh Museum, 118 W. Johnson Ave., has pioneer artifacts and archaeological exhibits.

STUTTGART, Arkansas County. US 79.

Arkansas County Agricultural Museum, 921 E. 4th St. Displays feature pioneer life and prairie farming. A one-room schoolhouse is on the grounds.

VAN BUREN, Crawford County. US 64. Albert D. Richardson, the peripatetic journalist for Horace Greeley's N.Y. *Tribune,* was out of action during many months of the Civil War imprisoned by the Confederacy; he had been a passenger on the Butterfield

Stage in its early days. In *Beyond the Mississippi* (Hartford, 1867), he wrote: "All day we were among mountains with farm-houses few and far between; and at evening we looked down upon a pleasant picture. At our feet the village of Van Buren nestled among shade trees; immediately beyond, the shining waters of the Arkansas river wound through a rich green valley; still further, the deep many-hued foliage of the Indian Territory dotted with blue mountain peaks melted into the deeper blue of the sky."

At Van Buren stages of the Butterfield line were ferried across the river and then rolled five miles down the valley to Fort Smith. Many old brick buildings of the 19th century are still standing on Main Street.

WASHINGTON, Hempstead County. State 4. Not long after the Louisiana Purchase, settlers came down the Southwest Trail, known locally as the Chihuahua Trail, and began the town that became known as the "Cradle of Arkansas History." David Crockett stopped here on his way to Texas; Sam Houston was here for a time. Washington was a military field headquarters in the Mexican War. The Confederate government was moved here during the Civil War. James Black, an early smith, is said to have fashioned the knife for which James Bowie is famous. The old Chihuahua Trail followed the Main Street of town, now Franklin Ave.

Hempstead County Courthouse, Franklin Ave., restored, was built in 1833 and served as the Confederate Capitol from 1863 to 1865.

Old Washington State Park, on State 4, is a restored historical site with a number of excellently reconstructed or preserved houses as well as a schoolhouse, a tavern, and a gun museum.

WILSON, Mississippi County. US 61.

Hampson Museum, N. on US 61, has a large collection of Indian relics unearthed from the Mound Builder sites of northeastern Arkansas. The Nodena Site on the family plantation of Dr. Henry Clay Hampson II is now a registered national historic landmark. The museum has more than 41,000 items.

CALIFORNIA

The gold mines are producing one good result; every creditor who has gone there is paying his debts. Claims not deemed worth a farthing are now cashed on presentation at nature's great bank. This has rendered the credit of every man here good for almost any amount. Orders for merchandise are honored which six months ago would have been thrown into the fire. There is none so poor, who has two stout arms and a pickaxe left, but he can empty any store in Monterey.

Rev. Walter Colton, *The Land of Gold. Three Years In California, 1846–1849* [1850]

Hutchings is landlord and author; his illustrated "Scenes of Wonder and Curiosity in California" is a creditable and valuable work. A friend, visiting here for the first time, found his wife upon the riverbank , with one hand vigorously turning the crank of a patent washing-machine, and with the other holding the latest *Atlantic Monthly,* absorbed in one of its articles. Only Indian labor is attainable. If eastern ladies who suffer constant martyrdom in respect of "help," were compelled to live on the Pacific coast a few months and employ Chinamen and Indians in lieu of servant girls, they would learn who is well off.

Albert D. Richardson, *Beyond the Mississippi* (Hartford, 1867)

Did you ever hear tell of Sweet Betsy from Pike,
Who crossed the wide mountains with her lover Ike,
With two yoke of cattle and one spotted hog,
A tall Shanghai rooster and an old yellow dog.

They swam the wide rivers and climbed the tall peaks
And camped on the prairies for weeks upon weeks,

Starvation and cholera, hard work and slaughter,
They reached California spite of hell and high water.
Hoodle dang fol-di-do, hoodle dang fol-de-day.

John Lomax, *Cowboy Songs* [1910]

. . . the next morning we crossed the hill by the bridlepath to the old Mission of San Juan Bautista. The Mission was in a beautiful valley, very level, and bounded on all sides by hills. The plain was covered with wild-grasses and mustard, and had abundant water. Cattle and horses were seen in all directions, and it was manifest that the priests who first occupied the country were good judges of land. It was Sunday, and all the people, about a hundred, had come to church from the country round about. Ord was somewhat of a Catholic, and entered the church with his clanking spurs and kneeled down, attracting the attention of all, for he had on the uniform of an American officer. As soon as church was out, all rushed to the various sports. I saw the priest, with his gray robes tucked up, playing at billiards, others were cock-fighting, and some at horse-racing.

William Tecumseh Sherman, *Memoirs* [1875]

CALIFORNIA FACTS: Juan Rodriguez Cabrillo, Spanish explorer, saw the land in 1542. Sir Francis Drake probably landed at Point Reyes briefly in 1579. Sebastian Vizcaino discovered the Bay of Monterey in 1602–1603. King Charles of Spain ordered the colonization of California in 1768. Father Junipero Serra founded the first mission near San Diego, July 16, 1769. The Mexican Revolution cast off Spanish rule in 1822. The American flag was flown at Monterey and Sonoma for the "Bear Flag Republic"—briefly—in 1846. Commodore John D. Sloat raised the U.S. flag at Monterey, July 7, 1846. California admitted to the Union, September 9, 1850, as the 31st state. Capital: Sacramento. Nickname: Golden State. California has 8 national monuments: Cabrillo, Channel Islands, Death Valley, Devils Postpile, Joshua Tree, Lava Beds, Muir Woods and Pinnacles; 5 national parks: Lassen Volcanic, Yosemite, Sequoia & Kings Canyon, and Redwood. Also Whiskeytown-Shasta-Trinity National Recreation Area, Point Reyes National Seashore, and John Muir National Historic Site; 17 national forests.

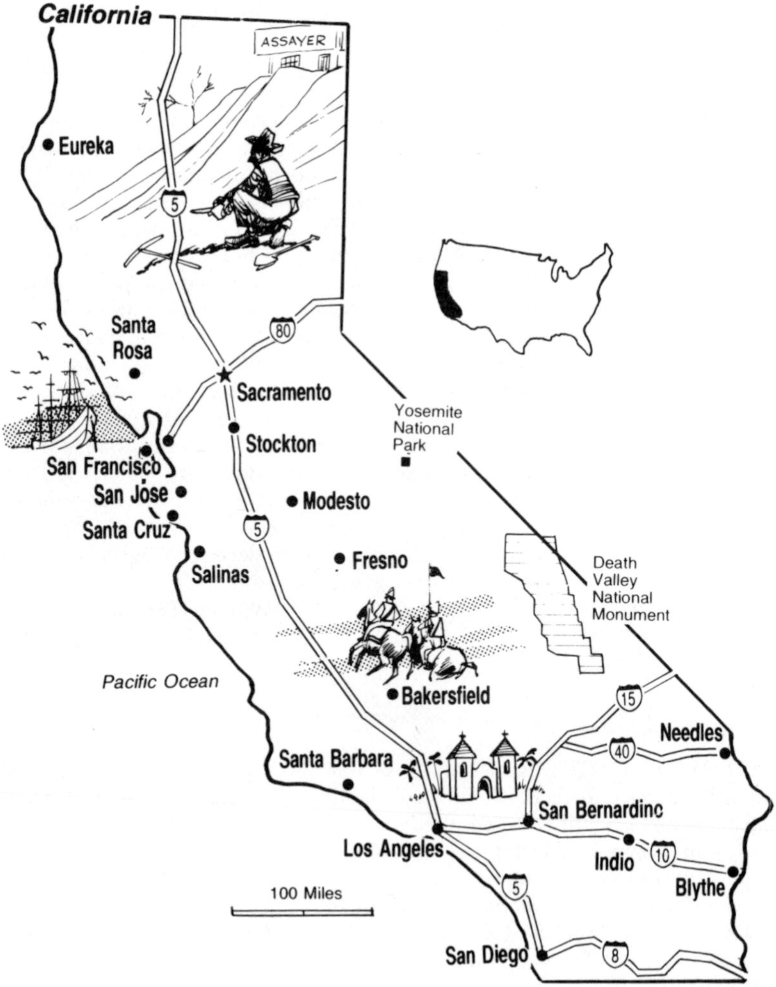
California
ASSAYER
Eureka
5
Santa Rosa
80
Sacramento
Stockton
San Francisco
San Jose
Santa Cruz
Salinas
Modesto
Fresno
Yosemite National Park
Death Valley National Monument
Pacific Ocean
Bakersfield
15
Needles
40
Santa Barbara
San Bernardino
Los Angeles
Indio
10
Blythe
100 Miles
San Diego
8

AGUANGA, Riverside County, State 79, was once a junction of old trails, the San Bernardino-Sonora Road, which went NE to the San Gorgonio Pass to the San Bernardino Valley and the Colorado Road which went NW.

Pechanga Cemetery, Indian Burying Ground on Pechanga Indian Reservation, ca. 4 miles NW of Aguanga, on State 79, on S. bank of the Temecula River which parallels the road. Juan Diego, shot because of a supposed horse theft, is buried here. He is the prototype of Alessandro, hero of *Ramona,* popular novel of its day by Helen Hunt Jackson, and later a 3-handkerchief movie starring Don Ameche of Kenosha, Wisconsin, as a highly romantic Indian.

Stage Station Ruins, on road running W. of highway ca. 2 miles N. of Aguanga. The first Butterfield Stage coach reached here in October of 1858, stopped twice weekly until 1861. Jacob Bergman and members of his family are buried in the small cemetery. Bergman drove the first Butterfield stage in the area.

ALTAVILLE, Calaveras County. State 4, 49. 2 miles N. of Angels Camp. The town was known as Cherokee Flat when Bret Harte wrote a poem about the "Pliocene" (Calaveras) skull found here, which provoked a storm of controversy and mockery. In 1903 the American Anthropological Society accepted the skull as a genuine relic but set no date on it.

Altaville Cemetery has a number of interesting old monuments from gold rush times. One which was photographed by historian Lambert Florin (*Ghost Town Album,* Superior, 1962) has the portrait of Alfredo Ribero on baked enamel. He is wearing a uniform thought to be that of local militia during the Civil War. Portraits on tombstones are common in Latin countries. Among buildings remaining: the Prince Hotel, the Prince and Garibardi Store (1857) and a brick school from 1858.

ALTURAS, Modoc County. US 395.

Modoc County Historical Museum, 508 S. Main St., has a large collection of Indian arrowheads, antique guns and other relics.

Modoc National Forest, via US 395 and State 299, comprises 1,500,000 acres. Headquarters are at Alturas, on Main St.

Modoc National Wildlife Refuge, 2 miles S. on US 395, covers 6,016 acres in three separate tracts.

Infernal Caverns Battle-Ground, ca. 17 miles S. on road going W. of US 395. Six marble headstones mark the graves of men killed September 26, 1867, in the Modoc Indian War. (See Lava Beds National Monument.)

AMADOR CITY, Amador County. State 49. At the bottom of a gulch on Amador Creek was the Ministers' Claim, where three preachers made the first quartz discovery although a camp had been established two years earlier. The Keystone Quartz mine made fortunes for its owners. Some original buildings remain.

Gold Rush Museum & Trading Post, on highway, has scale model of mining camp, and Wells Fargo display, housed in what was the Keystone Mine Company store, built in 1851.

ANGELS CAMP, Calaveras County. State 49. In the summer of 1848 a man named George Angel found gold in the creek. But the greatest fame came from Mark Twain's story *The Jumping Frog.* In the winter of

1864–65 Twain (Samuel Clemens) had tried pocket-mining at Angels Camp in the Mother Lode country. One entry in his notebook read: "Coleman with his jumping frog—bet a stranger $50.—stranger had no frog and C. got him one:—In the meantime stranger filled C's frog full of shot and he couldn't jump. The Stranger's frog won." And so did Twain. From the old story a tale-spinner named Ben Coon often told, came the frog named Dan'l and the start of Twain's fiction career. The New York *Saturday Press* printed it November 18, 1865; countless newspapers and anthologies have reprinted. Bret Harte's *Mrs. Skaggs' Husbands* also was set in Angels Camp.

City Park has a gate formed of mining relics and a statue of Mark Twain.

Angels Camp Museum, on State 49, 2 blocks N. of Angels Creek. Gold rush equipment and a large display of 19th century wagons and carriages.

Calaveras Hotel on the main street was built in 1857 as was the Stickle Store.

Rasberry Lane is named for Bennager Rasberry who was rabbit hunting, so the story goes, when his gun jammed, he tried a ramrod, which stuck in the barrel. When he shot at a rock the ramrod scuffed off the crust of the boulder and revealed gold beneath. He brought back a pick and shovel, made about $10,000 in the next several days and eventually became the richest man in town.

ANTIOCH, Contra Costa County. State 4. On the S. bank of the San Joaquin River. Settled by twin brothers, Joseph and W.W. Smith, carpenters and ordained ministers from Boston, who arrived via schooner in July 1849. Joseph died soon after but W.W. persuaded other New Englanders to settle here. (He must have been an eloquent persuader. Herbert A. Kenny, Boston poet and historian, tells of the astonishment registered by a fellow Bostonian who encountered a friend from home in Southern California and exclaimed, "Good heavens, how did *you* get here?" "Turned left at Dedham," was the response.)

Contra Loma Regional Park, Frederickson Lane, S. on State 4. 772 acres.

ANZA-BORREGO DESERT STATE PARK, San Diego and Imperial Counties. State 78. The highway bisects the nearly half-million acres of desert which look in many parts like the surface of the moon. One passable road takes off ca. 5 miles below Scissors Crossing in the San Felipe Valley and leads toward the pinnacle of Pinyon Mountain. The Crossing got its name because of the pattern made by converging roads; Pedro Fages, who named it, visited Indian villages of the area in 1782. Self-guiding auto tour available at headquarters, W. of Borrego Springs.

ARCADIA, Los Angeles County. I-210.

Los Angeles State and County Arboretum, 301 N. Baldwin Ave. at Colorado Blvd. Historical area has the Hugo Reid Adobe, with authentic furnishings of the 1840s; the Baldwin (or Queen Anne) Cottage, home of the mining king E. J. Baldwin, and his Coach House, fully restored. (Other buildings have been moved to the site and are appropriately furnished.)

ARCATA, Humboldt County. US 101, on the W. shore of Humboldt Bay. The town was named Uniontown by its founders in 1850, and has many Bret Harte associations. He arrived here to visit a married sister in the summer of 1857. The town was then a trading center and transshipment point for pack trains carrying supplies for the Trinity River mining camps. Harte worked as a tutor for a local family and sold poems to the *Golden Era,* a San Francisco literary weekly. Indians in the area raided smaller settlements and burned farms in the spring of 1858 and Harte in later life recalled how he had defended the frontier against the red men menace, but other settlers remembered only that he had dug a few postholes, tutored and wrote poetry. In the fall of 1858 the women and children of Union had been sent to stay in the only brick building while the men got ready for defense but no attack was launched. Harte became an editorial assistant for the *Northern Californian,* when it was established that December.

AUBURN, Placer County. State 49. First known as North Fork Dry Diggings, the town was the source of rich placer diggings in 1848 and became a shipping center for mining supplies and freight until the Central Pacific Railroad was built in 1865.

Old Auburn Historic District, at the head of Auburn Ravine, is bounded by Lincoln Way, Sacramento, Court and Commercial Sts. The Chamber of Commerce has literature on the history of the settlement. Among old buildings are the American Hotel, the Placer County Courthouse, the Post Office, the Union Bar, Lawyers' Row, and the Chinese Joss House.

Placer County Museum, High St. has old mining equipment among exhibits of the early days.

Two bad men of old Auburn were Tom Bell and Rattlesnake Dick who operated independently of one another. Bell with five friends held up a stage in 1856 carrying $100,000 in gold. But the stage driver whipped his horses when the gunmen were momentarily distracted by an approaching horseman and got away, though not before Bell had fired upon the coach, wounding several passengers and killing one woman. He was hanged for it. Dick was accused of stealing and decided to follow up the rumors. He became Rattlesnake Dick for stealing horses near Rattlesnake Bar and "the Pirate of the Placers," for robbing gold miners.

AVALON, Catalina Island, Los Angeles County. 29 miles SW of Los Angeles Harbor. The island was discovered in 1542 by Juan Rodriguez Cabrillo, a Portuguese navigator who was the first white man to see California. There was a brief gold rush in 1834.

Catalina Museum, Casino Bldg. Exhibits illustrate the history of the island; also natural history and archaeology displays.

BAKERSFIELD, Kern County. I-7. In 1885 when gold was discovered in the Kern River Canyon the town became a wild mining camp. A fire in 1889 destroyed much of the city. Oil was discovered in 1899 bringing another boom.

Kern County Museum and Pioneer Village, 3801 Chester Ave. 3 miles E. of State 99 and Pierce Rd. interchange. A 12-acre village of restorations with a log cabin, Victorian mansion, jail, hotel, saloon, locomotive, oil-drilling rig, vehicles. A museum has Indian artifacts with a diorama showing Yokuts and their basket-weaving techniques.

Walker Pass, 60 miles NE on State 178. The National Register of Historic Places officially lists the Pass as being in the "Bakersfield vicinity." 60 miles in some parts of the country is known as a "fur piece," and in other parts as being "no way a-tall." In still others a neighbor is "someone whose house you can get to in a half day." In Bakersfield, in any case, Nile St. becomes State 178 and leads to *Kern River State Park,* a 345-acre recreational area on high bluffs with a fine view of the river. The route then enters Kern River canyon, passes through Miracle Hot Springs, and Bodfish, a mining camp in the 1880s. (8 miles S. on Caliente Rd. is Havilah, another old camp.) Isabella Dam, at the junction with State 155, impounds the Kern River to form Lake Isabella. Kernville, which is 4 miles N. on 155, was known as Whiskey Flat. State 178 follows the route taken in 1834 by Joseph Walker, who was one of the guides of Capt. B. L. E. Bonneville's fur trapping expedition to the Rocky Mountains in 1833. Walker had left the Bonneville camp to explore the Pacific Coast. He was returning to the Rockies when he discovered the 5,248-ft pass. In 1843 he led the first emigrant train into California through this gap. It is now a national historic landmark. Bonneville, it might be noted, later complained that Walker and his men had made a long and frivolous expedition across California and had a very entertaining time in the Spanish settlements.

BARSTOW, San Bernardino County. I-40. State 58.

Calico Ghost Town Regional Park, 9 miles E. on US 91, I-15, then 3 miles N. on Ghost Town Rd., near Yermo. A restored mining town, with general store, schoolhouse, mine, saloon, and a western museum.

Calico Mountains Archaeological Project, on I-15, E. to Minneola overpass, then N. on local road to the museum camp.

BEAR VALLEY, Alpine County. State 49. The settlement first called Simpsonville was built by Capt. John C. Fremont as headquarters for his rich Mariposa mines. Fremont's Company Store, called Oso House, opened in 1851. The ruins of this and of his home (1851–61) may be seen on State 49, ca. 12 miles NW of town. In 1847 when Fremont bought a 44,000 acre ranch in the San Joaquin Valley (see Mariposa) he paid $3,000. Here and at his mines he survived many arguments with his partners and others and was eventually quoted as saying, "When I came to California I hadn't a cent. Now I owe two million dollars!" Many old stone and adobe structures, including saloons, stores, and hotels built in the 1850s remain.

BECKWOURTH PASS, Pluma County, State 70, was discovered in the spring of 1850 by James P. Beckwourth, son of a Revolutionary War officer and a slave mother. A fur trapping expedition brought him to the Rockies and he lived for a time among the Crow Indians. He led emigrant trains over the wagon road opened in 1851. A girl of 11, Ina Coolbrith, rode in one of the wagons. Mount Ina Coolbrith, S. of the pass, is named for her. She became California's first poet laureate.

The autobiography of James Beckwourth, as told to Thomas D. Bonner, was popular reading in the 19th century and will still entertain those who don't object to dollops of fiction mixed liberally with fact. *The Life and Adventures of James P. Beckwourth* was first published in 1856. William

Tecumseh Sherman said Beckwourth was one of the best chroniclers of events on the plains that he had encountered although "his reputation for veracity was not good." Francis Parkman, the historian, scribbled in his personal copy of the memoirs, "Much of this narrative is probably false." And J. Frank Dobie called him "the champion of all western liars." Certainly some of his tales seem as tall as the pass which bears his name, but he was a trail blazer and an original.

BELMONT, San Mateo County. US 101.

Ralston Home, College of Notre Dame campus. William C. Ralston helped develop the Comstock Lode mines in Nevada as well as industry and railroads in California. His mansion, built in the 1860s, is largely unchanged. It was built by Count Aconetto Cipriano and expanded by Ralston. In 1868 it could accommodate 120 guests. The ballroom is styled after the Hall of Mirrors at Versailles. Ralston's bank failed in August of 1875. His body was found next day. The house is a national historic landmark.

BENICIA, Solano County. I-80.

Benicia Capitol-Courthouse, 1st and G Sts. The third such structure to be built in California, the Benicia Capitol is the only one remaining from the first ten years of statehood. It was the seat of government from 1853 to 1854, and has been restored. A state historic landmark.

Benicia Barracks, E. edge of town. At the W. end of Suisun Bay, the infantry base was established in 1849, one of the first military posts in the California territory. Two years later to support troops scattered along the Pacific Coast of the new state (entered Union September 9, 1850), the Army founded an ordnance supply depot adjacent to the barracks, the first in the Far West. The barracks remained operative until 1898 when its troops left for the Philippines. At varying times in its early years the barracks was headquarters for Ulysses S. Grant, William Tecumseh Sherman, George Crook and other officers soon to become famous in the Civil War. The Army's camel experiment ended at the arsenal where the camels Edward Fitzgerald Beale had brought from Texas across the great southwest were sold at auction. The project was abandoned due to the emergencies created by the Civil War.

Economic footnote, from Grant's *Memoirs,* "Prices for all kinds of supplies were so high on the Pacific coast from 1849 until at least 1853 that it would have been impossible for officers of the army to exist upon their pay, if it had not been that authority was given them to purchase from the commissary such supplies as he kept, at New Orleans wholesale prices. A cook could not be hired for the pay of a captain. The cook could do better. At Benicia, in 1852, flour was 25 cents per pound; potatoes were 16 cents; beets, turnips, and cabbage, 6 cents; onions, 37½ cents; meat and other articles in proportion."

BERKELEY, Alameda County. I-688.

Robert H. Lowie Museum of Anthropology, in Kroeber Hall, on Bancroft, University of California campus, has a vast collection of California and other American archaeology materials, with changing exhibits.

Bancroft Library, on campus, has the 1579 brass plate found at Drake's Cove indicating the explorer landed in that year. The extensive collection of historical material was given by historian Hubert Howe Bancroft, with more than 100,000 volumes on Spanish-American history.

Earth Sciences Building, University campus, N. gate entrance from Hearst Ave. Geological displays and relics, paleontology museum.

Grizzly Peak Boulevard is a winding drive along the crest of the city that affords an excellent view of the Bay area. Berkeley was named for George Berkeley, Bishop of Cloyne, an 18th-century philosopher and teacher who came to America and helped to educate Indians of California. He wrote a line often borrowed by those who like a bit of rhetoric: "Westward, the course of empire takes its way."

BISHOP, Inyo County. US 395. The town and Bishop Creek were named for Samuel A. Bishop, a Fort Tejon cattleman, who drove the first herd into the Owens Valley in 1861. He built two cabins on his St. Francis Ranch and was besieged by the Paiutes in the uprisings of the 1860s. The town was developed 3 miles NE of Bishop's ranch.

The Chamber of Commerce, 690 Main St., has information and self-guiding maps on petroglyph and ghost town tours. There is a 50-mile circle trip which passes five sites where petroglyphs were found near old deer trails. Deer and mountain sheep were regarded as having mystical powers, favorable to hunters. At Fish Slough Site there are signs of an ancient village. Pits in boulders are where Indian women used to grind food.

Laws Railroad Museum, 5 miles NE on US 6, then ½ miles E. on Silver Canyon Rd. Once the terminal of a branch of the Southern Pacific, this is an 11-acre restoration which has a depot, a station agent's house, the post office with appropriate furnishings, a narrow-gauge locomotive and sundry other relics of the 19th century.

BODIE, Mono County. E. of US 395, N. of Lee Vining and Mono Lake. The ghost town once had 20,000 citizens, with 60 saloons, three breweries, three newspapers and a jail. Over $100 million in ore was mined in the vicinity. "Bad man from Bodie" was a saying of the times. The area is now a state historic park. A self-guiding tour covers the main part of town, passing the church, jail, two-room school, Miners Union Hall, now a museum, and the cemetery that has a monument to President James A. Garfield.

Waterman S. Body, or William Bodey, died in a blizzard during the winter of 1859–60; with typical Western spelling, the town was named for him. A story that has always been popular in Western legend is that a little girl when told her family was boarding a wagon train headed to this camp began her prayers with: "Goodbye, God, I'm going to Bodie."

BRENTWOOD, Contra Costa County. State 4.

Marsh Ranch, less than two miles on Marsh Creek Rd. off Walnut Blvd., 5.3 miles S. of town. John Marsh came to California from Massachusetts, with a Harvard diploma, in January 1836 to practice medicine, with a license from the Mexican government. He bought the 17,400-acre Rancho Los Medanos (sometimes spelled Meganos) and built a small adobe. In 1856 he built the Stone House with a 655-foot tower. That same year he was murdered on the road to Martinez. He was 52. Marsh was kind to the Indians but tight-fisted with everyone else. When the Bidwell-Bartleson Party, the first to cross the Sierra, arrived at his place in 1841 he charged them for stopping over. With a true New Englander's sense of thrift, he is said to have charged a steer a mile for house calls and soon had a sizable herd. The Stone House had been built for a bride who died before it was completed. The house and 7 acres of the original ranch are now a county park.

CALABASAS, Los Angeles County. US 101.

Leonis Adobe, 23537 Calabasas Rd., is the restored ranch of Miguel Leonis, once known as the "King of Calabasas." Original 19th-century furnishings.

CALIFORNIA TRAIL, Placer County, etc. I-80 at Nevada line near Truckee. The old California Trail ran a few miles below the present highway and crossed it at several points. In the autumn of 1844, Caleb Greenwood, mountaineer and trapper, in his 80s, led 12 wagons of the Stevens-Murphy party along this route. They were the first on wheels to cross the Sierra. In 1846 the Donner Party came too late for the season and were caught by the snows and the hunger that made them forever famous.

CALISTOGA, Napa County. State 29. The Indians called it Colaynomo (oven-place). When Samuel Brannan, millionaire Mormon, arrived in 1859, he established a spa. For a choice description of the area, read *The Silverado Squatters,* by Robert Louis Stevenson, the gifted Scotsman who saw frontier America with a keen, amused and more-kindly-than-sardonic eye. He was in broken-health when he camped in the mountains north of San Francisco in 1880. Of Calistoga he wrote: "It must be remembered that we are here in a land of stage-drivers and highwaymen: a land, in that sense, like England a hundred years ago. The highway robber—road-agent, he is quaintly called—is still busy in these parts. . . . Only a few years ago, the Lakeport stage was robbed a mile or two from Calistoga. In 1879, the dentist of Mendocino City, fifty miles away upon the coast, suddenly threw off the garments of his trade . . . and flamed forth in his second dress as a captain of banditti. . . . I am reminded of another highwayman of that same year. 'He had been unwell,' so ran his humorous defense, and the doctor told him to take something, so he took the express-box."

Petrified Forest, 5 miles W., has redwoods which had been buried more than 6 million years under volcanic ash when they were uncovered in 1860.

Mount St. Helena, 8 miles N. on State 29, is an extinct volcano where the ailing Stevenson spent his belated honeymoon in 1880, and wrote *The Silverado Squatters.* The park named in his honor has a monument: a statue of the author at site of his bunkhouse.

CARMEL, Monterey County. State 1.

Carmel Mission (San Carlos Borromeo del Rio Carmelo), 3080 Rio Rd., was the second of those established by Fra Junipero Serra and was headquarters of the *padre presidente.* A year after Monterey was founded, Father Serra moved his mission away from the presidio. Restoration of the building began in 1884. It contains many original paintings and statues. A national historic landmark. The body of Father Serra was buried left of the altar in the adobe church existing at the time of his death. Father Jean Crespi, his associate, and Father Fermin Lasuen, his successor, were buried beside him. During a hundred years of neglect the graves were exposed to weather in the ruined church. Three times the bones of the priest have been removed, identified and replaced; the last occasion was when proceedings began for canonization of the mission founder. He lived in the simplest possible manner and chose to die the same way. He never saw the elaborate part of the church which contains his grave.

CHICO, Butte County. US 99E. In the late 1840s, John Bidwell, a member of the first overland wagon train to cross the Sierra Nevada, established a ranch here. Later he donated much of the land for the townsite. He was an individualist who began an experimental orchard which produced 400 varieties of fruit. He began wine making during the Civil War years but two years later gave up his vineyards. Still later he ran for President on the Prohibition Party ticket.

In *Bidwell Mansion State Historic Park,* 525 Esplanade, is the 26-room Tuscan-style Victorian Bidwell home, partially restored. A memorial to Bidwell was built by Maidu Indians. It is a granite monument on the site of the original Bidwell cabin.

Bidwell Park, E. 4th St., has an oak tree named for Joseph Hooker and said to be a thousand years old, on Manzanita Ave. The park comprises 2,400 acres with a stream, Big Chico, and greenery that was used as background for a movie, "The Adventures of Robin Hood."

Patrick Rancheria, 3 miles S. of town, is a pre-Columbian site consisting of a large mound of village midden with 36 surface depressions, the remains of aboriginal dwellings. The site marks the northernmost extension of the "Ghost Dance" cult which thrived in the late 19th century. (One of the major battles in the Apache Wars fought in Arizona was touched off by the killing of a medicine man who was teaching the "Ghost Dance" religion.)

CHINESE CAMP, Tuolumne County. State 49. The town was founded by Englishmen in 1849 who brought Chinese to work in the mines. It became a gathering place for Chinese tongs and a tong war took place in 1856 when 900 members of the Yan-Wo Tong faced 1,200 members of the Sam-Yap Tong and fought out their rivalries. Four were dead in the two-hour conflict, four wounded and 250 jailed.

The post office was built in 1854 as a general store. The St. Francis Xavier Roman Catholic Church was built in 1855. A plaque on the old post office honors Eddie Webb, born in Snelling, California, "the last of the old-time stage drivers."

CHINO, San Bernardino County. State 60.

Yorba-Slaughter Adobe, Pomono-Rincon Rd., was built by Raimundo Yorba with Indian labor in the early 1850s. When the Butterfield line passed here in 1859–63, the family furnished relay teams. House was purchased in 1868 by Fenton Slaughter, a Mexican war veteran, and restored by Slaughter's daughter with authentic period furnishings. A state historical landmark.

COLOMA, San Mateo County. State 49. (Cullumah, beautiful vale, in Indian language.) James Marshall's discovery of gold here in 1848 set off the

Gold Rush but it was not the first California gold discovery. The first find of commercial value was in Placerita Canyon, by a Mexican prospector, Francisco Lopez y Arballo. Later Francisco Garcia found gold in San Feliciana Canyon. The two yielded about $40,000 in a year and a half which would be chicken feed after Marshall's discovery.

Captain John A. Sutter, a merchant and landholder, hired James W. Marshall to erect a sawmill in the small Indian valley of Culluma, along an old river channel on the American River. Marshall inspecting the tailrace noticed something glittering, picked it up, found it was malleable when beaten between two rocks. He put the original stonelike piece and two others in the crown of his hat and reputedly announced to the workers, "Boys, I believe I've found a gold mine," a simple statement which would change countless lives and be misquoted as often as Farragut's statement at Mobile Bay about damning torpedoes.

Capt. Sutter told his part of the beginnings in Hutchings' *California Magazine* in November, 1857: "It was a rainy afternoon when Mr. Marshall arrived at my office. . . . He told me then that he had some important and interesting news which he wished to communicate secretly to me, and wished me to go with him to a place where we should not be disturbed, and where no listeners could come and hear what we had to say. I went with him to my private rooms. . . . I forgot to lock the doors, and it happened that the door was opened by the clerk just at the moment when Marshall took a rag from his pocket, showing me the yellow metal: he had about two ounces of it; but how quick Mr. M. put the yellow metal in his pocket again can hardly be described. . . . After having proved the metal with aqua fortis, which I found in my apothecary shop, likewise with other experiments, and read the long article "gold" in the Encyclopedia Americana, I declared this to be gold of the finest quality, of at least 23 carats. After this Mr. M. had no more rest nor patience, and wanted me to start with him immediately for Coloma."

The secret was out, and Sutter was soon a nearly ruined man. (See Sacramento.)

Marshall Gold Discovery State Historical Park on State 49. Marshall's cabin has been preserved; his statue points to the site of the find. The sawmill has been reconstructed and a museum has an interesting collection of relics.

COLUMBIA, Tuolumne County. Off State 49. First known as Hildreth's Diggings when Dr. Thaddeus Hildreath (sic) and his brother George and friends slept overnight in the gulch at the foot of what became Main St. Next morning when they dried out their blankets, soaked from a midnight storm, they found glitter that was gold.

Columbia Historic District has many original buildings including the Wells Fargo Office of 1857. The rich placer mines were productive until 1880; by then about $87 million in gold had been mined. The noisiest and some say the wickedest of mining camps, it is also the best preserved.

Hidden Treasure Gold Mine is still partly in operation, partly open for tours.

CRESCENT CITY, Del Norte County. US 101.

Point St. George, N. of beach. The *Brother Jonathan,* a side-wheeler, was wrecked in 1865. The 203 persons aboard (of 232) who died are buried in Brother Jonathan Cemetery, Taylor Rd. & 9th St.

Crescent City Lighthouse, on Battery Point, end of A St., is accessible only at low tide but has a museum maintained by the Del Norte County Historical Society.

Del Norte County Historical Museum, 577 H St., has Indian displays in what was the county jail.

McNulty Pioneer Memorial Home, 710 H St., has appropriate period furnishings, and is maintained by the historical society.

Redwood National Park, E. of town, has 55 miles of coastline. Headquarters at 2nd & K Sts. has exhibits, literature and lectures. The 58,000-acre park encompasses three state park areas: Prairie Creek, Jedediah Smith and Del Norte Coast Redwoods State Parks. Some of the tallest trees in the world are on the inside bend of Redwood Creek.

DAVIS, Yolo County. State 113. Early settler Jerome C. Davis was a large-scale farmer not a miner; he had 400 acres of wheat, barley, fruit trees and vines, as well as livestock.

Davis Campus of the University of California, on State 113, has a Memorial Union Art Gallery with changing historical exhibits. The office of the Memorial Union (Freeborn Hall) has information on visiting the California State Agricultural Experiment Station laboratories and fields.

DEATH VALLEY NATIONAL MONUMENT, Inyo County. State 190.

Visitor Center at Furnace Creek. The area was named in 1849 when a party of gold seekers became lost in its wild salt flats. Only one died though the hardships were nearly unendurable. Many places in the valley carry reminders of the emigrants; also Indian petroglyphs. The Monument was established in 1933 with 3,000 square miles of desert; 500 miles of improved roadways now available.

Museum, at Visitor Center, has exhibits of history, geology, zoology and botany. There are hourly ranger lectures in the auditorium; brochures and maps.

Borax Museum, at Furnace Creek Ranch, is housed in what probably was the valley's first frame house, moved from its original site in Twenty-Mule-Team Canyon.

The Ghosttown of Rhyolite, Nevada, is on State 58, just outside the monument.

Titus Canyon, on a one-way dirt road entered from State 58, a 25-mile trip past the ruins of Leadfield and the Indian petroglyphs at Klare Spring.

Scotty's Castle, in the N. section of the monument, is a desert mansion, the incredible lodgings of the flamboyant Death Valley Scotty (Walter Scott) in his heyday. Hourly tours.

Harmony Borax Works, extensive ruins on State 190 N. of Furnace Creek.

Zabriskie Point, SE of Furnace Creek on State 190, an area of ancient lake beds, 5 to 10 million years old.

Dante's View, on crest of the Black Mountains, S. from 190, a spectacular scenic overlook at a point 5,755 feet above Badwater.

Badwater, reached via Artist's Drive off the main road S. of Furnace Creek, is considered the lowest point in the western hemisphere, minus 282 feet. Rock salt formations may be seen.

DEVILS POSTPILE NATIONAL MONUMENT, Madera County. W.

of US 395. Ca. 8 miles from Minaret Summit, in Inyo Forest. Thousands of basaltic columns are about 900 feet long and 200 feet wide. An easy trail leads to the top of the columns. Rainbow Fall is 2 miles down a river trail from the Postpile. Park rangers are on duty in summer months. Springs S. of the campground in the NE section of the monument produce a natural soda water.

DONNER MEMORIAL STATE PARK, Nevada County. I-80. The 353-acre park is a memorial to the wagon train emigrants, led by George and Jacob Donner and James F. Reed, who were stranded here in the winter of 1846. There were 45 survivors from a party of 81. They ate barks, twigs, mice and eventually their fellows who had died of starvation.

The Emigrant Trail Museum has exhibits on the Donner Party and other aspects of early emigration. A national and state historic landmark.

DOWNIEVILLE, Sierra County. State 49. The town, set in one of the most rugged areas of the state, was founded in 1849 with the discovery of gold. In 1852 and 1858 fire destroyed much of the settlement, which had more than 5,000 miners and many families. Each time the residents rebuilt. A few brick and stone buildings remain, some frame houses and two churches. The tree-lined main street has the look of the 19th century with old doors, shutters and trim.

Sierra County Museum, Main St., was built in 1851. A scale model stamp mill is among exhibits.

Sierra County Courthouse, built in 1855 on Durgan's Flat. Behind the courthouse on Piety Hill is an old gallows. A movie house stands where the theater was in the days when such stars as Edwin Booth, Lola Montez and Lotta Crabtree toured and were showered with coins and gold dust pokes, according to local stories. Lotta was a talented child when Lola was past her prime (see Grass Valley), but both were popular performers in the culture-starved frontier.

EL DORADO, El Dorado County. State 49. The town was first known as Mud Spring and was a watering place, of what seems doubtful quality, on the Carson Branch of the California Overland Trail. When gold was discovered in 1849, a mining camp boom followed and the area became a freighting center, with considerably *more* mud most of the time. A few buildings remain.

El Dorado National Forest comprises 886,000 acres. Lake Tahoe Visitor Center is on State 89 between Camp Richardson and Emerald Bay. Orientation programs and information for self-guiding tours are here. Naturalist-guided tours in summer. The Stream Profile Chamber is a partially submerged structure that shows a live, in-action mountain stream.

ESCONDIDO, San Diego County. State 78.

Palomar Observatory, 35 miles NE has a visitors' gallery and a museum.

San Pasquel Battlefield State Historic Monument, 8 miles SE toward Ramona. In December 1848 the forces of Brig. Gen. Stephen Kearny attacked the army of Gen. Andres Pico, which had no one killed, although Kearny lost 19 men.

EUREKA, Humboldt County. US 101.

Fort Humboldt State Historical Monument, 3431 Fort Ave. Exhibits of logging and military operations. Capt.

Ulysses S. Grant was stationed here in 1853 when he was a young officer, unhappily separated from his family. Though he writes of visits to San Francisco in his famous *Personal Memoirs,* he has little to say about his service in California. As for Fort Humboldt, in his opinion, even the getting there wasn't easy:

"The death of Colonel Bliss of the adjutant-general's department, which occurred August 5, 1853, promoted me to the captaincy of a company then stationed at Humboldt Bay, California. The notice reached me in September of the same year, and I very soon started to join my new command. There was no way of reaching Humboldt at that time except to take passage on a San Francisco sailing-vessel going after lumber. Redwood, a species of cedar, which on the Pacific coast takes the place filled by white pine in the East, then abounded on the banks of Humboldt Bay. There were extensive saw-mills engaged in preparing this lumber for the San Francisco market, and sailing-vessels used in getting it to market furnished the only means of communication between Humboldt and the balance of the world."

Indian Island, in the bay, is the site where a massacre of Indians by white settlers took place in 1860. The whites chose a day when the warriors of the tribe were known to be away and killed the elderly, the women and the children.

William Carson House, 2nd & M Sts., is a Victorian house of the style cartoonist Charles Addams uses for background. It has gables, gingerbread trim, verandas, and a tower above what appears to be a widow's walk. Not content with one gingerbread palace he built another across the street for his son's wedding gift.

Clarke Memorial Museum, 240 E. St. Indian artifacts, old guns, mineral collection and other relics.

Shipwreck, 1938 Buhne Dr., 5 miles S. of King Salmon Exit on US 101. A marine museum is housed in a replica of a square-rigged sailing ship.

Six Rivers National Forest. Headquarters are at 710 E. St. The forest comprises 1,065,954 acres.

FIDDLETOWN, Amador County. E. of State 49, on E. 16. The town was settled by Missourians who had brought their fiddles and played *Turkey in the Straw,* until one of the elder members of the group named the town, probably in some exasperation; Bret Harte called one of his short stories, *An Episode of Fiddletown.*

The Purinton House was the home of Judge Purinton who made frequent visits to San Francisco and Sacramento and hated to sign Fiddletown on the register book at hotels. It always brought laughs. He had the name changed to Oleta, but Harte's fame probably caused the townspeople to change it back.

Schallhorn Blacksmith and Wagon Shop was built in 1870 of Valley Springs rhyolite tuff. Chris Schallhorn sawed most of the blocks; the building now serves as a part-time museum.

FOLSOM, Sacramento County. US 50. Brick stores built in the 1850s and 1860s line the highway. Negro miners dug for gold on the American River, and their camp was laid out on the onetime Mexican ranch in the area that had been acquired by William A. Leidesdorff, U. S. Vice-Consul in 1844. A trail led across the land when it was traced by Captain Sutter from his fort to his sawmill on the South Fork of the Rio de los Americanos (American River) and became the

Coloma Road, the first route to the gold fields after Marshall's discovery. Capt. Joseph L. Folsom bought the land from Leidesdorff's heirs in 1848. He became the richest man in the area. A former assistant-quartermaster of Stevenson's New York Volunteers, Folsom also made purchases of properities in San Francisco that, combined with his holdings here, made him one of California's wealthiest citizens as well.

In 1857 the work began on the California Central Railroad. For a decade beginning in 1856 the town was a point of departure for the mines. And an important freight depot on the railroad. On April 4, 1860, Harry Roff galloped through town on the first run of the Pony Express.

Old Powerhouse is on the American River at the foot of Riley St.

FORT BIDWELL, Modoc County. In the town of Fort Bidwell, NE corner of state near Oregon and Nevada lines. E. of US 395. The Fort was founded in 1865 by volunteer troops to protect emigrants and settlers from Indians. Its garrison fought with Gen. Crook at the nearby Battle of Infernal Caverns in September, 1867, and during his Snake campaign of 1866–1868, and in the wars against the Modocs of 1872, 1873, the Nez Perces (1877) and the Bannacks (1878). A stable, school and other buildings are in varying states of preservation. The parade ground and a graveyard also remain. The site is now occupied by the headquarters for the Fort Bidwell Indian Reservation. It is a registered state historic landmark and is marked by a monument.

FORT BRAGG, Mendocino County. State 1.

Fort Bragg, 321 Main St. The post was established in 1857 on the Mendocino Indian Reservation. In 1858 its troops took part in the Indian war campaign in eastern Washington. When the Civil War began, regulars left the post to participate but were replaced by the California Volunteers who became active against the Apache Indians in Arizona and against the Confederate invasion of the southwest. A state marker commemorates the Fort (named for Gen. Braxton Bragg who fought in the Seminole, Mexican and Civil Wars. He was a Confederate general), which is a registered state historic landmark, near the hospital site. Main St. bisects the old parade ground, bounded on the north by Laurel St. between Franklin and McPherson, on south at a point about 100 feet S. of Redwood St.

California Western Railroad, foot of Laurel St. A 40-mile scenic trip through redwoods to Willits, following the Noyo River. Round trip is about 6 hours.

State Parks: most have naturalist programs and are worth visiting in an area rich in old western memories.

MacKerricher, 3 miles N. on State 1.

Russian Gulch, 9 miles S. on State 1.

Van Damme, 14 miles S. on State 1. A 1,825-acre park with Pygmy Forest in its boundaries. Trees nearly a century old are on a Tom Thumb scale.

Noyo, 2 miles S. on State 1 at the mouth of Noyo River is an old fishing village.

FORTS AND CAMPS, various sites.

Anderson, Humboldt County, on the right bank of Redwood Creek, was established in March, 1862, by the 2nd California Infantry. Never officially designated, the fort was abandoned late in 1862, later used as a camp during the Indian "troubles" of 1864.

Abandoned again in August, 1866.

Baker, Humboldt County. 23 miles E. of Hydesville on the W. bank of the Van Dusen Fork of the Eel River. Established in March, 1862, by the 3rd California Infantry. Named for Col. Edward D. Baker who was killed in the Battle of Ball's Bluff very early in the Civil War, October 21, 1861. This was a grievous loss to Lincoln, whose friend Baker had been. The post, never officially designated, was abandoned on September 7, 1863, and replaced briefly by Camp Iaqua.

Baker No. 2 (see San Francisco).

Crook, Shasta County. On N. bank of the Fall River, 7 miles above its confluence with the Pit River. Established July 1, 1857, by Capt. John Gardiner, 1st U.S. Dragoons. Originally called Camp Hollenbush, for Assistant Surgeon Calvin Hollenbush, the post was designated Fort Crook, in 1857 for George Crook, 4th U.S. Infantry, then a first lieutenant, later a Civil War general who became the most skillful Indian fighter of the southwest. Post was abandoned July 1, 1869.

Gaston, Humboldt County. Established December 4, 1858, in the Hoopa Valley on the W. bank of the Trinity River, ca. 14 miles above junction with the Klamath River. Named for 2nd Lt. William Gaston, 1st U. S. Dragoons, killed May 17, 1858, during the expedition against the Spokane Indians in Washington. Transferred to the Interior Department, February 11, 1892, for use of Indian Service.

Gaston, No. 2, Imperial County. Established on the W. bank of the Colorado River, ca. 45 miles N. of Fort Yuma. A supply depot to serve in connection with Fort Mojave, Arizona. For a time it served as an outpost to Fort Yuma and was garrisoned briefly at various times until 1867.

Guijarros (Castillo Guijarros), San Diego County. Established in 1795 on the E. side of Point Loma near the entrance to San Diego Bay. The viceroy of New Spain wanted a fortification similar to Castillo de San Joaquin which guarded San Francisco Bay but he didn't want to pay for it. Timber was sent from Monterey; Santa Barbara sent axletrees and wheels for ten carts. Bricks and tile were made at the San Diego presidio and delivered by flatboat across the bay. When U. S. forces occupied San Diego the fort, which had been abandoned in 1838, was in poor condition. Fort Rosecrans later occupied the site.

Humboldt, Humboldt County. Established in 1853, on a bluff overlooking the bay at Bucksport, now part of Eureka. Abandoned 1867. (Also see Eureka.)

Independence, Inyo County. Established July 4, 1862, on the N. side of Oak Creek, near its source in the Owens River Valley on the east slope of the Sierra Nevada Mountains. Ca. 2 miles N. of Independence. The 2nd California Cavalry were here to protect the mining district. The post was never officially designated and was abandoned in 1864, reoccupied the following year. Transferred to the Department of the Interior on July 22, 1884.

Jones, Siskiyou County, established in 1852 on the E. bank of the Scott River, to protect the mining district. Abandoned in June 1858. Never officially designated. A flagpole and commemorative marker at site, a registered State historic landmark.

Lippitt, Humboldt County, was a temporary post but occasionally is referred to in letters, diaries and memoirs. It existed for less than three months at Bucksport, now part of Eureka, from January, 1862 to March or April.

Lyon, Humboldt County. Established March, 1862, on the R. bank of Mad River, ca. 20 miles E. of Arcata. Named for Brig. Gen Nathanial Lyon, killed August 10, 1861, in the Battle of Wilson's Creek, Springfield, Missouri. The loss of Lyon was a major blow to Federal forces early in the war. The post, never officially designated, was abandoned late in the year.

McDowell, on Angel Island in San Francisco Bay, established in September 1863. *Camp Reynolds,* on W. side of island, was established in 1864 and served as post headquarters, both were part of the coastal defences during the Civil War. The post was officially designated Angel Island; in 1900 it was named Fort McDowell, for the Civil War general. The island which at times has been a prison camp is now a state park.

Mason, San Francisco County, on San Francisco Bay, Point San Jose. In 1797 the site was occupied by a Spanish-garrisoned Battery San Jose. The post was designated Fort Mason in 1882, named for Col. Richard Barnes Mason, 1st U. S. Dragoons, who was military governor of California from 1847 till 1849. The post now serves as headquarters for the San Francisco Port of Embarkation and passenger terminal.

Miller, Madera County. E. of State 41 on San Joaquin River. The post site has been buried by Millerton Lake. It was established in May, 1851, in an area where Camp Barbour had been set up in April of the same year, for the purpose of allowing treaty negotiations to be carried on between the Indian commissioners and the rebellious Indians of the area. Members of the 2nd California Cavalry were the last to occupy the post; it was abandoned in October, 1864.

Montgomery, at San Francisco then called Yerba Buena. This was a very temporary fort established during the early months of the Mexican War when rumors flew that the Mexican Army was advancing on the city.

Moore, Los Angeles County. Established in 1847 when U.S. forces occupied Los Angeles. The garrison was withdrawn in 1848, the buildings never finished and even the hill it stood on is gone, but the name lingers in old accounts of the occupation.

Piute, San Bernardino County. Established in 1859 near Piute Springs in the Piute Mountains, ca. 25 miles W. of Fort Mojave, Arizona, to protect the desert route used by the military and emigrants. For a period in its history the post was called Fort Beale for Edward F. Beale, the camel leader.

Reading, Shasta County. On W. side of Cow Creek above present town of Redding. Established in 1852 to protect the mining district. Abandoned in 1870.

Rosecrans, on site of Castillo Guijarros (which see), the military reservation was established in February, 1852, to protect the entrance to San Diego Bay. Named for Civil War General William S. Rosecrans.

Seward, Humboldt County, on the Eel River. Established in 1861. Named for Secretary of State William Seward, whose later act of purchasing Alaska was known as "Seward's Folly." The post was abandoned in 1862.

Stockton, San Diego County. Established in 1838 on Presidio Hill, built by householders of San Diego fearing an attack from Los Angelenos when a conflict existed between the supporters of Juan Bautista Alvarado and Carlos Cabrillo. Occupied by the U.S. in July, 1846. Called Fort Du Pont for Capt. Samuel F. Du Pont, then Fort Stockton for Commodore Robert F. Stockton, the post was occupied for two years.

Ter-waw, Del Norte County. Established 1857 on the N. bank of the Klamath River about six miles above its mouth, by 1st Lt. George Crook, then of the 4th U. S. Infantry. The post endured several floods, with many of its buildings washed away, but was not abandoned until June, 1862.

Weller, Mendocino County. Established 1859 on the Mendocino Indian Reservation near the head of the Russian River in Redwood Valley. Named for John B. Weller, a California governor. The post was abandoned within the year.

Winfield Scott, San Francisco County. Established in 1861 (building had begun in 1854) on Fort Point, at the S. anchorage of the present Golden Gate Bridge. The post was designated Fort Point until 1882 when it was renamed in honor of Maj. Gen. Winfield Scott who was in charge of Union forces at the outbreak of the Civil War. The present fort is ca. ½ mile S. of the old fort. (See San Francisco.)

Wright, Mendocino County, was established in December 1858 to control and support the Indians of the Nome Cult Agency, later the Round Valley Indian Reservation. It was transferred to the Department of the Interior for the Indian Service in July 1876.

FORT ROSS STATE HISTORIC PARK, Sonoma County. State 1. Fort Ross was the largest single Russian trading center S. of Alaska. John Sutter bought the fort in 1841. Now a national and state historical landmark. Several restored buildings are open to visitors, among these are the Manager's House, the Russian Orthodox Chapel, two blockhouses and surrounding stockade. There is a small museum in the former Commander's House. The Indians gave up 1,000 acres, by some reports, to the Russian-American Fur Co. in exchange for 3 blankets, 2 axes, 3 hoes, and a bunch of beads.

FORT TEJON, Kern County. I-5 (State 99). 38 miles S. of Bakersfield. Near Lebec. The post was established August 10, 1854, to guard the pass through the Tehachapi Mountains. The famous camel corps, led by Edward Beale across the Southwest, was based here for a time. Beale had been appointed Superintendent of Indian Affairs for California and Nevada in 1852. When the fort was abandoned on September 11, 1864, by order of Maj. Gen. Irvin McDowell the land and buildings became part of his ranch, a Mexican grant he had purchased.

In 1858 the post was a station on the Butterfield route. Its troops served as escort for the stages passing through perilous territory. It is now a state historical monument. Some buildings have been restored.

Rancho El Tejon, in Kern and Los Angeles Counties, US 99, at Lebec. There is a monument here for Beale's ranch. Beale, as a young navy lieutenant, served with distinction in the Mexican War. When he became Superintendent of Indian Affairs for the southwest area, he instituted a new Indian policy that called for a series of small reservations where Indians could be taught trades and farming in order to be independent. This was the first of the reservations, set up in 1853. When Beale lost his job because of political reasons in 1854, he became a rancher here. He bought 4 ranchos for about five cents an acre to make a 195,000-acre ranch. When the Tejon Reservation was abandoned in 1863, Beale invited the Indians to share the ranch. By 1870 he had more than 100,000 sheep, tended by 300 Indians.

FREMONT, Alameda County. State 17.

Jose de Jesus Vallejo Adobe, Niles Blvd. at Nursery Ave. Now the California Nursery Company, the Rancho Arroyo de la Alameda was granted to Vallejo in 1842. It comprised 17,705 acres. Vallejo was an administrator at the Mission San Jose and commander at the Pueblo de San Jose, 1841–1842. In 1850 he also became postmaster at the mission. The adobe has been restored. It is a registered historical building.

Mission San Jose de Guadalupe, 43300 Mission St. The original building is gone but relics are in the parish church. Part of the padre's house is a museum.

FRESNO, Fresno County. State 99.

Roeding Park, W. Belmont Ave. & State 99, has the old Fort Miller Blockhouse, built in 1841, which was moved here in 1944 when Friant Dam flooded the townsite of Millerton (once Rootville) and the old fort site.

Fresno Museum of Natural History and Junior Museum, 1944 N. Winery Ave., has a Yokuts Indian Room.

Courthouse Square, Van Ness Ave. at Mariposa. On the fountain is an unusual statue, the figure of a boy holding a worn shoe, given by the Salvation Army in 1895, called *The Boy With the Leaking Boot.*

Kearney Mansion, in Kearney Park, has late 19th-century furnishings, in the home of Martin Kearney, president of the first California Raisin Growers Association.

GHOST TOWNS of the Mother Lode. Just as a lot of mining camps came and went in the 19th century so the little towns flourish or decline in the years of restoration and replica-making, marking and preserving the vanished frontier. Some forgotten villages are bright with new calico curtains, checkered tablecloths and potted plastic ferns in flossy ice-cream parlors, with machine-made "heirloom" bedspreads in hotel rooms, and new brass spittoons in the lobby. But some are whistle-stops only for the wind. A few are in business, new and old; nearly all have a cemetery, some walls, the ruins of a Wells Fargo office, or a jail.

The Mother Lode country is about one hundred and fifty miles long and a few miles wide; it runs through the Sierra foothills. State 49 touches many of the old boom towns of the Gold Rush. US 40 and 50, State 88, 4, 108, 120 and 140 cross the gold area. Some of the names history hunters and photographers who roam the back roads will find: Strawberry Valley, Poverty Hill, Smartville, Poke Flat, You Bet, Yankee Jims, Chicago Park, Grizzly Flats, Shingle Springs, Michigan Bar, Jenny Lind, Ben Hur, and Melones, once Slumgullion.

GRASS VALLEY, Nevada County, State 20, 49. Placer gold was discovered in Boston Ravine in 1849 and gold-quartz at Gold Hill in 1850. The first stamp mill in California was in operation here in 1850. By 1880 the population was more than 5,000. The town gained as much fame from the presence of actress-dancer Lola Montez as from its gold.

Rough and Ready, 4 miles W. on State 20. The gold strike here was given the nickname of Gen. Zachary Taylor. His devoted followers once tried to secede from the Union and form a republic to be called Rough and Ready.

Pelton Wheel Mining Exhibit, S. end of Mill St. Hard rock mining display and relics. A 31-ft. waterwheel.

Empire Mine, on Empire Rd., one of the world's great gold mines still is in operation. It has more than 190 miles of tunnels; its deepest shaft is ca. 4,000 ft. Visitors may tour, with a pass from the mine office.

Lola Montez Cottage, Mill & Walsh Sts. The life of Lola has been the subject of a number of books. She was born in Ireland, had an unhappy childhood in India, and in Scotland, became a close friend of many famous people of her day, including Alexander Dumas (Pere), Franz Liszt, George Sand, and King Ludwig I of Bavaria, who built her a palace and made her Countess of Landsberg.

In Grass Valley she tried to lead a relatively quiet life but got into frequent quarrels, particularly with the press. She had a small menagerie of dogs, a pet bear and a parrot. Before she took this house she stayed briefly at a boarding house where she met the Crabtree family whose daughter Lotta would become a stage favorite in time. Lola brought carpenters and other workmen from San Francisco to embellish the cottage to make it a fitting setting for treasures she had saved from her travels. A bust of Ludwig I stood in a niche in the entrance hall. The late Ishbel Ross, one of her biographers, described the actress in her Grass Valley days (in *The Uncrowned Queen,* Harper & Row, 1972):

"Lola added a wing at the back of the cottage for the kitchen, bathroom and wine cellar. The bathtub caused almost as much talk as Millard Fillmore's at the White House. It was a novelty for California, although it was still of the primitive order and kept her servants running back and forth with cans of water. . . . She gave a Christmas party . . . playing carols on her melodeon, singing with some abandon and drinking champagne. Rubies glittered against her white skin. Her gown was of ruby-red velvet, cut low, and the men gathered around her could not take their eyes off the enchantress."

HORNITOS, Mariposa County. J 16. The name means "Little Ovens," and the town was founded by Mexican miners in 1850. They had been driven out of Quartzburg by an American vigilance committee, but when the placers at Quartzburg gave out the Americans suddenly overcame their prejudice and moved to the charming Mexican-style town. Many original buildings remain. The Well-Fargo office, a Masonic Hall and ruins of the D. Ghirandelli Store.

St. Catherine's Church, on hill top, still has old kerosene lamps. Nearby cemetery had unusual burials. The body was placed in a board coffin which was laid on the ground and a tomb of rock and adobe built around and above it. These resembled *hornitos* and led to the naming of the town.

Fandango Hall, on main street, was an adobe saloon where the notorious bandit Joaquin Murieta (often spelled Murrieta) is said to have made an escape via a tunnel under the street.

Probably more stories have been set afloat about Murieta than about any other villain in California's history. Presumably he was ambushed and killed at the mouth of Arroyo Cantova, near Priest Valley, by a posse of rangers under Capt. Harry Love in the midsummer of 1853. His severed head was brought to Hornitos for identification, displayed all over the area, and stored in a glass jar for posterity. Whether Joaquin Murieta was as real as Pancho Villa or made up of paper and film like Zorro, he lives in legend.

INDEPENDENCE, Inyo County. US 395.

Eastern California Museum, 3 blocks W. of the courthouse, on Grant St., has historical, anthropological, botanical and geological exhibits.

Ruins of Fort Independence, NE of town on dirt road. The post helped to quell the Inyo County Indian uprisings of the 1860s.

The Commander's House, 303 N. Edwards, was built for the commander at Ft. Independence in 1872, moved to this location in 1883. Some of the antique furniture was made by soldiers at the camp.

LANCASTER, Los Angeles County. State 14.

Burton's Tropico Gold Mine & Mill Tours, 14 miles N. and W. via State 14, N. on Mojave-Tropico Rd. in Rosamond. Ruins of a gold-mining camp have been restored and rebuilt with underground tunnels and the look of the 1880s. Museum has relics.

Antelope Valley Indian Research Museum, 15701 E. Ave. M, 18 miles from downtown, has displays showing the culture of the Anasazi. (Some artifacts are ca. 10,000 years old.)

LASSEN VOLCANIC NATIONAL PARK, Lassen County. State 44, 89. Lassen Park was named for Peter Lassen, a Danish immigrant and pioneer, who led parties from Nevada into the Sacramento Valley and often became lost. The Lassen Trail is a winding one. Some say that he used the peak, which now has his name, as a landmark. Another story is that on one occasion when he was hopelessly lost his party forced him at gunpoint to climb the peak and have a look at the territory. A museum and interpretive programs are available at Manzanita Lake. (See Susanville.)

LAVA BEDS NATIONAL MONUMENT, Siskiyou and Modoc Counties, via State 139 and secondary roads. 46,162 acres of rugged terrain formed by volcanic activity, ancient and recent. One of the largest cinder cones is Schonchin Butte, named for a Modoc chief; there is a trail to the top. The trail to Big Painted Cave and Symbol Bridge lead to Indian petroglyphs. Among the caves are Sentinel, Catacombs, Merrill, and Skull Cave. Headquarters are in the southern section near Indian Well and Cave Loop Rd. Museum is here.

The Modoc Indian War of 1872–1873 was fought within the monument area. For five months a band of Modoc warriors held off more than a thousand soldiers. The cost of the war for whites was more than half a million dollars and 83 lives. Captain Jack, a Modoc leader, had a stronghold, which may be visited today, where he was able to entrench his forces. The lava trenches and rock fortifications look much as they did in the 1870s. Nearby is Canby Cross where Gen. E. R. S. Canby was murdered when he tried to hold a peace conference. About 100 soldiers are buried in Gillem's Graveyard near Gillem Bluff.

LEE VINING, Mono County. State 120.

Mono Lake, E. of town. Jedediah Smith, the trapper and explorer, visited here in 1825. John Fremont and Kit Carson came nearby in 1825. LeRoy Vining, a prospector, led a party into the area in 1852. That year a Lt. Tredwell Moore and fellow soldiers chased a group of Indians around the lake and found gold. Mark Twain wrote about Mono Lake in *Roughing It,* published in 1872, and if there had been a Chamber of Commerce they might have tried to drown themselves:

". . . the 'Dead Sea of California.' It is one of the strangest freaks of Nature to be found in any land. . . . Mono Lake lies in a lifeless, treeless, hideous desert, eight thousand feet above the level of the sea, and is guarded by mountains two thousand feet higher, whose summits are always clothed in clouds. This solemn, silent, sailless sea—this lonely tenant of the loneliest spot on earth—is little graced with the picturesque." But in a better mood he found something favorable about it: ". . . its sluggish waters are so strong with alkali that if you only dip the most hopelessly soiled garment into them once or twice, and wring it out, it will be found as clean as if it had been through the ablest of washerwoman's hands."

LOCKE HISTORIC DISTRICT, Sacramento County. Sacramento River, Locke Rd., Alley St. and Levee St. Following the completion of the transcontinental railroad in the 1870s, the Chinese laborers were put to work on constructing a levee system in the delta area of SW Sacramento County. They established the town of Locke which has remained unchanged for decades. A four-block area comprises the historic district.

LONG BEACH, Los Angeles County. State 7.

La Casa Del Rancho Los Cerritos, 4600 Virginia Rd. Built in 1844, the adobe ranch house is now a museum and reference library. John Temple, original owner, was a New Englander who came to California in 1827. His house was ranch headquarters. A national historic landmark.

Rancho Los Alamitos, 6400 E. Bixby Hill Rd., one of the oldest adobes still in use, with antique furnishings and a blacksmith shop in the barn. It was built ca. 1784 by Manuel Nieto, 70, who had a 16-year-old bride.

LOS ANGELES, Los Angeles County. I-5.

The Pueblo de Los Angeles State Historical Park, area where the city was founded by settlers from San Gabriel Mission, has a Visitor Center at 100 Calle de la Plaza. Guided tours are arranged here. *The Plaza* is the center of the original settlement, Sunset Blvd. & Los Angeles St. *Nuestra Senora La Reina de Los Angeles,* 100 W. Sunset Blvd., the church from which the city takes its name has been restored. *Olvera Street* has a marker to Kit Carson, who would surely be lost among today's paper flowers and bright shops. Also on Olvera is a carved wooden cross commemorating the founding of the pueblo in 1781. *Avila Adobe,* 14 Olvera, once the home of Don Francisco Avila, *alcalde,* was occupied by Commodore Robert Stockton in 1847, damaged by the earthquake of 1857, and has been restored, with period furnishings.

Southwest Museum, 234 Museum Drive, at Marmion Way in Highland Park, Pasadena Freeway, exit 43, has handicrafts and exhibits which give the history of American Indians. Dioramas, artifacts include Hohokam and Anasazi Indian items.

Natural History Museum of Los Angeles County, 900 W. Exposition Blvd., in Exposition Park. Exhibits of early and regional state history. A diorama shows a Chumash village on the coast, Hohokam and Anasazi materials.

Lummis Home State Historical Monument, 200 E. Ave 43, 5 miles off Pasadena Freeway, State 11. Charles Lummis, who founded both the California History and Landmarks Clubs, and the Southwest Museum, built this unusual rubble stone house, beginning in 1897, completed in 1912.

Pico House, 500 N. Main St., was built in 1870 by Pio Pico, the last Mexican governor of California. Partially restored.

Casa de Adobe, 4605 N. Figueroa St. Replica of a ranch home of 19th-century Spanish-California. Two rooms are a museum.

Rancho La Brea Tar Pits, Wilshire Blvd. and Curzon Ave. in Hancock Park, 6 miles W. of downtown. 32 acres of black bogs. Indians used this substance to make their pottery vessels watertight. In 1792 Jose L. Martinez collected specimens of mammals which had been lost in the pits for perhaps 40,000 years. The area is considered one of the best sources of Pleistocene or Ice Age specimens in the world. An observation pit shows how the specimens looked when found.

Pico Adobe, 10940 Sepulveda Blvd. in Mission Hills, was originally part of San Fernando Mission. It was the home of Eulogio de Celis in ranch days, then the home of Romulo Pico, a nephew of the Mexican governor, Pio Pico.

Los Angeles Public Library, 5th St. between Grand Ave. and Flower St. has an outstanding collection of California reference material, sculpture and murals.

MARIPOSA, Mariposa County. State 140. In 1844 Gov. Manuel Micheltorena made a land grant of this area to Juan Alvarado who sold to John C. Fremont, in August, 1849. The location was in the San Joaquin Valley but was "floated" to the Mother Lode country when the land boom came following the gold strike at Coloma. This was done by shifting boundaries. Fremont's ranch, Rancho Las Mariposas, comprised 44,386 acres and was "floated" about 50 miles E. to include mountain territory that might contain gold. In the summer of 1848, gold-bearing quartz veins were discovered at his ranch, new location, on the S. end of the Mother Lode country. He hired 25 Mexican miners and in August, 1850, began operating a quartz mill, around which a small town developed. (See Bear Valley.) By 1862 he had acquired about $3 million in gold but profited little because of litigations and what most historians refer to as chicanery on the part of his associates (though it does seem as if the Little Pathfinder tried to move a path or two for his own betterment). In 1863 Fremont lost control of his holdings, but mining in the vicinity prospered as did the town of Mariposa. A few early buildings remain. Fremont's quartz mine is the Princeton, just S. of the town of Mount Bullion, ca. 6 miles SW of Mariposa on State 49.

Courthouse, oldest in the state, was built in 1854. The old clock in the quaint steeple was brought around Cape Horn. The second floor contains original furnishings.

Mariposa County Museum and History Center, State 140 at Jessie St. Local history (which was spectacular) is featured.

Schlageter Hotel, Trabuco Warehouse, and the Jail are all 19th-century originals.

MARTINEZ, Contra Costa County. State 21.

John Muir National Historic Site, 4440 Alhambra Ave. Muir, who was an authority on glaciers and the mountains of the West and a great conservationist, lived here from 1880 until his death in 1914. He was the first to verify the origin of Yosemite Valley by glacial erosion. A national historic landmark.

MARYSVILLE, Yuba County. US 99E. In 1842 Theodore Cordua built a trading post that became a station on the Oregon-California trail. Stephen J. Field, who became a Lincoln appointee to the Supreme Court, arrived in 1849, bought land for $16,250, and was elected mayor three days after he got here. The town was named for Mary Murphy Covillaud, a survivor of the Donner party.

Field's Home, 630 D St., an adobe.

John C. Fall House, 706 G St., was built in 1855.

Jose Ramirez House, 222 5th St., built ca. 1850.

Mary Aaron Museum, 704 D St., is housed in an 1854 home with relics of gold rush times, chapel, sheriff's office, and machine shop.

Chamber of Commerce, 429 10 St., has information on pioneer homes of the vicinity.

Hock Farm, 8 miles S. of Marysville on Garden Highway is a memorial to the farm which was established by John A. Sutter in the winter of 1841–42 on the W. riverbank of the Feather River, in Sutter County, near State 99, 8 miles S. of Yuba City. The actual site is a registered historic landmark though no buildings remain. Sutter lived at the farm from 1849 to 1865 when a fire destroyed the house.

MENDOCINO, Mendocino County. State 1. The town was named for Cape Mendocino which Juan Rodriguez Cabrillo discovered in 1542 and named for Don Antonio de Mendoza, 1st viceroy of New Spain (Mexico). Many old buildings remain.

First Presbyterian Church faces the Pacific Ocean and looks oddly displaced. It is New England in a land of Spanish-style missions. It was built in 1859; its bell came from Troy, New York, via Cape Horn. The church served as New England authentic for the background of the movie "Johnny Belinda."

Masonic Hall has a cupola with a group of figures carved from a single redwood log.

MISSION CHAIN, various sites, listed in chronological order. Some are also listed in connection with cities.

1. Mission San Diego de Alcala, July 16, 1769, founded by Father Junipero Serra, as were all of the first nine. Seven miles N. of San Diego in Mission Valley. Restored.

2. Mission San Carlos Borromeo del Rio Carmelo, June 3, 1770, on the Monterey Peninsula at Carmel. Historically the most important as Father Serra from this mission managed and developed the chain. He is buried here.

3. Mission San Antonio de Padua,

July 14, 1771, near Jolon, W. of US 101. Restored, with an aqueduct, olive gardens and winepresses.

4. Mission San Gabriel Arcangel, September 8, 1771, 537 Mission in San Gabriel. Restored after earthquake damage. First California winery is here.

5. Mission San Luis Obispo de Tolosa, September 1, 1772, in center of San Luis Obispo.

6. Mission San Francisco de Asis (Dolores Mission), October 9, 1776, in downtown San Francisco.

7. Mission San Juan Capistrano, November 1, 1776, US 101, in San Juan Capistrano. Original church was destroyed in an earthquake, has been restored in part.

8. Mission Santa Clara de Asis, January 12, 1777. On campus of the University of Santa Clara, only part of the old wall and cloister garden remain. Relics in present church.

9. Mission San Buenaventura, March 31, 1782, the last which Father Serra established in person. Located near Ventura where there is a statue of the priest and a great cross which he ordered raised on a hill.

10. Mission Santa Barbara, December 4, 1786, overlooks the city, E. Los Olivos & Upper Laguna. Called the "Queen of Missions."

11. Mission La Purisma Concepcion, December 8, 1787, at Lompoc, restored as a state historical monument.

12. Mission Santa Cruz, September 25, 1791, in Santa Cruz, is a one-half size replica of the original mission, near the original site.

13. Mission Nuestra Senora de la Soledad, October 9, 1791, 3 miles W. of US 101 at Soledad. Restored.

14. Mission San Jose, June 11, 1797, 15 miles NE of San Jose. One adobe remains; others are being rebuilt.

15. Mission San Juan Bautista, June 24, 1797, largest of the chain, a state historic monument.

16. Mission San Miguel Archangel, July 25, 1797, 9 miles N. of Paso Robles, off US 101, is the only mission remaining entirely in its original state.

17. San Fernando Rey de Espana, September 8, 1797, in the San Fernando Valley and the town of the same name, at 15151 Mission Blvd. Restored.

18. Mission San Luis Rey de Francia, June 13, 1798, ca. 4 miles E. of Oceanside. Known as the "King of Missions," it is one of the largest in the chain.

19. Mission Santa Ynez, September 17, 1804, off US 101 at Solvang. It is a historical museum.

20. Mission San Rafael Arcangel, December 14, 1817, 13 miles N. of Golden Gate Bridge at San Rafael. A replica of the original mission.

21. Mission San Francisco de Solango, July 4, 1823, the last and the farthest north of the chain is on the plaza in Sonoma. Restored.

MODESTO, Stanislaus County. State 132.

McHenry Museum, 1402 I St. Period rooms with relics, doctor's office, blacksmith shop.

Children's Park, S. Morton Blvd. in Beard Brook Park, has a frontier town and an old locomotive.

Miller Horse and Buggy Ranch, 9425 Yosemite Blvd. 10 miles E. on State 132, has 19th-century fire-fighting equipment and a variety of vehicles from pioneer days.

MOKELUMNE HILL, Calaveras County. State 49. Prospectors from Oregon Territory found gold here in 1848. By the 1850s the town was

The famed and lovely Mission Dolores in San Francisco.
Basilica in backround
(San Francisco Convention & Visitors Bureau)

booming with business and vice. (Chinese girls were sold as slaves or "rented out.") The town began to decline about the time of the Civil War as the placers were depleted. A number of buildings remain and the town has the authentic look of the old days. It even has a Joaquin Murieta legend: A young and foolish miner who happened to be winning at poker in the local saloon was flush with success and boasted that he had $500 he'd bet that he'd kill Murieta the first time he came face to face with him. Whereupon Murieta himself stood up at another table, grabbed the poke the miner had tossed on the board and departed, saying, "I'll take that bet."

Mayer Building constructed of local rhyolite tuff stands in ruins, with Chinese Trees of Heaven growing inside the onetime saloon.

Cemetery on Mokelumne Hill has old tombstones, iron fences and Italian cypress.

Leger Hotel, now an annex to the present hotel. Calaveras served as County Court House from 1852–1879. Joaquin Murieta is said to have stopped at the hotel, which would not have been this building. He was killed in 1853 by most accounts.

Congregational Church was built in Greek Revival style, 1856.

I.O.O.F. Hall, built in 1854, was an express office before it was acquired by the Odd Fellows in 1861.

MONTEREY, Monterey County. State 1. Spanish explorer Sebastian Vizcaino named this picturesque area for the Count of Monte-Ray, Viceroy of Mexico, in 1602. It was discovered again in 1770. From 1776 to 1849 it served as the Spanish and Mexican capital of California. In 1846 Commodore John D. Sloat raised the American flag over the city.

Old Town Historic District, bounded by Dutra, Madison, Polk and Jefferson Sts. in the southern district, and by Pacific, Scott, Alvarado and Decatur in the north district, is a national historic landmark. 43 adobe structures date from the 19th century; among them are the Casa Alvarado, 510 Dutra, which was the home of Gov. Don Juan Bautista Alvarado; Larkin House, 464 Calle Principal, where William Tecumseh Sherman had headquarters during his stay here in the 1840s; the Old Customhouse, 115 Alvarado St. and the First Brick House, 351 Decatur, built in 1847–48.

A "Path of History" is marked by an orange-red line down the center of streets leading to old houses of note. Each is marked by a descriptive plaque.

Chamber of Commerce, 2030 Fremont St., has maps and literature. Monterey is one of the few American cities preserved, maintained and marked as well as areas under the jurisdiction of the National Park Service. Visitors can do their own leisurely exploring with rich rewards.

Royal Presidio Chapel, 550 Church St., is the only remaining presidio chapel in California, and the sole existing structure of the original Monterey Presidio. Royal governors worshiped here and many state ceremonies were held in this building. A wing, transept and altar are 19th-century additions. The main structure is unchanged. A national historic landmark.

Allen Knight Maritime Museum, 550 Calle Principal, has exhibits on the naval history of the area.

MURPHYS, Calaveras County. State 49. Daniel and John Murphy discovered placer gold beds on Angel's

Creek in the summer of 1848. The town was first known as Murphy's Diggings, then Murphy's Camp, and finally as Murphys, no apostrophe. Where possible early names and spellings are provided. A great naming contest seems to have been going on throughout the 19th century as settlers tried to honor favorite candidates, or to describe the locale. Apostrophes in names came and went. Names came and went and often returned. Henry Smith Turner, who came to California with Gen. Stephen Watts Kearny and wrote a journal about it, was the champion phonetic speller. Some of his variations were Callaveras, Trucky, McCallami (for Mokelumne) and Towallomie (for Tuolumne).

Mitcher Hotel, built in 1855, still has iron doors and balcony. Among other old buildings are the Wells-Fargo office, a schoolhouse, and Thorpe's Bakery.

Peter L. Travers Building and Oldtimers' Museum is housed in the old express office, originally a store.

Vallecito is a ghost town S. of Murphys and directly E. of Angels Camp, on Coyote Creek where the Murphy brothers made their first diggings. Mexican prospectors arrived next and named the settlement. Several old buildings remain.

NEVADA CITY, Nevada County. State 49. Gold was discovered in September 1849, a small rush began, by year's end there were more than 400 buildings. Many stone and brick buildings date from the mid-19th century, including Fire House No. 1, the National Hotel, and the Assay Office where the ore specimens from the Comstock Lode of Nevada were originally identified. The town has many lovely old homes with a look of New England along some of the tree-lined streets.

Chamber of Commerce, 132 Main St., has booklets describing pioneer buildings and sites for a walking tour.

Nevada County Historical Society Museum, 214 Main, is housed in the old fire house.

Old Nevada Theater is the oldest theater building in California; it opened for the first performance in July, 1865.

Malakoff Diggings State Historic Park, 10 miles NE off State 49. A museum has mining exhibits.

OAKLAND, Alameda County. I-680.

Oakland Museum, 10th & Oak Sts., has history exhibits which cover centuries of California living. Archaeology materials from Bay area sites.

Joaquin Miller Park, Joaquin Miller Rd. & Warren Freeway, is the site of the former home of Joaquin (Cincinatus Hiner) Miller who was called "Poet of the Sierras." There is a mixed bag of statuary: monuments to Moses, John C. Fremont and Robert Browning, erected by Miller. The poet's house was three structures of one-room each, connected, and rather grandly called The Abbey. Miller was here from 1886 until his death in 1913. The Abbey is a national historic site.

OCEANSIDE, San Diego County. US 101.

Rancho Las Flores, 2 miles N. on Camp Pendleton Marine Corps base, was the home of Pio Pico, Mexican governor of California. In 1841 the Mexican government granted 100,000 acres to Pio and Andres Pico which became this and the San Margarita ranches. The old ranchhouse here has been slightly remodeled by the Marine Corps but maintains its former appearance. A national historic landmark.

Mission San Luis Rey de Francia, 3½ miles E. on State 76, was founded by Father Fermin Lasuen, named for Louis IX. It was 18th in the chain of missions begun by Padre Serra. It has a large collection of Spanish vestments, a cemetery, and many relics. A national historic landmark.

OROVILLE, Butte County. State 70. Originally Ophir City.

Lake Oroville Visitor and Information Center, 7 miles NE off State 70 has an observation tower and a history center with exhibits from Oroville's gold mining days.

Lott Home and Sank Park, between 3rd and 4th Aves. on Montgomery St. The house was built in 1856 and has period furnishings.

Chinese Temple, Elma and Broderick Sts., contains furnishings given by the Emperor of China. The temple was built in 1861.

PALO ALTO, Santa Clara County. US 101.

Leland Stanford Junior University, near State 82, is built on land where hay was still being raised in the 1890s by a tee-totaler named Timothy Hopkins who gave up his farm with a proviso that if liquor were ever sold on it the land would revert to the original owners. Early students used to patronize a town named Mayfield (allegedly named because a near-sighted postal clerk mistook an H for an M) where there were 27 drinking parlors. The university is named for the son of Gov. and Mrs. Leland Stanford who died at the age of 16. Stanford, an early railroad builder, and later a U.S. senator, gave an endowment fund of $30,000,000. The Leland Stanford Junior Museum, on Lomita Drive, has fine archaeological and anthropological collections as well as many other priceless items.

Stanford Guide Service Information Center is located at main entrance to the quadrangle. Campus tours leave daily at 2 P.M. A map and descriptive folder with self-guiding tour for walking or driving, also available.

PETALUMA, Sonoma County. US 101.

Petaluma Adobe State Historic Park, 3325 Adobe Rd., 3 miles E. The Petaluma Adobe was the headquarters of Gen. Mariano Guadalupe Vallejo's 666,000-acre ranch. He was commandant of the Sonoma Pueblo. It is the largest known existing domestic adobe in the U.S. A national historic landmark.

PINNACLES NATIONAL MONUMENT, 35 miles S. of Hollister (San Benito County) off State 25. The monument comprises 10,000 acres where millions of years ago volcanic eruptions created mountains and canyons. The area is crisscrossed with adventure trails. One self-guiding trail is a 1-mile round trip following the bottom of Bear Gulch canyon. High Peaks Trail is exactly what it sounds like, and Chalone Peak Trail climbs to 3,305 feet the highest point in the monument. Visitor Center is 2 miles from the entrance on the E. side of monument.

PLACERVILLE, El Dorado County. State 49. First called Dry Diggings, or Diggins; later Hangtown, after several supposed thieves had been hanged without a trial. Gold was discovered in 1848 and by 1854 the town had 1,944 residents; two years later the deposits were being used up and two large fires helped to discourage newcomers. But by 1860 the rebuilt town was a gateway to the Comstock Lode in nearby Nevada. The first transcontinental telegraph came here and so did the Carson Branch of the California Overland Trail, the Central Overland Mail and Stage Line and even the Pony Express. Three citizens became world famous: Mark Hopkins sold groceries, J. M. Studebaker built wheelbarrows for miners, and Philip Armour had a butcher shop. The town is now the headquarters for the Eldorado National Forest.

The Ivy House, the Methodist Church, St. Patrick's Catholic Church are among the early buildings which remain.

Gold Bug Mine, Bedford Park. Restored gold stamp mill, and mine.

Marshall Gold Discovery State Historic Park (which see) is 8 miles NW on State 49.

Camino, Cable & Northern Railroad, 8 miles E. on US 50 in Camino. A 2-mile ride in the Sierra Nevada Mountains and a display of railroad engines.

Chamber of Commerce has a pioneer museum.

POMONA, Los Angeles County. I-605.

Adobe de Palomares, 491 E. Arrow Highway, restored 1850s adobe with period furnishings. Indian artifacts. Don Ygnacio Palomares lived here before the house served as a stage station and tavern. A registered historic place.

RANCHO EL ENCINO (LOS ENCINOS STATE HISTORIC PARK), Los Angeles County. 16756 Moorpark St. The restored (1840) De La Osa Adobe, a campsite used by Padre Crespi and the spring where Gaspar de Portola stopped in 1769 are part of the memorial, as well as buildings from the American period.

RED BLUFF, Tehama County. US 99.

William B. Ide Adobe State Historical Monument, 1 mile N. on Old US 99, then 1 mile E. on Adobe Rd., has many relics of pioneer times. The house is restored. William Ide was the only president of the short-lived California Republic, known as the Bear Flag Republic. It existed for 25 days in 1846. Ide left Independence, Missouri, intending to go to Oregon but got sidetracked and arrived at Sutter's Fort in 1845. He was hired by Peter Lassen to work as a ranch hand in Tehama County. He did not last long at the job and started his own ranch here where the California-Oregon Trail crossed the Sacramento River.

Kelly-Griggs House Museum, 311 Washington, is an 1880s house with period furnishings. Indian artifacts and historical exhibits.

REDDING, Shasta County. I-5.

Redding Museum, 810 Rio Drive, has a pre-Columbian collection, Indian artifacts of a later date, and historical exhibits. Also Columbia River stone sculpture.

Shasta State Historic Park, 6 miles W. on State 299. A gold rush town with many original buildings and historical museum. On Shurtleff Hill is the fine old 1851 residence of pioneer physician Dr. Benjamin Shurtleff.

Chamber of Commerce, 1345 Liberty St., has additional information.

REDLANDS, San Bernardino County. I-10.

San Bernardino County Museum, California St. & I-10, has excellent archaeology displays, as well as many other historical items.

Asistencia Mission de San Gabriel, 26930 Barton Rd. The mission was built in the 1830s and restored a century later. Indian and pioneer exhibits, miniature historic scenes.

Lincoln Memorial Shrine, in Smiley Park.

Sepulveda Adobe, 5 miles SE. on I-10, then 5 miles E. to Yucaipa, restored house is at 32183 Kentucky St. Period furnishings; house was built in 1842.

RIVERSIDE, Riverside County. US 60.

Mission Inn, 3649 7th St., has many relics in a building of the 1890s, which is a registered historic place. Daily guided tours.

Riverside Municipal Museum, 3720 Orange St., has anthropological, natural history and historical displays.

Mount Rubidoux Memorial Park, W. end of 9th St. A cross on the peak is in memory of Fray Junipero Serra, founder of the California missions.

SACRAMENTO, Sacramento County. I-5.

State Capitol and Annex, 10 St. at Capitol Mall. Guided tours leave rotunda 4 times daily.

Governor's Mansion, 16 & G Sts., the house was once owned by Joseph Steffens, father of author Lincoln Steffens. Now a museum.

Sutter's Fort State Historic Park, 27 & L Sts. Restored, with exhibits depicting Sutter's life, a spectacular one. Gen. John Sutter had several thriving enterprises going well when the gold strike occurred and ruined him. In his own words, as told to Hutchings' *California Magazine* for November, 1857:

"From my mill buildings I reaped no benefit whatever, the mill stones even have been stolen and sold.

"My tannery, which was then in a flourishing condition, and was carried on very profitably, was deserted, a large quantity of leather was left unfinished in the vats; and a great quantity of raw hides became valueless as they could not be sold; nobody wanted to be bothered with such trash, as it was called. So it was in all the other mechanical trades which I had carried on; all was abandoned, and work commenced or nearly finished was all left, to an immense loss for me."

State Indian Museum, 2618 K St., has changing exhibits with displays of dugout canoes, baskets, pottery, and weapons.

SAN DIEGO, San Diego County. I-5, I-15.

Cabrillo National Monument, Catalina Blvd. on tip of Point Loma. Juan Rodriguez Cabrillo first saw the coast of what is now the U.S. at this point. Visitor Center and museum with interpretive displays and literature.

Old San Diego, Mason St. & San Diego Ave. A green line painted on the street leads to many early landmarks. Guided walking tours for 25 historical sites in Old Town depart from Whaley House, 2482 San Diego Ave. at Harney St. on Saturdays at 1:30 P.M. Other tours leave mornings from 4601 Wallace St.

San Diego Union Newspaper Museum, 2626 San Diego Ave. Restored home of the San Diego Union, first published in 1868. Scale model of Old Town in 1870.

Casa de Estudillo, San Diego Ave. at Mason St., home of Jose Maria Estudillo, commandante of San Diego, has been restored. Period furnishings.

Presidio Park, Presidio Dr. off Taylor St., is the site of the original Presidio and fort where the city was founded.

Serra Museum, Presidio Park, has a history of the city since 1562, displayed in artifacts. There is also an archaeological excavation of the Royal Presidio on display.

Derby-Pendleton House, 4017 Harney St., was at one time the home of Lt. George H. Derby, who wrote humorous essays under the name of "Phoenix," and was an officer in the Civil War. The house was built in Portland, Maine, disassembled, and shipped around Cape Horn to be put together at this site.

San Diego Museum of Man, in Balboa Park, has changing exhibits; a large collection of bows and arrows.

Barracks Monument, at Kittner and California Sts. on the site of the "New San Diego Barracks," with descriptive plaque.

SAN FRANCISCO, San Francisco County. I-80. So many books (not to mention songs) have been written about San Francisco from its beginning to the present, there is little need to sing its praises or to try to include all the history that remains visible in the city. The San Francisco Convention & Visitors Bureau, 1390 Market St., an active, enthusiastic, and vastly well-informed bureau, is worth a call. Their maps and brochures are explicit, up to date, well worth reading, and free.

Even in the 19th century it took Karl Baedeker the often querulous king of guide writers, nine pages of fairly fine print to describe the city. He was pleased with the Presidio: "Its walks and drives afford beautiful views, the finest, perhaps, being that from *Fort Point* or *Winfield Scott.* A military band plays at the Presidio nearly every afternoon." But of "Nob Hill," he wrote complainingly. Its large private houses "are of wood, and no expense has been spared to make them luxurious residences, but a great opportunity to develop something fine in timber architecture has been lost in an unfortunate attempt to reproduce forms that are suitable for stone buildings only."

There is a decorative gateway to Chinatown at Grant Ave. and Bush St. which was completed in 1969 at a cost of more than $75,000, and was made by Chinese artisans in the Orient, but Baedeker's China Town of 1893 sounds even more interesting:

"One of the chief features of China Town is the Theatres (adm. 10–25¢; for white visitors, who are taken on to the stage, 50¢), remarkable for the length of the performances (a single play often extending over days or even weeks), the primitive scenery and absence of illusion, the discordant music, the curious-looking audience, the gorgeous costumes, and the seeming want of plot and action."

California Historical Society, 2090 Jackson, has a small museum housed in an 1896 red sandstone palace.

Cable Car Barn, Mason & Washington, has a visitor's gallery and a museum with 19th century-displays. Cable cars on three routes are the only national landmarks on wheels.

Old Mint, 5th & Mission Sts., was built in 1873–74, is now a museum.

Mission Dolores, Dolores and 16th Sts., 6th in the mission chain was established by Father Serra in 1776, the church was built in 1782; a cemetery garden adjoins. The mission appears in many memoirs of the city and was the subject of a nostalgic essay by Bret Harte.

Portsmouth Square, Clay & Kearny St., is a small park where the U.S. flag was raised in July 1846.

Chinese Historical Society of America, 17 Adler Place, has displays telling the role of the Chinese in the settlement of the West.

Old St. Mary's Church, Grant Ave. & California St. in Chinatown, was dedicated in 1854, destroyed by fire in 1962. The new cathedral is at Geary and Gow Sts.

Presidio, Presidio Blvd. & Letterman Drive. The U.S. military reservation comprises 1,476 acres. Maps may be obtained at the Military Police Station, Presidio & Letterman.

Fort Point National Historic Site, on grounds of Presidio, was a post established during the Civil War and was designed in the style of Fort Sumter, South Carolina. It has a two-room museum and is being restored.

San Francisco Maritime Museum, State Historic Park & Museum foot of Polk St., has ships, a steam schooner, a ferryboat and other historical craft.

San Francisco Fire Department Pioneer Memorial Museum, 655 Presidio Ave., has fire-fighting displays and relics, including a hand pumper from 1849.

Alcatraz Island, in San Francisco Bay, was declared a military reservation in 1858, garrisoned in December, 1859. It served as a fort, military prison, disciplinary barracks and a federal penitentiary. "The Rock" is now a part of the Golden Gate National Recreation Area. Boats leave at half-hour intervals from Pier 43 for 1½ hour tours.

Golden Gate Promenade is a 3½-mile footpath in areas which were previously inaccessible to the public at the Presidio and Fort Mason. Begin at Fort Point or the Golden Gate Bridge Toll Plaza parking lot. Path follows the shoreline east to Aquatic Park.

Society of California Pioneers Museum & Library, 456 McAllister St. Displays trace state history.

Wells-Fargo Bank History Room, 420 Montgomery St. Old stagecoach and other memorabilia of stageline days.

California Division of Mines & Geology Mineral Exhibit, Ferry Building, has a vast collection of rocks and minerals with special displays of California specimens.

Josephine D. Randall Junior Museum, Museum & Roosevelt Ways. Displays feature Indians of northern and central California.

M. H. deYoung Memorial Museum, in Golden Gate Park, Lincoln Way, Stanyan and Fulton Sts., features art prior to 1850.

Prayerbook Cross, Kennedy Dr., commemorates the first religious service in English held on the Pacific Coast. It was conducted by the chaplain of Drake's expedition.

Jackson Square, Jackson St., has many restored buildings of the Gold Rush period.

San Francisco Maritime State Historic Park, Hyde and Jefferson Sts. Four vessels moored here all played a part in Pacific Coast maritime history, a three-masted schooner from 1895, a side-wheel ferry boat, a steamer and a scow. All but the scow may be boarded.

Museum of Money of the American West, Bank of California, 400 California St. at Sansome St., lower level.

Presidio Army Museum, Lincoln Blvd. and Funston Ave. in the Presidio, focuses on the role of the military in the development of San Francisco.

Site of Broderick-Terry Duel, Sloat Blvd. at S. end of Lake Merced, marked by two granite shafts. David Broderick, Tammany trained in politics, arrived in San Francisco in 1849, organized a fire company and was elected to the state legislature; at 31 he was serving as president of the state senate. He was elected to the

U. S. Senate in 1857. David Terry, southern-born, was Chief Justice of the California Supreme Court, a foe of Broderick's in politics. On a cold morning in September they met here to settle their disputes in a duel. Broderick's bullet hit the ground; Terry's bullet hit Broderick who died of his wound on September 16, 1859, and was widely mourned. About 30,000 mourners attended the funeral oration in Portsmouth Square. There were repercussions. Terry had resigned before the duel but talk followed that he had practiced with the pistols used and that Broderick's had a hair-trigger which caused the gun to discharge prematurely. He was known to be a good shot. Terry assaulted a jurist 30 years later when traveling on a train; a marshal shot him down.

SAN FRANCISCO BAY DISCOVERY SITE, San Mateo County. State 82. Four miles W. of San Bruno via Skyline Drive and Sneath Lane. Gaspar de Portola's explorers first sighted the bay from the crest of Sweeney's Ridge on November 4, 1769. A national historic landmark.

SAN JOSE, Santa Clara County. US 101.

The town was founded as Pueblo de San Jose de Guadalupe for Charles III of Spain. When Captain Thomas Fallon with 19 men entered the town on July 14, 1846, he raised the flag over a sleepy pueblo. It became a boom town in the Gold Rush as a supply center. The first California legislature convened here on December 19, 1849.

San Jose Historical Museum, 635 Phelan Ave., has exhibits on the history of the Santa Clara valley, Indian, Spanish and pioneer times.

New Almaden Museum, 21570 Almaden Rd. At New Almaden, 13 miles S. The museum is housed in an 1854 adobe.

Frontier Village, 4885 Monterey Rd., State 82, 1 mile N. of junction with US 101, is a replica of pioneer town, stagecoach and train rides.

Lick Observatory, at summit of Mount Hamilton, 19 miles E. of town. James Lick, pioneer who endowed the observatory, is buried here.

Mission San Jose de Guadalupe, State 238 and Washington Blvd. in Fremont, was founded June 11, 1797.

SAN JUAN BAUTISTA, San Benito County. Off US 101.

San Juan Bautista State Historic Park, 2nd St., 3 miles E. of US 101. The Plaza Hotel was built in 1813–14 as a Spanish barracks; the stable houses horse-drawn vehicles and blacksmith equipment. Castro-Breen House has self-guiding tours. Several other historic buildings are in the park.

Mission San Juan Bautista, in park, was the 15th of the chain of early missions built by the Franciscans; it was completed in 1812 and is still in use.

Fremont Peak State Park, on Gabilan Peak above the city, the area where John C. Fremont retreated in March 1846, defying the Mexican orders to leave the country. He flew the U.S. flag for three days before he withdrew to Sutter's fort.

SAN LUIS OBISPO, San Luis Obispo County. US 101.

Mission San Luis Obispo de Tolosa, Monterey & Broad Sts. was the fifth of the mission chain. It has an 8-room museum.

San Luis Obispo County Historical Museum, 696 Monterey St. adjacent to the mission, has a collection of California items and Indian artifacts. A

As the Mission Dolores looked in earlier days
(San Francisco Convention & Visitors Bureau)

map for a self-guiding tour of the city may be obtained here.

Ah Louis Store, 800 Palm St., was founded in 1874 and is still operated by the Ah Louis family.

Sinsheimer Brothers Store, 849 Monterey, has been restored to the look of the 19th century including gas lights. It has a cast-iron front.

Dallidet Adobe, 1309 Toro St., was built in the 1850s. Period furnishings.

SAN MARINO, Los Angeles County. State 19.

Huntington Library, 1151 Oxford Rd., has one of the world's great collections of rare books and manuscripts and has been a "workshop" for many prestigious Western historians.

El Molino Viejo, 1120 Old Mill Rd., is one of California's first grist mills to be operated by water. It has changing historical exhibits.

SANTA ANA, Orange County. US 101.

Charles W. Bowers Memorial Museum, 2002 N. Main St. Collections include anthropology materials and Pacific Coast natural history, also archaeological finds from all the cultures of Orange County as far back as 8,000 years. Dioramas show village life on the Great Plains.

SANTA BARBARA, Santa Barbara County. US 101.

Mission Santa Barbara, E. Los Olivos & Upper Laguna Sts. Founded in 1786, the present church was completed ca. 1820. The 10th mission, founded by Father Fermin Francisco de Lasuen, houses the archives of the California missions. Self-guiding tours.

Santa Barbara Museum of Natural History, 2559 Puesta del Sol Rd., has exhibits featuring prehistoric life of the coastal area. Dioramas depict California cave dwellers and desert village life.

Lobero Theater, 33 E. Canon Perdido St., was founded in 1872 by Jose Lobero. The original adobe has been rebuilt.

Santa Barbara Historical Society Museum, 136 E. De la Guerra St., exhibits on city and state history.

Fernald House, 414 W. Montecito St. 1 block S. of US 101, and the *Trussell-Winchester House,* 412 W. Montecito, are historical homes maintained by the Historical Society.

El Presidio de Santa Barbara State Historic Park, 122 E. Canon Perdido St., still has one structure of the original presidio, Adobe El Cuatrel, from 1782. Chapel is being excavated. Old foundations are visible.

Chamber of Commerce, 1301 Santa Barbara St., has a list of many old homes in the area that may be visited.

Casa de la Guerra, 11 E. de la Guerra St., was the home of a Spanish grandee. In *Two Years Before the Mast,* Richard Henry Dana wrote of a visit here. Dana's classic mid-19th-century narrative is rich in California scenery and customs. He often landed along the coast in his two years at sea and wrote eloquently of wedding fiestas, fandangoes, and pioneer eccentrics.

Hill Cabrillo Adobe, 11 E. Cabrillo St., and *Casa de Covarrubias,* 715 Santa Barbara St., are fine early houses.

SANTA CRUZ, Santa Cruz County, State 1.

Mission Santa Cruz, Emmett & High, is a half-size reproduction of the original church of 1794 which collapsed in an earthquake more than a century ago.

Santa Cruz Mission State Historical Monument, 130 School St. Casa Adobe was built in 1791 and served for a time as barracks for Spanish soldiers.

Santa Cruz City Museum, 1305 E. Cliff Dr., has California Indian exhibits as well as other natural history displays.

University of California at Santa Cruz, NW of town, overlooks Monterey Bay. Self-guided walking tours; campus overlooks the historic area where the expedition of Don Jasper de Portola's expedition arrived in 1769 and were disappointed to find no Indians but plenty of redwoods.

Roaring Camp and Big Trees Narrow-Gauge Railroad, 6 miles N. on State 9 in Felton. The 1890 steam locomotives draw even more antiquated cars up steep grades through a redwood forest.

SOLEDAD, Monterey County. I-5, US 101.

Mission Nuestra Senora de la Soledad, 3 miles S. of town, was founded in 1791 by Father Fermin de Lasuen. The chapel has been restored. A museum is planned.

Los Coches Rancho, US 101, was the ranch home of William Brunner Richardson who built the adobe on land granted to his wife by the Mexican government in 1841. Capt. John Fremont camped here in 1846 and 1847. Later the house was used as a stage station and post office. A state historic monument.

SONOMA, Sonoma County. State 12.

Sonoma Plaza, town center, is the site where the Bear Flag was raised on June 14, 1846, representing the start of an American revolt against Mexican rule. 33 men took possession of Sonoma and elected William Ide to represent them. The Mexican War brought a fast end to the revolt. Most of the original buildings are still surrounding the square, which has a bronze statue of a pioneer holding the staff of the Bear Flag. A national historic landmark.

Sonoma State Historic Park preserves the Mission San Francisco Solano,

Spain and 1st Sts., which was the northernmost of the mission chain, founded in 1823. It has been restored. General Mariano Guadalupe Vallejo's home is here also. Vallejo founded the town.

Buena Vista Rancho, 1 mile NE, was the home of Count Agoston Haraszthy, a Hungarian who planted the experimental vineyards which led to a vast wine industry. Wineries are open to visitors here, where the stone cellars are said to be the oldest in the state and the eucalyptus trees the biggest.

Sonoma Gaslight and Western Railroad Train Town, 1 mile S. of plaza on Broadway. A 15-minute train trip which passes a miniature town.

SONORA, Tuolumne County. State 49. Mexican miners discovered placer deposits of gold on Woods Creek in August of 1848. The boom town was made up of racist Americans, Chinese, Mexicans, Chileans and a few church-goers who maintained the St. James Episcopal Church and three others on Piety Hill. The town was filled with violence and senseless acts based on greed and prejudice. At the Big Bonanza, $160,000 in gold was mined in one day.

Columbia State Historic Park, 4 miles N. via State 49 and county road. Stage coach rides and all the trappings of a boom settlement, including a Wells-Fargo office, firehouse, schoolhouse, and many others.

Rail Town 1897, 5th Ave., 3 miles SE in Jamestown. A 19th-century railroad, depot, roundhouse, blacksmith shop, museum.

Moaning Cave, 5150 Moaning Cave Rd. 12 miles N. near Vallecito, was discovered in 1851. Museum has Indian and mining displays.

Mercer Caverns, 10 miles N. on State 49, then 5 miles NE on State 4, were discovered in 1885. Guided tours.

Twain Monument, at Jackass Hill near Tuttletown, 16 miles NE via State 108, is near the site of the restored cabin where Twain lived. Both Mark Twain and Bret Harte used Sonora as settings for stories.

SUSANVILLE, Lassen County. State 36.

Roop Fort & William Pratt Memorial Museum, 75 N. Weatherlow St. Fort was built in 1854 by Isaac Roop and served as the capital of the Nataqua Republic; a log cabin with a shake roof, it was called Fort Defiance during what was named the Sagebrush War in 1864, a boundary dispute with Nevada.

The town is headquarters for the Lassen National Forest, which is an area of 1,045,226 acres. The grave of Peter Lassen—pioneer settler for whom a county, a forest and a volcano are named—is 6 miles S. on an unpaved road. Site is marked by a monument.

VENTURA, Ventura County. US 101.

Mission San Buenaventura, 211 E. Main St. The last mission founded by Father Junipero Serra was 9th in the mission chain. It has been restored. Museum has the original wooden bells.

Ventura County Pioneer Museum, 77 N. California St. Spanish and pioneer artifacts, Indian relics, mineral and weapons collections.

Olivas Adobe, Olivas Park Drive off US 101 Victoria Ave. exit, was built in 1837. House has been restored. Original furnishings. Don Raimundo Olivas called his ranch on the Santa Clara River the Rancho San Miguel.

VISALIA, Tulare County. I-7.

Mooney Grove Park, 27000 Mooney Blvd., on 155 acres near Cameron Creek a pioneer village has been reconstructed with original cabins moved from other California locations. Ten buildings are furnished appropriately for early times and their original use; a log cabin built ca. 1854 on Elbow Creek by Isaac Harmon is here, the Cramer House once stood on the N. fork of Tula River, another house is from the Woodville area. The Tulare County Museum has a variety of pioneer relics from the early 1800s.

VOLCANO, Amador County. Off State 88. Gold was discovered in 1848 at what was called Soldiers' Gulch, renamed when the mining camp was established. Among old buildings are the St. George Hotel, the Odd Fellows Hall, the Adams Express Office, two saloons and a store, Sing Kees, which is now a museum.

Indian Grinding Rock (Chaw'se), ca. 2 miles SW on Pine Grove-Volcano Rd., is the largest known bedrock mortar concentration in the United States. The limestone outcropping has more than 1,100 pits formed by the Indians as they pounded acorns and seeds. Several hundred petroglyphs also are on the rock. Two middens mark former village areas nearby. The site was used by Northern Miwok Indians. A national registered place and state historic landmark.

WEAVERVILLE, Trinity County. US 299. With thousands of Chinese joining the gold rush as traders, laborers and miners, it was perhaps inevitable that disputes would grow. The first tong war broke out in Weaverville (a second one in Chinese Camp) where there were five or six Chinese companies. The war here was encouraged by whites and erupted in the 1850s; eight Chinese and one Dutchman were killed in the battle.

John Weaver had discovered gold on Weaver Creek in 1849; by the middle of the 1850s the town was established and became the county seat. Several original buildings remain.

Weaverville Joss House State Historic Park, Main & Oregon Sts. on State 299, was a temple built in 1874. It contains tapestries of great value and gilded scrollwork. Guided tours.

J. J. Jackson Memorial Museum, Main St., has local gold-rush exhibits.

WILLITS, Mendocino County. US 101. Once Willitsville for Hiram Willits of Indiana who opened a store in 1865.

Mendocino County Museum, 400 E. Commercial St. Indian artifacts, transportation exhibits, period rooms.

Black Bart Rock, ca. 11 miles SW., marks the site where Black Bart robbed the mail stagecoach. He robbed at least 27 coaches from 1875 to 1883 and always wore an immaculate linen duster and mask. He hated horses and did his work on foot. His tidiness brought his downfall: the laundry mark on one of his handkerchiefs, dropped near a robbery in Calaveras County, led to trail's end, and he was unmasked as one Charles C. Bolton, a seemingly respectable mining engineer of San Francisco. He spent the next two years at San Quentin.

WILMINGTON, Los Angeles County. State 1.

Banning Home, 401 E. M St. General Phineas Banning, who founded the town, dealt in transportation both land- and ocean-going. Some original furnishings are in the 30-room house which was built in 1864 and is a registered historic place. Banning Park is a 20-acre tract, part of the original estate. Banning developed the harbor and ran stages to meet the steamers. The railroad came in 1869.

Drum Barracks, 1053 Carey St., was established in 1862 as U.S. military headquarters for the southwest. It was garrisoned and served as a supply base. It was also a terminus for the camel pack trains led by Edward Beale. The original officers quarters and powder magazine remain. A state historic landmark.

YOSEMITE NATIONAL PARK, Mariposa, Tuolumne Counties. State 120, 140.

Visitor Center, in Yosemite Village, open all year, with an information desk open from 8 to 6 daily. Exhibits and an audio-visual program interpret the history of the park. Visitor Centers at Mariposa Grove, Glacier Point and Tuolumne Meadows have park naturalists on duty in summer. The park comprises ca. 1,200 square miles; some areas can be visited only via horseback or hiking. Upper Yosemite valley is closed to cars but accessible by foot, bicycle, or shuttle bus.

Pioneer Yosemite History Center, a few miles from Mariposa Grove, in Wawona. Historic buildings include homesteader cabins of the 1880s and a Wells-Fargo office, covered bridge, old wagons and other pioneer relics.

Travel Museum, 12 miles below Yosemite Valley on State 140, in El Portal, has a locomotive, caboose and other smaller vehicles.

YREKA, Siskiyou County. US 99. Originally known as Black Gulch Canyon, then Thompson's Dry Diggings, and as Shasta Butte City. A prospector named Albert Thompson struck it rich at Black Gulch camp in March of 1851. The town is now headquarters for the Klamath National Forest.

Siskiyou County Gold & Gem Display, in county courthouse lobby. Ores and nuggets mined in the area.

Siskiyou County Museum, 910 S. Main St., has Indian and pioneer artifacts on display.

COLORADO

In September the Government commissioner held a conference with the Arapahoes, Cheyennes, and Comanches at Bent's Fort. The leading chiefs were 'Little Raven,' 'Storm,' 'Big Mouth,' 'Left Hand,' 'White Antelope,' 'Black Kettle,' 'Old Woman,' 'Black Bird,' and 'Strong Arm.' . . . The commissioner distributed medal likenesses of Buchanan, then occupying the presidential chair, and of Douglas and Lincoln, rival candidates for it. The warriors received them with infinite pride. Little Raven having lost his Buchanan offered ten horses for the recovery of the priceless treasure!

Albert D. Richardson,
Beyond the Mississippi,
Hartford, 1867

'T was a balmy summer evening, and a goodly crowd was there
Which well nigh filled Joe's barroom on the corner of the square,
And as songs and witty stories came through the open door,
A vagabond crept slowly in and posed upon the floor.

"Say, boys, if you give me just another whiskey, I'll be glad,
And I'll draw right here a picture of the face that drove me mad.
Give me that piece of chalk with which you mark the baseball score—
And you shall see the lovely Madeline upon the barroom floor."
Another drink, and with chalk in hand, the vagabond began
To sketch a face that well might buy the soul of any man;
Then, as he placed another lock upon the shapely head,
With a fearful shriek he leaped and fell across the picture—dead.

H. Antoine D'Arcy, "The Face Upon the Floor"

One cannot always discern the true character of one's neighbors in the West. . . . There were four very rough-looking men of different ages sitting at a table near me in one of the restaurants or "eating-houses" of Creede. They had marked out a map on the soiled table-cloth with the point of an iron fork, and one of them was laying down the law concerning it. There seemed to be a dispute concerning the lines of the claim or the direction in which the vein ran. It was no business of mine, and there was so much of that talk that I should not have been attracted to them, except that I expected from their manner they might at any moment come to blows or begin shooting. I finished before they did, and as I passed the table over which they leaned scowling excitedly, the older man cried, with his finger on the map:

"Then Thompson passed the ball back to me—no, not your Thompson; Thompson of '79 I mean—and I carried it down the field all the way to the twenty-five yard line."

Richard Harding Davis,
The West from a Car Window, New York, 1892

COLORADO FACTS: There were very early nomadic hunters, followed by Basketmakers and Pueblo people of southwestern Colorado, village-makers in the eastern part of the present state, and farmers in the northwest. The Cheyenne, Arapaho, and Ute tribes roamed and hunted in historic times. Coronado and his expedition came on their long search for cities of gold but did not find the ore though many who came later did. Captain Zebulon Pike explored the area in 1806. He was followed by other explorers, trappers, fur traders, and miners. Colorado admitted to the Union August 1, 1876, as the thirty-eighth state. Capital: Denver. Nickname: The Centennial State. Colorado has two national recreation areas: Curecanti and Shadow Mountain; Rocky Mountain and Mesa Verde National Parks; Bent's Old Fort National Historic Site; and seven national monuments: Black Canyon of the Gunnison, Colorado, Dinosaur, Great Sand Dunes, Fossil Beds, Yucca House, and Hovenweep.

Names That Made Colorado History.

The Bent Brothers	The Tabors
Baby Doe	Kit Carson
Ouray	Chipeta
Zebulon Pike	John C. Fremont

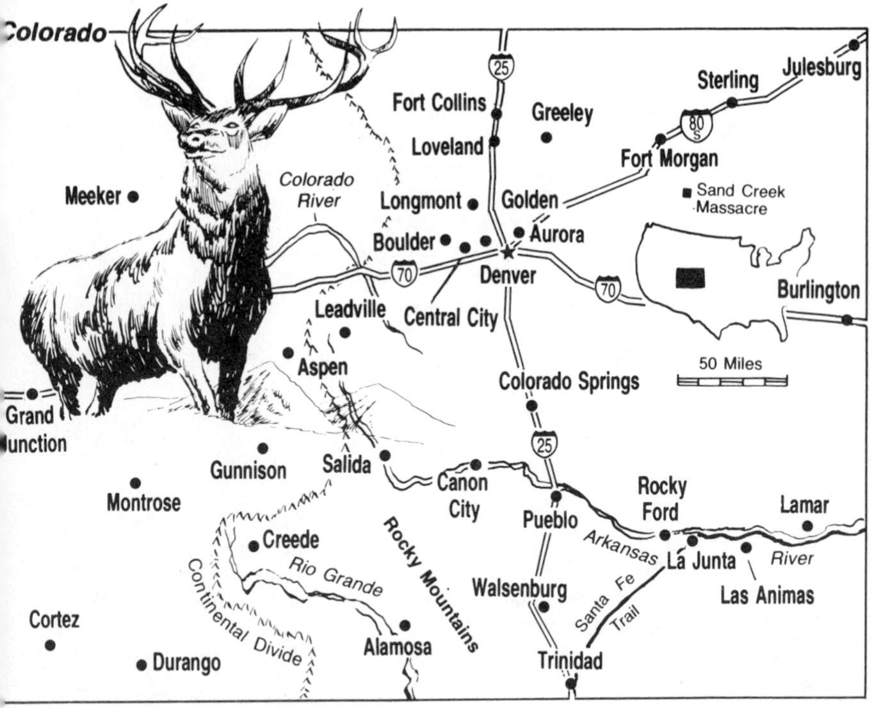

Colorado
25
Fort Collins
Loveland
Greeley
Sterling
Julesburg
80 S
Fort Morgan
Sand Creek Massacre
Meeker
Colorado River
Longmont
Golden
Boulder
Aurora
Denver
70
Central City
Leadville
Aspen
Burlington
50 Miles
Colorado Springs
Grand Junction
Gunnison
Salida
Canon City
Montrose
Pueblo
Rocky Ford
Lamar
Arkansas
River
La Junta
Las Animas
Creede
Rio Grande
Rocky Mountains
Continental Divide
Walsenburg
Santa Fe Trail
Cortez
Alamosa
Durango
Trinidad

Ceran St. Vrain	Nathan Meeker
W.H. Ashley	Philip Sheridan
Jim Beckwourth	Fred Beecher
Jules Beni	Black Kettle
The James Browns	John Chivington
William F. Cody	John Gregory
John Gunnison	George Jackson
David Moffat	Alfred (Alferd) Packer
Henry Teller	

AGUILAR, Las Animas County. Just off US 87, 160. Alt.: 6,400. The town was founded on the Apishapa River in 1867 by Agapita Rivali as a trading post for Indians and Spanish-American settlers. It was named for Jose Ramon Aguilar, a southern Colorado pioneer. Apishapa, Indian for stinking water, was a fitting term for the river in stagnant season. SW of town are the Spanish Peaks, which the Indians and the Spanish called Huajatolla (breasts of the world). Ute Indians believed they were the home of gods to be feared. Stories are told of the early, early days when gold was discovered here and used to placate the deities in their temples. Coronado reportedly came this way searching for Quivera.

AKRON, Washington County. US 34.

Washington County Museum, on highway, in the oldest rock building in town, once used as the town hall, has historical displays.

ALAMOSA, Alamosa County. US 160, 285, State 17. Alt.: 7,544. Incorporated in 1878, its name, and that of nearby creek, is Spanish for "cottonwood."

Cole Park, 425 4th St., has a Denver & Rio Grande Western narrow-gauge train on display.

Pike's Stockade, in Conejos County, 14 miles S. off US 285, just N. of State 136. When Zebulon Pike was sent to explore the SW corner of the Louisiana Purchase and to establish peaceful relations with the Indians, he mistook the Rio Grande for the Red River, and in February 1807 built a stockade in Spanish territory here. It was cottonwood log with a water-filled 4-foot ditch around it. Dr. John Robinson of the expedition went on to Santa Fe more or less to scout the country. The Spanish authorities soon arrived at Pike's stockade and demanded that he leave, under escort to the head of the Red River. He hauled down the flag, surrendered the fort—having no alternative—and went to Santa Fe, nominally under arrest. He was later taken to Chihuahua and released. His roundabout and arduous trip in and out of Louisiana Purchase bounds gave the U.S. government its first real knowledge of some of Spain's holdings in the southwest. Pike died in battle in the War of 1812. The reconstructed fort is a state and national historic landmark.

ANTONITO, Conejos County. State 17, US 285. 28 miles S. of Alamosa. Altitude: 7,888. The town is the southern entrance to the Rio Grande

National Forest (which see). It is also the Colorado terminus for the Cumbres & Toltec Scenic Railway. The last narrow-gauge luxury line had originally connected Denver with the gold and silver mines of the San Luis Valley. Scheduled runs were stopped in 1951, but railroad buffs organized an appeal which resulted in the line's being bought by Colorado and New Mexico to prevent its being scrapped.

APACHE, Huerfano County, I-25, is named for Apache Indians who lived here at one time. A wagon party of the 1840s was on the Taos Trail from Greenhorn to New Mexico when it was attacked near Apache Creek. Mrs. John Brown, riding with her small son John, fell behind the men of the group, including her husband, who shouted to her to jump an arroyo they had already crossed. She made the jump but clutched little John's neck so hard he suffered a spine injury and grew up with his head bent forward. Nobody recorded what Mrs. Brown said to her husband when the family was reunited.

ARAPAHO NATIONAL FOREST, several counties, mainly in Grand. I-70. There are many ghost towns within the 1,001,850-acre forest. The Moffat Road crosses the Continental Divide over Rollins Pass. It is open in summer until Labor Day. A 4-hour trip, which also passes through part of the Roosevelt National Forest, is recommended only for drivers accustomed to mountain roads. (See also Rollinsville.)

ASPEN, Pitkin County. State 82. Altitude: 7,908. During the silver boom the town had a population of 10,000. It is now a recreational and culture center, with many handsomely restored homes. The late Walter Paepcke, a Chicago industrialist, started the second boom, bringing in music, art, and distinguished speakers. He also painted a house pink:

The Webber House was built in 1881 for Mayor Henry Webber, whose wife committed suicide—gossips said—because of his infidelity. Restored, pink brick with a mansard roof and a lacy iron fence.

The Hotel Jerome, Pitkin County Courthouse, the *Wheeler Opera House* and other structures which were here in the 1890s when nearby mines gave forth $10 million in silver each year have been refurbished.

Aspen Historical Society Museum, 620 W. Bleeker St., has exhibits which pertain to area history.

Lenado, ca. 16 miles NE, N. via State 82 to Woody Creek, then E. to Lenado (locally pronounced Lenade-o, correctly pronounced Len-yah-do, meaning "wooded"). Once a silver camp, then a ghost town, the settlement has been revived by a sawmill.

Ashcroft, ca. 10 miles S. of Aspen, had a population of 1,000 in 1883 and 50 in 1890. In the spring of 1883, when H.A.W. Tabor arrived with his bride Baby Doe on an inspection tour, a 24-hour celebration was held with free drinks at thirteen saloons.

BAILEY, Park County. US 285, in the Platte River canyon, surrounded by the Pike National Forest. Altitude: 7,750. The highway goes across an old narrow-gauge bed of the Colorado & Southern Railroad. In 1873 it was the Denver, South Park & Pacific Railroad, with plans to run to the coast. By 1880 it reached almost to Leadville. Rates were high: passengers paid 10¢ a mile; freight rates ran to $29 per ton, which was considerably more than the cost of shipping from the eastern coast to California via Cape Horn. Stage accommodations at the terminus were so haphazard that passengers sometimes found themselves being sent back to Denver to wait for another train. The Union Pacific, backed by millionaire Jay Gould, bought the line. It went bankrupt after the Leadville boom collapsed.

BEECHER ISLAND BATTLEGROUND, Yuma County. Ca. 17 miles S. of Wray, US 34, 35. US 36 is 9 miles S. In September of 1868, Maj. George Forsyth led 50 men in a pursuit of marauding Indians. Forsyth, a Civil War veteran, had appealed to Gen. Philip Sheridan, now commander of the department of the Missouri, for a field command. Sheridan wired him to select 50 hardy frontiersmen to be used as scouts against the Indians of the area who were hostile. Lt. Frederick Beecher was to be Forsyth's subordinate. Many versions of what happened have been recorded, but it is certain that the men were enlisted at Fort Hays and Fort Harker in Kansas and reached Fort Wallace, Kansas, early in September 1868. They were on the trail of Indians who had been raiding livestock when they found themselves nearly surrounded. Forsyth's men entrenched themselves on a small sandy island in the Arikaree River and held out during a nine-day siege. Their suffering was intense as the only doctor had been shot in the back of the head while he attended to one of the wounded. He was delirious for the three days he lived. The losses were heavy on both sides. Forsyth was hit four times, half the men were wounded. Lt. Frederick Beecher, a nephew of the famous minister Henry Ward Beecher, was killed with four other defenders. An obelisk and individual stones commemorate those of Forsyth's command who died here. Chief Roman Nose of the Cheyennes was killed riding at the front of his line. He was 6′2″ tall, wearing war paint and feathers and, some said, sure of his own immortality. The tide of battle was broken with his death. Not far away is a rise of ground known as Squaw Hill where Cheyenne women and children watched the battle.

BENT'S OLD FORT NATIONAL HISTORIC SITE, Otero County. State 194, 8 miles NE of La Junta. The most important outpost on the Santa Fe Trail was a rendezvous for traders, Indians, trappers, and emigrants. William and Charles Bent were brothers. Charles formed a partnership with Ceran St. Vrain, another frontiersman and trader, and later the three made their headquarters at the fort William had built. It was named Fort William but became known as Bent's Fort. In 1835 William married the daughter of a prominent Cherokee and became influential in Indian matters, not only because of his family ties, but because of his fairness in dealing with everyone and his strict honesty. The post served as a gathering place for any number of wagon trains and government officials hoping to make peace terms with Indian leaders. The Cheyenne, Arapaho, Comanche, and Kiowa Indians traded with Bent. Kearny's Army of the West was welcomed here in the 1840s but their visit was the beginning of the end for the fort. When the army arrived, the Indians stayed away. The government never adequately paid Bent for its provisions, and grasslands were used up by government teams and cavalry horses. William Bent felt as if a horde of locusts had descended. Charles, married to a member of a leading New Mexican family, was made the first American governor of New Mexico territory but was killed by Taos Indians during a rebellion in 1847. William tried unsuccessfully to get a fair price for the fort when the government wanted to buy it. Angered by the purchase offer, he lost patience and burned his fort, then moved downstream to a new location. The national historic site is being restored.

BENT'S NEW FORT, Bent County. On secondary road ca. 2 miles S. of US 50, 7 miles W. of Lamar. In 1852, William Bent replaced a temporary stockade at this site with a stone structure, smaller than his old fort but similar in arrangement. The post was never successful. Bent leased it to the Army, which had begun construction of Fort Wise, later Fort Lyon, just SW of his new location. Earthworks and a marker remain.

BLACK CANYON OF THE GUNNISON NATIONAL MONUMENT, Montrose County. 14 miles NE of Montrose on US 50, State 347. The Gunnison River from a point near Sapinero cuts a gorge for about 50 miles. The narrow chasm of the monument got its name from the gloom that prevails most of the day. From the sunlit rim on fine days visitors can look down at lichen-covered black walls of a wild area at depths ranging from 1,730 to 2,425 feet. Altitude at the rim is ca. 8,000 feet. There are pictographs and petroglyphs in surrounding valleys. Ute Indians were hunting and camping in the area when the first white explorers arrived. Juan Maria de Rivera, under orders from the Spanish Governor of New Mexico, visited the site about 1765. After the Mexican War when the land was American territory, Capt. John W. Gunnison led an expedition through the region (1853) taking care to bypass the canyon. In 1874 the Hayden Survey expedition traveled along the north rim, setting up several survey stations. Headquarters are at 334 S. 10th St., Montrose. The monument comprises 22 square miles.

BLACK HAWK, Gilpin County, State 119, was incorporated in 1864. Altitude: 8,042. The Dory Hill cemetery has a number of interesting old gravestones. The community was one of the first settlements in the county. At the boundary between Black Hawk and Central City is the site of the first gold lode discovery in Colorado with a granite monument honoring John H. Gregory who made the claim, May 6, 1859. After mining $900 from the outcrop he sold his claim for $21,000. It turned out to be one of the richest in the state. The town was known as "The Mill City." A Professor Hill built a stamp mill here in 1867. Most of Central City's ore was processed in the mill and reduction furnaces at Black Hawk and made into a matt (a mass of gold, silver, copper and iron), which was sent to Swansea, Wales, where the precious metals were extracted.

BOGGSVILLE, Bent County. State 101. Marker on highway two miles S. of Las Animas. The town, named for Thomas O. Boggs, was established in 1860. It was the site of the first workable irrigation experiment in the SW part of the state. Boggs and his partner John Prowers, a Missourian, brought the first cattle herd to the area and with Robert Bent constructed a 7-mile irrigation canal called Tarbox Ditch on the Purgatoire River, a tributary of the Arkansas. Boggs sold his produce to nearby Fort Lyons, and the town thrived until 1873 when the Kansas Pacific Railroad went to Las Animas, leaving Boggsville stranded. Kit Carson lived here in 1867 after having been injured in a hunting accident. He had got caught in his own lariat and been dragged by his horse, and from here he could visit the doctor at Fort Lyon for treatment. In April 1868 a daughter was born to the Carsons, but the mother died soon after. Carson also died and was buried at Boggsville. The Carsons were later removed to Taos for reburial.

BOULDER, Boulder County. State 121, 119, 7. The city gets part of its water supply from Arapaho Glacier, which it owns. Most "Annual Events" listed by Chambers of Commerce in any given area tend to read somewhat alike, give or take a rodeo or a Frontier Days, but Boulder has the unique advantage of offering a Glacier Hike on the second Sunday in August. It is so well attended by hikers from what used to be the far corners of the world that reservations must be made in advance with the C. of C.

University of Colorado Museum, Henderson Bldg. on campus, has relics of early man and more contemporary displays.

Pioneer Museum, 1655 Broadway, regional historical displays.

Flagstaff Scenic Highway climbs 1,600 feet to the summit of Flagstaff Mountain. (Boulder is at 5,354 feet.)

Tungsten, Nederland, Cardinal and Caribou are old camps and towns due W. of Boulder via State 119. Caribou had the richest silver mine of the Front Range; its bullion formed the silver brick walkway for President U.S. Grant when he visited the Teller House at Central City in April 1873.

BRECKENRIDGE, Summit County. State 9. Altitude: 9,603. Gold was discovered in the Blue River in 1859 and set off a small rush which grew into a boom town. Lincoln City, Swandyke, Dyersville, and other ghost towns are nearby. Only automobiles can now traverse the once famous path of the Denver, South Park & Pacific Railway, a narrow gauge which ran from Denver over Kenosha Pass, across South Park to Como, where it then scaled the Boreas Pass on the Continental Divide, looped down to Breckenridge and went on to Frisco. At the summit of Boreas Pass is an old log section house. The highest post office in the U.S. was here in the late nineteenth century.

Breckenridge has no glacier hike in August but it has "no man's land" days. The story is that Breckenridge and nearby areas, through legal oversight, were never officially admitted to the Union. In 1936 a women's club arranged to have the Governor declare the area a part of the U.S., but by special proviso retained the right for Breckenridgers to remain subjects of a "free and independent kingdom for three days each year." The independent settlers named their town Breckinridge for the Vice President of the U.S. (1857–1861); when John Cabell Breckinridge became a Confederate general they renamed the village Breckenridge in patriotic protest.

BUENA VISTA, Chaffee County. US 24, N. of junction with US 285. Altitude: 7,954. Many buildings remain from the big days of silver mining. The Spaniards named the town Beautiful View and were not guilty of overstatement. It lies where the Continental Divide reaches the highest point in North America. Mt. Yale, Mt. Princeton, and Mt. Harvard are visible from here; there are sixteen peaks more than 14,000 feet high in the area (but, alas, not one is Mt. University of Texas). When the town was the terminus for the railroad, before an extension was built to Leadville, it saw many wild Saturday nights as gamblers, desperadoes, and miners on weekend holiday gathered for rest and relaxation.

The Episcopal Church was built in 1888–89 despite the general lawlessness of the region.

Winfield, NW of Buena Vista, 15 miles N. via US 24, then left ca. 12 miles past Vicksburg. Historian Caroline Bancroft says the Clear Creek district of Chaffee County had seven rival mining camps in 1881, but only Vicksburg and Winfield have survived and become resort areas. One of the mines in Winfield was the Augusta, owned by Jacob Sands, Baby Doe's lover before she met Horace Tabor. Curiously enough, the mine has the same name as the first Mrs. Tabor.

CANON CITY, Fremont County. US 50, State 115. Ute Indians camped in this area, as did Captain Zebulon Pike in December 1806 enroute to explore the Arkansas River. Joaquin Miller, who was the Rod McKuen of his day for popularity as a poet, was town judge, mayor, and minister during gold-mining times. He thought the town should be named Oreodelphia but miners protested that they could neither spell nor pronounce it. Spelling never seemed to boggle miners anywhere else, but the name stayed Cañon City for the nearby Royal Gorge. (It is possible that if Miller had his way, that famous line of W. C. Fields might have been "On the whole I'd rather be in Oreodelphia.") The anecdote-packed WPA-sponsored state guide says that Cañon City was offered a choice of the state penitentiary or the state university in 1868 and chose the former on the grounds that it would be better attended. *Cañon City Municipal Museum,* 612 River St., has weapons, Indian relics, mounted buffalo, and murals among its displays.

Rudd Cabin, built in 1860, is maintained by the museum. Some original furnishings.

Robinson Mansion, 12 Riverside Dr. at S. 1st St., is a restored Victorian home with period furnishings.

Pike's Block House Site, on the Denver & Rio Grande Western Railroad right-of-way, is marked by a boulder of native granite.

Henry Harkens Grave, in Deadman's Cañon on highway between Cañon City and Colorado Springs. Stone has the carved inscription: "Henry Harkens murdered Wednesday Eve, March 19th, 1863." The unfortunate Henry was an old man when he was hacked to death near his sawmill on Little Fountain Creek. He had no known enemies and his murder remains a mystery.

The Royal Gorge of the Arkansas River, eight miles W., narrows at some points to 30 feet, with cliffs of 1,200 feet. The Gorge is now spanned by the world's highest suspension bridge. Visitors can ride to the bottom of the gorge via the steepest incline railway in the world. A three-mile ride on a scenic railway is offered at whatever price the visitor thinks it is worth. A spacious Visitor Center with trained Park Rangers available as guides is near the NE end of the bridge on the N. rim of the gorge.

CENTRAL CITY, Gilpin County. State 279. Altitude: 8,496. Once known as the richest square mile on earth, Central City, a historic district, now digs successfully for tourist silver and greenbacks. John Gregory, a miner from Georgia, "struck it rich" in 1859. More than $75,000,000 in gold and other ores have been produced from area mines.

Central Gold Mine and Museum, 126 Spring St., has a variety of relics from early days of the region.

Adventure in History, Armory Bldg. Dioramas depict the town's history.

Site of First Gold Lode Discovery, on boundary between Central City and Black Hawk.

"Old 71," Spring St., is one of the early narrow-gauge trains.

Colorado Central Narrow Gauge Railway, on State 119, has a twenty-minute ride along the original roadbed.

Central City Opera House, Eureka St., has been restored.

Bobtail Tunnel, 1 mile E. on State 279 in Black Hawk, offers a mine tour in a train pulled by a burro.

The Teller House, Eureka St., is one of the most famous old hotels of the west. *The Face on the Barroom Floor* was painted years after the song. Some claim the original ditty was "The Face Upon the Floor." It had seventeen verses, written by H. Antoine D'Arcy. The painted face is preserved by a little brass rail in the barroom of the Teller House. Henry M. Teller ordered the finest rosewood and walnut furnishings, and they were hauled by oxcart, burro, and narrow-gauge railroad from the east. The hotel has been restored to its original elegance. Grant's bedroom has massive furniture and a large portrait of the President.

The Glory Hole, ca. one mile from the center of town, is a man-made crater. Tours are available, but visitors are warned not to stray too close to the edge of the crater. Glory Hole is a mining term for the type of operation which uses the crater and tunnel method.

St. James Methodist Church is said to be the oldest Protestant church in Colorado. It was organized in July 1859.

Nevadaville, S. of Central City, once had 13 saloons. In 1861 it was larger than Denver and is now a ghost town. American City, Nugget, Kingston, and South Kingston are on jeep roads NW of Central City.

CHALK CREEK CANYON, Chaffee County. State 162. A number of gold mining towns were established in the Arkansas River Valley in the 1870s. They were on the Denver, South Park & Pacific Railroad line. Alpine was settled in 1875 to support the Tilden Mine; ore was shipped to Pueblo for smelting. St. Elmo dates from 1880. Romley and Hancock are ghost towns not far from St. Elmo. The Mary Murphy Mine at Romley yielded $14 million and was active until the end of the first World War.

CHIMNEY ROCK ARCHAEOLOGICAL SITE, Archuleta County. In San Juan Forest, 2 miles E. of the Piedra River and 1.5 miles N. of State 151. On a mesa overlooking the Piedra River are pueblo ruins, kivas, and pit house dwellings. A national historic site.

CHIVINGTON, Kiowa County. State 96.

Sand Creek Massacre, ca. nine miles NE. One of the outrages of the Indian wars took place here in November of 1864 when troops led by Col. John M.

Chivington attacked Cheyenne and Arapaho Indians who were camped peaceably on the Arkansas River, having been assured of protection from Fort Lyon. Chivington, who favored extermination of Indians, led the charge although Black Kettle, Cheyenne chief, hastily raised the U.S. and white flags to show his peaceful purpose. His unprepared and poorly armed people were slaughtered and mutilated, among them many women and children; but Black Kettle managed to escape. Many settlers approved the action but Congress denounced Chivington for the wanton slaughter and he resigned. The massacre brought nearly all Plains Indians back into renewed warfare. A stone marker with descriptive plaque is on State 96, ten miles N. of town. The city fathers who chose the town name presumably might have honored Attila the Hun in another age.

COLORADO NATIONAL MONUMENT, Mesa County. State 340. Ten miles W. of Grand Junction, off US 6, 50. Spanish explorers came this way in August 1776. French trappers established a trading post near present Delta, S. of the monument, in the 1830s. The Visitor Center is near the W. entrance; it has a museum and travelogue of the Rim Rock Drive. The monument comprises 17,669 acres. There are a number of self-guiding trails and lookout points.

COLORADO SPRINGS, El Paso County. US 85, 87, 24. Altitude: 6,-012.

Pikes Peak, ten miles NW on US 24 to Cascade, then 19 miles on toll road, which climbs 7,309 feet to summit. Open from May till the end of October, depending on weather conditions. Offices of the U.S. Forest Service are in Summit House. A cog railway runs from Manitou Springs to the summit twice daily in season.

Pioneers' Museum, 25 W. Kiowa St., has historical and archaeological displays. Three rooms of the former home of Helen Hunt Jackson (author of *Ramona*) have been restored, with original furnishings.

El Pomar Carriage House Museum, Lake Ave. and Lake Circle, facing the Broadmoor Hotel, has a variety of old vehicles, including a Conestoga wagon.

Buffalo Bill's Wax Museum, 400 W. Manitou in the Briarhurst Center, features Old West scenes as they may never have been. Stanton Peckham, a longtime *Denver Post* editor, found the original Madame Tussaud's waxworks in London a disappointment after Colorado's museums, which are *really* scary. This one has the Gunfight at O.K.Corral (a Tombstone, Arizona, occurrence) and the Hanging of Blackjack Ketchum (he lost his head in Clayton, New Mexico).

Garden of the Gods, three miles NW on US 24, then right on 35th St. Red sandstone outcroppings, long a tourist's and photographer's delight.

McAllister House, 423 N. Cascade Ave., was built in 1875, with bricks brought from Philadelphia. Period furnishings. Major Henry McAllister assisted General William Palmer in the development of the city. McAllister had served under Palmer in the Civil War. Palmer, though a Quaker, commanded a cavalry corps and was a prisoner of war in 1862–63. He founded Colorado Springs, Colorado College, and aided Hampton Institute.

CORTEZ, Montezuma County. US 160, 164. Altitude: 6,200. *Four Corners Museum,* in the city library, has Indian artifacts, pottery, and two Pueblo Indian skeletons.

Hovenweep National Monument, ca. 40 miles W. of town, (also partly in San Juan County, Utah) is made up of six groups of Anasazi ruins. The Colorado sites contain numerous towers and pueblos. At Goodman Point is a large unexcavated pueblo and several smaller sites. The Pueblo Indians inhabited the sites from about 400 to 1300 A.D. The national park service area comprises 345.43 acres.

Yucca House National Monument, 12 miles S. of town via US 666 and secondary roads. Two large rubble and earth mounds may represent the ruins of a three- or four-story building. Indians inhabited the site ca. 1000 to 1300 A.D. The national park service maintains 9.6 acres but the site is not accessible to the public at this time.

Towaoc, thirteen miles SW, is a modern village of the Ute Indian Tribe.

Lowry Pueblo Ruins, US 666 to Pleasant View, nine miles W. on gravel. Anasazi ruins are 1,000 years old. Forty excavated rooms.

CRAIG, Moffatt County. US 40. Altitude: 6,185.

Moffatt County Museum, in the courthouse on US 40, has Indian relics, rock collection, and historical items of the area.

Private Railroad Car, entrance of City Park, E. on US 40, was owned by financier David H. Moffat; now houses the Chamber of Commerce.

CREEDE, Mineral County. State 149. Altitude: 8,854. Once a wide-open mining camp, then a ghost town, the settlement has been restored to the look of its best bad days. It was named for Nicholas C. Creede, who discovered gold at the head of West Willow Creek in 1889 with his partner George L. Smith. Population boomed; some say Creede acquired 10,000 new settlers overnight, including a number of the most colorful characters of the old West.

Soapy Smith, a longtime confidence man, swindled miners and any other gullible persons he could find. In Denver he had hired Bat Masterson to run a faro table; in Creede he put him to work in another saloon. Bob Ford, who had shot Jesse James and collected a $10,000 reward from Missouri governor Thomas Crittenden, bought a saloon in town and tried never to turn his back on the crowd. An upstairs room in the Creede Hotel has a notice which says "Bob Ford Slept Here." James was not asleep when Ford shot him but his back was turned.

Bat Masterson was 38 in his Creede days and a flashy dresser who favored lavender corduroy suits. Among the women gamblers in town were Killarney Kate, Poker Alice, and Calamity Jane. A new man, Ed. O. Kelly, arrived and lost no time in gunning down Bob Ford as he entered a saloon with his common-law wife Nell Watson. Creede citizens had not particularly liked Ford but they were ready to lynch his killer chiefly because he had used a shotgun. Kelly went to prison, then was pardoned. Ford was buried in Boot Hill above town but his remains were later removed to Missouri by the faithful Nell.

CRESTED BUTTE, Gunnison County. State 135. Altitude: 9,000. Once a picturesque and lively mountain mining town, and still picturesque. Some 2,000 feet higher than

Mexico City. Now a resort area, at the confluence of Slate and Coal Creeks. There are many old buildings in town with false fronts; the firehouse is still here. A snow slide in February of 1891 buried workers who were trying to uncover graves which had been buried in an earlier slide of the winter. For the many history hunters who like to read old tombstones, there are interesting headboards in the local cemetery. The ghost towns of Gothic, Bellvue, Schofield, Ruby, and Irwin are all in the vicinity of Crested Butte. Consult local maps and/or authorities for directions. Some involve climbing by foot, some can be reached by car.

CRIPPLE CREEK, Teller County. State 67. Altitude: 9,591 feet. The Gold Camp Road from Colorado Springs has 36 miles of incomparable mountain scenery; the paved highway leads through Ute Pass and around Pikes Peak. The Cripple Creek district was once the top of a volcano. It is the site of the largest known gold deposit in the world and has yielded over $430 million in precious ore. Among former residents who cared about gold, though not raw form, were Texas Guinan, who started her career here, and Jack Johnson, prizefighter. Jack Dempsey also worked here early in his career; Lowell Thomas was a newspaperman. The mines are said to have produced 28 millionaires.

Imperial Hotel, built in 1896, maintains much of its luxurious look.

Cripple Creek & Victor Narrow Gauge Railroad, at Cripple Creek Museum on Bennett Ave., has a four-mile trip through an area of abandoned mines to the ghost town of Anaconda and return, in tourist season.

The Mollie Kathleen Mine, one mile N. on State 67, has guided tours from June through August.

El Paso Gold Mines, three miles SE on State 67, tours from June through August.

Old Homestead, 353 E. Myers Ave., despite its name, was a brothel which was prosperous in gold rush times; some original furnishings.

DEL NORTE, Rio Grande County. US 160. Altitude: 7,880. The town, named for the Rio Grande del Norte which runs nearby, is one of the oldest on the Navajo Trail (US 160).

Rio Grande Museum, in County Courthouse, has relics from the Conquistadores who traveled this way in search of Quivera, the land of gold.

La Ventana, N. of town, is a window in rock which gives a view of the Continental Divide. Wagon tracks made by pioneers and Indian pictographs made long before emigration days may be seen in the vicinity.

DELTA, Delta County. US 50. The town, at the confluence of the Uncompahgre and Gunnison Rivers, was settled by Antoine Robidoux, a French trapper from St. Louis who built a fort here in 1830.

Delta County Historical Museum has pioneer and Indian relics.

DENVER, Denver County, I-70. The Mile-High City is filled with history in almost any form: manuscripts, books, paintings, buildings, replicas, statuary, wax, and even money. A good place to start sight-seeing is the Convention and Visitors Bureau, 225 W. Colfax Ave., which has folders, maps, and hostesses to answer questions.

State Capitol, E. Colfax Ave. and Sherman St. The thirteenth step in front is exactly one mile above sea

The Durango-Silverton Narrow Gauge draws rail buffs to Colorado

level and has a plaque for visitors to pose beside. The rotunda has paintings by Allen True and poems by Thomas Hornsby Ferril, long the editor of the *Rocky Mountain Herald* and western essayist and poet.

Colorado State Historical Museum, E. 14th Ave. and Sherman St., has outstanding exhibits of the early West. Scale models, paintings, artifacts covering Colorado's past from stone-age hunters to railroad-builders. On the third floor one of the main attractions is the $7,000 (now probably $35,000) wedding dress of Elizabeth Bonduel (Baby Doe) Tabor, and other mementos which were found in the trunks of H.A.W. Tabor's remarkable second wife who went from middle-class insecurity to riches to poverty. A helpful sign is posted (or was at last visit) on the stairs to this floor: "Visitors From Low Elevations. Warning: you are now a mile high. Exertion is magnified in this rare atmosphere especially with the excitement of traveling and the change in normal living habits. Please, do not exert yourself! If you feel faint, the first floor attendant will show you to a cot where you may lie down."

Denver Art Museum, 100 W. 14th Ave., in Civic Center, has an excellent collection of Western and North American Indian art.

Larimer Square, Larimer between 14th and 16th, is a shopping and entertainment area restored to the appearance of the 19th century.

The Wax Museum, five blocks S. of Civic Center, 919 Bannock St., gives the visitor the chance to meet Mark Twain, Jim Bridger, Chief Ouray, Brigham Young, in wax if not in person, and to see Alfred (often spelled Alferd) Packer, the cannibal, at one of his meals.

United States Mint, 320 Colfax, W. of Civic Center, has gold displays on mezzanine.

Molly Brown House, 1340 Pennsylvania St., was the home of Margaret Tobin, who was born in a cabin in Hannibal, Missouri. Some stories which seem reliable say that Molly was a waitress who learned about gold and silver while waiting on Mark Twain. With her boyfriend Daniel, she came to Colorado; though discreetly she persuaded him to proceed first to Leadville, where she followed him. She left Daniel as soon as she met James J. Brown, manager of the Louisville Mine. Brown struck it rich and the family moved to Denver. On one of Mrs. Brown's trips to Europe she survived the sinking of the *Titanic* and became a newspaper heroine and a legend, and eventually her life became a musical comedy libretto. Guides in costumes from 1900 conduct visitors on a tour of the house. A museum is in the Carriage House.

Forney Transportation Museum, 1416 Platte St., has 19th-century vehicles and costumed figures.

Civic Center has a number of statues of interest to students of Western history: an equestrian statue of Kit Carson, "On the Warpath," and the Bucking Bronco. The latter two are by A. Phimister Proctor. The Carson figure tops the "Pioneer Monument," which marks the terminus of the old Smoky Hill Trail, which gold seekers used to reach the Cherry Creek settlements in 1859 and 1860. Around the $75,000 fountain are figures of a hunter, a prospector, and a pioneer mother; it was designed by Frederick MacMonnies, and unveiled in 1911.

Denver Museum of Natural History, in City Park, has a collection of minerals and an exhibit of the prehistoric peoples of the Americas in addition to natural history exhibits.

Buffalo Bill Museum, top of Lookout Mountain, off US 40, has mementos of William Cody, the flamboyant nineteenth-century adventurer and showman, who is buried here.

DINOSAUR NATIONAL MONUMENT, Moffatt County. Off US 40. Also in Utah. Entrance 1½ miles E. of Dinosaur.

Headquarters and Information Center, at park entrance in Colorado, has an audio-visual program and displays. The 325-square-mile monument preserves the area where dinosaurs lived about 140 million years ago. The plateau has been cut by two rivers, the Yampa and the Green. The Canyon of the Ladore is more than 2,500 feet deep. Any visit to the monument should include the Quarry Center, which is in Utah, seven miles N. of Jensen.

DURANGO, La Plata County. US 550, 160. Altitude: 6,512. The town was founded by the Denver & Rio Grande Railroad and was a settlement with its share of wild characters. Billy the Kid is said to have been a frequent visitor; the Stockton-Eskridge gang fought the local law for nearly an hour in the main part of town.

The Silverton Depot, 479 Main St. A narrow-gauge passenger train still runs between this station and Silverton, using passenger coaches and steam engine that have been in service since 1882.

Southern Ute Tourist Center, 23 miles SE via US 550, 160, State 172, in Ignacio, has weapons, artifacts, and craft displays, among other exhibits.

San Juan National Forest, N. of town on US 550, comprises 1,897 acres, with some mountain peaks more than 14,000 feet high.

ESTES PARK, Larimer County. State 36. Altitude: 7,522.

Roosevelt National Forest surrounds the town on three sides. It covers 781,919 acres.

Aerial Tramway, 296 Riverside Drive, two blocks S. of Main St. A trip to the summit of Prospect Mountain affords a view of the Continental Divide the conquistadors, Zebulon Pike, and many others would have enjoyed.

The Chamber of Commerce, 215 E. Elkhorn, has information on a number of local sites and road conditions.

Rocky Mountain National Park, three miles W. (which see).

FAIRPLAY, Park County. US 285, State 9. Altitude: 9,953.

South Park City Museum; in this living ghost town some buildings stand on their original sites. Others were brought intact from ghost towns in less accessible areas. Twenty-two buildings house exhibits of all phases of frontier life, from the 1860s to the 1910s.

Prunes, a Burro is a statue of a pack burro which carried supplies to the mines until its death in 1930 at the age of 63. On Front St. next to the Hand Hotel.

Buckskin Joe, ca. seven miles NW, was a placer camp discovered in August 1859 by eight prospectors led by "Buckskin Joe" Higganbottom, who wore tanned deer skin. Silver Heels was a dancehall girl who stayed to nurse the miners stricken in a smallpox epidemic though all the other women left town. She disappeared, stories claim, because the disease ruined her looks. Mount Silverheels was named for her by grateful miners.

Leavick, Mudsill and Horseshoe were camps, then towns, SW of Fairplay. Many of Leavick's buildings are now in South Park City.

FLORENCE, Fremont County. State 120. Florence began as a coal town and converted to oil, which was found bubbling to the surface of Oil Creek, three miles W. of town. In 1862 A.M. Cassedy discovered oil at 50 feet in the canyon, hauled it to Pueblo, Denver, and Santa Fe by oxcart, and found its price reaching $5 a gallon during the Indian wars. The town has a Pioneer Museum and celebrates Pioneer Days each year. In very early days mountain Ute Indians fought the plains Arapahoes and Cheyennes near here. The town was first called Frazierville for Jesse Frazier, who set out an orchard in 1859; then named for the daughter of Sen. J.A. McCandless, who platted his 160-acre farm into the townsite.

FLORISSANT, Teller County. US 25, State 4. Altitude: 8,170.

Fossil Beds National Monument, S. on County 1. The 6,000 acres of the monument were covered by a prehistoric lake. Information station is two miles S. on County 1.

Petrified Forest Museum in town.

FORT COLLINS, Larimer County. US 287. Camp Collins was established by the 1st Colorado Cavalry near here in 1863 on the South Platte River. It was flooded in June 1864 and moved to higher ground on the Cache la Poudre River. The town grew up around it. The fort was set up to protect settlers and travelers on the Overland Trail; named for Lt.Col. William O. Collins, 11th Ohio Cavalry, commanding officer at Fort Laramie, Wyoming, and father of 1st Lt. Caspar W. Collins, who had a Wyoming fort, Fort Caspar, named for him.

Auntie Stone Cabin, 219 Peterson St., first dwelling in town, was built as a French trapper's home, later served as a mess room for officers. It has been moved from its original site and is now a pioneer museum.

FORT CRAWFORD, Montrose County. US 550, eight miles S. of Montrose, on the left bank of the Uncompahgre River about four miles N. of Los Piños Indian Agency. Established in July 1880 to control the Ute Indians after the White River massacre, the post was originally called "Cantonment on the Uncompahgre." In 1886 it was designated Fort Crawford for Captain Emmet Crawford, cavalry officer who died in 1886 of wounds received in Mexico while pursuing Geronimo.

Ouray-Chipta Park is four miles N. Chipta, wife of Chief Ouray, is buried here. Also a museum in park.

FORT GARLAND, Costilla County. US 160. Altitude: 7,936. The post was established in 1858, replacing Fort Massachusetts, which had been built in 1852 ca. five miles N. Massachusetts was the first U.S. military post in the present state of Colorado and the northernmost in the Department of New Mexico. The site in a seemingly sheltered valley on Ute Creek seemed favorable but proved swampy and dangerously situated for attack from insects and Indians. Fort Garland was named for Brig. Gen. John Garland, commander of the Department of New Mexico.

In 1863 a band of desperadoes known as the Espinosas were on a streak of terror and depredation through the San Luis Valley. Lt. Col. Samuel F. Tappan, in charge of Fort Garland, sent Tom Tobin, an old scout, with a detachment from the fort to find the marauders. Tobin not only found them, he brought back their heads in a sack, which he threw on the ground at Tappan's feet. Old scouts don't die, or even fade away. Tobin lived in the now peaceful San Luis Valley for many years and served as a member of the Costilla County School Board in 1896.

Kit Carson was in command of the post when General William Tecumseh Sherman paid a visit of inspection in 1866. Sherman conferred with Chief Ouray and later complimented Carson on his dealings with the Indians. Neither Sherman or Carson was ever the red man's best friend, however. On his journey back east Sherman had an adventure he recalled for his revised Memoirs in 1886. He reminisced about traveling in the West "before the days of the completed Pacific Railroad, with regular 'Doughertys' drawn by four smart mules, one soldier with a carbine or loaded musket in hand seated alongside the driver; two in the back seat with loaded rifles swung in the loops made for them; the lightest kind of baggage, and generally a bag of oats to supplement the grass, and to attach the mules to their camp. . . . Returning eastward from Fort Garland, we ascended the Rocky Mountains to the Sangre-de-Cristo Pass. The road descending the mountain was very rough and sliding. I got out with my rifle, and walked ahead about four miles, where I awaited my 'Dougherty.' After an hour or so I saw, coming down the road, a wagon, and did not recognize it as my own till quite near. It had been upset, the top all mashed in, and no means at hand for repairs." The seasoned general who'd had half a dozen or so horses shot from under him during the course of the Civil War merely repaired to the nearest cavalry camp and waited for his vehicle to be made road-ready again. [Note: The Sangre de Cristo Pass is essentially the same as La Veta Pass, crossed by US 160.]

Fort Garland is now restored and maintained by the Colorado Historical Society.

FORT LEWIS, La Plata County. State 140. Altitude: 7,610. A camp was established at Pagosa Springs on October 15, 1878, but Lt. Gen. Phil Sheridan recommended that the post be moved to a site on the La Plata River, SW of Durango, because of the White River Ute outbreak of 1879 with the threat of other Ute uprisings. The permanent post was established in July 1880.

FORT LOGAN, Denver County. US 85. Established in October 1887 on a site selected by Gen. Philip Sheridan, the post was meant to consolidate the troops. Several smaller posts were discontinued: Forts Garland, Crawford, Lewis, Lyon, and Uncompahgre. Fort Logan National Cemetery is here. The post was called Fort Sheridan unofficially in the Denver area; was designated Fort Logan, for Maj. Gen. John H. Logan, on April 5, 1889. "Black Jack" Logan, one of the few politicians who became a first-rate combat soldier in the Civil War, died in 1886. A then new fort north of Chicago was unofficially known as Fort Logan. Gen. Sheridan asked that this post be named for him; the names were traded. Fort Sheridan still stands on Sheridan Road in northern Illinois, and Logan, the Illinois lawyer, has the Denver post named for him. (A statue of Logan by the great sculptor Augustus Saint-Gaudens stands in Grant Park, Chicago, as does a Saint-Gaudens monument of Lincoln. Grant's statue stands in Lincoln Park.)

During Sherman's trip of inspection to western forts in 1866 he was besieged with petitions for new posts. He was against a military post here, feeling that Denver could raise 1,000 men for defense on short notice, and so reported to General Grant, then commanding the Army. Sherman noted that every Colorado town seemed to want a fort and that some petitions carried more signatures than he had soldiers in his department. As long as Sherman was in charge, no post was established at the capitol. When Sheridan succeeded him, matters changed. In recent years the Denver Arsenal site has been a parking lot, NE corner of 11th and Larimer Sts. Camp Wheeler became Lincoln Park, 13th and Osage. Fort Logan, on W. Oxford St., ca. eight miles S. of Sheridan, has been the Fort Logan Mental Health Center.

FORT LUPTON, Weld County. US 85. Built in 1836 as a trading post and also used as a stage station and stopover for settlers in times of Indian danger. First called Fort Lancaster. Present town is one mile S. of the old fort site.

FORT LYON I and II, Bent County. Arkansas River. US 50. The first Fort Lyon was established in August 1860 as Fort Fauntleroy, for a colonel of the 1st U.S. Dragoons, then named Fort Wise, for the governor of Virginia, which all too soon became a Confederate state. The post was renamed in honor of Brig. Gen. Nathaniel Lyon, killed in the Battle of Wilson's Creek, Missouri, in the first summer of the war. Fort Lyon II was established on the left bank of the river about 2½ miles below the mouth of the Purgatoire. In recent years it has been a U.S. Veterans Hospital.

FORT MORGAN, Morgan County. I-80, US 6, 34. The town was built on the site of the old fort, on the Overland Trail, and provided protection for emigrants and settlers. Formerly called Camp Tyler, then Camp Wardwell, finally Fort Morgan in 1866, for Maj. Christopher A. Morgan, 1st Illinois Cavalry, who established the post and died on January 20, 1866. After the Union Pacific Railway to Denver was completed, the garrison was transferred to Fort Laramie, Wyoming.

FORT REYNOLDS, Pueblo County. US 50, E. of Avondale. Marker on highway. The post, established July 3, 1867, was located on a plateau near the Arkansas River, a site previously selected by Colonel Randolph B. Marcy, early trailblazer and inspector general of the army. The fort was named for Maj. Gen. John F. Reynolds, killed on July 1, 1863, at Gettysburg.

FORT SEDGWICK, Sedgwick County. On South Platte River near the mouth of Lodgepole Creek. Granite marker on State 51 at site. The post was established in May 1864 to protect travelers on the Overland Trail and the Lodgepole Creek Emigrant route, and settlers. Originally Camp Rankin, designated a fort in September 1864 in honor of Maj. Gen. John Sedgwick, who was killed at Spotsylvania on May 9, 1864. The post was abandoned in the spring of 1871 when the Indians of the area were no longer a threat.

FORT VASQUEZ, Weld County. US 85, one mile S. of Platteville. Built ca.

1835 by mountain-men Louis Vasquez and Andrew Sublette of the Rocky Mountain Fur Company, the fort was not only an Indian trading post but a gathering place for early travelers. Other posts were soon erected in the South Platte region in competition with Vasquez for the fur trade. Fort Lupton (which see) is a few miles S. Peter Sarpy and Henry Fraeb built Fort Jackson nearby in 1837. Fort St. Vrain was established by Cerain St. Vrain and his partners, the Bent brothers, in 1838. Fort Vasquez fell into ruins but has been rebuilt in replica and maintained with a Visitor Center and museum, which tells the history of the Colorado fur trade.

GEORGETOWN, Clear Creek County. State 91. Altitude: 8,519. George and David Griffith found gold here in 1860 and the town was the leading mining camp until the Leadville strike of 1878. It is one of the best preserved early towns. In 1877 the narrow gauge Colorado Central reached the settlement and tourists began to gather at the "Switzerland of America." A Frenchman, Louis DuPuy, built a hotel which became one of the most famous in the West.

Hotel de Paris, 411 Alpine St., is a luxury establishment built in 1875 which attracted many notables of the nineteenth century. Now maintained by the Colonial Dames of America. Original furnishings.

Hamill House Museum, 3 and Argentine Sts. William A. Hamill's Victorian home has period furnishings, camel's hair wallpaper, restored carriage house, office with artifacts. Hamill was a silver king and state senator.

Maxwell House is a turreted Victorian relic of 1880, brightened with fresh paint, said to be one of the ten best examples of American Victorian architecture.

Alpine Hose #2 Fire House, founded in 1874, the bell tower was erected in 1880 making this one of the most elaborate firehouses in Colorado. Other historic buildings in midtown are the Clear Creek County Court House, the jailhouse, the old Missouri Fire House, and the Star Hook and Ladder Fire House. Several churches also have been restored.

Georgetown-Silver Plume Historic District takes in a railroad between the two towns and several mines, as well as historic houses of the area. The Georgetown Loop was built in 1884 for hauling silver ore. Its roadbed is part of the national historic landmark. The Silver Plume Depot is a national registered historic place built in 1884 as the terminus of the Colorado Central, which connected Denver with the Clear Creek mining region. It has been moved twice because of Interstate 70 contruction.

GLENWOOD SPRINGS, Garfield County. I-70, US 6, 24. Captain John C. Fremont explored the area, John Jacob Astor traded furs, and Doc Holliday, of Tombstone notoriety, died here. His tombstone notes that he died in bed in 1887. He was 35.

The Frontier Historical Society Museum has relics pertaining to the colorful past.

White River National Forest is N., E. and S. of town. Headquarters for the 1,938,633-acre tract are at 9th and Grand.

Ghost towns and pioneer settlements are nearby in almost any direction. Some are hard to reach in bad weather. S. on State 82, Cattle Creek is ca. 8 miles, Carbondale, 13 miles. S. from Carbondale on State 133 are

Redstone, Placita, Marble, and Crystal City. SW from Placita—in good weather only—try McClure Pass to Paonia. Marble, 30 miles S. of Carbondale, was founded in the early 1880s by prospectors who discovered gold and silver. Marble quarries were opened in 1890 and produced the marble used in the Lincoln Memorial and the Tomb of the Unknown Soldier. Crystal City had its boom days in the 1880s when its mines produced a fortune for many prospectors in silver, lead, and zinc. E. on US 68, 24 from Glenwood Springs are Shoshone, Dotsero, Gypsum, and Eagle. SE from Eagle are Lower and Upper Fulford, originally two camps, Camp Nolan and Polar City. Between Cattle Creek and Fulford, partly on State 82 and a secondary road, are Basalt, Ruedi, Meredith, and Thomasville.

GOLDEN, Jefferson County. US 6, State 68. Capital of Colorado Territory from 1862 to 1867.

Lariat Trail, US 6, leads to Buffalo Bill's Grave and Museum on Lookout Mountain.

Colorado Railroad Museum, 17155 W. 44th St., on State 58, has the largest historic railroadiana in the Rockies. Displays are housed in an 1880-style railroad depot.

Geological Museum, at Colorado School of Mines, main entrance to campus at Illinois Ave. and 15th St.

American Indian Museum, 705½ Joyce St. Indian artifacts including prehistoric.

Mount Vernon House (Robert W. Steele House), ca. one mile S. of city limits at the junction of I-70 and Mount Vernon Canyon Rd., is the mid-nineteenth century house of R.W. Steele, who was the governor of the extralegal territory of Jefferson. He was elected by local citizens in an effort to get some kind of government and served until June 1861, when President Lincoln's gubernatorial appointee arrived. The house also was used as a stage station, saloon, and general store. Privately owned, the house is listed in the Historic American Buildings Survey but is not accessible to the public at present.

Golden Museum and Jefferson County Library are housed in the Municipal Building, 911 10th St.

GRAND JUNCTION, Mesa County. I-70. Founded by George Crawford, Territorial Governor of Kansas in 1881, when the Ute Indians moved from the region.

Historical Museum and Institute of Western Colorado, 4th and Ute Sts. Displays tell the history of the Western Slope; a dinosaur skeleton is among the many relics here.

Grand Mesa National Forest, 18 miles E. off US 50, includes Grand Mesa, the world's largest flat-top mountain. The forest comprises 346,143 acres. Headquarters are in Delta.

Colorado National Monument (which see) is ten miles W.

GREAT SAND DUNES NATIONAL MONUMENT, Alamosa and Saguache Counties. State 150. The area lies in a ten-mile stretch along the base of the Sangre de Cristo Mountains, and includes 57 square miles. Zebulon Pike entered the San Luis Valley through the Medano Pass in the winter of 1806–07. He wrote about the dunes in his journal. Fremont visited the area in 1848, using the Mosca Pass. John W. Gunnison also wrote about the dunes. The Visitor Center is separated from the dunes by Medano Creek. Guidebooks supplied at the Center lead visitors on the Montville

Trail Tour with numbered stakes for reference.

GREELEY, Weld County. US 85, 34.

Meeker Memorial Museum, 1324 9th Ave. Nathan C. Meeker, who built the house, was a founder of Union Colony, later Greeley. He had been agriculture editor of Horace Greeley's *New York Tribune* before he took the boss's most famous piece of advice and went west. The adobe house was built in 1870 on the site of a frame shack erected on land given him by the city. Restored to its original appearance, with some original furnishings. Meeker was appointed Indian agent for the Ute Indians at the White River Agency. The rebellious Utes murdered Meeker and others in 1879. (See also Meeker.)

Municipal Museum, 919 7th St., has pioneer exhibits.

GUNNISON, Gunnison County. US 50. Altitude: 7,703.

Pioneer Museum, E. edge of town on US 50, has historical items from the county's past.

Curecanti National Recreation Area, nine miles W. on US 50, along the Gunnison River, includes Blue Mesa, Morrow Point, and Crystal Lakes. Visitor Center, 16 miles W.

Ghost Town Tours: a Visitor Center at 500 E. Tomichi Ave. provides free maps for a twenty-circle tour. Tincup, one of the wildest early mining camps, along with Creede and Leadville, is forty miles away along the Taylor River. At Parlin, E. of Gunnison on US 50, take a gravel road N. to Ohio City and Pitkin, not quite ghosts. A graded dirt road runs N. over Cumberland Pass to Tincup. For circle trip, continue past Tincup on the same road, past Taylor Reservoir, returning to State 135 at Almont. State 135 from Almont runs NW to Jacks Cabin, Crested Butte, and Gothic, or SW back to Gunnison. Gothic, nine miles N. of Crested Butte on improved county road, was founded in 1879 and served as supply depot for many small camps, with a population of 8,000 in its heyday.

Gunnison National Forest, NE and S. of town on US 50, has 27 peaks more than 12,000 feet high, includes 1,663,279 acres.

HOVENWEEP NATIONAL MONUMENT, Montezuma County. Access is by graded dirt roads. Monument is nearly due W. from Cortez (State 789); it comprises six groups of prehistoric towers, pueblos, and cliff dwellings. Two are in Utah, the remainder in Colorado. All date from the Great Pueblo Period of 1100 to 1300.

IDAHO SPRINGS, Clear Creek County. I-70. US 6, 40. Altitude: 7,540. A mining and resort town lying along a narrow canyon, which has had several names in its history. Before 1860 it was Sacramento City, Jackson Diggings, Idahoe, and finally Idaho Springs. Chief Idaho brought his sick and wounded warriors to the Radium Hot Springs here, which are still beneficial. In Blue Ribbon Tunnel is refreshing mineral water.

Site of the First Major Gold Strike in Colorado, US 40. A boulder marks the spot where George Jackson, Indian trader and relative of Kit Carson, who was working his solitary way down Chicago Creek, made camp on a sandbar and found gold.

Colorado School of Mines—Edgar Mine, Colorado St. and 8 Ave. An experimental mine operated by students, and by the government for training, has a 45-minute guided tour.

Bells of Granite Glen Museum, Upper Bear Creek, seven miles W. on I-70, then four miles S. on State 74 in Evergreen, bells from 1000 B.C. to the present. Until 1877 Evergreen was known as The Post, then named by pioneer D. P. Wilmot for the evergreens that supplied the sawmills during the logging era. There are interesting old buildings in town.

Mount Evans, SW on State 103, 14 miles to State 5, is 14,260 feet high. The highest auto road in the U.S. is open only in summer; inquire at Idaho Springs about road conditions —the road is fine but obviously is in steep country. The State 103 route passes the Arapaho National Forest Ranger Station Information Center and the Jackson Gold Discovery Monument, then travels through Chicago Creek Canyon to Echo Lake. An alternate route by way of Bergen Park and Squaw Pass to Echo Lake, then State 5 to the top, has many overlooks. Either route offers spectacular views. The summit has an incomparable view of the Great Plains. If your heart can stand it, your adjectives will still fail.

Loveland Pass on the Continental Divide is at 11,988 feet. 28 miles SW on US 6.

St. Mary's Glacier, 12 miles NW via I-70, Fall River Road to Alice, a ghost town once rich in placer gold. Visitors can park less than a mile NW of Alice; from here, Shank's mare only. The old Alice Glory Hole is less than a mile SW of town.

JULESBURG, Sedgwick County. I–76. The fourth and only surviving town named for Jules Beni, stationmaster for the Overland Stage and later an outlaw, who was killed by Jack Slade, another tough pioneer. The town was founded in 1881 during the construction of the Union Pacific cutoff to Denver.

Fort Sedgwick–Julesburg Museum, maintained by the Historical Society, interprets the history of the fort and the four towns. Early in 1865 southern Plains Indians, reacting to the Sand Creek Massacre (See Chivington), attacked the post, which was poorly garrisoned, and sacked the town. About one thousand Cheyennes, Arapahos, and Sioux made up the force. In February they again attacked the town (then at a different site) and burned it to the ground. The privately owned sites of the earlier towns are located in plowed fields. A monument marks the original site.

Italian's Cave, S. of town ca. 1.5 miles to graveled road, turn right, then 3.6 miles to the cave. Legend has it that Jules Beni once hid out here. Later Uberto Gabello, a Cripple Creek miner, enlarged the fissure and charged visitors. Although it was never proved, several survivors of stagecoach attacks attested that white men were in some of the Indian war parties. Beni was suspected of being in league with the marauders. Jack Slade was his replacement when Beni was fired as stationmaster. Beni shot Slade, who recovered to swear that he would cut off Beni's ears and wear them as watch fobs. He did catch up with his victim near Fort Laramie, Wyoming, and may have tortured him before finishing him off. Slade later was hanged by vigilantes in Virginia City, Montana, for "disturbing the peace." (See also Fort Sedgwick.)

KIT CARSON, CHEYENNE WELLS, FIRSTVIEW and WILD HORSE, Cheyenne County. US 40, 287.

Kit Carson was a supply post in the 1800s, burned to the ground by Indians and relocated a few miles N. of original site. Historical Museum has history of the area. During construction of the Kansas Pacific Railroad, the town saw wild times and much business from wagon trains headed west.

Cheyenne Wells, 25 miles E. on highway, was a station on the Butterfield Overland Line. The Wells, which were of great importance to wagon trains, were ca. 12 miles N. Bayard Taylor, travel writer and correspondent for the *New York Tribune,* visited here in 1866 and found the local mules better housed than the residents. There was, in his report, "a large, handsome frame stable," but the people lived "in a natural cave extending for some thirty feet under the bluff."

Firstview, a hamlet between Cheyenne Wells and Kit Carson on highway, got its name from the circumstance that on clear days travelers headed west get their first look at the mountains from here.

Wild Horse, 20 miles W. of Kit Carson, was a watering place for wild horses, which may have come from horses first brought to the area by Spanish explorers. Zebulon Pike saw a great herd of them in 1806.

KOKOMO, Summit County. State 91, 12 miles N. of Climax. Indiana prospectors found silver deposits in the vicinity in 1878 and thought of home when naming the settlement. A partial ghost town today, but the Masonic Hall and the Community Church are among the surviving buildings.

LAKE CITY, Hinsdale County. State 149, at the base of the San Juan Mountains, in the heart of the Uncompahgre and San Juan National Forests. Altitude: 8,671.

Lake Fork Recreation Area, S. and W. of town, 81,000 acres developed by the Bureau of Land Management for mining, grazing, and watershed protection as well as recreation. There are a number of ghost towns, abandoned mining sites, stamp mills, and countless spectacular views in the area. Lake San Cristobal, one of Colorado's largest lakes, was formed by the Slumgullion Earthflow in 1200 A.D. Cannibal Plateau near the lake is where Al Packer and five unfortunate companions were on a prospecting trip and only Packer survived. He was tried for murder, but it was known that he had been guilty of cannibalism. He was sentenced to hang but was granted a new trial on a technicality. He was paroled after serving only a few of the forty years he was given in the second trial, and died in Denver in 1906.

Uncompahgre Peak, trail starts at Nellie Creek a few miles W., elevation 14,306, a ten-mile trip to summit by horseback or on foot.

Jeep trips: The Hinsdale County Chamber of Commerce, at Lake City, has maps and information on a number of scenic drives and jeep trips in a 50-mile radius of town. Cinnamon Pass is 13,009 feet, Engineer Pass, 13,175 feet. Going on to Silverton and Ouray, returning by way of Henson Creek is a trip which follows the old Henson Creek and Uncompahgre Toll Road of 1877 which connected with the Animas Fork Road. North Henson, Carson City, Sawmill Park, and Slumgullion Pass also are worth visiting.

Ghost towns: Capitol City can be reached by car, ca. 9 miles W. of town. Road passes the Ute-Ulay Mine at 3.8 miles. Capitol City was the dream of George S. Lee, mill and smelter operator, who wanted his village to be the state capital and his home the governor's manse. Caroline Bancroft, an excellent and enthusiastic Colorado historian, described Lee's settlement in 1960: "Above the junction of North Henson Creek with Henson Creek there were some log cabins in what used to be the upper end of town. On the townsite proper there was only the derelict mansion which was being destroyed from every angle. Henson Creek had altered its course and was eating away the embankment on which the Lee house stood while at the same time human hands were carting away souvenirs. At the lower end of town only the foundations could be seen of the smelter on which George Lee had based his great dream. . . ." The ruins of Rose's Cabin are farther up Henson Creek on the old stagecoach route. Corydon Rose built a hotel and bar with stables here in 1874, which served as a stop for travelers over the Engineer Pass, which was in a different location from the jeep trip of today. Henson Creek was named for Henry Henson, an early prospector. Carson (sometimes Carson City) is ca. 15 miles S. of Lake City; the last 4 miles are by jeep only. J.E. Carson discovered a mine atop the continental divide in 1881 on the headwaters of Wager Creek and staked claims on both sides of the divide. Sections of Carson are very well preserved; but the slope toward the Atlantic is considerably more weathered. The little town of Sherman is on the Lake Fork road to Cinnamon Pass, due W. of the point where the jeep road to Carson begins. And beyond Sherman is Whitecross.

LA JUNTA, Otero County. US 50, State 6. The Santa Fe Trail and the old Navajo Trail met here.

Bent's Old Fort National Historic Site (which see) is eight miles NE on State 194.

Koshare Indian Kiva Museum, 18th St. and Santa Fe Ave. Indian artifacts and present-day crafts.

LAMAR, Prowers County. US 50, 287, 385.

The Madonna of the Trail monument, Main St. and the Santa Fe tracks, is dedicated to the pioneer mothers of covered-wagon days. The Chamber of Commerce, next door, has information on sites of the area. Mural carvings of southern Colorado cattle brands embellish the courthouse.

LAS ANIMAS, Bent County. State 101, US 50.

Kit Carson Museum, 225 9th St. The old jail and house are part of the display: restored period bedroom, living room, trapper's corner, with other exhibits pertaining to the early cattle industry and Indians of the area.

Cemetery has the grave of William W. Bent with the dates of his original burial, May 19, 1869, and his reburial here, May 23, 1909.

Santa Fe Trail, markers on US 50 and State 183.

LA VETA, Huerfano County. 16 miles SW of Walsenburg on State 10, 12. La Veta Pass is at 9,382 feet.

Francisco Fort Museum has historical artifacts of the area. The town was founded in 1862 by Colonel John M. Francisco and was known as Francisco Plaza.

San Isabel National Forest, 11 miles S. on State 12. Cuchara Canyon leads to Monument Lake.

LEADVILLE, Lake County. US 24. Altitude: 10,152. The highest incorporated city in the U.S., the town could have been Goldville, Silverville, or Scandalville, to fit its lively and productive past. Since placer mines were opened in 1860 in nearby California Gulch more than $600 million in ore has been produced. The largest molybdenum mine in North America is in operation at Climax, 12 miles away.

Healy House-Dexter Cabin Museums, 912 Harrison Ave. Healy House is a state historical monument with furnishings and mannequins dressed to fit its period (1878), and pictures of the 1890s when Leadville was at its mining peak. Dexter Cabin was built by mining millionaire and sportsman James V. Dexter to resemble an ordinary cabin on the outside with luxury inside. It was one of five hunting lodges he owned and served for poker sessions for "the stiffest and most exclusive private poker club" in town. Both houses are maintained by the State Historical Society.

Tabor Home, 115 E 5th St., was the residence of the romantic and successful H.A.W. Tabor and his dour first wife, Augusta, who lived here until they moved to Denver in 1881. Restored.

The Matchless Mine, two miles E. on E. 7th St., was the property the dying Tabor told his second wife, Baby Doe, to hold on to. Tabor's wives are almost as well-known as the womenfolk of Henry VIII and Bluebeard, but not everyone knows that the virtuous Augusta held on to her money instead of a played-out mine and died comfortably—though possibly still as miserable in spirit as she had lived—whereas the once hot-blooded beauty, Baby Doe Tabor, was found frozen to death in the cabin near the mine where she had lived for thirty-six years. Though Baby Doe was snubbed by high society, if not by President Chester Arthur who attended her wedding, and by her oldest daughter, the years have been kind to her legend. She emerges a heroine, not merely a gold-seeker, and a survivor—in her way—against incredible odds.

Tabor Opera House, 308 Harrison St., was built and elegantly furnished in 1879 and attracted the best in traveling thespians, musicians, and opera companies. It has been restored.

House with the Eye, 127 W. 4th St., has a stained glass "eye" in the roof. Period furnishings and relics, antique carriages and fire equipment. Guided tours.

Heritage Museum and Gallery, 9th and Harrison Sts., diorama and exhibits pertaining to colorful local history.

The Chamber of Commerce does a booming business in brochures and maps which give information about jeep and industrial tours and a trip along the "Routes of the Silver Kings." Among interesting old camps and settlements of the vicinity are Stumptown, 3½ miles E.; Stringtown and Malta, less than 3 miles S. on US 24; and Independence, SW via US 24 and State 82. (Stumptown is where the later "unsinkable" Molly Brown lived in a cabin as a miner's wife. Jim Brown was the manager of the Little Jonny mine. Molly may have lost a fortune in paper money, hidden in a stove, which went up in smoke.)

LONGMONT, Boulder County. US 287. Named after Major Stephen H. Long, who explored the valley in 1820.

Pioneer Museum, 3rd and Kimbark.

MANITOU SPRINGS, El Paso County. US 24, at the foot of Pikes Peak. Altitude: 6,412. Named for the Indian God Manitou, who the Indians believed lived underneath the waters of the soda springs.

Cliff Dwellings Museum, US 24 Bypass, in Phantom Cliff Cañon, a major archaeological preserve, representing the Great Pueblo period of 1100–1300.

Cave of the Winds, 2 miles NW on US 24. One mile of passageways through a series of sculptured prehistoric rooms, with stalactites, stalagmites, and other formations.

Manitou and Pikes Peak Railway Company, depot at 515 Ruxton Ave. Trains daily to the summit of Pikes Peak from May to October.

Mount Manitou Scenic Railway, the longest and highest railway of its kind in the world, leads to the summit of Mount Manitou daily May to October.

MEEKER, Rio Blanco County. State 13. Altitude: 6,249.

Meeker Massacre Site, just off State 64, ca. 3 miles W. The Ute uprising of 1879 began here at the White River Agency which had been founded in 1873 for several bands of Utes who had agreed to settle on a reservation. Nathan C. Meeker, the idealistic Indian agent who had founded Greeley, attempted to teach farming and to educate the children, but a quarrel took place, Meeker sent for troops, and before they could arrive the agency was attacked and burned. Meeker and at least nine employees were killed; his wife, daughter, and another girl were held captive for twenty-three days. A monument marks the site where Meeker died.

Courthouse park was the parade ground of the military post established four years after the massacre. At N. end of park are three log cabins used as barracks.

Meeker Hotel was Theodore Roosevelt's headquarters on one of his western hunting trips. Specimens of White River animals are on display.

Milk Creek Battlefield, in Moffatt County, on an unimproved road, ca. 20 miles NE of Meeker. After the Meeker massacre, Ute Indians ambushed a column of troops under Major Thomas Thornburgh here on the N. edge of the White River Reservation. The troops were headed toward Meeker, in response to a call for help, having marched from Fort Fred Steele, Wyoming; they sent a messenger for help and were reinforced ultimately by 35 black cavalrymen from Fort Lewis. A relief expedition of 350 men under Colonel Wesley Merritt from Fort D.A. Russell, Wyoming, finally broke the siege. The Army lost 13 including Major Thornburgh. Ute leaders were imprisoned and the tribe was removed to a new reservation in Utah. A monument on the site lists the dead.

MESA VERDE NATIONAL PARK, Montezuma County. Park entrance off US 160, between Corte and Mancos.

Visitor Center, 21 miles S. of entrance, should be visited first; open from late June to Labor Day. The paved highway climbs 1,500 feet to the summit of the flat-topped mountain where museums and park headquarters are located. En route the road passes Mancos Valley Overlook, with parking, and Knife Edge Overlook at the head of Prater Canyon. Free ranger guide service is provided for the ruins from early May to late October. The park includes 52,000

Cliff Palace, Mesa Verde National Park in southwestern Colorado, dates back to the 14th century

acres of mesas and canyons and has incomparable cliff dwellings left by Pueblo Indians of centuries ago. Park Point Fire Lookout, at 8,572 feet, halfway between the park entrance and the mountaintop, offers a splendid view of the Four Corners area of Colorado, Arizona, Utah, and New Mexico.

MONTROSE, Montrose County. US 50, 550.

Ute Indian Museum, two miles S. on US 550. Dioramas, relics, maps, and photographs depict the Ute tribal history. Museum is maintained by the State Historical Society. Chief Ouray and his wife Chipeta are featured in many of the exhibits. Among the items associated with the great leader is the beaded shirt he wore to Washington for peace talks in 1880–81, also his saddles, full-dress costume, and the desk the government gave Ouray, who had about as much use for it as President Garfield had for a feathered headdress—he could neither read nor write.

Uncompahgre National Forest is W., SW, S. and SE of town; Gunnision National Forest is NE; and Grand Mesa National Forest is N.

Black Canyon of the Gunnison (which see) is 14 miles NE via US 50, State 347.

OPHIR, San Miguel County. State 145. Altitude: 9,280. Old Ophir may serve as one of the many ghost camps still unlisted, which only the most dedicated ghost collector will visit. A jeep road which connects with State 145 at Ophir runs N. into Telluride. It is fifteen miles and the driving time is just under three hours. Another jeep trail to Telluride begins at 11,018-foot-high Red Mountain Pass, off US 550 N. of Silverton, where snows on the N. side never melt, and is slightly more difficult than the Ophir Pass route; a sign observing that the twelve-mile trip will take two hours adds: "You don't have to be crazy to take this trip, but it helps." The Ophir Pass road, descending from US 550 4 miles N. of Silverton, crosses an old burro bridge over Mineral Creek, passes through meadows and rock piles to reach the 11,700-foot summit, with the San Miguel Valley below. Descent takes a shelf road hacked out of rock, steep and frighteningly narrow, but it once served as the highway to the mining camps of the area in the 1870s. Old cemeteries in all ghost towns including Ophir are great places to visit, even if you wouldn't want to live there.

OURAY, Ouray County. US 550. The town is at the foot of the "Million Dollar Highway," US 550, which was blasted from sheer rock walls, and paved with gold-bearing gravel. Ouray, named for the Ute chief, was incorporated in 1876, the year Colorado joined the Union. It was a supply center for rich mines, with the Denver & Rio Grande Railroad arriving in 1888. The discovery of Camp Bird Mine by Thomas Walsh eventually led to his daughter's diamond. Evalyn Walsh McLean's "Hope diamond" was probably the most famous American rock since Plymouth. The Camp Bird Mine and Idarado Mining Co. still are the backbone of local industry.

Bear Creek Falls, three miles S. on US 550. Road crosses a bridge over the 227-foot falls with an observation point nearby.

Box Canyon, less than a mile S. on US 550, is 20 feet wide and rises 221 feet.

Jeep trips: rentals available from two companies in town, with experienced drivers to take visitors to old ghost towns, mines, passes, and areas above the timber line. One trip runs up Red Mountain on a road built in 1888, carved out of a canyon wall 1000 feet straight up.

Rutomipa Mine, one mile N. on US 550, has displays featuring mining history; rock exhibits. Guided tours.

Western Hotel Museum has local history exhibits. The ornate Beaumont Hotel was built in 1885 with a grand staircase that faces a hand-carved registration desk.

PAGOSA SPRINGS, Archuleta County. US 160, 84. Altitude: 7,079. (The Navajo Trail.) The town, named for the hot springs which the Indians believed had healing powers, were rediscovered by white men in 1859, who also believed they had healing powers. Now surrounded by the San Juan National Forest, Pagosa Springs was a favorite Indian camping ground and a military post in 1878.

PIKES PEAK, El Paso County. Pikes Peak Highway starts at Cascade, a few miles up Ute Pass off US 24. It climbs 7,309 feet in 18 miles. Open May 1 to October 31, depending on weather conditions; recommended only for experienced mountain drivers. Cog railway vista top cars run twice daily in season from Manitou Springs.

Summit House is headquarters for the U.S. Forest Service. Chauffeur service is available in emergencies for drivers affected by altitude and unable to make the return trip. Explorer and trailblazer Zebulon Pike was not worried about the return trip in 1806 when he discovered the peak; he did not reach the summit.

Pike National Forest takes in 1,107,000 acres in the Front Range of the Rockies. Gold Camp Road and Rampart Range Road offer other scenic drives besides the one to the most famous peak in America.

PUEBLO, Pueblo County. US 50, 85, 87.

El Pueblo State Museum, 905 S. Prairie, adjacent to fairgrounds. The museum depicts the rich history of Pueblo with dioramas and displays. Many famous names of the Old West touched base here. The area was an Indian crossroads long before Europeans visited America. Fur traders, including James Beckwourth, built an adobe fort in 1842. The town was stampeded by gold-seekers in the 1859 rush. These times and others are all excellently presented; the museum is maintained by the State Historical Society.

Pueblo Metropolitan Museum, 419 W. 14th St., a 37-room mansion houses period furnishings, Americana collections; a blacksmith shop and general store are also on display. The building was constructed by John Albert Thatcher, pioneer merchant and banker, with fresco ceilings, hand-carved banisters, and other Victorian embellishments.

Pueblo is headquarters for the San Isabel and Pike National Forests which comprise 1,107,500 acres.

RIFLE, Garfield County. I-70. Settled in 1882, the town is now the southern gateway to the Dinosaur National Monument (which see) and to White River National Forest. N. and W. of town are the Book Cliff Mountains, rich in oil shale.

Rifle Creek Museum has displays of local history.

White River National Forest was occupied by Utes and was their hunting ground before it was declared a national area by President Benjamin Harrison in 1891. John Fremont entered southern parts of the forest in 1845. Some peaks are 14,000 feet. There are a number of ghost towns within the boundaries. There are District Ranger stations in Minturn, Carbondale, Eagle, Meeker, and Aspen as well as in Rifle. The forest supervisor's office is at 9th and Grand in Glenwood Springs.

RIO GRANDE NATIONAL FOREST, in several counties. Crossed by US 160, State 149. The forest includes 1.8 million acres, enclosing the San Luis Valley on three sides. Some peaks are 14,000 feet high. Within boundaries are the Upper Rio Grande Primitive Area, La Garita Wild Area, and Wheeler Geologic Area with sandstone formations looking rather like an ancient cathedral, which can be reached only by pack trail from Creede.

ROCKY MOUNTAIN NATIONAL PARK, several counties in north-central Colorado. US 36, 40, State 66.

Headquarters, three miles W. of Estes Park off State 66. W. entrance at Grand Lake (US 34). The park comprises 410 square miles and straddles the Continental Divide. Information and maps are available as well as an interpretive movie. Moraine Park Visitor Center, 1 mile inside park from Beaver Meadows entrance, has museum, maps, slides, brochures. Tape tours are available for self-guided auto trips. The Alpine Museum is so named because one-third of the park is within the Alpine Zone with a climate approximately that of the Arctic Circle. Maps are essential and can be bought at the park or at the Government Printing Office in Washington, D.C. In 1859 Joel Estes and his son were the first white men to see the area. They settled and later the Earl of Dunraven bought the land and helped to preserve it. In 1868 Major John Wesley Powell and his party climbed Longs Peak, 14,256 feet high. It still can be climbed by the hardy, a full day's trip.

Shadow Mountain National Recreation Area includes ca. 29 square miles at the SW edge of the park.

ROLLINSVILLE, Gilpin County. State 119. Altitude: 8,420.

The Moffat Road was once a railroad bed in part. It climbs to 11,660 feet on a twisting 35-mile route over the Continental Divide. The E. approach is ca. 30 miles W. of Denver on State 72 at Tolland Drive Inn. W. approach is at Winter Park, US 40. The road was to be a temporary railroad line, laid down by David Moffat, until the Moffat Tunnel could be constructed. (In 1947 the Moffat railroad, the Denver & Salt Lake Railway, was merged with the Denver & Rio Grande Western, and runs through the Moffat Tunnel, finished by state funds in the late 1920s.)

Among sites to be seen are ghost towns, Yankee Doodle Lake, Rollins Pass, Riflesight Notch, Pumphouse Lake, and Deadman's Lake.

ROOSEVELT NATIONAL FOREST, in several counties, crossed by US 36, etc., occupies 1,080,540 acres on the eastern slope of the Rockies. A scenic route of Cameron Pass leads to Routt National Forest, 1,124,938 acres, which adjoins Roosevelt.

Pawnee National Grassland comprises 193,000 acres in Roosevelt National Forest.

SAGUACHE, Saguache County. US 285, State 114. Altitude: 7,697. At the foot of Monarch Pass, the settlement was a rendezvous for fur trappers and traders. *Saguache County Museum* has relics of early times.

SALIDA, Chaffee County. US 50, State 291. Altitude: 7,036. Founded in 1880 by the Rio Grande Railroad and known as South Arkansas. Explored by the Spanish in 1779. Pike, Fremont, and others came in the early part of the nineteenth century.

Frontier Museum, in Hot Springs Pool Bldg. on US 50. Indian and pioneer artifacts.

Jeep tours, 10165 US 50, four miles W., for viewing the Continental Divide, ghost towns, abandoned mines, and the Arkansas River Valley. Turret, once a gold town, is N.; Poncha City is W.; Alder, Villa Grove, and Bonanza are also in the vicinity to the S.

SILVER CLIFF, Custer County. State 69. Altitude: 7,982. The town had a population of 15,000 in its gold rush days of 1881, the year the Denver & Rio Grande Railroad reached the settlement. Its fire department was established in 1879, in the Town Hall, now a museum. Some fire hydrants are 90 or so years old. The town cemetery has interesting old tombstones, and stories persist that strange flickering lights can be seen in the graveyard. Legends say they were first seen in 1880 by a late-partying bunch of miners coming home from a big night in nearby Rosita. A blue flame glowed on the site of a new tombstone. It was thought that lights from the town reflected on the stones, but an experiment was tried in which all local lights were shut off and still the grave lights shone. Another theory is that phosphorescence of the ores in the area causes the spookiness. Silver Cliff, in the Wet Mountain Valley, is not a true ghost town but there are several in the vicinity: of varying populations are Hillside and Texas Creek on State 69 to the NW; Querida and Rosita to the E., and Greenwood, Wetmore, and Florence on State 67 going N. to Pueblo and US 50.

SILVERTON, San Juan County. US 550. Altitude: 9,318.

San Juan County Historical Society Museum, N. Greene St. in county jail building, has displays which feature mining, railroading, and pioneer days.

Silverton Historical District, a national historic landmark, includes some mines, a number of early buildings—the Imperial Hotel (1882), the Congregational Church (1881), and the city hall and courthouse.

Durango-Silverton Narrow Gauge Railroad, also in La Plata County, is a national historic landmark. It was built to haul ores from isolated mountain areas to smelter points. Silverton is the end of the line.

STEAMBOAT SPRINGS, Routt County. US 40. Altitude: 6,695.

Routt National Forest is NE and S. of town.

Tread of Pioneers Museum, Oak and 5th Sts., in a turn-of-the-century house built by Ernest Campbell. Museum displays mining, pioneer, and other local interest items from the 1870s.

Ghost towns, N. of town, are Mad Creek Village, Clark, Hahns Peak, and Columbine. Columbine had two famous gold mines, the Royal Flush and the Master Key.

STERLING, Logan County. US 6.

Overland Trail Museum, 1½ miles E. on US 6. Cattle brands, Indian artifacts, archaeological and paleontological exhibits.

STRASBURG, Adams County. State 36.

Comanche Crossing of the Kansas Pacific Railroad, on the Union Pacific Railroad tracks E. of the depot. It was here on August 15, 1870, that the final spike was driven connecting the west and east coasts entirely by continuous rail track. The golden spike at Promontory, Utah, driven in May 1869, did not complete a continuous rail link between oceans. Comanche Creek is spanned by the tracks. A registered historic landmark.

SUMMIT SPRINGS BATTLEGROUND, on Logan–Washington County line, ca. ten miles SW of Atwood on unimproved road. On July 11, 1869, troops led by Major Eugene A. Carr from Fort McPherson, Nebraska, and 150 Pawnee scouts under Maj. Frank North and Capt. Luther North, guided by "Buffalo Bill" Cody, surprised the Cheyennes at this site and killed 50 Indians, including Tall Bull, capturing 117. Only one cavalryman was wounded. Chief Tall Bull and his "Dog Soldiers" had been plundering Kansas and Colorado settlements for many months. The battlefield is marked by a stone monument near the springs.

TELLURIDE, San Miguel County. State 145. Altitude: 8,745.

Telluride Historic District, a national historic landmark. Several buildings date from the late nineteenth century: City Hall, 1883, Sheridan Hotel, 1890s, the Opera House, 1900. Claims were staked in 1875; later the Smuggler was struck, uncovering a vein that assayed at $1200 per ton. The town, which is known as "The City of Gold," has been one of the leading mining camps since the first operation. Sarah Bernhardt, Lillian Russell, and other celebrities of the past played at the Sheridan Opera House. The area was used as background for the motion picture *The Unsinkable Molly Brown,* starring the unsinkable Debbie Reynolds.

TRINIDAD, Las Animas County. I-25, US 85, 87. Altitude: 6,025. During the eighteenth century Spanish patrols crossed the mountains through the 7,834-foot Raton Pass, 15 miles S.

Bloom House, Main St., is restored and furnished in the 1880s period, with Victorian rose garden.

Baca House Pioneer Museum, 300 E. Main, opposite post office. Maintained by the State Historical Society, the adobe building houses pioneer relics, Indian artifacts, items pertaining to the active days of the Santa Fe trail, Kit Carson, and other pioneers. The house was built in 1869 by Felipe Baca, a rancher and freighter.

Kit Carson Park has an equestrian statue of the famous scout.

Santa Fe Trail, at junction of US 85 with US 350, tablet on Columbian Hotel is descriptive of the trail from Bent's Fort, which joined the mountain branch here from 1840–79. Granite shaft and plaque are also in Kit Carson Park.

IDAHO

One character we met at Keenan City deserves a notice. He was the traditional forty-niner. In most outside mining camps at least one is found. This one was in the last stages physically, an attenuated, wild-eyed skeleton, long haired and long-bearded, with stooping shoulders and hands like eagle's claws. His voice was weak and piping, and his footsteps slow and febble, but the spirit of an invincible nature possessed him still. The old fellow looked upon me and my party as imposters, smarties, and swore that we had come up the river instead of down, until I happened to mention one day that my first experiences in California dated from May, 1849.

Battle Drums and Geysers; The Life and Journal of Lt. Gustavus Cheyney Doane, Soldier and Explorer of the Yellowstone and Snake River Regions (Swallow, 1970)

We crossed three rivers we didn't know,
Out on the trail to Idaho.
It was a long and lonesome go
Out on the trail to Idaho.

On the Trail to Idaho, collected by John A. Lomax and Alan Lomax

IDAHO FACTS: Lewis and Clark brought the first explorers in 1805. Fur companies and the military came next. Missionaries came from both Catholic and Protestant churches, and from Brigham Young's Mormon church. When Idaho Territory was created in 1863, the land included much of Montana and Wyoming, but President Lincoln had trouble finding anyone willing to take the governorship. One appointee, Gilman Marston, never arrived, nor did Alexander Conner. But William H. Wallace took office in the territorial capital of Lewiston in December 1863. Idaho became the 43rd state on July 3, 1890. Nickname: Gem State. Capital: Boise. Idaho has Nez Perce National Historical

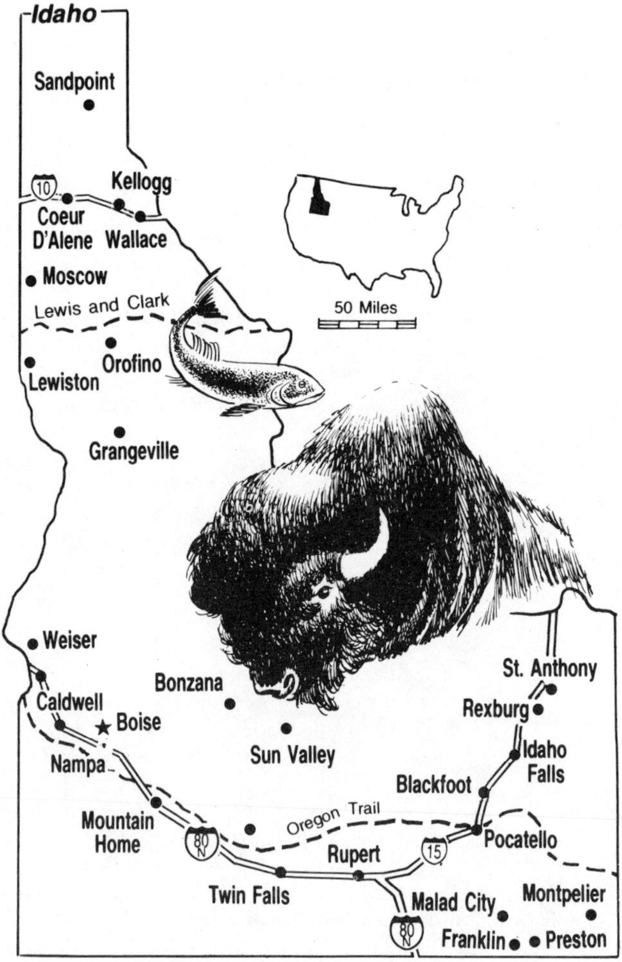
Idaho
Sandpoint
10
Kellogg
Coeur D'Alene
Wallace
Moscow
Lewis and Clark
50 Miles
Orofino
Lewiston
Grangeville
Weiser
Caldwell
Boise
Bonzana
Sun Valley
St. Anthony
Rexburg
Idaho Falls
Blackfoot
Nampa
Mountain Home
Oregon Trail
80 N
Pocatello
15
Rupert
Twin Falls
Malad City
Montpelier
Franklin
Preston

Park, Craters of the Moon National Monument, Sawtooth National Recreation Area, and 11 national forests.

Chief Tribes. Nez Perce, Flathead, Kutenai, Pend d'Oreille, Tukuarikas (Sheepeaters), Shoshoni, Bannocks, Colville, Spokane and Lemhis.

Names That Made News.

Meriwether Lewis	Joseph De Lamar
William Clark	The Kings
Chief Joseph	William Dillon
Chief Nampuh	E.L. Bonner
The Whitmans	William Judson Boone
The Spaldings	Alexander Ward
The Asa Smiths	Father De Smet
David Thompson	Father Ravalli
The Davis Family	A.J. Prichard
L.E. Bonneville	Cherokee Bob
Nathaniel Wyeth	Henry Plummer
Andrew Henry	Ezra Meeker
Thomas Smart	Tim Goodale
Benoni Hudspeth	Noah Kellogg
Donald Mackenzie	John Mullan
Lawyer	O.O. Howard
E.D. Pierce	Sacajawea
Chief Tendoy	

AMERICAN FALLS, Power County. I-15W. US 30N. A party of trappers for the American Fur Company was swept over the falls on the Snake River, thus the name for the falls and the community, according to many stories. A state highway marker says that the name was given in contrast to "Canadian Falls" now Shoshone Falls. The town, in any case, was founded when the railroad arrived in 1882.

Register and Massacre Rocks State Park, 20 miles SW on US 30N. Shoshone Indians ambushed a wagon train bound for Oregon here on August 10, 1862. Early journals called the area "Devil's Gate," "Gate of Death," etc. One chronicle says that nine were killed, six were scalped and many wounded. There is a monument at the site. Emigrant, or Register, Rock has the names of many early travelers.

Crystal Ice Cave, 6 miles NW on State 39, then 22 miles W. on N. Pleasant Valley Rd. Caves in a volcanic rift with stalactites and stalagmites. Guided tours. The cave is within the Great Rift National Landmark and is the only fissure cave in the world open for visitors.

ASHTON, Fremont County. US 20, US 191.

Targhee National Forest, N. on US 20,

191. The majority of the Forest lies within Idaho; part of the 1,687,761-acre tract is in Wyoming. Big Springs, Upper and Lower Mesa Falls are features of the area.

BLACKFOOT, Bingham County. US 20, 191. Blackfeet Indians call themselves Siksika because their feet were blackened by wading in ashes; for what reason is lost with the rest of the legend.

Tressi's Frontier Town, 4 miles NE off I-15 on Groveland Rd. is a replica of original town with buildings and farm equipment.

BLISS, Gooding County. US 30. Named for a settler not a state of mind.

Fossil Beds, marker on highway for site where fossil bones of zebras, beaver, otter and water birds are found in sediments left from a 3,400,000-year-old pond. Zebra-like horses used to graze these plains.

BOISE, Ada County. I-80. (BOY-see) The capital and largest city in Idaho still has trees that early French trappers called *les bois.*

State Capitol, 8th & Jefferson, has changing exhibits.

Julia Davis Park, N. of Boise River on E. side of US 30. The I. N. Coston and Ira B. Pearce cabins were built in the year Idaho was organized as a separate territory. Coston's cabin was made of driftwood, held together with pegs, Pearce's cabin of logs transported by oxen from the mountains. Both were moved here from their original sites. Stagecoaches and early fire engines are here as is "Big Mike," a Union Pacific locomotive from the days of steam railroads. Julia Davis was the wife of pioneer rancher, Tom Davis, in whose log cabin the town was platted.

Idaho State Historical Society Museum, 610 N. Julia Davis Dr., in park, has pioneer and Indian artifacts and displays illustrating Idaho history. One feature is "Fighting Bob," a stuffed ostrich that once boxed all comers in frontier sports, sponsored by gamblers.

Fort Boise (which see), 5th and Fort Sts., now occupied by a veterans' hospital. Nearby is the O'Farrell cabin, built in 1863, possibly the first family dwelling in town.

Boise National Forest, headquarters at 210 Main St. in the old assay office which opened in the 1870s to test Idaho gold. The building is a national historic landmark. The Forest, 18 miles SE on State 21, includes 2,642,-413 acres; features are the headwaters of the Boise and Payette Rivers, many old mining camps and ghost towns, and access to the Sawtooth Wilderness Area. (See Stanley.)

Table Rock, 4 miles E. at end of Shaw Mountain Road, gives a fine view of the historic valley.

Department of Commerce & Development, in the capitol, Room 108, has helpful advice for rugged terrain; maps and tour suggestions.

Moore-De Lamar House, 807 Grove St., was built in 1879 by Christopher W. Moore, banker and merchant. In 1891 Joseph R. De Lamar, a friend of President Benjamin Harrison and a millionaire, purchased the house. It was later a hotel, more recently a rooming house. It is a registered historic place.

BONANZA & CUSTER, Custer County. US 30N. Off US 93.

Marker for Bonanza Bar, on US 30N., points out site of old ghost town across the Snake River. Diggings began in 1878. A romantic and varying story is associated with the two camps on the Yankee Fork of the Salmon River. Historian Lambert Florin holds that in 1878 Agnes Elizabeth King arrived with her companion and perhaps husband, Richard King, having fled from Bodie, California, for reasons unknown. The local hotel owner, Charles Franklin, who had just built the Franklin house in Bonanza, a town he had founded, took more than a casual liking to the "golden beauty" called Lizzie. Meanwhile King went into local real estate with one William Dillon; they had an argument in midsummer of 1879, in a saloon which Lizzie managed, and Dillon fatally shot King. Residents objected to the Kings or their kind being buried in the new Bonanza Cemetery; so Franklin fenced off a separate plot with room for himself and his two friends, only one of whom was ready to take up residence. Then Robert Hawthorne came to town and swept the new widow off her pretty feet into marriage. A week after the wedding Lizzie and her new groom were mysteriously gunned down in her home, and Franklin had them buried beside Richard King in the tiny Boot Hill under the pines trees. Franklin became a recluse, though not a fugitive from justice as no one seemed to pursue the case or solve the mystery. He was found dead several years later in his lonely cabin, clutching Lizzie's photo in a gold locket and was buried miles from graveyard he had prepared and with no picket fence to enclose him. Bonanza's respectable cemetery has fallen into worse shape than the segregated one.

Custer, 2 miles above Bonanza, has a museum in the old schoolhouse and a mill. The twin camps were settled two years after the discovery of the General Custer Mine on the E. side of the Sawtooth Mountains in 1876. The Bannock, Shoshoni and Sheepeater Indians had prevented too many prospectors from exploring the area earlier. Any lands along the Salmon River were patrolled by them. Bonanza and Custer served as centers for the new Idaho boom, with Challis as supply base. A road was built in 1880. The old Boot Hill Cemetery is near the Bonanza Guard Station of Challis National Forest.

BONNERS FERRY, Boundary County. US 95. Highway marker points out the site of the ferry established by E.L. Bonner in 1864. Earlier, gold miners headed for Wild Horse in British Columbia were taken across the river by Indians paddling canoes. A trading store established by the ferry served B.C. pack trains. The Great Northern Railway arrived in 1892. At a nearby site, depicted by marker, David Thompson, explorer, map-maker and trader for the North West Company, in 1808 found the route which US 95 follows N. In 1809 he established Idaho's first trading post on Lake Pend d'Oreille.

BRUNEAU, Owyhee County. State 51.

Bruneau Canyon running the length of the Bruneau River varies from 450 to 2,000 feet in depth. Some visitors find it far more awesome than Grand Canyon. A bumpy road leading W. across desert for a short way is well worth traveling to see the narrow gorge which according to Indian legend of recent times caused the death of more than one beautiful copper-skinned maiden. Visitors can lie flat on the rim and look down 2,000 feet at some areas to see where Jarbridge, a Shoshone word for devil, was supposed to hang out waiting for sacrifices. When Jarbridge roared too often the village medicine man was called upon to select the prettiest girl in town and lay her dead body on the brink for the devil to consume. It was discovered after too many ceremonies that Jarbridge's roars were those of a mountain lion.

Settler's Cave, SE via a graveled road, which passes an old cemetery, one of the first in Idaho. Settlers dug a tunnel into a bluff here more than 85 years ago to escape pursuing Indians. The cave may still be visited. Hot Creek, with boiling springs, may be reached by continuing on the same road, taking the right fork (the left fork goes up the E. side of the river and leads to a view of the canyon) across a bridge, with a left turn at a point ca. 11.5 miles from Bruneau, then 1 mile to the creek and to the Indian Bathtub. The Bathtub was created by erosive action of the hot water. Indians actually bathed here and drew pictographs on the stone walls. Site is now owned by the government.

BUHL, Twin Falls. US 30.

Balanced Rock, 12 miles SW on county road, follow signs from Castleford.

Banbury Hot Springs, 12 miles W. on US 30.

Thousand Springs, 6 miles N. of US 30 on Clear Lakes Rd., once a natural site, is now a rainbow trout farm.

BURLEY, Cassia County. US 30.

Cassia County Historical Museum, county fairgrounds.

Minidoka National Wildlife Refuge, with headquarters N. of Rupert, extends ca. 20 miles up the Snake River from Minidoka Dam.

CALDWELL, Canyon County. US 30. US 20,26.

College of Idaho, Cleveland Blvd. at SE edge of town. Established in 1891 by William Judson Boone who was president for 45 years. The first faculty had 8 members, two of whom became governors and one a chief justice. There were 19 students in 1891. The science center has a mineral collection.

Odd Fellows Historical Museum has relics pertaining to state history.

Memorial Park, S. 6th Ave. & Irving St., has a pioneer display. The Johnson Cabin was owned by three bachelor brothers.

Dorion Monument, US 30 at W. edge of city, just N. of Canyon Ford Bridge over the Boise River. (Old Fort Boise is one mile from the mouth of the river.)

Oregon Trail-Ward Massacre Site, marker on US 20, 26, E. of Caldwell. Only two boys of the wagon train headed for Oregon survived an Indian attack on August 20, 1854. Alexander Ward's emigrant party had 20 members. The slaughter set off a chain of disasters; the military retaliation for the massacre brought on further Indian depredations. Hudson's Bay Company had to abandon its posts at Fort Boise and Fort Hall. Eight years of guerrilla warfare followed until the Idaho gold rush brought too many white men, civilian and military, to be overcome by the native Indians.

CAMP CONNOR, Caribou County. US 30N. Marker on highway. The post, E. of Soda Springs on the N. bank of the Bear River, was established to protect the overland route and the settlement of Morrisites, a group of apostate Mormons. Brigadier General Patrick Edward Connor, for whom the post was named, arrived on May 17, 1863, bringing the settlers from Utah. Never officially a fort, the post was abandoned in 1865.

CATALDO MISSION, Kootenai County. I-90, ca. 28 miles E. of Coeur d'Alene. Formerly called the Sacred Heart Mission. The oldest structure in the state was constructed by Indian laborers using simple methods and tools, axes, augers, small knives, ropes, pulleys and persistence in 1848–49. Jesuit missionaries working with the Indians here converted some nomadic hunting bands into farmers. In 1831–32, a party of three Nez Perce and one Flathead visited St. Louis to inquire about the white man's religion; two of the group died and were buried in a Catholic cemetery. In 1840 the Bishop of St. Louis authorized Father De Smet to look for sites for missions. Cataldo is one of those. Jesuit Father Ravalli supervised the building. It has been restored and is a registered national historic landmark.

CHALLIS, Custer County. US 93.

Challis National Forest, NW and S. of town, crossed by US 93, has an area of 2,447,707 acres, with ghost towns, hot springs, primitive areas, and nature trails.

Bayhorse, ca. 8 miles S. on US 93, then 3 miles W. on unimproved road, had its boom time in the last quarter of the 19th century. Beehive charcoal ovens still are to be seen. They were used to make charcoal for fuel in the large smelter at Bay Horse. A small cemetery is just below town. Several buildings remain in varying states of ruin.

CITY OF ROCKS, Cassia County. State 77, W. of Almo. City of Rocks State Park is one of the natural landmarks of the California Trail, now a national historic landmark, as well. The site was named for the rock formations in the valley of Circle Creek. Thousands of emigrants camped here; wagon train tracks are still visible. The Joseph B. Chiles party may have been the first train to take this route, in 1842.

At Twin Sisters Rocks, in 1863, a wagon train of 300 persons were massacred; only five escaped. Monument at site.

COEUR D'ALENE, Kootenai County. US 95. The name for the local Indians, who once lived across an area that nearly touched present-day Spokane, means Heart of Awl, or "Stingy-hearted," and probably came from their shrewd dealings with traders. The Coeur d'Alenes lived south of the Kalispels—around Lake Coeur d'Alene and its streams—and were friendly with that tribe and with the Flatheads. All three groups were converted by the Jesuit missionaries.

Lake Coeur d'Alene, in Idaho Panhandle National Forest, is 32 miles long, covers 50 square miles. A dam of glacial ice once blocked the northward passage of the rivers which form the lake.

Old Fort Sherman Chapel, Woodland Drive & Hubbard St. General William Tecumseh Sherman picked the site for the fort, and the town grew up in the same area. Sherman visited the far West after the war, in 1876, as a member of a committee appointed by President Andrew Johnson to try to establish peace with hostile Indian tribes, particularly along the line of the railroad being constructed to the Pacific coast.

Two local mines became world famous, the Bunker Hill and Sullivan

Mine, a leading producer of lead and silver, and the Sunshine Mine, a silver producer. A. J. Prichard first discovered placer gold deposits along the banks of the Eagle and Prichard creeks, in April, 1882. The panhandle of Idaho is still an important mining area.

CRATERS OF THE MOON NATIONAL MONUMENT, Custer and Blaine Counties. 20 miles SW of Arco on US 20, 93A. Lava fields and crater walls in ruins spread across the 83-square-mile monument, looking like a moon surface. Visitor Center has geological and historical exhibits. There is a seven-mile Loop Drive; also a four-mile round trip to Great Owl Cavern, and nature trails. The Devils Orchard Nature Trail leads through a weird arrangement of cinder fields and crater walls and is aptly named. An ancient Indian trail followed the Great Rift. Indian Tunnel indicates they used the formations for wind protection or firebreaks. Arrowheads and other implements were found in this area. Early travelers avoided crossing the rougher areas of the present monument. The old wagon road from Arco to Carey, skirting the lava flows, was 76 miles long. Crossing the rugged terrain directly, now possible, is only 43 miles.

DE LAMAR, Owyhee County. Off US 95. The ghost town is NE of Jordan Valley, Oregon, on unimproved road and 9 miles W. of Boot Hill, Silver City. The town has many old buildings on a street that is as crooked as the creek. It is best reached by four-wheel drive and was once a stop on the four-wheel-plus-horses stage line. Named for Captain De Lamar who bought the Wilson mine and adjacent claims. He also built the schoolhouse and hotel, which has an empty lobby, bar, and pigeon-hole mailboxes.

Camp Lyon, ca. 10 miles NW, on unimproved road that branches off from US 95 at N. edge of Sheaville, Oregon. The post was active from 1865 to 1869. In January, 1867 the garrison served in General Crook's campaign against the Snakes, escorting him on a trip along the Owyhee River which led to a victory at Steens Mountain. The troops also protected the Ruby City-Owyhee Crossing of the stage line. A marker at site; no remains of the eight buildings that made up the small camp.

ELK CITY, Idaho County. State 14. In May 1861 prospectors from Pierce discovered rich placer deposits that brought on a gold rush during the summer. Building began in August and within a month 40 stores and cabins were ready for winter. Late in 1861 about 2,000 miners were here. By 1864 most of them were gone and Chinese replaced them. Today nearly everyone is gone. Marker at site.

FLORENCE, Idaho County. In the Nez Perce National Forest. Ca. 14 miles E. of US 95, N. of Salmon River. This early but brief-lived mining camp boomed in October, 1861, after gold placers were discovered on Miller Creek, which flows into the Salmon River. Hordes of miners descended upon the area until the snows set in, trapping the new-arrivals who were virtually starving when the first pack trains reached them in the spring. By autumn of 1862 vigilantes were needed to handle the lawlessness. Here as elsewhere in northern Idaho gold camps, the placers were giving out about the time news came in that Boise Basin was a good place to dig. Chinese replaced the first miners. In six years the area had yielded about $9,600,000 in ore.

The Chinese, disliked by other miners, were barred from nearly all Idaho mining districts until 1864 when the Territorial Legislature actually began to encourage their interest in working abandoned mines, but placed a tax of $4 a month on them. Formerly unfriendly "white" miners now were eager to sell their played-out placer sites to the Chinese who could live on a smaller income and were able to make a profit with lower yields. An estimate has been made at today's values indicating that more than $18 million in gold was mined at Florence.

Florence Cemetery is little more than a wooden marker for the grave of Cherokee Bob. Once part of a Montana gang, Bob had killed two soldiers in Walla Walla, fled to Lewiston where he organized his own mob of desperadoes, then followed the gold-seeking crowd to Florence where on an unlucky night he sprang to the defense of his mistress who had been thrown out of a dance hall, and was killed by another bandit.

Highway Marker for "Fabulous Florence," on US 95. Most visitors should be content to read this and pass on. The road to Florence is perilous-to-impassable depending on the season. A fortune may lie in the canyon, but it's been there more than a hundred years: during the busiest days of Florence a man named Doc Noble was paid a dollar an ounce to guard and transport gold to Lewiston. Highwaymen attacked one of his trains and got $75,000 which they hid in the rocks near the trail (on E. side of old pack trail along the Salmon S. of White Bird). After tucking away their treasure, the gang headed for Seven Devils but all were killed before they got back to the cache. Presumably it's still there. Even the excellent myth-destroying state guide written by the Federal Writers' Project states: "There can be little doubt that this fortune still remains among the rocks in the canyon."

FORT BOISE, Ada County (Old Fort Boise). Near the junction of the Boise and Snake Rivers just W. of US 95. The post was established in 1834 by the Hudson's Bay Company which had a monopoly on the fur trade in the Northwest at that time, and wanted to challenge Nathaniel Wyeth's newly established Fort Hall for American trappers. As the fur trade dropped off in the 1840s the fort aided travelers on the Oregon Trail. In 1846 the boundary dispute with England was settled and Fort Boise came under U.S. jurisdiction, as did Fort Hall. A flood in 1853 washed away the adobe buildings; Indian troubles set in and the post was abandoned in 1855. Marker on State 18 indicates the site.

New Fort Boise, 5th and Fort Sts. in Boise, was established July 4, 1863, on a creek N. of the Boise River to control the Shoshoni Indians, protect the overland route to Oregon and serve as supply depot. Renamed Boise Barracks in 1879. Now occupied by a veterans hospital.

FORT BONNEVILLE, Lemhi County. US 93. There is a highway marker for the site where Captain Benjamin L.E. Bonneville, soldier and explorer, erected a temporary fort on Carmen Creek in 1832. His winter quarters were described as "a miserable establishment" by a rival but they were the first structures built on the Salmon River. *Note:* there is also a Fort Bonneville in Wyoming.

FORT HALL, Bannock County, off unimproved road, ca. 11 miles W. of the town of Fort Hall was a fur trading post established by Nathaniel J. Wyeth in 1834. The stockade of cottonwood logs with two blockhouses stood near the confluence of the Snake and Portneuf Rivers. Wyeth was in competition with, but much less influential, than his rival, the Hudson's Bay Company, which built (Old) Fort Boise, or Snake Fort, 260 miles W. Within a few years the latter had purchased Fort Hall from Wyeth. When the territory became U.S. property the post served to aid travelers on the Oregon Trail. A monument marks the site on the Fort Hall Indian Reservation. A national historic landmark. Marker on I-15.

Fort Hall I, established August 5, 1849, was located ca. 3 miles above the Hudson's Bay Company's Fort Hall (see above). It was a military post intended to guard Oregon Trail travelers and provide a rest stop. The garrison was called "Cantonment Loring" but the post was referred to as Fort Hall, as well.

Fort Hall II, E. of the old Hudson's Bay Company Post, given above, was established in May, 1870, ca. 8 miles S. of Blackfoot, to control the Shoshoni and Bannock Indians after they had been placed on reservations. The military reservation was transferred to the Interior Department in 1883 for the use of the Indian Service. At the town of Fort Hall today is the agency for the 528,000 acre reservation to the east. Tribal office has handicrafts on display. Marker on I-15 for reservation site.

Old Fort Hall Replica, in Ross Park, S. 2nd Ave., is a careful reproduction of the old trading post. In 1906, by covered wagon, 75-year-old Ezra Meeker, who had traveled the Oregon Trail in 1852, retraced the route to map the trail and point out existing landmarks. But he was not certain of the site of Fort Hall until a second trip in 1916. A dedicated group who assisted Meeker in his search worked to restore or build a replica of the fort. Dr. Minnie Howard and others found all available information regarding the old post and its history and a complete set of plans from the Hudson's Bay Company gave the original layout.

FORT HENRY, St. Anthony County. On unimproved road W. of US 20, 191. The fortification was built on the Snake River when the Missouri Fur Company sent Andrew Henry to explore the area in 1810. In 1927 a rock was found which had the inscription "Al the cook, but nothing to cook," with two other inscribed rocks from the old camp; these are now in Rexburg. A monument to the fort is on the bank of the Snake River where US 191 crosses the bridge. Descriptive marker indicates the location of the camp.

FORT LEMHI, Lemhi County. State 28. The adobe and log fort was built by Mormons in 1855, and named for a king in the Book of Mormons. Bannock Indians in the area raised such a fuss at the intrusion that the fort was abandoned. Now marked by a stone monument.

FRANKLIN, Franklin County. US 91. Marker on highway for the first permanent white settlement in present Idaho. The town was founded as part of a Mormon expansion plan by colonists from Utah, led by Thomas Smart, April 14, 1860.

Pioneer Relics Hall has a large collection of early tools and relics.

Old house in Idaho's oldest town: Franklin
(Idaho Dept. of Commerce & Development)

First Railroad descriptive marker is on US 91 for the narrow-gauge Utah Northern Railroad which stopped in 1874 at Franklin; later Jay Gould took over and rails reached Montana in 1880. Brigham Young, much earlier, had bought a steam engine which he shipped up the Missouri to Fort Benton, then overland to Franklin by wagon. The 10,000-pound engine was used in a local sawmill, then abandoned and put on display in Franklin Hall.

FREEZEOUT HILL, Gem County. State 16. Marker on highway for the Oregon Trail cutoff which Tim Goodale opened in 1862. Later that same year a gold rush to Boise Basin also took the route across the Payette Valley just W. of highway. When farmers settled the area they were plagued by horse thieves from Pickett's Corral. In 1864 a vigilante committee made up of settlers drove the bandits out of town.

GHOST TOWNS, various sites.

Placerville and Quartzburg, in the Boise National Forest, W. of Idaho City, in 18 square miles here was the richest find in the U.S. A church and the Magnolia saloon are among a number of buildings still standing.

Placerville Cemetery on the dirt road to Quartzburg has many interesting gravemarkers.

Vienna and Sawtooth City were competitors at the base of the Sawtooth Range. Vienna, with nearly 1,000 residents, was the largest, but the last citizen left town in 1892; Sawtooth City kept on until 1897 when the postmaster resigned. In another year everyone had gone elsewhere.

Leesburg, W. of Salmon City, was settled by southerners, had a thousand residents and a Chinatown; now has less than 100 in residence. Many picturesque old log cabins.

Warren, S. of the Salmon River, NE of McCall, 15 miles E. on Warren Road from Burgdorf. Road crosses two summits. Ghost town has many old ruins and mines. Farther down the road Alec Beaton's Place, once a stage stop, still has some ruins.

GLENN FERRY, Elmore County. US 20, 30. Highway marker for site of the Bannock War begun here on May 30, 1878. Buffalo Horn and his men fought to preserve lands which had been given them by treaty but were encroached upon constantly by new settlers.

GRANGEVILLE, Idaho County. US 95. The town, founded in 1876, was in the front battle lines of the Nez Perce Indian War. A descriptive marker on US 95 pertains to the action of July 4, 1877. Another sign, S. of town on highway, describes the opening battle, June 16, 1877, near its site. Between battle site and Grangeville is a historical marker for Camas Prairie, the land the Nez Perce had occupied for centuries and were being crowded out of by whites. When gold ore was found in the Florence area in the 1890s Grangeville became a boom town. It is a point of access to the largest wilderness area in the U.S.

Nezperce National Forest Headquarters, 319 E. Main St. The forest comprises 2,196,043 acres with the River of No Return (the Salmon) part of its magnificent scenery.

Pioneer Park, E. Main and Park Sts.

Mount Idaho, gravel road SE of town, ca. 3 miles. Ruins of Indian-fighting fort used in the Nez Perce War are on top of nearby hill. The town founder, Loyal Brown, is buried here. This was the first town built on Camas Prairie, and the county seat in 1875. The first Republican Convention in Idaho territory was held here. In 1922 no one could be found to take the postmaster's job and the town became another ghost village.

HAGERMAN, Gooding County. US 30. A tablet on highway commemorates Marcus Whitman, pioneer missionary who brought the first wagon across the Oregon Trail. Dr. Whitman had only a two-wheeled cart after the front axle broke east of Fort Hall, but he persevered, reaching Fort Boise in August of 1836. Dr. Whitman and Reverend Henry N. Spalding (a name originally spelled Spaulding) crossed the Rockies with their wives by the South Pass in 1836. The two women were the first white females to make the trip. The Whitmans and their children were among a group of settlers massacred by Cayuse Indians in Oregon in 1847.

HAILEY, Blaine County. US 93. Marker on highway describes the 1879 rush to the lead-silver mines of the valley.

Blaine County Historical Museum, N. Main St., has pioneer relics and a vast collection of American political items.

HELLS CANYON, in Oregon and Idaho. I-80N, State 201. Highway marker on I-80N describes the Valley of the Snake River, historic passage for emigrant trains. The construction of Hells Canyon Dam, Oxbow Dam, and Brownlee Dam has altered the look of the land. The possibility of another dam, which has been the subject of controversy for years, would eliminate the long-famous white waters of the Snake. The area still is virtually impassable in many stretches but incomparable for scenery. Hells Canyon-Seven Devils Scenic Area extends on both sides of the river for 22 miles, lying partly in the Wallowa-Whitman National Forest in Oregon and the Nez Perce and Payette National Forests in Idaho. Hardy explorers can arrange for boat trips in Lewiston (which see). To reach the dams and recreation areas, start from Weiser, US 30. Chamber of Commerce, 16 E. Idaho St., has information on roads and weather conditions.

HOPE, Bonner County. State 200.

Kullyspell House, E. end of Lake Pend Oreille. Site is described by highway marker. Only stones remain of the first trading post W. of the Rockies in U.S. territory. David Thompson, the North West Company's explorer-trader, selected the site in September 1809.

HORSESHOE BEND, Boise County. State 55. Highway marker describes the line of traffic brought on by a discovery of gold in the Boise Basin in 1862. In 1864 stages came this way and a toll road ran up Harris Creek.

HUDSPETH'S CUTOFF, Cassia County. State 81. Highway marker denotes site of the historic and much argued about shortcut to the main Oregon Trail. On July 19, 1849, Benoni Hudspeth and John Myers led their party west from here through rough country, hoping to save time and strength.

IDAHO CITY, Boise County. State 21. The town was Idaho's leading camp, with Placerville, Hogem, and Centerville next in importance toward the end of the century. Almost every known kind of mining was tried and water was sold by the inch. Private companies were organized to carry water to the placer operations for hydraulicking and other mining methods that needed it.

Gold Hill, 1 mile N. on Main St., was rich in ore.

St. Joseph's Catholic Church, Wallula St., was built in 1867.

Boot Hill, restored, has many gunfight losers.

Masonic Hall, Montgomery St. The Grand Lodge was formed here in 1867.

Odd Fellows Pioneer Lodge, first in Idaho, was established in April 1864. Original furnishings.

IDAHO FALLS, Bonneville County. US 191. The falls extend for 1,500 feet along the Snake River.

Island Park, off Broadway facing Snake River, has historical relics.

Taylor Toll Bridge, across Snake River, was built in 1866–67 with timbers hauled from Beaver Canyon 80 miles north and iron from old freight wagons and a wrecked steamboat. Only stone abutments remain.

KELLOGG, Shoshone County. I-90. Discoveries of silver and lead ores brought a second boom to a town where gold had been found in 1882 and the placers were soon played out. Noah Kellogg found silver ore mixed with zinc and lead at Milo Creek Gulch in 1885. Bunker Hill Mine resulted. It still can be visited in summer months, surface area only. When unions were formed in 1891 Kellogg saw the bloodiest times since the end of the Indian Wars. Federal troops were sent to settle the disturbance in 1899.

KOOSKIA, Idaho County. State 13.

Nee Mee Poo Indian Museum, on Star Route. Historical markers on highway for Nez Perce War and the Kamiah Monster, an Indian legend.

LAPWAI, Nez Perce County. US 95. A subagency of the Fort Lapwai Reservation, set aside for members of the Nez Perce tribe. In Nez Perce National Historic Park.

Lapwai Mission, highway marker denotes site of the earliest Idaho mission, established by Harmon Spalding November 29, 1836, at a spot chosen by the Nez Perce.

Site of Fort Lapwai is 4 miles N. of Spalding on US 95. Established by volunteer troops in 1862, occupied until 1884 when it became headquarters of the Nez Perce Indian Agency.

LEWIS AND CLARK TRAIL, various counties. US 12. In 1803 President Thomas Jefferson sent a secret message to Congress requesting authority to sponsor a transcontinental exploration. Meriwether Lewis, 28, Jefferson's private secretary, was selected to head the expedition. He chose his old friend William Clark, age 32, to be his associate commander to explore the land acquired by the Louisiana Purchase of 1803 from the Mississippi River to the Rocky Mountains and beyond to Oregon territory. The trip began in the spring of 1804; the following year the expedition had reached what is now Idaho and took the Lolo Pass, an Indian trail used by the Nez Perce on buffalo hunts. The Lolo Trail is ca. 150 miles long; in general it takes the high backbone of the mountain N. of the Lochsa River, in wilderness area from the mouth of Lolo Creek near Missoula, Montana, to Pierce, Idaho. It is a national historic landmark.

The Lewis and Clark Highway (US 12) has been worked on by prison laborers from Leavenworth, Kansas, and by Japanese detainees in World War II. More than $12 million was spent on 100 miles of the route between Kooskia and the Montana line since 1946. Lola Pass at the state line is 5,233 feet high; from here the highway follows the Lochsa River to Lowell where the stream connects with the Selway River to form the Middle Fork of the Clearwater River. Other Lewis and Clark historical areas are pointed out by highway markers: two are in Lemhi County on State 28 where Lewis camped with a Shoshoni band in August 1805, and where Clark explored the canyon of the Salmon River trying to find an easy river trip to the Pacific. In Clearwater County on State 11 there is a marker describing Clark's meeting with the Nez Perce on September 20, 1805.

LEWISTON, Nez Perce County. US 95. The town at the junction of the Clearwater and the Snake Rivers was a supply point for early camps at Orofino City, Elk City, Florence and Pierce, and had the usual attractions for criminals to fight over. Henry Plummer of the then secret but later well known Plummer Gang of robbers operated two roadhouses on highways out of Lewiston. Travelers were asked to give up their property, including horses, and in return offered forged bills of sale. Anyone who refused didn't live to regret it. The town threw Plummer out when a well-liked tavern owner turned up among the murdered. Plummer went to Florence, which already had plenty of problems; but later he went to Bannack, Montana, in time to be hanged by the vigilantes. Other Lewiston troublemakers were hanged without benefit of trial and some took to their heels; then times quieted.

Luna House Museum, 310 Third St., on the site of the Luna Hotel, a pioneer inn and courthouse. Articles of Idaho history are featured. The Luna County Historical Society has headquarters here with maps for a walking tour of historical buildings.

Chamber of Commerce, in Ponderosa Lewis-Clark Motor Inn, has maps for auto tours which include the Lewis and Clark trail. Clearwater National Forest and Nez Perce National Historic Park are in the Lewiston vicinity, as is Hells Canyon. Ask here about arrangements for canyon boat excursions.

Lewis-Clark State College, 6th St. & 8th Ave., was established in 1893.

Mackenzie's Post, marker on US 95. In August 1812 Donald Mackenzie set up an American Fur Trading Post for John Jacob Astor's company. He found that the Nez Perce thought trapping was woman's work and had little luck with his venture. The site was abandoned in May 1813.

First Capital, marker on US 95. The first two legislatures of Idaho territory met here. In 1864 the capital was moved to Boise.

MC CALL, Valley County. State 55.

Headquarters for Payette National Forest, which is E. and W. of town on State 55. Forest covers 2,307,415 acres.

Chamber of Commerce, State 55, has information on pack trips into the Primitive Area.

MALAD CITY, Oneida County. US 191.

Oneida County Relic Room, corner of Main and Bannock Sts., has historical displays. The town has a history of stage robberies, lynchings and murders. Here the Overland Stage had a terminus. Gold was freighted by this route from the northern mines to Utah smelters, with corresponding violence. The town streets are haphazard, following old paths and cow trails. The East Malad Mountain, 9,332 feet, provides a shelter against extreme weather. John C. Fremont camped ca. 16 miles SE in August 1843 while looking for the Great Salt Lake.

MARSING, Owyhee County. State 55.

Froman's Ferry, marker on highway. In 1888 George Froman built a ferry ca. one mile downstream. The barge was connected with ropes to a pulley which slid along a cable across the river. The alert ferryman had to operate the tricky contraption to avoid spilling his passengers in the swift current, but the mode of transportation was used on many western rivers in the 19th century. Froman's ferry was in operation until 1921.

City Museum has historical relics.

MONTPELIER, Bear Lake County, US 30. First called Clover Creek, then Belmont, and finally named by

Brigham Young for the capital of Vermont.

Daughters of Utah Pioneers Historical Museum, 430 Clay St.

Cache National Forest is 17 miles S. on US 89, then W. on local roads. Minnetonka Cave in the Forest is 10 miles W. of St. Charles off US 89. Guided tours through nine rooms.

MOSCOW, Latah County. US 95.

Latah County Pioneer Museum, 110 S. Adams, is in the William J. McConnell house built in 1881–86. McConnell was Idaho's first senator and third governor. Museum has 19th-century furnishings.

University of Idaho, W. off US 95, was founded in 1889 by the territorial legislature. Classes began in the fall of 1892. There is a museum on campus.

Site of Old Fort Russell, 88 B St. Monument marks the area where the stockade stood.

MULLAN ROAD AND FOURTH OF JULY CANYON, Shoshone County and Kootenai County. US 10. I-90.

Mullan Monument, at W. end of town of Mullan, on highway. Historical markers on I-90 describe the route Captain John Mullan took in 1862 when he completed the job of building a road through wilderness and Indian territory. The first route had to be changed because of floods. I-90 follows Mullan's road N. of Coeur d'Alene lake.

Fourth of July Canyon, Kootenai County, I-90. Marker on highway. On July 4, 1861, Captain Mullan and his men camped here and raised an American flag to the top of the tallest white pine. The tree stands in the center of a 50-acre park.

MURPHY, Owyhee County. State 45.

Owyhee County Historical Museum, 1 block behind courthouse, has Paiute artifacts.

NAMPA, Canyon County. US 30. Town is named for a Shoshone chief who is said to have had a foot 17 inches long and 6 inches wide.

Cleo's Ferry Museum, 311 14th Ave, S. The adobe served for 58 years as the home of the local ferry master, who operated his boat on the Snake River at Walter's Ferry. It was also a hotel. Restored, with period furnishings and pioneer displays.

Deer Flat National Wildlife Refuge, 5 miles SW off I-80N. The 11,400 acre refuge includes Lake Lowell.

Indian pictographs, 14½ miles S. on State 45, then 6 miles W. along the N. bank of the Snake River.

NEZ PERCE NATIONAL HISTORIC PARK is made up of 22 parcels of land in northern Idaho. The U.S. owns, or will own, only 4 of the sites, with others in private ownership under government administration and care. From Spalding on the W., to Lolo Pass at the Montana State line, and S. as far as the White Bird Battlefield on US 95. Visitor centers will be constructed at Spalding, East Kamiah and White Bird. Park headquarters are in Spalding.

Spalding Site, Nez Perce County, at the junction of US 12 and old US 95, and at the junction of Lapwai Creek and Clearwater River, ca. 10 miles E. of Lewiston. Lewis and Clark passed here in 1805. Included in the historical area are the remains of the Spalding Mission established in 1836, the graves of Henry and Eliza Spalding, and the site of the original Nez Perce Agency. In 1836 the Spaldings (also spelled with a u, particularly in early accounts) were headed for Oregon with the Marcus Whitmans. In November they established Lapwai Mission on Lapwai Creek. The Spaldings stayed. The Whitmans went on to Oregon and were massacred there. The Mission Cemetery contains more than 100 graves, including the Spaldings'.

White Bird Battlefield, on the N. slope of the White Bird Canyon, W. of the creek on US 95 ca. 3 miles N. of White Bird. It was here in 1877 that the first battle of the Nez Perce War was fought; it was a victory for the Indians. In 1919 the skeleton of a soldier was accidentally excavated and the county erected a memorial granite shaft in honor of the soldiers who died. Historian Alvin M. Josephy, Jr., who wrote a definitive history of the Nez Perce and the opening of the Northwest (Yale, 1965) understandably objects to the wording of the memorial marker, which reads: "Before you to the westward lies the historic White Bird battle ground of the Nez Perce Indian War in which 34 men gave their lives in service for their country June 17, 1877. Beneath this shaft lies one of these men who rests where he fell." Josephy feels that the wording should be clarified, pointing out that "while the whites died bravely in the service of their country, the Indians fought bravely *for* their country."

East Kamiah Site, US 12, an area occupied by Nez Perce since prehistoric times. A historical marker on State 9 points out the Kamiah Monster: Nez Perce legend made the rocky outcrop a bad-tempered monster who ate up all the animal and people in his neck of the woods. In 1806 Lewis and Clark set up their "long camp" in Kamiah Valley. Historical marker points out site on the Lolo Trail E. of US 12.

First Presbyterian Church (Indian), US 12, two miles S. of the bridge over Clearwater River at Kamiah, was built in 1874 and still serves the Indian community. The cemetery behind the church is worth a visit; among graves are those of missionaries Susan and Kate McBeth and of Lawyer, a local Indian who was part Nez Perce, part Flathead, highly intelligent and a good debater—which is how he got his American name. His name was Hallalhotsoot, and he was involved in the signing of the peace treaty.

Coyote's Fishnet, historical marker on US 95, 12, ca. 6 miles E. of Lewiston and 4 miles W. of Spalding, points out a natural formation on the bluff face and relates a Nez Perce legend telling how a coyote and a black bear had an argument while fishing here. The Nez Perce stories and accounts of their life, as told in the journals of the Lewis and Clark expedition, are timeless and wholly engaging. William Clark found the Nez Perce "chearfull" and most pleasant although he got sick from eating fish and roots too freely. Another Nez Perce legend is recorded on a historical marker at a point ca. 9 miles E. of Lewiston on US 95, just W. of Spalding. A rock formation bred a story about an ant and a yellow jacket who had a dreadful surprise when they failed to settle their argument about who had the right to eat the dried salmon.

Craig Donation Land Claim, US 95, ca. 4 miles S. of Lapwai (which see), has been called the first homestead in Idaho. It was the property of William Craig, mountain man, who settled among the Nez Perce here in 1840. Interpretive sign on W. side of highway.

St. Joseph's Mission, at Slickpoo on

Mission Road, 4 miles S. of Jacques, was founded by Father Cataldo.

Camas Prairie, descriptive marker on US 95 S. of Grangeville.

Site of Cottonwood Skirmishes, interpretive markers along US 95 in Cottonwood and S.

Clearwater Battlefield, on bluffs adjacent to State 13, on E. bank of the S. Fork of the Clearwater, ca. 1½ miles S. of Stites. The biggest battle of the Nez Perce War within Idaho was fought here on July 11 and 12, 1877, when troops under General O.O. Howard engaged five bands of Indians led by Joseph, White Bird, Looking Glass, Toohoolhoolzote and Husishusis Kute. Howard's command included cavalry and numbered 400 regulars with more than 150 civilian scouts, volunteers and packers. After two days of hard fighting in broiling weather Howard claimed a victory, but he had lost 15 men; the Indians had lost four.

Weippe Prairie, State 11, is the site where Lewis and Clark, coming down from the high ridges of the Bitteroot range heading west in September 1805, met the Nez Perce for the first time.

There are a number of other historical areas within the park. Headquarters are at present in Watson's Store at Spalding.

OROFINO, Clearwater County. US 12.

Lewis and Clark Canoe Camp, 3 miles W. on US 12, is one of the 23 sites of the Nez Perce National Historic Park. Descriptive marker on highway.

Clearwater Historical Museum, College Ave.

OWYHEE COUNTY, US 95. Historical marker S. of Homedale explains how the county and the nearby mountains got a name that sounds Indian but is Hawaiian, more or less. In 1818, the peripatetic Donald Mackenzie brought Hawaiian natives, called Owyhee, here to trap; they had come to America on fur-trading ships, but they never went back to the islands.

PARIS, Bear Lake County, US 89, was founded not by French explorers but by a wagon train of Mormons. Descriptive marker on highway.

PIERCE, Clearwater County. State 11. The town was founded in 1860 after the discovery of gold. In the same year the U.S. signed an access treaty with the Nez Perce tribe, an Indian trader, Captain Elias Davidson Pierce, found gold at Canal Gulch, Oro Fino Creek, along the Clearwater River. The boom came in 1861 with 10,000 miners here, and at Oro Fino, Elk City and Florence, apparently ignoring the war that was going on in the East. When the placers gave less yield the first bunch of miners moved on and the Chinese came in. By 1866 most old workings were owned by the Chinese. In Pierce's heyday lots sold from $100 to $200, log houses for $1,000, and some weeks carpenters as well as ferry masters made as much money as the miners. Authors Howard and Lucille Sloane, who wrote a lively and fact-packed history of American mining which is engrossing even to a claustrophobe, discovered that the Chinese were also doing business in opium smuggled in tobacco tins.

Chinese Hanging, historical marker on highway, describes the incident of September 18, 1885, when five Chinese—charged with having hacked a local merchant to death—were hanged by a group of masked armed vigilantes who forced the deputy sheriff and his posse to surrender their prisoners. A marked trail leads to the hanging site.

POCATELLO, Bannock County. US 191.

Idaho State University, 5 Ave., SE side of town on US 30N. An Indian collection is in museum, on 2nd St.

Bannock County Historical Museum, Center St. and Garfield Ave. Pioneer relics and Shoshone Indian display.

Old Fort Hall Replica (see Fort Hall).

Caribou National Forest, S., W. and E. of city. Headquarters are in Pocatello; the Forest extends into Wyoming and Utah. The ghost towns of Keenan and Caribou City are within its boundaries.

PRIEST RIVER, Bonner County. State 57. The area was explored by Jesuit priest Father Peter John De Smet, who was known as "Great Black Robe" by friendly Indians. Priest Lake and the Priest River are named for him.

Idaho Panhandle National Forest, SE and around Priest Lake.

Chimney Rock, E. of Priest Lake, was formed by a glacier. A local landmark, it can be climbed (200 feet high).

SALMON, Lemhi County. US 93.

Sacajawea Monument, 17 miles SE on State 28. Memorial to the Indian (Shoshoni) woman who served as an interpreter for Lewis and Clark.

Salmon National Forest, N. and S. of town on US 93. Visitor Center at Lost Trail Pass, 44 miles N. Headquarters are in Salmon. The forest comprises 1,767,787 acres.

Leadore and Gilmore, State 28 S. ca. 49 miles to Leadore, a town of false fronts and picturesque ruins. Gilmore is ca. 17 miles farther S. on State 28, then 1 mile to the right, a partial ghost town with pioneer buildings.

SHOSHONE, Lincoln County. US 93.

Shoshone Indian Ice Caves, 16 miles N. on US 93. Cave is 3 blocks long. Museum on grounds with Indian artifacts, mineral and gem displays.

SILVER CITY, Owyhee County. On unimproved road 25 miles SW of Murphy. Gold discoveries of 1863 brought a crowd of some 2,500 miners. Later in the year silver was discovered and thousands more headed this way. Boonville, Ruby City and Silver City were all rapidly settled. A number of buildings remain in the now ghost town including the Idaho Hotel, which was a sort of 19th-century pre-fab. It was built, all 50 rooms of it, a mile away in Ruby City, and brought here by ox teams in 1865. Here, as elsewhere in Idaho territory, the Chinese were taxed four dollars a month for residency, but they reworked the quartz tailings and repanned placers and doubtlessly would have reconstituted lemon juice if there'd been any handy. In the end they persevered and prospered, or at least survived. Silver City street names range from Avalanche, Morning Star, and Jordan to the prosaic Washington and Clinton. The buildings vary; there are a church and a school, Masonic and Odd Fellows Halls, post office, bar, barber shop, ice house, the Stoddard Mansion, the Miners' Union Hospital, and a Chinese laundry. Recently some of the old structures have been spruced up for vacation residences.

SODA SPRINGS, Caribou County. US 30N. The town was founded by

Brigham Young and the Mormons. The mineral-charged springs in the area caught the attention of every early traveler who kept a journal, it seems, or wrote a letter home. Its name reoccurs frequently in early accounts of the far Northwest.

Steamboat Spring, 2 miles W. off US 30N. Now drowned by dammed (and to some damned) water, the spring still boils up.

Hooper Spring and Champagne Spring, 1 mile N. on State 34.

Cemetery has a "wagon-box grave of 1861," with monument inscribed for a family killed by Indians on Little Spring Creek ½ mile S. of the burial site. They were buried in their own wagon box.

STANLEY, Custer County. US 93.

Sawtooth and Challis National Forests surround the town.

Sawtooth Wilderness Area. Chamber of Commerce has information on wilderness hiking and mountain climbing.

TENDOY, Lemhi County. State 28.

Lemhi Pass, 12 miles E. off State 28, is a national historic landmark. It is the point where the Lewis and Clark expedition crossed the Continental Divide and where it left the U.S. as

Silver City, where gold was found in 1863, once had 5,000 inhabitants
(Idaho Dept. of Commerce & Development)

represented by the boundary of the Louisiana Purchase. The cooperation of the Shoshoni Indians, who lived on either side of the crest, made possible the journey to the navigable waters of the Columbia River. The Pass is 8,000 feet high.

Grave of Shoshoni Chief Tendoy is on a hillside above his former ranch, visible from State 28. White settlers erected the memorial shaft. He was influential in protecting whites of the region from Tukuarikas, Sheepeaters and other hostile tribes.

Monument to Sacajawea, interpreter for Lewis and Clark, is N. of town. She was born here.

Cameahwait's Village: one site was ca. 7 miles N. of town on the E. bank of the Lemhi River, just N. of Sandy Creek; a second location was ca. 3 miles S. of this on E. bank of the Lemhi near the mouth of Kenney Creek. Both sites are ca. ¼ mile W. of secondary road that follows the E. bank of the river; the road branches off State 28 ca. 3¼ miles N. of Tendoy. Cameahwait was the brother of Sacajawea and was Chief of the Shoshonis who entertained Lewis and an advance party of three men in August 1805, after they had crossed the Lemhi Pass. When Clark and the main body of the expedition joined the others, Sacajawea was delighted to be reunited with the brother she had not seen in years. The party spent some of late August in the Shoshoni camp. It is believed that from the time of Clark's first visit on August 20 to Lewis's second visit on August 26 the village had moved the 3 miles S. from the first site. Neither are marked at present. A monument to Sacajawea is just N. of town.

TWIN FALLS, Twin Falls County. US 30.

Shoshone Falls, 5 miles NE on Snake River.

Twin Falls Historical Society Museum, 3 miles W. on US 30, 93. Early frontier shops, household displays and farm machinery.

Herrett Arts & Science Center, 1220 Kimberly Road. Museum has Indian collections.

WALLACE, Shoshone County. US 10, I-90.

Coeur d'Alene District Mining Museum, 509 Bank St. Displays on the history of mining and equipment; also has information on mine tours and old ghost towns in the area.

WEISER, Washington County. Headquarters for the Idaho part of Hells Canyon.

Historical Museum and National Fiddlers' Hall of Fame, 44 W. Commercial St. A large collection of historical relics, featuring fiddling and folk music items.

KANSAS

The town of Hays City, near us, was a typical Western place. The railroad having but just reached there, the "roughs," who fly before civilization, had not yet taken their departure. There was hardly a building worthy of the name, except the station-house. A considerable part of the place was built of rude frames covered with canvas; the shanties were made up of slabs, bits of drift-wood, and logs, and sometimes the roofs were covered with tin that had once been fruit or vegetable cans, now flattened out. A smoke rising from the surface of the street, might arrest your attention, but it indicated only an underground addition to some small 'shack,' built on the surface of the earth. The carousing and lawlessness of Hays City were incessant. Pistol-shots were heard so often it seemed a perpetual Fourth of July. . . .

Elizabeth B. Custer,
Following the Guidon, 1890

I woke up one morning on the old Chisholm trail,
Rope in my hand and a cow by the tail. . . .
With my knees in the saddle and my seat in the sky,
I'll quit punching cows in the sweet by and by.

The Old Chisholm Trail,
anonymous cowboy song

Not a habitation is seen; for the Kansas Indians build their log-houses only in the woods which here skirt the low creeks. Wagon roads, revealing the jet-black soil, intersect the deep green of graceful slopes, where waves the tall prairie grass. . . . Upon our beaten road are immigrants with their household goods and household gods packed in long white covered ox wagons, teams hauling freight from the river, speculators working their way upon refractory mules, half-breed girls with heavy eye-lashes and copper-brown cheeks, jogging

> steadily along upon horseback, Indian boys mounted on black ponies, their hair decorated with feathers and their tattered garments streaming in the breeze as they dash by us, yelping "How?"—the universal "How-d'ye do?" of their race, and footmen with cane upon the shoulder and carpet sack suspended from it, who look up wearily and ask "How much further to Lawrence?"
>
> Albert D. Richardson,
> *Beyond the Mississippi,* 1867

KANSAS FACTS: Francisco Vasquez de Coronado and his conquistadores came in 1541 looking for Quivira and gold. The Louisiana Purchase brought many explorers: Lewis and Clark, Zebulon Pike, Stephen Long. The Kansas-Nebraska Act of 1854 created Kansas Territory. Kansas entered the Union as a free state in 1861. The 34th state. Capital: Topeka. Territorial Capital: movable from Fort Leavenworth, to Shawnee Mission, to Big Springs (Free Staters), and elswhere; in 7 years 6 governors and 5 acting governors came and went. *Kansas* from the Indian tribe called Escansaque by the Spanish, Kansa by the French, has been spelled 55 ways on record. Nicknames: Sunflower State, Jayhawker State. Kansas has Fort Larned National Historic Site and Cimarron National Grasslands.

Chief Tribes. Pawnees, Osages, Kaws, Wichitas; moved to the lands of the Kaws and Osages were the Shawnees, Delawares, Ottawas, Quapaws, Cherokees, Chippewas, Kickapoos, Iowas, Sac and Foxes of Missouri, Potawatomis, Miamis, Sac and Foxes of Mississippi, Wyandottes and the Munsees.

Early Routes. The Santa Fe Trail, the Oregon Trail, the Chisholm Trail, Cimaron Cutoff, Butterfield Overland Stage Line, the Pony Express, the Atchison, Topeka & Santa Fe Railroad, Union Pacific Railroad.

ABILENE, Dickinson County. US 40. In the 1860s, the terminus of the Kansas Pacific, later the Union Pacific, Railroad and the nearest shipping point for cattle driven north along the Chisholm Trail, Abilene was known as a lively cowtown. Wild Bill Hickok was one of the marshals in the 1870s. He succeeded Tom Smith.

Dickinson County Historical Museum, 412 S. Campbell St. Early pioneer exhibits, old vehicles.

"Old Abilene Town," 201 SE 6 at Kuney St. is a replica of the cattle boom days, with some original buildings in the exhibit.

Eisenhower Center, 201 SE 4th St. President Dwight D. Eisenhower was a 20th-century man but he is one of three presidents buried W. of the

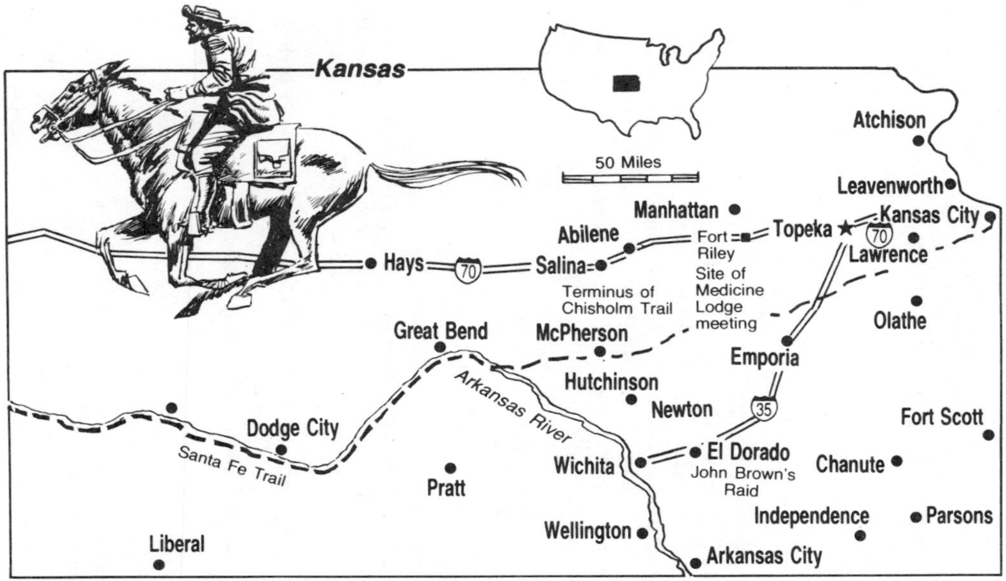
Kansas
50 Miles
Atchison
Leavenworth
Kansas City
Manhattan
Topeka
70
Lawrence
Abilene
Fort
Riley
Site of
Medicine
Lodge
meeting
Hays
70
Salina
Terminus of
Chisholm Trail
Olathe
Great Bend
McPherson
Emporia
Hutchinson
Arkansas River
Newton
35
Fort Scott
Dodge City
Santa Fe Trail
El Dorado
John Brown's
Raid
Wichita
Chanute
Pratt
Independence
Parsons
Wellington
Liberal
Arkansas City

Mississippi River. The Center includes library, home, museum, and burial site (in Meditation Chapel).

Chisholm Trail Boulder, on post office lawn, denotes the end of the trail over which more than 3 million head of cattle were driven in the 1860s and 1870s.

ALMA, Wabaunsee County. State 99. In the Flint Hills of Kansas, the town has many stone buildings, churches, homes, and even fences of stone.

Mill Creek Museum, 7 miles W., features pioneer farm items.

ARKANSAS CITY, Cowley County. US 77. (Ar-KAN-sas).

Cherokee Run Site, marker on US 77 S. of town where the historic run began at high noon on September 16, 1893, when 75,000 to 100,000 homesteaders ran for land in the newly opened Cherokee Strip. The number of runners seems to increase with the years—a goodly crowd, in any case.

Cherokee Strip Living Museum, 2 miles S. on US 77.

Buffalo Bill Boulder, E. edge of town at end of Madison Ave. on the E. bank of the Walnut River. Cody carved his initials into a granite boulder at the campsite where he stayed in 1869–1870 with cavalry to patrol the border. The vicinity of the bluff was once the property of Cherokee Two-Boys-Stray-Shadow, also known as James Hightower. Where two old trails met, pole tracks are still visible. Kansas Indians traveled by dugout and by travois—an arrangement of poles to which a dog was hitched for dragging cargo.

ASHLAND, Clark County. US 160. Two great cattle trails crossed here: one from Texas to Fort Dodge, one from Santa Fe to Sun City.

Pioneer Museum, W. of Main St. on US 160., has many items used by the settlers of the area. Displays include furnished shops, bank, hospital, blacksmith, and even an undertaker's workroom.

Santa Fe Museum, in renovated depot, has railroadiana.

ATCHISON, Atchison County. US 73. As a landing site on the Missouri, the settlement attracted many early travelers including Lewis and Clark in 1804, and Major Stephen Long on his way to the Yellowstone in the 1850s.

Atchison County Historical Society Home, 409 Atchison St. 19th-century period rooms, country store.

Atchison County Museum, 1440 N. 6th St., has Indian artifacts.

Lincoln Plaque, in courthouse square, marks the spot where Abraham Lincoln first delivered the speech he gave later at Cooper Union.

Santa Fe Memorial, a monument in front of Memorial Hall, 819 Commercial St., commemorates the organization of the railway; a locomotive stands in the park adjoining Union Station.

AUGUSTA, Butler County. US 77, State 96.

Augusta Historical Society Museum, 300 State St., is housed in the town's first log cabin (1868). Hundreds of pioneer relics. The structure also served as post office, church and schoolhouse as well as country store.

BALDWIN CITY, Douglas County. US 56.

Old Castle, Baker University, 513 5th St., built in 1858, now houses a museum with many pioneer exhibits, including Santa Fe Trail displays. Old Castle Hall which served the university until 1871 is a registered historic place.

Black Jack Park, 3 miles E. on US 56, was the site of skirmish between the abolitionists and the forces of proslavery in 1856.

BAXTER SPRINGS, Cherokee County. US 66, 166. In 1850, A. Baxter arrived and built a shack and a sawmill and someone spread the word that the spring waters had restorative powers; traffic got heavy and Baxter built a tavern. Stores and a bank were soon established. In the 1860s, Texans sent their longhorns to pasture here. The military road from Fort Leavenworth to Fort Gibson followed Military Avenue.

Site of Baxter Springs Massacre, E. 7th St. On October 6, 1863, a small Union garrison of cavalry and black infantrymen were attacked by Quantrill's men while part of the unit was away. Nine were killed. Quantrill lost two men. But the day was not over. Major General James G. Blunt and a detachment of troops, approaching the post en route to Fort Gibson, mistook the marauders for a welcoming escort. Soon surrounded by Quantrill's men, 87 were killed and a number taken captive. Blunt and a few of his party escaped.

Baxter Springs National Cemetery has the graves of many who were lost in the massacre. Monument.

BELOIT, Mitchell County. US 24.

Little Red School House, a museum, with local history artifacts. The town is in the heart of the rock fence post area where settlers used limestone instead of wood, which was scarce.

BONNER SPRINGS, Wyandotte County. State 7, US 73.

The Agricultural Hall of Fame and National Center consists of three buildings with exhibits on the evolution of agriculture. *The Wyandotte County Historical Society Museum,* E. of Agriculture Hall, has artifacts of state and county history and archaeology.

BROOKVILLE, Saline County. State 140. The town was the scene of an Indian raid soon after it was founded in 1871. Settlers took refuge in the roundhouse. Indians easily had the building surrounded and were piling railroad ties for a burning out when an engine under steam crashed through the doors, rolled across the turntable and took off for Salina with whistle shrilling and bells clanging. The Indians departed. Jesse James and his gang used the nearby hills as a hide-out in his day.

Brookville Hotel served cattlemen in the town's busy days as a stopping place on the trail. It is still in operation. Upstairs bedrooms and parlor are furnished with a number of frontier period originals.

BUFFALO, Wilson County. US 75.

Fort Belmont, ca. 2 miles E. on State 39, a stockade and stagecoach station until the 1860s. Somewhere in the area is the unmarked grave of Hapo, Chief of the Osage, and that of his daughter who died while the Osage were in camp here. Hapo was on the Union side in the Civil War and once went to Washington to seek aid for his starving people from President Lincoln. He died before he got an answer.

CALDWELL, Sumner County. US 166, State 49. A booming cowtown on the Chisholm Trail. Marker is 1 mile S. for site where the trail entered Kansas. The old cowboy song, about the Chisholm Trail has a once common complaint:

We hit Caldwell and we hit her on
the fly,
We bedded down the cattle on the
hill close by.
No chaps, no slicker, and it's pouring down rain,
And I swear, by god, I'll never
night-herd again.

Buresh Archaeology Site, NW of town, excavations have exposed three house floors and a number of storage pits. A registered historic place.

CHANUTE, Neosho County. US 169.

Safari Museum, 16 S. Grant, is the main attraction in town, but pertains to Africa and Polynesia. Osa Johnson, explorer with her husband Martin, was born here.

Site of Canvill Trading Post, SW of town in country churchyard, has a monument for the site where the Osage negotiated their Withdrawal Treaty in 1865. A monument also marks the site of the Neosho Mission, founded in 1824, by the Reverend Benton Pixley and Samuel Bright, the first mission in Kansas. Hopefully directional markers will have been established. These two sites have been overlooked in recent years.

CHENEY, Sedgwick County. W. of Wichita on US 54.

Pioneer Village, 1 miles SW of town.

CHERRYVALE, Montgomery County. US 169.

Bender Museum is a replica of the infamous Bender home with mannequins to reenact one of the several crimes the family committed. William Bender and his wife and daughter Kate and son John moved to Kansas on the old trail from Independence to Osage Mission and set up a sort of shop-farm on a hill. The front part of their establishment was a store; they also gave meals to travelers. Often the last meal. Between 1870 and 1873 so many persons disappeared at this stop in the route, others began to bypass it. When settlers gathered to begin an investigation, the Benders took part, but vanished soon after. Eleven bodies had been left behind buried in the orchard and garden behind the house. The Benders were never seen again.

CIMARRON, Gray County. US 50.

Cimarron Crossing Park, on the Arkansas River, marks a shortcut on the old Santa Fe Trail. Replica of a covered wagon in park.

COFFEYVILLE, Montgomery County. US 166, 169. Colonel James A. Coffeey built a house and store near the Verdigris River in July 1869. The railroad came to town and so did the Dalton gang in a raid on October 5, 1892. Three Daltons and two pals tried to double-up the day's work by robbing two banks at once. This resulted in a running battle with armed locals. Several citizens were killed and only Emmett Dalton of the raiders survived.

Dalton Museum, 113 E. 8th St. Raid memorabilia. Museums make strange bedfellows and fame is fleeting (to double up on cliches as the Daltons did on banks): Wendell Willkie mementoes are also here and so are displays pertaining to Walter Johnson, the major league pitcher. Willkie was a schoolteacher in Coffeyville.

Brown Mansion, 2019 Walnut St., was designed by Stanford White, with original furniture and hand-painted wall coverings. It is operated as a museum by the local historical society.

COLBY, Thomas County. US 24.

Sod Town Prairie Pioneer Museum, 2 miles E. on highway. Reconstructed sod buildings with furnishings, costumes, tools, and other items of the sod-house era.

COLDWATER, Comanche County. US 160.

Comanche County Museum features an extensive collection of household items, clothes, and tools of the first settlers.

CONCORDIA, Cloud County. US 81. A plaque marks the homestead of Boston Corbett the man who claims to have fired the fatal shot into John Wilkes Booth, hiding out in Maryland after Lincoln's assassination. His dugout was a few miles SE of town. Corbett announced that God had directed the shot, to which a Secret Service man reportedly snapped: "I guess He did, or you could never have hit Booth through that crack in the barn." After the war Corbett, who had been a member of the 16th New York Cavalry, got religion instead of returning to the hat business where he had been a hatter's apprentice and became an evangelist, showing magic lantern slides of Booth and the conspirators.

Cloud County Historical Society, in courthouse.

Brown Grand Opera House is a registered historic place, as is the Nazareth Convent & Academy.

COTTONWOOD FALLS, Chase County. State 177, just S. of US 50.

Chase County Courthouse, town square, is a beautiful old structure of tooled limestone with a red mansard roof and a clock tower, the oldest courthouse in Kansas still being used. It is a registered historic place well worth preserving, from its flagpole to its lightning rods. Young Americans who have seen countless housing developments with "mansard roofs" popular in the last decade can see the real thing in the heart of Cottonwood Falls.

Roniger Memorial Museum, on courthouse square, has Indian and pioneer relics.

COUNCIL GROVE, Morris County. US 56.

Council Grove Historic District, in the heart of the Flint Hills where the Kansas Prairie Parkway crosses the Santa Fe Trail. Two marked trees on the N. side of Main Street are the Post Office Oak, where letters were left for passing wagon trails in a cache, and the stump of the Council Oak, where the Osage Indians signed a treaty in 1825 giving the U.S. the right-of-way for the old Santa Fe Trail.

Madonna of the Trail, near Post Office Oak, 16-foot memorial to pioneer women.

Pioneer Jail, 502 E. Main St. on US 56, was the only lockup on the trail in its day (since 1849).

Hays Tavern, 112 W. Main, a trading post and restaurant, later a saloon, supply house and inn. Also known as Last Chance Store.

Custer's Elm, Neosho St., 6 blocks S. of Main St. May have sheltered George Armstrong Custer in 1867 when he was leading an expedition in western Kansas.

Kaw Methodist Mission, 500 N. Mission St. at Huffaker St. A museum is housed in the 1851 building where Methodist Church members once held school for Indians.

Farmer and Drovers Bank, 201 W. Main, dates from 1892.

Council Grove because of its water and pastureland as well as timber was an important supply point for the Santa Fe Trail. It is a national historic landmark. (Also see Herington.)

DODGE CITY, Ford County. US 56. Like Tombstone, Arizona, this frontier town lives in its bawdy past and collects from it. And some of the same names are the most "cashable." Wyatt Earp was a marshal, and so were Bat Masterson, Bill Tighlman, Dave Mather, Prairie Dog Dave Morrow and Luke Short. Both towns have Boot Hill cemeteries spruced up to the tourist minute, with headstones more readable than authentic.

Front Street, 500 W. Wyatt Earp Blvd., is a two-block reproduction of where it all began in the 1870s. The Long Branch Saloon and other onetime buildings are here again. Beeson Museum has memorabilia. *Hardesty House* is the restored home of a cattle king, with period furnishings. After Wyatt Earp Boulevard what comes next—Wyatt Earp Airport?

Home of Stone, 112 E. Vine, was built in 1881. Guided tours in summer months. It has been furnished with original pieces belonging to the John Mueller and Adam Schmidt families who were early occupants. Mueller, a bootmaker, built the house; Schmidt bought it in 1890.

Fort Dodge, 5 miles E. on US 154, was an army outpost on the N. bank

You remember Dodge City?
(Kansas Dept. of Economic Development)

of the Arkansas River to protect travelers on the Santa Fe Trail. The site was selected by Major General Grenville M. Dodge in 1864. It was used as a base for operations against the Arapaho and the Cheyenne Indians; among officers stationed here were George A. Custer, Nelson A. Miles and Philip Sheridan. The garrison was withdrawn in 1882. Several buildings are in use as the Kansas Soldiers' Home.

Point Rocks, 7 miles W. on US 50, mark the corner of the old United State-Mexico boundary on the 100th meridian, the NW corner of the Osage Ceded Lands.

Fort Mann, on N. bank of the Arkansas River, ca. 5 miles W. of town, was garrisoned because the government needed a post between Fort Leavenworth and Santa Fe for the changing of horses and wagon repairs. Captain Daniel Mann, master teamster, erected the fort which was abandoned in 1850 when Fort Atkinson was established.

Fort Atkinson, ca. 4 miles W. of town, on the left side of the Arkansas River, was created in August 1850 to control Indians and protect the trail. It was constructed of sod and known as Fort Sod and even Fort Sodom. Stone marker on N. side of US 50 commemorates the fort sites; no remains have survived.

Santa Fe Trail Remains, 9 miles W. of town on US 50. The longest continuous stretch of the trail is preserved in a rangeland which remains unplowed. The hill, overlooking the river, forms a two-mile arc. The trail divided upstream at Cimarron Crossing (see Cimarron) where some travelers chose the Cimarron Cutoff and others chose to follow the river. A national historic landmark.

EDGERTON, Johnson County. US 56.

Lanesfield School is maintained as a museum by the Lanesfield Historical Society.

EL DORADO, Butler County. State 177.

Butler County Historical Museum, Central Ave. and Star St., has a scale model of a Wichita Indian grass lodge and pioneer relics.

ELLSWORTH, Ellsworth County. US 40.

Mother Bickerdyke Home, at S. edge of town, was founded for nurses and female relatives of Civil War veterans. Mary Bickerdyke was an outstanding nurse in the war.

Hodgden House, 104 W. South Main St., was built in the 1870s of natural sandstone. Now a museum with period furnishings and pioneer relics.

EMPORIA, Lyon County. US 50.

Red Rocks, 927 Exchange St., was the home of newspaperman William Allen White, who bought the *Emporia Gazette* in 1895. His 1896 editorial "What's the matter with Kansas?" got international attention. The house was built in the 1880s; damaged by fire in the 1920s and reconstructed in part, with plans drawn by Frank Lloyd Wright. A registered historic place. Peter Pan Park, Kansas Ave. and Neosho St., was given to the city by the White family. The Gazette Building, at 517 Merchant St., has many White mementoes. Tours on request.

Emporia Kansas State College, 12th Ave. and Commercial St., has a one-room schoolhouse museum.

EVEREST, Brown County. State 10.

Kimberlin Hill Cemetery has the oddity of the largest known cedar tree in

Kansas growing from the grave of Missouri Kimberlin, buried in 1854.

Miller Cemetery has the grave of a child who was a smallpox victim while traveling in a wagon train. Ruts are still visible along the old trail.

FAIRWAY, Johnson County. US 50, 56.

Shawnee Mission, 3403 W. 53rd St. at Mission Rd. The Methodist Mission and Indian Manual Training School, established in the 1830s by the Rev. Thomas Johnson, was located on the Santa Fe and Oregon Trails and considered an outpost of civilization. Three brick buildings still stand on the site chosen in 1838. A national historic landmark.

FLORENCE, Marion County. US 50. City Park, the old Harvey House, now a museum, and the LLL Ranch, 2 miles E. on highway, are worth a visit. Buffalo roam at the ranch, as well as deer and elk.

FORT RILEY, Geary County. State 18. The historic fort was the home of the cavalry for 83 years and is now the base of the 1st Infantry Division. On the 100,000-acre military reservation is the First Territorial Capitol of Kansas, 2 miles W. of E. gate of the Fort, maintained as a public museum with many artifacts pertaining to the Old West. The United States Cavalry Museum is in Bldg. 30 which dates from 1855. Memorial to the Cavalry has been erected on the lower parade ground. Chief, the last cavalry horse on official rolls, is buried in front of the memorial.

Camp Funston Monument and Leonard Wood Memorial, near the E. entrance, are on the site of Camp Funston. A Battle of Wounded Knee Monument and a monument in memory of Major E. A. Ogden, who planned and supervised the first permanent construction of the post are near the W. entrance to Main Post on State 18.

Custer's Headquarters, adjacent to the Cavalry Museum, has many items of civilian historical interest as well as military relics. Many of the memoirs written by the lively and observant Elizabeth B. Custer, after her husband's death, center on their life here. Life was arduous, full of perils and at times of boredom; there were prairie fires and hurricanes and heavy snowfalls to cope with but mostly there were tedious periods of waiting, between letters, for her husband's return. Mrs. Custer still found matters amusing. In *Tenting on the Plains* she describes her days: "Now that we were alone, it was necessary to make the needle fly . . . the riding-habit was fortified with patches, and any amount of stout linen thread disappeared in strengthening the seams; for between the hard riding and the gales of wind we encountered, the destruction of a habit was rapid. Diana, with the elastic heart of a coquette, had not only sped the parting, but welcomed the coming guest; for hardly had the sound of the trumpet died away, before a new officer began to frequent our parlor. It was then the fashion for men to wear a tiny neck-bow, called a butterfly tie. They were made on a pasteboard foundation, with a bit of elastic cord to fasten them to the shirt-stud. I knew of no pasteboard nearer than Leavenworth; but . . . I found Diana with her lap full of photographs, cutting up the portraits of the departed beaux, to make ties for the next. Whether the new suitor ever discovered that he was wearing at his neck the face of a predecessor, I do not know."

FORT SCOTT, Bourbon County. US 69. The fort, built to preserve peace among the Osage, Cherokee, and other tribes in the territory, served as a halfway stop between Fort Leavenworth and Fort Gibson. Several buildings date from the 1840s. During the 1850s the area was the hot spot of the Bleeding Kansas furor when proslavery forces clashed with Free-Soilers. In the period of the Civil War the post was a Union supply depot and was reactivated in the following decade to keep order during settler-railroad troubles. A national historic landmark.

Carroll Plaza, Marmaton, Blair, Benton and Lincoln Aves., was the parade ground. Fort Blair is a renovated Civil War blockhouse. Officers' Quarters are at 11 Blair Ave. The area is being restored.

Fort Scott National Cemetery, E. National Ave., was established in 1862, one of the first in the country.

GARDEN CITY, Finney County. US 83.

Finnup Park, S. city limits, on US 83, has a museum with pioneer relics.

Windsor Hotel was built in 1886 and was known as the Waldorf of the Prairies with Buffalo Bill Cody, Eddie Foy and Lillian Russell among the many guests.

GENESEO, Rice County. Between State 4 and US 56.

Tobias-Thompson Complex, 4 miles SE of town, is a Wichita Indian village which reveals European presence here in the time of Coronado. Fragments of Indian glaze pottery from the Southwest were found in the excavations, probably brought by the Spanish explorers. A national historic landmark not accessible to the public at present.

GOODLAND, Sherman County. State 27, N. of I-70.

Pioneer Museum has frontier artifacts, Indian displays and other exhibits.

GREAT BEND, Barton County. US 56, 156.

Fort Zarah, historical marker 3 miles E. on highway. The post was established E. of Walnut Creek, about 3 miles from its confluence with the Arkansas River, in September 1864, to guard the Santa Fe Trail. It was set up by Major General Samuel R. Curtis and named for his son Major Henry Zarah Curtis who was killed on October 5, 1863, in the Baxter Springs Massacre. General Curtis is credited with winning the battle of Pea Ridge in the Civil War. After the war he served as Indian commissioner and as examiner of the Union Pacific Railroad until his death in Council Bluffs, Iowa, in 1866.

GREENSBURG, Kiowa County. US 54.

Burketown, U.S.A., on US 54, is a replica of a western town with saloon, opera house, country store, and live-steam railroad trips. Museum.

Big Well, Sycamore St., 3 blocks S. of US 54, is the "world's largest hand-dug well" with a meteorite in the adjoining "Celestial Museum." The well was excavated in 1888 by the Santa Fe Railway.

HANOVER, Washington County. US 36.

Hollenberg Pony Express Station, 6 miles N. of US 36, via State 15E and 243. Built by G. H. Hollenberg in 1857, houses a pioneer museum, and is the only unaltered Pony Express Station extant. A national historic landmark.

HAYS, Ellis County. I-70.

Fort Hays, Frontier Historical Park, the parade ground and three original buildings remain from the fort which was established in June, 1867. Museum in the blockhouse. Many officers who gained fame in the Civil War were in command here at varying times: Hancock, Pope, Custer, Sheridan and Miles. Originally called Camp Fletcher, the fort later served as a quartermaster's depot supplying other posts in the Southwest. A registered historic place.

Sternberg Memorial Museum, on campus of Fort Hays Kansas State College, W. edge of town, has geological, historical and other collections.

HERINGTON, Dickinson County. US 56.

Padilla Monument, in city park, honors Father Juan Padilla, the soldier-priest, who was killed by Indians in 1542 when he was on the Coronado expedition. The memorial was erected by the Quivira Historical Society, but the city of Council Grove also claims the site where Father Padilla was murdered and has a monument on a rocky hill outside of town that stood on the Santa Fe trail. Legend has it that two Indian laymen were allowed to return to the spot where Father Padilla fell and to dig a shallow grave for him. A group of priests later came back, found the rock cairn atop the grave, and took the body in a coffin to New Mexico where it was buried in the mission chapel at Isleta. The cairn was replaced and has been diminished by souvenir hunters over the years and replaced again, more than once. Here and there grisly collectors are perhaps proudly displaying stones selected by anonymous citizens of Council Grove.

HIAWATHA, Brown County. US 36.

Iowa, Sac and Fox Presbyterian Mission, 15 miles E. on US 36, then N. on State 136, was an early mission and the first permanent white settlement in the county. Museum. Restored chapel and Indian artifacts.

Mount Hope Cemetery has the unique and grandiose tomb of the John M. Davises. Eleven life-size statues under a marble canopy depict Mr. and Mrs. Davis at various times of their lives. They sit somberly on the "porch" of the monument, tidily costumed in marble, looking at nothing.

HILLSBORO, Marion County. State 15.

Pioneer Adobe, in city park, is a replica of early homes built by Mennonite settlers of the 1870s. Attached barn has more than 10,000 museum pieces.

INDEPENDENCE, Montgomery County. US 75.

Montgomery County Historical Society Museum, in Riverside Park. Log cabin of 1869 has pioneer displays.

Independence Museum, 8th and Myrtle Sts. Indian crafts and antiques; changing exhibits.

IOLA, Allen County. US 169.

Funston Memorial, 4 miles N. on highway, is the restored 19th-century home of General Frederick Funston, a military leader in the Phillipine campaign of 1901.

Courthouse, in town square said to be the world's largest, has a year-round museum maintained by the Allen County Historical Society.

Old Jail Museum, 201 N. Jefferson, was the county jail from 1869 to 1959; restored. Open May through September. A registered historic place.

KANOPOLIS, Ellsworth County. State 141.

Fort Harker, once a military supply depot, now has a museum in the old guardhouse. The fort was established in August, 1864, first located on the Smoky Hill River at a point where the Santa Fe stageline crossed, ca. 3 miles E. of present town of Ellsworth. In 1867 it was moved to Kanopolis. First called Fort Ellsworth, it was later designated Fort Harker to honor Brigadier General Charles G. Harker, killed June 27, 1864, in the Battle of Kenesaw Mountain, Georgia.

KANSAS CITY, Wyandotte County. I-70.

Wyandotte County Museum, now in Bonner Springs (which see).

Indian Cemetery, Huron Park, Center City Plaza between 6th and 7th Sts., was the tribal burying ground of the Wyandots, 1844–1855, now in the business district.

Grinter House, 78th and State 32, was built by Moses Grinter in 1857. Restored, with relics. A registered historic place. Grinter came to Cantonment Leavenworth, Kansas, in 1828 and soon operated a ferry across the Kansas River. It became part of the Fort Leavenworth-Fort Scott military road; Grinter's trading post at the landing was in business from 1855 to 1860.

KENDALL, Hamilton County. US 50.

Fort Aubry, at the head of Spring Creek ca. 2½ miles N. of the Arkansas River between Kendall and Syracuse, was established in September, 1865. The site was recommended by Francis X. Aubry, trader and scout, for whom the post and the town at that time were named. (Aubry had been killed in Santa Fe in a saloon argument in 1854.) The post was intended to protect part of the Santa Fe Trail and the Aubry Cutoff during the Indian troubles of the mid-1860s. Old Indian graves are near the fortsite. Aubry, who used to win bets in how fast he could get from Santa Fe to Independence with relays of horses, had found the shortcut which later bore his name. The name of the town was later changed.

KINGMAN, Kingman County. US 54.

Historical Museum, in old city hall, has pioneer exhibits. A game refuge W. of town has buffalo herds.

KINSLEY, Edwards County. US 50, 56.

Edwards County Historical Society Museum and Pioneer Sod House, at junction of highways.

KIOWA, Barber County. State 2, 14. Carry Nation swung at her first saloon here in July, 1900, and S. of town a monument marks a spot where homesteaders began their Cherokee Strip run in 1893.

LA CROSSE, Rush County. US 183.

Barbed Wire Museum, 614 Main St., displays more than 500 specimens of the "wire that fenced the West."

Post Rock Museum has limestone fence posts of the type settlers had to use in lieu of wood.

LARNED, Pawnee County. US 156.

Fort Larned National Historic Site, 6 miles W. on US 156. This important post guarded the Santa Fe Trail and served as a base of operations against hostile Indians on the central plains. It is one of the best preserved Western forts; among original buildings are the commissary storehouse, quartermaster warehouse, workshops, barracks and officers' quarters. The national park covers 681 acres. Other buildings are being restored. Conducted tours and interpretive talks are available. Native Kansan Robert Frizell, who was born in the commandant's house, where Custer, Buffalo Bill and Sheridan had been guests at times, and members of his family were in large part responsible for the excellent condition of the post and were supportive of the federal takeover. But in the days when it was untouched by reconstruction and identification a visitor wandered through the barracks, commissary, blacksmith shop, quartermaster's quarters, and emerged from the officers' quarters to ask, "Where's the fort?" No wooden poles, no blockhouses, no fort, for this Hollywood oriented tourist.

Santa Fe Trail Center, 3 miles W. Museum and library.

LAWRENCE, Douglas County. US 59.

Haskell Institute, 23rd St. and Barker Ave., was first called the Indian Training School. It dates from 1884 and is a national historic landmark.

Ludington House, 1613 Tennessee St., was built in 1860 for a local businessman and remodeled in 1872. Judge Solon Thacher, ambassador to Central and South America and Mexico, had the house enlarged when he received his appointment. A registered historic place, not open to the public.

Old Lawrence City Hall, 1047 Massachusetts St., built in 1887 is a registered historic place.

Oak Hill Cemetery, 13th St. A monument marks the graves of 150 victims of the Lawrence Massacre, which took place on August 21, 1863, when the town was plundered and burned by William Clarke Quantrill and his raiders. Senator James Lane, a man whom Quantrill hoped to kill personally, is buried here; he was a suicide but he escaped Quantrill. He had led atrocious attacks on proslavery groups.

Massacre Site, 935 New Hampshire St. Stone marker is near the area where Quantrill's men shot 20 unarmed boys.

The Chamber of Commerce, 901 Tennessee, has information on local tours.

LEAVENWORTH, Leavenworth County. US 73. Ironically a federal prison has long been located in a town that was established illegally on land belonging to the Delaware Indians. Town officials later met strong protests by agreeing to pay a government-set price.

Fort Leavenworth, 3 miles N. on US 73, established in 1827 to protect the wagon trains and the settlers, played an important role in the development of the trans-Mississippi, and in the Indian, Mexican and Civil wars. It occupied the center of a line of forts along the Indian frontier. When the Territory of Kansas was organized in 1854, the fort served as temporary capitol. Some original structures remain. A national historic landmark. Self-guiding tour pamphlets are available at museum, which features early vehicles. A national cemetery is on the grounds.

Leavenworth County Historical Museum, 334 5th Ave. Early rooms and furnishings with local mementoes are displayed.

LEAWOOD, Jackson and Johnson Counties. US 69.

Alexander Majors House, 8145 State Line Road. Majors, who was field co-

Every building at old Ft. Larned still stands
(Kansas Dept. of Economic Development)

ordinator for the freighting firm of Russell, Majors and Waddell, in 1856–1858, lived here. The house, which straddles the state line, is a registered historic place.

LECOMPTON, Douglas County. SW of Perry (US 24) on secondary road.

Constitution Hall, Elmore St. between Woodson and 3rd. A proslavery constitution drafted by the territorial legislature here was rejected by the electorate.

LIBERAL, Seward County. US 54.

Coronado Museum, 567 E. Cedar St., has some exhibits pertaining to Coronado's historic search for Quivira and his route through the present state of Kansas.

LINCOLN, Lincoln County. State 18, 14. A monument to buffalo hunters and settlers attacked by Indians is in the courthouse square.

Historical Museum, in courthouse, has pioneer and Indian relics. Quartzite quarries from which the Indians obtained flint are still in business SW of town.

LINDSBORG, McPherson County. State 4.

McPherson County Old Mill Museum, 120 Mill St., on the Smoky Hill River, has Indian and pioneer artifacts.

Coronado Heights, 3 miles NW, has a shelter house at summit, where the Spanish explorer is said to have camped in 1541.

LYONS, Rice County. US 56.

Rice County Historical Museum, E. of courthouse square, 221 East Ave. S., has artifacts of the Coronado expedition and the Quiviran Indians.

Padilla Cross, 4 miles W. of town, honors Father Juan de Padilla who returned to Kansas after the Coronado expedition had gone back to Mexico and was killed. Descriptive marker beside the 30-foot granite cross. (Also see Herington.)

MANHATTAN, Riley County. US 24. State 18.

Goodnow House, 2301 Claflin Rd., was built in the 1860s by pioneer educator, Isaac T. Goodnow. Period furnishings. Next door is a restored house which was brought to Manhattan via the river by Free-Staters who hoped to establish an antislavery community.

Riley County Historical Museum, 11th and Poyntz Ave. Pioneer and Indian exhibits, clothing, weapons, furnishings, etc.

Kansas State University, 17th and Anderson Sts., NW edge of town, was the first land-grant college in the U.S., established in 1863. Buildings are of limestone.

City Park, between 11th and 14th Sts. on Poyntz Ave., has a 30-foot statue of Johnny Kaw, legendary wheat farmer.

MARYSVILLE, Marshall County. US 36.

Pony Express Barn Museum, 108 S. 8th St., is housed in one of the buildings used to stable horses at this home station of the Pony Express.

Koester House Museum, Broadway, is restored, with relics.

MEADE, Meade County. State 23.

Dalton Gang Hideout Museum and Park, 4 blocks S. of sign at Pearlette St. at junction of US 54 and 160. Furnishings used in the hideout in the 1880s and a tunnel to the barn where escape horses were stabled. Museum in barn.

MEDICINE LODGE, Barber County. US 160. In the hot dry summer of 1867 a great meeting of Indians and U.S. peace commissioners took place at the "medicine lodge" on the Medicine River, which the Indians had peacefully shared for many years. Araphaho, Apache Cheyenne, Comanche and Kiowa were the major tribes to sign the treaty on October 21, 1867, after weeks of negotiations. Among the Indian leaders were Black Kettle, Little Robe and Little Bear of the Cheyenne; Satanta, the great Kiowa, who liked to drink and play a bugle but awed the white men who met him; Satank, an eloquent Kiowa when he chose to speak; Silver Brooch and Ten Bears of the Comanche, who wore white shirts and black vests for the occasion but were not fooled by the white men; and Little Raven of the Arapaho. For all the weeks of work in often stifling weather in the valley of the Timbered Hill River, the treaty did not put an end to the Plains wars; nor to the end of white-men's broken promises. It was the first treaty that did not ask the Indians to give up their homes and move farther west to a government reservations. It asked them to give up their lives as nomadic hunters and take up farming. They were to be given a mule and a plow and wooden roof over their heads, along with schools and teachers to instruct them how to endure it. The treaty site is a national historic landmark. A 400-acre Memorial Peace Park overlooks the area.

Carry A. Nation Home Memorial, 211 W. Fowler Ave. at Oak St. is a W.C.T.U. shrine, and museum with original furnishings.

Medicine Lodge Stockade, adjoins the Carry Nation home, on US 160, 281. Replica of the stockade and peace site. Museum with Indian relics.

NEWTON, Harvey County. State 15, US 50. The town became the terminus of the Chisholm Trail in 1871 when the railroad extended its line here. Mennonites emigrated from Russia in the 1870s, bringing Turkey Red hard winter wheat to Kansas aiding the state's claim of being "Breadbasket to the World."

Warkentin House, 211 E. 1st St. Victorian dwelling built in 1886–1887, the home of Bernhard Warkentin, Russian immigrant who became a wheat magnate. A registered historic place.

Kauffman Museum, on campus of Bethel College, 1 mile N. on State 15 in North Newton. Indian artifacts and Mennonite memorabilia are among the collections.

NICODEMUS, Graham County. S. of US 24, ca. 17 miles W. of Stockton, 12 miles E. of Hill City, on unmarked road. This Negro ghost town was one of three all-black Kansas Colonies founded by the "Exodusters," organised in 1873 by Benjamin Singleton, who tried to establish a rural foothold in a community which resented the intrusion. The town was named for the legendary Nicodemus who came to America on a slave ship and bought his freedom. Historical marker describes the community.

NORTON, Norton County. US 36.

Station 15, 200 Horace Greeley Ave. 1 mile S. of junction of US 36, 283. Replica of a stagecoach depot of 1859 with mannequins.

Gallery of Also Rans, 105 W. Main St. First State Bank mezzanine, photos of not-so-famous losers who were unsuccessful presidential candidates.

OBERLIN, Decatur County. US 83.

Last Indian Raid Museum, 268 S. Penn. Site of Cheyenne raid of September 1878. Period rooms and relics. Wire collection.

Oberlin Cemetery has memorial monument to settlers killed in the raid.

OSAWATOMIE, Miami County. US 169.

John Brown Memorial Park, 10th and Main, has a log cabin used by, and a statue of, the abolitionist who raided Harper's Ferry and was executed. The cabin was owned by Samuel Adair, Brown's brother-in-law; the abolitionist came to Kansas at the request of his five sons who had preceded him. On May 23, 1856, Brown and six others terrorized and murdered victims in the Potawatomi Indian country. In August, Osawatomie was sacked and burned, in retaliation. The cabin has been moved from original site.

Old Stone Church, 6th and Parker, a restored pioneer structure, dedicated in 1861.

Original Land Office, Lincoln Ave. and 6th St. Restored. Now occupied by the Chamber of Commerce, which has keys to stone church.

OTTAWA, Franklin County. State 68.

Ottawa University, 10th and Cedar, was established in the 1860s on land to which the Ottawa Indians owned rights until 1873.

Ottawa Indian Burial Grounds, NE of town. Jotham Meeker, a minister who established the Baptist Mission in 1837, is buried here. The Ottawa Indians were given 34,000 acres of land in this area in 1832 in exchange for their Ohio lands.

Centennial Cabin Museum, in City Park, Main and 5th, is reconditioned and furnished in 19th century period.

Old Depot Museum, Tecumseh St., ½ block W. of Main. County historical museum has relics and a transportation room.

PAWNEE ROCK, Barton County. Just N. of US 56. Santa Fe Trail landmark of red sandstone, now a state park with shelter house and monument on the summit.

PHILLIPSBURG, Phillips County. US 36.

Old Fort Bissell, City Park, W. edge of town on highway. Replicas of Indian fort and sod house, authentic log houses and a gun collection.

Kirwin National Wildlife Refuge, 5 miles S. on US 183, then 6 miles E. on State 9.

PITTSBURG, Crawford County. US 69.

Crawford County Historical Museum, Madison and Joplin, has a replica coal mine and pioneer artifacts.

PLEASANTON, Linn County. US 69.

Battle of Mine Creek was fought 2 miles S. of the present town which did not exist at that time, October 25, 1864. The town was named for Major General Alfred Pleasonton with the change of one letter. Marker at roadside park near the site. Relics of battle at museum in City Park.

John Brown Fort Massacre Memorial Park occupies the site where farmers were massacred by Missouri border ruffians. The only survivor, Amos Hall, lived to be a banker.

Mound City, ca. 8 miles SW of Pleasanton, has marked the school where the wounded were cared for; some victims of the Mine Creek battle are buried in the cemetery, as is Col. James Montgomery, one of John Brown's men. The home of Col. Charles (Doc) Jennision, leader of the Jayhawkers, is marked in the E. part of town on State 52.

QUINTER, Gove County. I-70.

"Wagons Ho," 600 Main St., is a commercial enterprise that provides covered wagon trips along the old Smoky Hill Trail, during summer months. A wagonmaster, Trail Boss, wranglers, and other personnel of the pioneer wagon trains are part of the experience. Saddle horse riding in rotation, pioneer costumes, Indian Raid, Pony Express rider with personal mail, and many other reenactments of historical goings-on.

REPUBLIC, Republic County. State 266.

Pawnee Indian Village Site, on the Republican River, 8 miles N. of US 36. A Republican (Kithehahki) Pawnee village was here in the 1820s and 1830s with as many as 1,000 people living in 30 or 40 earth lodges. The only such site to be excavated in Kansas. A registered historic place. Modern museum with artifacts.

RUSSELL, Russell County. US 281.

Fossil Station Museum, 331 Kansas St., has displays on the history of the oil development and pioneer artifacts.

Oil Patch-Russell, I-70 and US 281, outdoor display of oilfield artifacts. Replica of first derrick in area.

RUSSELL SPRINGS, Logan County. State 25.

Old Logan County Courthouse houses the Butterfield Trail Historical Museum.

SALINA, Saline County. State 140.

Prehistoric Indian Burial Site, 4 miles E. The Whiteford (Price) Site is a national historic landmark. A cemetery in which some 146 skeletons of the Smoky Hill Indian culture are protected by a building. Part of a nearby village has been excavated.

Smoky Hill Historical Museum, Oakdale Park, Mulberry St. and S. 2nd Ave. Period rooms, Indian and pioneer relics, some Stone Age exhibits.

SCOTT CITY, Scott County. US 83.

Scott City State Park, 12 miles N., has the ruins of El Quartelejo, a Pueblo ruin attributed to a group of Picuris Indians from the Southwest, in the 17th century. A national historic landmark.

SENECA, Nemaha County. US 36.

Fort Markley and Indian Village, W. on US 36. Replica of old frontier town with buffalo herd, not in replica. Among exhibits is a buffalo cafe which once served the Pony Express line, other original artifacts are on display.

SMITH CENTER, Smith County. US 36.

Home on the Range Cabin, 8 miles W. on US 36, then 8 miles N. on State 8 and less than a mile W. Restored cabin where Dr. Brewster Higley, as a homesteader, wrote the lyrics for the ever-popular song, in 1872.

Continental Sculpture Hall, 18 miles S. on US 281. Guided tours for studio of sculpture from 3 varieties of rock.

STOCKTON, Rooks County. US 24. A replica of the original log hotel in Stockton is now a museum. Twin Mounds and Sugar Loaf Mound near town were Indian lookout posts.

TOPEKA, Shawnee County. I-70.

State Capitol, center of town, design is based on the national Capitol. On the grounds are statues of Lincoln and the Pioneer Woman.

Kansas State Historical Society, Memorial Building, 120 W. 10th St. Historical museum has period rooms and a variety of exhibits including a Spanish sword of the Coronado period, found on Kansas plains. Indian items.

TRADING POST, Linn County. US 69.

Marais des Cygnes Massacre Site, 5 miles NE A memorial park is the site of the massacre of 1858 which stirred up the North and broke the antislavery movement in Kansas. On May 19, 1858, a band of proslavery sympathizers led by a former resident of Trading Post came from Missouri to capture and kill a number of Free-Staters. Five were killed, five wounded and one unhurt. Only one raider was ever caught and punished. A registered historic site. The Marais des Cygnes Wildlife Refuge is nearby.

ULYSSES, Grant County. US 160, 270.

Wagon Bed Springs, 11 miles S., on US 270 was a popular stop on the Santa Fe Trail; now a national historic landmark. Also called Cimarron Springs, it served as an oasis on a dry 60-mile stretch of the Cimarron Cutoff. Ruts of the trail are still visible. Near the highway marker is a memorial to explorer and trader, Jedediah Smith, mountain man who led the first Americans to reach California overland.

Grant County Library and Museum, 215 E. Grant, has pioneer items.

WALLACE, Wallace County. US 40.

Fort Wallace, ca. 2 miles SE, at the junction of Pond Creek and the S. fork of the Smoky Hill River, near the then Pond Creek Station on the Butterfield Overland route to Denver, was established in September, 1865. Originally called Camp Pond Creek, it was named in honor of Brigadier General H. L. Wallace, who died in April, 1862, after the battle of Shiloh. Some troops remained at the post until 1882.

Fort Monument, established in November 1865, was in Gove County on the Kansas Pacific Railway route, between Fort Wallace and Fort Hays, near monument-shaped rocks that gave it this name; often called, Fort Pyramid. Officially it was Monument Station. Troops were to protect the stage and the mail route.

Fort Wallace Museum, ½ miles E. of town on US 40 at Rest Area, has pioneer articles and military relics.

Cemetery, 2 miles SE of Wallace, across from fort site, has a monument erected by Custer's Seventh Cavalry to their lost men. Military interments have been transferred to national cemeteries.

WABAUNSEE, Wabaunsee County. State 18.

Beecher Bible and Rifle Church, SE corner of Chapel and Elm Sts. The Reverend Henry Ward Beecher of Connecticut persuaded his congregation to support a westward expedition made by a group of antislavery men who wanted to settle in Kansas and promote their hope of making it a free state. The Brooklyn church supplied money for rifles. Some 70 colonists founded Wabaunsee in April, 1856. Their church, completed in 1862, is a registered historic place.

WELLINGTON, Sumner County. State 81, 160.

Chisholm Trail Museum, on Washington, is a 3-story building with mementoes of trail driving days.

Sellers Park has a steam locomotive on display.

WICHITA, Sedgwick County. US 54. First settlers were the Wichita Indians in their grass lodges in 1863. James Mead set up a trading post in 1864 and the following year sent Jesse Chisholm on a trading tour of the southwest. His route became historical after longhorns from Texas followed it to the Union Pacific at Abilene.

Wichita Historical Museum, 3751 E. Douglas. Indian relics, period rooms, minerals, etc.

Fellow-Reeve Museum, on campus of Friends University, University and Hiram Sts. has Indian and pioneer exhibits including a covered wagon. The university is operated by the Society of Friends.

Museum of Man, McKinley Science Hall, Wichita State University.

Cowtown, 1717 Sim Park Dr. A 30-building reproduction of old Wichita, with the restored first house and church and Wyatt Earp's jail among displays. Five buildings are more than a century old.

Wichita Art Museum, 619 Stackman, has one of the largest collections of Charles M. Russell paintings.

Great Plains Railroad Museum, Room 207 of Union Station Bldg., has artifacts, models, maps and other items of railroadiana but is open only on Sunday afternoons and some Friday evenings. Inquire locally.

WINFIELD, Cowley County. US 160, 77.

Cowley County Historical Museum, 1011 Mansfield, depicts the history of southern Kansas in exhibits, period rooms.

First National Bank has a mural portraying the town's history.

MISSOURI

He would sit out on the porch, resting his chin on his cane, with his face towards the West—a lonely figure. He liked to talk of his life on the Plains, and I remember his saying once, at a time when his eyesight was almost gone, "I wish I was back there among the mountains again—you can see so much farther in that country."

J. Cecil Alter, *Jim Bridger,*
1962, quoting a neighbor

O Jesse had a wife, a mourner all her life
And the children they were brave,
But the dirty little coward that shot Mr. Howard
He laid Jesse James in his grave.

Capt. Lewis killed a Rabit. Sgt. Floyd, June 25, 1804, Vic. of Mill Creek Jackson County, Missouri.

The town of Boonville, where George worked in the cabinet-maker's shop, was much like the town of Franklin. The two towns originally stood almost across the Missouri River from each other. In fact, a popular toast "drank standing" at public dinners was "Boonville and Franklin, they smile o'er the waters."

By 1828 Boonville smiled alone. In one of its unpredictable shifts of channel, the Missouri River began to chew away at the north bank. . . . Business buildings and homes in Franklin began to slide into the river. . . . But Old Franklin, as it is now called in the histories, has never been forgotten . . . it was the boyhood home of George Caleb Bingham. It was also the boyhood home of Christopher Carson, more often called Kit. When the famous frontier scout and plainsman ran away from Franklin and his apprentice status, his master advertised for his return, offering a reward of ONE CENT! Josiah Gregg, explorer, artist, and author of *Commerce on the Prairies* . . . lived in Franklin. So did John Hardeman, botanist; Alphonse Wetmore, first Missouri playwright; and William Becknell who opened up the Santa Fe trade.

Alberta Wilson Constant
Paintbox on the Frontier; The Life and Times of George Caleb Bingham, 1974

MISSOURI FACTS: French explorers came down the Mississippi River in the late 17th century. The territory was acquired by the United States with the Louisiana Purchase of 1803. Missouri entered the Union on August 20, 1821, the 24th state. Capital: Jefferson City. Missouri has the Jefferson National Expansion Memorial, the Ozark National Scenic Riverways, Wilson's Creek National Battlefield, and the George Washington Carver National Monument. There are 2 national forests. Nickname: Show Me State.

Early Trails. Santa Fe, Lewis & Clark, Butterfield Stage Line, Wire Road.

Major Indian Tribes. Woodland and Mississippi cultures, Sauk, Fox and Illinois, Oto, Iowa, Osage, Missouri, Quapaw, and Kansa.

ARROW ROCK, Saline County. State 41.

Arrow Rock State Park preserves and commemorates the beginning of the Santa Fe Trail and other historical sites. By 1817 a ferry was already in operation for traffic across the Missouri River. William Becknell's pioneering Santa Fe expeditions of 1821 and 1822 were organized here. The rock cliff, remains of the old ferry road, the Santa Fe Spring used for rendezvous are part of the national historic landmark.

Also in the park is the George Caleb Bingham home, built in 1837. Bingham, who became one of America's foremost frontier painters, was born in Virginia, came to Missouri with his family when he was 9. Bingham bought the lot in Arrow Rock for $50 from Claiborne Fox Jackson, a character in his own right. Jackson had three wives who were daughters of Dr. John Sappington; when he asked for the hand of the third girl, Sappington is said to have replied, "You can take her but don't come back after the old woman." Bingham lived for his painting but he also got involved in politics and one of his works stirred up more emotions than a hundred editorials. After the bloody border battles and the sacking of

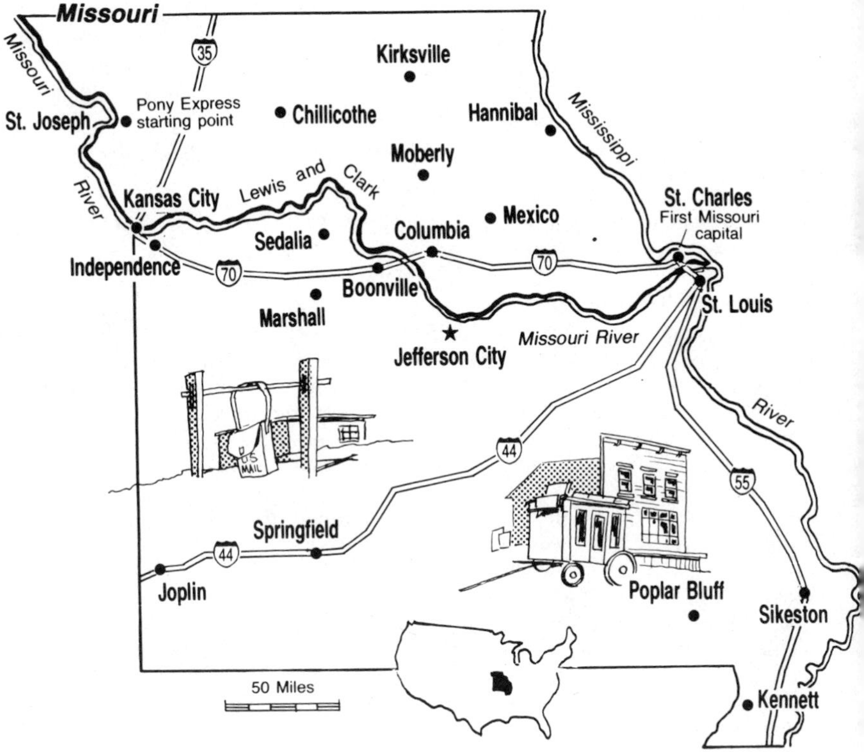

Missouri
Missouri River
Missouri River
Mississippi River
Kirksville
Pony Express starting point
St. Joseph
Chillicothe
Hannibal
Moberly
Kansas City
Lewis and Clark
St. Charles
First Missouri capital
Mexico
Columbia
Sedalia
Independence
Boonville
St. Louis
Marshall
Jefferson City
US MAIL
Springfield
Joplin
Poplar Bluff
Sikeston
Kennett
35
70
70
44
44
55
50 Miles

Lawrence, Kansas, Brig. Gen. Thomas Ewing issued Order No. 11 which ordered all persons in three Missouri counties (outside of cities) to evacuate. Bushwhackers, and probably Quantrill's men among them, got help from farmers of the area, but the remedy was nearly as bad as the ailment. Many families were set up on the road with their household goods and nowhere to go. Bingham's painting, "Martial Law," always called the "Order No. 11," helped to fan the flames of public feeling. On Ewing's side there were Kansas families who were dragged from their homes and murdered for favoring the Union by these same guerrilla fighters who were aided by Missouri farmers. Ironically, and tragically, a building owned by Bingham's wife collapsed in Kansas City, killing and injuring women of Rebel sympathies, who were being kept "prisoners of war" there. Among the dead was a sister of "Bloody Bill" Anderson, one of Quantrill's most fanatic followers. Historian Alberta Wilson Constant says that Bingham did much of the work on the Arrow Rock house himself; he had been trained in cabinet-work and was able to lay the oak floors, frame the walnut doors and windows, and possibly set the brick walls.

Old Tavern of early Arrow Rock has been restored, with period furnishings and exhibits.

Walking Tour takes in the restored log courthouse, gun shop, chapel, jail and private homes in the old town, which was platted in 1829, called New Philadelphia, until the named was changed by an Act of the Legislature in 1835. Three governors came from Arrow Rock: Meredith M. Marmaduke, who donated the 50-acre tract for the town; the much-married Claiborne Jackson, who was serving at the highly controversial time of the Civil War when Missouri was torn in sympathy and support, and John S. Marmaduke.

Sappington House, 3 miles SW of town on County Route, TT, was the home of William B. Sappington, who discovered quinine as a treatment for malarial fever. He was a son of Dr. John Sappington, whose daughters married Jackson. A registered historic place, not open to the public at present.

BETHEL HISTORIC DISTRICT, Shelby County. State 15. The area is bounded by 4th, King, 1st, and Main and Liberty Sts. The town was founded by Dr. William Keil, a German, as a communal settlement in 1844 and was successful. In 1874 some of the population was drained away because Keil started a second colony in Oregon. After his death in 1877, both colonies lost interest in communal organization; quarrels resulted. Bethel was incorporated in 1883. The 50 buildings of the original colony are of handmade brick and stand close to the sidewalks.

Elim, 1.5 miles E. of town, was the home of Dr. William Keil; a registered place not open to the public. In the 1840s, members of the society erected the brick house that served as administrative quarters and an herbarium which Dr. Keil, used for cure and store medicinal herbs.

BLUE SPRINGS, Jackson County. US 40. This was James Brothers territory. The *Jackson County Democrat* for September 27, 1901, wrote up a sentimental reunion that would have been worthy of national television coverage in this day. Headlines announced: "Qauntrell's (sic) Men

Meet, The Annual Reunion Brought Twenty-Five Survivors Together" despite the obvious that reunions do bring survivors together; but newspapers had more space in those days and this one had room for a couple more subheadlines: "Frank James Here, Too. Remembered All the Boys and Exchanged Jokes with Them." The yearly get-togethers were held on the grounds of the old Blue Church. Frank James gave a speech on this occasion and asked that a monument be erected to the "noble women" who stood by the raiders in the dark days of the War. He started the fund with $50. The group, which included Sam Whitset, and the Webb boys, were photographed behind a large portrait of Quantrill.

BONNE TERRE, St. Francois County. State 47.

Washington State Park, 15 miles NW on State 47, 21, has a variety of Indian petroglyphs and a nature museum. The park covers 1,101 acres.

Bonne Terre Mines, State 47, 33 N. Allen, were opened in 1870. Guided tours, along lighted walkways in underground caverns, exhibits of old mining equipment.

BOONESBORO, Howard County. State 87.

Boonslick State Park, 1 mile N. on State 87. A natural salt lick, the spring was used by Indians and settlers until 1833. It was named for Nathan and Daniel Boone, sons of the great pioneer explorer and hunter, who boiled salt here in 1805. A registered historic place.

BOONVILLE, Cooper County. US 40, State 41. Hundreds of wagon trains of the Western expeditions got provisions here. Many historic buildings remain. Two battles of the Civil War were fought locally. The first battle took place on June 17, 1861, ca. 4 miles E. of town. Captain, later General, Nathaniel Lyon (his death in the Battle of Wilson's Creek, ended a brief but brilliant career) routed the Missourians under Col. John S. Marmaduke. The 2nd Battle of Boonville in the fall of 1863 occurred at the E. end of Morgan St. on the grounds of what is now St. Joseph's Hospital. Some old trenches remain.

Thespian Hall, also called Lyric Theatre, NE corner of Main and Vine Sts., was built in 1855–57, and is the oldest continuously used theater W. of the Alleghenies. During the Civil War troops used the building for quartering, then as a hospital and even as stables, and military prison.

Kemper Military Academy, 3rd St. and Center Ave., the oldest boys' school and academy of its sort W. of the Mississippi, founded June, 1844.

Vest House, 745 Main St., was the home of Sen. George G. Vest, a state representative who later served in the Confederate Congress and in the U.S. Senate.

Harley Park, on river bluff, has a pre-Columbian archaeological site which contains 4 well-preserved mounds. A registered historic place.

BRANSON, Taney County. US 65.

Old Matt's Cabin, State 76, Shepherd of the Hills Farm, was the homestead of the J. K. Ross family who were the main characters in Harold Bell Wright's novel *The Shepherd of the Hills,* a best-seller in its day and a popular movie. Original furnishings in cabin; museum has Indian relics, and pioneer items.

Ralph Foster Museum, 3 miles S. of

town at Point Lookout, on campus of the School of the Ozarks, has a large collection of Indian pottery from the Mississippian culture. Also artifacts made by Ozark Bluff Dwellers and others.

Silver Dollar City, 9 miles W. on State 76. Restored pioneer settlement of the 1880s has a general store, blacksmith shop, newspaper office, and a 180-foot swinging bridge.

CAMDENTON, Camden County. US 54.

Camden County Historical Museum, NE on US 54, in Linn Creek, has antique tools, arrowheads, and other early day items.

CAPE GIRARDEAU, Cape Girardeau County. I-55. Louis Lorimier, an Indian agent for the Spanish in Louisiana, set up a trading post here in 1792. Four Civil War forts were located in the area.

Court of Common Pleas Building, Spanish and Themis Sts. The main body of the structure was built ca. 1854 to replace a log building. During the Civil War the basement was used as a military prison. Museum on 2nd floor.

Cape Rock, Cape Rock Drive, which circles the city, is the site of Lorimier's trading post.

Trail of Tears State Park, 10 miles N. on State 177, commemorates the migration of the Cherokee Indians in 1838. The forced march from Georgia to Indian Territory, now Oklahoma, passed here. Princess Otahki, one of the many who perished on the arduous journey, and who was the daughter of Chief Bushyhead, is buried in the park. Memorial marker at her grave. A large Woodland village area, on a hill at the . edge of park, was occupied in Woodland times and was used by other tribes including the Cherokee. A registered historic place.

Burfordville, W. on US 61, then SW on State 34 to County HH, just S. of highway, has two registered historic sites: The Burfordville (Bollinger) Mill has occupied this spot for 176 years; the present gristmill was built on the stone foundations of an earlier one; Burfordville Covered Bridge, E. edge of town on County HH, spans the Whitewater River and was built in the mid-19th century.

CARROLLTON, Livingston County. US 65.

William Baker House, 5 miles S. on Missouri River, was the home of a river captain who built a mansion that became a hotel for steamboat passengers and was known as River House. It is rumored to be haunted by the ghost of a Union soldier, James McMurtry, who was killed after he and two friends crashed a New Year's Eve party here in 1865.

St. Mary's Cemetery, NE edge of town, has the grave of General James Shields, who once challenged Abraham Lincoln to a duel; they later became friends. He was appointed governor of Oregon Territory and served as the first U.S. Senator from that state. A life-size bronze statue of Shields stands on the E. side of courthouse grounds. Shields, who had served in the Black Hawk and Mexican wars, commanded a division in the Shenandoah Valley in the Civil War and served as U.S. Senator from Illinois, Missouri and Minnesota as well as from Oregon.

CARTHAGE, Jasper County. US 66. Belle Starr, the "Bandit Queen" of Indian Territory, was born on a farm somewhere in this area, unless it was somewhere else, which is about the only safe way to say anything about the colorful Myra Belle Shirley. Her tombstone stated flatly that she was born in Carthage on February 5, 1848. As recently as 1975 a new authority puts her birthplace in Washington County, Arkansas. In any case she lived and loved, often, in the second half of the 19th century. She did not marry quite as many of her lovers as dime novels of her day reported. But she had many interesting affairs though her photographs give no clue as to why so many outlaws and handsome Indians found her fatally attractive. Her father became an inn-keeper in Carthage who lost his source of income when the Union soldiers burned the town in 1863. The Shirleys went to Texas. Ed (or Bud) Shirley was a Missouri bushwhacker. Neither Belle nor Ed rode with Quantrill as was often reported, but Belle did marry Jim Reed, who was one of Quantrill's men.

Markers in town describe the Civil War battle of July, 1861, which was the first of 13 skirmishes in the area.

Kendrick House, US 66 and 71, N. of town, has Civil War and other relics. The house was occupied by both armies during the Civil War.

Old Fort Osage: America's first outpost in the Louisiana Territory built by Lewis of Lewis and Clark *(Missouri Division of Tourism)*

CASSVILLE, Barry County. State 248, 76.

Butterfield Overland Mail Relay Station, 6 miles N. of town. Marker in town for the John D. Crouch stop. The town served as the Confederate Capital for a time in November 1861, when Confederate members of the Missouri general assembly met here and rewrote the ordinance of sucession which had been approved at Neosho, Missouri by 11 senators and 44 representatives. The revised ordinance was signed here. During the hostilities both sides attacked the town.

CENTRALIA, Boone County. State 22. In September, 1864, a massacre took place here when 30 Confederate guerrillas under Bloody Bill Anderson plundered the town, held up the Columbia stagecoach, then laid ties across the tracks of the North Missouri Railroad and held up the St. Louis train. Union soldiers who were passengers on the train were forced to strip off their uniforms then were lined up and shot. On the same day another group of Union soldiers, under Maj. A.V.E. Johnson was captured by Anderson's guerrillas. Johnson was shot by Jesse James, who was only 17 at the time.

Anderson and his men hung human scalps from this affair on their horses' bridles. When they rode into Boonville two weeks later to assist Gen. Sterling Price, he refused to talk to Anderson until the "trophies" were thrown away. Afterwards, however, he accepted a gift of pistols from Anderson and told him that if he had 50,000 such men he could hold Missouri forever. The guerrilla leader was assigned to destroy key bridges on the North Missouri Railroad but failed to carry out his orders with any success and was killed by Federals near Albany, Missouri, in October. His head was cut off and mounted on a telegraph pole.

CLARKSVILLE, Pike County, State 79, was founded in 1807 and named for William Clark; he wintered here in 1815. Though Meriwether Lewis died in 1806, either a suicide or murdered, Clark became superintendent of Indian affairs at St. Louis in 1807 and governor of the Missouri Territory in 1813, having concluded treaties with the Indians after the War of 1812.

Lookout Point, at Pinnacle Park on State 79, is the highest area on the Mississippi River between New Orleans and St. Paul. The park has a 50-foot observation tower for a panoramic view of the valley. Skylift.

COLUMBIA, Boone County. US 63, 40.

University of Missouri-Columbia, Elm and 8th Sts., has several museums on campus; Art, Archaeology, State Historical Society and Rare Books are in Ellis Library; Anthropology is in Swallow Hall with American Indian dioramas and displays. Journalism Historical Museum, between Neff and Williams Halls.

DANVILLE, Montgomery County. State 161.

Graham Cave State Park, 2 miles W. off I-70 and County TT, A sandstone shelter contains archaeological evidence of the earliest known Indian habitation in Missouri.

DEFIANCE, St. Charles County. State 94.

Daniel Boone Home, ca. 5 miles W. on County F, was built between 1803 and 1810. Authentically furnished with museum. Boone himself supervised the construction and lived here until his death in 1820. He was buried beside his wife Rebecca Bryan Boone, who died in 1813, in the Bryan-Boone Cemetery near Marthasville, W. of here via County F and D, in Warren County. Monument at gravesite, but in 1845 the bodies were removed to Frankfort, Kentucky. The Flanders Callaway House, 1 mile S. of Marthasville off State 94, was the home of Jemima, one of the Boone daughters, married to Flanders Callaway.

DE SOTO, Jefferson County. State 110.

Washington State Park Museum, S. via State 21. Petroglyphs and a museum of archaeological exhibits. Directions for the petroglyph sites available at park headquarters.

DIAMOND, Newton County. US 71A.

George Washington Carver National Monument, W. on County V. Carver, born a slave, became a noted scientist. Visitor Center has Carver memorabilia. His log cabin birthplace is part of the monument.

EAST PRAIRIE, Mississippi County. State 80.

Towosahgy State Archeological Site, 6 miles E. on State 80, then S. on County FF for Indian village of the Mississippian Indian culture. A museum is being developed.

ELDON, Miller County. US 54.

Enchanted Caverns, 3 miles S. on US 54. Indian burial ground with artifacts on display.

EXCELSIOR SPRINGS, Clay County. US 69.

Jesse James Farm, 6 miles NW via US 69, State 92, then 1 mile NW. House where the outlaw brothers were born has many original furnishings. Alexander Franklin (Frank) was born ca. 1843; Jesse Woodson James in 1847. In June 1863, a band of volunteers hanged Dr. Reuben Samuels, Jesse's stepfather, until he was near death and gave Jesse a beating. A bomb, thrown by Pinkerton men in 1874 trying to capture Jesse at the farm, ripped off the arm of Jesse's mother. Frank had joined the Confederate army early in the war, was taken prisoner at Wilson's Creek and released on his word not to join the rebel forces, but he joined Quantrill's guerrillas, and took part in the sacking of Lawrence, Kansas. Long after his war and outlaw days were over Frank worked as a shoe salesman in St. Louis, then lived at this old home and died here in 1915. He is buried in a private cemetery near Kansas City but only a few people know its location so that his tombstone will not suffer the mutilation Jesse's did. Jesse was too young for the war but managed to join Quantrill's men before it was all over. Many stories have him being used as a spy in women's clothing. After he was killed in St. Joseph in 1882 he was buried at the farm but later removed to Mount Olivet Cemetery, Kearney.

Watkins Woolen Mill State Historic Site, 6½ miles N. on US 69. Woolen Mill of 1860 contains original machinery. Owner's home, built in 1851; smokehouse and cemetery. Waltus Watkins had founded a Utopian community in the county in 1838. An octagonal schoolhouse is included in the state park. A national historic landmark.

FARMINGTON, St. Francois County. US 67.

Village of St. Francois, ca. 5 miles S. on US 67, SW. on County H and County AA. Twenty six Ozark buildings have been moved here to form a village representative of mountain life in the 18th and 19th centuries; museum with pioneer relics.

FLORIDA, Monroe County. State 107.

Mark Twain State Park, State 107, contains the birthplace of Samuel Clemens within a modern museum building. Several first editions and the original manuscript of the English edition of *Tom Sawyer* are among many Twain memorabilia on display. The park covers 1,192 acres.

HANNIBAL, Marion County. US 36.

Mark Twain Museum and Boyhood Home, 208 Hill St. Twain relics and the Clemens family home with period furnishings.

Becky Thatcher House, 211 Hill St. Home of Laura Hawkins, the girl Twain fashioned Becky after, has period furnishings.

Pilaster House, Hill and Main, contains a restoration of oldtime drugstore, doctor's office and living quarters where John Clemens, Samuel's father, lived and died.

Molly Brown House, 600 Prospect St. (Us 36) was the birthplace of the girl who became the "unsinkable Mrs. Brown," wife of a successful Colorado prospector and a Titanic survivor whose adventures made a popular stageplay and motion picture.

Chamber of Commerce, 320 N. Main, has a 30-minute documentary on Hannibal in Twain's day, and other information on local sites. The Mark Twain Cave and statues of Twain characters and Twain himself are in the area.

HERMANN, Gasconade County. State 19.

Old Stone Hill Historic District contains the grounds and buildings of the Stone Hill Win Company established in 1847. Tours. A registered historic place.

German School Building, 4th and Schiller, houses museum with early settler artifacts. River Room has exhibits pertaining to early river traffic. Children's museum has toys and furniture of the 1890s.

Bottermuller House, 205 E. 8th St., restored with period furnishings, was built in 1852; a country store next door has pioneer implements and clothing; *Pommer-Gentner House,* 108 Market St., was built about 1841; *Strehly House,* 129 W. 2nd St., period furnishings; *Klenk House,* 432 E. 3rd St., built ca. 1846, has smokehouse and summer kitchen.

Graham Cave State Park, 13 miles N. on State 19, then 5 miles W. off I-70. Excavations indicate Indians occupied cave as early as 7850 B.C.

INDEPENDENCE, Jackson County. US 24.

The Harry S. Truman Library and Museum, Delaware St. and US 24, has a mural by Thomas Hart Benton in the entrance area that depicts the history of Independence and the opening of the West. Truman is buried in the courtyard.

1859 Jackson County Jail and Marshal's Home, 217 N. Main St. Restored. The jail house was one of the first buildings put up by the first county court in 1827 (cost was ca. $400). In 1841 after a fire, another was built on the same site. The present building was erected in 1858. William Quantrill and Frank James were among prisoners. There are 6 cell-blocks and a rear courtyard where the gallows once stood. A one-room schoolhouse is here now. The Marshal's quarters have been authentically furnished. Pioneer history museum.

Temple Site, corner of Lexington Ave. and River Blvd. The Mormons came to Independence in 1830, the town having been revealed to Joseph Smith, prophet, as the future city of Zion for his people. The Temple Site was dedicated on August 3, 1831, although construction never began because of conflict between Mormon and non-Mormon citizens. The Mormons fled to Clay County across the Missouri River. A marker stands at site.

World Headquarters, Reorganized Church of Jesus Christ of Latter-day Saints, River and Walnut Sts. Museum and art gallery. Guided tours.

Vaile Park, 1500 N. Liberty St. and 1518 N. Osage, mansion, built ca. 1871, was the home of Col. Harvey M. Vaile from 1881 until his death in 1895. Horse barn and carriage house. A registered historic place, now a nursing home.

Jackson County Courthouse, 107 W. Kansas Ave., was built of logs in 1827, the oldest courthouse W. of the Mississippi.

Bullene-Choplin House, 702 N. Delaware, restored Victorian home with period furnishings. Tours.

Fort Osage, 11 miles NE on US 24 to Buckner, then 3 miles N. to Sibley. The old trading post and stockade has been reconstructed. It was established in 1808 by William Clark. Blockhouses, officers' quarters, a factory building, and barracks. A registered historic landmark.

Missouri Town, E. side of Lake Jacomo, directional signs on I-71, 70, is made up of historical buildings moved from original sites and reconstructed in a setting as similar to the first location as possible. Among the buildings are the Blue Springs Law Office, the Riffie House from Marysville, the Flintlock Church, the Samuel-Chevis Tavern, the Luttrell Cabin, a log structure typical of the 1850s, the Withers House built ca. 1840, from near Liberty, with slave cabins and summer kitchen.

The Old Spring, Truman Rd. and Noland Rd., is of the type used by early residents and western emigrants. A furnished log house is at site.

The McCoy House, 410 W. Farmer, was built by Samuel Owens in 1849 and completed in 1856 by William McCoy, first mayor of Independence. Handsomely restored by Mr. and Mrs. Forest Ingram who make it their home; not open to the public.

The Truman House, Truman Rd. and Delaware, was built by Mrs. Bess Truman's grandfather in the 1860s and was the Trumans' home from the time of their marriage in 1919. Not open.

The Flournoy House, Lexington and Short, is one of the earliest dwellings in town, built of hand-made brick in 1826, period furnishings.

JEFFERSON CITY, Cole County. US 54.

State Capitol, High St. and Broadway. Statuary includes the figures of Lewis and Clark. Murals tell state history. Jefferson City was established as the capital soon after statehood was approved in 1821. St. Charles served as the capital until the first Capitol building was completed here in 1827; it was destroyed by fire in 1837. A second Capitol burned in 1911.

Executive Mansion, overlooking the Missouri River, has been occupied since 1871.

Missouri State Museum, in Capitol,

has a firearms collection, an Indian burial restoration, and many other items of Missouri history.

Cole County Historical Society Museum, 109 Madison St. Old maps, photographs, war relics, antique furnishings among exhibits. Missouri's Governor B.G. Brown built the house in 1871.

Lincoln University, 830 Chestnut St. , is a land-grant college established by Union soldiers for Negro students in 1866. Members of the 62nd Colored Infantry are said to have conceived the idea of the university while at Camp McIntosh near Galveston, Texas.

National Cemetery, 1042 E. McCarty St., has the graves of Union soldiers killed in battle near Centralia. *Woodland Cemetery,* adjoining, has the grave of Confederate Gen. John S. Marmaduke.

Lohman's Landing Building, W. corner, Jefferson and Water Sts. was built in 1834–36, and was used as a depot for passengers and freight until the 1850s, later as an inn and warehouse. A registered historic building.

KANSAS CITY, Jackson County. I-35.

Kansas City Museum of History and Science, 3218 Gladstone Blvd., has regional history, weapons, Indian artifacts, geology and natural history displays, dioramas, period costumes. The museum is housed in the 72-room mansion once the home of R. A. Long, a lumber baron.

Union Cemetery, 2801 Warwick Trafficway, has the graves of more than 1,000 Civil War soldiers, George Caleb Bingham, and Alexander Majors, founder of the Pony Express. The Sexton's Cottage, is a restored Victorian home, built in 1883.

Wornall House, 61 Terrace at Wornall Rd., is the restored mansion of John Wornall, once part of a 500-acre farm. It has been furnished with antiques of the 1850s when it was built. During the Battle of Westport, October 1863, the house was used as a hospital by both armies.

Majors House, 8145 State Line Rd., was occupied by Alexander Majors from 1856 to 1858. Nearby, wagons were outfitted to supply army posts on the frontier. The firm of Russell, Majors and Waddell had a monopoly on freighting for a time but went into bankruptcy in 1861.

Convention and Tourist Council, 1212 Wyandotte, has maps and information on many old buildings in the area which are of historical and architectural interest and may be seen on walking or auto tours.

Line Creek Park, Waukomis Drive, N. of US 71, an 80-acre park that contains the archaeological preserve of the Hopewell Indian civilization and a small herd of buffalo.

Native Sons Room, 25th floor, City Hall, an excellent collection of Westport and Kansas City relics.

Westport Inn, 500 Westport Rd., was once an outfitting store for the Santa Fe Trail, built in 1837.

Drips Park, 16th and Jarboe, was the first park in town and was given to the city in 1882 by William Mulkey and his wife in honor of her father, Andrew Drips, an early fur trapper.

Pacific House, 4th and Delaware, was a hotel built in 1867 and was a popular stopping place for famous people of the day. It burned in 1867 and was rebuilt the following year; now houses a business firm.

Kansas City Stockyards, 16th and Genesee, were organized in 1871. Boston's Charles Francis Adams, surprisingly, was president of the Stockyards company from 1875 to 1902.

Penn Valley Park, Pershing Rd. and Main, two outstanding statues: an Indian Scout modeled after the son of Kicking Bear, an Oglalla Sioux; and a pioneer mother and family.

Delaware Indian Mission and Burial Ground, in Fairway, Kansas, between the Missouri River and US 70, was established in May 1832. Graves of Indian chiefs and councilors are here.

Mt. Washington Cemetery, Truman Rd. between Kansas City and Independence, has the grave of Jim Bridger, mountain man, scout, and explorer. He was first buried in a family plot near what is now 101st and Jefferson Sts. But in December, 1904, a hundred years after Bridger's birth, Gen. Grenville Dodge had his body moved to a select spot in Mt. Washington Cemetery and a 7-foot monument placed at the grave.

Westport Landing was a large flat rock at 1st and Grand, where steamers brought merchandise to be hauled overland to Westport ca. 4 miles S.

KINGSTON, Caldwell County. State 13.

Far West, 5.5 miles W. of town via County D and H. When the Mormons were driven from Jackson County, they established a townsite here in August 1836. This was the first time the Mormons had controlled a local government and the town prospered, achieving a population of several thousand. In July 1837, the cornerstone for a Temple was laid but only the cellar was completed. The Mormons were forced to leave the state in 1839 and 1840 and the town died.

KIRKSVILLE, Adair County. State 6.

Northeast Missouri State University, Normal, Marion, Franklin and Davis Sts., was founded in 1867.

Kirksville College of Osteopathic Medicine, 204 W. Jefferson, called the "birthplace of osteopathy" opened in 1892.

Thousand Hills State Park, W. of town, has pre-Columbian petroglyphs.

Memorial Park, Hickory St. at Florence Ave., is the site of a Union assault on a Confederate position in the Battle of Kirksville, August 1862.

LACLEDE, Linn County. US 36.

Gen. John J. Pershing Boyhood Home, State and Worlow Sts., was built in 1857, purchased by the Pershings in 1866. Some furnishings from the Pershing occupancy. After graduating from West Point, Pershing served as a cavalry officer in campaigns against Geronimo in 1886 and against the Sioux in 1890–1891.

Locust Creek Covered Bridge, 3 miles S. of town on US 36, then NE on gravel road. The 1868 bridge is one of four surviving covered bridges in Missouri.

LEBANON, Laclede County. State 64.

Laclede County Museum, 3rd and Adams Sts., an 1872 building which was used as a county jail.

Bennett Spring State Park, 12 miles W. on State 64, excellent nature museum.

LEXINGTON, Lafayette County. US 24.

Battle of Lexington State Historic Site, NW edge of town at 10th and Utah Sts. Anderson House, center of the battle of September, 1861, is restored. Guided tours.

Museum of Yesturyears, US 24, State 13. Twenty-two old-time stores, blacksmith shop, dental office, barber shop, schoolhouse, other relics.

Lafayette County Courthouse, built in 1847–49, is the oldest in use in the state today. A cannonball fired during the Civil War battle here in 1861 is lodged in the east column.

LIBERTY, Clay County. State 10.

Historic Liberty Jail, 1 block N. of square, restored and housed in museum, was built in 1833. Joseph Smith, the Mormon prophet, was confined here for a few months in 1838–39.

Clay County Historical Museum, W. side of square, has prehistoric displays of the Nebo Hill culture, which may date from so long ago as 5000 B.C. The museum is housed in a pioneer drugstore and has many early day farm tools, Indian relics, guns, and Clay County family heirlooms.

Clay County Savings Association, NE corner of Franklin and Water St., has a bronze plaque at the site of the first daylight bank hold-up in the U.S. in February 1866. But neither of the James brothers was involved, as has been often reported. A student on his way to William Jewell college was shot by the robbers. The building now houses the Jesse James Bank Museum although Jesse seems to have been ill at home on the day of the heist.

LONE JACK, Jackson County. US 50.

Museum has diorama and displays pertaining to the Battle of Lone Jack, August 16, 1862. Confederate and Union soldiers were buried near here. A marble shaft at the site of the Confederate burial ground that was marked by a solitary blackjack tree in the 1860s. The Union gravesite is also marked but the soldiers have been re-interred at Leavenworth.

MARSHALL, Saline County. State 41.

Utz Site, 12 miles N. of town, adjoining Van Meter State Park, is believed to have been the principal settlement of the Missouri Indians from the 1670s until 1728. A national historic landmark.

MEXICO, Audrain County. US 54.

Audrain County Historical Society Museum, 501 S. Muldrow St. Restored 1857 mansion with period furnishings, a Currier and Ives collection, American Saddle Horse Museum.

NEVADA, Vernon County. US 54.

Bushwhacker Museum, 231 N. Main St., in building used as jail for more than 90 years. Osage Indian collection and other relics.

Carrington Osage Village Site, N. of town on W. edge of Green Valley Prairie, was visited by Zebulon Pike in 1806. Excavations have uncovered large amounts of aboriginal and later materials. A national historic landmark not open to the public at present.

OSAGE BEACH, Camden County. State 42.

Indian Burial Cave, 3 miles NE on County V. Archaeological museum, incline railway to cave entrance and boat ride on underground river. Guided tours.

Arrow Point Cave, 9 miles E. on State 42, near Brumley. Indian relics in museum.

PILOT KNOB, Iron County. County 21.

Fort Davidson State Historic Site, earthwork on County 21 S. of County V, was occupied by Federal Troops. The Battle of Pilot Knob was fought in September 1864.

RICHMOND, Ray County. State 13.

Richmond Cemetery, N. Thornton St., has the grave of "Bloody Bill" Anderson who was killed in ambush in Ray County by Union troops in October 1864. He was a savage and merciless outlaw who had his own version of the rebel yell; he rode with Quantrill and then organized his own band of guerrillas. Cole Younger came to town years after Anderson had been buried here without a funeral and hired a preacher, used his own band from his traveling show, and staged a belated ceremony. Still later in 1967 the efforts of an interested citizen got a headstone, government issue, placed on the Anderson grave. Anderson, who was born in Huntsville, Randolph County, which takes no pride in the fact, usually went his own way but he did receive orders from Gen. Sterling Price and was therefore a soldier, no matter how wayward.

ROLLA, Phelps County. US 63.

Minerals Museum, Norwood Hall, on campus of University of Missouri-Rolla.

Ed Clark Museum of Missouri Geology, in Buehler Park, W. edge of town, on US City 66. Displays of regional geological history.

Maramec Spring and Remains of Old Iron Works, 8 miles E. to St. James then 6 miles SE on State 8. Iron works were built in 1826; furnace in 1857. Museum. Historic structures of the Ironworks District are the stack of the cold-blast furnace, five refinery forge stacks and three dwellings: the Maramec House, the McDole Cabin, and the Jolley Cabin. A registered historic place.

ST. CHARLES, St. Charles County. I-70.

First Missouri State Capitol, 208–214 S. Main St. Restored with 1820 period furnishings.

St. Charles Historic District, Madison St., Missouri River, Chauncey St. and an alley from Boonslick Rd. to Madison. The town was founded in 1769 by Louis Blanchette, settled by French traders, hunters, farmers and became an outfitting area for river and overland travelers on the Boonslick Road that ran to Arrow Rock where it joined the Santa Fe Trail. In May 1804, this was the final embarkation point for the Lewis and Clark expedition that had wintered at their base camp in Camp Wood. They went upriver on the afternoon of May 21. In September 1806, coming home they stopped here overnight. There are nearly 100 structures in the district. The Capitol, listed above, and Stone Row, 314–330 S. Main are on the National Register.

Bushnell Pioneer Museum, 4 miles W. off I-90, has blacksmith shop, general store, railroadiana and many other historical items.

Fort Zumwalt State Historic Site, 13 miles W. on I-70. Built as a cabin by Jacob Zumwalt in 1798, enlarged into a fort during the War of 1812. Stone chimney and a few other ruins remain.

St. Charles Borromeo Cemetery, W. of Blanchette Park, has many interesting early graves, among them: Jean Baptiste Point du Sable, an early explorer whose father was French and mother a slave and for whom a Chicago high school is named; Major James Morrison, trader and salt manufacturer, and Rebecca Younger, wife of Cole Younger of Liberty, the outlaw. There is a monument to Louis Blanchette, founder of St. Charles, whose exact gravesite is unknown. He built the first church, of logs, and was first buried beside it with his Pawnee wife, but later was moved.

SAINTE GENEVIEVE, Sainte Genevieve County. US 61. The author approaching this town for the first time made a bet with a friend as to whether it would be given a French or an Americanized pronunication by the natives. The first resident approached was serving hamburgers and was startled to be asked. "Huh?" he responded. "Oh, you mean Saint GIN-uh-veeve?"

The town was the first permanent settlement in Missouri and developed, from lead-mining activities, on the banks of the Mississippi in 1732. After a flood in 1785 it moved to higher ground, 3 miles upstream.

Sainte Genevieve Historic District: Bolduc House, 123 S. Main, was built about 1785, has been restored; Amoureaux House, St. Mary's Rd, has antique furniture and a doll collection; Dr. Benjamin Shaw House, 2nd and Merchant Sts., has fixtures from a wrecked steamboat; Greentree, 224 St. Mary's Rd., was once a tavern; Ste. Genevieve Church, 49 DuBourg Pl. Three French governors are buried here. Historical Museum, Merchant St. and DuBourg Pl., has a display of birds stuffed by John J. Audubon during the time he was in business here. Indian artifacts and other historical relics.

ST. JOSEPH, Buchanan County. US 36.

John Patee House, 12th and Penn Sts., was one of the best-known hotels in the area; built in 1858, it served as headquarters for the Pony Express, operated by Russell, Majors and Waddell. Now a registered historic landmark, it contains the reconstructed offices of the freighting firm. A shot fired April 3, 1860, sent the first rider westward on the gallop. The last of the relay would arrive in Sacramento. The building was used as a provost marshal's office and a recruiting office in the Civil War.

Pony Express Stables Museum, 914 Penn St., houses relics of the service which was in operation for only 18 months before the completion of the telegraph put it out of business. The stables were rebuilt in 1886.

St. Joseph Museum, 11th and Charles St., in 1879 mansion. Indian, historical, and natural science exhibits.

Site of Joseph Robidoux Houses, 219–225 Poulin St., may still be standing or have fallen to urban renewal. It was part of an extensive "Robidoux Row," built in the 1840s. Here the founder of St. Joseph died in 1868. A house Robidoux built for his daughter stood at the NW corner of 2nd and Michel Sts. Both Joseph and his father (Joseph, Sr.) had been important fur traders. In the first decade of the 19th century, he established a post at Council Bluffs where Manuel Lisa of St. Louis, the great scout and trader, and John Jacob Astor's American Fur Company were his competitors.

Jesse James House, Belt Highway, 1 mile N. of US 36. James had been living under the name of Howard in the one-story frame cottage where he was killed on April 3, 1882, by Bob Ford, a former associate. Ford, in turn, was killed in his own saloon, which he bought with the reward money, in Creede, Colorado, by a man named Ed O. Kelly (often printed incorrectly as O'Kelly) who did not serve much time in penalty. Ford was generally disliked, partly for having shot James in the back, an act which produced the ditty that went the rounds about the dirty little coward that shot Mr.

The Pony Express: one of the most exciting episodes in the history of the Old West
(Missouri Division of Tourism)

Howard, and partly for killing him from any direction. James was a fairly popular outlaw with many who never had been his victims. The home was moved to this location from 1318 Lafayette and in the early 1940s was operated in conjunction with a gas station and cafe. "Admission free with purchase of gasoline; 15¢ otherwise." A statement which may evoke more nostalgia now than Jesse himself.

ST. LOUIS, St. Louis County. I-70. The city was founded by Pierre Laclede as a fur-trading post and was named for Louis IX of France. The first steamboat docked in 1817. The first constitutional convention was held in 1820.

Jefferson National Expansion Memorial, a symbolic starting point of the westward expansion. The author was once enroute to Wilson Creek and Pea Ridge Battlefields with a group of Civil War historians when the plane pilot got tower permission to fly lower than usual over the arch. One fellow declined to glance down; in response to an "Aren't you going to look?" he yawned and said, "Not unless he decides to fly *through* it. It wasn't there in Sherman's day." But it's there now and the Visitor Center in Old Courthouse, 11 N. 4th St. (built in 1839–64) houses Indian and westward expansion exhibits. *Old Cathedral,* 2nd and Walnut, has a museum.

Missouri Historical Society, Lindell Blvd. and DeBaliviere Ave. Western history exhibits, firearms, and river relics.

Riverfront Information, in riverboat Becky Thatcher.

Eads Bridge, Washington Ave. at river, was designed by the engineer and inventor Capt. James B. Eads. He was a purser on a Mississippi River steamboat when he invented and patented a diving bell. During the Civil War he proposed and supervised the building of a fleet of gunboats for use on Western rivers, a most important contribution to the Union war effort. His plan for the bridge here was approved by Congress which had almost abandoned as impracticable a project to bridge the river. It was completed in 1874.

Museum of Science and Natural History, in Oak Knoll Park, Clayton and Big Bend Rds.

Campbell House Museum, 1508 Locust, 19th-century mansion.

Jefferson Barracks Historical Park, 10000 S. Broadway, 10 miles S. on State 231. The post was the successor to Fort Belle Fontaine, several miles upstream which had been established in 1805. The Barracks were founded in 1826 by troops from that Fort under Capt. Stephen W. Kearny and Col. Henry Leavenworth. Leavenworth founded an infantry training school; a few years later Col. Henry Dodge organized the 1st Dragoons. The post was the starting point for many military and exploring expeditions. The historical park covers 490 acres in the N. part of reservation; restored buildings include stables and a laborer's house, built in 1851, used later as a guardhouse and barracks. Museum at site, in restored powder magazine. A national cemetery is W. of the parade grounds.

National Museum of Transport, 20 miles W. at 3015 Barretts Station Rd. in Kirkwood, locomotives and many other early vehicles.

Bissell House, 10225 Bellefontaine Rd., restored home of Gen. Daniel Bissell, military commander on the

Mississippi frontier, built ca. 1814, with period furnishings.

Chatillon-DeMenil House, 3352 S. 13th St., built ca. 1849. Period furnishings.

Eugene Field Birthplace, 634 S. Broadway, Field memorabilia. The house built about 1845 was part of a solid block known as Walsh's Row. The poet and journalist was born here September 3, 1850.

Six Flags Over Mid-America, I-44, US 66, 50, has a narrowgauge steam engine railroad which encircles the park, mock trading posts, etc.

City Art Museum, on Art Hill in Forest Park, has George Caleb Bingham paintings in its collections.

Grant's Farm, Grant and Gravois Rds., a 281-acre area with cabin and land formerly owned by Ulysses Grant. Has buffalo, elk, deer in park. Tours by miniature trains.

Bellefontaine Cemetery, 4947 W. Florissant Ave., has the graves of Gen. William Clark, Francis P. Blair, politician of Civil War fame, Sen. Thomas H. Benton, who was the father of Mrs. John C. Fremont in addition to his own fame as one who worked for westward expansion, Manuel Lisa, Gen. Sterling Price, one of the most respected of Confederate generals, and James B. Eads, Gen. B. L. E. Bonneville, Gen. Stephen Kearny.

Calvary Cemetery, 5239 W. Florissant Ave. Gen. William Tecumseh Sherman is buried N. of the entrance. Also in the cemetery are the graves of Alexander McNair, Missouri's first governor, and Auguste Choteau, early trader and explorer who was one of the founders of the city.

Florissant, 10½ miles NW on I-70, then 5 miles N. on Florissant Rd., is a city with many historic old buildings. Visitors Bureau at 1060 Rue St. has maps for a self-guiding tour. Green markers are on the right side of the pavement. The first settlers came in 1786; most were French. St. Ferdinand's Shrine, at St. Francois and St. Charles Sts., was built in 1819. Father Pierre Jean DeSmet, also active in the settlement of the Old West, was ordained here in 1827. A convent and historical museum adjoin the church.

SPRINGFIELD, Greene County. I-44.

Wilson's Creek National Battlefield, 13 miles SW via US 60, State ZZ. Information Trailer at entrance has information on the battle of August 10, 1861, in which Union General Nathaniel Lyon was killed. Map for self-guiding tour. Thirty Union officers became generals before the war was over. The Confederate forces were led by the able Sterling Price and Ben McCulloch.

National Cemetery, 1702 Seminole St. Monuments honor Gen. Lyon and Price who are not buried here. Price is in St. Louis's Bellefontaine Cemetery. Lyon is buried in Eastford, Conn. Henry Walters, a scout with John Singleton Mosby, is here as are more than 700 unknown soldiers among the total of 1,514 Union graves. The Confederate Cemetery was established in 1870, with a number of unknown soldiers among the 463 gravesites. The unfortunate Lyon's body was captured twice: first in the field by Gen. McCulloch's troops who returned it to the Union army under a flag of truce, and second, in its coffin in the courthouse when the tide of battle turned and the Union soldiers fled town.

Bentley House, Calhoun and Washington Sts., was built about 1852, one of the finest houses in the area. Period furnishings.

Springfield Art Museum, 111 E. Brookside Drive, has American paintings, antique furnishings and pioneer relics.

STANTON, Franklin County. US 66.

Meramec Caverns, 3 miles S. on County W. off US 66, I-44. Was used for the manufacture of gunpowder during the Civil War and as a hideout by Jesse James in the 1870s. In 1864 Confederates captured the gun powder mill. A brochure distributed at the caverns states that the "Quantrill Irregulars, under the command of General Price" were made up of Frank and Jesse James, Frank Dalton, and the Younger brothers. Gen. Sterling Price of the regular Confederate Army had an uneasy alliance with Quantrill, who—after all—was fighting for the southern cause, and had indeed served in Price's army in the siege of Lexington. But as the army retreated in September of 1861, Quantrill made his own way to Kansas City where he set up in business as a bushwhacker, and no one controlled his "Irregulars" except Quantrill himself. In October of 1863 he sent his first and last written report to Price, telling of the Baxter Springs (Kansas) massacre and signed it W. C. Quantrill, Colonel, Commanding, etc. Price and other southern generals tried to persuade Quantrill to abandon his outlaw style of war. He did not listen, and they were forced to accept his help no matter how they disapproved of the savagery, particularly of Bloody Bill Anderson and his psychotic killers.

Jesse James Wax Museum, US 66. Life-size outlaws, gun collection.

SULLIVAN, Franklin County. State 185, US 66.

Onondaga Cave, 10 miles SW on US 66, then SE on County H. near Leasburg, was discovered by Daniel Boone. 1,000-acre park. Guided tours through lighted caves.

WARSAW, Benton County. US 65.

Benton County Museum, Van Buren St. N. of center of town, has antique furnishings, farm implements, and other historical items. The town was a stop on the Butterfield Line, and an important shipping point on the Osage River. The "Slicker War" of 1841–45 took place between the law-abiding and the horse thieves and cattle rustlers of the area. The townspeople and farmers "slicked" hickory switches and used them on those they suspected of breaking the law. But thieves infiltrated the respectable and a reign of terror set in with nine lives lost before it was all over. The ambushing, night riders, raids, bloodshed and general idiocy were similar to Ku Klux Klan activities.

WESTON, Platte County. State 45. A leading 19th-century riverport.

Weston Historical Museum, Spring and Main Sts., on site once owned by Benjamin Holladay of the Overland stagecoach line.

Historical Homes: a number of places are open for tour including a country store, tobacco warehouses, the C. Emmett Riley House, built in 1853, the Robert B. Jones House, of 1844, the George Z. Hull House, of the 1840s, the Charles Sebus Home of the 1840s and the Warren E. Hall House of 1844. Detailed pamphlets are given with tickets at any building on tour.

VAN BUREN, Carter County. US 60.

Ozark National Scenic Riverways, off US 60. More than 57,000 acres on the Current and Jacks Fork Rivers have been developed by the National Park Service. Powder Mill Visitor Center, on State 106, has information on the area, as does the Alley Spring Visitor Center, 5 miles W. of Eminence.

MONTANA

May 28, 1867

At 2½ o'clock I was awakened by "Knocking on my chamber door." Proceeding to the stage office of Huntly's Line and waiting "dilligently" for half an hour we were duly arranged, myself and five others—I upon the seat with the driver. . . . The crack of the driver's whip started four splendid American horses. . . . My credentials, consisting of a bottle of whiskey and a bunch of cigars, being duly presented to the driver, he enlivened the *very early* hours of the morning by describing to me his various exploits in the "Jehu" line of business. A very pleasant man he seemed to us at starting. But, alas for appearances, our smiles were turned to frowns, our good humor to wrath, our good opinion to positive dislike—long before we reached Fort Benton. With the most diabolical persistency he continually sang out upon reaching any mud hole: "Now gentlemen if you will be so kind as to give me a lift for only 20 steps," this meaning that we were to walk through the mud and water from one to two miles, and in one case, four. . . . in crossing a slough near the end of the Kanyon, our vehicle "stuck fast." "All out," was the cry, including myself . . . the ground gave way and I was in an instant engulphed into the water, saving my hat in dryness *alone* of all my garments. I crawled forth amid a hearty peal of laughter from the passengers.

The Road to Virginia City; The Diary of James Knox Polk Miller
(Norman, 1960)

I'd like to be a packer
And pack with George F. Crook,
And dressed up in my canvas suit
To be for him mistook.
I'd braid my beard in two long tails
And idle all the day
In whittling stick and wondering
What the New York papers say.

Anonymous

To the Editor of the Herald:
Helena, MT.T., July 25th, 1875 [1876]
In the presence of so great a disaster as that which overtook the regular troops on the Little Horn, and the consequent excited state of the public mind and its eagerness to get hold of every detail, however minute, of that unfortunate affair, it is to be expected that many stories of a sensational character having no foundation in truth would obtain currency in the newspapers and credence with the public. Of such a character is that now going the rounds of the press, to the effect that the Sioux had removed Custer's heart from his body and danced around it. . . .

In my capacity as Commander of the Scouts, accompanying General Gibbon's column, I was usually in the advance of all his movements, and chanced to be upon the morning of the 27th of June . . . the body of a horse attracted our attention to the field of Custer's fight, and hastening in that direction the appalling sight was revealed to us of his entire command in the embrace of death. This was the first discovery of the field. . . . Later in the day I was sent to guide Colonel Benton [Benteen] of the 7th Cavalry, to the field, and was a witness to his recognition of the remains of Custer. Two other officers of the regiment were also present, and joined in their identification; and as all had known him well in life, they could not be mistaken and the body so identified was wholly unmutilated. Even the wounds that caused his death were scarcely discoverable (though the body was entirely naked) so much so that when I afterwards asked the gentlemen whom I accompanied whether they had observed his wounds they were forced to say that they had not.

Letter by Lt. James H. Bradley, killed August 9, 1877, in the Battle of Big Hole, Montana

MONTANA FACTS: First white arrivals were French traders, Pierre and Francois Gaultier in 1743, then Lewis and Clark, followed by Manuel Lisa and other traders, trappers, miners and ranchers. In 1841 Father Pierre Jean De

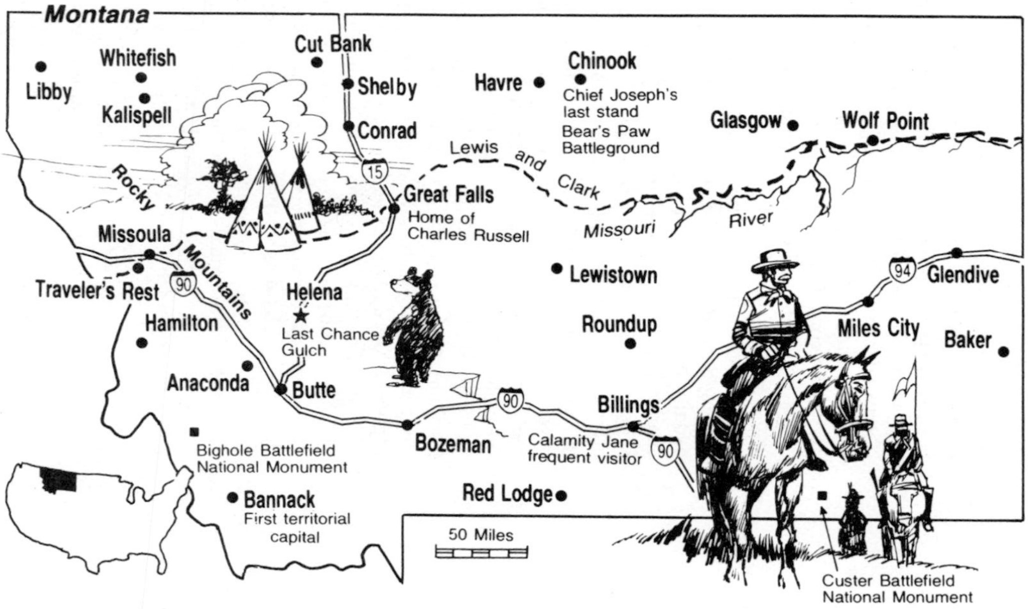
Montana
Libby
Whitefish
Kalispell
Cut Bank
Shelby
Conrad
Havre
Chinook
Chief Joseph's last stand
Bear's Paw Battleground
Glasgow
Wolf Point
Lewis and Clark
Rocky Mountains
15
Great Falls
Home of Charles Russell
Missouri River
Missoula
Traveler's Rest
90
Helena
Last Chance Gulch
Hamilton
Lewistown
Roundup
94
Glendive
Miles City
Baker
Anaconda
Butte
Billings
Bozeman
Calamity Jane frequent visitor
Bighole Battlefield National Monument
Bannack
First territorial capital
Red Lodge
50 Miles
Custer Battlefield National Monument

Smet built the first mission. Gold was discovered in 1852 but the rush began in 1858. Texas cattle were driven north to establish herds by 1866. The still controversial battle of Little Bighorn took place in June 1876, wiping out George Armstrong Custer's command of a 7th Cavalry contingent. Montana became a territory in 1864. Entered the Union November 8, 1889 as the 41st state. Capital: Helena. Territorial Capitals: Bannack, Virginia City. Montana has Big Hole and Custer National Battlefields, Glacier National Park, 3 of 5 entrances to Yellowstone National Park, part of the Bighorn National Recreation Area, 11 national forests, 13 primitive and wilderness areas. Nickname: Treasure State.

ABSAROKEE, Stillwater County. County 420, 307.

Jorgen Elesius Madson, County NRS 288-B, 6 miles S. Historical marker on highway for pioneer Lutheran minister who rode the circuit in the foothills of the Crazy Mountains in 1895, in an area that included the open range and mountain valleys from Hardin to the Snowies near Lewiston, to the Belts and Beartooth Mountains. When the Crow Reservation was opened he homesteaded across the highway from marker, naming his pioneer home "Fagerheim" (Beautiful Home), more for the scenery than for the house.

ANACONDA, Deer Lodge County (5,288 feet). US 10A. Chosen as a smelter site by Marcus Daly in 1883, the town is still a copper mining center. The Anaconda Copper Company has been in business since 1892. The town was temporarily called Copperopolis until the postmaster discovered another Montana town already had that name. Some old log cabins and framehouses of the pioneer days are in the original section of town.

Atlantic Cable Quartz Lode, 11 miles W. on US 10A. Marker on highway for the mining property that was located on June 15, 1867, and was named for the second transatlantic cable. In 1889 a chunk of ore from this mine was bought for $10,000 and was said to be the largest gold nugget ever found. The town of Cable, 4 miles N. on gravel road, now a ghost; some old buildings remain.

Southern Cross, on border of Deer Lodge and Granite Counties, 2 miles off US 10A. NW of Anaconda. Ghost town on hillsite has several old buildings.

Anaconda Reduction Department has tours in summer months.

Lost Creek State Park, N. of US 10A, go 3 miles E. of town, then N. on County 273, take a left turn to park. Lost Creek Falls cascades over rock in a verdant setting of evergreens, willows, aspens and other greenery. The creek flows through a 3,000-foot-deep canyon.

ARLEE, Lake County. US 93.

The Jocko Valley, descriptive marker on highway. Phonetically named for Jacques (Jacco) Raphael Finlay, fur trader and trapper in the Flathead and Kootenai Indian country in the early years of the 19th century.

AUGUSTA, Lewis and Clark County. US 287.

Sun River, 3 miles N. of town on US 287, was called the Medicine River in the time of the Lewis and Clark travels (1804–06). The Blackfeet Nation lived here in pioneer days. Descriptive marker on highway.

BAINVILLE, Roosevelt County. US 2.

Fort Union Trading Post, National Historic Site, historical marker on US 2, 2 miles E. of town. The Fort was ca. 14 miles SE, near the mouth of the Yellowstone, on the Missouri River. First called Fort Floyd in 1828 by Kenneth McKenzie, agent for Astor's American Fur Company. The first steamboat, *Yellowstone,* arrived from St. Louis on June 17, 1832. George Catlin, the artist, was among the passengers. The next year Prince Maximilian of Wied-Neuwied arrived on the *Assiniboine.*

The area is now under development. In 1868 the government dismantled the old trading post and used the materials for the building of Fort Buford, down the Missouri River.

BAKER, Fallon County. US 12, State 7.

Medicine Rocks State Park, 26 miles S. on State 7. Caves and rock formations. Some sandstone formations were used by Indians in tribal ceremonies.

O'Fallon Historical Society Museum, 1 block W. of junction of State 7 and US 12. Regional relics.

Wagon Road, State 7, N. of town. Historical marker on highway describes the old trail between Ft. Lincoln on the Missouri River in Dakota Territory and Ft. Keogh on the Yellowstone in Montana.

BANNACK, Beaverhead County (5,510 ft.). S. of State 278. The first territorial capital is now a state monument. A gold strike in 1862 brought settlers. One of the most famous signs in the Old West was nailed up at the confluence of the Beaverhead River and Rattlesnake Creek; it was a rough board with a message in axle grease that looked like lines from Chaucer, but were directions:

Tu grass Hop Per digins
30 myle
Kepe the trale nex the bluffe

And the reverse said:

To Jonni Grants
One Hundred & twenti myle.

In the next few years plenty of emigrants and prospectors kept to the trail next to the bluff to reach Bannack, which had been Grasshopper Diggings. Johnnie Grant was a Deer Lodge Valley rancher who welcomed travelers.

Among sites to be visited on a well-marked walking tour of Bannack are the *Court House,* built ca. 1875, which was remodeled and became the *Hotel Meade.* Bannack lost its position as county seat when the railroad from Salt Lake City reached the area and Dillon was founded. *Skinner's Saloon,* owned by Cyrus Skinner, a friend of Sheriff-Outlaw Henry Plummer. Several sites are connected with Plummer who moonlighted as a road agent after his regular day as sheriff was ended; on January 10, 1864, his two jobs were over at the same time. A Vigilante Committee made up of miners and merchants hanged him in Hangman's Gulch. Gallows and Gulch are marked.

Bachelor's Row was lined with wickiups in mining days. Yankee Flat was named by Unionists. Southern sympathizers had Jeff Davis Gulch. A number of houses are being restored or have been completed, and among these are the Governor's "Mansion," an assay office, the jails, Masonic Temple, Apex Mill, First Church, Bootlegger's Cabin. First Territorial Meeting Place, and early day cabins.

BIGFORK, Flathead County. State 35.

Village Square Art Center and Information Booth, State 35, exhibits of early Montana history and information on western Montana.

Biological Station of University of Montana, 14 miles S. on State 35. Museum of the natural sciences.

BIG HOLE BATTLEFIELD NATIONAL MONUMENT, Beaverhead County. State 43, near Idaho border. The monument covers 666 acres including a portion of the ground where the battle of August 9, 10, 1877, took place when U.S. troops aided by civilian volunteers made a surprise attack on Nez Perce under Chief Joseph. The Nez Perce were trying to flee to Canada, having been forced from their lands. The attack force led by Col. John Gibbon was outnumbered two to one but the element of surprise aided their unholy cause. The Indians were pursued by Gibbon and his troops through a part of present Yellowstone National Park, then N. to Bearpaw Mountain, where within miles of the border they were forced to surrender in October, 1877. This affair is an unsavory episode in our history; and it seems important to note that the U.S. Department of the Interior, which has been accused by a number of writers of attempting to whitewash the mistakes of the past, in this instance tells the story correctly in its brochure given to all who visit the battlefield. Chief Joseph's face, not Gibbon's, is on the cover of the pamphlet. Visitor Center and museum, self-guiding trail goes past memorials to the soldiers and to Chief Joseph's men.

BIGHORN, Treasure County. US 10. The townsite has been occupied almost continuously by white men since Lt. William Clark camped in the area on July 26, 1806. Manuel Lisa built a trading post here in 1807. Lisa, a St. Louis man, was as much traveled in the Old West as many more famous persons. For some reason his name is not generally known although it appears in a great many early accounts of areas related to the Missouri River. He was the first private trader to ascend the Missouri with an organized group to trade and trap, after Lewis and Clark, who were government-sponsored. His biographer, Richard Edward Oglesby, points out that it was not only the first private trip but Lisa also made the second, third and fourth; the history of the Missouri River from 1807 to 1820 was virtually the narrative of Lisa's voyages and dealings with the natives. A keen competitor, a 19th-century supersalesman, he acted as subagent for the Indians in the War of 1812 and retained their friendship for America versus the British, who tried to win their support. In 1822 Col. W. H. Ashley built another trading post here. Fort Van Buren stood 2 miles below the mouth of the Big Horn River. Gibbon, who was to surprise Chief Joseph at Big Hole in 1877, passed this point in June 1876 when he was en route to aid Custer but was too late.

Junction of Big Horn and Yellowstone Rivers, marker on US 10, 1 mile W. of Big Horn Station, denotes spot from which Gen. Terry and Gibbon started up the Big Horn and Tullock Creek to aid Custer in meeting the hostiles, but Custer did not wait for this support. The Battle of Little Bighorn was fought on June 25th. Gibbon arrived two days later.

BIG TIMBER, Sweet Grass County. US 10.

The Bonanza or Bozeman Trail, W. city limits, on US 10. Descriptive marker points out the site of the old trail that crossed the Yellowstone near this point. Chief Red Cloud and his Sioux fought the trail that crossed Indian hunting grounds, for six years and forced the Government to close it in 1868. John Bozeman had found the shortcut to Montana goldfields in the spring of 1863. Five military posts guarded it, but the Indians maintained their rights in often bloody encounters.

BILLINGS, Yellowstone County. US 10, 87, I-94.

Chief Black Otter Trail, begins at E. end of town, runs past Boothill Cemetery, where bad guys, good guys and the in-betweens are buried in shallow graves. Marker for grave of Luther Sage Kelly, who was called "Yellowstone" Kelly, is on the trail. He was an Indian scout.

Yellowstone County Museum, across from airport, on top of the Rims, has Indian artifacts, steam locomotive, old vehicles, diorama of Indian sacrifical ceremony. Range Rider of the Yellowstone, cowboy statue, nearby.

Western Heritage Center, 2822 Montana Ave. Old West paintings and artifacts, a Will James collection and Stetson hat display.

Indian Caves, 5 miles SE off US 87, 212, excavations reveal evidences of habitation as long as 5,000 years ago. A museum here was vandalized but the many excellent pictographs remain. A national historic landmark.

Custer National Forest, W. via US 212, covers 1,097,769 acres. Beartooth Primitive Area comprises 230,000 acres. Among other features are Rock Creek Vista Point; Granite Peak, which is the highest point in the state at 12,799 feet; Woodbine Falls and Grasshopper Glacier.

Pompey's Pillar, 28 miles NE off US 10, 312. (Called Pompy's Tower by William Clark for Sacajawea's son whom he had nicknamed Pomp.) Clark wrote in his journal ". . . Indians have carved the figures of animals and other objects on the sides of the rock. On the top are two pillars of stone. I marked my name and the day of the month and year." (July 25, 1806). A national historic landmark.

Gallery '85, on Emerald Drive in Billings Heights, has Old West exhibits as well as contemporary displays.

Calamity Jane: there seems to be no particular site marked for Martha Jane Cannary (often spelled Canary) who was called Calamity Jane, but she was often seen in Billings' streets and saloons; and on at least one memorable occasion in a drygoods store. The Billings *Gazette* for November 21, 1902, reported she was in jail again for more than usual unruly conduct and "several overt breaches of the peace." "Without any apparent reason, save that suggested by a mind more or less overstimulated by her favorite tipple, Jane armed herself with a hatchet and invaded Yegen Brothers store and attempted to put an end to one of the young ladies employed in the drygoods department. She advanced toward her with hatchet uplifted and said she was going to chop her to pieces then and there. It may have been only one of Jane's practical jokes, but the victim, having little sense of humor, screamed for help. One of the male clerks disarmed the belligerent Calamity and assisted her from the battlefield. No complaint was made and she retired in order. This morning she visited another store on the south side and again threw down the gage. She was promptly arrested and will be tried this afternoon should she be sober enough to face the bar of justice. It is deemed likely that she will receive a sentence long enough to give her time to sober up."

In her earlier days Jane and a 16-year-old Ben Greenough cut logs at Canyon Creek, W. of town, and hauled them in for the many wood-burning fireplaces of the Northern Pacific Hotel, one of the most popular places of early Billings.

BIRNEY, Rosebud County. On County 332, ca. 15 miles SW of town, is the Wolf Mountain (Tongue River) Battlefield where Col. Nelson Miles, who had pursued the Sioux after the Battle of Little Bighorn, captured 2,000 and sent them back to the reservations in October 1876. He remained here despite a bitter winter. In January he camped beside the Tongue River on the S. flank of the Wolf Mountains. Crazy Horse and 800 men made a surprise attack on the morning of January 8. Miles, disguising his howitzers as wagons, repulsed the Indians. (In the battle of Apache Pass, Arizona, the Apaches had their first encounter with howitzers and Cochise later said, "You would never have beaten us if you had not shot wagons at us.") The Indians here took refuge on the bluffs, withdrew under cover of a blizzard, and many surrendered with Crazy Horse and Dull Knife's Cheyennes the following spring at Fort Robinson, Nebraska (which see). The Battlefield is on the E. side of the Tongue, beneath Pyramid Butte. A gravel road goes across the river and the valley where Miles camped. Pyramid Butte was the Indian retreat position.

BOZEMAN, Gallatin County. US 10. John M. Bozeman blazed a highly controversial trail from Wyoming, leading emigrants who settled here in 1864.

Museum of the Rockies, on campus of the State University, S. 7 Ave. and Kagy Blvd S. Indian and pioneer exhibits. Prehistoric items from Montana excavations.

Ketterer Art Center, 35 N. Grand, is housed in a restored pioneer home, with changing exhibits.

Missouri River Headwaters State Monument, 31 miles NW on I-90, at spot where Lewis and Clark discovered the source of the Missouri River. (See Three Forks.)

Madison Buffalo Jump State Monument, 30 miles NW off I-90. Indian hunting skills and methods are demonstrated. (See Logan.)

Gallatin National Forest, N. and S. of town, 1,700,160 acres, including the Absaroka Primitive Area, Spanish Peaks Primitive Area, and Gallatin Gateway to Yellowstone. In summer months, park rangers offer interpretive programs at the Madison River Canyon Earthquake Area which has exhibits. Headquarters are in Federal Bldg., Bozeman.

Sunset Hills Cemetery, which overlooks the city, S. from the highway, has been a burial ground since 1864. Bozeman is buried here (he was killed by Piegan Indians near Springdale in April 1867), with a marble monument erected in 1883 after cows had knocked down the pine headboard that first marked the grave. Near

Bozeman is the grave of Henry T.P. Comstock, a suicide in 1870, after he had used up the paltry $10,000 he received for his share in discovering the Comstock Lode of Virginia City, Nevada. A pyramid marks the burial place of Lady Blackmore, of Britain, who was traveling with her husband Lord Blackmore to visit the Yellowstone geyser area with a group of geologists when she died. Lord Blackmore bought 5 acres and gave them to the city for a cemetery.

Site of Fort Ellis, via State 187, then unimproved road, N. of town. William Clark and party camped here in July 1806; and in August 1867, the fort was established to protect the Bozeman and the Bridger and Flathead passes. It was named for Col. Augustus Van Horn Ellis of the 124th New York Volunteers who participated in the Sioux Wars of 1876–1881. The Washburn-Langford expedition of 1870, which led to the creation of Yellowstone National Park, outfitted here in August 1870. A monument is on US 10 nearby.

Gallatin Valley, US 10, 1 mile E. of town, descriptive marker on highway for route taken by Capt. William Clark and his party in July 1806, and other early travelers Bozeman and Bridger.

Fort Elizabeth Meagher, 8 miles E. at the mouth of Rock Creek, was established in May 1867. A picket post was also set up on the approaches to Bridger Pass. Gallatin Valley settlers were worried that the Crow and Sioux hostiles were about to invade their territory after John Bozeman had been murdered. The post was named for the wife of Thomas F. Meagher, secretary of the territory.

BRIDGER, Carbon County. US 310.

Bridger Marker, on highway 2 miles S. of town, honors the mountain man for whom the town is named. Montana historical markers written by R.H. Fletcher are among the liveliest in the U.S., as well as informative. All are worth stopping to read.

BROADUS, Powder River County. US 212. Historical marker 2 miles N. on highway.

Mac's Museum of Natural History, at Powder River High School, more than 4,000 Indian relics; many prehistoric items, some believed to date from 2500 B.C. Montana material from bison traps in the Powder River country.

BROWNING, Glacier County. US 2, 89.

Museum of the Plains Indian and Crafts Center, W. of town at junction of US 2, 89. Dioramas and excellent displays, with an audio-visual presentation. The museum is maintained by the Bureau of Indian Affairs with exhibits executed by the Smithsonian Institution.

Bob Scriver Museum of Montana Wildlife, W. edge of town on US 2. Dioramas, models, mounted animals.

Blackfeet Indian Reservation, headquarters are in town for the Blackfeet Tribal Business Council and Bureau of Indian Affairs Blackfeet Agency. Historical marker on US 2, 89, 1.3 miles E. of town. The reservation covers 1.5 million acres.

Two Medicine Fight Site, ca. 25 miles SE in Pondera County. In the summer of 1806, Lewis and three companions camped with eight Piegan Indians at Two Medicine Creek. The next morning the Indians were trying to steal guns and horses when the explorers awoke. The Indians were driven off and the four members of the expedition raced to the mouth of the Marias River fearing pursuit by a large war party. This was the only armed conflict of the Lewis and Clark travels. The area looks much as it did with buffalo remains, tipi rings and a piskun. A registered historic site.

Camp Disappointment, 12 miles NE of Browning on the Blackfeet Reservation. The northernmost point reached by the Lewis and Clark expedition. Meriwether Lewis and nine of his men made a side trip on their return from the Pacific on July 23, 1806. A national historic landmark.

BUTTE, Silver Bow County (5,716 feet). US 10, 91. Located on the "Richest Hill on Earth," the Butte Mining District has been active for more than a century. It developed from gold placer mining in 1864; since 1885 has been producing copper, and is the largest copper mining region in the world. An area less than 5 square miles has produced more than $2 billion in mineral wealth; the Butte Historic District is a national historic landmark.

Copper King Mansion, 219 W. Granite St., restored 1884 residence built by William Andrews Clark, copper magnate and U.S. senator. Fine furnishings include nine imported French fireplaces.

Mineral Museum, in library on campus of Montana College of Mineral Science and Technology, Park St. at W. edge of town. Mining displays include a geological relief map of Montana deposits.

World Museum of Mining, W. Park St. 1 mile W. at Orphan Girl Mine. Indoor and outdoor displays, oldtime mining town, railroad tour.

Lewis and Clark Caverns State Park, 47 miles E. via US 10. Underground rock formations.

Marcus Daly Statue, N. Main St. between Copper and Gagnon Sts. Bronze by Augustus Saint-Gaudens of the copper king with his coat on his arm and his battered hat in hand, a position he did not have to take in life. He was an Irish immigrant who landed in America with nothing but his Irish smile, according to biographers. He arrived in Butte in 1876, having learned about mining in Nevada silver camps. He sank a shaft in what experts thought was valueless land and was disappointed to find no copper until at 400 feet he reached a vein which was 50 ft. wide. In less than 20 years he was head of one of the world's greatest monopolies.

Copper mining; open-pits can be viewed from an observation platform and free tours scheduled by the Butte Chamber of Commerce, Finlen Hotel, 100 E. Broadway. "Old No. 1," an early open streetcar runs a tour that includes the Berkeley Open Pit Mine, Montana Tech and the World Museum of Mining, in summer months.

Deerlodge National Forest, via US 10, 91, State 38, covers 1,134,504 acres. Headquarters in Federal Building.

Meaderville, historical marker on US 91, 1 mile N. of town, was named for Charles T. Meader, a '49er who came from California in 1876. Many mines in the area.

CASCADE, Cascade County. US 91. Marker on highway 16 miles S. for Lewis and Clark campsite of July 17, 1805.

CHESTER, Liberty County. US 2. Marker on highway 5.6 miles E. of town for the Sweet Grass Hills or Three Buttes, which Indians used as watchtowers to locate buffalo.

CHINOOK, Blaine County. US 87.

Chief Joseph's Battleground of the Bear's

Paw (Bearpaw Mountain Fight), ca. 15 miles S. of town on country road. In the flight of the Nez Perce, the Indians were overtaken here by troops commanded by Gen. Nelson A. Miles. A battle took place on September 30 that lasted until October 5 when the Nez Perce surrendered. "From where the sun now stands, I will fight no more forever" are the unforgettable words of Chief Joseph made here on that sad day. A registered historic place, and state monument, which includes 160 acres; two monuments are in the park. Miles escorted the 418 captives to Fort Keogh, from where they were sent to Fort Leavenworth, then to a reservation in Indian territory and 8 years later were settled on the Lapwai Colville Reservation in Idaho.

CHOTEAU, Teton County. US 89. Historical marker, 5 miles N., for Blackfeet and Buffalo country. The town is named for Pierre Chouteau, Jr., one of the family of fur traders who worked with Astor's American Fur Company. There is a Chouteau County in Montana. The town dropped the first 'u' to avoid confusion. Choteau was once headquarters for big ranches whose herds ranged far and wide.

COLUMBIA FALLS, Flathead County. US 2. A gateway to Glacier National Park.

Bad Rock Canyon, marker on highway 2 miles E. of town describes the Indian origin of the name. The Flathead River enters the valley through this canyon.

CONRAD, Pondera County. US 91.

The Whoop-Up Trail, on US 91, marker on highway. In the latter part of the 19th century, supplies brought up the Missouri River from St. Louis were transferred to wagons at Fort Benton to be transported overland to a trading post in Canada. The traders swapped booze for furs and the Canadian post soon became known as Fort Whoop-Up with the trail of the same name.

COOKE CITY, Park County (7,535 feet). US 312. Once a gold rush area with ca. $1 million panned from the streams. Descriptive highway marker on US 312, 1 mile W. Chief Joseph and his Nez Perce came this way in 1877 and burned the gold mills. Before railroads arrived in the northern mountains Cooke was the receiving point for freight shipped up the Missouri and Yellowstone Rivers. They were forwarded by stage and pack train on a trail that led through Red Lodge.

CULBERTSON, Roosevelt County. State 16.

Medicine Lake National Wildlife Refuge, ca. 24 miles N. on State 16, covers 31,458 acres. Self-guiding 18-mile trail. Headquarters 3 miles SE of Medicine Lake.

CUSTER, Yellowstone County. US 10.

Junction, historical marker on highway just E. of Custer, a frontier town now wholly a ghost except for a few graves on the hillside. Calamity Jane stayed here at one time in her free-swinging life.

CUSTER BATTLEFIELD NATIONAL MONUMENT, Big Horn County. 2 miles SE of Crow Agency. Entrance 1 mile E. of US 87. Visitor Center, museum and National Park Service personnel to interpret the most controversial military conflict of the 1870s, or perhaps of all the Indian wars, the Battle of Little Bighorn which took place June 25, 26, 1876. The Custer National Cemetery, near Visitor Center, was established in 1876. Four days after the fight, General Terry's men buried officers in shallow graves and partially covered enlisted men, with little time to do more as the conquering Sitting Bull and his Sioux and Cheyenne warriors were still at large. When a detail from Fort Keogh came back nearly a year later, many skeletons had been exposed and picked clean by prairie animals. Custer's remains were sent to West Point for reburial. A granite memorial shaft marks the mass grave of enlisted men on Custer Hill. From this point the visitor can see most of the battlefield and the valley in which the Indian village was located. Interpretive signs describe the action and locate positions.

In a detached section SE is the Reno-Benteen defense perimeter, accessible by a road leading through the Crow Indian Reservation. From Reno Hill the path of retreat may be seen. Several members of the 7th cavalry described this position as looking like a saucer with one side broken out. Major Marcus Reno faced a court of inquiry at the Palmer House in Chicago in January, 1879, requested by himself because of charges made in a then current book about Custer. The court's finding was in part "while subordinates in some instances did more for the safety of the command by brilliant display of courage than did Major Reno, there was nothing in his conduct which requires animadversion from this Court." Reno faced two court martials, one in March, 1877, and again in November, 1879, both concerned with his boozing and womanizing and not with his conduct on those fateful days in June, 1876. Historian Don Russell, who probably knows more about the Old West than anyone else alive, says: "The charges probably were worth $1 and costs in police court, but in those days an officer was supposed to be a gentleman, and apparently Reno was not." Reno was given a dishonorable discharge and after an apparently lively life was buried in what the newspapers called "a pauper's grave" in a Washington, D.C., cemetery from which many years later he was removed for reburial in the National Cemetery with full military honors and restored to full military rank. The last hearing of the Reno case far from taking place at a Chicago hotel was held in the Pentagon.

DARBY, Ravalli County. US 93.

Ross' Hole, 18 miles S. on US 93. Marker for campsite of Alexander Ross, of the Hudson's Bay Company, with 55 white and Indian trappers, 89 women and children, on March 12, 1824. The party was en route from Spokane House to the Snake River country. Ross called this the "Valley of Troubles," as they spent a month trying to break through deep snow.

Medicine Tree, S. of town on US 93, marker for the Ponderosa Pine which has stood at the bend of the river for more than 400 years. For many years the horn of a Big Horn ram was imbedded in the tree. Indians decorated it with wampum and beads believing the whole affair had medicinal properties; a story in Salish Indian lore explains how the horn got rooted: Old Man Coyote had challenged the sheep to butt down the tree. The horn is long gone but the tree is still honored.

DEBORGIA, Mineral County. US 10.

Mullan Road, 2 miles E. Marker for winter camp of Capt. John Mullan and his road-builders in 1859–1860. Congress authorized the road to connect Fort Benton on the Missouri with Fort Walla Walla on the Columbia.

DEER LODGE, Powell County. US 10A.

Grant-Kohrs Ranch, edge of town, began in 1853 and is significant in the history of the range cattle industry. John Grant, original owner, is credited with being a founder of the industry in Montana. Conrad Kohrs, who bought the ranch in the 1860s, was a cattle king. He had been a butcher boy in Bannack. The frame house, erected in 1862, still stands, with alterations made in the 1890s. Other buildings date from the 1850s and some old corrals still exist. A national historic landmark; not accessible to the public at present. The Grant family was an interesting lot. Capt. Richard Grant, said to be of Falstaffian size, was a factor of the Hudson's Bay Company, having supervised a number of trading posts including Fort Hall, Idaho. He lived in a log cabin in the upper end of the Jefferson Valley, where the Stinking Water, now the Ruby River, flows into the Beaverhead. His wife was a convent-bred daughter of Red River mixed bloods; their two sons, Johnny and James, lived in elkskin tipis nearby and these homes became the hub for what became a settlement. Cottonwood, nearby, became Deer Lodge. The Grant men accumulated their first herd of cattle by trading on the Mormon Trail between Fort Bridger and Salt Lake City. A monument stands on the site of Johnny Grant's cabin. He was the "Jonni Grant" of the "Tu grass Hop Per digins" sign; historical marker is on US 10A, 5 miles E. of town.

DILLON, Beaverhead County (5,100 feet). US 91.

Beaverhead County Museum, 15 S. Montana, Indian artifacts, mining and pioneer relics. Ca. 5,000 items.

Beaverhead National Forest, off US 91, I-15, covers 2,130,775 acres. Headquarters at Skihi St. & US 91. Bannack State Monument (which see) is in the forest. The Anaconda-Pintlar Wilderness of 157,803 acres is in the NW section of forest, SW of Anaconda.

DRUMMOND, Granite County. US 10.

Bearmouth Ghost Town, 14 miles W. via US 10, 12, across the St. Regis River, was a supply camp for many nearby camps and was a stage stop on the Mullan Road. Many old structures remain, including stage station, inn and stables.

Beartown & Other Ghost Towns: from Bearmouth on US 10 take dirt road N. up Bear Gulch 6 miles. This was once the hangout of the "Beartown Roughs." Some ruins remain. Other ghost towns in Granite County will be found near *Philipsburg,* S. just off US 10A. Philipsburg, not quite a ghost, has Victorian buildings. *Granite* is 2 miles away on a dirt and gravel road which is steep; inquire locally for conditions. The old town offers a spectacular view and has a number of old buildings nearly intact, and the ruins of a mill. *Black Pine,* ca. 1 mile N. of Philipsburg on US 10 A, take gravel road W. ca. 12 miles. Mine operators have taken over the area but some old ruins from the 19th century remain. *Southern Cross,* on border of Deer

Lodge and Granite Counties, 2 miles on dirt road off US 10A. The old town high on a hill has a fine view and several ruins. *Garnet* is 5 miles above Beartown on a hill called Chinee Grade. Many weathered pine buildings and false fronts on main street, with the 3-story Hotel Garnet still standing when last seen. But the road is recommended for dry weather only.

EAST GLACIER PARK, Glacier County. State 49, US 2. Eastern entrance to Glacier National Park in Two Medicine Valley, with the look of the Old West as Indians and cowboys trade in town.

EKALAKA, Carter County. State 7. Descriptive marker on highway 1 mile N.

Carter County Museum, in high school, has dinosaur skeletons and other exhibits including Indian and pioneer relics.

ELKHORN, Jefferson County. (5,430 ft.) On unmarked road NE of Boulder, which is on County 281, just off US 91. A ghost town with more than 30 buildings standing. A Montana mule skinner looking for lost mules at the base of Elkhorn Peak discovered rocks with silver; this drew prospectors and among them a Swiss named Peter Wys who struck the Elkhorn lode. More than $14 million in silver was mined before the boom was over. In its busiest days Elkhorn had a thoroughly mixed population of 2500; this included Danes, Cornishmen, Irish, Germans, French, Swedes and Norwegians.

ENNIS, Madison County. US 287, State 287.

Raynald's Pass (6,834 feet), 35 miles S. of town on State 287, marker on highway denotes site of the pass over the Continental Divide through which Jim Bridger guided an expedition of scientists in June, 1860. The party was led by Capt. W.F. Raynalds of the U.S. Corps of Engineers.

EUREKA, Lincoln County. US 93.

Tobacco Plains, 1 mile E. of town, historical marker on highway for plains where posts were established in the early trading days and where experiments were made in tobacco raising by the missionary priests.

FORT BELKNAP RESERVATION, Blaine County. US 2. Marker on highway 4 miles SE of Harlem for reservation which was established in 1887 for the Assiniboine and Gros Ventre Indians. An early trading post of the Northwest Fur Company had the same name and was located near present Chinook.

FORT BENTON, Chouteau County. US 87. Capt. Clark and members of the expedition camped here in June, 1805. A trading post was established by the American Fur Company in 1847 and was known as Fort Lewis. This was the eastern terminus of the Mullan Road and the head of navigation on the Missouri River. In goldstrike days of 1862 much traffic came this way.

Ruins of Old Fort Benton, on riverfront, near Main St. In 1846 the post was rebuilt of adobe and named for Sen. Thomas H. Benton. One building and parts of others remain.

Fort Benton Museum, 1800 Front St., in City Park, has dioramas and exhibits of early traffic and trading.

FORT C. F. SMITH, Big Horn County. On County 313. Established

August, 1866, on a bluff of the Big Horn River, ca. 8 miles above the mouth of Rotten Grass Creek, now on the Crow Indian Reservation, then the E. edge of Crow land. The northernmost post of three set up to protect the Bozeman Trail from the Sioux, it was so remote that not a message got through from November 30, 1866, to June, 1867. The commanding officer had resigned on January 7 but wasn't able to leave the fort for five dreary months. Mounds indicate where a row of barracks once stood.

FORT CUSTER, Big Horn County. On unimproved road, ca. 1 mile W. of I-90 and 2 miles SE of Hardin. Established July 4, 1877, on the bluff above the confluence of the Big Horn and Little Big Horn Rivers, to control the Sioux and other Indians. Originally called Big Horn Post or Big Horn Barracks, designated Fort Custer in November, 1877. A D.A.R. marker designates the site which is on the Crow Indian Reservation.

FORT PECK, Valley County. State 24. In 1871 an Indian agency was established at the fort which had been founded in 1867, near the present dam site. Later the agency was moved near Poplar. The post was active until 1893 when the Bureau of Indian

Only the ghosts are left in Elkhorn, near Boulder
(State Advertising Unit, Montana Dept. of Highways)

Affairs acquired it for use as an Indian boarding school. No original buildings remain but the site is a registered historic place.

FORT SHAW, Cascade County. State 21. Descriptive marker on highway just W. of town, for *Fort Shaw,* which was established here on the right bank of the Sun River, ca. 25 miles above its junction with the Missouri in June, 1867. Originally called Camp Reynolds, the post was ca. 5 miles above the point where the Fort Benton-Helena stage road crossed the Sun River and was intended to protect the route and the settlement southward. It also guarded miners in NW Montana. After the army gave up the fort in 1891 it became an Indian school run by the Department of the Interior. Later the buildings were acquired by the Fort Shaw school district. Some original buildings remain. The first commander of the post was Col. and Brevet Maj. Gen. Philippe Regis Denis de Keredern de Trobriand, son of a French baron; a division commander in the Civil War, De Trobriand also liked duelling, poetry and was a novelist of sorts. Published one, at least. In America he married an heiress, survived the Civil War and the marauding Indians of northern Montana to succeed to his father's title in 1874. He wrote an excellent history of his four years in the Army of the Potomac.

GALLATIN GATEWAY, Park County. US 191.

Gallatin Pioneers Museum, in the courthouse, pioneer relics, old guns, Indian items, and furnishings.

Lorene's Antique Museum, US 191, in town, has early day furniture.

GARDINER, Park County (5,287 feet). US 89. Northern entrance to Yellowstone National Park, the only approach which is open all year.

The Devils Slide, old rock formation, 5 miles NW on US 89.

Emigrant Gulch, US 89, 29 miles N. Historical marker on highway describes the route used by emigrants in August, 1864, which led to a mining strike and boom.

GARRYOWEN, Big Horn County. US 87. Marker on highway points out the area where the Battle of Little Big Horn began on June 25, 1876. "Garryowen" was the regimental marching song of the 7th U.S. Cavalry. They also favored "The Girl I Left Behind Me."

GLACIER NATIONAL PARK, Glacier County. US 2, covers 1,600 square miles. The scenery is much as it was when Meriwether Lewis saw it. The major roads are well marked. Visitor Center and exhibits at Logan Pass, which gives a spectacular view at 6,664 feet. St. Mary, US 89, also has Visitor Center and museum. 700 miles of trails.

GLASGOW, Valley County. US 2.

Pioneer Museum, US 2, Indian artifacts and pioneer photographs.

Fort Peck Dam and Reservoir, 20 miles SE on State 24, has information center, museum, and guided tours. There are fossil beds nearby.

GLENDIVE, Dawson County. US 10.

Frontier Gateway Museum, 1½ miles E. of town, has regional historical displays.

Hagen Site, 5 miles SE on secondary road, a late prehistoric lodge village believed to have been a Crow settlement. A national historic landmark.

Makoshika State Park, 3 miles S. of US 10, I-94, has fossils, eroded sandstone cliffs, with scenery of the kind emigrants saw and wrote home about.

Clark Yachting Party, US 10, 1 mile W. of town. Marker for Clark's boating experience of August 1, 1806, with six of his men, Sacajawea and her year-and-a-half-old son. Historian Donald Jackson, in a bibliographical essay on the many volumns about Lewis and Clark, and the ones by them, said: "Nobody ever managed to write anything absolutely dull about Lewis and Clark." A remark which even covers this highway sign. As Montana's "Bob" Fletcher says, the group floated past "navigating a craft made by lashing together two hollowed out cottonwood logs. It was Clark's birthday and the outfit had to land that afternoon to let a herd of buffalo swim the river ahead of them."

GREAT FALLS, Cascade County. I-15.

Charles M. Russell Museum and Studio, 1201 4th Ave. Models, watercolors, bronzes, illustrated notes and letters of the cowboy artist, in the museum. The log cabin studio has Russell memorabilia. In an age when few white men had respect, let alone liking, for Indians, Russell had both, and his feelings were evident in his paintings and sculptures. He came to the far west by railroad from St. Louis, Missouri, arrived in Corinne, Utah, then North to Red Rock in Montana Territory. At Fort Hall, Idaho, he got his first look at western Indians and found Flatheads in Helena. Early in his western life two Piegans held a gun on him, made him cook them a meal and walked out, after assuring him he was a good chef. He had many Indian friends who would often drop in at his home here and tell him how life used to be in such detail he could make his paintings authentic down to the smallest items such as the tip of a hunting lance. A national historic landmark.

Great Falls Portage, US 87, 89, and 91, SE of town, where Meriwether Lewis and a small party reached the falls of the Missouri on June 13, 1805; the first white men to see the spectacle. A national historic landmark.

Lewis and Clark National Forest, E. on US 87, 89, State 200. 1,862,018 acres, including part of the Scapegoat Wilderness and the Bob Marshall Wilderness. Headquarters in Federal Bldg., Great Falls.

Giant Springs, 4½ miles NE on the S. bank of the Missouri River, one of the world's largest fresh-water springs with a flow of 388,800,000 gallons every 24 hours. Water temperature is always at 52 degrees.

Visitor Center, 10th Ave. S. near 47 St., summer touring information.

GREYCLIFF, Sweet Grass County. US 10. Marker on highway 4 miles E. for site where the Thomas covered wagon party from Illinois was killed by Indians and buried in a mass grave by other emigrants, in 1866.

HAMILTON, Ravalli County. US 93.

Fort Owen State Monument, 20 miles N. off US in Stevensville (which see).

Bitterroot National Forest, via US 93, State 38, headquarters at 316 N. 3rd St. for the 1, 113,813 forest which includes part of the Selway-Bitterroot Wilderness, the largest in the U.S. (1,239,840 acres). and extends into Idaho; parts of the Anaconda-Pintlar Wilderness and the Salmon River Breaks Primitive Area.

Ricketts Memorial Museum, 1 miles

NW off US 93. Exhibits trace history of spotted fever research, mid-June to mid-August. Highway marker. The first fever occurred here in 1873.

Painted Rocks State Recreation Area, 20 miles S. on US 93, then 23 miles SW. on State 473, in the Bitterrot Mountains.

Sleeping Child Hot Springs, 3 miles S. on US 93, E. via State 38, then 11 miles SE. on County 501.

HAVRE, Hill County. US 87.

Fort Assiniboine, 6 miles SW on US 87, established in May, 1879, on the left bank of Beaver Creek, ca. 4 miles above its meeting with the Milk River, to prevent the return of Sitting Bull and his warriors from Canada and to control the Indians of the area, mainly Blackfeet. Though Sitting Bull never showed up either as a threat or in belated friendship, the post was an elaborate one with a large garrison. Some buildings remain though many were torn down in the careless years of the 1920s. A D.A.R. commemorative marker on the parade ground.

H. Earl Clack Memorial Museum, ½ miles W. on US 2, on county fairgrounds. Regional history exhibits, geology, archaeology.

HELENA, Lewis and Clark County. US 91. In 1864 four Georgians prospected in an area they named "Last Chance Gulch," now Helena's main street, having yielded, with surrounding area, more than $20 million in gold.

State Capitol, Lockey & Roberts Sts. The building faces the Prickly Pear Valley. The entrance is embellished by the equestrian statue of Gen. Thomas Francis Meagher, Civil War soldier and acting territorial governor, who here brandishes a bronze sword with his one time dashing style. In the entrance room to the executive suite is the painting, "Scouting for Custer," by E.S. Paxson. "Driving of the Golden Spike" mural above the grand staircase.

Montana Historical Museum & C.M.Russell Art Gallery, in Veterans-Pioneers Memorial Bldg., 225 N. Roberts St. Dioramas present Montana history, excellent Russell collection, Territory Junction is a recreation of an 1880s scene. Military History Room and Montana Historical Library are also in building.

Last Chancer Tour Train, leaves from Historical Museum to tour major historical sites of city from June 15 to Labor Day.

Governor's Old Mansion, 304 N. Ewing St. Restored, 1884, 20-room house used by 9 governors. Victorian style furnishings.

Pioneer Cabin, 208 S. Park Ave., authentic furnishings.

Gold Collection, Northwestern Bank & Union Trust Co., 350 N. Last Chance Gulch, has gold in many forms including nuggets.

Reeder's Alley, near S. end of Last Chance Gulch, once a hangout for miners, muleskinners, drifters, and Chinese laundrymen, now an artists' center.

Canyon Ferry Arms Museum, 2 miles N. of Canyon Ferry State Recreation Area, on State 284, has military displays, Indian artifacts.

Frontier Town, 13 miles W. on US 12, is a replica of early Montana village, hewn out of rock and giant trees. The Continental Divide may be seen from the grounds.

Gates of the Mountains, 16 miles N. off US 91, I-15. A 2-hour Missouri River cruise runs through a deep gorge of the Helena National Forest discovered and named by Lewis & Clark. On July 19, 1805, Lewis wrote:

". . . this evening we entered much the most remarkable cliffs that we have yet seen, these cliffs rise from the water's edge on either side perpendicularly to the hight of 1200 feet . . . the tow(er)ing and projecting rocks in many places seem ready to tumble on us . . . from the singular appearance of this place I called it the *gates of the rocky mountains.*"

Helena National Forest, surrounds town, covers 966,654 acres, with headquarters at 616 Helena Ave. Includes part of the Scapegoat Wilderness and the Gates of the Mountains Wilderness.

Fort William Henry Harrison, now a Veterans Administration Hospital, was established in 1892, garrisoned three years later with troops from Fort Assiniboine. It was part of a program for concentrating troops in large establishments, abandoning smaller, scattered posts.

Kluge House, 540 W. Main St., was built in the 1880s, half log and half timber construction in Prussian style. Emil Kluge came from Germany in 1873. Registered historic place.

Ghost towns: *Clancey,* 10 miles S. on US 91; *Alhambra,* 2 miles S. of Clancey; *Lump City,* 2 miles W. of Clancey; *Corbin,* S. on US 91 to Jefferson City then SW 2 miles W. of Clancey; *Corbin,* S. on US 91 4o Jefferson City then SW 2 miles on gravel road, old mining camp has the white-chinked log type of structure which was common to early Montana camps; *Rimini,* ca. 9 miles W. of Helena on US 10N, then via dirt road S. 7 miles, old false fronts on main street. *Wickes,* S. from Helena on US 91 to Jefferson City, then SW 4 miles on dirt sideroad, ruins of a large mill and other buildings; *Unionville,* 4 miles S. 2 roads begin at the S. end of W. Main St. and wind up Grizzly and Oro Fino Gulches, joining before reaching town. Old gold mines in the area and ruins of early stamp mill.

Site of First Strike, 6th and Fuller, plaque on building honors the gold discovery of 1864 in Last Chance Gulch.

Mullan Road, 21 miles W. on US 12, descriptive plaque tells the route of the famous road.

Prickly Pear Diggings, 6 miles S. on US 91. Marker at site with description of first camp in area.

HOBSON, Judith Basin County. US 87. Marker on highway for the Judith River where Capt. Clark had a sentimental moment in 1805 and named the waterway for a girl he'd left behind, teenager Julia Hancock who later became his first wife. Locations of Pig-eye Basin and Yogo Gulch in the Little Belt Mountains are pointed out.

HUNGRY HORSE, Flathead County. US 2.

Hungry Horse Dam and Power Plant has self-guiding tours in summer and exhibits. 4 miles SE on unnumbered road.

KALISPELL, Flathead County, US 2.

Fort Kalispell, 3 miles E. on US 2. Replica of frontier town with Indian village, many other features including stagecoach rides.

Flathead National Forest, NE & SE via US 2, 93. 2,336,400 acres include part of the Bob Marshall Wilderness, the Mission Mountains Primitive Area. Headquarters are at 290 N. Main.

KIRBY, Big Horn County. County 314.

Rosebud Battlefield, just off unimproved road ca. 9 miles SW of town.

On land which is now a private ranch, the second battle of the 1876 campaign against the Sioux and Cheyenne was fought. A monument is near the gravel road E. of battleground. Crazy Horse led some 1500 warriors to stop the advance of General Crook's 1,774 troops. Crook drove the Indians back but returned to his supply depot and base on Goose Creek to await reinforcements.

LA HOOD, Jefferson County, US 10, Lewis and Clark Campsite of August 1, 1805, is described by marker on highway. Meriwether Lewis and three others went scouting to try to find Sacajawea's people.

LAME DEER, Rosebud County. US 12. Headquarters for the Northern Cheyenne Indian Reservation, with Cheyenne crafts at tourist center.

Lame Deer Battlefield, ca. 1⅓rd miles SW of town just off unimproved road. On May 7, 1877, Col. Nelson A. Miles' troops from the Tongue River Cantonment defeated Lame Deer's band of Miniconjou Sioux here. The chief, his son, 12 warriors and 4 soldiers were killed. Battlefield, marked by historical sign, is on the creek called Lame Deer, on a privately owned ranch.

LAURIN, Madison County. (5,058 ft.) State 287.

Robbers' Roost, 2½ miles N. of town, marker on State 34, was built in 1863 by Pete Daly as a roadhouse. The two-story log building faced the stage route between Virginia City and Bannack. The bar and gambling room were on the ground floor; a dance hall took up the second story. Here and elsewhere—at Rattlesnake Ranch, Dempsey's Cotton wood Ranch, and hideaways in Bannack and Virginia City—Henry Plummer and his "Innocents" made their plans for robberies. Plummer was a sheriff by day for part of his career. At the age of 15 he had migrated from Connecticut to California via Cape Horn and was marshal of Nevada City in 1856. He shot his way to notoriety in several parts of western territory, and eventually was hanged in Bannack (which see). From Robbers' Roost the gang used to mark men and stagecoaches for plucking—using a cipher in their messages. Alder and Nevada City are nearby. At Nevada City on State 34, historical marker takes note that George Ives, notorious road agent, was the first Vigilante execution. He was a leading member of Plummer's "Innocents."

LEWISTOWN, Fergus County. US 87. First known as Reed's Fort, according to a state guide published in 1939 the town was renamed to honor a Major Lewis who established a fort nearby in 1876. Major A. S. Reed had opened the first post office in 1881. No official Fort Lewis is listed in the usual records; a Fort Lewis was erected in 1846 by John Jacob Astor's agent, Kenneth McKenzie, at the mouth of the Marias River. When this post was rebuilt it became Fort Benton. In any case, Lewiston was not named for Meriwether Lewis.

Fort Maginnis, 15 miles E. on US 87, then 10 miles N. Established in 1880 to protect settlers and stockemn, named for Major Morton Maginnis, territorial delegate to Congress. When the post was disbanded in 1890, local settlers carried off the buildings in pieces. Even so, a few ruins remain.

Maiden, marker on US 191, 10 miles N., then 6 miles E. was a mining camp, now a ghost town. Gold was found here in May, 1880, by "Skookum Joe" Anderson and several other prospectors. Over $3 million in gold was taken from Maiden. *Kendall,* 16 miles N. on US 191, then 6 miles W. on gravel is another ghost; *Gilt Edge* is 14 miles E. on US 87, then 6 miles NW. Calamity Jane was here for part of her adventurous life.

Central Montana Museum, E. Main St. Indian artifacts, dioramas of Montana history.

LIBBY, Lincoln County. US 2.

Kootenai National Forest, surrounds the town. 1,769,618 acres, includes part of Cabinet Mountains Wilderness. Giant Cedars Nature Trail. Headquarters at 418 Mineral Ave.

LIVINGSTON, Park County. US 10.

Park County Museum, 5th & Callender Sts. Old West exhibits.

Bozeman Pass (5,712 feet), 13 miles W. on US 10. Historical marker tells of Sacajawea guiding a party of the Lewis and Clark expedition over an old buffalo road and through the pass in July 1806. Another marker honoring John M. Bozeman will be found on US 10, 14 miles E. of town, and on US 10 W. city limits of Big Timber. Bozeman was killed by Piegan Indians in April, 1867, and buried near Springdale, later reburied in Bozeman.

LOGAN, Gallatin County. US 191.

Madison Buffalo Jump, 7 miles S. of town on local road to Visitor Center. Several hundred places have been found on the E. approaches to the Rocky Mountains where Indians killed bison by driving them off cliffs. Many of these are in Montana. The animals not killed by the fall were done in by arrows or lances at the bottom of the cliff. This buffalo jump is located on a 30-foot limestone bluff above the Madison River valley. The jump area includes the site of an Indian village, slaughter area, Indian trail and gravesite, as well as a lookout point. A registered historic place.

LOLO, Missoula County. US 93.

Traveler's Rest, marker on US 93, just S. of town. The Lewis and Clark party camped at the mouth of Lolo Creek on their way W. in September, 1805, and named the spot. They again camped here on their way back to the states in June and early July, 1806. Lewis set out from here with a small party to explore the country between this area and the Great Falls of the Missouri River, in order to follow President Jefferson's orders to find the shortest and best route between the Missouri and the Columbia. A national historic landmark.

Fort Fizzle, ca. 5 miles W. of town, was located where the Lolo Trail entered the Bitterroot Valley in 1877. When word of Chief Joseph and his Nez Perce on the run reached the commanding officer, Capt. Charles Rawn, he organized his small command and a group of volunteer citizens to block Joseph's way. The Indians came and went without stopping and the fort was thereafter known as Fizzle.

LOMA, Chouteau County. US 87.

Maria's River, historical marker on US 87, just S. of town. Lewis and Clark campsite of June 3, 1805. In 1806 on the return trip Capt. Lewis explored the river almost to its source. In 1831 James Kipp of the American Fur Co. built Fort Piegan at the mouth of the river, as a trading post for Blackfoot Indians.

MALTA, Phillips County. US 2.

Bowdoin National Wildlife Refuge, 8 miles NE on old US 2. 15,500 acres. Self-guiding auto trail.

Cree Crossing, marker on US 2, 15 miles E., points out site of old Indian ford for the Milk River. *Sleeping Buffalo Rock,* in same area, is also marked.

MARYSVILLE, Lewis and Clark County (5,035 feet). NW of Helena, on loop road off County 279, 356. The town, founded in the 1870s, was a great gold-producer with a population of 2,000 in 1887. Drumlummon Mine was one of the wealthiest. Several old buildings remain, including the Drumlummon mill, churches, schoolhouse and stone and brick structures.

MELROSE, Silver Bow County (5,173 feet). US 91.

The Big Hole River, 2 miles N. Marker on US 91. Named the Wisdom River by Lewis and Clark. They passed here in August 1805.

MILES CITY, Custer County. US 10. In the town's early days the S. side of Main Street was a solid block of saloons, gambling rooms and dance-halls.

Range Riders Museum & Pioneer Memorial Hall, US 10, 12, W. end of town. Displays and memorabilia of pioneer days. Geological and archaeological items.

The Huffman Pictures, 1600 Main St. in Coffrin's Old West Gallery, early days in photographs.

Fort Keogh, US 10, SW edge of town. The post on the S. bank of the Yellowstone River at the mouth of the Tongue River was known as the Tongue River Cantonment for its first year. Col. Nelson Miles founded it as a base for patrolling the Yellowstone to prevent the Cheyenne and Sioux who had defeated Custer from escaping to Canada. The U.S. Range Livestock Experiment Station occupies the site now. The superintendent lives in the residence occupied by Miles, at the W. point of the diamond-shaped parade ground. Tongue River Cantonment, 1 mile E. in a field on S. side of highway, marked by mounds of earth and one wall.

MILLTOWN, Missoula County. US 10.

Junction of the Hell Gate and Big Blackfoot Rivers, marker on highway, just W. of town. Site of an important Indian road. The Indians called the Big Blackfoot the Cokalahishit, meaning "river of the road to the buffalo." Capt. Lewis followed this road in July 1806. Capt. John Mullan had a construction camp nearby in the winter of 1861–1862, named Cantonment Wright. He was the first engineer to bridge the river.

MISSOULA, Missoula County. US 93, 10.

City-County Library, Pine & Pattee Sts., has collection of Montana and Northwest history.

Paxson Paintings, County Courthouse, 200 W. Broadway, murals depicting Montana history.

Lolo National Forest, surrounds the town. 2,076,641 acres. Lewis and Clark Highway (US 12) follows the famous route over the Bitterroot Mountains. Headquarters at 2801 Russell. Ranger stations at Huson, Plains, Superior, Thompson Falls, and Seeley Lake. The Visitor Center of the Aerial Fire Depot, 7 miles W. on US 10, I-90, Forest Service headquarters for aerial fire attack in northern area has information on 16 national forests in the region.

Fort Missoula, SW edge of town, just off US 93, was founded in 1877 on the Bitterroot River. Its garrison took part in the battle of Big Hole in August, 90 miles S. Captives were held at this fort. The stone magzine, laundresses' quarters (usually known as Suds Row), and an officers' quarters remain. Stone marker and plaque.

MOORHEAD, Powder River County. US 12.

Powder River Battlefield, ca. 4 miles NE of town on unimproved road. The river, a tributary of the Yellowstone, was named Redstone by Clark in 1805; later got its present name because the fine black sand along its banks resembles gunpowder. The opening battle in the 1876 campaign against the Sioux and Cheyennes took place here. At dawn on the 17th of March, Col. Joseph Reynolds and 6 troops of cavalry charged an Indian village. The natives fled to the bluffs and fired on the troops below. Reynolds burned most of the village, captured ponies and retreated. This setback caused Gen. George Crook, already hampered by a shortage of food and deep snow, to return to Fort Fetterman to reorganize. The battlefield is now a private ranch. The mesa and bluffs from which the Indians fired is unchanged. A marker is near the N. edge of Moorhead.

MOSBY, Garfield County. State 200.

Fort Musselshell, 1.5 miles E. of town , historical marker describes the trading post of the 1860s where River Crows and Gros Ventres Indians traded. The Assiniboines and Sioux often lay in ambush and picked off careless whites of the area. Note: the town of Musselshell is ca. 35 miles SW on US 12. Melstone (US 12) is directly S. of Mosby on a road which follows the Musselshell River. Turn W. as the river turns, follow US 12 about 5 miles for the town which was named for the old stockmen's landmark, Musselshell Crossing, where the herds of Texas longhorns driven north in the 1880s were bedded down for the last time before being separated into smaller lots for Montana ranches. The crossing, established in 1877 on the N. bank of the river. opposite the present town, was on a trail used for travel between Fort Custer and Fort Maginnis.

PARK CITY, Stillwater County. US 10.

Captain Clark Campsite, highway marker at site, 2 miles NE on highway. Clark was here from July 19, 1806, until July 24. The party used cottonwoods nearby to make canoes, which were lashed together with buffalo hides. From here the seven men of the group, Sacajawea and her baby, went downriver arriving at the mouth of the Yellowstone August 3rd.

PRYOR, Big Horn County. State 416.

Chief Plenty Coups Memorial, 1 mile W. off State 416. The chief was a Crow Indian who did much to aid friendly relations with the white men. He was born near Billings in 1848 and lived till the 1930s. He served with Gen. George Crook as a scout and took active part in his tribal affairs while running a store on the reservation. The memorial is on the site of his former farm. The two-story log house was his home. Plenty Coups and two of his wives are buried here. A registered historic place.

RED LODGE, Carbon County (5,548 feet). US 212.

Beartooth Scenic Highway, US 212, from Red Lodge to the NE. entrance of Yellowstone National Park rises to 10,942 feet. Usually open from end of May through September. Panoramic views all the way.

Big Sky Historical Museum, S. on US 212, western weapons, Indian artifacts.

Red Lodge Zoo, 1 mile S. on US 212, has Montana animals and birds and a prairie dog town. More than 200 kinds of native wildlife.

ROSEBUD, Rosebud County. US 10. Descriptive marker on highway 2 miles W. of town. Capt. Clark made note of the stream in his journal for July 28, 1806, when he was descending the Yellowstone. In June, 1876, Generals Gibbon and Custer met here to confer aboard the steamer "Far West" (which in a short time would carry the wounded to Fort Lincoln, N.D., after the massacre at Little Bighorn, under pilot Captain Grant Marsh, one of the great river pilots of all time).

RONAN, Lake County. US 93.

National Bison Range, SW via US 93 and County 212, entrance at Moiese. Great herds of buffalo, elk, antelope, deer and mountain sheep are on the 18,540-acre range. Self-guided tours in summer months. Visitors must remain on the tour road (19 miles), in or near their cars.

Ninepipe and Pablo National Wildlife Refuges, 7 miles S. and ca. 9 miles N., have a combined area of 4,500 acres.

St. Ignatius Mission, ca. 15 miles S. on US 93, SW edge of the town of St. Ignatius, was established in 1855 by Father Adrien Hoeken, to carry out terms of a treaty by which the government provided the Flathead Indians with schools, mills, and blacksmith and carpenter shops, in return for ceded lands. Some original structures remain. Dry-fresco murals.

Fort Connah, US 93, S. of Ronan, ca. 6 miles N. of St. Ignatius, highway marker at site of the last Hudson's Bay Company trading post established within the present borders of the U.S. Built in 1847, it remained in operation until 1872.

SIDNEY, Richland County. State 200.

J. K. Ralston Museum, 221 5th St. SW. Scale model of Fort Union and other exhibits pertaining to Montana frontier days.

Old Fort Gilbert, on highway 5 miles N. of town, marker denotes site of the 1864 fort, used as a trading center in the lower Yellowstone Valley. This point was also the S. boundary of the Fort Buford Military Reservation. A side road just N. and W. leads to Fort Gilbert Lookout Point on the bluffs which affords an excellent view of the Yellowstone Valley.

STEVENSVILLE, Ravalli County. US 93.

Fort Owen, ca. ½ mile NW of town, was never an official post but a trading center established by John Owen in 1850. Archaeological investigations have located the foundations of the fort's walls and other structures. A state historic monument.

St. Mary's Mission and Church, North Ave., was built in 1867 and still functions. The log church is the oldest mission in the Northwest. A museum houses historical items related to its work. Father Pierre Jean De Smet was here in 1840 and returned the following year to found a mission in Bitter Root (now Bitterroot) Valley. The first St. Mary's mission prospered for a time under Father Anthony Ravalli but had to be closed when traders incited drunken Indians against the priests who were trying to keep peace. The mission church shelters many art objects sculptured by the courageous and talented Father Ravalli; he was skilled in medicine as well as art and the practical matters of forging farm tools and repairing broken ones. When the first mission had to close Ravalli served elsewhere but returned to erect the present church. He served here until his death in 1884 and is buried in the cemetery behind the church.

THOMPSON FALLS, Sanders County. US 10A. Marker on highway 2 miles E. describes the area. The falls were named for David Thompson, explorer for the North West Company, who built a trading post opposite the mouth of Prospect Creek in 1809.

THREE FORKS, Gallatin County. US 10.

Missouri River Headwaters State Monument, 3 miles E., then 3 miles N. of US 10 at Trident Junction. Discovered July 27, 1805, by the Lewis and Clark party, who named the Madison, Gallatin and Jefferson Rivers which join here. An overlook building at site. A national historic landmark.

TOWNSEND, Broadwater County. US 12. Three runaway Confederate soldiers who hit a pay streak here in the fall of 1864 called the site Confederate Gulch. Marker on highway, 8 miles W. of town. Lewis and Clark came up the Missouri River through this valley in July, 1805.

Diamond City, Meagher County, 23 miles NE of Townsend, on unpaved road. The mining camp at the head of Confederate Gulch in the Big Belt Mountains produced $10 million in gold. The town grew from a few cabins to a population of 10,000; by 1870 it was all over and only 64 persons remained by 1871. A few foundations are still here.

TWIN BRIDGES, Madison County. State 41. Descriptive marker on highway 5 miles N. of town for Lewis and Clark route of August 1805, looking for the Shoshones, Sacajawea's tribe. Clark came this way again on the return trip in 1806.

Beaverhead Rock, ca. 12 miles SW of Twin Bridges; the Beaverhead River curves around rock's base. Old town of Blaine is opposite rock, across river. On August 8, 1805, Sacajawea saw the rock and recognized it as a landmark near the summer camp of her people. Soon afterwards Lewis and Clark met the Shoshones and got horses which were essential to their crossing the Bitterroot Mountains. A registered historic place.

VIRGINIA CITY, Madison County (5,822 feet). State 34.

Thompson-Hickman Memorial Museum, Wallace St. Gold camp relics.

Virginia City-Madison County Historical Museum, Wallace St. Montana relics.

Rank's Drug Store Museum, 211 Wallace St. A 19th-century drugstore in basement of present store is now a museum.

Boot Hill, five Plummer gang road agents who were hanged by vigilantes are buried here in a row. The hangings of George Lane, Boone Helm, Frank Parrish, Haze Lyons and Jack Gallagher took place at Wallace and Van Buren Sts. on January 14, 1864.

Bale of Hay Saloon is still operating

with one of the oldest backbars in Montana. Stereopticon slide shows and mechanical music makers are added features.

Virginia City Historic District, Wallace St., includes most of the area once known as Alder Gulch where gold was found in 1863; from 1865 to 1875 this was the territorial capital. The vigilantes here were formed to get rid of the much-traveled Henry Plummer and his gang, and hanged several of them. Among reconstructed buildings are the territorial capital and the *Montana Post* building, a brewery, Wells-Fargo Express office, livery stable, barbershop, and a general store. A national historic landmark.

Nevada City, just W. on State 287, has a railroad museum and many replicas of early stores, homes, school, etc.

WEST YELLOWSTONE, Gallatin County (6,665 feet). US 191.

Targhee Pass, (7,075 feet), 9 miles W., across the Continental Divide, is named for an early Bannack chief. Chief Joseph led his Nez Perce through the pass in 1877 while pursued by Gen. O. O. Howard's forces.

WHITEHALL, Jefferson County. I-90. Historical marker on US 10, 6 miles E. of town for route of Lewis and Clark in August, 1805. In August 1840, Father Pierre Jean De Smet, camped near the mouth of the Boulder River with the Flathead Indians and celebrated Mass.

WHITE SULPHUR SPRINGS, Meagher County (5,200 feet). US 89.

The Castle, on US 12, 89, 310 Second Ave. NE, was built in 1892. Period furnishings.

Castle Ghost Town, 6 miles E. on US 12, then 15 miles S. on unimproved road. Calamity Jane lived here for a time. Some old buildings remain. Check locally for road conditions before trying the last several miles. The route is rougher than Calamity on her worst days.

Fort Logan, ca. 17 miles NW. Camp Baker-Fort Logan was established in 1869 and served as the main base for protecting the freight route from Fort Benton. The original blockhouse remains but is not in its original location. A registered historic place. Named for Capt. William Logan, killed in the Battle of Big Hole, August 9, 1877.

WIBAUX, Wibaux County. US 10. Historical marker on highway 4 miles E. of town. Pierre Wibaux ran one of the biggest spreads in Montana. His will provided for a statue of himself which now overlooks the land 1 mile W. of town. The town, on the banks of Beaver Creek, was a really wild western frontier settlement where cowhands gathered for end-of-the trail sprees that often involved shooting up the ceilings or worse. Wibaux's cattle were wiped out in the blizzards of 1886–87 but he managed to get help from France and made it rich again.

WILSALL, Park County (5,048 feet). US 89.

Shields River Valley, marker on highway 3 miles S. Capt. Clark named the river for John Shields of the expedition. The party camped here in July, 1806. Jim Bridger took this route in the 1860s when guiding emigrant wagon trains.

WOLF POINT, Roosevelt County. US 2.

Wolf Point Historical Society Museum, 220 S. 2nd Ave. Ranching, relics, weapons and Indian items.

Lewis and Clark, marker on US 2, 1.3 miles W. of town. The expedition passed here in 1805.

YELLOWSTONE NATIONAL PARK, Park County. US 89. Most of the 3,472-acre park established in 1872 is in Wyoming but a portion is in Montana. The Absaroka Primitive Area is just N. of the park.

Nevada City, one of the great Gold Rush towns
(Travel Promotion Unit, Montana Dept. of Highways)

NEBRASKA

The homesteader got most of his outside items through mail order catalogues, including, sometimes, his wife, if one could call the matrimonial papers, the heart-and-hand publications, catalogues. They did describe the offerings rather fully but with, perhaps, a little less honesty than Montgomery Ward or Sears Roebuck. Unmarried women were always scarce in new regions. Many bachelor settlers had a sweetheart back east or in the Old Country, or someone who began to look a little like a sweetheart from the distance of a government claim that got more and more lonesome as the holes in the socks got bigger. . . . But many bachelors had no sweetheart to come out, and some of these started to carry the heart-and-hand papers around until the pictures of the possible brides were worn off the page. In those days the usual purpose really was marriage, not luring the lonely out of their pitiful little savings, or even their lives. 'We married everything that got off the railroad,' old homesteaders, including my father, used to say.

Mari Sandoz, *Sandhill Sundays and Other Recollections* (Lincoln: 1970)

Farewell to my homestead shanty;
  I have my final proof;
The cattle will hook down the walls,
  And someone will steal off the roof. . . .
Farewell to my tea and my crackers;
  Farewell to my water and soap;
Farewell to my sorghum and buckwheat;
  Farewell to lallacadope.

Anonymous, "Farewell to My Homestead Shanty"

I taught school in the Predmore district and earned enough money to build a photograph gallery 18 by 28 feet, made as follows: We placed six-inch fencing boards up edgewise every two feet, then lathed them both sides, piled clay up around a post, caught a couple of steers, walked them round and round on the clay, adding water until the mud was mixed to the proper consistency, after which we filled in between the laths, making a wall six inches thick. The building was roofed with sheeting. . . . I borrowed some money to get my photographic apparatus together and was soon prepared to take tintypes. The next move was to manufacture a background from an old wagon cover that had several holes gnawed in it by the rats. . . . Finding a couple of coiled wire bed springs, we fastened them to the ceiling, hung the background on them, set them in motion, which blurred the patches so that they were not visible in the picture. Such an outfit! —dirt floor, cloth windows, and an old wagon cover for a background—it made us sick at heart. We often wondered what some of our stylish friends back east would think if they should peep in and see us.

Solomon D. Butcher,
Pioneer History of Custer County, Nebraska

NEBRASKA FACTS: The land was acquired by the Louisiana Purchase of 1803. French and Spanish explorers came briefly; Lewis and Clark camped on bluffs above what is now Omaha and held the first council between representatives of the U.S. and Nebraska Indians. Zebulon Pike and Maj. Stephen Long came on explorations. The Missouri River was a highway for fur traders, trappers, and emigrants. Peter Sarpy set up a trading post. Manuel Lisa, John C. Frémont, Kit Carson, Capt. William Drummond Stewart, Prince Maximilian, Jim Bridger, Alfred Bierstadt—all the adventurers of the pioneer days sought the regions of the Upper Missouri River. The Mormons migrated across the state and were nearly lost in the winter of 1846; '49ers and others took the Oregon Trail. It has been estimated that more than 350,000 persons crossed the state in covered wagons. Territorial status was gained in 1854. The Union Pacific came in the 1860s. Nebraska entered the Union on March 1, 1867, the 37th state. Capital: Lincoln. Nickname: Cornhusker.
Nebraska comes from the Omaha Indian word *nibthaska,* meaning "flat water." Nebraska has three national monuments: Scotts Bluff, Homestead and Agate

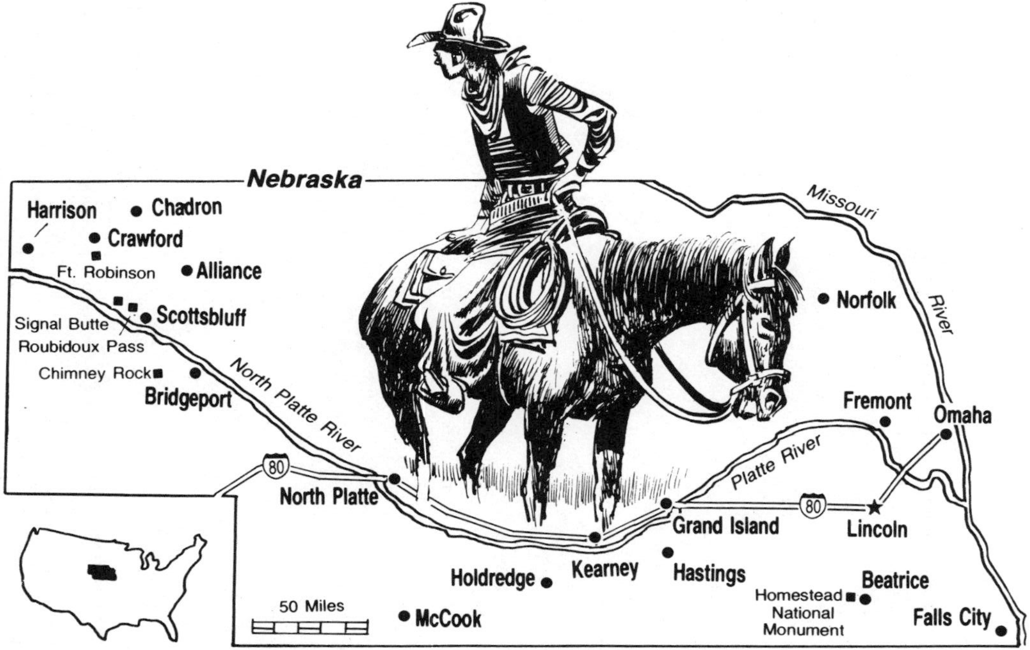
Nebraska
Harrison
Chadron
Crawford
Ft. Robinson
Alliance
Signal Butte
Roubidoux Pass
Scottsbluff
Chimney Rock
Bridgeport
North Platte River
80
North Platte
Missouri
River
Norfolk
Fremont
Omaha
Platte River
80
Lincoln
Grand Island
Kearney
Hastings
Holdredge
McCook
50 Miles
Homestead
National
Monument
Beatrice
Falls City

Fossil Beds; Chimney Rock National Historic Site, Oglala National Grassland and a national forest divided into three sections.

Chief Tribes. Omaha, Oto, Ponca, Pawnee, Cheyenne, Dakota (Sioux), Arapaho.

AGATE FOSSIL BEDS NATIONAL MONUMENT, Sioux County, State 29, has a visitor center with fossil remains of mammals that inhabited the area 20 million years ago. In the 1,970-acre area are other concentrations of well-preserved fossils of mammals that occupied the Great Plains between 13 and 25 million years ago. The monument is named for the bed of blue agate nearby. Self-guiding trails for the outdoor natural museum, much of which is covered with prairie grasses and wildflowers such as the first settlers found.

ASH HOLLOW STATE HISTORICAL PARK, Garden County. US 26.

Fort Grattan, at the mouth of Ash Hollow on the North Platte River, was a sod fort built in 1855, named in honor of Lt. John Grattan, killed by the Sioux near Fort Laramie when he tried to retrieve a stolen cow for a Mormon.

Ash Hollow Cave, 2 miles SE of Lewellen, is a rock shelter which was occupied by prehistoric hunting parties for more than 3,500 years. A national historic landmark, not accessible at this time.

Old Graveyard, at mouth of Ash Hollow. Marker describes the old trail. Near here was a popular camping place on the Oregon Trail, often mentioned in early journals of travelers who usually had trouble getting their wagons down the hill. The grave of Rachel E. Pattison, who was shot by Indians here on June 19, 1849, while traveling with a wagon train headed for Oregon, has been marked. The original small headstone has been incorporated into the memorial placed at the grave by the American Legion. Joe Clary, also buried here, was the first settler in the Hollow. His cabin stood half a mile below the crest of the hill.

Battle of Blue Creek, just N. of US 26 from the point where the highway crosses the creek immediately W. of Lewellen. Troops under Gen. Harney defeated the Sioux here in 1855. Several Oregon Trail markers on highway.

BELLEVUE, Sarpy County. US 73, 75. Established as a trading post by John Jacob Astor's American Fur Co. ca. 1820, Bellevue is the oldest continuous settlement in Nebraska.

Sarpy County Historical Society, 1805 Hancock, in log cabin believed to have been built about 1835; moved from its original site and furnished with pioneer items.

Hamilton House, 2003 Bluff St., was the home of Rev. William Hamilton, from 1856 to 1867. He came to Nebraska in 1853 to direct the Presbyterian Indian Mission at Bellevue.

Fontanelle Bank, 2212 Main St., was built in 1856. After failing as a wildcat bank in the 1857 panic, the building was used as the county courthouse from 1861 to 1875; then became the

Upper gardens, Arbor Lodge
(Nebraska State Historical Society, Lincoln)

town hall for nearly 80 years. Marker on lawn.

Presbyterian Church, 2002 Franklin St., is believed to be the oldest in Nebraska still used for religious services. Built in 1856–58.

Fontenelle Forest Nature Center, between Bellevue and the Missouri River at 1111 Bellevue Blvd., has displays of regional habitats.

Astorian Expedition Monument, on Elk Hill, commemorates the expedition of June 23, 1810, organized by Astor's American Fur Co. The plaque gives the group credit for discovering the Oregon Trail in Nebraska, but the trail in this area was not the Oregon.

Merrill Mission, US 75 at intersection with road to Papillion, 2 miles from town. Marker for site where the first permanent white settlement and the Moses Merrill Baptist mission were located. Rev. Moses Merrill was sent by the Baptists in 1833 to teach the Otoes. With his wife he erected a house that combined school, church and home. He kept a diary until his death in 1841. The stone chimney stands under a group of cottonwoods.

Mormon Hollow, N. of town beyond the pioneer cemetery, is the place where a detachment of the Mormon migration spent the winter of 1847.

Chief Big Elk Burial Site, near entrance of Clarke Hall, at the former Bellevue College. The chief of the Omaha tribe who owned lands here signed a "Peace and Friendship" agreement in 1815 with the explorer Manuel Lisa as a witness. The lands were ceded to the United States in 1854 in a treaty signed by Logan Fontenelle, Joseph LaFleshe and other Omaha chieftains and by George W. Moneypenney, Commissioner of Indian Affairs. The hill above town was called Elk Hill because the chief and his family were buried there. The bodies were disturbed during excavation for the college and reburied near the entrance. The college closed in 1917.

Logan Fontenelle Burial Site, marker at intersection of Svoboda Rd. and Bellevue Blvd., left-hand side of road points the way to the site which also is marked. Fontenelle was the last chief of the Omahas, from 1825–55, and was influential in establishing peace with the U.S.

BIG SPRINGS, Deuel County. US 138. On a night in September 1877 six bandits dressed as cowboys rode into the town which consisted of a little wooden depot with a water tank, section house, and two other dwellings. The station agent who was also the telegrapher was waiting for the eastbound express when he was surrounded by the Sam Bass gang and forced to flag down the train which they robbed with spectacular success, though not without a few hitches. The Wells-Fargo messenger in the baggage car was unable to open the safe which contained $200,000; it had a time lock set in San Francisco to be opened in Omaha. They banged him about but gave up on the safe, found $1,600 in silver ingots, decided these were too heavy to carry and then noticed three small heavy boxes which contained $20 gold pieces fresh from the San Francisco mint. Each box held $20,000 but they still took time to rob the passengers. A Texas cattleman managed to hide a roll of $3,100, another man threw his wallet and watch on the floor where they went unnoticed. The gang did not bother any women passengers and some male passengers hid their valuables in nearby workbaskets and handbags. One fellow got his money back when

Bass saw that he had only one arm. A reward of $10,000 was offered for their capture but they took their time leaving the country and camped overnight at their headquarters in Ogallala. Bass reckoned there was no hurry—the James boys already were being blamed for the stickup. After the gang parted ways, four were captured and dead within a year. Sam Bass survived—to die in another robbery on his 27th birthday, July 21, 1878. He is buried in Round Rock, Texas.

Pony Express Monument, just outside of town, marks the site of the South Platte Station.

BLAIR, Washington County. US 73.

Territorial Military Trail, US 30 at SW edge of town, marker for the old trail between Omaha and Decatur established by the government in 1855.

De Soto National Wildlife Refuge, across the river at Missouri Valley, Iowa, has relics salvaged by the National Park Service from the steamboat *Bertrand* which sank April 1, 1865, en route to Fort Benton. Steamboat traffic reached a peak shortly after mid-century when the major Colorado gold rush was over and the Civil War was on, with more railroads coming into service. The sternwheeler *Bertrand* was one of the largest to ply the river north of the Platte. She apparently struck a snag north of Omaha and sank with a cargo of mercury destined for the mining operations in the Dakotas or Montana. The wreck was located near the Iowa border by the use of metal detectors.

BRIDGEPORT, Morrill County. US 26, 385.

Pioneer Trails Museum, 205 Railroad Ave., on US 385.

Mud Springs Station, State 19, ca. 15 miles SW, marker at site of old stage and pony express stop which was attacked by Indians in February 1865.

Oregon Trail Markers, on US 26 and in town. At a site on US 26 between here and Broadwater the reverse side of marker carries an inscription which once marked the prairie grave of Amanda Lamin, who died of cholera in June 1850; she was 28, the wife of M. J. Lamin of Devonshire, England.

Camp Clarke Bridge Site, US 26S, W. of town, monument marks site of crossing on the Sidney–Black Hills trail which was defended by a blockhouse.

BROKEN BOW, Custer County. State 70, 21.

Custer County Historical Society Museum, 1138 N. C St.

Haumont House, Rural Route 3, NE of town, was a two-story sod belonging to Isadore Haumont. It was built in the 1880s and has been neglected, although it is a registered historic place.

BROWNVILLE HISTORIC DISTRICT, Nemaha County. US 136. The town was settled by Richard Brown in 1854 and became a major steamboat landing, river crossing, freighting and milling center. Most of the buildings in the historic district are from the 1855–75 period. The area is bounded by the river on the E., Allen and Richard Sts. S. 7th St. W., and Nemaha and Nebraska Sts. N. The Methodist Church was built in 1859, the Brown–Carson House, 1860, the Furnas House, ca. 1868, the Muir House, 1868–72, and the Bailey House, 1877. Legend has it that Jesse James used to play poker at the Lone Tree Saloon. The town has been restored by the Brownville Historical

Society which maintains the museum. The *Belle of Brownville* excursion boat offers river cruises on weekends in summer months.

BRULE, Keith County. US 30.

Diamond Springs Stage Station, 1 mile W. of Brule exit on I–80. Built by the freighting firm of Russell, Majors & Waddell, the stop was used by the Pony Express, and the Overland Stage, after the telegraph made the earlier line obsolete. An Indian raid of 1865 put it out of business. A registered historic place.

CALIFORNIA OVERLAND TRAIL, Hall County. Markers on county line of Hall and Merrick counties, ½ miles S. of US 30, on US 281, 18 miles S. of US 30, and on N. side of Platte River near Shelton.

CHADRON, Dawes County. US 20, 385. This was the starting place of a newsmaking 1,000-mile horse race to Chicago in 1893. Nine starters included Doc Middleton, a former outlaw, but John Berry beat everyone else to the door of Buffalo Bill's Wild West Show at the World's Columbian Exposition in 13 days and 16 hours. The Humane Society kept a humane eye on the horses all the way.

Museum of the Fur Trade, 4 miles E. on US 20. History of the trade from 1600 to 1900 in displays; Indian and weapon exhibits, restored trading post, a storehouse used by French trader James Bordeaux, a garden of

Chimney Rock
(Nebraska State Historical Society, Lincoln)

crops of the early period is an unusual added feature.

CHIMNEY ROCK, Morrill County. 16 miles W. of Bridgeport off US 26, State 92. A landmark of the West which rises 500 feet above the S. bank of the North Platte River provided a moral boost for tired travelers headed for Oregon; even though much rougher terrain lay ahead the dreariness of the prairies was behind them. The Rock appeared in nearly all journals, letters, and sketches of those who came this way and left a record. The 80-acre site is administered by the national park service. A roadside park just N. of the formation provides a good lookout.

COTESFIELD, Howard County. State 11.

Coufal Site, 6 miles NW on Davis Creek, is a major village of the central Plains Indian culture, where 22 houses were excavated and more than 17,000 specimens collected. A national historic landmark not accessible to the public at present.

COZAD, Dawson County. US 30.

Platte River Museum, 203 E. 6th St., has materials excavated from the Platte River area and from Wyoming sites.

CRAWFORD, Dawes County. US 20.

Fort Robinson, 3 miles W. on US 20, now in state park. Established March 8, 1874, on the White River near Soldier Creek, the post was a center for control of Indians at the Red Cloud Agency and the Pine Ridge Agency. Chief Crazy Horse, the great leader of the Oglala Sioux, was killed here in September 1877. He came to the fort reluctantly for a talk with authorities; when he was taken to the guardhouse he saw that he had been tricked, drew a knife and struck out at his captors. He was fatally wounded by a soldier's bayonet while an Indian held his arms. Touch-in-the-Clouds, who was 7 feet tall, carried Crazy Horse into the adjutant's office where he died. The post surgeon had administered a painkiller but only two Indians were with him at the end. Later his parents removed the body in a wooden coffin to the Spotted Tail Agency, which was soon to be vacated as the Indians were being removed to Missouri. His parents, with the chief's body on a travois, broke away from the main group and managed to bury him privately, wrapped in a buffalo robe, somewhere beyond Pine Ridge, South Dakota, in the valley of Wounded Knee Creek. Like Cochise in Arizona, Crazy Horse lies hidden in the Dakotas. The fortsite is now a national historic landmark; the adjutant's office and guardhouse have been reconstructed. Many original buildings remain and a fine museum is in the original post headquarters. Another tragedy occurred at this fort in 1879 when the sad remnants of Cheyennes under Chief Dull Knife, who had escaped from an Oklahoma reservation, chose to die here rather than be returned to the area where many of their families had died of disease. They died against the bluffs behind the fort, fighting the soldiers, after the Army had telegraphed they were to be marched south immediately.

Nebraska National Forest, Pine Ridge Division, 8 miles S. on State 2.

Crazy Horse Museum, in Crawford City Park, end of W. Main St. Pioneer and Indian relics.

Sidney-Black Hills Trail, State 2, 17 miles S. of Crawford. Descriptive marker on highway for the 1870s trail.

DAKOTA CITY, Dakota County. US 73.

Emmanuel Lutheran Church, 1500 Hickory St., was built in 1860. The bell, cast in 1856, is original. An historical American building.

FAIRBURY, Jefferson County. US 136, State 15.

Jefferson County Historical Society Museum, 701 F. St.

Whiskey Springs and Virginia Stage Station, ca. 5 miles N. and ¾ miles W. of town, a sandstone marker in a granite rock with bronze plaque notes the burial site of George Winslow of Newton, Massachusettes, who died of cholera at this point in his travels toward Oregon in June 1849. The springs and stage station were 1¼ miles to the SE.

Homestead Cabin, in City Park, was the home of Edward Hawkes in 1864. Moved from original site.

Fremont and Kit Carson Names, in Quivera Park, ca. 7 miles SW on the P.W.F. highway, in sandstone, are still legible. They were carved in June 1842, when the expedition camped here. Facsimile on a D.A.R. plaque.

Site of Rock Creek Station, ca. 2 miles due E. of Quivera Park. The much-disputed shooting of David McCanles by Wild Bill Hickok occurred near a well, which is to be found in replica on the W. side of the county courthouse in Fairbury, unless souvenir hunters have made off with it. County markers, as well as many books, misspell the victim's name.

FORT CALHOUN, Washington County. US 73.

Fort Atkinson, 1 mile E., was one of a line of forts guarding the western frontier in the 1820s, and was a center of the fur trade. In 1819 Col. Henry Atkinson and his troops of the 6th Infantry had constructed Cantonment, Missouri, at the river bottom near the bluffs which had been visited by Lewis and Clark early in the century and recommended as a trading post. After a winter of disease and summer floods, they moved to the top of the bluffs. The fort operated as a social center as well as a garrison. It sheltered a number of travelers, teamsters, Indians, trappers, hunters and even Prince Paul, Duke of Württemberg, who liked the cabbage, beans, onions and melons he found in the gardens in 1822. The site is a national historic landmark, though few remains are visible. Archaeological excavations have produced many artifacts and exposed building foundations. The Fort Calhoun Museum has a number of these relics on display.

Lewis and Clark Boulder, in village park, said to be the earliest monument erected in the state to mark a historic spot and the spot marked is the site of the first council of the U.S. with Indians west of the Missouri River.

FORT HARTSUFF, Valley County. State 11. The post on North Loup River was intended to protect settlers in the Northern Loup Valley and the Pawnee Indian Reservation, now in Nance County, from the raiding Sioux.

A number of buildings are being restored. The fort was constructed in 1874, the year of the grasshopper invasion which proved worse than the Sioux, who never made the threatened attack. Settlers who had lost their crops to the insects were happy to have government jobs building the post.

FORT MCPHERSON, Lincoln County. State 107. The post on the S. side of the Platte River was built to protect emigrants and stage coaches on the Oregon Trail in 1863. First named Cantonment or Fort McKean, then Fort Cottonwood, it became Fort McPherson in 1866 for the Union Major General who lost his life at the Battle of Atlanta in July 1864. The Grand Duke Alexis of Russia, escorted by Buffalo Bill, accompanied by Gen. Sheridan and Gen. Custer, and a hundred Indians, visited here in 1872, in a great and much publicized hunting expedition. The fort also served as headquarters for Maj. Frank North and his Pawnee Scouts who never quite got used to their uniforms and were famous for wearing nothing but breech-clouts during battle and often cut the seats out of their pants so they could ride better. A marble shaft occupies the site of the camp's flagstaff. A lonely marble soldier stands fenced in, a tribute to the Iowa 7th Cavalry. A pony express marker is nearby. The National Cemetery is a half mile W. on State 107.

FREMONT, Dodge County. US 30.

Dodge County Historical Museum, Bell St. at 14th.

Townsite and California Rd. marker in Masonic Park, Broad St. and US 30.

FULLERTON, Nance County. State 14, 22

Pawnee Memorial, at entrance to county courthouse, a granite boulder honors the Pawnee Confederation which ceded lands to the United States in 1857. The four tribes, Skidi, Tshaivi, Litkwhaki and Pitahawirat, were removed to Indian Territory in 1873–75.

GENOA, Nance County. State 39.

Genoa Site, 1 mile S. of town on State 39, represents three villages occupied by the Pawnees under Chief Pitalesharo in the 1860s. In ten years from 1862 more than a thousand tribesmen had died of a population of 3,400, from fighting or starvation. From this area the North brothers recruited their famous Pawnee scouts. A registered historic site.

GERING, Scottsbluff County. State 92.

North Platte Valley Museum, 1349 10th St., has a reconstructed sod house and log cabin as well as many relics.

Fort John, 9 miles SW in Helvas Canyon, marker at site of trading post established by the American Fur Co. in 1850. It had a number of distinguished visitors including Jesuit Father DeSmet and Prince Paul of Württemberg.

GOTHENBURG, Dawson County. US 30, State 47.

Pony Express Station, on State 47 in Ehmen Park, was the Midway Station, one of 36 stops and the least altered of three remaining. Midway was halfway between Atchison, Kansas and Denver. Later it was used by the Overland Stage. Memorabilia.

GRAND ISLAND, Hall County. I-80.

Stuhr Museum of the Prairie Pioneer, 3 miles N. at junction of US 34, 281. A two-story museum, designed by Edward D. Stone, is on an island reached by a causeway in an 800-foot artificial lake. It has more than 30,000 items pertaining to pioneer life. The outdoor museum began with 12 historic buildings from the surrounding countryside which were arranged along a meandering stream starting with an Indian village and ending with a 19th-century small town and an operating horse-drawn farm.

GUIDE ROCK, Webster County. State 78.

Pike Pawnee Village Site, 4 miles SW, is believed to be the site of Kitkehahki where Zebulon Pike raised the American flag in 1806, ending Spanish authority in Nebraska. There is archaeological evidence to support the belief. Among artifacts uncovered were a Spanish peace medal from 1797, an American one of the 1800s and a military button bearing the battalion number of Pike's infantry. A national historic landmark, not accessible to the public at present. (Also see Republic, Kansas.)

A letter written by Zebulon Pike to Henry Dearborn from the Pawnee Republic, October 1, 1806, complained that the Osage escort had led his party miles out of the way because of their fear of the Kansas Indians: ". . . In my opinion not less than 100 miles; this was entirely owing to the pusillanimity of the Osage, who were more afraid of the Kans, than I could possibly have imagined." There has long been a dispute as to where the village Pike reached is located. Both Kansas and Nebraska have interesting sites. In 1901 Kansas erected a monument on their "village," but later historians tend to support Nebraska's claim. Because Zebulon Pike raised the American flag in the village and took down the Spanish colors, the site is of more than usual importance. In his journal for September 29, a Monday, he recorded:

> . . . The Spaniards had left several of their flags in this village; one of which was unfurled at the chief's door the day of the grand council, . . . amongst various *demands* and *charges* I gave them, was, that the said flag should be delivered to me, and one of the United States' flags be received and hoisted in its place. This probably was carrying the pride of nations a little too far, as there had so lately been a large force of Spanish cavalry at the village, which had made a great impression on the minds of the young men, as to their power, consequence, & c. which my appearance with 20 infantry was by no means calculated to remove. After the chiefs had replied to various parts of my discourse, but were silent as to the flag, I again reiterated the demand for the flag, adding that "it was impossible for the nation to have two fathers; that they must either be the children of the Spaniards or acknowledge their American father." After a silence of some time, an old man rose, went to the door, and took down the Spanish flag, and brought it and laid it at my feet. . . .

Pike, diplomatically, before leaving the village gave them back the Spanish colors in case the Spaniards might return in force. Said Pike on that day long ago: "I did not wish to embarass them with the Spaniards, for it was the wish of the Americans that their red brethren should remain peaceably round their own fires, and not embroil themselves in any disputes between the white people. . . ."

HASTINGS, Adams County. US 6, 34.

Hastings Museum, 1330 N. Burlington Ave., natural history, Indian and pioneer displays, sod house, country store, farm vehicles and weapons.

First Well and House, 1218 W. 2nd St., low stone marker with descriptive plaque.

32-Mile Station, 4 miles S. and 4 miles W. on Oregon Trail and 32-Mile Creek. A stopping place which offered the last running water on the trail before reaching the Platte River.

HAYES CENTER, Hayes County. State 25.

Duke Alexis Campground, ca. 10 miles NW of town, marker at site where Duke Alexis of Russia and his hunting party of 1872 camped. The grand affair was sponsored by Buffalo Bill Cody, Gen. Sherman, Gen. Custer, Capt. Hays and Capt. Egan, with Spotted Tail and Tribe and "other noted buffalo hunters" as guests.

HOLDREGE, Phelps County. US 183, State 23.

Phelps County Historical Society Museum, 512 East Ave. Early farm equipment, Indian tools and pottery, period rooms.

HOMESTEAD NATIONAL MONUMENT, Gage County. 4 miles NW of Beatrice, off State 4. One of the first areas settled under the Homestead Act of 1862; 160 acres, a quarter section went for a nominal fee to anyone who would live on it and farm it for five years. The government made 120 million acres available to landseekers. Daniel Freeman, an Illinois farmer, filed this claim when he was on furlough during the Civil War. Visitor Center has pioneer tools and interpretive displays. A log cabin is furnished in style typical of the period. A self-guiding trail passes the Freeman homestead.

KEARNEY, Buffalo County. I-80. (CAR-nee.)

Fort Kearny State Historical Park, 8 miles SE on State 10. The original fort, a two-story log blockhouse, was located on the right bank of the Missouri about 50 miles below Omaha at the mouth of Table Creek, now site of Nebraska City. Col. Stephen Watts Kearny (often called "Soldier of the West") and Col. George Brooke selected the site in 1846. The post was meant to protect the Oregon Trail but was too distant to be effective, and was abandoned in 1848. Fort Kearny II at this site was established in June 1848, by two companies of Mounted Riflemen and was an important post on the trail, until 1871 when the transcontinental railroad was well established, lessening travel on the old trail. (Note: Fort Phil Kearny is in Wyoming.) Interpretive center with displays and audio-visual program, restored stockade and sod blacksmith-carpenter shop in 40-acre park.

Fort Kearney Museum, 311 S. Central Ave., has historical items from a number of countries, and offers glass-bottom boat rides which would have astonished most emigrants on the old trail.

LEXINGTON, Dawson County. US 283.

Dawson County Historical Museum, 805 N. Taft, is housed in a one-room school of 1888 and a furnished Union Pacific depot.

Plum Creek Massacre, 15 miles SE in Phelps County, near the mouth of Plum Creek. Monument marks the site in a small fenced plot where a group of frontier men and women lost their lives on August 7, 1864, in an Indian raid. A Pony Express marker is nearby.

LINCOLN, Lancaster County. I–80.

State Capitol, 14th and K Sts. Bas

relief and mosaics depict state history. Guided tours.

University of Nebraska State Museum, 14th and U Sts. in Morrill Hall, features prehistoric and modern animal life and geology in the Great Plains.

State Historical Society Museum, 15th and R Sts., state history from earliest Indians to the pioneers. Dioranas. Period rooms.

City Hall, 920 O St., built in 1874–79.

Nebraska Statehood Memorial (Thomas P. Kennard House), 1627 H St., was built in 1869. Kennard was one of three chosen by the state legislature in 1867 to select a capital city. His home has been furnished in the 1870s period. (All three commissioners had homes designed by architect John Keys Winchell of Chicago; only the Kennard one remains.)

Lewis–Syford House, 700 N. 16th St., was built ca. 1878.

Fairview, 4900 Sumner St., built in 1902 was the home of William Jennings Bryan. Original furnishings and memorabilia. Now part of Bryan Hospital grounds.

LYMAN, Scottsbluff County. State 92.

Horse Creek Treaty, US 26, 2 ½ miles NE of town in angle formed where Horse Creek flows into the North Platte River. Descriptive marker for site where Father DeSmet, Jim Bridger and many others were present for the signing of a treaty in 1851. The Oregon Trail crossed the highway at this point.

MC COOK, Red Willow County. US 83.

Museum of the High Plains, 423 Norris, regional pioneer artifacts, furniture and clothing.

Norris House, 706 Norris Ave., is the restored home of Senator George W. Norris, built in 1886, original furnishings and a small museum.

MINDEN, Kearney County. US 6, 34.

Harold Warp Pioneer Village, on highway, covers three city blocks. An early town is recreated in 24 buildings from an authentic soddy to the depot that was the western terminus of the Burlington Railroad from 1872 to 1882.

MURRAY, Cass County. State 1.

Walker Gilmore (Sterns Creek) Site, 5 miles SE of town, is a key archaeological site for the prehistorical culture of the central plains woodland area. A national historic landmark, not open to the public at present.

NEBRASKA CITY, Otoe County. US 73, 75. Site of the first Fort Kearny, an active trading post, a stop on the Oregon Trail and the Pony Express, a town which grew big and boisterous, with both river and overland traffic. There are a number of markers and monuments in the area pertaining to the early days and many trail markers.

Arbor Lodge, Arbor Lodge State Park, just W. of city limits, was the home of J. Sterling Morton, territorial governor, early journalist and horticulturist who served as Secretary of Agriculture under President Cleveland and is known today as the founder of Arbor Day, which was first celebrated in Nebraska in 1872. The house, a registered historic place, was built in 1855, enlarged several times. The 52-room mansion is furnished with antiques and relics of pioneer days.

Wildwood Period House, in Steinhart Park, NW of town, has furnishings from 1856. The 10-room house was built in 1869.

John Brown's Cave, State 2, near 20th St., was a major station on the Underground Railway. Museum.

Steam Wagon Monuments, at Burlington Depot, and at sites W. and NW of town, for the steam wagon invented by Joseph R. Brown which arrived on the steamer *West Wind,* July 12, 1862. The contraption started for Denver ten days later, broke down and was abandoned 7 miles on its way. A great little dream that ran out of steam.

NELIGH, Antelope County. US 275.

Neligh Mill, 111 W. 2nd St., was built of locally produced brick for John D. Neligh, founder of the town. He was forced to sell the mill in the panic of 1873. A registered historic place. Restored but not in operation.

NORTH PLATTE, Lincoln County. US 83.

Buffalo Bill Ranch State Historical Park, 1 mile N. on Buffalo Bill Ave. Cody's ranch and winter quarters when he traveled with his rodeo. Original barn and outbuildings. Interpretive film. Original Victorian furnishings in house; the wallpaper was designed by the indefatigable frontiersman himself.

OGALLALA, Keith County. US 26. The town was named for the Oglala Dakota Sioux, despite the spelling.

Front Street, 519 1 St., is a re-creation of an Old West town with Cowboy's Rest, Crystal Palace, watering tank and windmill.

Mansion on the Hill, is the oldest brick landmark in the area, now a museum maintained by the Keith County Historical Society. The house was built in 1887.

Boot Hill has descriptive state historical marker at site. The first burial was a mother and child but the lawless came soon after. As a terminus for the Western Trail, on the Union Pacific Railroad, the town was often filled with cowboys who camped on the river banks and raised hell after their long drives were over. Many graves are associated with the cattle days. The trail was used until 1895 although Dodge City, Kansas, became the main terminus in the 1880s.

OMAHA, Douglas County. I-80. The Omaha Indians had a village here in the days when the great traders and explorers, such as Manuel Lisa and Baptiste Charbonneau, were working the area, along the highway of the West, the Missouri River. Lewis and Clark, the Astor expeditions, the Stephen Long outfit, all used the river and saw Omaha but kept on going. Settlers came in the 1850s.

Joslyn Art Museum, 2200 Dodge St., has a magnificent collection of the Maximilian–Bodmer paintings and documents from Prince Maximilian's expedition of 1833–34, and the Stewart–Miller collection of Great Plains paintings of the 1830 period, as well as Indian arts.

Mormon Cemetery, Northridge Dr. and State St. About 600 Mormons failed to survive the bitter winter of 1846–47 in camp here. A monument by Avard Fairbanks commemorates their hardship; it depicts a father and mother standing before the grave of a child.

Creighton University, 24th St. between Cass and Burt Sts., is named for Edward and John Creighton, Ohio farm boys, who pioneered as cattlemen on the Plains, and later surveyed the western telegraph route and helped build the line. The University opened in 1878.

Union Pacific Historical Museum, 1416 Dodge St. A variety of railroadiana in the Union Pacific headquarters includes a Lincoln display and a replica of his funeral car. Both railroad and Western buffs will be interested in the equipment displays which are detailed from large pieces such as a sauerkraut stomper down to a section of the rail and rail chair used in the original construction of the Union Pacific in 1867.

Bank of Florence, 8502 N. 30th St. The town was platted in 1854 on the site of the Mormon's winter quarters eight years earlier. The bank was chartered by the territorial legislature in 1856; a registered historic place.

Fort Omaha, main entrance on Fort St. off 30th. Established as headquarters of the Department of the Platte in December 1868, it was called "hindquarters" by Gen. Sherman, who thought it too far from the frontier. Building No. 1 has a plaque which says Sherman slept there and for a time it was called "The Sherman House," but lately it has been called the Crook House for Gen. George Crook, who is not yet as famous as Sherman, Sheridan or Custer, but who may still be, as interest in Western history deepens and modern writers sort the evidence. Crook served here as head of the Department of the Platte from 1875 to 1882 and again from 1886 to 1888. He had served in the Pacific Northwest before the Civil War and was wounded by a poisoned arrow in 1857. He led the 36th Ohio early in the war, commanded a division at South Mountain and Antietam, and served capably in various campaigns but suffered the indignity of being captured in a hotel in Cumberland, Maryland, in February, 1865, by Confederates in Union uniforms. After the war he became one of the Army's toughest but most fair-minded Indian fighters. He was called "Gray Fox" by the Indians.

Chamber of Commerce, 1620 Dodge St., Suite 2100, has information on other local points of interest. There are many markers and monuments throughout the area for early trails and territorial sites, though some are lost in the growing city.

PALMER, Merrick County. State 92.

Palmer Site, 4 miles N. and 1 mile W. of town on Loup River, in Howard County, is a Skidi Pawnee Indian village which the Lewis and Clark expedition made note of in 1804. Zebulon Pike was here in 1806. A national historic landmark, not open to the public at present.

Phelps Hotel, NE corner of 2nd and Pine, was built in 1885 and was an important 19th-century landmark of the area, a center of activity and a popular stopping place for travelers. A registered historic place.

RED CLOUD, Webster County. US 281.

Willa Cather Pioneer Memorial, Webster St., honors that author and has tour maps for routes past many of the sites in her books. She lived in Red Cloud for six years as a girl. The house, at 3rd and Cedar Sts., operated by the Memorial, has family furnishings. Wallpaper she put up in the 1880s is still there.

RULO, Richardson County. State 4.

Leary Site, 4 miles SE on State 7, is a large prehistoric village and burial site of the Oneota Indians and was mentioned by Lewis and Clark in their travels of 1804. It has been partially excavated. A national historic landmark, not open to the public at present.

SCOTTS BLUFF NATIONAL MONUMENT, Scottsbluff County. State 92. The bluff rises 800 feet above the plains, although to many emigrants it seemed to reach even nearer to heaven for it signified that the long dull crossing of the prairies was nearly ended. Even though the terrain beyond would prove far more difficult, it was a welcome change. All early expeditions came this way. An Oregon Trail museum is at the Visitor Center. A paved road to the summit passes through three tunnels and is closed earlier in winter months than in summer, also in bad weather.

Roubidoux Pass, ca. 3 miles W., was another natural landmark on the trail, and a popular stop nearby was the Joseph and Antoine Roubidoux trading post in 1849–50 when the pass was opened to travel. A national historic landmark.

Signal Butte, 10 miles W., is a national historic landmark. Deposits here show occupation from ca. 2500 B.C.

Mitchell Pass, just W. of monument, was used by the emigrants. Oregon Trail marker at site.

Fort Mitchell, 3 miles W.; markers here show the fortsite and trail. Also the Pony Express Route is marked in this area. The fort lay about 2 miles NW of the monument and consisted of stockade, blockhouse, rifle ports and flagpole. Originally Camp Shuman.

SIDNEY, Cheyenne County. US 30.

Fort Sidney, built in 1867 for the protection of construction workers on the Union Pacific Railroad, was maintained until the end of the Indian wars in 1894. The post commander's quarters have been restored. This and two old barracks are on 6th Ave., 1 block S. of US 30.

THEDFORD, Thomas County. US 83. A marker on highway just E. of town describes the historic Sandhills which cover ca. 24,000 miles and were created by glacial erosion.

Nebraska National Forest (Bessey Division), 15 miles E. on State 2, then ca. 2 miles S.

TRENTON, Hitchcock County. State 25.

Massacre Canyon, 3 miles E., marked by a 35-foot pink granite shaft to commemorate the Sioux-Pawnee battle of August 5, 1873, which nearly wiped out the Pawnees. Cavalry from Fort McPherson stopped the battle. Among the Pawnee chiefs were Sky Chief, Sun Chief and Fighting Bear; among the Sioux were Spotted Tail, Little Wound and Two Strike.

VALENTINE, Cherry County. US 20, 83.

Sawyer's Sandhills Museum, US 20, 4 blocks W. of US 83. Pioneer and Indian artifacts.

Fort Niobrara National Wildlife Refuge, 5 miles NE on State 12, has a museum of natural history. There are prairie dog towns and buffalo herds in the refuge, which covers 19,122 acres on the site of the former Niobrara Military Reservation established in 1879. At headquarters are exhibition pastures where bison, Texas longhorns and a number of other once-free animals may be viewed.

Valentine National Wildlife Range, 17 miles S. on US 83, then W. on State 16B.

WAR BONNET (HAT) CREEK BATTLEFIELD, Sioux County. 17 miles NE of Harrison (US 20), marker at Montrose. After the great Indian victory at the Battle of Little Bighorn,

Cheyenne and Sioux gathered to join the victors under Sitting Bull and Crazy Horse. Here on July 17, 1876, Gen. Wesley Merritt and his 5th Cavalry drove back a party of Indians who were trying to intercept couriers. Buffalo Bill Cody, who had rejoined the fighting forces leaving show business behind, shot Chief Yellow Hand and scalped him. The consequent publicity made much of this as "the first scalp for Custer," in retaliation. Yellow Hand's Indian name, Hay-o-wei, had been incorrectly translated by a 5th Cavalry scout. "Yellow Hair" was correct, but never used.

WEEPING WATER, Cass County. State 50A.

Heritage House Complex portrays the history of the Weeping Water River Basin with fossil remains, Indian and pioneer relics.

WYNOT, Cedar County. State 12.

Wiseman Massacre Site, monument commemorates the site of the Henson Wiseman pioneer home where five Wiseman children were massacred by Yankton and Santee Sioux Indians on July 24, 1863, when their father was away serving with the 2nd Nebraska regiment in the Civil War.

NEVADA

Frame shanties, pitched together as if by accident; tents of canvas, of blankets, of brush, of potato-sacks and old shirts, with empty whisky-barrels for chimneys; smoky hovels of mud and stone; pits and shafts with smoke issuing from every crevice; piles of goods and rubbish on craggy points, in the hollows, on the rocks, in the mud, in the snow, every where, scattered broadcast in pell-mell confusion. . . . A fraction of the crowd, as we entered the precincts of the town [Virginia City], were engaged in a lawsuit relative to a question of title. The arguments used on both sides were empty whisky bottles. Several of the disputants had already been knocked down and convinced, and various others were freely shedding their blood in the cause of justice. . . . Some two or three hundred disinterested observers stood by, enjoying the spectacle, several of them with their hands on their revolvers, to be ready in case of any serious issue; but these dangerous weapons are only used on great occasions—a refusal to drink, or some illegitimate trick at monte.

J. Ross Browne, *A Peep at Washoe,* 1875

Mornin' on the desert, and the wind is blowin' free,
And it's ours, jest for the breathin', so let's fill up,
You and me.
No more stuffy cities, where you have to pay to
breathe,
Where the helpless human creatures move and
throng and
strive and seethe. . . .
All day through the sagebrush here the wind is
blowin' free,
And it's ours jest for the breathin': So let's fill up,
you and me.

Anonymous poem found nailed to door of southern Nevada cabin.

> The great mineral wealth of Eastern Nevada has not been exaggerated. In fact I did not expect to find so rich or so many Silver Mines. There is not so much wild reckless extravagance among the people of the towns & the miners as in the early days of California. There are not as many homicides according to the numbers, but there is perhaps more highway robberies committed. We have here as twenty years ago numbers too lazy to work not too lazy to steal & some too proud to work & not afraid to steal. The laws of Nevada license gambling & here at Hamilton, in Treasure City & Shermantown are some ten or twelve licensed gambling tables. The next session of the Legislature may perhaps license Highway robbery. There are two banking establishments, two Express offices, Wells & Fargo, & Union Express, some ten or twelve Assay offices & a small army of Lawyers. The District Court has been in session ever since I arrived. . . .
>
> Henry Eno, in letter from Hamilton, August 21, 1869 (*Twenty Years on the Pacific Slope,* 1965)

NEVADA FACTS: In the 1770s several Spanish explorers came near, but the report of Father Silvestre Velez de Escalante was discouraging as was the look of the arid land. However, fur traders came in the next century and Jedediah Smith crossed the territory in 1827 on his way to California. In 1828 Peter Skene Ogden, of the Hudson's Bay Co., discovered the Humboldt River, and Joseph Walker crossed the Sierra Nevada. Capt. John C. Frémont explored the region in 1843–45. Gold was discovered at Carson City in 1850 bringing more settlers. But the Comstock Lode discovered in 1859 brought the greatest boom. Nevada was originally part of Utah Territory; became a separate territory in 1861. On October 31, 1864, Nevada entered the Union as the 36th State. Nickname: Battle Born State.

Capital: Carson City. Territorial capital: Mormon Station, Genoa. Nevada has Lake Mead National Recreation Area, Lehman Caves National Monument, a section of Death Valley National Monument, the Humboldt and Toiyabe National Forests.

Chief Trails and Routes. Spanish Trail, Fremont Trail, Donner Trail, Death Valley Emigrant Trail, Pony Express Overland Mail, Bidwell–Bartleson Trail,

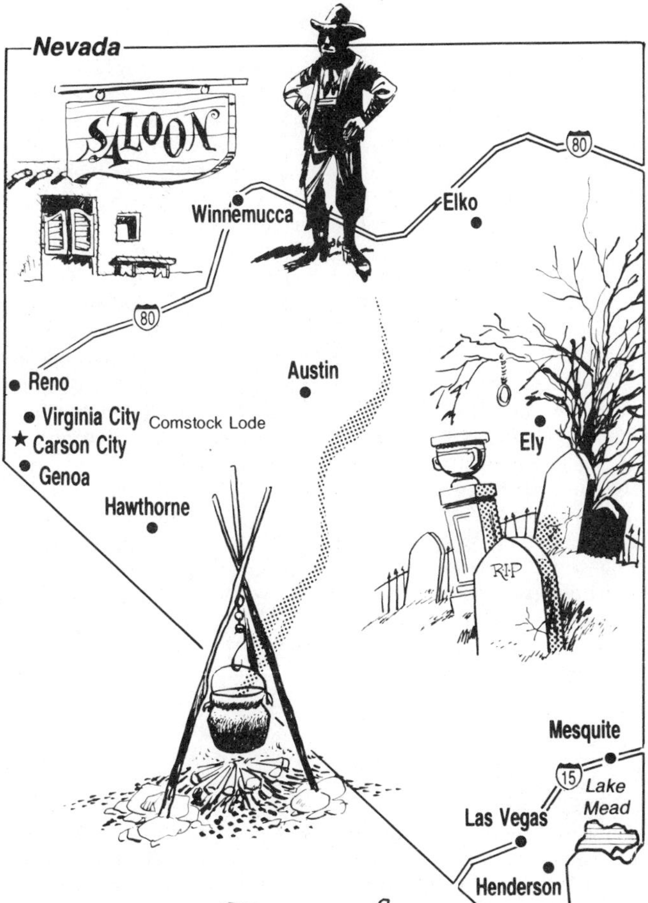
Nevada
SALOON
80
Winnemucca
Elko
80
Reno
Austin
Virginia City
Comstock Lode
Carson City
Genoa
Ely
Hawthorne
R·I·P
Mesquite
15
Lake Mead
Las Vegas
Henderson
50 Miles

Applegate–Lassen Cut-off, Jedediah Smith Trail, Goose Creek–Humboldt Emigrant Trail, San Bernardino–Salt Lake Wagon Road.

AUSTIN, Lander County. (6,635 feet). US 50. A silver rush began in 1863, bringing 10,000 miners into the area. In 1868 mines yielded more than $3,574,000, the peak of production. After that, the population began to drift to other towns. The Central Pacific Railroad missed Austin by 92 miles to the north. By century's end there were only 600 citizens. Thirteen brick buildings on Main St. include three churches, a hotel, the courthouse, some stores, a newspaper office and a museum in Reuel C. Gridley's former store.

Gridley, a grocer with Southern sympathies, lost an election bet with Dr. H. S. Herrick, a Unionist. The loser was to carry a 50-pound sack of flour a mile down the canyon to Clinton. The whole town turned out to watch the payoff. A parade was led by town officials on horseback, followed by Herrick carrying the loser's coat and cane, then Gridley and the flour sack which was gaily decorated with flags and ribbons. His son marched beside him waving a flag and the band played "Dixie." Speeches were made on delivery at the Bank Exchange Saloon in Clinton, thirsts were quenched and everyone went back to Austin where the sack of flour was auctioned off and resold until more than $10,000 had been raised for the Sanitary Commission fund for war relief. Austin adopted the flour sack design for the city seal. Gridley went on tour from coast to coast, raising more than $175,000 for the aid of war wounded, but went home broke. The sack is in the Nevada State Historical Society Museum at Reno. Gridley is buried in Stockton, California, with a G.A.R. monument.

A former keeper bought nine of the camels which had been used by Edward Beale in his army experiment when they were sold at auction in California and brought them to Austin to carry salt from the marshes to a quartz mill. Camels were found straying in the area years later.

Lander County Courthouse was built in 1869.

Stokes Castle, once the home of financier Anson Phelps Stokes, was built in 1879.

The Reese River Reveille has been published continuously since May 16, 1863, and is edited from the original desk. Complete files are in the courthouse vault. William C. Phillips, the first publisher, had been a neighbor of the Lincolns in Illinois.

Hickson Petroglyph Recreation Site, 24 miles E. on US 50. The Indian drawings are on a 6,500-foot cliff. An old pony express trail is nearby.

Chamber of Commerce, in Austin, has self-guiding tour maps. US 50 enters town through an old cemetery and follows the Overland stage route. There are many old headstones worth reading.

BATTLE MOUNTAIN, Lander County. US 40. The town was established in 1868 as a station to serve the camps of the Battle Mountain Mining District. The area got its name from one of the early skirmishes with Indians, who had attacked a wagon-train in 1861 at Gravelly Ford, killing several persons and making off with loot. The Indians were pursued and beaten in two subsequent attacks. Open pit copper mining is in nearby Copper Canyon.

BEATTY, Nye County. US 95. A onetime supply base for mining camps in the Amargosa River Valley, Beatty is the Nevada gateway to Death Valley National Monument in California. Rhyolite nearby, via State 58 and graveled road, was a booming mining town after the turn of the century when the Bullfrog Mine was active. The depot, which once served three railroads connecting with the Southern Pacific and the Atchison, Topeka and Santa Fe, is a curious structure which looks as if the builder had intended to erect an adobe but forgot what he had in mind. In recent years it has housed a rock shop. (Minerals, not music.)

Johnnie Mine, SE of town via US 95, then State 16, ruins of the old mill and town are still standing. It was named for Indian Johnnie, a Paiute guide, who pointed out the site in 1890 to two prospectors.

BELMONT, Nye County. State 82. Ca. 14 miles NE of Manhattan. A ghost town with a number of buildings remaining. Among them are the Nye County Courthouse and the Cosmopolitan Opera House. In 1865 an Indian discovered silver quartz veins and word got around. The Philadelphia Mining District was organized, and by 1867 there were 10,000 residents. Three stamp mills opened and mining reached a peak in 1873–74; by 1885 the mines had played out. Ruins of the old Highbridge ore mill are off the main road and near a tall round chimney thought to have been part of the clay firing works.

BOUNDARY PEAK, Esmeralda County. In Toiyabe National Forest, at California State Line, W. of State 3A. The highest point in Nevada, elevation 13,140 feet. Lida and Gold Point are ghost towns in the area.

CANDELARIA, Mineral County. From Coaldale on US 6, 95, go N. 12 miles on US 95 to dirt road going W. 7 miles. A ghost town with ruins and an old cemetery with a number of well-preserved markers. Silver ore was found here by Mexicans in 1864, but the area was not developed until 15 years later when the Northern Belle was put in operation, and produced $20 million in a few years.

CARSON CITY, Ormsby County. US 50. Named for Kit Carson.

State Capitol, N. Carson St. The cornerstone was laid in June 1870. Daily tours.

Nevada State Museum, N. Carson and Robinson Sts. in the former U.S. Mint, has coins, guns, minerals, pioneer relics, mining items and Indian artifacts. There is a life-size Indian camp scene; also a replica of an underground mine.

Warren Engine Company Museum, 111 N. Curry St. antique fire-fighting equipment.

Bowers Mansion, 10 miles N. in Washoe Valley, was built in 1864, for more than $400,000, profits from a Comstock Lode gold and silver mine. Many original furnishings. Guided tours.

Chamber of Commerce Information Bureau, 1191 S. Carson St. Map and brochure for self-guiding city tour.

CATHEDRAL GORGE STATE PARK, Lincoln County. 16 miles N. of Caliente on US 93, 2 miles N. of Panaca. A 1,607-acre park features odd-shaped rock formations formed as the result of centuries of erosion. At twilight some of the area resembles Gothic church towers.

CRYSTAL BAY, Washoe County. (6,250 feet). State 28.

Ponderosa Ranch, on Tahoe Blvd. (State 28) in Incline Village, is the structure seen in the "Bonanza" television western. Lake Tahoe provides a scenic backdrop.

DAYTON, Lyon County. US 50. Gold was found in nearby Gold Canyon in 1850.

Sutro Tunnel, ca. 2 miles E., 1 mile N. of US 50. Adolph Sutro, who operated a stamp mill in the Carson Valley, proposed to the legislature that he dig a tunnel under the Comstock Lode to solve problems of drainage, ventilation and access as well as safety. The legislature granted him a 50-year franchise in 1865. He began construction in 1869 after many difficulties in raising the money. The main tunnel was completed in 1878 and was considered one of the great engineering feats of the 19th century. But it was too late for the Comstock mines which were failing. Sutro resigned as president of the company and disposed of his stock before it was valueless. He invested in real estate and served as mayor of San Francisco from 1894 to 1898.

Dayton Post Office, built in 1891, still serves the town. So does the Dayton Public School, built in 1865. The Comstock Lode began here at the intersection of Gold Canyon Creek and the Carson River. The settlement was called Spafford Hall's Station by the '49ers, then Ponder's Rest. The Pony Express stopped here in 1860.

ELKO, Elko County. US 40.

Northeastern Nevada Museum, 1515 Idaho St. Indian, pioneer and nature displays.

Chamber of Commerce, 1601 Idaho St., has information on touring the area. Horseback-hiking trips to the high country can be arranged.

Elko County Ghost Towns: Aura, Charlestown, Cornucopia, Columbia, Deep Creek, Gold Creek, Jarbridge, Midas and Tunscarora.

Humboldt National Forest, 8 miles S. on State 46, then 15 miles SE is in nine sections, covers 2,523,243 acres. Old mining camps are in some areas. Visitor Center near Wheeler Peak. Headquarters in Elko.

ELY, White Pine County. US 6.

White Pine Public Museum, 2000 Aultman St. Mineral display, early vehicles and other relics.

Ward Charcoal Ovens Historic State Monument, 5 miles SE on US 6, 50, 93, then 10 miles S. on unnumbered road. Six stone beehive charcoal ovens used during the mining days of the 1870s.

Liberty Copper Pit, 6 miles W., one of the largest open pit mines in the world. Observation point has a recorded narrative of mining operations.

Ghost towns of the area: Hamilton, ca. 37 miles W., 12 miles S. of US 50 on unpaved road. Prospectors found silver here in 1865 and developed Cave City, renamed in 1868. The mines yielded about $6 million. The two-story hotel walls are still standing among the ruins. *Cherry Creek,* N. off Alt. 50 on State 35. *Fort Schellbourne,* on Schell Creek, was a military post in the 1860s at the site of a relay station used by the Pony Express and the Overland Stage Route from 1859 to 1869. Ruins of the stage station and the post are still to be seen. Inquire locally for road conditions and directions. The old mining camps of Osceola, Lane City and Taylor are also in the county.

EUREKA, Eureka County, (6,500 feet) US 50. In its first two decades the Eureka mining district produced $100 million in silver, gold and lead. Many old buildings remain, among modern ones. In the town's heyday, the Colonnade Hotel, the Jackson House and the Opera House were popular spots. Mt. Prospect, nearby, reaches 9,604 ft. Ruby Hill is an old district 2 miles W. Secret Canyon is S. Spring Valley SW and the Pinto or Silverado district SE. Eureka was headquarters for the stage lines. The Eureka and Palisades Railway was completed in 1875, all 84 miles of it, but it gave access to the transcontinental line.

In the winter of 1888 the whole town was talking about a storekeeper named Phil Paroni who was suspected of rape but was found innocent in two trials and a grand jury investigation. A mob, dissatisfied with the decisions, called on Paroni at his home, took him to a lime kiln where they stripped him to the waist, covered him with hot tar and shredded paper. Some wanted to set fire to the tar but cooler heads prevailed, as the saying goes, and he was sent down the railroad tracks, his hands tied behind his back, with orders not to return. He arrived at Diamond Station about 12 miles away where a section boss for the railroad took him, cleaned him up and gave him clothes. Paroni went back to Eureka and lived to serve as county commissioner. This incident recalls the Lincoln story. When an enemy threatened to have him tarred and feathered and run out of town on a rail, "Abe" is supposed to have said: "If it weren't for the honor, I'd rather walk."

FORT CHURCHILL, Lyon County. US 59A. 8 miles S. of US 50. Established in July 1860, on the N. side of the Carson River, because of the Paiute uprising in western Nevada. The post was situated between the Pyramid Lake and Walker River Indian reservations, established not long after the fort was erected, and controlled both. On the central Overland Mail Route, it protected the mails and the first transcontinental telegraph. Some adobe buildings have been reconstructed and are in a state park. The area is a national historic landmark.

FORT HALLECK, Elko County. State 11 at Secret Canyon, ca. 11 miles SE of Halleck. Established in July 1867, on the right bank of Cottonwood Creek at the foot of the N. end of the Humboldt Mountains, 12 miles S. of the Humboldt River. It was set up to protect settlers and the Central Pacific Railway route, as well as stage and telegraph lines. Most of its garrison served in the Nez Perce War of 1877. Stone marker at site which is in a meadow, owned privately. Earth mounds show the location of fort buildings.

FORT RUBY, White Pine County. Ca. 8 miles S. of Cave Creek on unimproved road; inquire locally about exact directions and road conditions. The fort was established September 1862, on the W. side of the Ruby Valley near the S. end of Ruby Lake, by Col. Patrick Connor, 3rd California Infantry. He was later stationed in Utah, when the government wanted to keep an eye on Brigham Young and his people during Civil War times. (There is a monument to Connor and his volunteers in the post cemetery at Fort Douglas, Salt Lake City. (Which see.) Fort Ruby's garrison was important in guarding transportation and communication routes and also took part in Indian wars. William Rogers, first white settler in Ruby Valley and an assistant Indian agent, built a cabin which became a station for the Central Overland Mail, the Pony Express and a relay station on the transcontinental telegraph. Troops from this garrison took part in the Gosiute War of 1863; in 1864 the California volunteers were replaced by Nevada troops. Two original buildings, the post office and a house remain. The site is a national historic landmark, on private property at present, not accessible to the public.

GABBS, Nye County. State 23.

Berlin–Ichthyosaur State Monument, 23 miles E. via State 91. Fossilized remains of enormous sea reptiles, also called "fish-lizards," are in the park as is the ghost town of Berlin, once a mining camp.

Ione, N. of town take graveled road E., 3 miles to Stokes Iron Mine, continue on dirt road 13 miles to another dirt road intersection, go 7 miles NE on this. A ghost town with many old

A saloon in Gold Hill near Virginia City
(Pro-Am Photo Labs, Reno)

stone buildings, some with sod roofs, of the 1860s. *Grantsville,* another ghost town, will be reached by turning right on the fork above instead of left for Ione. Grantsville is ca. 6 miles on the right (or SE) fork. Large ruined mill, stamp mill, brick schoolhouse, dug-out houses, stone houses.

GENOA, Douglas County. US 395.

Mormon Station Historic State Monument, 3 miles W. of US 395. The site of the first capital of Nevada Territory. The first permanent white settlement was established in 1849 when Hampden Beatie and six other Mormons were sent from Salt Lake City to set up a trading post. Emigrants on the Humboldt part of the California Trail made it a stopping place. By 1857 most of the Mormons had returned to Utah, ordered to do so by Brigham Young. The territorial capital was established in 1859 but was moved to Carson City in 1861. The two-story log cabin, which also served as a Pony Express and Overland Stage station, was built in the 1850s when Col. John Reese and 18 other Mormons arrived in 10 wagons. Reese bought the original cabin built by Beatie and added the larger structure and a stockade. Fire destroyed the building in 1910. Replicas are in the state park on the original site.

GOLDFIELD, Esmeralda County. US 95. For the purposes of a 19th-century guide the gold rush came here three years too late, but it's a ghost town that looks for the most part very like earlier ones set on a desert with Joshua trees to throw ghostly shadows. *Gold Point,* S. from Goldfield 15 miles on US 95 to State 3, turn right, 4 miles on dirt road, turn left (S.) 4 miles to the ghost town, once called Hornsilver. More Joshua trees and ruins. *Silver Peak,* another old town, is on State 47, reached by going W. from Tonopah on US 6, 95 then S. on State 47. It is almost due W. from Goldfield and not far as the crow flies but a long haul by good roads. It should be noted that all official highway maps caution travelers to inquire locally about roads; this is particularly true when visiting the many ghost towns. A relief map is also a useful item in this terrain. Goldfield Summit has an elevation of 6087 feet. To the SW Montezuma Peak reaches 8,376 feet. Stonewall Pass, SW via State 71, off US 95, is 4,686. To the east of Goldfield a large area is occupied by the Nellis Air Force Range and AEC Nuclear Testing Site, with the Indian Springs Gunnery Range to the S. of this and Danger Areas N. of Las Vegas. The Indians are subdued but Nevada is still not a state to wander around in without a road map.

HAWTHORNE, Mineral County. A Western desert town in what was a gold-mining area.

Walker Lake, 4 miles N. on US 95, named for Joseph Walker, trapper and scout, is a home for cutthroat trout.

Aurora, ca. 30 miles SW via State 31, on the state line, is a ghost town which was founded in 1860 when three California prospectors found silver ore in the area. In 1863 it had 6,000 residents, 17 quartz mills, 20 stores, 12 hotels and plenty of saloons. Mark Twain tried gold mining with considerably less profit than he achieved with his pen.

HENDERSON, Clark County. US 93, 95.

Southern Nevada Museum, 240 Water St., has Indian artifacts, mining and gambling equipment, historical exhibits.

LAKE MEAD NATIONAL RECREATION AREA, Clark County. 4 miles E. of Boulder City on US 93, 466. A 3,000-square-mile tract along the Colorado River. Petroglyphs will be found in Grapevine Wash on the Christmas Tree Pass, reached from State 77, W. of Bullhead City, Arizona, or from US 95 S. of Searchlight, Nevada.

LAS VEGAS, Clark County. I–15, US 95.

University of Nevada, 4505 Maryland Pkwy., has on campus the Museum of Natural History, with Indian collections, mining history and pioneer artifacts; there is a mineral collection, in the Chemistry Bldg. Rm. 119.

Desert National Wildlife Range, 28 miles NW on US 95. Bighorn sheep are on display.

Mormon Fort, N. Las Vegas Blvd. at Washington, was established in 1855 by Mormons under William Bringhurst, sent by Brigham Young. In 1857 the Mormons were recalled to Salt Lake City. Overland Mail continued to stop at Vegas Springs and Fort Baker was established here early in 1862. The post was named for Col. Edward D. Baker killed in the Battle of Ball's Bluff, Virginia. A part of the fort is still standing inside a high wire fence on private property but may be visited.

LEHMAN CAVES NATIONAL MONUMENT, White Pine County. 5 miles W. of Baker on State 74. On the E. side of Wheeler Peak in the Wheeler Peak Scenic Area in the Humboldt National Forest. The monument covers 640 acres. A Visitor Center is near the tunnel entrance. Guided tours.

LOVELOCK, Pershing County. US 40.

Leonard Rockshelter, 12 miles S. off State 95, is a site which dates from ca. 9000 B.C., and has provided important information on the Indian occupation of the Great Basin. Petroglyphs. A national historic landmark.

Ghost towns: Seven Troughs, NE on State 48; Rochester, 25 miles NE on US 40, to Oreana, E. on unnumbered road, mill ruins and a wrecked onetime dancehall-saloon, several other buildings in varying last stages.

MCDERMITT, Humboldt County. US 95, at Oregon state line.

Fort McDermit, on unimproved road ca. 2 miles W. of US 95 and town. Established August 1865, near the mouth of canyon in the Santa Rosa Mountains on the Quinn River, to control the Paiute Indians of the area and to protect travel routes. First called Quinn River Station, then Camp McDermit, designated a fort in April 1849, named for Lt. Col. Charles McDermit, of the 2nd California Cavalry, who was killed by Indians in the Quinn Valley in 1865. Gen. George Crook used the fort in his 1866–68 campaign against the Snake Indians. Troops from here also took part in the Bannock War of 1878. The Indian Bureau took over the fort buildings when the garrison was withdrawn. Remaining buildings serve as headquarters for the Fort McDermit Indian Agency.

MOAPA, Clark County. Off I–15.

Valley of Fire State Park, State 40, off I–15, covers 34,200 acres, with a number of prehistoric petroglyphs in the area.

NORDYKE, Lyon County. Just W. of State 3.

Wovoka Hut, on unimproved road, along the NE side of Mill Ditch. A hut lived in by "Jack Wilson," or Wovoka, the Indian who founded the Ghost Dance religion of 1890. There had been a Ghost Dance of 1870 in several tribes. Wovoka's religion was based on the coming of a millennium in 1891 and on invoking the help of the supernatural to set the world right again for Indians. Wovoka was a Paiute of 14 when his medicine man father died and he was taken on the ranch of David Wilson to work as a hand, was taught Christian religion and the white way of living. But he left the ranch to travel through several other Western states. In Washington he saw some tribes practicing a Shaker-type religion. In 1889 after a long illness he had a vision in which white men would disappear, buffalo and Indians would return in their old strengths and life would be good again. This belief with its ceremonies spread from the Great Basin to the plains, and to other western tribes. The frenzy it created caused part of the troubles which beset many Indian tribes in the early part of the 1890s. Sitting Bull's death was indirectly due to his participation in the Ghost Dance movement. The owner of the Nordyke ranch has protected the hut, but it is not open to the public. Wovoka is buried in the Schurz Cemetery, ca. 20 miles NE of Nordyke.

OVERTON, Clark County. State 12.

Lost City Museum of Archaeology, on restored site of the Pueblo Grande de Nevada, extensive collection of fossils, semiprecious gems, Indian artifacts. Tourist information available at Community Center.

PARADISE VALLEY, Humboldt County. State 8B, E. of US 95.

Camp Winfield Scott, at the foot of the Santa Rosa Mountains, near the head of the valley, ca. 5 miles E. of town, was established in December 1866, for Indian control. The camp was maintained until 1871; it was never officially designated a fort. Gen. George Crook used the camp as a base in his 1866–68 campaign against Northern Paiutes. Some adobe buildings remain but are in use as part of a ranch.

PIOCHE, Lincoln County. US 93, State 85. A Paiute Indian discovered silver ore at Meadow Valley in the winter of 1863–64. The Meadow Valley Mining District was soon formed. In 1869 miners founded Pioche on the slopes of Ely Mountain. By 1874 there were about 6,000 residents. Production reached $12 million in the early 1870s then began to decline. Some early buildings remain. The nearby camps of Frisco and Silver Reef founded later than Pioche were rivals. Pioche was a wild town which took a certain pride in its outlaws. Until fairly recently a signboard advertised that 67 men were buried in Pioche's Boot Hill before one died a natural death. Murderer's Row has about 100 killers in an area fenced off from the "respectable."

The brick county courthouse was condemned as unsafe in 1933, three years before it was paid for. It had been built in 1871 for $75,000.

PYRAMID LAKE, Washoe County. State 34. On Pyramid Lake Indian Reservation N. of Reno. Capt. John Frémont named the lake in 1844. The Southern Paiute Indians fought two engagements with troops at a point N. of the Carson River Valley, ca. 4

miles SW of the lower end of the lake and directly S. of Nixon. Emigrants saw the green valley as a fine place to settle but the Indians resented the intrusion. The Buckland and Williams Stations on the Central Overland Mail and the Pony Express lines were located near here to supply goods for miners as well as emigrants. In May 1860, traders abducted two Indian girls at the Williams Station. Indians burned the station in retaliation and killed five men. Miners from several communities organized as the 105 Nevada Volunteers under Maj. William Ormsby, marched N. into Paiute country around Pyramid Lake and fell into an ambush that took a toll of 46 volunteers. This defeat halted stage and mail service for a time. Then regular troops led by Col. Jack Hays, a former Texas Ranger, encountered the Paiutes on June 3 in a three-hour battle. Twenty-five Indians were killed and the rest fled. The following month Fort Churchill was established near Buckland Station to keep the peace. The battlesite looks much as it did when the hostilities took place. A marker is across the street from the Nixon Post Office. Fort Storey was a temporary breastwork set up by the Washoe Regiment during the second battle with the Paiutes on June 3, 1860. Named for Capt. Edward Faris Storey of the Virginia Rifles, who died on June 7, from wounds received in this engagement.

RENO, Washoe County. I–80, US 40, 395.

Nevada Historical Society Museum, 1650 N. Virginia St. Prehistoric and modern Indian artifacts, pioneer materials.

Mackay School of Mines Museum, on campus of University of Nevada, Reno, has fossils, rocks, etc.

Toiyabe National Forest, 10 miles W. on US 40, then S. on I–80, covers 3,128,960 acres; part of forest in California, headquarters at Reno.

Newlands House, 7 Elm Court, built in 1889 was the home of Sen. Francis G. Newlands. A national historic landmark not open to the public at present.

STAR CITY, Pershing County. State 50, ca. 12 miles S. of Mill City. Once the largest mining town in the NW part of the state. In 1861 Isaac Miller and Jose Thacker found silver here and started a rush of miners who then founded the Star City Mining District. By 1864 there were 1,200 residents, a stamp mill, two hotels, a Wells-Fargo office, post office and telegraph. Only mining scars remain.

TONOPAH, Nye County. (6,050 feet). US 6, 95.

Lunar Crater, near US 6 between Tonopah and Ely. Steep-sided pit of 400 feet in depth created by volcanic action ca. 1,000 years ago.

Mizpah Hotel, 100 Main St. Two early-day saloons.

Chamber of Commerce has on its emblem "Me and Jim Found Tonopah." This pictures a prospector, Jim Butler, leading a burro. Butler is said to have picked up a rock to throw at his burro, which proved to have minerals in it and led ultimately to the mining strikes.

UNIONVILLE, Pershing County. State 50, S. of I–80. California prospectors found silver in 1861 bringing a rush that resulted in the Buena Vista Mining District and a camp called Dixie. During the Civil War the name was changed to Unionville. Six original miners' houses are still in use.

Mark Twain Cabin, stone cabin used by the author, is still standing. A *Pioneer Museum* has nickelodeons and a rock display.

VIRGINIA CITY, Storey County. State 17. 26 miles SE of Reno. The entire town is a national historic landmark. The Comstock Lode, one of the richest deposits of lode gold and silver ever found, gave Virginia City unequalled prominence among mining towns. Bret Harte and Mark Twain were reporters on the *Territorial Enterprise.* There are many surviving homes and public buildings, many restorations and relics. A Visitors' Bureau on C St. has a 15-minute film on the history of the town and information on the sites and tours of the district. Piper's Opera House, at B and Union Sts., is one of the most famous old theaters in America.

Mark Twain was here
(Pro-Am Photo Labs, Reno)

NEW MEXICO

They buried poor William H. Bonney, just a bit more than old enough to vote, dressed in a borrowed white shirt that was much too large for him, in a coffin of plain wood, in the little cemetery of Fort Sumner. . . . No more around Fort Sumner did William H. Bonney, through protruding front teeth, sing and whistle bars of the song hit of the day, "Silver Threads Among the Gold," a few words of which, because he knew only a few of them, he sang over and over again, even when on missions which he knew would end for someone in death or disaster.

With William H. Bonney out of the way, Patrick Garrett's fame increased to substantial proportions . . . [he] traveled to Santa Fe to collect the $500 reward that he thought had been offered for the killing of the desperado by Governor Lew Wallace, on behalf of the Territory of New Mexico. Politicians in Santa Fe pointed out that Lew Wallace had worded the offer of a reward "for the delivery" of Billy the Kid to the Sheriff of Lincoln County, not for killing him. Chagrined, Garrett spent nearly five hundred dollars buying drinks in Santa Fe for members of the 1882 Legislature, before they passed an act making it possible for him to draw down his reward from the Territorial Treasury.

William A. Keleher, *The Fabulous Frontier* (Santa Fe: 1945)

Dobe Bill, he went a-ridin'
    From the town of Santa Fe
On a quiet Sunday morning,
    Goin' happy on his way,
Ridin' happy on that pinto
    That he dearly loved to straddle,
With his six-gun and sombrero
    That was wider than his saddle. . . .

Anonymous

Here I fell in with Candelaria, an aged shepherd, who in the palmy days of mining stumbled upon a lump of gold worth $750. "Straightaway,' he told me, recounting his luck, 'straightaway all the men bowed to me, the women courtesied, the *comerciantes* took off their hats when they met me. My name grew like a gourd. From Candelaria it became Don Juan, Don Juan Candelaria, Señor Don Juan Candelaria, Señor Don Juan Candelaria, Caballero! This lasted three weeks. My gold lasted twenty days. On the twenty-second day my name was flattened out to *Old* Candelaria, and now I herd sheep. Adios, compadre.'

James F. Meline, *Two Thousand Miles on Horseback; Santa Fe and Back,* 1866

NEW MEXICO FACTS: The Folsom Man and the Sandia Man are the oldest traced inhabitants of the Western hemisphere. Pueblo Indians were here in prehistoric times, and still are. The Spanish explorers came in the 16th century. Coronado and his conquistadors found no gold and eventually returned to Mexico. Missionaries and settlers came from the South. The Indians rebelled in 1680 driving the Spaniards away. The Santa Fe Trail opened in the 19th century bringing traders and more settlers. New Mexico became a province of Mexico until Col. Stephen W. Kearny and troops occupied Santa Fe in 1846 and declared the territory a part of the United States. In 1848 it was formally ceded to the U.S. and in 1850 became the Territory of New Mexico. The 47th state, New Mexico entered the union January 6, 1912.
Capital: Santa Fe. Nickname: Land of Enchantment.

New Mexico has one national park, Carlbad Caverns, ten national monuments, five national forests and one national grassland, 19 Indian Pueblos and four non-Pueblo reservations.

New Mexico Indians. Basket-makers, Pueblo, and Nomads; Ute, Navajo, Apache. Tribes, subtribes and families are confusing even today and the Spanish writers gave different names to the Apache. Subdivisions in New Mexico, of the Athapascan or Apache: Querecho or Vaquero, Navaho, Chiricahua, Pinaleno, Coyotero, Arivaipa, Gila, Tonto, Jicarilla, Mescalero, Faraon, Llanero, Lipan, White Mountain, Pinal, Gileno, Mimbreno, Mogollon.

Pueblos. The Western Keres: Acoma, Laguna; The Eastern Keres: Cochiti, Santo Domingo, San Felipe, Santa Ana, Zia; the Tanoans: Isleta, Sandia; the

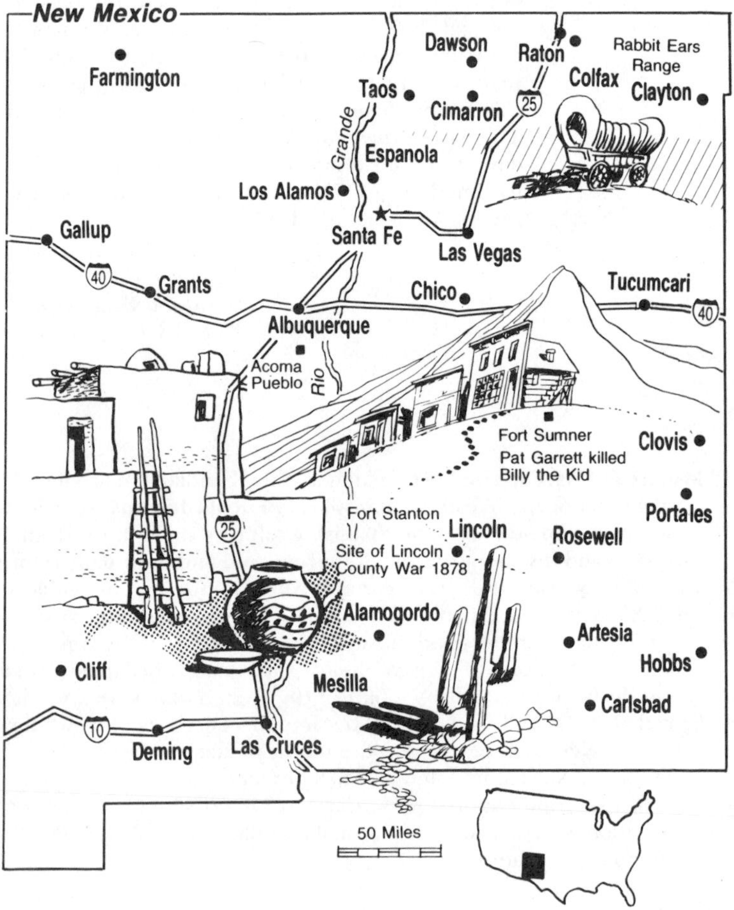
New Mexico
Farmington
Dawson
Raton
Rabbit Ears Range
Colfax
Clayton
Taos
Cimarron
25
Grande
Espanola
Los Alamos
Gallup
Santa Fe
Las Vegas
40
Grants
Chico
Tucumcari
40
Albuquerque
Acoma Pueblo
Rio
Fort Sumner
Pat Garrett killed Billy the Kid
Clovis
25
Fort Stanton
Lincoln
Site of Lincoln County War 1878
Rosewell
Portales
Alamogordo
Artesia
Hobbs
Cliff
Mesilla
Carlsbad
10
Deming
Las Cruces
50 Miles

Northern Tiwa: Picuris, Taos; the Tewa: San Juan, Santa Clara, San Ildefonso, Nambe, Tesuque; the Towa: Jemez; the Zunian: Zuni.

Early Routes. Santa Fe Trail, Cimarron Cutoff, Goodnight–Loving Cattle Trail, Butterfield Trail, El Camino Real, Coronado Trail, Chisum Trail (not the Chisholm), Jim Stinson Trail.

ABBOTT, Colfax County. US 56.

Dorsey Mansion, ca. 12 miles NE of Abbott at Chico, on secondary road. Stephen Dorsey, a soldier, businessman, rancher and politician, built the house in 1878–84 with locally quarried stone. Sculpted portraits of the builder, his wife and his brother appear on the octagonal tower, which may explain why the construction took so long. Above these are an eagle and two gargoyles, representing Dorsey's political opponent, James G. Blaine. A registered historic place. Dorsey was U.S. Senator from Arkansas (1873–76); this house and his ranch were sold at a foreclosure sale in 1893. Present owners are restoring the mansion.

ABIQUIU, Rio Arriba County. (5,930 feet). US 84.

Ghost Ranch Museum, 14 miles NW on US 84, in Carson National Forest, has live local animals and plants, a miniature forest, geology and paleontology exhibits and a beaver museum; operated by the Forest Service. The forest covers 1,411,113 acres including Wheeler Peak, 13,161 feet, Wheeler Peak Wilderness, part of the Pecos Wilderness and 8 miles of the Rio Grande Wild River. Also part of the Sangre de Cristo Mountains. Headquarters in Taos.

ABÓ, Torrance County. US 60. An Indian village among the Salinas pueblos E. of the Manzano Mountains, occupied from late prehistoric through early Spanish times. By the 1620s many of the Indians had been converted to Christianity. A national historic landmark, the site is administered by the Museum of New Mexico. The ruins of the adobe pueblo, church and convent are preserved.

ACOMA PUEBLO, Valencia County. (7,000 feet). Ca. 12 miles S. of I–40, or 13 miles S. of Casa Blanca on State 23. The pueblo is possibly the oldest continuously occupied settlement in North America. It was established ca. 1075 on a flat, 40-acre mesa which rises 350 feet above the plains. To reach the village means to climb a stone trail. Most of the villagers live in three parallel communal houses. When first constructed, these could be entered only by ladders which could be drawn up in case of attack and were windowless.

Mission of San Estevan Rey, founded by Fray Juan Ramirez in 1629. All materials were carried by Indians to the mesa. Some beams are 40 feet long. The church was completed in 1642; repaired in 1799–1800. A national historic landmark.

Enchanted Mesa, 3 miles N. on State 23, is 430 feet high and can be climbed by experienced persons without special equipment but amateurs should not try it.

ALAMOGORDO, Otero County. US 70.

Lincoln National Forest, E. of town, comprises ca. 1,100,000 acres. Headquarters are here.

Three Rivers Petroglyph Site, 29 miles N. on US 54, then 5 miles E. on county road. Interpretive shelter. The more than 500 rock carvings were made from 900 to 1400, by the Jornado Branch of the Mogollon Indian culture. Bureau of Land Management at Las Cruces administers the site and has added information.

Mescalero Apache Indian Reservation, 29 miles N.

Caravan Tours, to ancient Lake Lucerne in the White Sands National Monument, are infrequently conducted by Chamber of Commerce. The only access leads through the missile range. The National Park Service sponsors the tours and provides a ranger to interpret the site. The bed of the lake is gypsum and would be of commercial value if it were not for the location. No more than 30 cars can make the trip and are under guard. Tour times can be found at the C. of C. here, or the White Sands National Monument, or White Sands Missile Range, Las Cruces.

Otero County Historical Society Museum, in town, has regional relics.

ALBUQUERQUE, Bernalillo County (5,314 feet). I-40, US 66. I–25.

Old Town, 1 block N. of Central Ave, at Rio Grande Blvd. The original settlement, with a plaza, was founded in 1706. Now an art center with Spanish style shops and galleries.

Church of San Felipe de Neri, NW corner of Old Town Plaza, was established in 1706. The building has been enlarged and remodeled several times.

Museum of Albuquerque, Yale Blvd., SE. Regional history displays; also art and science exhibits.

Rio Grande Zoological Park, 903 10th St., SW. Animals are bred here to stock state game preserves. Children's section has a prairie dog town.

Cibola National Forest, headquarters here, covers 1,660,631 acres.

University of New Mexico, 2 miles E. on Central Ave., was founded in 1889. On campus: *Maxwell Museum of Anthropology,* Roma Ave., NE. and University, features southwest exhibits; *Museum of Geology,* 200 Yale Blvd., NE.; *Jonson Gallery,* 1909 Las Lomas, changing exhibits and paintings; *University Art Museum,* Redondo and Cornell, NE, changing art exhibits.

Historical Society of New Mexico Museum, on University Hill, NE.

Sandia Peak Museum, base terminal of tramway in Cibola National Forest, has history of transportation and Southwest trade told in exhibits.

Sandia Crest, 16 miles E. on US 66, 6 miles N. on State 14, 44, 7 miles NW on State 44, then 6 miles W. on State 536, is at 10,678 feet. There is an observation tower; nature talks in summer months. Another way to get to the summit is aboard the Aerial Tramway. The cables are strung through two towers built into the mountain. The span from Tower No. 2 to Sandia Crest is 7,750 feet, one of the longest single-cable spans in the world. The first man to scale the mountain and make a note of it was Jules Marcou, a Swiss geologist, in 1853. The tram was built by the Swiss.

Sandia Frontier Town, just E. of town, has covered wagon and stagecoach rides, with the usual replica scenery.

Coronado State Monument, NW via I-25 to Cuba-Farmington exit, then 5 miles W. on State 44. Anasazi Indians

Billy the Kid, the tiny desperado killed by Sheriff Pat Garrett
(New Mexico Dept. of Development, Mark Nohl photo)

were here about 1300, in a pueblo known as Kuaua (KWAH-wah). The Spanish came in 1540. The Visitor Center has artifacts from the area.

Petroglyph Park, W. edge of town, is an area set aside by the developer of Volcano Cliffs. The Indian drawings are in canyons. Signs in the area. Some may be reached by a road which turns left from Paradise Blvd. at a point opposite the Paradise Hills Golf Club. The petroglyphs show kachinas, birds, animals, flute players and handprints.

ARTESIA, Eddy County. I-8, US 285.

Historical Museum & Art Center, 505 Richards Ave., pioneer and Indian artifacts, changing art exhibits.

AZTEC, San Juan County (5,686 feet). US 550.

Aztec Ruins National Monument, 1 mile N. of US 550. One of the best preserved pueblo ruins in the Southwest, occupied between 1100 and 1400 and built by ancestors of today's Pueblo Indians was mistakenly called Aztec by European settlers. The great kiva has been handsomely restored. Interpretive museum and self-guiding tours.

Aztec Community Museum, 125 N. Main St. 2 blocks S. of US 550, has archaeological displays and pioneer material.

BANDELIER NATIONAL MONUMENT, Sandoval County. State 4. The many ruins here are typical of the prehistoric dwellings of the later Pueblo period. In the cliffs of Frijoles Canyon are cave rooms. The National Park Service area covers 29,661 acres. Slide programs are presented in the Visitor Center. A museum has geological and Indian exhibits. Self-guiding walking tours of the principal ruins, Guided tours in summer months.

BELL RANCH HEADQUARTERS, San Miguel County. NE of the Conchas Reservoir (State 104). The original ranch was made up of the Pablo Montoya grant of 1824. and other properties. Wilson Waddingham, an Englishman, recorded the Bell Grant in 1875. The brand and name came from a landmark in the vicinity, a small bell-shaped hill called "La Campana." The ranch covers 130,855 acres. The original ranch building, center of the main house, consists of two adobe-walled rooms built ca. 1860. Other buildings include a post office, manager's office, mess hall, barns, corrals. Pablo Montoya, who received the first land grant, was alcalde of Santa Fe. In its greatest days the ranch covered 2 million acres and its owners and managers lived like royalty. New Mexico historian, Erna Fergusson, writing of the ranch in the mid-1960s said:

> Its manager, George Ellis, lives in the rambling old adobe house that has known its Indian fights. A day on the ranch now is probably not unlike any day within the last fifty years. Cowboys ride in to the chuck wagon for dinner; and if the chuck wagon is now a pickup truck, it is driven by the same old "hooligan," who also fetches wood and water, peels potatoes and polices camp . . . most of these young men had served in the Navy. Cowboys are afraid that in the Army they might have to walk.

The ranch is a registered historic place.

BERNALILLO, Sandoval County. US 85.

Church of the Pueblo of San Felipe, 11 miles NE on the Rio Grande, was erected ca. 1700.

Sandia Cave, 11 miles E. on State 44, in Cibola National Forest, represents one of the earliest occupations of the continent. Three distinct prehistoric groups were revealed by excavations, the earliest from ca. 9000–8000 B.C. A national historic landmark, not open to the public at present.

Zia Pueblo and Mission, 16 miles NW on State 44. The mission was established in the 17th century. The Zia sun symbol is used as the design of the state flag, but the Zia people do not always welcome visitors. Their pottery is distinctive in color and design and excellently made. No photography or sketching allowed in the Pueblo.

Big Bead Mesa, W. of Casa Salazon in Cibola National Forest on Secondary roads. The Utes in the first half of the 1700s with the aid of the Comanches drove the Navajos from their homes on the Upper San Juan River. The Navajos settled in this area in the mid-18th century and soon formed an alliance with the Gila Apaches, harassing the pueblos of Laguna and Acoma. The mesa is a national historic landmark.

BLANCO, San Juan County. State 44.

Francés Canyon Ruin, inquire locally for road directions, By tree rings archaeologists reckon the structure was built between 1716 and 1742; it is believed that Navajos fortified their village against raiding Utes and Comanches. This is the largest known village of the "refugee" sites. There were 40 masonry-walled surface rooms. A registered historic place.

Other ruins in Rio Arriba County will be found at *Tsiping,* 1.3 miles S. of Canones on Pueblo Mesa; *Puye Ruins,* 14 miles W. of Espanola on State 5, 30, Santa Clara Indian Reservation, among the largest of the prehistoric Indian settlements on the Pajarito Plateau, a national historic landmark; *San Gabriel De Yungue-Ouinge,* 4 miles N. of Espanola via US 64 and secondary roads, the ruins of a Tewa Indian Pueblo on the site of the first Spanish capital of New Mexico. Excavated remains include the earliest European church and house ruins found in continental U.S. to date, a national historic landmark not yet open to the public.

CAPULIN MOUNTAIN NATIONAL MONUMENT, Colfax County. State 72. An extinct volcanic cinder cone on a 775-acre monument rises 8,215 feet above sea level. Capulin Mountain is about 7,000 years old. Visitor Center has an audio-visual program and other interpretive information. Ranger on duty in summer months. Self-guiding leaflets available at parking area.

CARLSBAD, Eddy County. US 62, 180.

Carlsbad Caverns National Park, 27 miles SW on US 62, 180. Visitor Center near entrance has plenty of literature on the many facets of the cave. There is a three-story observation tower and an exhibit room with the geology, biology and archaeology of the site depicted in displays. Trips are available daily. The complete Walk-In trip is 3 miles long, takes from 2½ to 3 hours; shorter trips are available. An elevator returns visitors to the surface. Part of the Big Room may be visited by persons in wheelchairs.

Temperature is 56° at all times. Rangers patrol the cave for information and protection. Bat Flight programs start ca. 7 P.M. during the summer. Inquire at information desk. (And *vaya con Diós*—my investigative tour guiding stops at all cave entrances).

Carlsbad Municipal Museum, 101 S. Halagueno St. in Public Library. Prehistoric relics and mineral exhibits.

Million Dollar Museum, 20 miles SW on US 62, 180 to White's City, W. on State 7. Pioneer and Indian displays.

Zoological-Botanical State Park of the Southwest, 1½ miles NW off US 285. Large cactus collection, small animal exhibits.

CARRIZOZO, Lincoln County. (5,-425 feet). US 380.

Valley of Fires State Park, 3 miles W. on US 380. The park covers 463 acres on the Mal Pais lava flow which is 1½ miles wide and ca. 60 miles long. An interesting terrain.

My House of Old Things, 24 miles N. on US 54, then 2 miles E. State 462 to Ancho, is a museum in a frontier-style home. Restored railroad office.

Smokey Bear Historical State Park, E. of town on US 380 at Capitan. Smokey Bear has been a longtime resident of the National Zoo in Washington, D.C., and is alive at this writing but he's 26. Congress in 1974 authorized the return of his remains, on that sad day when he is only a happy memory, to Capitan in sight of the Capitan Mountains of Lincoln National Forest where he was born. The museum which began in a one-room log building has plans for expansion.

CERRILLOS, Santa Fe County. State 10.

Cerrillos Mining District, S. of Santa Fe, along State 10, in the Cerrillos Hills, Ortiz Mountains, and the northern foothills of the San Pedro Mountains, has yielded silver, gold, turquoise, coal and other minerals and has been worked since prehistoric days when the Pueblo Indians mined turquoise. In the New Place area a small gold rush occurred in 1839. *Tuerto* mining camp developed and died out in mid-century. In 1879 *Bonanza City* and *Carbonateville* grew because of the discovery of sulphide, zinc, silver and lead. Many relics of the old days are in the area. Abandoned mineworks are in the fringe areas of the old towns. The Ortiz Mine is behind the little town of *Dolores* off State 10 just S. of Cerrillos, unpaved road winds S. ca. 9 miles to old gold town in a high valley in the Ortiz Mountains.

Other ghost towns of Santa Fe County: *Golden,* State 10, has a fine old Pueblo church and picturesque cemetery; *Madrid,* State 10, deserted frame houses on main streets of the old coal-mining camp. Adobe and other buildings are also still standing. Boot Hill at edge of town; *San Pedro,* State 10, to dirt road 14 miles N. of Tijeras, then less than a mile. One-time gold-mining camp. *Waldo,* just W. of Cerrillos, has adobe ruins. This was once the junction point of the rail spur to Madrid.

Cerrillos has had another "boom" in tourism when Walt Disney chose the site for the background of *The Nine Lives of Elfego Baca,* which brought spectators and business. Disney additions to the town decor are still around. The Tiffany Saloon, at a main intersection, served as a Mexican cantina and courtroom in the movie. The original 22-foot walnut bar has a real brass footrail that has supported many a miner's boot in times past and still does service.

CHACO CANYON NATIONAL MONUMENT, McKinley County. State 57. Preserves the remains of a Pueblo culture of 600–1200. Pueblo Bonita was built with five stories on a floor plan that exceeded 3 acres and could house ca. 1200. The National Park Service area covers 21,509 acres, 12 large ruins and more than 400 smaller ones are in the monument. There are three self-guiding trails, conducted tours and evening programs in summer months. Visitor Center with museum.

CHAMA, Rio Arriba County (7,850 feet). US 84.

Cumbres & Toltec Scenic Railroad, a one-day trip on an 1880s narrow-gauge steam railroad to Antonito, Colorado, with return by motor coach. The route through the Cumbres Pass (10,000 feet) crosses and recrosses the state line and passes through backwoods terrain. As advertised by brochure, there are "pitch-black tunnels, lofty bridges & antique snowshed, abandoned way stations and spring-fed water tanks." Open observation cars.

CHIMAYO, Santa Fe County (6,872 feet). State 76.

Santuario de Chimayo, E. end of town. Chapel built in 1816. Original religious paintings. The church is still active. A national historic landmark.

CIMARRON, Colfax County (6,427 feet). State 21. The town was once part of the Lucien B. Maxwell land grant on the Santa Fe Trail.

Philmont Scout Ranch and Explorer Base, 6 miles S. on State 21 for headquarters of the 138,000-acre ranch. *Kit Carson Museum* is 7 miles S. of headquarters; more than 7,000 Indian artifacts are in the *Ernest Thompson Seton Memorial Library & Museum* on ranch. Buffalo, deer, elk and antelope are here also.

Old Mill Museum, in Old Town on US 64, was a gristmill in 1864. Historical displays.

St. James Hotel, built in 1870, now a museum. Lobby and bedrooms restored with antique furnishings. Among those said to have stayed here: Annie Oakley, Buffalo Bill Cody, Wyatt Earp and Zane Grey.

Cimarron County Courthouse, now deserted, looked upon wild days in the 19th century, and many legendary Old Westerners. The Maxwell Grant covered 1,714,765 acres. Lucien B. Maxwell was a hunter and trapper from Kaskaskia, Illinois, who became the son-in-law of Carlos Beaubien. Beaubien in 1841 with Guadalupe Miranda acquired land in what is now NE New Mexico extending into Colorado and disputed in litigation for many years after the U.S. gained the land from Mexico in 1848. Maxwell's adobe mansion was richly furnished; he hired 500 peons and cultivated thousands of acres with cattle and sheep grazing in vast herds in other parts of his territory. The discovery of gold on his land brought his downfall; he invested a fortune in the mining enterprise and it failed. The town was the center for cowboy revels in their spare time and was the agency for the Ute Indians. Buffalo Bill Cody owned a sheep ranch with Maxwell nearby. The Don Diego Tavern, built in the 1870s, was the scene of 26 killings, by some reports; now a hotel. There is a rather incredible statue of Lucien Maxwell in concrete in the plaza of "New Town." He is holding a rifle on his knobby concrete knees. New Town straddles US 64, just N. of the Cimarron River. There have been a number of books written about

Maxwell and his adventures. A lively tale of old Cimarron is in *Haunted Highways,* by Ralph Looney (Hastings House, 1968) which deals with many but by no means all New Mexico ghost towns. The state Bureau of Mines and Mineral Resources recently published a map of New Mexico ghost towns which lists more than 700, also shown on map, and nearly as many unmapped.

Other ghosts in the general area of Cimarron are *Colfax,* ca. 12 miles N. on US 64 at intersection with Dawson Rd. Old Dickman Hotel still standing, a school and other buildings; *Dawson,* take gravel road N. of Colfax ca. 5 miles, ruins and a Boot Hill; *Koehler,* from Cimarron on US 64, N. 24 miles to paved spur W. 6 miles. Old stone buildings.

CLAYTON, Union County. US 56.

Rabbit Ears, N. and W. of Clayton, a natural landmark, which resembles the name, for westbound travelers on the Cimarron Cutoff of the Santa Fe Trail. The twin-peaked eminence is a national historic landmark. It was a focal point for camps and other landmarks, grouped as the Clayton Complex: McNee's Crossing, Turkey Creek Camp, Rabbit Ears Creek Camp, Mount Dora and Round Mound. These sites had year-round springs of vast importance to early travelers.

CLIFF, Grant County. State 211.

Kwilleylekia Ruins Monument, 2¾ miles E. on State 211, is a site once inhabited by the Salado Indians, now vanished. Visitor Center has displays showing implements left when the inhabitants fled from a 16th-century flood. Guided tours.

Woodrow Ruin, 5 miles NE of Cliff off State 293, on a high bench overlooking the W. bank of the Gila River. The most untouched relic of the Mimbres Branch of the Mogollon Culture. The village probably measured some 500 by 900 feet. A registered historic place.

DEMING, Luna County. US 180. Marker on highway N. of town for route of the Butterfield Trail.

Fort Cummings, on unimproved road ca. 21 miles NE of town and ca. 6 miles NW of State 26, make local inquiry. Gen. James H. Carleton's California Volunteers founded the post in 1863 to guard Cooke's Spring and the road to California. The previous year the site, which was a stop on the Butterfield line, had been attacked by Apaches. D.A.R. plaque at site. Some remains of officers' quarters, adobe walls, on private ranch.

Rockhound State Park, 14 miles SE via State 549 then unmarked road. Agate and other semiprecious stones for rock collectors. Free for the finding.

DULCE, Rio Arriba County (6,769 feet). US 64.

Jicarilla Apache Indian Reservation, US 64, is on a mesa from 6,500 to 8,500 feet high, with unrestored Indian ruins, hiking trails, open to the public.

ELIZABETHTOWN, Colfax County (ca. 8,500 feet). State 38. Once a gold-mining center of the Sangre de Cristos. The gold, first discovered in the 1860s, was giving out in 1875 when the Indians were beginning to give trouble and the town began to decline. Several old buildings and a cemetery remain. Other ghost towns in Colfax County (also see Cimarron) are *Gardner,* S. of Raton on US 64; *Brilliant,* 1 mile from Gardner, which was first known as Tinpan. A cluster of old sites around Brilliant has such names as Pend Flor, Elkins, Blossburg.

EL MORRO NATIONAL MONUMENT (INSCRIPTION ROCK), Valencia County. State 32, 53. The Rock of Zuni sandstone bears hundreds of names inscribed over the centuries. From prehistoric petroglyphs to the explorers, soldiers, settlers, nearly everyone registered his name in passing except the Indians of the historic times who were probably too busy trying to keep a piece of the land. (Not to say a piece of the Rock.) The national park service area covers 1,277.7 acres. Visitor center.

ESPAÑOLA, Rio Arriba County (5,590 feet). State 5. Pueblo and pottery country.

Pojoaque Pueblo, 8 miles SW. Nambé ware is made here.

San Idlefonso Pueblo, ca. 13 miles S. Black pottery and ceremonial dances in season.

San Juan Pueblo, 4 miles NE. In 1598, Governor Juan de Onate named this pueblo San Juan de los Caballeros and occupied the pueblo across the river, naming the latter San Gabriel de los Espanoles. Stone marker and mounds at site of San Gabriel.

Santa Clara Pueblo, 2 miles S. on State 30. Before the Spanish arrived, this village was called Kapo. In prehistoric times the Santa Clara Indians lived on the Pajarito Plateau near Puye.

FARMINGTON, San Juan County (5,395 feet). State 17.

The *Salmon Ruin,* 9 miles E. off State 17, near Bloomfield, a steep-sided ruin of the Chacoan culture dating back to the 11th century. Museum with artifacts from excavation.

San Juan County Museum, 100 E. La Plata, local history.

FOLSOM, Union County. State 72.

Folsom Museum, many ruins and a cemetery are worth visiting. *The Folsom Site,* 8 miles W. of town on the banks of Dead Horse Gulch, dates from ca. 13,000–8,000 B.C. Although Early Man finds are more common now than in the 1920s when this archaeological discovery was made, the site is a significant national historic landmark.

FORT BASCOM, San Miguel County. Via unimproved roads from Logan and State 39. In the SE corner of the county. Inquire locally. The fort was established on the S. bank of the Canadian River during the Civil War to help control Kiowas, Comanches and any other hostiles of the area. The Goodnight–Loving Cattle Trail and the Santa Fe Trail were watched over by soldiers from this fort. Kit Carson, leading troops from here, fought the Battle of Adobe Walls, Texas, against Kiowas, in 1864. When the post was abandoned in 1870, troops and supplies were moved to Fort Union, New Mexico. No remains of buildings on site which is on a private ranch.

FORT BAYARD, Grant County. Ca. 1 mile N. of Central (State 90) on unimproved road. Established in August 1866, 10 miles E. of Silver City, near the base of the Santa Rita Mountains, to protect the Pinos Altos mining district against hostiles, particularly the Warm Springs Apaches. Named for Brig. Gen. George Bayard, fatally wounded at Fredericksburg in 1862. Old post cemetery is on a hill nearby. Buildings now a Veterans Administration Hospital. This was a base in the Apache wars, particularly in the 1879–80 campaign against Victorio. *Fort Butler* appears on old maps on the Gallinas River near Santa Rosa, or on the Canadian River, ca. 12 miles W. of Bascom; plans had been made but the garrison never existed.

FORT CRAIG, Socorro County. E. of US 85, ca. 4 miles S. of San Marcial. Established in April 1854, when Fort Conrad, which had been located in 1851 ca. 9 miles N. on the right side of the Rio Grande was abandoned, the new post protected miners and the Santa Fe–El Paso Road. Soldiers from here took part in the Navajo and Apache troubles of the 1850s and in the Apache wars of 1861–86. The post was strengthened at the outbreak of the Civil War; its troops took part in the battle of Valverde, February 21, 1862. The Texans won that conflict and Federal troops withdrew to this base. Walls and some earth mounds remain. A registered historic place.

FORT STANTON, Lincoln County. On secondary road, ca. 5 miles SE of Capitan. Established in 1855 to control the Mescalero and White Mountain Apaches, the post was held briefly by the Confederates. Reoccupied by Kit Carson, 1st New Mexico Infantry, in 1862. Now a tuberculosis sanaterium.

FORT SUMNER, De Baca County. US 60. Established in 1862, in the Bosque Redondo on the E. bank of the Pecos River S. of the present town of Fort Sumner. An Indian trading post had used the site since 1851. Col. Kit Carson brought the Navajos from Canyon de Chelly, Arizona, here; there were 8,000 to make the "Long Walk," forced upon them by the decision to remove them from their own lands. They were half-starved before the journey began; at the end of it there were the Mescaleros who detested them already in Bosque Redondo, and prison-like conditions of overcrowding and disease. In 1865 the 400 Mescaleros departed. Eventually the Navajos were allowed to return to Arizona. From 1866 into the 1870s the fort was a way station on the Goodnight–Loving Cattle Trail. When the garrison was removed and the post put up for auction in 1869, it was bought by Rancher Lucien Maxwell. His son inherited it. In 1881 Pat Garrett shot Billy the Kid in the remodeled ranch house. Fortsite on private land now. State marker at junction of US 60 and State 212. Cemetery off State 212 ca. 1 mile E. has the grave of Billy the Kid, also Lucien Maxwell and other pioneers.

FORT UNION NATIONAL MONUMENT, Mora County. US 85. Established on the W. side of the valley of Wolf Creek on the Mountain Branch of the Santa Fe Trail in July 1851 to protect the route and to serve as a depot of supplies. The original log buildings were too close to the mesa on the W. rim of the valley to be considered secure so Col. Edward R. S. Canby ordered a new post on the valley floor ca. 1 mile from the first site and E. of Wolf Creek. He feared a Confederate attack and began construction in August 1861. This was an earthwork which was damp and easily deteriorated. The third and last Fort Union was built just N. of the second, of adobe and brick. The original post was used as an arsenal. As Canby had feared, the Confederates attempted to capture the fort in 1862 but were cut off by Union troops 70 miles SW. The post was officially abandoned in 1891. Many of its adobe walls remain. A museum in the Visitor Center has many relics. The National Park Service has a problem maintaining the surviving adobe structures and is working with the Archaeological Center of the University of Arizona to try to find a means of halting deterioration. Chemical sprays, epoxies and other preservatives are studied. Silicone treatments have been made but last only from one to five years. Visitors are cautioned not to try climbing on existing structures.

FORTS, various sites:

Cantonment Burgwin, on the Rio Grande del Rancho, near the mouth of the Rito de la Olla, ca. 10 miles S. of Taos. Named for Capt. John H. K. Burgwin, 1st I.S. Dragoons, who died in 1847 of wounds received in the Taos uprising. Burgwin had occupied the Post of Albuquerque in 1847. Never officially a fort, the post was referred to as the Fort Fernando de Taos. Abandoned in 1860, now reconstructed and occupied by the Fort Burgwin Research Center. Museum.

Fort Fillmore, on the left bank of the Rio Grande, ca. 6 miles S. of Mesilla, river has since changed course S. of Las Cruces today. The post was part of the frontier defense system and named for President Millard Fillmore. Union troops abandoned the fort in the summer of 1861; Confederate soldiers from Texas under Col. John R. Baylor moved in, but departed the following July as the California forces approached. The 1st California Cavalry arrived in August 1862, but were moved to Mesilla in October and the fort was not permanently garrisoned again. Lydia Spencer Lane, who wrote *I Married a Soldier,* claimed to have run the fort when the garrison, except for a sergeant and ten men were away. The sergeant made his daily report to the redoubtable Lydia.

Fort Lowell, on the Chama River, SW of Tierra Amarilla, established November 1866, to protect the area against Ute Indians, originally called Camp Plummer. Designated a fort in 1868 and named for Brig. Gen. Charles Lowell, who died in 1864 of wounds received at Cedar Creek, Virginia. In 1872 the agency for some Ute and Apache tribes was sent from Abiquiu to Fort Lowell which had been abandoned in 1869.

Fort McLane, 15 miles S. of the Santa Rita copper mines at Apache Tejo on the W. side of the Santa Rita River. Established in 1860 and called Fort Floyd, Camp Webster and Fort Webster before the post was officially designated in January 1861, and named for Capt. George McLane of the Mounted Riflemen was killed in Indian fighting in 1860. The post garrisoned infrequently during the Civil War was abandoned at the conflict's end.

Fort McRae, ca. 5 miles W. of the Jornada del Muerto, 3 miles E. of the Rio Grande, near Ojo del Muerto. Established April 1863, named for Capt. Alexander McRae, 3rd U.S. Cavalry, killed on February 21, 1862, in the Battle of Valverde. Abandoned in 1876.

Fort Marcy, adjacent to the Palace of Governors, Santa Fe. Established by Brig. Gen. Stephen Watts Kearny in 1846. Named for Secretary of War William Marcy. Kearny had taken over New Mexico as a U.S. territory during the War with Mexico and declared himself governor. Post was used intermittently and finally abandoned in 1894. Group of mounds on hilltop overlooking Santa Fe marks the site.

Camp Ojo Caliente, on the right bank of the Alamosa River, near the foothills of the San Mateo Mountains, ca. 18 miles N. of present Winston. An advanced picket post of Fort Craig, the camp established in 1859 was abandoned during the Civil War. In late 1860s became the agency headquarters for the Warm Spring Apache Reservation.

Fort Selden, S. end of the Jornada del Muerto, ca. 1½ miles E. of the Rio Grande, ca. 12 miles above Dona Ana, established in 1865 to protect settlers of the Mesilla Valley and travel routes.

Fort Thorn, on the right bank of the Rio Grande at Santa Fe, now Hatch, established in December 1853, to guard the El Paso–Santa Fe route and the San Diego Rd. Abandoned in 1859, one storeroom and the hospital was left for travelers. Other property was used at Fort Fillmore. Confederates occupied the old post in 1861–62. Union came back in July 1862, but the fort was never regarrisoned after the war.

Fort Tularosa, on left bank of Tularosa Creek, ca. 15 miles N. of Reserve, established in April 1872, to protect the Apache Reservation, just opened. The post was soon moved to Horse Creek, ca. 18 miles E. In 1874 the post was abandoned as the Indians had been removed to Ojo Caliente, Arizona.

Fort Webster was a movable post, having three or possibly four locations. An old Mexican fort had protected the Santa Rita copper mines since 1804. The boundary commission who occupied these buildings called the site Cantonment Dawson; the Army came after the boundary commission departed and named the post Fort Webster for Secretary of State Daniel Webster. In 1852 it moved to the Rio Mimbres, ca. 14 miles NE of the mines and a new post was built but the old name kept. In 1853 the garrison was removed to Fort Thorn. Two more temporary posts were given the name Fort Webster.

Fort West, E. side of the Gila River in the Pinos Altos Mountains, N. of present Silver City, existed from January 1863 to January 1864.

Forts Wingate I & II, first established in October 1862, at El Gallo at present San Rafael, abandoned in 1868; garrison transferred to Wingate II, established 1860, at Ojo del Oso, N. end of the Zuni Range, near the Rio Puerco of the West. First called Fort Fauntleroy, for Thomas Fauntleroy of the 1st U.S. Dragoons who joined the Confederacy, renamed Fort Lyon for Brig. Gen. Nathaniel Lyon, killed at Wilson's Creek, Missouri. Garrison was withdrawn in September 1861, when the Texans approached. Confederates called the post Fort Fauntleroy throughout the war. U.S. troops reoccupied the post in June 1868, and it was designated Fort Wingate. Now Fort Wingate Ordnance Depot, but this was moved in 1925 closer to the railroad. Unfortunately for the history-minded, the old post which was one of the best preserved in the Southwest was razed and replaced with modern buildings. A two-story barrack, rebuilt after a fire in 1896, is the only surviving building of any importance. The site of Fort Wingate I has no remaining structures but will be found just off State 53, ca. 1 mile W. of San Rafael in Valencia County.

GALLUP, McKinley County (6,515 feet). US 40.

Museum of Indian Arts & Crafts, 103 W. 66th Ave. Hopi, Navajo and Zuni artifacts; slide program.

GILA, Grant County. State 211. The LC Ranch Headquarters were here in the 1870s when the range covered 1 million acres.

Gila Cliff Dwellings National Monument, State 25, 527, contains five well-preserved dwellings in natural caverns of an overhanging cliff. The national park service area covers 533 acres. The ruins are near the West Fork of the Gila River, reached by a half-mile trail. Visitor Center at monument, with park ranger on duty. Self-guiding trails.

Gila National Forest, S. of Gila, US 180, 90. Headquarters in Silver City. The forest covers 2,694, 471 acres, including the Gila Wilderness, a primitive area in the Mogollon Mountains. *The Gila and Black Range Primitive Areas.* Visitor Center on State 25 and 527. The wilderness areas were used by outlaws of the 19th century as hideouts. Butch Cassidy and his gang, Tom Ketchum, Billy the Kid and others had nesting places in the canyons.

GRAN QUIVIRA NATIONAL MONUMENT, Socorro and Torrance Counties. State 14. Mogollon Indians occupied the area from ca. 800 to 1675 when dry weather and Apaches drove them away. The national park area comprises nearly 611 acres. There are pueblo and mission ruins. Self-guiding trail and a small museum-visitor center, with archaeological and historical exhibits. The 30-minute walk begins here. Guided tours may be arranged for groups.

GRANTS, Valencia County (6,464 feet). I–40. A Navajo Indian discovered uranium ore here in 1950.

Laguna Pueblo, 33 miles E. off US 66, on a land grant made by the Spanish king in 1689. *Mission of San Jose,* still in use, was erected in 1699. The Laguna Tribal Council Hall was built with profits from the uranium mine on the reservation.

Zuni-Cibola Trail, State 53, S. from Grants runs along the W. edge of the lava flow (*mal pais,* or bad lands) to Perpetual Ice Caves, 26 miles SW; to Bandera Crater, El Morro National Monument and the Zuni Pueblo.

Chamber of Commerce Museum, 500 W. Santa Fe, Indian artifacts and frontier relics. Mineral display.

HILLSBORO, Sierra County (5,238 feet). State 90. In 1877 two prospectors found gold on the E. side of the Black Range and started the Opportunity and Ready Pay Mines. The mines eventually produced more than $6 million in gold and silver. Many old stone and adobe buildings remain. The ruins of the large stone jail and part of the Sierra County Courthouse are still here. Large cottonwood trees add to the picturesque scene. The Black Range Museum has regional artifacts.

Other ghost towns of the area: *Kingston* is reached by State 90 which was once the main route for stagecoaches and attendant Apache raiders and assorted robbers, through the narrow but scenic Percha Creek Canyon. It doesn't seem possible that any frontiersman would have named a hotel for an Apache chief but the old Victorio Hotel still stands in Kingston. After the lucky strike at Hillsboro, prospectors fanned out to find more pay dirt. One group found silver on Thief Creek in November 1880. The Iron King and Empire Mines were established. The following spring Victorio drove the prospectors back to civilization but a year later a strike was made here that brought a small boom. New Mexico historian Ralph Looney gives credit for the strike to a drunk named Jack Sheddon, who had gotten rich in Leadville, Colorado, then lived up half a million dollars before he sobered up long enough to look for more mines. At Lake Valley, 20 miles S. of Hillsboro, he stayed in the saloon until a marshal loaded him onto a burro with food and whiskey and sent him out of town. He stopped for a bourbon break near Middle Percha Creek and found silver. At Kingston's peak there were 27 mines in operation, a brewery, opera house, three newspapers, three hotels, a G.A.R. post and even a schoolhouse.

Cemetery at Lake Valley has interesting headstones or markers. State 27, S. of Hillsboro.

Andrews and Gold Dust are N. of Kingston and Hillsboro; inquire locally. Tierra Blanca and Macho Springs are S. toward Lake Valley.

ISLETA, Bernalillo County. State 45, 47, S. of Albuquerque.

Mission of San Agustin de Isleta was built in the period of 1621–30 by Fray Juan de Salas. During the Pueblo rebellion the mission was partially burned and used as a corral. Restored and in use today. On the Isleta Indian Reservation.

JEMEZ STATE MONUMENT & VICINITY, Sandoval County. State 4. At N. edge of Jemez Springs, preserves the San Jose de los Jemez Mission and the ruins of the Guisewa Pueblo. Franciscans built the mission in the 17th century. A museum has artifacts.

San Juan Mesa Ruin, in the Jemez Springs vicinity, along the E. edge of the San Juan Mesa, is a registered historic site of pre-Columbian to 17th-century times.

Note: Photographers will find an abandoned church in Cabezon, nearby, a fine target with Cabezon Peak for background. Geologists have called the peak a volcanic plug, the neck of an old volcano. The "Giants Head," as it was called, marked the E. edge of the Navajo tribal world; the Spanish came in the 18th century, then Kit Carson and the Army. By 1875 the old town was a stage stop on the Star Line Mail & Transportation Co. which also stopped at Pena Blanca, San Ysidro, (Cabezon), Willow Springs, San Mateo, San Antonio Springs, Bacon Springs and Fort Wingate, then continued W. to Prescott, Arizona. Stages made the 76-mile trip in ca. 9½ hours in good weather.

LAS CRUCES, Dona Ana County. US 70. Named for the crosses which marked the graves of an oxcart caravan destroyed by Indians and buried days later by a freighting group from Dona Ana who found the bodies.

Mesilla, 2 miles SW, was the Confederate capital of the Territory of Arizona for a time. The Gadsden Treaty was signed here and Billy the Kid was on trial for his life in an adobe building at the SE corner of the plaza. The old town was an important stop on the El Paso–Fort Yuma stageline and the Butterfield Overland Mail. The site is now a state monument and a national historic landmark. Museum with many historical relics of the area.

Chamber of Commerce, 760 W. Picacho Ave., has tour plans for seven scenic trips of the area, taking in volcanoes, old forts and ghost towns.

LAS TRAMPAS, Taos County. State 76.

Las Trampas Historic District preserves the 18th-century town and is a national historic landmark. The Church of San Jose de Garcia on N. side of the Plaza was built in 1760–76 and is still in use.

LAS VEGAS, San Miguel County (6,420 feet). I–25. Santa Fe trail ruts can still be seen near town.

Rough Riders' Memorial & City Museum, Municipal Bldg. 720 Grand Ave. Relics.

LINCOLN, Lincoln County. US 380.

The Lincoln Historic District includes the sites of the famous Lincoln County War of 1878 one of the famous cattle-empire conflicts. The Murphy–Dolan crowd fought the Tunstall–McSween outfit. Cattle baron John Chisum (who has been portrayed by John Wayne on the screen) and Gen. Lew Wallace, territorial governor of New Mexico at the time, were also involved in the argument. The town is well preserved and is a national historic landmark. Headquarters of both warring parties are still standing. Historical markers are plentiful.

The courthouse from which Billy the Kid made his escape has been restored and is a state museum featuring frontier history. John H. Tunstall, a Britisher, was murdered by a posse, setting off the chain of violence. (Four horse thieves were blamed for the actual killing.) Billy the Kid, born Henry McCarty, first took the surname of Antrim; then William Bonney became his pseudonym. He was riding with Tunstall and ranch hands when the murder occurred; he had been fond of the Englishman and went on a spree of revenge. There was a showdown in July 1878 when Billy and his friends and the McSweens held out for three days against a small army of lawmen and gunmen. McSween and others were killed but Billy the Kid escaped. Mrs. McSween also survived. In February 1879 more shootings connected with the affair occurred, Billy was arrested and escaped to live as an outlaw for two more years before Sheriff Pat Garrett arrested him at Stinking Springs, two days before Christmas 1880. Tried for murder at Mesilla, he was freed on a technicality; convicted and sentenced to hang for another murder, he was held in an upstairs room of the courthouse which had been a store when the Lincoln War began. He managed to shoot two deputies and make his escape again. Two months later Pat Garrett shot him at Fort Sumner.

LORDSBURG, Hidalgo County. I–10. A onetime stop on the Butterfield Stageline, and the Pony Express.

Ghost towns of the area: *Shakespeare,* on gravel road S. from US 80 ca. 2½ miles. Boot Hill on left at edge of town. Several old adobe buildings, hotels, stores, etc. Gold was discovered in the nearby Pyramid Mountains in 1872; both gold and silver mines were soon in operation; *Ulmaris,* just S. of the old Butterfield Trail and SW of Lordsburg. *Gary, Conrad, Mondel* and *Steins* are all on the old trail W. to the state line. The route is now followed by I-10.

LOS ALAMOS, Los Alamos County (7,300 feet). State 4.

County Historical Museum, 1921 Juniper St. Displays trace local history since prehistoric times. The town was once the hideout of Vicente Silva and his "40 Thieves." He was an unusually vicious outlaw.

Village Cemetery has many interesting headstones.

MOGOLLON, Catron County. State 78. A partial ghost town on the edge of the Gila Wilderness, once a big silver producer. *Alma,* with a small Boot Hill to the W. just above Glenwood is nearby. Several marble slabs mark the graves of soldiers killed by Apaches. *Cooney and Clairmont* are N. of Mogollon. *Graham, Cleveland, Pleasonton* and *Lone Pine* lie S. and SW. Victorio and his Apaches made most of this area hazardous for miners for years in the 1880s. Miners had trapped and killed a son-in-law of the Apache Chief near Alma in April 1880—a vast mistake.

MORIARITY, Torrance County (6,200 feet). State 66.

Longhorn Ranch & Museum of the Old West, on State 66. Ranch and other frontier relics, in reconstructed buildings.

MOUNTAINAIR, Torrance County (6,550 feet).

Quarai State Monument, 6 miles N. off US 10. Ruins of the Mission de la Purisma Concepcion, built about 1628. Visitor Center with interpretive exhibits.

PECOS NATIONAL MONUMENT, San Miguel County. 2 miles S. of Pecos and E. of I-25. There are 340 acres, with pueblo ruins and the old Pecos Mission ruins, excavated and partially stabilized. Self-guiding trail, interpretive services at the ranger station. The large church and convent were built in the 1620s and destroyed during the Pueblo Rebellion of 1680. The convent was reconstructed and a new church built after the Reconquest, probably in the early 1700s.

PINOS ALTOS, Grant County. State 25. Several original buildings of the town which developed when gold was discovered in 1860 are still standing. In 1861 Mangas Colorados led 500 Apaches against the town. Most of the miners departed but one remained and formed the Pinos Altos Mining Co. By the turn of the century ca. $4,500,000 in gold had been produced. The town sits astride the Continental Divide. An old Mormon church and the first schoolhouse are among picturesque buildings. The town cemetery has many interesting headstones and fancifully carved crosses.

PORTALES, Roosevelt County. US 70.

Eastern New Mexico University has several museums on campus with Southwest archaeological exhibits, Early Man on the High Plains displays, etc. The Roosevelt County Museum, also on campus, has old machinery and tools as well as historical artifacts.

Oasis State Park, ca. 8 miles NE off State 467, has sand dunes which have yielded mammoth and mastodon bones.

Blackwater Draw Museum, 7 miles N. on US 70. Fossils and other artifacts from nearby site, displays include murals with history of prehistoric man.

QUARAI, Torrance County. 1 mile S. of Punta de Agua on secondary road. The Tiwas Indian Pueblo and mission date from the years of 1300–1670. A national historic landmark. Quarai was abandoned in 1672 after a series of Apache raids.

RATON PASS NATIONAL HISTORIC LANDMARK (7,800 feet). US 88, 87. On Colorado–New Mexico border. Colfax County in New Mexico. The pass was an alternate route to the Cimarron Cutoff segment of the Santa Fe Trail. During the Mexican War it was a route for the invaders.

ROSWELL, Chaves County. US 285.

Chisum Ranch, on the Bosque Redondo, ca. 4 miles S. John Chisum, from Tennessee, was a cattle baron. He had driven a herd up the Pecos River over the Goodnight–Loving Cattle Trail at a time when he was facing bankruptcy after a packinghouse in which he held an interest in Little Rock failed. He established headquarters in the Pecos Valley at South Spring, sold his first herd at Fort Sumner and got a government contract to deliver more. He made his permanent quarters in the Pecos Valley but maintained two cow camps elsewhere and by 1880 had one of the largest cattle holdings in the world. His ranch reached from Fort Sumner to the Texas line, 200 miles S. No original buildings remain. The ranch is operated as the South Spring Dairy Ranch today.

Roswell Museum & Art Center, 11th and Main Sts. Medical instruments of early times; Peter Hurd paintings and other exhibits.

Bitter Lake National Wildlife Refuge, 13 miles NE off US 70.

RUIDOSO, Lincoln County (6,900 feet). US 70. In the Sierra Blanca Mountains and the Lincoln National Forest.

Mon Jeau Forest Service Lookout Tower (10,056 feet), N. on State 37, 9 miles to Alto, turn left through gate, take right fork ca. 7 miles.

Old Dowlin Mill, in town, a 20-foot waterwheel more than a century old.

Mescalero Indian Reservation, 18 miles S. on US 70. Trading post and store. Ceremonial dances in summer; inquire at store.

SANTA FE, Santa Fe County (6,990 feet). US 85, 285.

Chamber of Commerce, La Fonda Hotel, publishes a fine map of the area. Walking tour starts at the Plaza, the square where the Santa Fe Trail ended; marker at SE corner. Kearny Proclamation marker on N. side. Soldiers' Monument in center.

Palace of the Governors, oldest public building in America, built in 1610, now a museum with exhibits which tell more than 2,000 years of the area's history. Territorial Gov. Lew Wallace wrote *Ben Hur* here. The Hall of Ethnology has artifacts, costumes and reproductions of living areas of early settlers.

Fine Arts Museum on N. side of plaza. Changing exhibits.

Laboratory of Anthropology, 1½ miles from plaza, in the 1100 block of Old Santa Fe Trail. Potter displays, basketry and other crafts.

Museum of International Folk Art, adjoining the above. Costuming and folk craftsmanship; many artifacts from New Mexico's Spanish Colonial era.

Museum of Navajo Ceremonial Art, next to the above, in octagonal building symbolic of a Navajo ceremonial hogan. Sand paintings, carvings and many other exhibits.

San Miguel Mission, Old Santa Fe Trail and De Vargas St. Oldest church in the U.S. built ca. 1610. Restored.

Oldest House, E. on De Vargas, now a shop.

State Capitol, De Vargas, built in

Territorial style in 1966. The Rotunda is faced with marble quarried from the Laguna Indian Reservation.

College of Santa Fe, 3 miles SW at Cerrillos Rd. and St. Michael's Dr., has a restored 18th-century storehouse built by Tarascan Indians, on campus.

Our Lady of Light Chapel, (Loretto Chapel) 219 Old Santa Fe Trail, dedicated in 1878, has an unusual spiral staircase to the choir loft.

Santa Fe National Cemetery, 1½ miles N. of plaza on US 285, has graves of soldiers killed in the Battle of Valverde and the Battle of Pigeon's Ranch, also called Pidgin's Ranch.

Santa Fe National Forest covers more than 1,526,489 acres, including the Pecos Wilderness Area and the San Pedro Parks Wilderness Area. Trails with ranger stations.

St. Catherine's Indian School, Griffin St., W. of Rosario Chapel, across from the Rosario and National Cemeteries. Katharine Drexel, a Philadelphia heiress, became a nun in 1889 and later founded the Order of the Sisters of the Blessed Sacrament for Indians and Colored People. She helped support the school built in 1886 and in 1894 came from the east to help manage the school. Some structures from the early years are still in use.

Glorieta Pass Battlefield, San Miguel

The Palace of the Governors at Santa Fe, built in 1610
(New Mexico Dept. of Development, Mark Nohl photo)

and Santa Fe counties, US 84, 85, 10 miles SE of Santa Fe. On March 28, 1862, the Union destroyed the Confederate ammunition and supply train without Union loss. Confederates retreated to Santa Fe. The battlesite is now a national historic landmark.

SANTA RITA, Grant County (6,325 feet). State 90.

Santa Rita Copper Mine, on State 90, is the oldest active mine in the Southwest to be developed within present boundaries. An Apache chief guided José Manuel Carrasco, commandant of a Spanish post, to the site in 1880, according to old stories. Carrasco sold the property to a Chihuahua merchant who obtained a grant to develop the mine. Using convict labor, Elguea built a smelter and an adobe fort to discourage the ever-raiding Apaches. The mine has had many owners and is now operated by the Kennecott Copper Company, which with a careless disregard for the past recently removed the only surviving original structure, an adobe fortress tower, to make room for new construction. There is an observation point for the open pit process.

SANTO DOMINGO, Sandoval County. State 22.

Church of the Pueblo of Santo Domingo, erected in 1886, replaced an earlier mission washed away by the flooded Rio Grande. Paintings and old records are displayed.

SHIPROCK, San Juan County. US 666.

Shiprock Peak, SW of town off highway, on Navajo Indian Reservation, is a 1,865-foot butte. A long-time landmark.

SILVER CITY, Grant County (6,000 feet). State 90. Once an Apache camp later a boomtown of gold, silver and zinc-mining camps.

Silver City Museum, 312 W. Broadway, early tools, American Indian artifacts.

Western New Mexico University, NW part of town, was founded in 1893. Museum on campus.

Phelps Dodge Copper Mine, 12 miles SW on State 90 in Tyrone. Open-pit mine has observation point. Tours conducted by arrangement.

Gila National Forest comprises 2,790,986 acres, headquarters here.

SOCORRO, Socorro County. US 60, I–25. Once a Piro Indian village.

Old San Miguel Mission, 403 El Camino Real, 2 blocks N. of plaza, has one wall which was part of the 1598 mission. Recently restored, artifacts and other exhibits.

Mineral Museum, in Workman Center on campus of New Mexico Institute of Mining and Technology.

Gallinas Springs Ruin, near Magdalena, a partial ghost town W. of Socorro on US 60, 27 miles. The pottery found at Gallinas Springs is related to the Mesa Verda ware, black-on-white. The village site in the foothills of the Gallinas Mountains may have had as many as 500 multistoried homes. A registered historic place.

Kelly, 1 mile S. of Magdalena, another ghost town with a cemetery worth seeing. Mill ruins above town. In Magdalena, Pythian Hall, once a town center, is still standing although boarded up.

SPRINGER, Colfax County. US 56. Town is just N. of the old Cimarron Cutoff of the Santa Fe Trail.

Mills House, 509 1st St. was built for

Melvin W. Mills, a Canadian who came to New Mexico in the 1860s and became a miner, rancher and lawyer. In 1875 he was elected to the state legislature. House is a registered historic place.

Old Towns on the Cimarron Cutoff, S. of Springer are Taylor Springs, Robinson and Colmor. Vernon, on the railroad S. of the trail, and Abbott and Palo Blanco are in the S. part of Colfax county.

TAOS, Taos County (7,050 feet). US 64, State 3. Spanish colonists were here in 1615. A church was built two years later. Since 1880 Taos has been an artists' colony.

Kit Carson House and Museum, E. of the plaza on US 64. Carson's home from 1843 to 1868. Period furnishings and artifacts on display. His last wife was an heiress, Josefa Jaramillo. The house is a national historic landmark.

Kit Carson Memorial State Park, 2 blocks N. of the plaza, includes the cemetery where the famous scout, and his wife, and Padre Antonio Jose Martinez are buried.

Taos Pueblo, 2½ miles N. on Pueblo Rd. Two-terraced communal dwellings are five stories high, the highest pueblos in the Southwest. A national historic landmark.

Ruins of the Mission of San Geronimo de Taos, near pueblo entrance. Established ca. 1598, burned by Indians in the 1680 pueblo rebellion, restored, then destroyed by U.S. troops putting down a revolt in 1847. Sections of wall and part of the original bell tower remain.

Picuris Pueblo, 26 miles SW at Penasco, was probably established in the mid-13th century.

Mission of San Lorenzo at Picuris was built after the reconquest and has been used for more than two centuries.

Millicent A. Rogers Memorial Museum, 4 miles N. of Taos, has authentic Spanish, Indian and pioneer relics.

Mission of St. Francis Assisi, 4 miles S. of town on US 64. Built in 1710–55 in cruciform shape. Art objects and statuary. The church, considered one of the most beautiful in America, was rebuilt in 1772.

Governor Bent House Museum & Gallery, Bent St. 1 block N. of plaza, was the home of New Mexico's first American governor and the place where he was scalped alive and then murdered. House has early west items. Charles Bent was the brother of William Bent of Bent's Fort, Colorado. He married an older sister of Kit Carson's wife and was appointed governor by Gen. Stephen Watts Kearny. His death came during an uprising in 1847.

Harwood Foundation of the University of New Mexico, Ledoux St. Indian artifacts, a library of the Southwest, paintings, etc.

Carson National Forest, headquarters in town, covers 1,492,110 acres.

Blumenschein House, Ledoux St., former home of the cofounder of the Taos Art Colony in 1898, Ernest L. Blumenschein. An 11-room adobe built in the 18th century. A national historic landmark.

TRUTH OR CONSEQUENCES, Sierra County. I–25. Called Hot Springs before television.

Geronimo Springs Museum, 325 Main St. Artifacts and photographs. Mineral display.

TUCUMCARI, Quay County. US 54.

Tucumcari Historical Museum, 416 S. Adams St. Western relics include Indian items, minerals, fossils.

WAGON MOUND, Mora County. US 85. The last landmark of the high plains section of the Cimarron Cutoff of the Santa Fe Trail. It was visible from Point of Rocks and served as a guidepost for wagon caravans headed W. from the Rock Crossing of the Canadian River. Santa Clara Spring 2 miles NW was an important watering place. Frequent Indian ambushes took place in this area. Ruts of the old trail are visible S. and W. of Wagon Mound. A national historic landmark.

WATROUS, Mora County. US 85. The Mora and Sapello Rivers at their junction were the rendezvous point for organizing wagons trains for the open plains. Watrous, also called La Junta, was also where the mountain and Cimarron Cutoff routes divided the Santa Fe Trail. The Watrous Store and Ranch, Sapello Stage Station and the Fort Union Corral are all part of the national historic landmark, not accessible to the public at this time.

WHITE OAKS HISTORIC DISTRICT, Lincoln County. State 349, 12 miles NE of Carrizozo. A mining town of the 1880s when gold was discovered on Baxter Mountain. Several structures remain, old mine shafts are still here, and the Cedarvale Cemetery is well kept. A registered historic place.

WHITE SANDS NATIONAL MONUMENT, Otero County. US 70, 82. 146,535 acres of gypsum sand. Visitor Center with exhibits of the history of the area. There is a 16-mile round-trip drive from entrance. (Also see Alamogordo.) The mice turn white in this area.

ZUNI PUEBLO, McKinley County. State 53,32. One of the Pueblos which Fray Marcos de Niza saw from afar in 1539 and mistook for a city of gold in the sunset. Coronado was extremely disappointed when he arrived the following year. Some rock and adobe walls remain. A national historic landmark.

NORTH DAKOTA

The companies each gave a ball in turn during the winter, and the preparations were begun long in advance. There was no place to buy anything, save the sutler's store and the shops in the little town of Bismarck, but they were well ransacked for materials for the supper. The bunks where the soldiers slept were removed from the barracks and flags festooned around the room. Arms were stacked and guidons arranged in groups. A few pictures of distinguished men were wreathed in imitation laurel leaves cut out of green paper. Chandeliers and side brackets carved out of cracker-box boards into fantastic shapes were filled with candles, while at either end of the long room great logs in the wide fireplaces threw out a cheerful light. . . . We were escorted out to the supper room in the company-kitchen in advance of the enlisted men. The general delighted the hearts of the sergeant and ball managers by sitting down to a great dish of potato salad.

Elizabeth B. Custer, *Boots and Saddles,* 1885.

I am looking rather seedy now, while holding down my claim,
And my victuals are not always served the best;
And the mice play slyly round me as I nestle down to sleep,
In my little old sod shanty on the claim. . . .
The hinges are of leather and the windows have no glass,
While the board roof lets the howling blizzard in;
And I hear the hungry coyote as he sneaks up through the grass,
Round my little old sod shanty on the claim.

F. J. Smith, *Fort Abercrombie Scout,* July 1, 1887.

Not long ago I returned to Bismarck. . . . I visited the graves of my parents and slave-born grandmother I never knew. I drove by the rented farm west of Driscoll where we Thompsons last lived as a family. The frame house, the barns and outbuildings have disappeared. Even the windmill was gone. . . . In the intervening years I had . . . crossed the the equator a dozen times, fought bushflies in the Australian outback, planted a tree in Israel and meditated in Indian with Maharishi Mahesh Yogi at his ashram high above the Ganges.

So what is North Dakota?

It is the state of the International Peace Garden and the ever-burning coal mines. It is where Teddy Roosevelt ranched and where General Custer fought and in which Sakakawea joined the Lewis and Clark expedition. It is the home of the rodeo and the rare, black-footed Ferret; of Buffalo Bill and Lawrence Welk and that couple I met while crawling through a Maori cave in New Zealand. . . ."

Era Bell Thompson,
North Dakota Horizons,
1973.

NORTH DAKOTA FACTS: Pierre Gaultier de Varennes, Sieur de la Verendrye, was the first explorer. After him came trappers and settlers from Canada and Spanish explorers from the south. In 1803 part of the land became U.S. territory by the Louisiana Purchase. Lewis and Clark passed the winter of 1804–05 at the Mandan villages on the Missouri River. The Dakota Territory was organized in 1861. The state entered the Union November 2, 1889; 39th state. Capital: Bismarck. Territorial capital: Yankton.
Nicknames: Sioux State, Flickertail State.

North Dakota Indians. Mandan, Sioux, Arikara, Assiniboine, Dakota, Hidatsa, Cheyenne and Chippewa.

Some of the Names That Made News

Meriwether Lewis	John James Audubon
William Clark	John Jacob Astor
Sakakawea (Sacajawea)	Jean Nicollet
H. H. Sibley	James Fisk
Alfred Sully	Toussaint Charbonneau

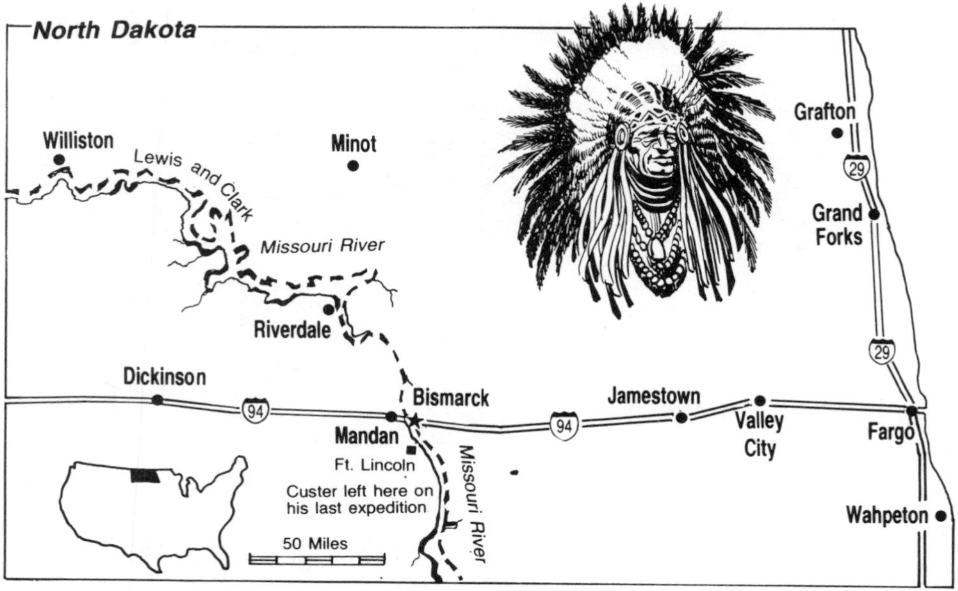
North Dakota
Williston
Lewis and Clark
Minot
Missouri River
Riverdale
Dickinson
94
Bismarck
Mandan
Ft. Lincoln
Custer left here on
his last expedition
50 Miles
Missouri River
94
Jamestown
Valley
City
Grafton
29
Grand
Forks
29
Fargo
Wahpeton

Sitting Bull	The Cooper brothers
Alexander McKenzie	Henry Minot
Theodore Roosevelt	Pierre Bottineau
The Marquis de Mores	Medora de Mores
George Armstrong Custer	Elizabeth Custer
Pierre de la Verendrye	David Thompson
Alexander Henry, Jr.	Charles le Raye
John C. Fremont	

ALEXANDER, McKenzie County. US 85. Alexander McKenzie, a political boss of his day, was one of the incorporators of the town named for him. The old log building that served as first county courthouse is still standing.

Lewis and Clark Museum has antique farm machinery and other pioneer artifacts.

ANTELOPE, Morton County. US 10. The highway follows the trail made by Custer's 7th Cavalry on their way to the Little Big Horn territory in June 1876. They were coming from a stay at Fort Abraham Lincoln. Deep ruts cut in the prairie by the wagons of the expedition and others making use of the trail have long remained visible N. of highway and running parallel in the area of Young Men's Butte. Legend says that here two young Arikara Indians wanting to go home to their girls deserted a group headed for the Northwest and new hunting grounds. The major party was never heard from again. (Who ever heard of *any* of them again? But that's the name of the butte.)

Site of Gen. Sully's Temporary Camp, for the Battle of Killdeer Mountain, S. of Antelope on an unimproved road to the Heart River, .8 mile. Heading for the Yellowstone River in 1864, Sully made a corral of his wagon train at this point and launched a surprise attack on a camp of 5,000 Sioux to the N. (Also see Killdeer.)

BELCOURT, Rolette County. US 281. Headquarters for the Turtle Mountain Indian Reservation. The town was named for Rev. George Antoine Belcourt, a priest who helped to establish the community. The reservation comprises 72 square miles.

BELFIELD, Stark County. US 10.

Fort Houston Museum has a variety of items pertaining to the "Last Frontier" of America and claims to have the largest collection of Badlands artifacts in the world. Open daily April through October.

BEULAH, Mercer County. State 49.

Site of Charles Le Raye's Camp, marked by the Mercer County Old Settlers' Association. Le Raye, a French explorer, camped here in the early 1800s. He was a captive of the Brulé Sioux and is said to have been the first to mention the Knife River and, while still a captive, was one of the earliest white men to see the Rockies.

BIRCH CREEK HISTORIC SITE, Barnes County. Off State 1. The first U.S.-sponsored exploration party into this area was headed by Jean Nicollet and John Frémont in the late 1830s. They camped here in 1839. In August 1863, part of the Sibley Indian expedition under Col. Samuel McPhail camped here and named the site Camp Johnson.

BISMARCK, Burleigh County. I–94. Many colorful figures of early West history were in and out of Bismarck on their travels, expeditions or merely on the run. Lewis and Clark camped nearby; they had used a keelboat to carry most of their gear to Fort Mandan, near today's Bismarck. From here they used more manageable dugout canoes. Gen. George Armstrong Custer was in command of Fort Abraham Lincoln nearby; his troops often came to town. From this fort he set out on his last campaign.

State Capitol, N. 6th St., a modern structure which has caused much controversy: why go high when you can go wide and handsome? But the skyscraper has its admirers. Fort Abraham Lincoln and the State Penitentiary can be seen from its observation tower.

State Historical Society Museum, in Liberty Memorial Bldg. SE of the Capitol, has an excellent collection of Indian artifacts; pioneer and military relics. Display gives the history of the North Dakota Indian, from prehistoric times. Theodore Roosevelt memorabilia also are on display. Roosevelt said, in what seems more than a campaign-stop speech, that if it hadn't been for the time he spent in North Dakota he never would have been president. He was a frail youth with asthma and many childhood fevers; in North Dakota he learned how to excel in rugged outdoor life, becoming a good cowhand and even knocking out a bully who mistook him for a dude.

Sakakawea Statue on lawn between statehouse and Memorial Building. The Shoshone "Bird Woman," who with her husband accompanied Lewis and Clark to the Northwest, served as their interpreter at times. Her husband, Toussaint Charbonneau, was hired as interpreter; she proved valuable, too. Part of her reason for going on the arduous trip even with a newborn child was to find her own people from whom she had been taken as a child by another tribe of Indians. (Her name is spelled Sacajawea in most early accounts; spelled variously by modern writers.)

Pioneer Family Statue, at foot of Capitol Mall, is by Avard Fairbanks.

Camp Hancock Museum, 1st and Main Sts., has historical displays pertaining to the early fortification and the city which began at this site.

Site of Alexander McKenzie Home, 722 5th St. McKenzie, a successful entrepreneur of the region, is usually given credit for having the capital moved from Yankton to Bismarck. He was a 19th-century mover, in any case, in private and public matters, and should not be confused with Sir Alexander MacKenzie, Canadian fur trader and explorer who crossed the continent to the Pacific in the 18th century. McKenzie only held the office of sheriff of Burleigh County but his influence was enormous and his followers were known as the "McKenzie Ring."

St. Mary's Cemetery, NE edge of city, has many graves of pioneers; Alexander McKenzie is buried here, as is Gen. E. A. Williams, representative to the territorial assembly. One of the most interesting monuments in the cemetery is that which marks the grave of Capt. Grant Marsh, pioneer pilot on the Missouri River, who brought the steamer, *Far West,* with the wounded from the Battle of Little Big Horn to Fort Lincoln in 54 hours. It was a journey of 710 miles and Capt. Marsh set a steamboat record for the distance.

Bismarck River Warehouse and Historic Site, River Rd. N. of the old highway bridge. A large river warehouse built in the 1870s was active here for years. Interpretive markers.

BOTTINEAU, Bottineau County. US 281.

J. Clark Salyer National Wildlife Refuge, 22 miles W. on State 5. Self-guiding auto tour, also canoe trail on Souris River.

Lake Metigoshe State Park, 12 miles N. on unmarked road 1 mile E. of fairgrounds, is in the Turtle Mountains, with marked trails and looks much as it must have when Indians were free to roam. The park lodge has a collection of Indian artifacts and fossils of the Turtle Mountain area. On the W. bank of Oak Creek is a stone cairn marking the site of the first white man's home in the county and the original townsite. It is a few miles NE of town not far from the bridge over Oak Creek, via the Lake Rd. which also leads to the park.

BOWMAN, Bowman County. US 85. Town and county are named for E. K. Bowman, a territorial legislator.

Yellowstone Trail Museum has many items pertaining to homesteading days of the area.

BUFFALO CREEK, Cass County. US 10. Gen. H. H. Sibley and his troops came this way on August 16, 1863, returning from chasing Indians across the Missouri River. Bronze marker on highway.

CAMP ARNOLD, Barnes County. State 32, 4 miles N. of Oriska. Site of Sibley's camp in 1863. The graves of James Ponsford and Andrus Moore have marble headstones. Descriptive marker at site. There are a number of state historic sites pertaining to Sibley's far-flung campaign against the Sioux in the midsummer of 1863 and it may seem as if every place he stopped to water his horses became historic. But the importance of his expedition to the scattered and often stranded settlers should not be underestimated. As historian Robert G. Athearn pointed out in *Forts of the Upper Missouri,*

> While Minnesotans found solace in the hanging of thirty-eight "war criminals" at Mankato on December 26, Dakotans heard no creaks of stretching rope in their part of the country. They were convinced, as settlers in many parts of the West would be each year for several decades to come, that "when the grass grew in the spring" the Indians would be on the move and blood would flow.

CAMP ATCHESON HISTORIC SITE, Griggs County. State 1. Marker for Sibley's base camp, July 18, 1863, is at the junction with a prairie trail. The actual site is less than half a mile down the trail to the NE shore of a small lake. Sibley had informers among the Chippewas who told him the Sioux were leaving the Devils Lake area and heading for the Missouri River. He made a fort here for his wounded and the baggage train and pursued the Indians with his main column. On a hill nearby, overlooking the lake from the NE, a marble headstone marks the grave of a private who died while in camp here.

Lake Jessie, ca. 4 miles N. on highway, 2 miles E. The lake of pioneer days became an alkali dustbowl (motorcycle races were run on it in the 1930s). But long ago Nicollet and Frémont camped here (1839) and the gallant captain named the body of water for his fiancée, Jessie Benton, daughter of Thomas Hart Benton. Ironically, a lot of Frémont's dreams also turned to dust.

In 1853 I. I. Stevens, home from the Mexican War, was en route to serve as Governor of Washington Territory when he camped at Lake Jessie. Stevens was one of the few Union generals almost everyone admired. He was killed at Chantilly in 1862. When he was here, his guide was Pierre Bottineau, an excellent scout, for whom the city and county are named. Capt. James Fisk, taking gold hunters to Montana, camped here in 1862 and again in 1863 when Sibley was a short distance away and the two parties exchanged visits.

CAMP CORNING HISTORIC SITE, Barnes County. State 1. Another stop in Sibley's campaign against the Sioux. Named for one of his officers, the camp was set up on July 16, 1863. Granite monument marks site.

CAMP GRANT HISTORIC SITE, Stutsman County. State 36, 6 miles N. of Woodworth. A bronze tablet marks the site of a Sibley camp in 1863.

CAMP HAYES HISTORIC SITE, Ransom County. Off State 27, from Lisbon 4 miles E. to graveled road, turn right 2 miles to the junction with another graveled road; left to another junction at 3 miles; right to the old camp on the first rise above the Sheyenne (sic) river. Sibley and his men camped here a week in July 1863 waiting for supplies from Fort Abercrombie. Breastworks are still visible. Old Indian mounds are on the hills bordering the river opposite the campsite. Okeidan Butte is the largest of the hills. Sisseton Sioux warriors are said to have attacked a band of Arikara Indians here and won the battle. Okeidan, meaning "place where they all rushed together," refers to that long ago skirmish. In the 1880s Brevet Gen. H. M. Creel had his soldiers surrounded, but by bison, not Indians.

Cheyenne Indian Village Site, ca. 3 miles S. of State 27 on unimproved road, 8 miles E. of Lisbon. Across the road is the Strong Memorial Park, land given to the state historical society by pioneer Frank Strong.

CAMP KIMBALL HISTORIC SITE, Wells County. Off State 30, 8 miles SW of Carrington. Sibley and his forces camped here on July 22 and July 23, 1863. From here the expedition moved SW to the Battle of Big Mound. Hawksnest on the same road was a camping place for the Sioux traveling between Fort Totten and Fort Yates.

CAMP SHEARDOWN HISTORIC SITE, Barnes County. State 32, 3 miles SE of Valley City. Bronze marker at the site of another Sibley camp of July 1863.

CAMP WEISER HISTORIC SITE, Ransom County, State 46, 13 miles W. of Enderlin. The camp was named for the Sibley expedition surgeon who was killed while the opponents were holding a parley near Big Mound (see McPhal's Battle). His death set off the battle.

Roosevelt's Maltese Cabin, southern entrance to the Theodore Roosevelt National Park
(North Dakota Travel Division, Russ Hanson photo)

View of the Soldiers Monument in Whitestone Battlefield State Historic Park
(North Dakota Travel Division)

CANDO, Towner County. US 281.

Towner County Pioneer School Museum has a collection of oldtime school relics.

CARRINGTON, Foster County. US 281.

Arrowwood National Wildlife Refuge, 10 miles S. on US 281, then 7 miles E. on State 9, on shores of Arrowwood Lake and James River.

CAYUGA, Sargent County. State 11.

Tewaukon National Wildlife Refuge, 4 miles S. on the Sisseton Indian Reservation. 7,844 acres of lakes, marsh and rolling prairie. For guided tours see the manager at headquarters on Lake Tewaukon.

CHASKA HISTORIC SITE, Burleigh County. US 10, 3½ miles N. of Driscoll. Named for one of Sibley's scouts who died on the return trip from the Missouri River in the campaign against the Sioux. Granite stone memorial with bronze tablet. Sibley camped here on the night of August 2, 1863.

COOPERSTOWN, Griggs County. State 7. The Cooper brothers struck it rich in Colorado mines and came to North Dakota to farm. They helped build the Sanborn, Cooperstown and Turtle Mountain Railway, later a branch of the Northern Pacific. The terminus was Cooperstown. Many old buildings remain. On the courthouse grounds is the Opheim Log Cabin with handmade furnishings.

Griggs County Historical Society has antique farm machinery, weapons and other relics in its museum.

CROSBY, Divide County.

Divide County Pioneer Village and Museum, W. on State 5, has a pioneer church and school, as well as small historical items.

DAWSON, Kidder County. State 3.

Slade National Wildlife Refuge, 2 miles S. on State 3. 3,000 acres. Lake Isabel Recreation Area is ½ mile E. and 1 mile S. of the refuge entrance sign; headquarters 1 ½ miles E. of entrance.

DEVILS LAKE, Ramsey County. US 2.

Fort Totten Historic Site, 15 miles SW on State 57, in Benson County on the Fort Totten Indian Reservation. The post, established July 17, 1867, was on a site chosen by Brig. Gen. Alfred H. Terry on the S. side of Devils Lake with the purpose of guarding the emigrant route and as part of the plan to put all Indians of the area on reservations. The fort, named for Brig. Gen. Joseph Gilbert Totten, chief engineer of the U.S. Army, was unusually attractive in layout and geographical situation. It was abandoned in 1890 and transferred to the Interior Department. It became the headquarters for the Fort Totten Indian Agency and industrial school. In 1960 the Bureau of Indian Affairs transferred much of the site to the state. The park comprises the excellently preserved post with nearly all of the original buildings much as they were in the 1870s. The Pioneer Daughters maintain a museum.

Sullys Hill National Game Preserve, 12 miles SW on State 57. 1 mile NE of Fort Totten. A self-guiding auto tour and a nature trail in the more than 1,600 acres of the preserve. There is a big game enclosure which has bison as well as smaller animals.

DOUBLE DITCH INDIAN VILLAGE STATE PARK, Burleigh

County. US 83. Marker on highway. One of the largest Mandan villages in the state was here on the E. bank of the Missouri River and had already been abandoned when Lewis and Clark came this way. Outlines of earth lodges, refuse dumps and a couple of dried-up moats still are visible. There is a shelter to protect maps and descriptive material.

DRISCOLL, Burleigh County. US 10.

Battle of Stony Lake, on old US 10, 2 miles W. of town, descriptive marker on highway for the site of a skirmish on July 28, 1863, when troops under Gen. H. H. Sibley were pursuing the Sioux. Sibley's camp was on the E. side of the lake.

EPPING, Williams County. State 42.

Buffalo Trails Museum has fine displays of regional history with three life-size dioramas of early times, a homesteader's cabin and schoolhouse. Not only the social culture but the geology and natural history is interpreted by displays.

FARGO, Cass County. I–94.

Cass County Historical Society Museum, in Minard Hall on campus of North Dakota State University, N. University Drive and 12th. Indian artifacts.

Forsberg House, 815 S. 3rd Ave. Pioneer relics and furnishings of the 19th century, in the Victorian home of early Fargo resident Anna Marie Bergan, a native of Norway, who lived here with her three children after the death of her Swedish husband, Peter Gustav Forsberg. Four floors of rooms display a variety of Americana, including the children's onetime playroom.

FORT ABERCROMBIE STATE HISTORIC SITE, Richland County, US 81. The first federal military post in North Dakota has been partially rebuilt. The post was first occupied in August 1857, on the left bank of the Red River of the North at Graham's Point above the confluence of the Otter Tail and Bois de Sioux rivers. In July 1859 the post was abandoned but Indian troubles made it necessary to garrison the post again. In June 1860 the fort was moved to a point on higher ground which became its permanent location. The original guardhouse and reconstructed blockhouses and stockades make up the fort; a museum has pioneer and military relics.

FORT ABRAHAM LINCOLN STATE PARK, Morton County. State 80, ca. 4 miles SE of Mandan. Lt. Col. George Armstrong Custer commanded the post from 1873 to 1876. It was the base for his 1874 expedition into the Black Hills with the announcement afterwards that brought trouble. Prospectors who were too late for the California gold rush and too late for the best of the Colorado, Nevada, Montana and Idaho placer finds had long wanted to try the Black Hills region. Indian tales indicated that gold was there in abundance and one discovery had already made the Black Hills seem the next best place to try to strike it rich. Gen. William Sherman, commander of the Division of the Mississippi, expressly declared the area off-limits for prospecting as this was Indian territory, but so many protested it looked as if civil and military authority would soon be disregarded. This was the major purpose for sending Custer and 1200 troops and some scientists to the Hills during the summer of 1874. When he announced with dramatic bombast that gold did exist in the Hills, the rush was on. And the Sioux and Cheyenne made ready to go to war.

From this Fort, Custer also set forth on his last expedition. His vivacious wife rode part of the way with him on the first day, May 17, 1876. She returned to the fort to wait with other wives. Her description of the departure: "The wagons themselves seemed to stretch out interminably. There were pack mules well laden and the artillery and infantry followed, the cavalry being in advance of all. The column totaled 985 men, including citizens, employees and Indian scouts. As the column passed by the barracks, the band struck up, 'The Girl I Left Behind Me.' . . ." Within the month 26 widows were among those left behind.

The post, originally called Fort McKeen for Col. Henry Boyd McKeen killed at the Battle of Cold Harbor, was built on the site of an ancient Mandan settlement known as Slant Village, and was located on the river bluffs. It has been partially restored. The museum has Indian artifacts and model of Indian life, military relics and early tools.

FORT BERTHOLD, McLean County. State 37. Originally a trading post, Fort Atkinson, 1858–59, on the left bank of the Missouri River, now covered by the waters of the Garrison Reservoir. The fort was renamed in 1862 when purchased by the American Fur Co. The post was evacuated in 1867, when Fort Stevenson was established, and became the agency headquarters for the Arikara, Gros Ventre and Mandan Indians, operating as a trading post until 1874. The Fort Berthold Indian Reservation, Lake Sakakawea State Park and the Audubon National Wildlife Refuge are all in the vicinity. The Powerhouse lobby of Garrison Dam has displays; free guided tours. Four Bears park on the E. shore of the reservoir has a monument to Chief Four Bears and other Indian leaders, including Knowing Goes Along, Never Retreats and Carries Moccasin Tied. The Four Bears museum has a collection of Indian items.

FORT BUFORD STATE PARK, Williams County. Unimproved road ca. 1 mile SW of Buford. Near Montana line. The post was on the left bank of the Missouri, just below confluence of the Yellowstone and 2½ miles below the American Fur Co.'s Fort Union (which see). The Sioux greatly resented the intrusion of the garrison in the heart of buffalo country. On June 15, 1866, when the post was established, Indian troubles were far from over. Among army brass who visited the post were Gens. Sherman, Sheridan, Miles, Custer and "Black Jack" Pershing. Sitting Bull and his men harassed the builders of the fort, and it was here that he surrendered. About 36 acres are a state historic site. The officers' quarters and the powder magazine are original buildings.

FORT CLARK STATE PARK, Oliver County. State 25. The fort was established by the American Fur Co. in 1829. The site is maintained by the state historical society, and is being developed. A nearby Mandan Indian earth-lodge village was abandoned in 1837 after a smallpox epidemic and was later taken over by the Arikara until the 1860s. Primeau's Post was built on the site in mid-century, in competition with Fort Clark for several years.

FORT DILTS STATE PARK, Bowman County. Just N. of US 12, between Rhame and Marmarth. Capt. James L. Fisk's wagon train headed for Montana gold fields was corralled here in a siege in September 1864, held relatively captive by the Hunkpapa Sioux, who had attacked the camp. Sixteen volunters, however, slipped through the lines and brought help from Fort Rice. The Sioux departed for bison-rich fields as soon as the fortification was well established. The state historical society owns part of the area. Within a fenced section are the ruins of the fort and graves of eight who died in the affair. Interpretive marker.

Note: there have been stories throughout western history of the white man trying to poison Indians. Here it seems to have been a fact, although any writer is taking a chance making flat statements about nearly any event of the Indian wars. Reportedly, at least 25 Indians died from eating poisoned hardtack left at Fort Dilts.

FORT MANDAN, McLean County. 14 miles W. of Washburn, on the N. bank of the big bend in the Missouri River. The fort was built by Lewis and Clark in the winter of 1804–5 when they camped on their way west. Here they took on the services of Sacajawea and her husband Toussaint Charbonneau. Earlier explorers, including Alexander Henry, Jr., of the North West Co., had visited the Mandan Indians shortly after the turn of the 19th century, as had David Thompson, James McKay and possibly Sieur de La Verendrye, Pierre Gaultier de Varennes. The Indians got on well with the visitors and received Lewis and Clark with friendliness. On April 7, 1805, the expedition went up river in two pirogues and six canoes. Clark came back in the late summer of the following year to see what "the old works" looked like and found all the houses except one had been burned accidentally. The fort is being restored. Interpretive marker.

FORT PEMBINA, Pembina County. Off I–29, US 81. In 1797 Charles Chaboillez established the state's first trading post where the Pembina River joins the Red River of the North. In 1801 it was replaced by another North West post under Alexander Henry, Jr., and was in competition thereafter with two other frontier posts not far away, one belonging to the always progressive Hudson's Bay Co. The Earl of Selkirk began to colonize the area with settlers from Scotland and Ireland. This was British territory until a boundary line was established in 1818. Historical marker on I–29. Pembina State Historical Site is in the state park, one block E. Exhibits pertain to the history of the area and explorations.

FORT RANSOM, Ransom County. N. of State 27, NW of Lisbon. Interpretive marker for the military post of 1867–72, which was established on the W. bank of the Sheyenne River by Gen. A. H. Terry, as one of a chain of forts for the protection of travelers west. The site is owned by the State historical society.

FORT RICE, Morton County. County 1806. In Fort Rice State Park. The post was established by Gen. A. H. Sully on his expedition of July 1864, against the Sioux, to protect navigation on the river. Several blockhouses have been restored. Descriptive marker.

FORT UNION TRADING POST NATIONAL HISTORIC SITE, Williams County. Ca. 1½ miles W. of Buford. S. of US 2. The post was the main Upper Missouri fur trade depot. Built in 1828, it opened John Jacob Astor's campaign to gain rich lands for the American Fur Co. The Army bought the post in 1866 and built Fort Buford nearby with some of Fort Union materials. A national historic site of 380 acres, with guided tours in summer months provided by the Park Service.

FORT YATES, Sioux County on Standing Rock Indian Reservation, State 24, was established late in December 1874 on the right bank of the Missouri River as headquarters for the Indian Agency. It was near here that Sitting Bull was killed.* He had been arrested at his home (the detachment was made up of 39 Indian police and 4 volunteers). A scuffle took place in which six of the police and eight Indians were killed. When the cavalry arrived, many of the angry Hunkpapas fled south toward the Cheyenne River and the whole affair led eventually to the Battle of Wounded Knee. The sacred Standing Rock of the Sioux is on a bluff above the river at the N. end of town. The Indian police who died in the Sitting Bull tragedy are buried in the town of Fort Yates at the Catholic Cemetery. Sitting Bull has not rested in peace. He was first buried in the post cemetery; then moved to a memorial overlooking the Oahe Reservoir near Mobridge, South Dakota. For a number of years his grave, ca. about 10 miles S. of Cannon Ball, had a concrete slab covering it; he was interred without ceremony.

*South Dakota maintains that Sitting Bull was killed in that state.

GRAND FORKS, Grand Forks County. I–29.

University of North Dakota, University Ave., museum in Babcock Hall has historical items.

Historic Campbell House has been restored with period furnishings.

Lincoln Park, Belmont Rd. at S. edge of town, is on the old Red River Oxcart Trail. The log building which housed the first post office is now part of the clubhouse.

HETTINGER, Adams County. US 12.

Sod House Museum, in City Park, is a furnished sod house.

Dakota Buttes Museum, in old Methodist church building, on highway, has small historical items pertaining to local history.

JAMESTOWN, Stutsman County. I–94.

Site of Fort Seward, indicated by a marker on US 281, at foot of bluffs on the NW edge of town. The post was built in 1872, partly with materials from Fort Ransom. First called Camp Sykes, then Fort Cross and then Fort Seward for Lincoln's Secretary of State, who was injured at the time of the President's assassination.

Frontier Village, I–94, E. edge of town, has an enormous statue of a buffalo; but the rest of the area is in scale to pioneer times: restored school, church, the inevitable log cabin, shops, railroad depot.

Stutsman County Historical Museum, 3rd Ave. SE and 4th St. SE. Indian and pioneer items.

KILLDEER MOUNTAIN BATTLEFIELD, Dunn County. Unimproved

road, ca. 11 miles NW of Killdeer. In the summer of 1864 Brig. Gen. Alfred Sully wound up his campaign against the Sioux and defeated the fleeing Chief Inkpaduta at the base of Killdeer Mountain. A marker and gravestones are on the battlefield.

Dunn County Historical Museum, in Old City Hall, town of Killdeer has historical items relating to the community history. Open only part-time.

LITTLE MISSOURI NATIONAL GRASSLANDS, in the W. section of the state, along the Little Missouri River and the South Dakota border.

Burning Coal Vein Area, ca. 15 miles NW of Amidon (US 85), is ca. 30 feet below the surface of the land and has been burning since before the first explorers came. It has advanced only a few hundred feet in the last century.

McPHAIL'S BUTTE HISTORIC SITE, Kidder County. Ca. 10 miles N. of Tappen (US 10) on unimproved road. The battle of Big Mound was one of the major encounters of Gen. Henry Hastings Sibley's campaign against the Santee Sioux in 1863. The Sioux had started trouble in the Minnesota River Valley in 1862 when most of the men of the state were away fighting the Civil War. Sibley was not a man to forget injury. He had been a fur trader in Minnesota, a territorial delegate to Congress, the first governor of the state, and a Union officer. During the Sioux outbreak of August 1862, he won a victory over Little Crow at Wood Lake and was commissioned a brigadier general soon after. The surviving Sioux fled to North Dakota and joined forces with the Tetons. Here on July 24, 1863, Sibley surprised nearly 3,000 Sioux, as they were hunting buffalo at Big Mound. One of Chief Inkpaduta's warriors shot Sibley's surgeon, Dr. Joseph Weiser, during a parley. Gen. Sibley and Gen. Sully kept up the chase and the fighting and eventually triumphed over the Indians. The battleground, also known as the Burman Historic Site and Camp Whitney site is mostly under private ownership at this time. A stone marker indicates where Dr. Weiser fell.

MANDAN, Morton County. US 10.

Beck's Great Plains Museum, 3½ miles S. on State 1806. Log house with early furnishings, shops, firearms, tools and farm machinery.

MANVEL, Grand Forks County. US 81, was originally known as Turtle River station on the Great Northern Railway. Before that it was one of the six stops on the Fort Abercrombie to Fort Garry trail and was a log hut with a sod roof.

Red River Oxcart Trail, marker on highway ca. 11 miles S., was first used by fur traders, later by nearly all travelers in this part of the country.

MEDORA, Billings County. US 10. The Marquis de Mores, an anti-Semitic and generally snobbish young Frenchman who, according to one of his biographers, was "obsessed with lineage," founded the town of Medora. He named it for his beautiful and wealthy wife whose father was a German baron doing very well on Wall Street. Using his father-in-law's money, the Marquis tried to make a killing in the meatpacking industry. He did kill one of the townsmen, a foolhardy youngster, Riley Luffsey, who had rashly joined with other braggarts in taunting the Frenchman into a fight. Luffsey is buried in the Medora cemetery. The

Marquis and his family left town one day in December 1886, and never returned. He was killed at 37 on an expedition in North Africa in 1896. His statue in North Dakota style of dress stands in De Mores Memorial Park.

Chateau de Mores, 1 mile W., off US 10, I–94. Guided tours daily, except in exceptionally bad weather, to see the house as the family left it. Also the ruins of the packing plant are here.

Rough Riders Hotel provided the name for Roosevelt's regiment in the Spanish-American War. There are many historic buildings in town. A Western Gallery and a museum have items associated with western North Dakota and its colorful past.

Medora Doll House was the Von Hoffman house built by the Marquis for his in-laws. It was later lived in by James Foley, a poet laureate of North Dakota, and became a museum featuring pioneer Dakota life.

Headquarters for the Theodore Roosevelt National Memorial Park (which see) has dioramas depicting life of the Badlands and Roosevelt memorabilia.

MENOKEN INDIAN VILLAGE SITE, Burleigh County. N. of Menoken in Verendrye State Park. A descriptive marker at site of village which occupied 14 acres. It probably was the first village reached by Pierre de la Verendrye's expedition of 1738. The moat is still visible; excavation has uncovered evidence of a palisade. A national historic landmark.

Molander Indian Village, which also had a moat, is N. of Mandan, on the W. bank of the Missouri River.

Huff Indian Village, S. of Mandan on County 1804, to Huff then 1 mile S. to site on W. bank of Missouri. Marker describes the housesites, palisade and moat.

Crowley Flint Quarry Site is 17 miles N. of Hebron (just above I–94). The site, administered by the State Historical Society, is on the N. side of the Knife River Valley.

MINOT, Ward County. US 2.

Northwest Historical Society Museum and Pioneer Village, state fairgrounds. First county courthouse and many other early buildings are there; museum with antiques.

PARSHALL, Mountrail County. State 37.

Paul Broste Rock Museum has an exceptionally fine collection of polished rock spheres from all over the world.

RUGBY, Pierce County. US 2.

Geographical Center Museum and Pioneer Village, 508 S.W. 2 St. Pioneer home, church, school, gun collection, farm tools, etc., at the center of North America. Monument at exact spot.

STANTON, Mercer County. State 48. On N. bank of the Knife River, 1 mile N. of town is the Big Hidatsa Village site, largest of five villages in the area which were once the center of northern Plains fur trade. Impressions of trenches and earth lodges remain. A national historic landmark.

THEODORE ROOSEVELT NATIONAL MEMORIAL PARK, Billings and McKenzie counties. The 70,374-acre park is divided into three units: the S. Unit is reached from I–94 at Medora Visitor Center (Roosevelt's Maltese Cabin is here); the Rough Rider's Elkhorn Ranch Site on the Little Missouri River is located on rough roads—inquire at park headquarters at Medora. The North Unit can be reached via US 85 from Watford City. Self-guiding trails in north and south sections. Within the park are the Badlands along the Little Missouri. Roosevelt's ranching operations took place here in 1883–87. The National Park Service maintains a small herd of buffalo. Several large prairie-dog towns also are of major interest. The President's experiences here contributed to his book, *The Winning of the West.*

VALLEY CITY, Barnes County. I-94.

Barnes County Historical Museum, in courthouse, 4 St. N.W., features Indian relics.

Gale Museum, 300 Viking Dr., Indian artifacts, tools and weapons; coins.

WAHPETON, Richland County. US 81.

Richland County Historical Museum, 2nd St. and 7th Ave. Pioneer displays trace county history. Fine Indian collection.

WASHBURN, McLean County. US 83.

Joseph Henry Taylor Cabin, on highway, in city park, has been restored. A one-room home built by Taylor, who was a trader, trapper, author, editor and Civil War veteran.

WATFORD CITY, McKenzie County. US 85.

Pioneer Museum, 109 Park Ave. W. Homestead kitchen and other household rooms furnished in 19th-century style. Country school and store.

WHITESTONE BATTLEFIELD STATE HISTORIC PARK, Dickey County. Off US 281. The Battle of Whitestone Hill took place on September 3, 1863, and was the first of Gen. Alfred Sully's victories over the Sioux Indians under Chief Inkpaduta. Army casualties were heavy. A monument in the center of the battleground is surrounded by 22 markers each listing the name of a soldier who died in the confrontation. An interpretive exhibit is in museum at the site.

WILLISTON, Williams County. US 2.

Frontier Museum, 3 miles N. on US 2. Two buildings house pioneer and Indian clothing, and other relics.

WRITING ROCK STATE PARK, Divide County. On county road SW of Fortuna from the junction of US 85 and State 5. The State Historical Society maintains a large glacial boulder on which are a number of Indian petroglyphs.

OKLAHOMA

The country is beginning to be hilly, dry, and covered with sparse, stunted oaks, among which are sometimes seen deer and a rather large number of polecats, which can be smelled before they can be seen. From the hilltops we could soon see the bloody banks of the Red River; The Red Fork of the Arkansas called the Cimmarron. We then soon reached the sandy shores of the Arkansas, whose waters look exactly like crayfish soup. Nowhere have I ever seen so many deer, moose, bear and turkey tracks. For our evening meal we had deer, moose, turkey, beef, pork, fritters, and coffee. For dessert we had wild grapes and "*plaquemines,*" which the Americans call persimmons. . . . There was nothing so pretty as our camp site with its fourteen fires which lit up the forest. The animated groups around the fires cast long, moving shadows against the tree trunks. Abundance was everywhere.

On the Western Tour with Washington Irving; The Journal and Letters of Count de Pourtalès (Norman: 1967).

The leaves forming the shady roof of the medicine house wilted. The heat of the sun preyed upon the naked dancers. To-haint (no-shoes), the great medicine chief, made medicine for clouds and rain. The rain came with a tempest of wind and the most vivid lightning. Peal after peal of thunder shook the air. The ground was literally flooded. Two Cheyenne women were killed by the lightning. The next morning To-haint apologized for the storm. He was a young man, and had no idea of making such strong medicine. He hoped the tribe would pass by his indiscreetness. He trusted that, as he grew older, he would grow wiser. The Cheyenne women were dead, not because of his medicine, but because of their wearing red blankets. All Indians know they should not wear red during the great medicine dance of the Kiowas.

Thomas C. Battey, *The Life and Adventures of a Quaker Among the Indians,* 1875 (Norman: 1968).

Anadarko is a town of six stores, three or four frame houses, the Indian agent's store and office, and the City Hotel. Seven houses in the West make a city. I said I thought this was the worst hotel in the Indian Territory, but the officers at Fort Sill, who have travelled more than I, think it is the worst in the United States.

Richard Harding Davis, *The West from a Car-Window,* 1892.

OKLAHOMA FACTS: In 1830 Congress decreed that all Indians east of the Mississippi River be relocated in an area designated as Indian Territory. From 1817 to 1840 the Five Civilized Tribes were moved from the southeastern woodlands. The march of the Cherokees from Georgia, in the winter of 1838–39, killed many of them and became known as the shameful "Trail of Tears." The Cherokee, Chickasaw, Choctaw, Creek and Seminole Indians were called civilized by English colonists who saw in their government a structure like the British. They had a chief, a House of Chiefs and a House of Warriors, who cooperated in governing. The nations, reestablished in what is now Oklahoma, had written constitutions, laws and other refinements of civilization; many Indians became wealthy or remained so. Some were plantation owners with slaves. Others were poverty-stricken. There was trouble among tribes; this was increased with the outbreak of the Civil War. Most tribes sided with the South; others went with the Union. In 1890 the western half of the area became Oklahoma Territory. Both sections sought statehood, but were united in 1907 when Oklahoma was admitted to the Union as the 46th state.
Capital: Oklahoma City. Territorial Capital: Guthrie. Nickname: Sooner State.

Indian Tribes. Absentee Delaware, Absentee Shawnee, Caddo, Cherokee, Chickasaw, Choctaw, Comanche, Creek, Delaware, Iowa, Kaw, Kickapoo, Kiowa, Miami, Modoc, Osage, Ottawa, Pawnee, Peoria, Ponca, Quapaw, Sac and Fox, Seminole, Tonkawa, Wichita and Wyandotte.

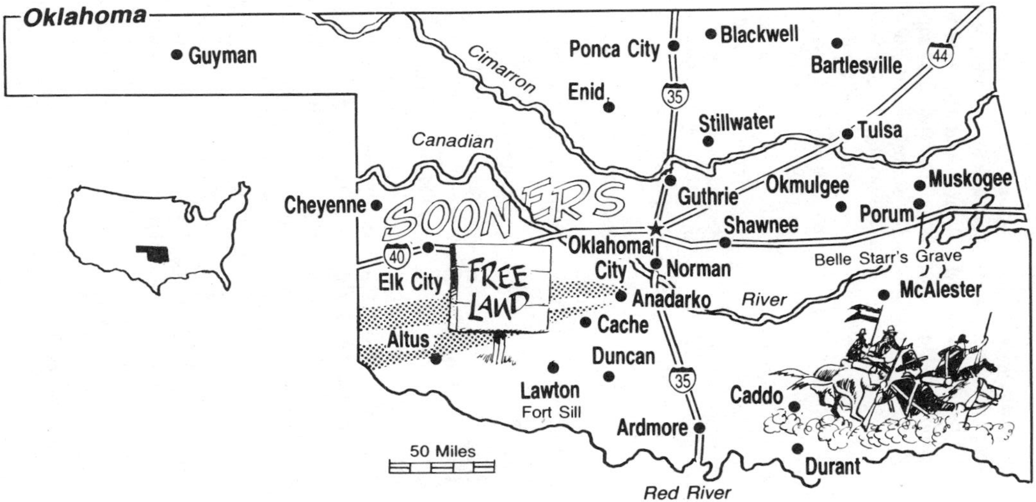
Oklahoma
Guyman
Cimarron
Ponca City
Blackwell
Bartlesville
44
Enid
35
Stillwater
Tulsa
Canadian
Cheyenne
SOONERS
Guthrie
Okmulgee
Muskogee
Porum
Shawnee
Oklahoma City
Norman
40
Elk City
FREE LAND
Belle Starr's Grave
Anadarko
River
McAlester
Cache
Altus
Duncan
Lawton
Fort Sill
Caddo
Ardmore
50 Miles
Durant
Red River

ADA, Pontotoc County. State 1, 19.

East Central University Museum, on campus, Main St. and Francis Ave. Hall of Primitive Man has prehistoric items; other displays illustrate cultures of the Plains Indians with domestic artifacts. Near entrance to university is the fossilized stump of a Callixylon tree of the Devonian Age.

ALTUS, Jackson County. US 62, 283.

Museum of the Western Prairie, 1100 N. Hightower. Pioneer exhibits, early farm equipment, early vehicles.

ALVA, Woods County. US 64, 281.

Cherokee Strip Museum, 508 7th St. in Public Library, Cherokee Strip relics, Lincolniana, flag and uniform collections.

Northwestern State College, Oklahoma Blvd., at junction of US 64, 281. Natural history museum with fossils, Carter bird collection.

ANADARKO, Caddo County. US 62. The site of a reservation in 1858, but the agency was destroyed during the Civil War. The Anadarko Area Office, in Federal Bldg., serves Indians of Oklahoma, Texas and Kansas. Murals by Kiowa artists.

Indian City—U.S.A., S. on State 8, reconstructed villages of seven Plains tribes (Pawnee, Caddo, Kiowa, Navajo, Pueblo, Wichita and Apache) with Indian guides and dance ceremonies.

Southern Plains Indian Museum and Crafts Center, E. on US 62. Exhibits feature Southern Plains Indian art.

National Hall of Fame for Famous American Indians, E. on US 62. Outdoor museum with bronze busts of leading Indians. Among these are Chief Joseph, Sacajawea, Quanah Parker and Jim Thorpe.

ARMSTRONG ACADEMY, Bryan County. US 70. Ca. 3 miles NE of Bokchito on unimproved road, it was founded as part of the Choctaw school system in 1843, with the supervision of Baptist missionaries. It closed at the beginning of the Civil War, then the building became the Choctaw national capitol, and capitol for members of the Civilized Tribes supporting the Confederate States. In 1883 the Choctaw capital was moved to Tuskahoma, while Presbyterian missionaries reopened the academy, cooperating with the Choctaw nation. It served as a school for Choctaw orphans. The building was nearly totally destroyed by fire in 1921. Extensive ruins remain.

ARNETT, Ellis County. US 283.

Antelope Hills, just S. of S. Canadian River, off US 283. The six peaks which rise dramatically above the plains were a landmark to many emigrants headed West.

ATOKA, Atoka County. US 69. Named for Capt. Atoka, a Choctaw ball player.

Boggy Depot State Recreation Area, 5 miles SW on US 69, 75, then eight miles W. An early settlement of the Choctaw nation. During the Civil War a Confederate Army post here kept a flagpole in midtown, flying the Stars and Bars. Choctaws liked to gallop around it, hollering and singing the Choctaw war song. The cemetery of old Boggy Depot has a row of Confederate graves. Markers for historical sites in park.

BARTLESVILLE, Washington County. State 123. Jacob Bartles established a trading post here in the 1870s.

Nellie Johnstone Oil Well, in Johnstone Park, at city limits, is an exact replica of the first commercial oil-well rig in Oklahoma.

Woolaroc Museum, 14 miles SW on State 123. Ranch has 11,000 acres of wooded land its lakes, hills and pastures stocked with many animals, some wild. Visitors are advised to stay in car until they reach the museum, which cost $5 million and features paintings of great Western artists, including Remington and Russell. Seven rooms contain exhibits on the Southwest. Also on grounds, the National "Y" Indian Guide Center has Indian crafts.

Phillips Exhibit Hall, Phillips Bldg., 5th and Keeler Sts. Displays trace history of petroleum development. Tours.

BIG CABIN, Craig County. US 69. The town and Big Cabin Creek got the name from a large cabin on the old Texas Rd., a popular stopping place for early day travelers.

BLACKBURN'S STATION, Pittsburg County. 6 miles S. of Blanco on State 63. A stage stop on the Butterfield Overland which crossed SE Oklahoma from 1858 to 1861. Casper Blackburn was the local trader.

BLACK MESA, Cimarron County. N. of State 325, in the Panhandle corner of the state near New Mexico and Colorado lines, the highest point in Oklahoma, 4,978 feet, created by a lava flow. Indian writings and pictographs in Black Mesa State Park, dinosaur excavation site, petrified wood. Ca. 12 miles SE of mesa.

BLACKWELL, Kay County. US 177. The town was settled in 1893 by A. J. Blackwell, an adopted Cherokee citizen. When the Cherokee Outlet was opened, Blackwell called upon his Indian rights to the land, formed a city government and sold homesites. One of America's largest zinc smelters is here.

BOISE CITY, Cimarron County. US 56.

Fort Nichols, near Cold Springs, ca. 4 miles E. of New Mexico line and 23 miles W. of Boise City, was established in June 1865. Also known as Cedar Bluffs and the springs as Upper Cimarron Springs. Kit Carson set up the post to protect travelers along the Santa Fe Trail.

BOKOSHE, Le Flore County. State 31.

Choctaw Indian Jail, constructed of native stone with walls 2-feet thick, still has original iron doors and barred windows. An elm tree nearby is where condemned Indians were shot by a friend of their choice.

BRIDGEPORT, Caddo County. N. of US 66, 5 miles N. of Hinton. Site of the old stage crossing of the Canadian River.

BROKEN BOW, Tulsa County. US 70.

Memorial Indian Museum, 2nd and Allen Sts. Prehistoric and historic Indian artifacts, collections of Caddo pottery, fossils.

Big Cypress Tree, off US 70 E. of town, is 2,000 or more years old, the largest in Oklahoma, near the historic home of Choctaw Indian Chief Jefferson Gardiner.

CACHE, Comanche County. US 62. The town, originally called "Quanah" for Quanah Parker, was built on the Spanish or Ozark Trail, an old Indian road connecting Santa Fe with the Arkansas River crossing at Fort Smith. The West Cache Indian Agency and Trading Post was nearby.

Quanah Parker's Star House, Eagle Park, Wichita Mountains Highway. Parker was the half-breed son of Cynthia Ann Parker, who had been captured by Indians when she was a child, and Peta Nokoni, a Quahada Comanche chief. Parker became a chief when he was grown and unsuccessfully led his people against the whites. In 1892 when the Comanches were given land allotments, Parker selected 160 acres S. of Eagle Mountain for his home. Now restored, with some original furnishings. A registered historic place. Old West General Store and Museum nearby.

Wichita Mountains Wildlife Refuge, N. of Cache on State 115. A preserve of 59,020 acres, it has one of the world's largest herds of buffalo, as well as wild turkeys, wild longhorn cattle and elk. Paved road to summit of Mount Scott where there is a panoramic view of area. *Charons Gardens Wilderness Area,* SW of refuge headquarters, was designated by Congress in 1970 as a wilderness area.

CANTON, Blaine County. State 51, 58.

Cantonment, on the North Canadian River, established by Col. Richard Dodge in March 1879. Northern Cheyennes under Dull Knife had caused much havoc in the area the previous summer and settlers asked for help. Troops remained here until 1882. Site later was used as an Indian school. One building remains, in ruins. Registered historic place.

CHEROKEE, Alfalfa County. State 8, 11.

Salt Plains National Wildlife Refuge, entrance 3 miles E. 32,000 acres with an observation tower near the entrance. Refuge headquarters is 1 mile W. of State 38 and 2 miles S. of State 11. Driving on salt flats not recommended no matter how easy it looks. Digging crystals is permitted on weekends and holidays from April 1 to October 15; access road 3 miles S. of entrance leads to a selenite crystal area.

CHEYENNE, Roger Mills County. US 283.

Battle of Washita Battleground, less than 2 miles W. on State 47A. Another controversial battle, brought on by the ambitious Lt. Col. George A. Custer, was fought here on November 27, 1868. Scouts discovered a fresh Indian trail on the morning of November 26 near the South Canadian River, Custer's column pursued it all that blizzardy winter's day and came upon an Indian camp along the Washita. He chose a surprise attack at dawn, dividing his command into four groups. The village Cheyennes under Black Kettle, were sleeping peacefully when the firing commenced. Black Kettle and more than 100 of his people were killed; the village was burned and the pony herd destroyed. Custer learned then that the village was only one of many. Cheyennes, Arapahos, Kiowas, Kioa-Apaches and Comanches began to assemble on the hills. Maj. Joel Elliott and a 16-man command did not return. According to reports by other officers, he had seen a group of Indians escaping along the valley, had collected a group of men and gone in pursuit calling out a movie-like last line: "Here goes for a brevet or a coffin!" Elliott ran into the hordes of rallying Indians and never got back. Many reports said that Custer, who got away by a ruse of mounting his lesser wounded and prisoners on ponies, unfurled regimental flags, had the band play, "Ain't I Glad to Get Out of the Wilderness," and marched forward surprising the enemy by this show of strength. Rumors also flew that he took to bed the lovely Monahseetah, the daughter of chief Little Rock, who had been killed in the battle, and that she later bore his child. Frederick Benteen, who was there, many Cheyennes and historians, such as Mari Sandoz, have said this happened.

Benteen (who was to command a battalion at the Battle of Little Bighorn, holding the defense perimeter with Marcus Reno) had no great love for Custer, it seems; Benteen wrote of Washita in the *Missouri Democrat* for February 9, 1869: "(Custer) exhibits his close marksmanship and terrifies the crowd of frightened, captured squaws and papooses by dropping the struggling ponies in death near them. Ah! He is a clever marksman. Not even do the poor dogs of the Indians escape his eye and aim as they drop dead or limp howling away."

Custer's orders from Gen. Philip Sheridan were in part: "To proceed south in the direction of the Antelope Hills, thence toward the Washita River, the supposed winter seat of the hostile tribes; to destroy their villages and ponies; to kill or hang all warriors and bring back all women and children." In his after the battle report Custer said all the dead were warriors. Others said there were many women and children among the slain. Sheridan sent a congratulatory telegram to Custer; and in his report to the War Department described Chief Black Kettle as "worn out and useless," (and presumably better off dead).

A granite monument overlooks the valley where the attack occurred. A national historic landmark.

Black Kettle Museum, at junction of US 283 and State 47, honors those massacred in the "battle." Items from the battlefield and other Indian artifacts are displayed. A diorama of the scene just before the attack may be viewed.

CHOUTEAU, Mayes County. US 69.

Union Mission, on unimproved road, ca. 3 miles SE of town. Established in 1820, it was a school for Osage Indians from 1821 to 1833. In 1835 the mission was reopened and served the Cherokees for a time. Site has a stone marker. A cemetery and some foundations remain. When Presbyterian missionary Rev. Samuel A. Worcester, who founded Park Hill Mission, was here, he used the equipment he had brought from Georgia to print textbooks and tracts and the first book printed in Oklahoma, *The Child's Book,* 1855.

CLAREMORE, Rogers County. US 66.

J. M. Davis Gun Museum, 333 N. Lynn Riggs Blvd. Weapons, saddles, Indian artifacts.

Will Rogers Memorial, Will Rogers Blvd., State 88, trophies, a diorama, Rogers memorabilia.

Long's Historical Museum, State 20 and 88, 1002 W. Will Rogers Blvd. Wax figures and other historical items.

CLEO SPRINGS, Major County. State 8.

Homesteader's Sod House (in Alfalfa County just over line), State 8. Marshall McCully staked a claim to the section on which the house stands in September 1893, soon after the area was opened. Some alterations have been made; furnishings are representative of the homesteader's day. A registered historic place.

CLINTON, Custer County. US 66.

Western Trails Museum, 2229 Gary Freeway. Early Oklahoma and Indian artifacts, old farming equipment.

COLONY, Washita County. State 69.

McLemore Site, 4 miles SE of town on State 69, is one of the excavated sites of the Washita River Focus, a Plains village which has provided the most data on the activities of the prehistoric Wichita-speaking Indians. A national historic landmark, not open to the public at present.

CUSHING, Payne County. State 108.

Cimarron Valley Railroad Museum, just S. of town.

DAVIS, Murray County. US 77.

Initial Point, ca. 7½ miles W. of town on the Garvin–Murray county line. Congress established a point of reference from which to carry on the division of the Chickasaw Nation in 1864. A stone post marks this initial point which was then in the center of the Chickasaw land. A registered historic place.

DEWEY, Washington County. US 75.

Tom Mix Museum, at Delaware and Don Tyler Ave. Memorabilia of the Western cowboy movie star.

The Dewey Hotel, built in 1899, has been restored and features an early baby grand piano.

Dewey Cemetery has the grave of outlaw Henry Starr.

DUNCAN, Stephens County. US 81. On the old Chisholm Trail.

Stephens County Historical Museum, 916 Main St. Indian, pioneer and Civil War relics. Early carriages.

EDMOND, Oklahoma County. US 77.

Old North Tower, Central State College, 400 E. Hurd St. The first structure to be built in Oklahoma for normal school training was built in 1893, 1894. A registered historic place.

ELK CITY, Beckham County. State 6.

Old Town Museum, 2 miles SW on US 66, replica of an early Western town. Museum has period furnishings and relics. Old schoolroom, doctor's office.

EL RENO, Canadian County. US 66.

Canadian County Historical Society Museum, Wade and Grand. Former Rock Island depot houses Indian and pioneer artifacts, railroadiana, steam train and log cabin on grounds.

Fort Reno, 5 miles W. on US 66,270, then N. Established in 1874, the fort guarded the Cheyenne–Araphao Reservation. The U.S. founded the reservation and the adjacent Kiowa–Comanche Reservation in 1869. It was reactivated in 1874 during a Cheyenne uprising. The Darlington Agency, named for Brinton Darlington, a Quaker representing President Grant's Peace Policy, was the first agent. The site of this is 1½ miles NE of Fort Reno on an unimproved road on the Darlington State Game Farm. Fort Reno was named for Jesse L. Reno, killed at Antietam during the Civil War, not Marcus Reno, who fought in the Indian wars. Several buildings remain and a cemetery. The site is now on the Fort Reno U.S. Livestock Research Station.

FORT ARBUCKLE, Garvin County. State 7. On State 7, ca. 7 miles W. off

Davis. The first fort with this name was located on the Arkansas River near the mouth of the Cimarron and was well built, although it was never officially a fort. Arbuckle II was established in August 1850, a few miles W. of Mustang Creek and 1 mile S. of the Canadian River, to safeguard the travelers on the New Mexico–California route and to protect relocated Chickasaw Indians from the plains Indians. It was later moved to the right side of Wild Horse Creek, ca. 5 miles from the Washita, on a deserted Kickapoo Indian village site. The Kickapoos had moved to Mexico. Capt. Randolph B. Marcy, who established the post, named it "Fort Near the Crossing of the Washita River"; on June 25, 1851, it was designated Fort Arbuckle for a colonel who had died two weeks earlier. In 1858 all but five of the garrison were sent to Utah in connection with the Mormon campaign. A threat of Comanche trouble led to the reoccupation of the post by volunteers in June 1858. Just after the beginning of the Civil War, the Union withdrew and the fort was taken over by Confederates the following day (May 6, 1861). Federal troops were back in 1866. The land reverted to the Chickasaw Nation in 1870 by treaty.

FORT COBB, Caddo County. State 9. E. edge of town of Fort Cobb. Established on the E. side of Pond Creek where it reaches the Washita, the post was to protect the Wichita Indian Agency and the newly established reservation for Penateka Comanches, Wacoes, Caddoes and Tonkawas, who had been removed from Texas. It is named for Secretary of the Treasury Howell Cobb of Georgia. As were most forts, the post was abandoned at the start of the Civil War and taken over by Confederate troops. On October 23, 1862, a band of Osage, Shawnee, Delaware and Caddo Indians attacked the post, killed most of the small garrison and set fire to the buildings. They turned next to the Tonkawas, who had sided with the South and whom they accused of cannibalism. Before they were done the Tonkawas were nearly wiped out and so was the fort. In 1868 Kiowa and Comanches were moved here from near Fort Larned, Kansas, with Col. William B. Hazen as agent. He had been an Indian fighter before the war, taught at West Point and commanded in many battles in the Western theater of the war (the Mississippi Valley, Shiloh, Perryville, Chattanooga and Chickamauga, etc.). He then returned to Indian fighting, was reprimanded by a court martial for a minor affair (criticizing a superior officer) and died on active duty as a chief signal officer and head of the weather bureau in 1880. Sheridan was based here in December 1868, but soon departed to establish Fort Sill. State marker at site but no buildings remain. Site is private property.

FORT GIBSON, Muskogee County. US 62.

Fort Gibson, N. edge of town, was established in April 1824, on the Neosho (Grand) River, 3 miles above its confluence with the Arkansas. The first fort in Indian Territory, it was active for many years with affairs relating to the Five Civilized Tribes and was a center of military and commercial traffic. In 1834 it was the base for the Dragoon Expedition, under Col. Henry Leavenworth, who died enroute to the Red River to negotiate with some of the Southern Plains Indians. His successor, Col. Henry

Dodge, was successful in persuading the tribes to send delegates to Fort Gibson which eventually led to peace treaties. Keelboats and steamers came up the river to unload passengers, freight and military supplies. The Texas Road passed by the fort, and troops provided escort service for road traffic. The Confederates held the fort at the beginning of the Civil War, but the Federals came in 1863. Regular troops replaced volunteers after the way; the fort was garrisoned until 1890. Several buildings have been reconstructed. Interpretive markers. Fort Gibson National Cemetery is 1 mile E. of the town, N. of US 62. Diana Rogers, Cherokee wife of Sam Houston, and Capt. Billy Bowlegs, Seminole warrior, are among those buried here. The fort is a national historic landmark.

Judge Garrett's House of History, in town, is housed in a former U.S. hospital built in 1871.

FORT SUPPLY, Woodward County. US 270.

Camp Supply, 1 miles E. of town on US 270, was established by Lt. Cols. Alfred Sully and George Custer in November 1868, near the junction of Wolf Creek with the North Canadian River, as an advance base in Sheridan's 1868–69 campaign. From here Custer moved to the Battle of the Washita and brought the captives back to this camp. It was designated a fort in 1878. The garrison had taken part in the Red River War of 1874–75. Now occupied by the Western State Hospital, some buildings remain from the Army period: a brick guardhouse, log fire station, and a few others. A registered historic district.

FORT TOWSON, Choctaw County. Off US 70, E. edge of town. The first fort, Cantonment Towson, was established in May 1824, on Gates Creek, ca. 6 miles N. of the Red River, with troops from Fort Jesup, Louisiana, to control the outlaws and Indians along the Red River, then the frontier between the U.S. and Mexico. Col. Matthew Arbuckle was commander. This encampment was abandoned in 1829. The new post (called Camp Phoenix, then Cantonment Towson and finally on February 8, 1832, Fort Towson) was 6 miles N. of the Red River, just S. of Gates Creek; the last troops left in June 1854. Fort Towson became the capital of the Choctaw Nation. During the Civil War it was occupied by Confederate troops and served as headquarters for the Confederate Indian Territory Department. Gen. Stand Watie surrendered here in June 1865. He was the last Confederate general to lay down his arms. U-shaped ruins remain. The fort cemetery is at the W. side of the grounds and includes some civilian graves. George Gooding, the post sutler, his wife and a daughter are buried here. About 120 military burials were removed to Fort Gibson National Cemetery. A registered historic place.

FORT WASHITA, Bryan County. SW of Nida on State 199. Established April 23, 1842, near the False Washita River, ca. 30 miles above its junction with the Red River, which was near the spot Col. Henry Dodge had selected for Camp Washita during his 1834 expedition. The site here was chosen by Col. Zachary Taylor, 1st U.S. Infantry, in response to a request from the Chickasaws and was a stopping place on the Overland Trail for protection from both Indians and Texans. This, like most other Oklahoma forts, was abandoned by the

Federals early in the war and occupied on the following day peacefully by the Confederates. Headquarters for the Indian Territory Department of the Confederacy was moved here late in the war. The buildings were burned on the night of August 1, 1865. In July 1870, the reservation, never formally declared, was made available for the use of the Chickasaws. Now a national historic landmark, some buildings remain. Modern gate with frontier-style guard tower. Gen. Douglas Hancock Cooper, who had been U.S. agent to the Choctaws and Chickasaws, became a Confederate commander in the area. He lies in an unmarked grave in the Fort Washita cemetery.

FREEDOM, Woods County. US 64, 50A.

Alabaster Caverns, in state park, 6 miles S. on State 50. The 200-acre park contains one of the largest known gypsum caves with a bat cave within the cavern as an added attraction (?).

Chimney Rock, 8½ miles SE of town, was a landmark to early travelers. It is a sandstone pinnacle in the Cimarron River Valley.

Portion of restored Fort Washita complex. Original site chosen by Gen. Zachary Taylor in 1841
(Oklahoma Tourism, Fred W. Marvel photo)

GEARY, Blaine County. US 281.

Jesse Chisholm Gravesite, 8 miles NE of town. Chisholm was the mixed-blood Cherokee trader and guide who established the trail named for him which was used for the big cattle drives from Texas to the railroad in Kansas. The trail ran from the Nueces River in E. Texas through Indian Territory. When Oklahoma celebrated the centennial of the trail in 1967, Chairman Henry B. Bass, a long-time Oklahoma booster and lover of history, had elegant stationery printed which reproduced a fine map of the trail. As pictured in this drawing, the trail ran almost due north from the Red River Station through Ryan, Waurika, Addington, Comanche, Duncan, Marlow, Rush Springs, Chickasha, Amber, Pocasset and Minco where it reached the South Canadian River and branched E. to pass Mustang and Piedmont, W. to Union City, El Reno, Fort Reno, Caddo, Okarche and Kingfisher; then at the Cimarron River, it joined again for Red Fork Ranch, Hennessey, Bison, Buffalo Springs Stage Station, Waukomis, Enid, Kremlin, Pond Creek (there crossing the Arkansas River), Medford and so to the Kansas Line.

GOODWELL, Texas County. US 54. In the "panhandle" which was created in 1850 when Congress bought the Western claims of Texas. The strip became known as "No Man's Land" because it was not included in the territories of Colorado, Kansas or New Mexico. Indian country at first it was later settled by cattlemen, sheepmen and squatters. In 1886–87 the section tried to get recognition from Congress for a Cimarron Territory but the effort failed. On May 2, 1890, Congress passed the Organic Act creating the Territory of Oklahoma which included this area.

No Man's Land Historical Museum, on campus of Panhandle State University, has anthropology, biology, geology and pioneer artifacts.

GRAND LAKE, Delaware County. US 59.

Cayuga-Splitlog Mission, on the Cowskin Arm of Grand Lake, was built in 1894 as a tribute to the wife of Chief Mathias Splitlog, chief of the Seneca–Cayuga Indians, one of the richest men in the Seneca Nation. *Loom House* in the same area has craftwork by weavers both Indian and white of the Council House Friends Church.

Har-Ber Village, 3½ miles W. of Grove on Lake Rd., is a reconstructed pioneer town.

Pensacola Dam, impounding Grand Lake, ca. 17 miles SE of Vinita, has a lookout house and tours.

GUTHRIE, Logan County. I–35.

Oklahoma Territorial Museum, 402 E. Oklahoma Ave. Site where the first state governor took office has historical displays.

When the territory was opened to white settlers at high noon on April 22, 1889, Guthrie was a booming tent city, 80 miles from the land-rush starting point on the Kansas border. With the Santa Fe coming through town, the village grew rapidly and was the capital from 1890 to 1910.

Langston University, in Langston, NE of Guthrie, was authorized for Negro students by the Territorial Legislature in 1897. The town and university are named for black educator and Congressman John M. Langston of Virginia.

HEAVENER, Le Flore County. US 59, 270.

Heavener Runestone, in Clem Hamilton State Park, 2 miles E. Stone bears an inscription in a Runic alphabet used in Scandinavian countries in ancient times. The inscription carries the date 1012 A.D. and is believed to have been carved by Viking explorers long before Columbus.

Peter Conser House, 4 miles S. and 3½ miles W. of town, was built in 1894 by Conser, a leading Choctaw citizen. Period furnishings. Conser was a homeless orphan, son of a Frenchman trader and a Choctaw mother, who died of smallpox when Peter was a boy. After the Civil War he worked hard to gain wealth and security for his family; he also became a deputy sheriff in the Choctaw Nation, and a captain in the Choctaw Lighthorsemen, tribal police force that served the Choctaws from 1834 to 1906.

HINTON, Caddo County. US 281.

Rock Mary, ca. 4 miles W. of town, was described by Lt. James H. Simpson of the U.S. Corps of Topographical Engineers when he was accompanying Capt. Randolph B. Marcy and an emigrant group in 1849. It was named for a lady in the group. A traveler's landmark and a registered historic place.

HOBART, Kiowa County. US 183. Local legend says Coronado came through in 1541 with his expedition, 1950 persons, plus horses, cattle, sheep and hogs.

Camelback Mountain, SW of town, has 4th-century Indian petroglyphs.

Indian Cemetery, and Chief Lone Wolf's Grave, 4 miles S.

HUGO, Choctaw County. US 70.

Rose Hill, off US 70, E. of town, was the home of Col. Robert Jones, wealthy Choctaw planter who had thousands of acres along the Red River and 500 slaves. The house is gone but the Historical Society maintains the family cemetery here.

Goodland Presbyterian Children's Home, 2 miles SW, was established in 1848 as an orphanage for Indian children. The chapel was built in 1852 and is still in use.

IDABEL, McCurtain County. US 70. Named for Ida and Belle, daughters of the Choctaw landowner of the townsite.

Harris House, S. of town, built in 1866 by Henry Harris has been restored; artifacts date back to the American Revolution.

Marker on highway for Courthouse and first post office, ca. 9 miles S. of town. The post office was established in 1824.

JAY, Delaware County. State 28.

Piney Indian Church, E. of town on State 20 at Indian Rd. Visitors are welcome for a service performed entirely in the Cherokee Indian language.

Hillside Church, NW of town, just off State 28, also has devotions in Cherokee. Hillside Burial Grounds next to church are reserved for full-blooded Indians.

KENEFIC, Bryan County. State 22.

Fort McCulloch, ca. 2 miles SW of town. Established in 1862 by Gen. Albert Pike, commander of all Confederate troops in the Department of the Indian Territory. Abandoned after the war. Earthen trenches and breastworks remain. A registered historic place.

KINGFISHER, Kingfisher County. US 81.

Chisholm Trail Museum and Governor Seay Mansion, 1 mile SW at 11th and Overstreet, 5 blocks W. of US 81. Chisholm Trail relics, pioneer and Indian artifacts. The restored home was built in 1892 and has period furnishings. Abraham Seay was associate justice of an Oklahoma court in 1890. In 1892 he was the second governor. A registered historic place.

KINTA, Haskell County. State 31.

Ruins of Choctaw Jail and Courthouse, 4 miles E. and 1 mile N. of town. Green McCurtain, Chief of the Choctaw nation, is buried here. The McCurtain house is a registered historic place, not open to the public at present.

LAKE MURRAY STATE PARK, Love County. State 77S. The 5,728-acre park has a museum in Tucker Tower.

LAWTON, Comanche County.

Fort Sill Military Reservation, 4 miles N. on US 277. A 95,000-acre field artillery and missile base now. Ironically, Geronimo, who had his own kind of missiles, is buried in the Apache cemetery. He was imprisoned here in 1894. Historic sites on the reservation are well marked. Among the sites within The Old Post National Historic Landmark, in continuous use since 1870: Sherman House, commandant's home. Not open to the public. On the porch here, Stumbling Bear of the Kiowas tried to kill Gen. Sherman, as many Southerners had before him, without success. The general died in bed 20 years later. Old Post Headquarters and the Post Chapel; U.S. Army Field Artillery Center Museum is comprised of the old guardhouse, McLain Hall, Hamilton Hall, Hall of Flags, and Old Stone Corral connected by Cannon Walk. Cavalry and Indian relics.

Fort Sill Cemetery has a Chiefs Knoll with the graves of Quanah Parker, Satanta and other Plains Indian chiefs, also the Comanche and Apache cemeteries are on the military reservation.

Museum of the Great Plains, in Elmer Thomas Park, 601 Ferris Blvd. Regional museum for Great Plains of North America. Relics of fur trading, cattle drives, Indian days and an outdoor museum of farm and ranch implements.

LEXINGTON, Cleveland County. US 77.

Camp Mason, on the N. bank of the Canadian River, was established in June 1835, by Maj. Richard Mason of the 1st U.S. Dragoons, to provide a council place for the Indians and whites. In August 1835, more than 5,000 Indians met with the representatives of Governor Montfort Stokes. Never officially a fort, the post area was used by Auguste Chouteau for trading and continued to be called Fort Mason. Chouteau's place was a popular stop on the California Rd. No remains.

LINDSAY, Garvin County. State 19, 76.

Erin Springs House, S. of the Washita River, was built in 1880. Frank Murray, the builder, was born in Ireland and settled in Oklahoma after he married a woman of Chickasaw background and migrated with her to the territory in the 1860s. He became a wealthy cattleman. The house is a registered historic place, restored with period furnishings.

McALESTER, McIntosh County. US 69. James J. McAlester established a tent store where the Texas and California roads crossed in 1870. He married a Chickasaw girl which made him a member of the Choctaw nation with Indian rights. (The tribes had mutual citizenship.) He used a geologist's memorandum book to find coal when the railroad came through the area and began mining. The Choctaws claimed his royalties, but a tribal court supported his case. Chief Coleman Cole then sentenced McAlester and three co-owners to death. They escaped with the aid of a guard and subsequently settled the affair by compromise. McAlester later became lieutenant governor.

Old Tobusky County Courthouse, 200 E. Krebs, of the Choctaw Nation, where Indian trials were held, was erected in 1876. Preserved in N. McAlester Park, 1 block E. of US 69.

MILLERTON, McCurtain County. US 70.

Wheelock Mission, off US 70 E. of town, established by Rev. Alfred Wright in 1832 was the first national academy founded under the Choctaw Nation's Education Act of 1842 and set the precedent for 35 academies and seminaries. The school closed in 1955, but Old Seminary, built in 1839, and several other old buildings remain. A national historic landmark. The church still is used.

MUSKOGEE, Muskogee County. US 69. An early trading post on the old Texas Road.

Five Civilized Tribes Museum, E. on Agency Hill in Honor Heights Park. Displays feature the history of the Cherokees, Chickasaws, Choctaws, Creeks and Seminoles. Exhibit Room, tribal photo gallery, reference library in Union Indian Agency was built in 1875.

Thomas-Foreman House, 1419 W. Okmulgee St. Grant Foreman came to Oklahoma in 1899 as an employee of the Dawes Commission which was to allot land in severalty to the members of the Five Civilized Tribes; he became one of the state's leading historians. Carolyn Thomas-Foreman also wrote of Indians and Oklahoma. The state historical society owns the home. Original furnishings. Indian artifacts.

Bacone College Museum, in Ataloa Lodge on campus of Bacone College is a repository of American Indian artifacts. NE off State 16.

NEWKIRK, Kay County. US 77.

Chilocco Indian School, ca. 8 miles N. on unimproved road. Founded in 1883 to provide education for children of the Plains tribes in western Indian Territory. Several old buildings remain in use.

Deer Creek Site, 6 miles NE of town, is believed to have been occupied by the Wichita Indians early in the 18th century. It also was the site of a French trading post known as Ferdinandino ca. 1725–50. A national historic landmark, not open to the general public at present.

NORMAN, Cleveland County. US 77.

Stovall Museum, on campus of University of Oklahoma, University Blvd. and Boyd St. Historical and scientific exhibits, fine collection of Indian art.

W. B. Bizzell Memorial Library, on campus, has special collections and much material on Oklahoma and Indian history.

NOWATA, Nowata County. US 169.

Historical Society Museum has "theme" rooms with many antiques and relics.

OKEMAH, Okfuskee County. State 48.

Territory Town Museum, Civil War and Indian relics in a frontier town setting.

OKLAHOMA CITY, Oklahoma County. I–40, 44.

State Capitol, NE. 23 St. and Lincoln Blvd. Tours.

Oklahoma Historical Society, in Wiley Post Bldg., opposite capitol, NE. 19th St. and Lincoln Blvd., a large collection of Indian material, Oklahoma history exhibits.

Chamber of Commerce, 1 Santa Fe Plaza, has information on sites and tours.

National Cowboy Hall of Fame and Western Heritage Center, 1700 NE. 63rd St., 6 miles NE on US 66. Museum of Western history, Fraser Studio collection of American sculpture, "West of Yesterday" exhibits depict pioneer life. Among many monuments is the famous "End of the Trail" statue.

Wildlife Department Building, in Capitol Complex, has dioramas.

Oklahoma Heritage Center, N. Robinson at 14th St., in the former mansion of Judge R. A. Hefner, has an Oklahoma Hall of Fame, family furnishings in restored rooms, archives and gardens.

Oklahoma State Firefighting Museum, 2716 NE. 50th St. Early equipment.

Heritage Hills, NW. 14th to NW. 21st Sts. between Walker and Robinson, and from Robinson to Classen Blvd. on NW. 14th and 15th, is an Historical Preservation Area of early Oklahoma homes.

Frontier City, I–35 and US 66. Recreated town and Santa Fe Railroad with trail rides, museum, the inevitable Last Chance Saloon, etc.

OKMULGEE, Okmulgee County. State 56.

Capitol of the Creek Nation, 6th St. between Grand and Morton Aves. A Creek Indian Museum features tribal history exhibits. The building is a national historic landmark. The first capitol was a two-story log structure built in 1868 housing the supreme court and the legislature. The new capitol was built in 1878.

OOLOGAH, Rogers County.

Will Rogers Birthplace, ca. 4 miles NE of town. Clem Rogers, father of the humorist and cowboy star, built a log home here which became the present two-story frame structure with alterations. Will Rogers was born here on November 4, 1879. Construction of the Oologah Dam flooded the original site. House was moved in 1960, now part of the state parks system, the birthplace is being developed as a 19th-century frontier ranch. A registered historic place.

OPTIMA, Texas County. US 54.

Stamper Site, 2.5 miles S. of town on the S. bank of the N. Canadian River. The excavation revealed a village culture of the Panhandle which dates from 1300. A national historic landmark, not open to the public at present.

PAWHUSKA, Osage County. US 60.

Osage Tribal Museum, Grandview Ave. Treaties, costumes, other artifacts.

Osage County Historical Society Museum, 700 Lynn Ave. Indian and pioneer relics; old Santa Fe depot.

PAWNEE, Pawnee County. US 64.

Pawnee Bill Museum and Mansion, on US 64, on Blue Hawk Peak. Prairie home of Gordon and May Lillie. Museum has many mementoes of "Pawnee Bill," wild west showman and "white chief" of the Pawnees, who drove cattle on the Chisholm Trail and toured with Buffalo Bill's show. Guided tours. Buffalo pasture seen by auto tour has buffalo and longhorns.

PERRY, Noble County. US 77, 64.

Cherokee Strip Museum, 1208 W. Fir Ave. Pioneer and land run items.

PLATT NATIONAL PARK, Murray County. Off US 177. 912 acres. The Travertine Nature Center has exhibits. There is a herd of buffalo in the park. Nature walks.

Arbuckle National Recreation Area is 8 miles SW.

PONCA CITY, Kay County. US 177.

Pioneer Woman Museum, 701 Monument Rd. Bronze statue, pioneer home and ranch artifacts.

Indian Museum, 1000 E. Grand Ave. Early day and Indian items, including costumes, in onetime home of Gov. E. W. Marland.

101 Ranch, just off US 77, ca. 10 miles SW of town, was founded by George Miller, a trader who came from Kansas in the 1870s with 10 tons of bacon which he parlayed into 400 Texas longhorns and herded N. to a range in Quapaw Indian Territory. He made friends with the Ponca Indians, who were living at the time with the Quapaws, and was able to make terms to graze his herds on their land. He got rich from his ranching, and just before his death in 1903, oil was found on his land. The White House which he was building in his last year is still standing; before that his headquarters was a dugout. White Eagle Monument is 2 miles W. of the ranch, erected by the Miller brothers in memory of the Ponca Indian chief who was their father's friend.

PORUM, Muskogee County. State 2. Once the home of Tom Starr, half Irish, half Cherokee, who had five sons, one of whom married Myra Belle Shirley Reed, thereby giving her the name Starr which she retained through other alliances. Belle, who became known as the Bandit Queen of Indian Territory, was killed nearby and buried in the yard of her home called "Younger's Bend" on the N. bank of the Canadian River, with a granite headstone engraved with a horse's head, her name, statistics and a verse. Nearly everything ever written about Myra Belle Shirley, from her birthplace to who killed her, is still controversial. She was born somewhere near Carthage, Missouri, perhaps in northern Arkansas. She died from a shot in the back which may have been inflicted by her son, or a discontented tenant, or a neighbor mistaking her for someone else, or the man she was seeing off at the time. She walked down a wooded trail near her home for the last time. A glamorized bronze statue of Belle Starr stands in Woolaroc in Bartlesville. The verse on her tombstone:

Shed not for her the bitter tear
Nor give the heart a vain regret,
'Tis but the casket that lies here,
The gems that filled it sparkles yet.

One of her biographers states that the headstone was paid for by Pearl Reed, her daughter, with money earned in the Pea Green Bawdy House at Fort Smith. Pearl Reed (whose father supposedly was Jim Reed but whose name is often spelled Read) is buried in Calvary Cemetery, Douglas, Arizona.

POTEAU, Le Flore County. US 271.

Kerr Museum, 6 miles SW on US 271, then 1 mile E. Home of former Senator Robert Kerr has exhibits

End of the Trail, in National Cowboy Hall of Fame and Western Heritage Center
(Oklahoma Tourism, Fred W. Marvel photo)

maintained by the Eastern Oklahoma Historical Society which tells the development of the area from prehistoric times through the Spiro Mound-Builders, the possible visit of the Vikings, the Choctaws and the other pioneers. A brochure given to visitors points out other sites in the area. (All listed separately in this guide.) The Talimena Scenic Drive passes Horse Thief Springs and other historic places along the Old Military Trail.

PRYOR, Mayes County, State 20, was named for Capt. Nathaniel Pryor, a scout with Lewis and Clark, who built a trading post here for business with the Osage Indians. He was their friend and his wife was an Indian. The Osages had many interesting names: Arrow-Going-Home, Walks-Badly, Bad-Tempered-Buffalo, Little-Eagle-That-Gets-What-He-Wants, Smells-Like-a-Man and many others. Seasons were such as Little-Flower-Killer Moon, Yellow-Flower Moon. There were the Place-of-the-Oaks Osages, the Place-of-the-Many-Swans, and even the They-Who-Do-Not-Touch-Blood gens. Whites were first called Long Knife and then Heavy Eyebrows.

QUARTZ MOUNTAIN STATE PARK, Kiowa County. US 283, State 44. An 11,053-acre scenic area.

Peace-on-the-Plains Site & Soldier Spring Battlefield, first site is ca. 5 miles SE of junction of US 283 and State 44; second is 2 miles E. of the first. They are accessible only by foot from the park. Make local inquiry. The first important peace conference between the U.S. and southern Plains Indians took place here. (Also see Fort Gibson.) The Dragoon Expedition left Fort Gibson under Col. Henry Leavenworth in 1834. When he died of fever, he was succeeded by Col. Henry Dodge who held the conferences here; the aim was to achieve unmolested travel on the Santa Fe Trail and security for the Five Civilized Tribes, toward whom other tribes were hostile.

At Soldier Spring on December 25, 1868, Maj. Andrew Evans and the 3rd Cavalry, from their base in Fort Bascom, New Mexico, attacked a Comanche village, much as Custer had done in the Battle of the Washita, about a month earlier. Both sites are on privately owned farmland. State historical marker at junction of US 283 and State 44.

Capital of Old Greer, in Mangum, just W. of the park, was an area claimed by 14 different governments from 1669 to 1907. For the oddball tourist, there is Bat Cave near town where hundreds of thousands of bats swoop and swirl in early evening.

RED OAK, Latimer County. US 270.

Butterfield Stage Stop, at Edwards Store, NE of town, was a favorite eating place. The pioneer store and trading post and Edwards home are still in use.

RENTIESVILLE, McIntosh County, also in Muskogee County. Off US 69.

Honey Springs Battlefield, N. of town, site of a well-mixed Civil War engagement in July 1863. Federals under Maj. Gen. James G. Blunt opposed Confederates under Gen. Douglas Cooper. The Confederates had two Creek regiments, one regiment made up of Choctaws and Chickasaws, and the 20th Texas Cavalry. Gen. Blunt had two cavalry and two Indian regiments, the 2nd Colorado Infantry and the 1st Kansas Colored Infantry. The North drove the South across Elk Creek. This was one of the first times black troops had been engaged. The battle itself was the most significant encounter of the war in Indian Territory. The area is little changed today. The foundation of the powder magazine remains. A registered historic place.

ROSE, Mayes County. State 33.

Saline County Courthouse, 1 mile E. and 1 mile S. of town on State 33, was built by the Cherokee National Council between 1884 and 1889 and is the only one remaining of nine original court buildings. Courtyard is the Cherokee Burial Grounds.

RUSH SPRINGS, Grady County. US 81.

Rush Springs Battlefield, just E. of US 81, ca. 5 miles SE of town. On October 1, 1858, Capt. Earl Van Dorn's Wichita Expedition from Fort Belknap, Texas, comprised of the 2nd Cavalry and Indian allies, destroyed a Comanche camp here killing 82 people. Five soldiers died and Van Dorn received severe wounds (but lived to be killed by an irate husband during the Civil War, who said the general had invaded the sanctity of his home). Buffalo Hump, leader of the Comanches, had come north from Texas to discuss peace with the authorities at Fort Arbuckle and was in temporary camp here when the massacre, a dawn attack, took place. The battlefield is now on a private farm.

SALINA, Mayes County. State 20. Marker shows site of early Chouteau trading post. At W. side of town is the Paradise Tree, planted in 1796 after being imported from France to shade the post, which also served as a meeting place for the Grand Peace Council of the Cherokee, Creek and Osage Indians in 1868.

Chouteau Memorial has family memorabilia and other historical displays. Jean Pierre Chouteau, of St. Louis, was an early trader of the frontier. Auguste Pierre Chouteau succeeded his father and built a home at the confluence of the Grand, Verdigris and Arkansas rivers, which Washington Irving visited in 1832 and described in his *Tour on the Prairies.*

SALLISHAW, Sequoyah County. State 101.

Sequoyah's Home, 11 miles NE on State 101. One-room log cabin built late in the 1820s by the Cherokee Indians, who created an 84-character alphabet for the language. Restored by the Oklahoma Historical Society using original sources and materials. Sequoyah's statue is in Statuary Hall in the U.S. capitol. The giant Sequoia trees of California are named for him. The cabin is enclosed within a stone shelter. Nearby is a relocated log building, dating from 1855, which once adjoined cabin. The home is a national historic landmark.

SHAWNEE, Pottawatomie County. US 270. Before the land was opened for settlement, the Sac and Fox, Kickapoo, Shawnee and Pottawatomie Indians were relocated here from the Great Lakes area. In 1876 on land donated by the Pottawatomies, the Benedictine Fathers established Sacred Heart Mission near the California Rd. Jim Thorpe, later a superb football player and an Olympic winner, was a student at the mission. Beard Log House, in city park, was the first house in town.

SPIRO, Le Flore County. US 271.

Spiro Indian Mounds, E. of town. The mounds and village site originally covered ca. 80 acres. A registered historic place.

Fort Coffee, on unimproved road, ca. 5 miles NE of town, was established April 22, 1834, on a bluff on the right side of the Arkansas River at Swallow Rock. It was to protect the newly relocated Choctaws and Chickasaws, partly by stopping whiskey shipments on the Arkansas River. The post was turned over to the Choctaw Nation in 1843. The Council established an academy for boys, operated under the direction of Methodist ministers. The school closed soon after the beginning of the Civil War and was occupied by Confederates. In October 1863, the fort was burned by Union troops.

Skullyville and New Hope Seminary, ca. 3 miles E. of town on US 271. The town of Skullyville began in 1832 as the agency for the relocated Choctaws, but did not get its name until 1860. (Means "Money Town" in Choctaw.) Tribal annuities were paid here. The Butterfield Overland Mail came through town in 1858 and established a station here. Federal troops occupied the village in 1863 and left it a shambles. New Hope Seminary, a boarding school, was founded in 1844 for Choctaw girls; closed during the war, it was rebuilt and reopened in 1870, then burned out in 1897. The foundation ruins of the agency and seminary remain. The town cemetery has the graves of many leading Choctaws.

SWINK, Choctaw County. US 70.

Chief's House, the oldest house in the state, built in 1832 for Choctaw chief Thomas LeFlore, restored by the Historical Society. N. of US 70 near town. The chief had a 1,000-acre farm tended by black slaves. A registered historic place.

TAHLEQUAH, Cherokee County. US 62, State 82.

Cherokee National Capital, Muskogee Ave. The brick building of 1869 presently serves as the courthouse of Cherokee County. A national historic landmark. The Supreme Court Bldg. and the National Prison are on Water St. The Cherokee Female Seminary is now the administration building of Northeastern State College. The library has a museum with regional artifacts.

Murrell Home, 4 miles S. on State 82, then 1 mile E. at Park Hill. Restored antebellum mansion has many original furnishings. George Murrell, a Virginian, traveled the Trail of Tears with the Cherokees. Though the house was looted during the Civil War, it was the only one in the community not destroyed. Registered historic place.

Tsa-La-Gi, 1½ miles SE on US 62, State 10, 82, then 1 mile E. Replica Indian village, authentically maintained by the Cherokee National Historical Society. *Trail of Tears,* a drama by Kermit Hunter, is presented nightly in summer months at the Tsa-La-Gi Theatre.

TISHOMINGO, Johnston County. State 99.

Chickasaw Council House, on courthouse grounds, was raised in 1856 and served as the tribe's capitol.

Tishomingo National Wildlife Refuge, S. of town, comprises 16,609 acres on the upper Washita arm of Lake Texoma. Observation post allows closeup viewing of waterfowl and other fauna. Refuge headquarters on gravel road from State 78 at E. edge of town.

TULSA, Tulsa County. I-44. In 1879 Tulsa was a post office on a pony mail route through Indian Territory. The office was in the home of Creek rancher, George Perryman, near present 41st St. His brother was the postmaster.

Philbrook Art Center, 2727 S. Rockford Rd., has American Indian paintings and crafts, a splendid collection of pottery, the Lawson Collection of American Indian costumes and artifacts.

Thomas Gilcrease Institute of American History & Art, 2500 W. Newton St., founded by Gilcrease, an oil magnate of Creek Indian descent, now belongs to the city. Many of the world's finest paintings of American Indians are here: works by Frederic Remington, Charles Russell, George Catlin, Alfred Miller and others. Sculpture, manuscripts, artifacts, maps. Archaeological displays represent all major epochs.

Creek Council Oak Tree, 18th and Cheyenne. Site of the council fire used by the first group of Creeks to arrive from Georgia in 1828. A tribal meeting place for the "Turtle Clan."

World Museum, I-44, at Peoria Exit. Among displays are some pioneer and Indian items, model ghost town, Wells-Fargo desk, antique carriages, spinning wheels and photographs of Indian chiefs, including Geronimo and Sitting Bull.

TUSKAHOMA, Pushmataha County. US 271.

Choctaw National Capital, 2 miles N. of town, has been restored and houses Choctaw artifacts. The building is used for Choctaw council meetings. Jackson McCurtain, Chief of the Choctaws from 1880 to 1884, is buried nearby. An earlier log structure at Nanih Waya was the first capitol. A registered historic place.

WANETTE, Pottawatomie County. State 102.

Log Cabin Museum, pioneer artifacts and other displays in restored home, built in 1894.

WATTS, Adair County. US 59.

Fort Wayne, originally located S. of the Illinois River, just W. of the Arkansas line, on the present townsite. Established in October 1838, with troops from abandoned Fort Coffee. Many men died from the unhealthy location. The dead included Captain John Stewart, who founded the fort, which had been called Camp Illinois for a time. A new site near Spavinaw (Flag) Creek, near present Marysville and the Arkansas state line, was selected and a post established there in July 1840, to protect the military road from Fort Snelling, Minnesota, to Fort Towson, near the Red River. When the post was abandoned in 1842, the garrison was sent to Kansas where it became a part of newly founded Fort Scott. During the first year of the Civil War, Confederate Gen. Stand Watie used the old post for recruitment.

WAURIKA, Jefferson County. US 81, 70.

Chisholm Trail Museum, US 70 in town, has cattle-industry artifacts and mementoes of the trail; also the history of Black Beaver, a Delaware scout who established the route which became the trail. He is buried near Anadarko.

WETUMKA, Hughes County. State 9. Settled by the Creek Indians and named for the Alabama town where they lived before being forced to move west. A living fire was carried from Alabama to the new tribal home by two braves. The first trading post was established here in 1858. The Levering Mission was built nearby on the North Fork of the Canadian River.

WEWOKA, Seminole County. State 59, 56. The Seminole tribal capital. A pecan tree on the courthouse grounds was used for tribal justice penalties as a whipping tree. An execution tree had been used earlier.

Seminole Nation Historical Museum, in Rock Community Building, has many displays featuring tribal history.

WILBURTON, Latimer County. State 2.

Robbers Cave State Park, 5 miles N. on State 2, covers more than 8,000 acres and is named for the cave which was used by outlaws and refugees from both Confederate and Union armies in the Sansbois Mountains. Belle Starr and her gang are among those said to have used the cave's protection.

WOODWARD, Woodward County. State 34, 34C.

Plains Indians and Pioneer Museum, 2009 Williams Ave. Historical material of northwest Oklahoma, displays of Indian life and pioneer days on the plains.

Boiling Springs State Park, on State 34C, 8 miles NE. The 820-acre park with cold water springs which "boil up" through white sand is on the N. bank of the Canadian River. The springs were a favorite stop for emigrants, and watering place for pioneers.

OREGON

. . . the mortuary ground of these [Yaquina Bay] Indians . . . occupied the only level spot we could get for the block-house. Their dead were buried in canoes, which rested in the crotches of forked sticks a few feet above-ground. . . . According to the custom of all Indian tribes on the Pacific coast, when one of their number died all his worldly effects were buried with him. . . . I made known to the Indians that we would have to take this piece of ground for the block-house. They demurred at first, for there is nothing more painful to an Indian than disturbing his dead, but they finally consented. . . . It was agreed that on the following day at 12 o'clock, when the tide was going out, I should take my men and place the canoes in the bay, and let them float out on the tide across the ocean to the happy hunting-grounds.

At that day there existed in Oregon in vast numbers a species of wood-rat, and our inspection of the graveyard showed that the canoes were thickly infested with them. . . . I have known them to empty in one night a keg of spikes in the storehouse in Yamhill, distributing them along the stringers of the building, with apparently no other purpose than amusement. We anticipated great fun watching the efforts of these rats to escape the next day when the canoes should be launched on the ocean. . . . When the work of taking down the canoes and carrying them to the water began, expectation was on tiptoe, but, strange as it may seem, not a rat was to be seen. . . . They had all disappeared; there was not one in any of the canoes, as investigation proved, for disappointment instigated a most thorough search. The Indians said the rats understood Chinook, and that as they had no wish to accompany the dead across the ocean to the happy hunting-grounds, they took to the woods for safety.

P. S. Sheridan, *Personal Memoirs,* 1888

Salute my mountains,—clouded Hood,
Saint Helens in its sea of wood,—
Where sweeps the Oregon, and where
White storms are in the feathered fir.

Joaquin Miller, "Songs of the Sierras," 1871

Two miles beyond Coles station we cross the State line, and, entering Oregon, begin the ascent of the Siskiyou Mountains. This ascent is a wonder of railway engineering. . . . Elevation at State Line—2,859 feet. . . . Length of Tunnel No. 13—4,160 feet. The mathematician has the advantage here. He can tell exactly the facts concerning this great work; but the descriptive writer strives in vain to convey to the reader the beauty and grandeur of the scene. The southern slope of the range is denuded of trees, while the northern side is covered with a dense growth of pine. . . . Lakes, rivers and valleys lie spread out before us like a map; and, in a word, for variety, grandeur, beauty and extent, this view has no equal on the continent.

Stanley Wood, *Over the Range to the Golden Gate* (Chicago, 1896)

OREGON FACTS: The land was first claimed by Spain in 1775, then by England, and after Capt. Robert Gray's 1792 discovery of the Columbia River, the young United States took interest, which the Lewis and Clark expedition encouraged. John Jacob Astor's Pacific Fur Co. sent two parties, one via Cape Horn, the other opening the Oregon Trail. Fort Astor, later called Astoria, was built in 1811. Astoria was reclaimed by the British in the War of 1812. Joint occupancy was achieved by the U.S. with Britain in 1818. Trappers, missionaries and finally settlers arrived. The boundary was fixed at the 49th parallel and the Territory of Oregon was recognized in 1849. Oregon was admitted to the Union on February 14, 1859, the 33rd state. Oregon has Crater Lake National Park, Oregon Caves National Monument, Oregon Dunes National Recreation Area, 13 national forests and a national grassland. Capital: Salem. Territorial capital: Oregon City. Nickname: Beaner State.

Early Routes. Lewis and Clark Trail, the Barlow Road, the Oregon Trail, the Applegate Road.

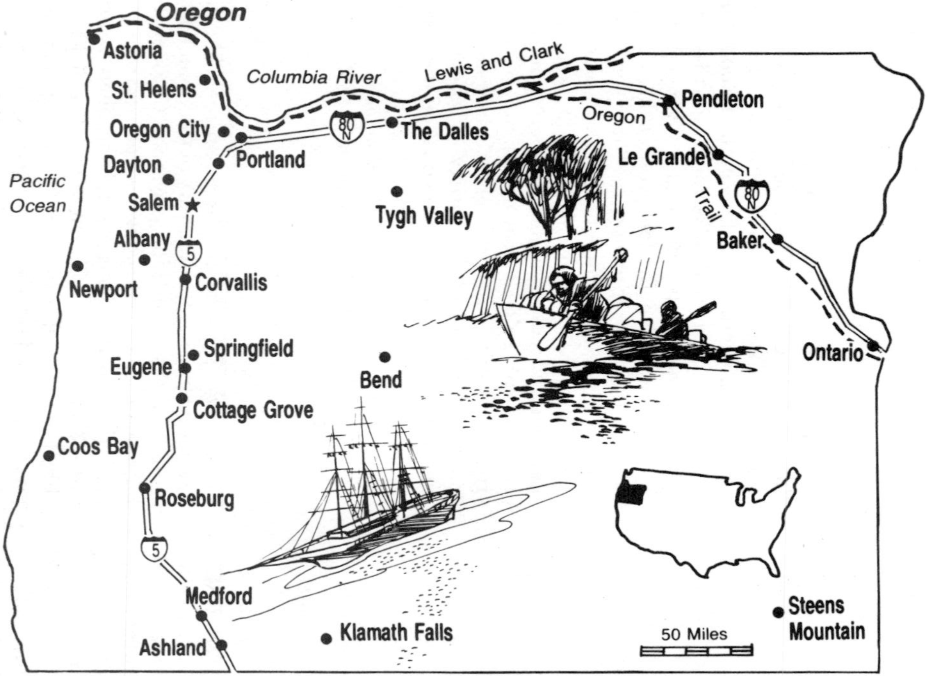
Oregon
Astoria
St. Helens
Columbia River
Lewis and Clark
Oregon City
80 N
The Dalles
Pendleton
Oregon
Trail
Portland
Dayton
Pacific Ocean
Salem
Albany
5
Newport
Corvallis
Tygh Valley
Le Grande
Baker
Springfield
Eugene
Cottage Grove
Bend
Ontario
Coos Bay
Roseburg
Medford
Ashland
Klamath Falls
50 Miles
Steens Mountain

Major Indian Tribes. Chinookans: Clatsops, Cathlamets, Multnomahs, Clackamas; Athapascans: Tlatskanai, Tututni, Upper Coquilles, Chastacostas, Chetcoes; Umpquas, Siuslaws, Tillamooks, Siletz, Yakonians, Kusan, Kalapooyan, Yamhills, Chemeketas, Santiams, Klamath, Modoc, Cayuse, Shastas and Karoks.

ALBANY, Linn County. US 99. The town was named by Walter and Thomas Monteith in 1848 for their New York hometown.

Monteith House, 518 W. 2nd St., was the first house in town and was built as a claim cabin in 1848 by the Monteith brothers. It faced Washington St. at 2nd. with the dividing line running through the structure so that each brothers could occupy his own claim.

Takenah Park, 4th & Ellsworth Sts. at the mouth of the Calapooya River. An Oregon Trail marker is in the park; the Weatherford Tablet honors an early school director.

Old Steamboat Inn, Water St. near Ellsworth, E. of the S. approach to the Ellsworth St. Bridge, was an important stopping place for river traffic and the stage lines which ran up and down the valley and E. across the Cascades.

ARLINGTON, Gilliam County. US 30. Named for the home of Robert E. Lee.

Oregon Trail Crossing, S. of town, 2 miles off US 30, on State 19. Marker honors W. W. Weatherford who was 17 when he followed this route barefoot across the plains, driving an oxteam, in 1861.

John Day River, ca. 26 miles W. on US 30, was called LePage's River by Lewis and Clark for a member of their expedition, but the name honors now one of the Astorians of whom Washington Irving said: ". . . [He walked] with an elastic step as if he trod on springs. . . . He was strong of hand, bold of heart, a prime woodsman, and an almost unerring shot." Unfortunately, Day dropped behind the main group with a companion named Ramsay Crooks and another man who fell ill and died in the winter of 1811–12 on the Snake River. The next spring Crooks and Day reached the mouth of the river (now the John Day), found what they thought were friendly Indians who gave them food, then stripped them of their clothing, took their rifles and drove them off. Months later, the two were found by a searching party and taken to Astoria. Day started back to the U.S. with Robert Stuart's party but became violently insane before reaching the Willamette. He was sent back to Astoria where he soon died. Marker at river.

ASHLAND, Jackson County. I–5. At the S. end of the Rogue River Valley on the banks of Bear Creek, the area looked so welcoming to tired pioneers who had crossed the Siskiyou Mountains some went no further. Lithia water from the mineral springs is now piped in for fountains on the city plaza. Abel D. Hillman named the town in 1852. Marble works were established in 1865.

Lithia Plaza has a fountain embellished by the heroic figure of a scout, and is dedicated to early settlers, H.

B. Carter and H. H. Carter. In Lithia Park adjoining the plaza are markers showing the sites of Ashland's early industries. Also in the 100-acre park are trails, walks and mineral springs.

ASTORIA, Clatsop County. US 101, 30. The first permanent settlement in Oregon was on a site selected by Lewis and Clark for winter quarters in 1805. John Jacob Astor's partners picked the spot for a trading post in 1811.

Clatsop County Historical Museum, in old Flavel Mansion, 441 8th St. Capt. George Flavel built the house in 1883–84. Regional historical items on display.

Astoria Column, on Coxcomb Hill, has an observation room atop the 125-foot tower which commemorates the first settlement. A spiral frieze illustrates Oregon history.

Fort Astoria, 15th and Exchange Sts. Fort outlines are painted on streets and sidewalks. In the tiny park are a reconstructed blockhouse and the graves of D. M. McTavish and Alexander Henry, Jr., both of whom had a fondness for Jane Barnes, the adventurous barmaid who was said to be the first white woman in Oregon. The two men drowned while crossing the Columbia River and Jane went on to other romances. Astor sold the post to the British when their warships were rumored to be in the area during the War of 1812; he acquired it again in 1818.

Fort Clatsop National Memorial, SW off US 101A. Lewis and Clark began construction of winter quarters here in December 1805. The fort has been reconstructed. Museum in Visitor Center.

Fort Stevens, in Fort Stevens State Park, 13½ miles W. on US 101. Construction of the fort was begun in 1863; it was garrisoned in April 1865, named for Isaac I. Stevens, first territorial governor of Washington who was killed at Chantilly, Virginia, in September 1862. The wreck of the *Peter Iredale* is on Columbia Beach in the park.

Columbia River Maritime Museum, 16th and Exchange Sts.

Samuel Elmore Cannery National Historic Landmark, on the waterfront at the foot of Flavel St. The original cannery which opened in 1881, storage building and bunkhouse which lodged Chinese laborers, are here. Conducted tours.

AURORA, Marion County. US 99. The town was settled by a colony of Germans under the leadership of Dr. William Keil, who had organized a successful communal living group in Bethel, Missouri (which see). Both communities eventually disintegrated. Dr. Keil died in 1877.

Ox Barn Museum and Kraus House, 2nd and Liberty Sts. The barn was a station on the stage line between Portland and Sacramento. The Kraus House, moved from its original site, has been restored, with many original furnishings of the 1860s.

BAKER, Baker County. US 30. Named for Lincoln's friend, E. D. Baker, U.S. Senator, who was killed at Ball's Bluff, Virginia, in 1861.

Wallowa-Whitman National Forest, State 7,86,203, covers 2,238,026 acres with headquarters in Baker. Eagle Cap Wilderness is within the forest.

U.S. National Bank, 2001 Main St., has an exhibit of native gold in all forms.

Auburn, ca. 7 miles S., on unpaved road ca. 3 miles W. of State 7. The ghost town of a mining camp, which was founded in 1861 when prospectors found gold along the Powder River; Auburn had a population of 5,000 within a year and was the second largest town in the state. When Baker became county seat in 1868, Auburn dwindled.

Express Ranch, E. of Durkee, ca. 21 miles SE of Baker. Marker on highway for the relay station on the Umatilla-Boise Basin stage and freight route.

BATTLE MOUNTAIN STATE PARK, Umatilla County. US 395. Commemorates the battle of Willow Springs, the last engagement with the Indians in Oregon. In 1878 Paiutes and Bannocks, from Idaho, who were trying to gain recruits in Oregon, engaged in a battle with troops under Gen. O. O. Howard. Chief Egan, Paiute leader, was defeated and was chased down the Malheur River and out of the territory. Chief Egan had been betrayed and his scalp was delivered to the army camp. Marker at site. There are other markers in the area for sites pertaining to the Bannock War of 1878: at Crooked Springs on US 95 and at West Suntex Mountain Station on Central Oregon Highway.

BEATTY, Klamath County. State 140.

Masekeske Cemetery, E. of town on road which crosses the Sprague River. Hundreds of aborigines are buried on a low hill beneath closely set white headstones.

Schonchin Cemetery, 5 miles W. of town on highway, then right, ca. 1½ miles, and again 1.5 miles to the right, is an old Indian burying ground named for Schonchin Jack, Modoc war chief. Winema, niece of Captain Jack is buried here. She was married to a white man, learned English and became an interpreter and intermediary in negotiations between the Modocs and their conquerors. During the Modoc uprising Winema saved the life of Reservation Superintendent A. B. Meacham, risking her own. Congress voted her a lifetime pension and the D.A.R. erected a tablet on her grave.

Bly, 9 miles E. of Beatty on highway, was named from the Indian word *P'lai,* which translates very roughly to "heavenly." The stream once called P'lai is now the Sprague, for Capt. F. B. Sprague, Indian fighter, who was in charge of Fort Klamath in 1866. The town was kept on the alert in the 1880s by a bear named Twisted Foot, which left a track as large as a sombrero and liked to kill cattle. He remained on the prowl for several years; when brought down by a hunter named Indian Dick he proved to be one of the largest bears ever found in Oregon, measuring 3 feet between the ears and 4 feet from the tip of his nose to the top of his head.

BEND, Deschutes County. US 20. For many years known as Farewell Bend, the town stands at the point where the old Oregon Trail leaves the Snake River and goes over ridges to Burnt River. Pioneers bade farewell to the river, not knowing where they might find verdant land and water again. Olds Ferry was here from 1862. A marker indicates the campsite of expeditions of Wilson Price Hunt, Captain Bonneville, Nathaniel Wyeth and John Frémont. Washington Irving wrote how the starving Astorians at this point had to kill two horses to make a canoe in order to cross the river.

Pioneer Park, Hill St. and the river.

Lava River Caves State Park, 12 miles S. on US 97. Lava tunnel is 1 mile long. Lanterns for rent.

Pilot Butte State Park, 1 mile E. on US 20, gives a view of 10 mountain peaks.

Home of Klondike Kate, 231 Franklin St., had a lava-rock foundation and stood among the pines at least 20 feet above the street. Reportedly after winning and losing two fortunes as a song and dance favorite of Alaska miners, Kate married a sourdough.

BONNEVILLE, Multnomah County. US 30. Marker on highway; town was named for Capt. B. L. E. Bonneville who stopped here in his travels of 1832.

Bonneville Fish Hatchery, I–80N and US 30, adjacent to the Bonneville Lock and Dam, has a museum with a variety of marine life.

Fort Rains Blockhouse, marker on highway at site, E. of town. A blockhouse was built in 1853 by Lt. H. C. Hodges to protect settlers and travelers along the old portage tramway. Replica.

BROWNSVILLE, Linn County. Near junction of I–5, State 228.

Linn County Historical Museum, pioneer history of the area. Indian relics.

Moyer House, 204 Main St., was built in 1881; restored with period furnishings.

Blakely Monument honors Capt. James Blakely, who with his uncle, Hugh L. Brown, a settler in 1846, platted the townsite in 1853. Among early citizens were George A. Waggoner, who came in 1852, served as one of the first railroad commissioners, and wrote Oregon stories, Rev. H. H. Spalding, who crossed the Rockies with the Marcus Whitmans; and Z. F. Moody, early governor of Oregon, 1882–87. The large city park is on the banks of the Calapooya River. There are two prehistoric mounds in the area; inquire locally for directions in North Brownsville and across the river in South Brownsville.

BURNS, Harney County. US 395, 20.

Harney County Historical Museum, N. on US 395 Indian and pioneer artifacts.

Malheur National Wildlife Refuge, 32 miles S. on State 205. 180,850 acres. Museum.

Malheur Cave, 55 miles SE just off State 78. A lava tunnel which should not be explored without lanterns.

Fort Harney, ca. 12 miles E. of town on Central Oregon Highway, was named for Gen. William S. Harney, who took command of the military department of Oregon in 1858. The post was established in August 1867, on the right side of Rattlesnake Creek. It was used for operations against hostile Indians in the Modoc and Bannock wars. Earlier in 1867 a depot on Harney Lake established by Lt. Col. George Crook was known as the "Camp on Rattlesnake Creek," then Camp Steele, Camp Crook and Camp Harney. Marker at site.

Buchanan Stage Station, ca. 24 miles E. on US 20, on the route from Vale to Burns, was kept by Thomas Buchanan in the 1880s.

Drewsey, 3 miles N. of US 20 on unimproved road 18 miles E. of Buchanan, is an old town on the onetime stage route, which saw many lively and sometimes fatal encounters among cattlemen, rustlers, gamblers, miners and adventurers of the Old West. Abner Robbins, who started a store here in the summer of 1883, aptly called the settlement Gouge Eye. The post office refused to recognize the town name, and it was changed to honor Drewsey Miller, a rancher's daughter.

CANYON CITY, Grant County. US 395.

Herman and Eliza Oliver Historical Museum, N. of post office. Regional displays and gun and gold collections.

Joaquin Miller's Cabin, adjacent to museum, home of the poet and his family has been restored with furnishings in the style used by the family.

Boot Hill has many interesting old headstones; some graves are those of persons killed by Indians, some were hanged by fellow white men. The town was a lively rendezvous for outlaws and miners after gold was discovered on nearby Whiskey Flat. By 1872, millions of dollars worth of gold had been mined. There were clashes between Unionist miners and pro-Southerners who had migrated to the gold fields from the California rush. The southerners, on a day when they had lost an important battle back home (July 4, 1863, Vicksburg) hoisted the Confederacy's Stars and Bars on "Rebel Hill." The northerners started a small Civil War to haul it down.

CANYONVILLE, Douglas County. US 99. The town developed from a station on the California-Oregon Stage route. The Hudson's Bay Co. trappers used this route to California in 1828. In 1851 Joseph Knott and Joel Perkins operated a ferry across the South Umpqua calling the settlement Kenyonville. When gold-bearing quartz was found nearby, a rush began. This became the main road to California until the arrival of the railroad.

CAVE JUNCTION, Josephine County. US 199.

Kerbyville Museum, 2 miles N. on US 199, in Kerby, is furnished in the period of the 1870s when the house was built. Outdoor museum has logging and mining tools, rock displays, log schoolhouse, blacksmith shop and other items.

Woodland Deer Park, S. on US 199, has a variety of small wildlife and buffalo.

CENTRAL POINT, Jackson County. I–5.

Crater Rock Museum, 2002 Scenic Drive. Indian artifacts and a large collection of rocks. An unusual honeybee display.

COOS BAY, Coos County. US 101.

Shore Acres, 13 miles SW on Cape Arago Highway, is a state park on a former estate which has many varieties of plantings representative of the area, trails and observation shelter.

House of Myrtlewood, 1125 S. 1st St., 1 mile S. off US 101, tours of log manufacturing plant.

Coos Bay Chamber of Commerce, 400 N. Bayshore Dr., has information for tours of the city, which is the world's largest lumber-shipping port.

CORBETT, Multnomah County. US 30. The Sandy River which flows nearby was discovered in 1792 by Lt. William Broughton. Lewis and Clark passed here in November 1805, and wrote in their journals: "We reached the mouth of a river on the left, which seemed to lose its waters in a sand bar opposite, the stream itself being only a few inches in depth. But on attempting to wade across we discovered that the bed was a very bad quicksand. . . ."

Crown Point State Park, ca. 5 miles E. on US 30, offers a fine view of the Columbia River Gorge from the Vista House.

CORVALLIS, Benton County. US 20. Originally Marysville.

Horner Museum, on campus of Oregon State University in Gill Coliseum, lower lever, has antiques, pioneer relics, Indian items, natural history and minerals.

Site of Territorial Capitol, SE corner of S. 2nd and Adams Sts. Plaque on building commemorating the brief time in 1855 when the city was the capital of Oregon. The legislature moved there in January, but Asahel Bush persuaded the government to return to Salem in June.

Corvallis City Park, S. end of 4th St., has old millstones, quarried in France, shipped around the horn, hauled here by oxteam in 1856 and used in Chambers' Mill on the Luckiamute River, NW of town.

Siuslaw National Forest, W. on State 34, has 50 miles of ocean frontage in the 625,126-acre area.

Fort Hoskins, ca. 12 miles NW of town, was established in July 1856, in Kings Valley on the Luckiamute River, near the mouth of Bonner Creek. The post was set up after Indians were gathered at the Siletz Agency, following the Rogue River War. A blockhouse on the Siletz River was connected by trail to the fort. The post was named for Lt. Charles Hoskins, killed in 1846 in the Battle of Monterey, Mexico. When Phil Sheridan was a young officer here before the Civil War, he had the duty of finishing the construction of the fort which included building a blockhouse. Being the self-assured fellow who later won laurels in the Civil War, he also felt confident about building a road across the mountains from King's Valley to the Siletz, a route he had explored: ". . . the ground was matted with huge logs from five to eight feet in diameter. These could not be chopped with axes nor sawed by any ordinary means, therefore we had to burn them into suitable lengths, and drag the sections to either side of the roadway with from four to six yoke of oxen." This done, Sheridan wanted to demonstrate the value of the road and dispatched a government wagon over it loaded with about 1,500 pounds of freight, drawn by six-yoke of oxen, escorted by soldiers. When it had gone no more than 7 miles the sergeant came back to report trouble, so Sheridan hastened to the scene:

> I found the wagon at the base of a steep hill, stalled. Taking up a whip myself, I directed the men to lay on their gads, for each man had supplied himself with a flexible hickory withe in the early stages of the trip, to start the team, but this course did not move the wagon nor have much effect on the demoralized oxen; but following as a last resort an example I heard of on a former occasion, that brought into use the rough language of the country, I induced the oxen to move with alacrity, and the wagon and contents were speedily carried to the summit.

"The whole trouble," Sheridan summarized in his *Memoirs*:

> . . . the oxen had been broken and trained by a man who, when they were in a pinch, had encouraged them by his frontier vocabulary, and they could not realize what was expected of them under extraordinary conditions until they heard familiar and possibly profane urgent phrases. I took the wagon to its destination. but as it was not brought back, even in all the time I was stationed in that country, I think comment on

the success of my road is unnecessary.

COTTAGE GROVE, Lane County. State 99.

Cottage Grove Historical Museum, Birch Ave. and H. St. Pioneer, Indian, mining displays in 19th-century church.

Railtown, U.S.A., at Village Green Station, off I–5 Cottage Grove exit, E. of town. Antique steam locomotives, passenger cars on display. A steam excursion train has rides, but the train is of 1914 vintage. A 2½-hour trip through the Row River Valley runs into the Calapooya Mountains. On some days a diesel makes the same run.

CRATER LAKE NATIONAL PARK, Klamath County. US 97, State 62, 47 miles N. of Klamath Falls, on the crest of the Cascade Range. The park covers 250 square miles, can be explored by car or on foot. Trails begin at Rim Drive and Rim Village.

DAYTON, Yamhill County. State 221.

Fort Yamhill Blockhouse, in city park. The fort was established in 1855 near the Yamhill River in the Grand Ronde Valley, ca. 25 miles SW of Dayton. The original post was the blockhouse. In 1856 it became a U.S. Army fort and was garrisoned to control the Indians of the Grand Ronde and Siletz agencies.

There are many old buildings in the town which was once a place of entertainment in off-duty hours for Phil Sheridan and other officers serving in Oregon before the Civil War. Sheridan had a particularly difficult time with the Indians during his stay at Fort Yamhill, although he spoke Chinook "fluently" by his own testimony in his memoirs. After sixteen Indians once shot an Indian "doctress" nearly at his feet, he went to deal with them in their own village. While he was explaining that the guilty persons must be delivered up for punishment, the situation grew sticky:

> The conversation waxing hot and the Indians gathering close in around me, I unbuttoned the flap of my pistol holster, to be ready for any emergency. When the altercation became most bitter I put my hand to my hip to draw my pistol, but discovered it was gone—stolen by one of the rascals surrounding me. Finding myself unarmed, I modified my tone and manner to correspond with my helpless condition . . . As soon as an opportunity offered, and I could, without too much loss of self-respect, and without damaging my reputation among the Indians, I moved out to where the sergeant held my horse, mounted, and crossing the Yamhill River close by, called back in Chinook from the farther bank that "the sixteen men who killed the woman must be delivered up, and my six-shooter also." This was responded to by contemptuous laughter, so I went back to the military post somewhat crestfallen. . . .

A deal was made later with one of the Indian leaders who said Sheridan could kill one of the 16 men who had probably fired the *fatal* bullet, although 16 bullets were in the victim's body. This unfortunate fellow was considered a bad Indian the tribe wanted to get rid of anyway. The other 15 surrendered to the Army, and were made to work at the post, but eventually went back to farm their own land.

DAYVILLE, Grant County. State 19. A former stage station.

Thomas Condon–John Day Fossil Beds State Park, 8 miles NW on State 19. The beds cover 4,345 acres and have yielded many remains of extinct animals including mastodons. Indian pictographs are in Picture Gorge, near junction of State 19 and US 26. Parts of the park may be seen from State 19 along the John Day River. There is a marker on Warm Springs Highway. Thomas Condon was a minister and geologist who is said to have carried his Bible in his pocket and his pick in his hand when he went on geological explorations. He may have been the first white man to see the pictographs in Picture Gorge. Capt. John M. Drake, a cavalryman stationed at Camp Maury on the Crooked River, wrote to Condon that while he was away chasing Snake Indians some of his men had found mammal fossils and marine shells. Condon learned that specimens from this site included shells from the last of the oceans of the Age of Reptiles. His explorations in Central Oregon in the 1860s led to discoveries which attracted scientists from all over the world.

DESCHUTES NATIONAL FOREST, on the E. slope of the Cascades, covers 1,600,460 acres and includes the Diamond Peak Wilderness, Mt. Washington Wilderness, Mt. Jefferson Wilderness and the Three Sisters Wilderness. Newberry Crater is 24 miles S. of Bend and ca. 13 paved miles E. of US 97. Lava Butte Geographical Area is 10 miles S. of Bend on US 97.

EUGENE, Lane County. I–5.

Lane County Pioneer Museum, 740 13th Ave. W. Wagons among other pioneer relics and furnishings.

Museum of Natural History, on campus of University of Oregon, 11th, 18th, Alder and Moss Sts., Indian artifacts include Northwest Coast Indian masks and primitive weapons; fluorescent mineral display. Library on campus has Oregon Collection on 2nd floor.

Willamette National Forest, E via US 126, State 58, covers 1,666,002 acres; among features are the Cascade Mountain Range summit; Pacific Crest National Scenic Trail; lava beds at summit of McKenzie Pass and Hot Springs.

FOREST GROVE, Washington County. State 8, 47.

Old College Hall, on campus of Pacific University, main entrance on College Way, has a museum of pioneer items. This is the oldest building W. of the Mississippi River in use for higher education. The university was the first to be chartered in Oregon Territory.

FORT UMPQUA, Douglas County. US 101. The fort was built on the S. side of the Umpqua River at Winchester Bay in July 1856, one of three set up to watch over the Indians of the Grand Ronde and Siletz agencies. The buildings had been moved from abandoned Fort Orford. One happening which contributed to the closing of the fort was on a summer day in 1862 when the paymaster arrived to find the post deserted—everyone had gone hunting.

GOLD BEACH, Curry County. US 101. A picturesque village at the mouth of the Rogue River was once a crossroads of a sort. Orientals, Indians and adventurers gathered at the log cabin saloon that was also the county courthouse in the 1850s. There were some placer gold operations but floods in 1861 swept many deposits into the ocean. Boat trips on the Rogue River are available in town.

Battle of Pistol River, marker at Pistol River ca. 12 miles S. 34 men were besieged here in March 1856 by Indians until relieved by troops.

Cape Sebastian State Park, 7 miles S. on highway. Landmark named for Capt. Sebastian Vizcaino in 1603. 1,104 acres.

GOLD HILL, Jackson County. State 234 just N. of I–5. Gold was discovered in the nearby uplands. The first quartz mill in Jackson County was opened in 1860.

Old Oregon Historical Museum, on Sardine Creek Rd., Indian artifacts, antique guns, mining tools and other relics.

Sams Valley, ca. 6 miles NE, was the home of Chief Sam of the Rogue River tribe. The *Table Rock Treaty Site,* ca. 2 miles N. on State 234 then 2.6 miles E. on unmarked road. On September 10, 1853, Gen. Joseph Lane concluded peace negotiations with the Rogue River Indians at this site,

In a fort very like this the Lewis and Clark expedition spent winter of 1805-06
(Oregon State Highway Travel Section)

after a series of battles in the surrounding area.

GRANTS PASS, Josephine County. I–5. The town was named when road builders heard the news of Grant's victory at Vicksburg ending the siege on July 4, 1863.

Fort Vannoy, was located on the right bank of the Rogue River ca. 4 miles W. of town. Exact site is not known. The post was established in 1855 and served as a base for the Oregon Volunteers in the Rogue River War of 1855–56. River trips on the Rogue River can be arranged in town. Chamber of Commerce, 131 NE. "E" St., has information.

Siskiyou National Forest, S. and W. off US 199, covers 1,082,500 acres. Headquarters are in Grants Pass. An 84-mile stretch of Rogue River between Lobster Creek Bridge and Applegate River is a National Wild and Scenic River area.

HAINES, Baker County. US 30.

Eastern Oregon Museum, 4 blocks off I–30E, has a reconstructed blacksmith shop, old saloon bar and pioneer items, including a horse-powered hay baler.

Lone Tree Crossing of Powder River, ca. 2 miles N. Thomas J. Farnham was one of several early travelers who took note of the tree. In September 1839, he observed: "Cooked dinner at *L'Arbeur Seul,* a lonely pine in an extensive plain." John C. Frémont, in 1843, looked for the pine he had heard about from fellow adventurers but "we found a fine tall pine stretched on the ground, which had been felled by some inconsiderate emigrant axe. It had been a beacon on the road for many years past."

Marie Dorion Marker, ca. 11½ miles N. of Haines on highway, at camp where Marie Dorion the wife of Pierre Dorion, the half-breed interpreter attached to the Wilson Price Hunt party, gave birth to another child. Pierre remained in camp with his wife and family until the following morning when the whole crew was on the road again. Mrs. Dorion, rode with the baby in her arms and her 2-year-old son wrapped in a blanket which was slung at her side. Washington Irving's Western travel writings include several stories about the Dorions.

HERMISTON, Umatilla County. US 395.

Cold Spring National Wildlife Refuge, 6 miles E. off State 32; 3,000 acres. Migrating waterfowl are here in season and are luckier than the turkeys which are big business in town, the home of the Eastern Oregon Turkey Association.

Butter Creek, which runs SW from town, W. of State 207, crosses the old Oregon Trail (as does State 207) ca. 10 miles S. The stream is said to have gotten its name when volunteer soldiers during the Cayuse Indian War of 1848 stole some butter intended for officers. Other stories featuring butter are equally plausible and trivial. One is that crocks of butter were left behind when the soldiers broke camp. In any case the country crossed by the creek was a favorite hideout for cattle and horse thieves in the 1880s. Stockmen had to organize vigilante committees, and there were some hangings but none of this got the publicity accorded the Johnson County War in Wyoming.

HILLSBORO, Washington County. US 26.

Washington County Historical Society Museum, 641 Main St. Pioneer relics.

HOOD RIVER, Hood River County. State 35.

Panorama Point, 6 miles S. on State 35. Lookout for splendid view of Mt. Hood and the valley.

Hood River County Historical Society Museum, in courthouse, 4th and State Sts. Indian collections, pioneer relics.

Chamber of Commerce, in Port Marina Park, has a relief map of the Columbia River region, with changing historical exhibits and tour information.

JACKSONVILLE, Jackson County. State 238. A gold rush began in 1852. Many historic buildings remain but one of the finest, the United States Hotel, built in 1884, was about to be knocked flat by the wrecker's ball in 1967 when help came from an unexpected source. The U.S. National Bank of Portland had plans to build a branch office in Jacksonville. Quick-minded preservationists got together with architects, museum directors and leading citizens, and persuaded the bank to use the restored hotel. A happy ending to what usually has been a dismal story in many communities. The Jacksonville Historic District is a national historic landmark.

Jacksonville Museum, in Old County Courthouse, 206 N. 5th St. Pioneer relics, photographs, Indian items, toys.

Beekman House, California St., was built in 1880. Original furnishings.

Beekman Bank, California and 3rd Sts. Built in 1862, restored, with early banking equipment on display.

Methodist Church, 5th and D Sts., was erected in 1854. *Parish House,* 4th and C. Sts., dates from 1860.

Rogue River Valley Railroad Depot, N. Oregon & C Sts. 1891.

Pioneer Village, 725 N. 5th St. on State 238, has old buildings, relics, stagecoach rides, etc.

JOHN DAY, Grant County. US 26, 395. A busy mining and cattle town in the 19th century.

Canyon Creek, S. on US 395, was so rich in gold dust it yielded $8 million in one decade in the 1860–70s. Scars are still on canyon walls.

Malheur National Forest, N. and S. on US 26, 395, covers 1,456,530 acres, contains fossil beds, and the Strawberry Mountain Wilderness.

JOSEPH, Wallowa County. State 82. Named for the two great Nez Perce chiefs, both named Joseph.

Old Joseph Monument, N. end of Wallowa Lake. Memorial to the Nez Perce chieftain, at his burial site.

Nez Perce War Marker, on State 82, W. of Enterprise. In May 1877, the Nez Perce under Chief Joseph (the younger) began their last resistance here. After a 1,000-mile retreat they were forced to surrender in October 1877.

JUNTURA, Malheur County. US 20.

Peter Ogden Skene Marker, E. of town on highway, denotes the route taken by the Hudson's Bay Co. trappers in 1828. Ogden, who was born in Quebec, was 24 when he headed a trapping party with headquarters at Fort George, now Astoria. He continued with the Hudson's Bay Co. after its merger with the North West Co. and led many expeditions. It has been said that of all the mountain men none trapped more beaver, played worse practical jokes or left his name on more places than Ogden (a distinction he could only win if Frémont is not classified as a mountain man).

Agency Ranch, on unpaved road, ca. 16 miles N. of Juntura, the headquarters of Henry Miller's cattle empire in the 1880s. T. M. Overfelt, a pioneer Oregon rancher, established a ranch on Trout Creek in the Silvies Valley. Miller was Pacific coast cattle king and shrewd enough to form a silent partnership with Overfelt. When the government opened the Agency Valley Indian Reservation for occupation the partners acquired the ranch. The original buildings no longer exist.

KLAMATH FALLS, Klamath County. US 97.

Klamath County Museum, 1451 Main St. Geological, historical, natural history and Indian displays.

Favell Museum of Western Art and Indian Artifacts, 125 W. Main. Extensive Indian collection, works of Western art, relics.

Collier Memorial State Park and Logging Museum, 30 miles N. on US 97. Tools and equipment of logging days.

Winema National Forest, N., E. and W., via US 97, State 62, comprises 907,240 acres and includes the ancestral lands of the Klamath Indians, part of the Pacific Crest National Scenic Trail and Mountain Lake Wilderness.

Klamath Basin National Wildlife Refuge, 22,800 acres, 15 miles S. off US 97.

Upper Klamath National Wildlife Refuge, 23 miles N. on Klamath Falls–Klamath Agency Rd. 12,500 acres.

Fort Klamath, near junction of State 62 and 232, was established on the E. side of the Wood River in September 1863, to protect routes and settlers from hostile Indians of the area. The Klamath Indian Agency was ca. 5 miles S. The fort was of major importance in the Modoc War of 1873. It was located near roads which led both to Idaho and California, which made it a natural base of operations, but more than that, the troops which lit the war fuse by trying to force Capt. Jack and his band of Modocs back onto the Klamath Reservation had set out from here. It became the principal supply, replacement and medical-receiving depot. After Capt. Jack surrendered in June 1873, he was imprisoned with his followers in a stockade built for the purpose, tried and hanged with three of his lieutenants in October 1873, at this fort. Replica of the guardhouse at site.

LA GRANDE, Union County. US 30.

Grande Ronde Valley, E. of town, marker on highway for the route followed by thousands of settlers and wagons which skirted the valley then crossed the Blue Mountains.

Hilgard Junction State Park, 8 miles W. Off I–80N, is on the old Oregon Trail.

Site of Ben Brown House, marker on highway W. of town, near the first house in the area, 1862.

LAKEVIEW, Lake County. US 395.

Schminck Memorial Museum, 128 S. "E" St. Weapons, Indian relics, pioneer furnishings.

Geyser and Hot Springs, 3 miles N. on US 395, said to be the largest continuous hot water geyser in the world. Emigrants' journals and letters home, understandably, never ceased to marvel at the hot water they encountered so rarely.

Fremont National Forest, N., E., and W. of town, via US 395 State 31. Headquarters are in town, for the 1,194,710-acre area which has many outstanding features such as the Abert Rim, the Gearhart Mountain Wilderness, Indian pictographs and petroglyphs.

LAUREL HILL, Clackamus County. US 26.

Government Camp, marker on highway W. of town for the most dangerous descent of the Barlow Rd. Capt. Samuel Kimbrough Barlow got off a nifty one-liner for the Oregon provisional legislature that has been often quoted and should be again, as it seems to sum up the attitude of far westerners: "God never made a mountain that he had not made a place for some man to go over it or under it—I am going to hunt for that place." He built a road that was difficult but many wagons, cattle, horses and sheep made the arduous trips over it.

LEBANON, Linn County. US 20. The town on the South Santiam River was an important stopping place on the Cascade Wagon Rd. Jeremiah Ralston platted it in 1851.

Pioneers of the Oregon Trail Tablet, Main and Tangent Sts.

LINCOLN CITY, Lincoln County. US 101.

Lacey's Doll House & Antique Museum, 3400 N. US 101, has old guns, coins, musical instruments, as well as dolls.

MADRAS, Jefferson County. US 97.

Round Butte Dam, 10 miles W. off US 97, on the Deschutes River. Observatory has geological, wildlife and relic displays.

MEDFORD, Jackson County. I–5.

Crater Rock Museum, 4 miles N. on State 99, then 1 mile N. and E. to 2002 Scenic Ave. in Central Point. Minerals, Indian artifacts, fossils, petrified wood, guided tours.

Rogue River National Forest, S. off I–5, comprises 631,451 acres. Part of the Pacific Crest National Scenic Trail is within the forest.

Fort Lane, ca. 9 miles NW of town, on Gold Ray Rd. The fort was situated on the S. bank of the Rogue River near the mouth of Bear Creek in 1853. Near Lower Table Rock troops won a victory in August 1853, that ended the first Rogue River War. At the end of the second war, the post served as a transfer point; most of the captives gathered here were sent to the Siletz Indian Reservation. During the 1850s, many expeditions used the small fort for a rendezvous point. Table Rock is across the Rogue River from the old site, which has no remaining buildings. A marker is nearby.

MILTON–FREEWATER, Umatilla County. State 11.

Marie Dorion Historical Park was developed to pay tribute to early area settlers. Pierre and Marie Dorion traveled with the Astorians under the command of Capt. Wilson Hunt.

MILWAUKEE, Multnomah County. State 51.

Milwaukee Historical Museum (Failing House), 2515 Lake Rd., believed to have been brought from Portland on a barge. The 1858 Victorian-style dwelling has been restored, with period furnishings.

MITCHELL, Wheeler County. US 26.

Camp Watson, S. of US 26, established in 1864 and named for Lt. Stephen Watson of the 1st Oregon Cavalry was intended to protect the Canyon City–Dalles route from raids of the Snake Indians under Chief Polini. The campsite, ca. 5 miles W. of Anatone, is accessible from the Mitchell–John Day highway. Marble markers remain in cemetery.

MOUNT HOOD NATIONAL FOREST, Hood River County. Crossed by US 26. The forest covers 1,118,360 acres. Mount Hood is 11,235 feet high. Headquarters for the area are in Portland.

MYRTLE POINT, Coos County. State 42.

China Flat Recreation Area, ca. 30 miles S. on South Fork of Coquille River Rd. is an old placer mining area. Trails. Scenic gorge.

NEWBERG, Yamhill County. State 219.

Minthorn House, 2nd and River Sts. Restored Quaker home, built in 1881, where Herbert Hoover lived with his uncle. Authentic furnishings.

Champoeg State Park, 7 miles SE off State 219, is the site where trappers and settlers met in 1843 to accept U.S. jurisdiction rather than that of the British-owned Hudson's Bay Co. Historical marker at site. In the area are the Newell House Museum, just outside park entrance, a reconstructed pioneer home. Pioneer Museum in park has many items of river life and pioneer relics. Pioneer Mother's Memorial Cabin, in park, is a replica of 1850s home. The town was never rebuilt after it was destroyed in the flood of 1861.

Willamette Post, marker near Willamette River Bridge, on US 99. First trading post in Willamette Valley was established by the Astor Fur Co. in 1811.

NEWPORT, Lincoln County. US 101.

Lincoln County Historical Museum, 579 SW 9th St. Indian artifacts, tools, carpenter shop, other historical relics.

Old Yaquina Bay Lighthouse, N. end of bridge of US 101. Historical maritime items.

Sailing Vessel, 325 SW. Bay Blvd., *The Sara,* 19th-century two-masted schooner, is typical of the ships that carried Pacific coast cargo.

Siletz Blockhouse, 6 miles E. on US 20, then 9 miles N. to village which was the site of agency headquarters and blockhouse in the 1850s. Lt. Phil Sheridan is credited with building the fortification when he served in Oregon before the Civil War. In his *Personal Memoirs,* he refers to a group of Indians being transferred from the Grande Ronde Reservation to the Siletz. The road he built while stationed in the area ran from Kings Valley to Siletz. (See Kings Valley.) No fort buildings remain.

NORTH BEND, Coos County. US 101.

Coos-Curry Museum, US 101, in Simpson Park, N. edge of town. Pioneer and Indian displays. Steam locomotive.

OREGON CAVES NATIONAL MONUMENT, Josephine County. State 46, 20 miles E. of Cave Junction. A hunter reportedly found the cave while following a bear. Tours.

OREGON CITY, Clackamas County. US 99.

McLoughlin House National Historic Site, 713 Center St. in McLoughlin Park. Dr. John McLoughlin was chief factor for the Hudson's Bay Co. in the early part of the 19th century. The house was built in 1845–46 for his retirement years. Some original furnishings.

Barclay House, 719 Center St., was the home of Dr. Forbes Barclay and was built in 1850, moved from its original site in 1936, historical documents, artifacts, antiques.

Capt. John Ainsworth House, 19195 S. Leland Rd., was built in 1850 by a steamboat and banking leader. Period furnishings.

Holly Knoll Museum, 7 miles SE on State 213, several pioneer buildings with artifacts and antiques.

McCarver House (Locust Farm), 554 Warner Parrott Rd. The lumber was brought around the Horn from Maine to San Francisco, then shipped here with Gen. Matthew McCarver who had platted Sacramento for John Sutter.

PENDLETON, Umatilla County. US 30. In the 1870s and 1880s, the town was the assembly point for cattle drives E. into Idaho, Montana and Wyoming. By 1889 the Oregon Short Line Railroad arrived. Fires in 1893 and 1895 damaged a lot of property but the town was rebuilt. It is headquarters for the 1,390,500-acre Umatilla National Forest. Fort Henrietta was established in 1855 near the W. bank of the Umatilla River at the present town of Echo, ca. 18 miles W. of Pendleton. It was abandoned the following year.

PLEASANT HILL, Lane County. State 58.

First Christian Church is the oldest of this denomination in Oregon and was organized by Elijah Bristow in August 1850, with 23 members. Bristow was a Virginia veteran of the War of 1812 who came to Oregon in 1846. He and many old settlers are buried in the Pleasant Hill Cemetery which is one of the oldest burial grounds in Oregon. Bristow Memorial Fountain was constructed of stones from his original home. The trough now overgrown with ivy once provided water for thirsty animals. Marker at fountain on highway.

PORTLAND, Multnomah County. I–80, US 30.

Oregon Historical Society, 1230 SW Park Ave. Northwest history library is excellent, with many early journals, maps, relics.

Oregon Museum of Science & Industry, 4015 SW. Canyon Rd. Varied exhibits include a mineral display.

Hoyt Arboretum, 4000 SW. Fairview Blvd., 214 acres with self-guiding trails.

Pittock Mansion, in Pittock Acres Park off NW. Irving, was built early in the 20th century.

Portland Art Museum, 1219 SW. Park, has Northwest Indian art.

Bybee-Howell House, 12 miles N. via US 30 and unnumbered road, on Sauvie Island. Restored early settler home; period furnishings.

Willamette Stone State Park, 4 miles W. of NW. Skyline Drive. The initial point of all government surveys of Oregon and Washington.

Western Forestry Center, 4033 SW. Canyon Rd. Forestry exhibits.

The Old Church, 1422 SW. 11th, city's oldest existing church. Self-guided tours.

Fort William, Sauvie Island, was the second unsuccessful attempt by Americans to set up a commercial colony in what was Hudson's Bay territory. The men who came to the area with Nathaniel Wyeth remained to set up their own farms in Oregon, whereas the Astorians gave up and returned east. When Wyeth set up a trading post here it was called Wappato Island. He sold the fort to Hudson's Bay Co. in 1837. Stone and plaque are ½ mile W. from original site.

PORT ORFORD, Curry County. US 101.

Battle Rock State Wayside, S. edge of town on US 101, honors pioneers who fought Indians here in 1851. The Indians were the victors against whites who were attempting to establish a settlement.

Stone Age Park, 7 miles N. on US 101, rock museum and Indian relics.

Fort Orford, established September 14, 1851, at the head of Trichenor Bay was not the same as the two blockhouses on Fort Point which were set up by settlers in June 1851. The military post was established because of hostile Indians and was to be used as a supply point for posts on the Oregon–California route and elsewhere. Plans proved impractical and the post was abandoned in July 1856.

PRINEVILLE, Crook County. US 26.

Prineville Historical Museum, in Pioneer Park, is a log cabin of 1880 housing pioneer relics.

Ochoco National Forest, E. on US 26, comprises 846,850 acres. Headquarters in Prineville.

REEDSPORT, Douglas County. US 101. Marker on highway for Jedediah Smith, trapper and explorer, who made the first recorded overland trip from California to Oregon in 1828.

ROSEBURG, Douglas County. I–5.

Douglas County Museum, off I–5 at fairground exit, displays of logging equipment, steam traction engine.

Joseph Lane House, 554 SE. Douglas Ave., was built in 1853–54, home of the first territorial governor, a U.S. senator and a candidate for vice-president. House has been restored and furnished as pioneer museum. President James Polk had hoped to secure a territorial government for this region before his term expired. On August 14, 1848, after two years of a boundary dispute, Congress passed a bill admitting Oregon as a territory. Polk signed it the next day then appointed Lane of Indiana as governor and Joseph L. Meek as U.S. marshal. Meek was in Washington to report the recent Whitman massacre near Walla Walla; he stopped on his way West to pick up Lane in Indiana. They hastened to the new territory and were in business by March 3, 1849, one day before Polk left office.

ST. HELENS, Columbia County. US 30. Marker at the Lewis and Clark campsite of November 5, 1805, and March 28, 1806, at Deer Island, W. of town.

SALEM, Marion County. I–5. The city was founded by Jason Lee, who was sent from New England as the Methodist "Missionary to the Flatheads." The Flatheads and Nez Perce Indians had sent four delegations to St. Louis to ask for missionaries in the 1830s. The Roman Catholic church sent "Black Robes" (Jesuits) to the Northwest in the 1840s, founding Lapwai Mission in Idaho, St. Mary's in Montana, and others. Eventually a number of Protestant missions were established, but Lee's was the first. He had arrived at Fort Vancouver, Hudson's Bay Co. post, in the fall of 1834 where Dr. John McLoughlin, the factor, advised him to avoid the more dangerous Flathead country (though it was Flatheads Lee had come West to convert) and to settle in the area of French Prairie. McLoughlin's purpose, in behalf of the British-held trading post, was to keep American settlers south of the Columbia.

Lee's first mission failed because sickness wiped out most of the Indians. His second one at Salem prospered in time but with changes and setbacks.

Methodist Mission Parsonage and Jason Lee Home, Thomas Kay Historical Park. Restored buildings of the 1834 mission, which was originally located 10 miles N. of present Salem on the Willamette River. Statue of Jason Lee stands on E. end of Capitol grounds.

Jason Lee Cemetery, N. end of 25th St. The Lee family rest in the Missionary Plot. Many other settlers also are here. Lee's wife, Anna Pittman Lee, has a headstone which states that she was the first white woman buried in Oregon, a distinction no woman of her day was likely to envy.

State Capitol, Court and Summer Sts. A modern structure topped by a statue of a "Pioneer." Statuary on the capitol grounds include two large groups at the entrance, one is a pioneer family on the Oregon Trail, the other shows the Lewis and Clark expedition led by Sacajawea. Murals on the Rotunda show scenes from Oregon history.

Bush House, Bush Park, 600 Mission St. SE. An 1877 Victorian mansion with authentic furnishings, former home of pioneer Asahel Bush, banker and newspaper publisher.

SEASIDE, Clatsop County. US 26. Oregon's oldest ocean resort lies at the end of the Oregon Trail.

End of the Trail Monument, End of Broadway, commemorates the Lewis and Clark journey's end.

Salt Cairn, S. end of Lewis and Clark Way, replica of the cairn built by the expedition to obtain salt from the sea.

SISTERS, Deschutes County. US 20. Highway historical markers point out the Lost Prairie, W. of town, named in 1859 by Willamette Valley settlers who were looking for a cattle trail to grazing lands E. of the Cascades. Santiam Toll Road Crossing, W. of town, built by pioneers across the Cascade Mountains in 1865, and Indian Ford, W. of town, across the Santiam River.

STEENS MOUNTAIN AND RELATED SITES, Harney County. State 205. The mountain is an upthrust of almost perpendicular lava, with virtually no foothills, towering nearly 10,000 feet. A trip around the base covers ca. 100 miles. Residents of Harney County take pride that it is bigger than any one of eight states: Rhode Island, Connecticut, Delaware, Hawaii, New Jersey, New Hampshire, Vermont or Massachusetts. The first permanent settler was John Devine in 1868. Peter French's Round Barn, off State 78, was built in 1883 and used to break and train wild horses. He was a big-time rancher, murdered in 1897. Frenchglen was the old headquarters of the P Ranch, named for Peter French. He had come to the area from California and was both liked and hated as a cattle baron. Many Old West yarns about the rimrock stem from the P Ranch in its gun-fighting days. Its vaqueros went armed, but were sometimes shot from ambush. The Brenton homesteading cabin still is standing in the Blitzen Valley. Pete Conley, from Ireland, built not only his house but his corral of stone; part of the walls remain. The Alvord Desert on the E. side of the mountain has some scattered old deserted cabins.

THE DALLES, Wasco County. US 30. (French, meaning "flagstones," named by French explorers.)

Fort Dalles, established in May

1850, was situated on the left bank of the Columbia River on Mill Creek. An earlier trading post owned by the Northwest Co. had been abandoned. The Whitman massacre of November 1847, and the subsequent Cayuse War, called for greater protection in the area. The post was first called Fort Lee, then Fort Wascopam, Camp Drum and designated Fort Dalles in July 1853. The surgeon's quarters, built in 1858, is now a museum, 15th and Garrison.

Winquatt Museum, E. of The Dalles Bridge in Seufert Park. Petroglyphs, Indian and Stone Age relics.

Chamber of Commerce, 404 W. 2nd St., has information for motor loop trips. The Dalles was an important meeting place for Indians for many years. In 1847 Dr. Marcus Whitman purchased the Methodist Mission here and established the Presbyterian Mission. He and his wife and 12 others were massacred by Cayuse Indians at his original mission in the Northwest at Waiilatpu, Washington (now a national historic site near Walla Walla). At The Dalles in the early days pioneers had reached the end of the wagon road and had to load their goods on boats to make the rest of the trip on the Columbia River. The falls and rapids so often written about in old reports are now beneath water backed up by dams.

TILLAMOOK, Tillamook County. US 101.

Tillamook County Pioneer Museum, 2106 2nd St. at Pacific Ave. Replica of pioneer home and barn with many exhibits. (More than 12,000 items.)

Three Arch Rocks National Wildlife Refuge, near Oceanside, is the home of Stellar sea lions. Pups born in the late spring may be seen playing in the surf near shore.

TYGH VALLEY, Wasco County. State 216.

Sherar's Bridge, at Deschutes River, began in 1860 when Maj. Steen designated the site as a crossing for military groups. Earlier Peter Skene Ogden had found 20 Indian families camped here (1826). There was a bridge "of slender wood" which the Indians were using for fishing. Five horses in Ogden's party fell from the bridge while trying to cross. In 1845 Stephen Meek's wagon train camped nearby. Ruts of wagon wheels may still be seen to the north. Historians and others pondered about the curiosity of a bridge in an area where the natives were not builders. John Todd, a cattleman and homesteader in the Tygh Valley, said the Indians had told him the span was a fishing platform built out from each side of the river which met in the middle. But not a bridge. Todd built his own bridge which was used by pack trains carrying supplies to the mines; it was wide enough for wagons, but there were no approach roads to the structure. The pack train was a lucrative operation. Mules were loaded with kegs of whiskey for which the miners paid premium prices. Todd made his bridge part of a toll road. When he moved to Farewell Bend, he sold to Joseph Sherar, who renamed the bridge and charged exorbitant prices. The Pony Express between The Dalles and the John Day gold fields used the route for ca. two years. Descriptive marker on highway.

UNION, Union County. US 30. E. of town on highway is a marker for the site where Wilson Price Hunt and his Astorians, who were the pathfinders of the old Oregon Trail, entered the Grande Ronde Valley in 1811. Across the state on US 30 will be found many historical markers for sites associated with the emigrants trains, trappers, Lewis and Clark and the Astorians. The present highway roughly follows the line of the trail.

YACHATS, Lincoln County. US 101.

Cape Perpetua Visitor Center, 2 miles S. on US 101 in Siuslaw National Forest, has interpretive displays of the natural history of the area. The forest comprises more than 1 million acres on Oregon's southern coast.

YONCALLA, Douglas County. US 99.

Jesse Applegate Site, N. of town on highway, marker denotes place where the pioneer statesman and emigrant leader, who came to Oregon in 1843, settled in the 1850s. He is buried there but the gravestone is on private property. Historian Lambert Florin quoted a letter written by Jesse Applegate's daughter Roselle Putnam in 1852 saying that the hill was named for an old chief "who came to beg for a crust of bread or an old garment." There were four cattlemen living in the area; Applegate's claim lay at the foot of Yoncalla, the hill: ". . . He keeps the post office and calls it after this hill—he is very fond of hunting and this is his hunting ground. He has killed two bears and upwards of forty deer on it since he has been living here."

SOUTH DAKOTA

The idea of a gigantic sculpture in the Black Hills originated in 1923 with Doane Robinson, State historian of South Dakota. In the beginning, he considered carving, on the granite formation known as the Needles, the figures of romantic western heroes such as Jim Bridger, John Colter, and Kit Carson. The proposal met with only moderate public acceptance. At times criticism of the project was severe, but . . . public opinion was changed and authorization for the memorial and funds to carry the work forward were obtained.

Mount Rushmore
brochure, U.S.
Department of the
Interior, 1974

Korczak told us what Harold Ickes had said when he'd been approached as Secretary of the Interior for permission to make a monument on Crazy Horse Mountain (then known as Thunderhead and owned by the National Park Service): "I don't care what the Indians want. I wouldn't cross the street to see Mount Rushmore, and no one is going to deface any more of *my* mountains."

. . . Ziolkowski and his project have antagonized the more conservative elements of the Black Hills ever since the first blast on the mountain back in 1948. . . . He has been widely criticized for playing a major role in transplanting the bones of Sitting Bull (Tatanka Iyotake) from their burial place at Fort Yates, North Dakota, to what he thought to be a more appropriate spot in South Dakota. Public officials considered the act grave robbing and were scandalized, but nothing came of the uproar. By the time the escapade was discovered the remains were resting under 20 tons of cement and a high pedestal weighing an additional 6 tons supporting an 11-ton granite bust of the great Indian leader (whacked out gratis by Ziolkowski). There was the further barrier of a high wire-mesh fence topped with barbed wire. This time Sitting Bull was in to stay.

Bill Ballantine, *High West*
(Rand McNally, 1969)

The murderer, Jack McCall, was captured after a lively chase by many of the citizens, and taken to a building at the lower end of the city, and a guard placed over him. As soon as this was accomplished, a coroner's jury was summoned, with C. H. Sheldon as foreman, who after hearing all the evidence, which was to the effect that, while Wild Bill and others were sitting at a table playing cards, Jack McCall walked in and around directly back of his victim, and when within three feet of him raised his revolver, and exclaiming, "damn you, take that," fired; the ball entering at the back of the head, and coming out at the centre of the right cheek causing instant death, rendered a verdict in accordance with the above facts. Preparations for a trial were then made. . . . The jury, after being out an hour and thirty minutes, returned the following verdict: "Deadwood City, August 3rd, 1876. We, the jury, find Mr. John McCall not guilty."

From *Black Hills Pioneer,*
August 5, 1876

SOUTH DAKOTA FACTS: The Verendrye brother, Louis and François, were probably the earliest white men to explore what is now South Dakota. The Missouri River soon proved to be highway for rugged early travelers including Lewis and Clark. Pierre Dorion, later a guide for the expedition, had settled among the Yankton Sioux and married one of their women in the 1770s. The land became U.S. territory when the Louisiana Purchase was concluded in March 1804. The territory was created in 1861. South Dakota and North Dakota were admitted to the Union on November 2, 1889. 39th State. Capital: Pierre. Nicknames: Coyote State, Sunshine State.

South Dakota Indians: The Mound Builders, Arikara (often known as Ree); the Sioux or Dakota Indians, making up the Sioux Nation have 13 tribes: among these are the Wahpeton, Sisiton (Sisseton), Teton, Yankton, Oglala and Hunkpapa.

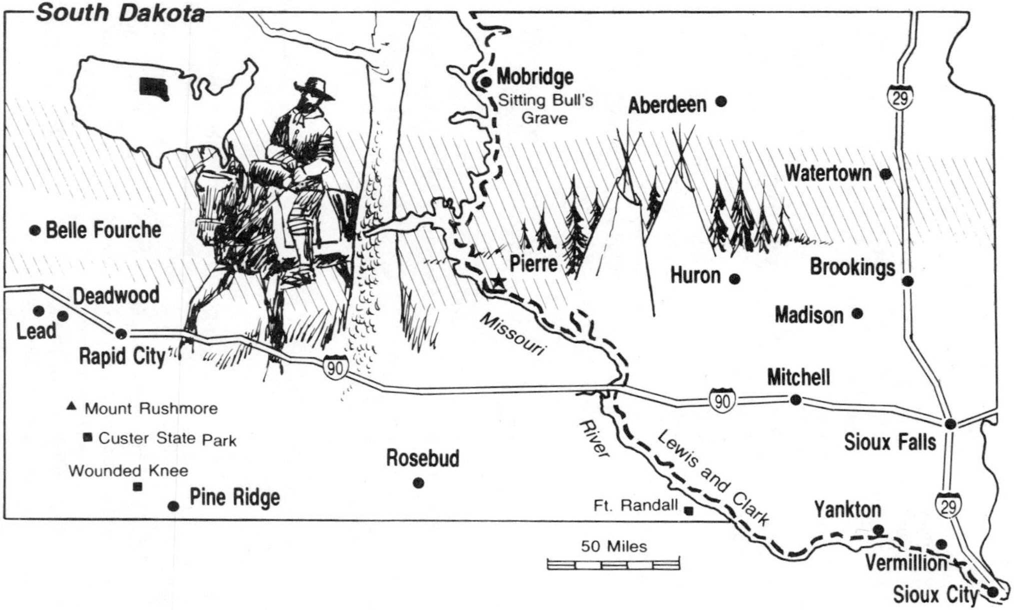
South Dakota
Mobridge
Sitting Bull's Grave
Aberdeen
Watertown
Belle Fourche
Pierre
Huron
Brookings
Deadwood
Lead
Rapid City
Madison
Missouri
Mitchell
90
29
Mount Rushmore
Custer State Park
Wounded Knee
Pine Ridge
Rosebud
River
Lewis and Clark
Sioux Falls
Ft. Randall
Yankton
50 Miles
Vermillion
Sioux City

Names That Made News:

Sitting Bull	George Armstrong Custer
Lewis and Clark	Pierre Dorion
Crazy Horse	Hamlin Garland
Poker Alice	Korczak Ziolkowski
Wild Bill Hickok	Jack McCall
John James Audubon	John Jacob Astor
Sacajawea	Red Cloud
Jean De Smet	Gutzon Borglum
Martha Jane Burke (Calamity Jane)	Mentor Graham
Annie Tallent	John Gordon
Moses Aaron	Alfred Sully
Andrew Faulk	Murdo McKenzie
Richard Pettigrew	George Crook
American Horse	Arthur Mellette

ABERDEEN, Brown County. US 12, 281. Authors Hamlin Garland and L. Frank Baum lived in Aberdeen. The Yellow Brick Road is in Kansas, but many local scenes are in Garland's novels.

Dacotah Prairie Museum, 21 S. Main St. Pioneer and Indian items.

BADLANDS NATIONAL MONUMENT, Meade County. 62 miles E. of Rapid City via I–90, US 14, 16, 16A.

Visitor Center, on 16A at Cedar Pass. Headquarters of the monument are also here. Exhibits trace Indian life in the Badlands from 10,000 years ago, through the Woodland culture of ca. 500, the Village Indians and the Sioux of 1800. The area was formed during Oligocene time, millions of years ago. There also is an audiovisual program to interpret the area. Guided trips in summer months. Another part of the center has exhibits pertaining to the Battle of Wounded Knee.

Prairie Homestead, at E. entrance to monument, is open from late May to September. A sod dugout furnished with pioneer items.

BELLE FOURCHE, Butte County. US 212, 85.

Tri-State Museum, 831 State St., on US 212. Exhibits of South Dakota historical interests; fossils.

Buckskin Johnny Cabin, 801 State St. Two-story cabin has tourist information.

Chamber of Commerce, 510 State St., has data on regional events. This is a Western-style "cowtown," with rodeos in season.

THE BLACK HILLS, several counties in W. part of state, comprises mountains, forests, ghost towns, the Mount Rushmore National Memorial, Deadwood and other sites. The Black Hills National Forest includes 1,224,604 acres with headquarters in Custer (which see).

Among the many prospectors who hoped to get rich here when the area was open to white invasion, Jerry Bryan of Illinois was one who kept a diary. His recordings are probably typical of many eager first-time dig-happy young men. On April 7, 1876, Bryan arrived in Custer with a friend from Illinois who had gone to Cheyenne with him:

> Drove in to Custer City makeing .23. miles Tired and Hungry. Being 15 days from Cheyenne pushing or pulling the Wagon half the way. After getting a good Square meal of Slapjacks and Bacon we went down Town to See the Sights They Say Custer has 400 Houses and I guess there is. and all kinds of Houses too. I of course would naturaly bring up at a Hurdy Gurdy Saloon. I find 4 or 5 old Blisters and all the men that could get in the Saloon half dozen games running But very little money in Sight A Ruff crowd is Custer

By May he had cheered up: "Worked to day on our own hook put in only ¾ of the day Did not way our Dust but think we have $75.00 evry body think we have a good thing This is good enough any how Charley feels Bully and I dont feel bad."

BLOOM, Hanson County. On James River, E. of Bloom. A well-preserved example of a prehistoric Indian site is on a terrace of the James River Valley. A fortification ditch protects the site in which there are 25 lodge depressions to be seen. Burial mounds are in the fields N. and W. A national historic landmark, not accessible to the public at this time.

BLUNT, Hughes County. US 14.

Mentor Graham House, W. edge of town, has been restored. Lincoln once stayed in Graham's home in Sangamon County, Illinois. Graham, who had been Lincoln's tutor, was invited to sit on the platform at the first inauguration.

BRITTON, Marshall County. State 10.

Prayer Rock Museum, Main St., open May to September has pioneer items, Indian displays, weapons, etc.

BROOKINGS, Brookings County. US 14, 77.

University Museum and Heritage Center, basement of Wenona Hall on campus in NE part of town. Midwestern household goods of early times and farming tools.

South Dakota Memorial Art Center, Medary Ave. at Harvey Dunn St., paintings of pioneers featured.

CHAMBERLAIN, Brule County. US 16, State 47.

Crow Creek Village, 15 miles N. on the E. side of the Missouri River near State 47, has been partially excavated. A national historic landmark not open to the public at this time.

Crow Creek Indian Reservation, 20 miles N. on State 47.

Old West Museum, 3 miles W. of town on I–90, has Indian artifacts, pioneer items, barbed-wire collection, horse drawn-vehicles and Wells-Fargo items.

CAMP EDWARDS, Brookings County. In Oakwood Lakes State Park, N. of Brookings. Troops were stationed here twice. In the winter of 1864–65 their chief purpose was to keep the Sioux from drifting back into Minnesota. Earthworks are visible. There is an interpretive marker at the site.

CUSTER, Custer County. US 16. Here is where the Dakota gold rush began when a prospector with Custer found dirt that would pay off. Since 1874 gold, quartz, beryl, mica and gypsum are among the ores that have been mined. But Jerry Bryan and Charles Hallenbeck, who came all the way from Cordova, Illinois, to seek their fortunes, were very unhappy here in the spring of 1876. (Bryan's brief but lively diary is printed in the Illinois State Historical Society Pamphlet Series [No. 2].) For April 8 Bryan writes: "Come to camp with our Spirits way down dont like the looks of the country. and I dont like the looks of the men dont believe there is a claim on the creek that will pay Wages have not Seen any money that was taken out here there is not Sufficient water and there is no fall to the creek Good Reports come from Spring Rapid & Dead Wood Creeks. . . . Good Bye to Custer."

Way Park Museum, Way City Park on Mt. Rushmore Road has mineral exhibits, some from early days, in an 1875 cabin.

Wiehe's Frontier Museum, 25 N. 5th St., items of historical interest from the Black Hills. Sioux Indian exhibits.

Black Hills Central Railroad—1880 Train offers a 32-mile round trip to Hill City in Dakota Territory vintage coaches behind a steam locomotive through genuine scenery, used as background for Walt Disney studio movies and TV's "Gunsmoke." Runs mid-June to August 3.

Borglum Ranch and Studio, 18 miles E. on US 16, State 36. Home, studio and memorabilia of Gutzon Borglum, sculptor of Mount Rushmore.

Black Hills Museum of Mining and Minerals, 624 Crook St., behind post office, has mining equipment and displays related to the early miners of the region.

Chamber of Commerce, 31 S. 5th St., has a brochure for a self-guiding tour of 20 historic sites in the area.

Crazy Horse Memorial, 5 miles N. off US 16, is a monument in progress, and now that Stone Mountain, Georgia, is finished, here is the only chance to see a gigantic piece of sculpture before it is completed. The sculptor, Korczak Ziolkowski, actually welcomes visitors to his studio. Admission goes to the memorial fund. The home and gallery and an Indian museum are open. The equestrian pose of Chief Crazy Horse will be the largest statue in the world when finished: some 563 feet high and 641 feet long, or to put it in more visual terms, workers declare an 8-room house would fit into one of the pony's nostrils.

Harney Peak, ca. 8 miles NE on State 89, is the highest point in the Black Hills (7,242 feet) and may be reached by riding and hiking trails which begin at Sylvan Lake. When Lt. Col. George Armstrong Custer and his expedition were here in 1874, they camped nearby, 3 miles below Custer, and Custer with his staff climbed the Peak nearly to the summit, leaving a copper cartridge shell with their names enclosed on a slip of paper to mark the spot. For all his vanity, Custer probably never foresaw what his autograph would be worth in sentimental value in the future. Many history hunters would have been as excited finding this shell as John Marshall was at Sutter's Mill when he picked up rocks of gold.

CUSTER STATE PARK, Custer County. 3 miles E. of Custer on US 16A. Comprising 72,000 acres, the area ranks as one of the largest state parks in the U.S. and is home to one of world's largest bison herds. The park museum has historical, geological and forestry exhibits.

Gordon Stockade, in the park, is a replica of the fortification built by a party of gold-hunters who came after Custer's expedition and had found evidences of paying ore in the Black Hills, or "color," as it was called. Several groups of gold-seekers mounted expeditions or smaller ventures to find riches. One was the group which departed from Sioux City, Iowa, in the autumn of 1874. It was named for its guide, John Gordon, who was hired by the people of Sioux City to lead prospectors to the gold fields. This was a practical enterprise from their point of view; a better route passed through Yankton where the outfit could get its supplies thereby causing the Iowa city to lose a great deal of business. Gordon, unfortunately, was not the expert he seemed to be; he was both bossy and bumbling. Some of his party were tenderfeet and one was a woman, Annie Tallent, who did her best—even to cooking an elk which all agreed was the worst meal they'd ever tried to swallow. The long winter in camp here brought on fights among the group, even to a shooting and a near-knifing. Moses Aaron, a Jew, died and had to be buried with an improvised Odd Fellows ritual, with the hope of keeping Indians from desecrating the grave. There is a statue to Annie Tallent at the stockade.

DEADWOOD HISTORIC DISTRICT, Lawrence County. US 14, 85. This gulch in the Black Hills was the

Legend says Jesse and Frank James evaded a posse by hiding in this cave after the 1876 bank holdup at Northfield, Minn.
(South Dakota Tourism photo)

scene of a gold rush in the fall of 1875 after a rich gold strike. By summer 25,000 people had settled in the town. There is one main street; additional houses have been built above it on both sides of the steep gulch. It looks like, and may well be, one of the worst towns in the world in which to kill a man and then try to get away. But Jack McCall almost did. He was acquitted by the local jury who tried him in a local theater for shooting Wild Bill Hickok in the back of the head. Cooler heads prevailed and he was retried and hanged (see Yankton). A fire in 1879 leveled much of Deadwood, but it has been rebuilt and is a national historic landmark.

Wild Bill Hickok Statue, by Korczak Ziolkowski, stands on Sherman St. and hopefully will remain there. Several monuments, including statuary, placed on Hickok's grave in Mount Moriah were chipped away by souvenir hunters in the years since he was interrupted at a card game, holding that world-famous hand of aces and eights.

Mt. Moriah Cemetery is not the dead end it might seem but probably one of the most popular sites in the Old West. Wild Bill is the main attraction. Calamity Jane, known to be a publicity hound in life, made sure she would not drop from sight after her funeral and insisted upon being buried next to Hickok, although he had a wife who might have wanted the space for herself. Hickok once caught the eye of no less a celebrity than Mrs. George Armstrong Custer, the pretty and perceptive "Libby," who stayed as near to her famous husband as was possible in his army career and met a lot of rough and ready characters who are the subjects of today's legends. Of James Butler Hickok when he was a scout during the Indian troubles, she wrote: "He did not make an armory of his waist, but carried two pistols. He wore top boots, riding breeches, and dark blue flannel shirt, with scarlet set in the front. A loose neck handkerchief left his fine firm throat free." Dashing or not he married a woman much older than himself and left her behind when he went to Deadwood perhaps to prospect, as he told her, but more likely to gamble.

Ghosts of Deadwood Gulch Wax Museum, in Old Towne Hall, Lee St., has more than 70 life-size figures of villains, miners, pioneers, Indians and others depicting 19 events.

Broken Boot Gold Mine, 1 mile W. on US 14A, was in operation from 1878 past the turn of the century. Underground guided tours.

Adams Memorial Museum, Sherman and Deadwood Sts., frontier times featured in exhibits.

Rock-land Covered Wagon Ride, 12 miles S. on US 385. A short trip over a Black Hills trail has surprise Indian attacks. Bloodless.

Theodore Roosevelt Monument, ca. 5 miles W. on Mount Roosevelt, has an observation deck at top of tower from which visitors can see four states. The Society of Black Hills Pioneers erected the monument.

The '76 Historical Museum, next to rodeo grounds, has exhibits of early transportation, and mining vehicles.

Deadwood Gulch Art Gallery, Main St., has mementos of the Deadwood Chinatown.

DeSMET, Kingsburg County. US 14. Named for the missionary-explorer priest Father Pierre Jean De Smet, a Jesuit, who seems to have known of gold in many territories and always advised the Indians not to speak of it. This is the *Little Town on the Prairie* of Laura Ingall Wilder's books. A memorial society provides daily tours which depart from a former railway construction-camp surveyor's shanty, his family home for a time. The later homestead is on the tour, as is a replica schoolhouse.

DeSmet City Museum, N. of city hall, has local history items.

EDGEMONT, Fall River County. US 18.

Painted Rocks, 2½ miles E. on US 18, then 7 miles N. on dirt road. Early Indian pictures of animals and tribal symbols.

Colgan's "Old General Store" Museum, on main street, has artifacts from the town's early days.

FAULKTON, Faulk County, US 212, was named for an early governor of Dakota Territory, Andrew J. Faulk.

Pickler House, in Pickler Park, was the 17-room home of a leading lawyer and congressman. It had a lantern in its tower to guide night travelers across the prairies; Maj. Pickler and his family entertained notables such as Theodore Roosevelt, Grover Cleveland and Susan B. Anthony. Restored.

FORT BENNETT, Stanley County. Now inundated by Lake Oahe. The post was established in May 1870, on the Missouri River, ca. 30 miles above Fort Sully, on the Cheyenne Indian Reservation, to protect the agency. First called Cheyenne Agency it was renamed for Capt. Andrew Bennett, killed in 1878 in a skirmish with Bannock Indians in Montana.

FORT DAKOTA, Minnehaha County. On the left bank of the Big Sioux River at Sioux Falls, it was established as one of a chain of posts to guard the frontier in May 1865. A plaque marking the site is on the brick wall of a theater at 218 N. Philips Ave. in downtown Sioux Falls. The fort was across the street; barracks on Philips N. of 8th St.

FORT HALE, Lyman County. State 47, on Lower Brulé Indian Reservation Area. The post was originally located on the right bank of the Missouri River; in July 1870, it was moved upstream to a spot opposite the mouth of Crow Creek. It was designated Fort Hale late in 1878, in honor of Capt. Owen Hale, 7th Cavalry, killed in 1877 in a skirmish with Nez Perce Indians. Opposite the site now is Big Bend Dam.

FORT JAMES, Hanson County. S. of Alexandria (I–90) on unimproved road, past the Hutterite Colony, on left side between road and the James River. A quartzsite slab nearly buried in a cornfield in corn season helps to mark the fortsite, near the junction of Fire Steel Creek with the James. Indians used to watch the post from a bluff, W. of site, and once fired on the garrison who shot back. The fort had various names but was called Fort James in its last days. It was established in September 1865 by Gen. Alfred Sully's orders as one of the chain of forts in the area guarding the settled areas from the still wandering and hostile Sioux who had fled Minnesota.

FORT LOOKOUT, Lyman County. Ca. 10 miles N. of Chamberlain on unimproved road. The fort was built in the summer of 1856 on the right bank of the Missouri River, near the site of an old trading post with the same name, which the Columbia Fur Co. had once occupied. The post was established by Capt. Nathaniel Lyon, later killed at the Battle of Wilson's Creek, Missouri, in the first year of the Civil War. When the post was abandoned in 1857, some of its material was shipped downriver to Fort Randall. Historian Herbert M. Hart points out:

> Fort Lookout had all the earmarks of becoming quite an elaborate layout. Its parade ground was a quarter of a mile long and its site on the southern bank commanded all steamboat traffic along the Missouri river. . . . When it was abandoned, the Army left behind the stone fireplaces, and married soldiers' cabins. The grave of a Sergeant Fiske remained on the hill to the west of the fort.

FORT MEADE, Meade County. State 34. The fort which was established in August 1878 replaced Camp Sturgis which was ca. 5 miles NE. Meade, on the E. side of Bear Butte Creek, was on a site selected by Lt. Gen. Phil Sheridan, ca. 14 miles NE of Deadwood and was intended to control the Sioux in the area of the mining camps. Called Camp Ruhlen for a short time, it was officially designated in December 1878, to honor Maj. Gen. George Gordon Meade, who led the Union forces at the Battle of Gettysburg. Since 1944 the buildings have been used as a veterans hospital. Bear Butte is 3 miles N., right side of State 79; Sturgis campsite is on the left side of the road. Historical marker at site.

Old Fort Meade Cavalry and Pioneer Western Museum, at hospital, has 7th Cavalry artifacts, military pictures, weapons and pioneer items.

FORT PIERRE, Stanley County. N. of US 14. Established as a trading post in the 1830s on the right side of the Missouri River ca. 3 miles above the mouth of the Bad (Teton) River, NW of the present town of Pierre. The U.S. purchased the post in 1855 but abandoned it two years later because of insufficient forage for horses and other unsatisfactory conditions. Some of its materials were used for Fort Randall's construction. Although nothing is left of the old post, it is important because it figured in the settlement of the state even before it was garrisoned. In 1817 Joseph La Framboise, a French fur trader, stopped at the mouth of the Bad River and erected a temporary shelter mostly of driftwood; this was the first white settlement in what is now South Dakota. It had several names, as did many early fortifications. Its last name was in honor of Pierre Choteau, Jr., an explorer and trader who eventually acquired John Jacob Astor's interests in the America Fur Co.

Verendrye Museum, on Deadwood St. in the town of Fort Pierre, has items of local history, ranching and homesteading.

FORT RANDALL, Gregory County. US 18. The post was first set up in 1856 and moved a short way downstream in 1870. It was intended to prevent the Sioux and other Indian tribes from molesting the settlers and was the last link in the chain of forts guarding the overland route along the Platte. Sitting Bull and his tribe were here as prisoners after their surrender at Fort Buford. The post was abandoned in 1890. The old parade ground, the remains of the chapel and other ruins of the fort are below the SW corner of the Randall Dam.

Fort Randall Visitor Center, at Fort Randall Dam at Pickston, features general history of the Missouri River area.

FORT SISSETON, Marshall County. State 10 in Fort Sisseton State Park. First known as Fort Wadsworth, the post was founded in 1864 to reassure settlers in the area that peace was to be maintained. The Sisseton and Wahpeton of the area were friendly. The campaigns of Sibley and Sully had quieted most of the Sioux. There are 16 buildings which have replaced the original log structures.

Fort Sisseton Visitor Center, in park, features local history.

FORT SULLY, Hughes County. State 34. Established by Brig. Gen. Alfred Sully in September 1863, on the Missouri River, during his Sioux campaign, the post was located ca. 6 miles below the present town of Pierre. It was relocated 28 miles above the city in 1866. Marker on State 34, 4 miles E. of Pierre, for the original fort.

Farm Island Visitor Center, at Farm Island State Recreational Area, E. of Pierre preserves Indian and Army artifacts at the site of the old fort.

FORT THOMPSON, Buffalo County. State 50. The post was established in September 1864 on the Missouri River at the mouth of Soldier Creek, on the Crow Creek Indian Reservation, and served as agency headquarters. In 1867 the garrison was sent to Fort Sully and the post abandoned.

Fort Thompson Mounds, near town of Fort Thompson on State 50, Crow Creek Indian Reservation, are burial mounds from the time of the Plains Woodland Indians. A national historic landmark.

GREGORY, Gregory County. US 18.

Soper's Sod House, on US 18 E. of town, is furnished in pioneer style.

HILL CITY, Pennington County. US 16. A once wild mining town with 13 saloons and hurdy-gurdy style of entertainment. A hurdy-gurdy was a saloon and dance house combined, popular in all the gold camps. Miners were expected to buy their own drinks and one for each of their partners at the end of every very short dance. Price of whiskey: 50¢ a glass.

The town was founded in 1876 when prospectors struck gold on Spring Creek. Most of its population departed when Deadwood had a strike, but some of the miners came back. Ranchers settled in the valley and in 1883 tin was discovered, and caused a small flurry of mining activity.

Black Hills Central Railroad—1880 Train, US 16, 385, offers a 32-mile, 2½-hour, round trip to Custer in old-style cars and steam locomotive from mid-June to August. (Also see Deadwood.)

HOT SPRINGS, Fall River County. US 18. The town with its old Victorian buildings of pink sandstone has been made a registered historic site.

Fall River County Historical Museum, 300 N. Chicago Ave. 22 rooms of displays.

Wind Cave National Park, 12 miles N. on US 385. Visitor Center has displays of Arikara and Mandan pottery and other artifacts. The park area covers 44 square miles. There are guided tours for the cave which are recommended only for the physically fit. A wildlife preserve on the grounds is stocked with bison, antelope, prairie dogs and other animals.

HURON, Beadle County. US 14.

State Fair Pioneer Museum, 8 blocks W. on US 14 at Fairgrounds, has pioneer exhibits and a log cabin. Open from Memorial to Labor Day.

JEWEL CAVE NATIONAL MONUMENT, Custer County. US 16. Entrance is ca. 14 miles W. of Custer on the E. side of Hell Canyon in the Black Hills. The monument includes 1,275 acres; guided tours in summer months.

KADOKA, Jackson County. US 16.

Red Cloud Indian Museum, W. off I–90, has Sioux clothing, weapons, tools, arrowheads.

Badlands Petrified Gardens, off E. Kadoka exit of I–90, comprises three acres of petrified wood. Museum has fossils and fluorescent minerals from the area.

KEYSTONE, Pennington County. US 16, US 16A.

Big Thunder Gold Mine, off US 16A. Guided tours mid-May to mid-September.

Cosmos of Black Hills, 3616 W. Main, 4 miles NE off US 16, is a "Mystery House," which has arranged optical illusions and gravitational effects and has little to do with the historical side of the Black Hills except that many miners, especially on Sundays, had optical illusions, self-induced and probably had some difficulties overcoming the force of gravity. Sunday was the traditional day off in times of much mining activity; it was used for shopping as well as for recreation. There were few or no churches and only occasional itinerant preachers to be listened to, but all the saloons were open in *all* the mining centers, not just Keystone.

Shrine to Democracy Wax Museum, on US 16A, has Betsy Ross, who never got near a gold mine, stitching the flag; and other figures depict other historic scenes.

Rushmore Cave, 6 miles E., has guided tours.

Rushmore Aerial Tramway, US 16A, offers 15-minute rides to view the Black Hills and Mt. Rushmore, in spring and summer months.

Rockerville Ghost Town, ca. 9 miles NE on US 16. Museum, old shops, saloon, stagecoach and other trappings.

LEAD, Lawrence County. US 85. Lead (Leed) was the end link in the chain of gold mines that began at Custer and ran through the Black Hills. The Homestake gold mine is the largest in the U.S. and was incorporated in 1877. Moses and Fred Manuel who had been prospecting for a year discovered the Homestake Ledge, or Lead, on April 9, 1876. They took out $5,000 in gold that spring.

Homestake Mine, Main St. between Mill St. and city limits, has a tour of surface workings.

LEMMON, Perkins, US 12.

Petrified Wood Park & Museum, 500A Main Ave. Petrified objects, fossils in park. Museum has minerals, pioneer artifacts and Indian displays.

MADISON, Lake County. State 34.

Lake County Historical Museum, on campus of Dakota State College, 6th St. NE.

Prairie Village, 2 miles W. on US 81, State 34, is a replica with 25 restored buildings on 140 acres: Thormodsgaard House is a two-story handhewn log structure built near Canton by four brothers and has some original furnishings; Smith Ranch House, one of the first permanent residences in Lake County built by a Civil War veteran, has family furnishings; Jacobs Sod House was a homesteader's place. Antique vehicles also are on display.

MARTIN, Bennett County. US 18.

Hill Top Museum is a sod house, with old farm machinery also on display.

Lacreek National Wildlife Refuge, 5 miles S. on State 73, then 9 miles E. Self-guiding tours.

MILBANK, Grant County. US 12.

Grant County Historical Society Museum, 1 block E. of Main St., local history items from 1890.

Old Windmill, near railroad depot on Main St., is a gristmill of 1886 with a restored country school next door.

MISSION, Todd County. US 18.

Buechel Memorial Sioux Indian Museum, 6 miles W. on US 18, then 16 miles SW on unmarked road in St. Francis Mission. Sioux artifacts, in a comprehensive and well-documented collection. From prereservation culture to relics of the Battle of Little Big Horn.

Rosebud Indian Reservation includes 60,000 acres along the Little White River. Craft shop at Rosebud with handicrafts and paintings by local Indian artists.

MITCHELL, Davison County. I–90.

The Corn Palace, Main St. and 6th Ave., originally built in 1892, rebuilt twice, has scenic murals in colored corn and grasses. Indian dances daily in summer season.

Museum of Pioneer Life, 1311 S. Duff, was sponsored by the Friends of the Middle Border, which included Hamlin Garland, John Dewey and James Truslow Adams. Displays include a one-room school.

Mitchell Site, at municipal golf course, has yielded archaeological materials of the Woodland Indian culture. Fortification trenches are visible as are more than 40 house depressions. A national historic landmark.

Hunter's Store, on I–90, has a display which claims to be the largest collection of "famous western rifles and handguns in the West. The authentic guns of the people who made the West, Wyatt Earp, Calamity Jane, Annie Oakley, Jim Bridger—U.S. Army Scout, Chief Sitting Bull, Chief Crazy Horse, Chief Standing Bear" and others. Mountain Man Jim Bridger apparently is the only man who helped make the West who needs identification for Herter's customers.

MOBRIDGE, Walworth County. US 12. Once the site of Arikara and Sioux villages.

Land of the Sioux Indian Museum, just S. of the city library at 511 N. Main, has many interesting relics including ghost shirt artifacts. In the last third of the 19th century, Indian leaders in scattered areas preached of the coming of a Messiah. In connection with the "new religion" were dances in which some of the participants kept going until they fell into trances. White Americans began to call this the Ghost Dance religion. One of the first outbreaks because of the movement was in Arizona where a Medicine Man was killed in the goings-on and the dispute between the Army and the Indians kept up through the Apache Wars. The Messiah, or Ghost Dance, religion seems to have touched many tribes from the Apache of the Southwest to the Teton here, and others elsewhere in North America. It was indirectly because of the Ghost Dance stirrings-up that Sitting Bull was killed, although he had been living fairly quietly on the Pine Ridge Reservation.

Sitting Bull Monument and Memorial Site, 3 miles W. on US 12, then 4 miles on unmarked road. This burial ground is the second for the great Teton chief who was first interred at the Fort Yates cemetery in North Dakota. Reburial took place in 1954. The bust of Sitting Bull was sculpted by Korcsak Ziolkowski, who is at work on the gigantic statue of Crazy Horse near Mount Rushmore. The gravesite overlooks the Oahe Reservoir which has inundated the Cheyenne River Agency and old Fort Bennett.

Sitting Bull had surrendered his band in 1881 at Fort Buford, North Dakota, and spent two years in prison at Fort Randall, South Dakota, and had then returned to live here with his own people at Standing Rock Agency near his birthplace on the Grand River of South Dakota. He resisted efforts of the authorities to turn his people into farmers, and became a leader in the Ghost Dance movement, but matters were well under control by the Standing Rock Indian agent. When Maj. Gen. Nelson Miles suddenly decided to arrest ringleaders of the movement, some 39 Indian police and a few volunteers were sent to pick up Sitting Bull. In the slight fracas of his resistance one of his men suddenly shot a policeman and brought on a real tragedy in which six police and eight Indians were killed, including Sitting Bull and one of his sons. The deaths occurred on the morning of December 15, 1890. It has been said that the warriors who fell in the struggle lay unburied for two weeks; relatives were afraid to come for their bodies. Then a minister volunteered to assist in the burial. They were placed in a common grave near the scene of the killing.

Sacajawea Monument, a short distance from Sitting Bull Memorial, near river, on the summit of a hill at State 8. The memorial honors the Shoshone woman who went to the far West on the Lewis and Clark expedition.

Molstad Village, 18 miles S. of Mobridge, in Dewey County, overlooking Oahe Reservoir, is prehistoric, now a national historic landmark, and has been excavated by the Smithsonian Institution.

MOUNT RUSHMORE NATIONAL MEMORIAL, Pennington County. 22 miles S. of Rapid City off US 16A. Washington, Jefferson, Lincoln and Theodore Roosevelt are the stone faces on the 6,000-foot mountain in the Black Hills which was carved by Gutzon Borglum in the years from 1927 to 1941. His son, Lincoln Borglum, managed the project after the sculptor's death in March 1941. Visitor Center and headquarters are on the grounds of the memorial. The national park service maintains 1,278 acres set aside as the memorial. Three tunnels on Iron Mountain Rd. approaching the area were blasted in order to frame the four faces on the scenic drive.

MURDO, Jones County. US 16, 83. The prairie town was on a branch of the Texas Trail in the days when thousands of cattle were brought north in the spring and was named for Murdo McKenzie, manager of the Matador Cattle Co. of Texas which ran about 20,000 head of cattle to the area.

Pioneer Auto Museum and Antique Town, Junction I-90, US 83, has a variety of horse-drawn early vehicles and farm equipment.

PIERRE, Hughes County. US 14, 83.

State Capitol, Capitol Ave. E., built in the early 20th century, has guided tours. The city is located on the site of the Arikara Nation's capital. Among the many murals and paintings of early day history is "Spirit of the People" on the W. wall of the conference room which tells the story of the settlers' advance into the Dakota Territory.

South Dakota State Historical Society, in Soldiers' and Sailor's War Memorial opposite the capitol, has memorabilia of pioneer and Indian life. Among Indian exhibits is the Verendrye Plate, a lead plate buried at Fort Pierre in 1743 by the first French explorers in the area.

Arzberger Site, ca. 7 ½ miles E. on the Missouri River, is a fortified billage site on a mesa and was the northern outpost of the Central Plains tradition. A national historic landmark.

PINE RIDGE, Shannon County. US 18. Headquarters for the Oglala Sioux Reservation.

Wounded Knee Battlefield, 8 miles E. on US 18, then 7 miles N. on unmarked road. The battle of December 29, 1890, was the last major clash between Indians and soldiers in North America. The oppressed and crowded Sioux, constantly being shoved by the encroaching white culture, followed the hope held out by the exponents of the Messiah or Ghost Dance religion. Army troops were called out to put down the newly rebellious groups by arresting their leaders. The battle was joined here. It is now a national historic landmark. A monument marks the mass grave of the many unarmed Indians, including women and children, who were killed in the sad affair. When Sitting Bull was killed resisting arrest at his camp on the Standing Rock Reservation, his followers fled southward and this contributed to the chain of events that brought on the Battle of Wounded Knee.

Oglala Sioux Tribal Museum and Historical Society, at the edge of the industrial park in Pine Ridge, has a fine collection of Indian artifacts, as well as geological and natural history displays.

PLANKINTON, Aurora County. US 281, I–90.

White Diamond Ranch Museum, SE of highway junction, has a large collection of horse-drawn machinery and other pioneer articles.

RAPID CITY, Pennington County. US 16, I–90.

Museum of Geology, O'Harra Building, on campus of South Dakota School of Mines and Technology, St. Joseph St. Minerals, fossils and other items of geological and Dakota interest. Exhibits of prehistoric skeletal remains are particularly fine.

Dinosaur Park, W. on Quincy St. to Skyline Drive, cement copies of the animals which once roamed the area.

Sioux Indian Museum & Crafts, 1002 St. Joseph, in Halley Park. Interpretive exhibitions of historic and modern Sioux Indian arts and pioneer artifacts.

Horseless Carriage Museum, 10 miles S. on US 16, pioneer buildings, vehicles and sundry relics.

Minnilusa Historical Museum, West Blvd. in Halley Park, historical relics of the Black Hills and the Dakotas.

Timber of Ages Petrified Forest, NW of town, open mid-May to mid-September, off I–90. Guided tours of forest.

General Custer won this one
(Travel Division, South Dakota Dept. of Highways)

ROCKERVILLE, Pennington County. US 16, ca. 12 miles E. of Hill City. The town was once second only to Deadwood in the value of its place mines. A rush began in 1876; by 1883 the camp was nearly deserted. Now a ghost town, rebuilt and furnished as it used to be in its busy days.

SIOUX FALLS, Minnehaha County. I–90. The falls were described by Jean Nicollet in 1839, when he was sent on a trip by the Canadian government to explore the area. Sketches of the falls drawn by Nicollet interested persons in Dubuque who organized a party to look for a townsite. The Dakota Land Co. was chartered in 1856–57 by an act of the Minnesota Territorial legislature which established the city by the same legislation. A log house was the first dwelling. In 1862 the town was deserted because of Indian troubles. It was reestablished three years later.

Richard Pettigrew House, 131 N. Duluth Ave., was the home of the first senator from the state of South Dakota. A museum has Indian natural history and other exhibits.

Sioux Falls College, 22 St. and Prairie Ave., has the Lorene B. Burns Indian Collection. There is an historical marker on campus where the Yankton Trail crossed the area. It was used by settlers fleeing from the Indians in the 1860s.

Minnehaha County Courthouse, Main Ave. and 6th St., has murals depicting early Sioux Falls, and the area before the city was settled.

Fort Dakota Site, marker on Philips Ave., between 7th and 8th Sts. (Also see Fort Dakota).

Smith Printing Press, marker on W. end of 8th St. bridge, was the first newspaper in Dakota Territory.

SLIM BUTTES BATTLEFIELD, Harding County. State 20, ca. 2 miles W. of Reva. On September 8, 1876, an advance unit of Brig. Gen. George Crook's command charged a band of Sioux under American Horse who were camped at Rabbit Creek nearby. The soldiers were outnumbered but captured the village and held on until the main body of the troops caught up. American Horse and his men were trapped in a cave and surrendered when the leader suffered mortal wounds. A monument and markers are at the site.

STURGIS, Meade County. US 34, State 79. Poker Alice, the cigar-smoking madam, had a popular brothel here where soldiers from nearby Fort Meade came to town in their off-duty hours and the many bullwhackers who brought in the supply trains for the post also made the town lively. Poker Alice, as well as Calamity Jane and Belle Starr, was a colorful character whose name was probably borrowed to lend spice to many a story presented as factual. If these women had been in all the places attributed to them, they would have had little time for anything but travel. Alice may or may not have been present when Bob Ford, the man who shot Jesse James, was also shot in Creede, Colorado, although some accounts of the Police Gazette variety had Alice, Killarney Kate and Calamity Jane all looking on. But she did have a brisk business in Sturgis, which had the nickname of Scooptown. Soldiers said that those who went to town were "scooped" or "cleaned out."

Black Hills National Cemetery, S. on US 14.

TYNDALL, Bon Homme County. State 50.

Midway Museum, 5 miles S. on State 37, has historical collection in log cabin.

VERMILLION, Clay County. State 19, 50.

W. H. Over Dakota, Clark St. on campus of University of South Dakota, has a vast collection of Indian items, historical and geological displays. The Hall of Man depicts the development of implements and their uses from Paleolithic times. A diorama of Scalp Creek village shows round earthlodges surrounded by the usual stockade and moat. There are exhibits from the Scalp Creek site showing a people who combined two cultures.

Austin-Whittemore House, 108 Austin, is a two-story brick dwelling with Victorian scroll-work and a cupola; the home of Horace Austin, who laid out the town and later served in the state legislature.

Spirit Mound, on State 19, is a spot the Indians held sacred. Lewis and Clark visited it when they came upriver by keelboat enroute to what is now the Bismarck area and their way west. John James Audubon was here on his travels of the early 1840s.

WALL, Pennington County. I–90.

Wall Drug Store has a free map of its territory, and free coffee for hunters, skiers and honeymooners. There is free ice water and this is probably the only drugstore W. of the Holland tunnel that has ever been written up in the *Wall Street Journal.* All kinds of gimcrackery, Western style, are on display or offered for sale. The Western Art Gallery Café has original oil paintings, some by Standing Soldier, Indian artist. The room is paneled in "American Black Walnut" with a life-size carving of Butch Cassidy and the Sundance Kid, made from a 187-year-old cedar tree, at least from a tree that was plenty old when the undated brochure was printed.

Frontier Acres Museum, 1 mile S., has old machinery and horse-drawn vehicles.

WATERTOWN, Codington County. US 81. This town had almost as much trouble from grasshoppers in the 1870s as other villages had from the Sioux Ghost Dancers. The grasshoppers invaded in 1874; a prairie fire devastated the area in 1878.

Mellette House, Memorial and Museum, 415 5th St. NW. Restored home of the last governor of the territory and first governor of the state, Arthur Mellette. A two-story brick Victorian manse, now a house museum with some original furnishings.

Olive Chateau, US 81, another Victorian brick dwelling with turrets and towers, built by H. D. Walrath, a banker and real estate man. Antique furnishings. May be opened by appointment; inquire locally.

WESSINGTON SPRINGS, Jerauld County. State 34.

Dunham Memorial Museum, in county courthouse, has Indian artifacts and early household items as well as a weapon collection.

YANKTON, Yankton County. US 81, State 50. First capital of Dakota Territory (1861–83) has wide streets, well planned, lined with homes from territorial times. Jack McCall was hanged here for the shooting of Wild Bill Hickok in Deadwood where McCall had been tried and found not guilty at his first, but not his second, judging by a jury of his peers.

Yankton County Territorial Museum, Douglas Ave. Restored building has historical displays; pioneer kitchen and schoolhouse, and office of the 1st governor.

Chief Eagle Feather "Wamblee Weyaka" Museum Area, W. end of Mount Marty College Campus, has Indian artifacts.

Lewis and Clark State Recreational Area Visitor's Center and Museum, 4 miles W. on State 52 which follows Yankton Trail, has Indian artifacts, cavalry, homestead and trapping items.

Jack McCall Sites have been marked by the state historical society. The gallows was two miles from town on March 1, 1877, when he was hanged. The story of his hanging is on plaque 2 miles N. of US 81, at corner of State Hospital grounds. The burial site is marked, with the comment that he was tucked away with the noose still around his neck.

TEXAS

. . . Three or four young punchers rode their hosses into a saloon when one of them overdressed Eastern drummers happened to be at the bar imbibin' his after-supper refreshments. Bein' considerably jostled by one of them hosses, he complained bitterly to the bartender 'bout all this goin's-on.

The barkeep, an old stove-up ex-cowpuncher, glared at 'im a minute and came back: "What the hell you doin' in here afoot anyhow?"

Ramon F. Adams, *The Old-Time Cowhand*

Now all of us were wounded, our noble captain
slain,
The sun was shining sadly across the bloody plain,
Sixteen brave Rangers as ever roamed the West,
Were buried by their comrades with arrows in their
breast.

The Texas Rangers

Bass steadfastly refused to give information, though he talked freely of the men who were killed, and of the facts that were well known.

On Sunday Bass's death became a certainty. Major Jones again tried to gain some information.

"No," said Bass, "I won't tell."

"Why won't you?" asked Major Jones.

"Because it's agin my profession. . . . If a man knows anything he ought to die with it in him." And he did. When Dr. Cochran told him the end was near, he said, "Let me go." And, as he went, he said:

"The world is bobbing around!"

Walter Prescott Webb,
The Texas Rangers; A Century of Frontier Defense
(University of Texas Press)

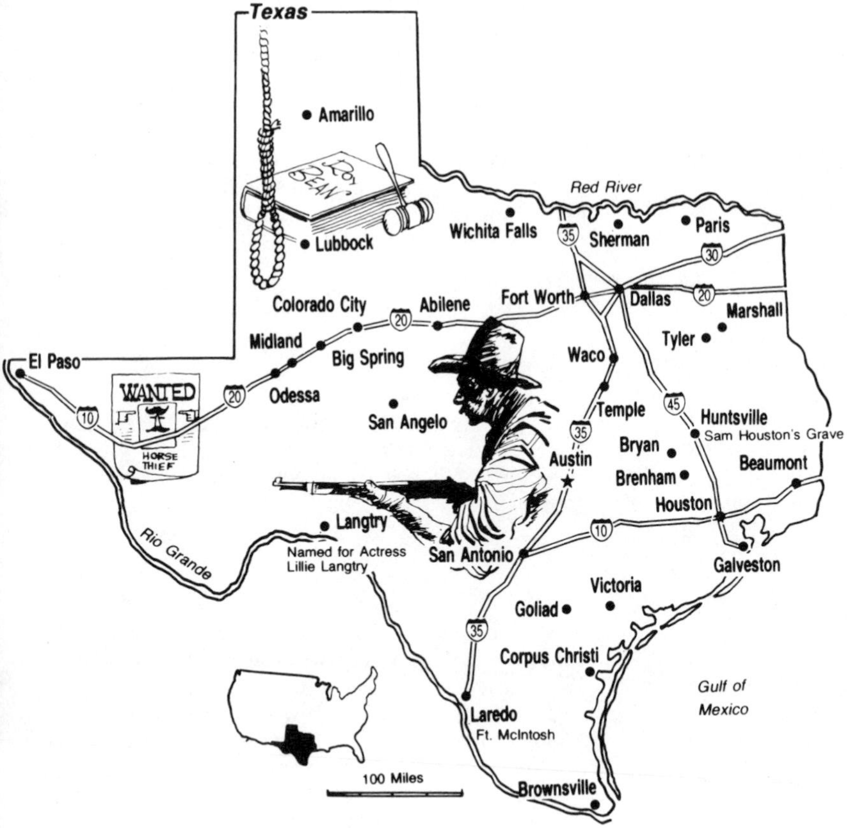
Texas
Amarillo
Lubbock
Wichita Falls
Red River
Sherman
Paris
Fort Worth
Dallas
Marshall
Tyler
Colorado City
Abilene
Midland
Big Spring
El Paso
WANTED
HORSE THIEF
Odessa
San Angelo
Waco
Temple
Huntsville
Sam Houston's Grave
Bryan
Austin
Brenham
Beaumont
Houston
Langtry
Named for Actress
Lillie Langtry
San Antonio
Galveston
Rio Grande
Victoria
Goliad
Corpus Christi
Gulf of
Mexico
Laredo
Ft. McIntosh
100 Miles
Brownsville
10
20
35
30
45

TEXAS FACTS: Cabeza de Vaca was probably the first white explorer in Texas in 1528. Coronado and De Soto came in the mid-16th century. In 1821 Mexico, which included Texas, gained independence from Spain. The Texas revolution for independence from Mexico began in 1835. In 1836 the Republic of Texas was created and lasted until 1845 when Texas was admitted to the Union as the 28th state. Texas seceded in 1861 and was readmitted in 1870.

Capital: Austin. Nickname: Lone Star State.

Texas has two national parks, four national forests, and a national seashore.

Early Trails. The Chisholm Trail, the Goodnight–Loving, Trail, the California Trail, the San Antonio–El Paso Road, the Butterfield Overland Mail Line, El Camino Real, the Mackenzie Trail, the San Antonio–San Diego Stage Line, the Comanche Trail.

Texas Indians. West Texas Cave Dwellers, Caddo, Kiowa, Comanche, Apache, Karankawa, Attacapa, Tonkawa, Cherokee, Alabama, Seminole, Kickapoo, Cooshatti.

ABILENE, Taylor County. I–20. Shipping point on the Texas and Pacific Railroad in 1881.

Old Abilene Town, 4 miles NE on I–20. Replica frontier town, museum.

Fort Phantom Hill & Lake, on the Clear Fork of the Brazos River. 14 miles N. on FM 600. Ruins of 1850s fort, built to protect gold miners en route to California. Guardhouse, powderhouse and some chimneys remain. Interpretive signs and literature.

Abilene State Park, near Lake Abilene, ca. 15 miles SW on FM 89. 507 acres where Comanche Indians once camped.

ALAMO, Hidalgo County. State 281.

Live Steam Museum (The Engine Room), ca. 2 miles N. of US 83 on FM 907. All kinds of steam engines from the 1880s on.

Santa Ana National Wildlife Refuge, just E. of intersection of US 281 and FM 907. Ca. 2,000 acres preserve species native to the S. Texas region. Jungle-like growth is typical of Texas area before it was converted to farms.

ALBANY, Shackelford County. US 67. Early supply point on the Western Trail to Dodge City.

Albany News, established 1883, has a valuable file of authentic frontier history from its own records and runs of other frontier-days publications.

Fort Griffin State Historic Park, 15 miles N. on US 283. Fort ruins are in the 503-acre park. Historical plaques. The first Fort Griffin was a Texas Ranger post on the Little River in 1839. Griffin II was established here in July 1867, to replace Fort Belknap. It was an important supply point for buffalo hunters and protected cattle trails. Abandoned May 1881. Museum.

Camp Cooper, in Throckmorton County, on ranch near Fort Griffin, is accessible by foot only. And only the most dedicated buff will make the trip to the site. Permission should be obtained from ranch owners; then to reach the camp one must wade across the hip-deep Clear Fork of the Brazos. The camp existed from 1856 to 1861 to protect settlers and control the 400 or more Comanches living on the nearby Comanche Indian Reservation. Robert E. Lee was a junior officer in 1856–57. One building from the early 1850s is near the S. edge of the parade ground.

Ledbetter Picket House Museum, Webb Park, in Albany, S. Jacobs St., has relics from the Ledbetter Salt Works. Restored ranch house with frontier furnishings. The house is a dog-run cabin built of pickets. Artifacts from the fort and homes of the area.

ALPINE, Brewster County. US 90.

Museum of the Big Bend, on campus of Sul Ross State University, has Indian, Spanish, Mexican and pioneer artifacts.

ALTO, Cherokee County. US 79. Once a stop on the Old San Antonio Rd.

Davy Crockett National Forest, 6 miles SW on State 21. 161,556 acres in Houston and Trinity Counties. Headquarters at Lufkin.

Mound Prairie (George C. Davis Site) 6 miles SW of town. Ceremonial mounds are the remains of Hasinai Indian culture. Archaeologists have found many artifacts here. A registered historic place.

AMARILLO, Potter County. US 66, I–40.

Tourist Bureau, on I–40, US 287 just E. of town.

Helium Monument and Tourist Center, Nelson St. at I–40. Historical data and information on local sites.

Ellwood Park, S. 11th Ave. between Washington and Jackson, has a monument to Fray Juan de Padilla, Franciscan of the Coronado travels, killed by Indians in 1544.

Buffalo Lake National Wildlife Refuge, 28 miles S. and W. via US 60, then 2 miles S. on FM 168.

ANAHUAC, Chambers County. State 65, 61.

Fort Anahuac, on Galveston Bay near the mouth of Trinity River, some traces remain of old Mexican fort and customhouse, built ca. 1831 by prisoners of the Mexican government. William B. Travis, who commanded and died at the Alamo, captured the fort early in the Texas Revolution. Outlines are still visible on a bluff just S. of town.

Chambers House, SE corner of Cummings St. and Miller Ave. was the antebellum home of Gen. Thomas Jefferson Chambers, once surveyor-general of Texas and a judge. He built the house so that only one person could ascend the circular stairway at a time, but he was killed in the east room downstairs by a shot through a window.

Anahuac National Wildlife Refuge, ask at office in town for directions. Refuge is 18 miles SE on East Bay.

ANDERSON, Grimes County. State 90. Established in 1834 on the La Bahia Rd., an ancient Indian trail that ran from Louisiana through Texas to the West. Route was used by the Spanish, Alonzo De Leon passed through in 1690; later became a cattle trail known as the Opelousas Road. During the Civil War Anderson was an assembly point for troops and supplies. Local Arms factory produced arms and ammunition. Many historic homes in town are open on a Sunday early in May with hosts in costume and a parade of 19th-century vehicles.

Everyone remembers the Alamo
(Texas Tourist Development Agency)

Steinhagen Log Cabin, two blocks S. of Main St. at State 90, is more than 100 years old with frontier furnishings, many early tools and farm equipment. Open only by appointment, at present.

Sam Houston National Forest, ca. 13 miles E. on FM 149. 158,235 acres in Montgomery, San Jacinto and Walker counties.

Old Fanthrop Inn, a stagecoach stop, bottle-shaped brick cistern in rear courtyard.

ANDREWS, Andrews County. US 385.

Andrews County Museum, 212 NW. 2nd St. Pioneer relics, Indian artifacts.

ANGLETON, Brazoria County. State 35. Many fine old plantations in this area. Gen. Albert Sidney Johnston was a planter here.

Varner–Hogg Plantation State Historic Park, 15 miles W. on State 35. An 1835 home with period furnishings in 65-acre park.

ANTHONY, El Paso County. State 20. The town is new but the highway follows the historic El Camino Real, Spanish royal road to connect Mexico with Texas and other areas. In 1598 Don Juan de Onate and colonizers traveled this route to settle Santa Fe.

Tourist Bureau, I–10 at New Mexico state line. The Texas Highway Department maintains nine Tourist Bureaus at points of entry to the state and in Austin and Langry. All are open daily with trained travel personnel. Free maps, literature and advice.

ARANSAS PASS, San Patricio County. State 35. The area was settled by Irish colonists in the 1820s. The enterprising W. A. Jones, deputy custom collector, seized the Union coast guard schooner *Twilight* in April 1861, when the war was scarcely begun. The Union navy attacked in February 1862, but in April, Confederates were again victorious in capturing U.S. navy launches off the pass.

ARCHER CITY, Archer County. State 25, 79.

Archer County Historical Museum, in county courthouse, pioneer items.

ARLINGTON, Tarrant County. State 360. Established as Johnson's County in 1843.

Six Flags Over Texas, Dallas–Fort Worth Turnpike midway between cities. Six sections of the entertainment park feature Texas history.

Southwestern Historical Wax Museum, 601 E. Safari Pkwy. At last count 48 scenes, 140 wax heroes and villains and bystanders, antique guns, Indian artifacts and barbed-wire collection.

AUSTIN, Travis County. I–35. Named for Stephen F. Austin, son of Moses Austin, leader of the first American colony in Texas. Buffalo hunters camping here in 1838 thought this would make an ideal capital for the republic. Mirabeau Lamar, one of the hunters, was then Vice-President. When he gained the presidential office he selected Austin.

State Capitol, N. end of Congress Ave. Built in 1888 of pink granite from Burnet; the town traded the stone for a railroad. Tourist information in Rotunda. Earlier capitols were at Columbia, Houston, Washington-on-the-Brazos and Austin. Guided tours.

Texas State Library, 1201 Brazos, on capitol grounds. Texas Declaration of Independence is among the many historical documents housed here.

Mural gives history of the republic and state. Guided tours.

Old Land Office, 112 E. 11, houses the Texas Confederate Museum and the Daughters of the Republic of Texas Museum.

Governor's Mansion, 1010 Colorado between 10th and 11th. was built in the 1850s, has housed more than three dozen governors, over 120 years. Sam Houston's bed is still in his chamber used in the 1860s. Stephen Austin's desk is in the Houston bedroom, and a coffee table made from—alas—a drum used at Shiloh. Houston memorabilia in the room.

Texas Memorial Museum, on University campus, 24th and Trinity Sts. Historical exhibits and many others including geological, anthropological, etc. *The Mustangs*, a bronze statue, at W. terrace.

University of Texas at Austin, San Jacinto, Guadalupe, 19th and 27th Sts. Observation Tower open daily except Sunday. Campus tours from Alpha Phi Omega office, Rm. 207, Union Bldg. Visitor Information Center in Sid Richardson Hall.

2009 ½ Guadalupe, temporary residence of obscure historian, Alice Hamilton, during senior year at University. No Indian artifacts, no pioneer relics, no coffee tables made from Shiloh drums.

O. Henry Museum, 409 E. 5th St. onetime home of William Sydney Porter, some original furnishings.

Old French Legation, 802 San Marcos St. The only Texas building erected for a representative of a foreign government (1840). The *Chargé d'Affaires* to the Republic lived here. House and gardens have been restored.

Treaty Oak, 503 Baylor St., legendary meeting place of historic conferences. And quite a few forgettable ones.

Texas Catholic Historical Society, Congress and W. 16th, has records and documents of Spanish rule and the establishing of missions.

State Cemetery, E. 7th and Comal Sts., has many statesmen and heroes, including tombs of Stephen Austin and Gen. Albert Sidney Johnston, killed at Shiloh.

Laguna Gloria, W. end of 35th St. on Lake Austin, is a site said to have been chosen by Stephen Austin for his home. The estate belonged to Clara Driscoll, who helped to preserve the Alamo. Now houses changing art exhibits.

Lake Austin, formed by the Tom Miller Dam, on the Colorado River, dates from 1893. A sternwheeler makes chartered cruises.

Austin Chamber of Commerce, 901 Riverside Dr., adjacent to Municipal Auditorium, has information on the many sites of the area.

Elizabet Ney Museum, 44th and Ave. H. One of the oldest sculptor's studios in America. Many exhibits.

Neill-Cochran House, 2310 San Gabriel St. The National Society of the Colonial Dames of America in Texas has headquarters here. Antique furnishings and historic documents. House was built about 1853.

Bremond Block Historic District, W. 8th, Guadalupe, W. 7th and San Antonio St.; from 315 to 610 consists of 13 Guadalupe, houses built from ca. 1870 to 1890, all once owned by members of the Bremond and Robinson families. A registered historic area.

Carrington House, 1511 Colorado St., is being restored, built in the 1850s by merchant and land speculator L. Davis Carrington. Run by State Historical Survey Commission.

Littlefield House, 24th St. and Whitis Ave. Built in 1894 by Maj. George W.

Littlefield, cattle baron and banker. Operated by the University of Texas.

North-Evans House, 708 San Antonio Ave. 1874 Victorian dwelling with garden. Operated by Austin Women's Club.

Swedish Pioneer Cabin, Zilker Park, 2220 Barton Springs Rd. Built ca. 1840, on the Colorado River, by an early Swedish settler. Pioneer furnishings.

Driskill Hotel, 117 W. 7th St., has been the scene of many state functions from its opening; in 1877 the first major affair was an inaugural ball for Governor Sul Ross. A registered historic place.

Gethsemane Lutheran Church, 1510 Congress Ave., services began in December 1868. Present church built in 1883; bricks came from the 1852 state capitol. Historic building.

The Old Bakery, 1006 Congress Ave. Charles Lundberg, Swedish immigrant, built the bakery in 1876.

U.S. Post Office (Old Post Office) and Federal Building (O. Henry Hall), 126 W. 6th St. A registered historic place built in 1878.

Woodlawn (Pease Mansion), 6 Niles Rd. Abner Cook built the house in 1853 for James B. Shaw, but Governor Elisha Pease lived here for many years. A registered historic building.

AUSTWELL, Refugio County. FM 774.

Aransas National Wildlife Refuge, 7 miles S. of town on Aransas Bay has 54,827 acres. Visitors must register before taking the self-guiding trips along hard-surfaced roads. The last flock of whooping cranes in the world are here. Boat tours to see the cranes from mid-October to mid-April may be arranged at the Sea Gun Lodge, 10 miles N. of Rockport on State 35.

BAIRD, Callahan County. US 283. Established in 1880 with the building of the Texas & Pacific Railroad, named for Matthew Baird, director who drove the first stake in 1885.

Callahan County Pioneer Museum, basement of courthouse, has farm and ranch implements from the old days, barbed wire, household items.

BALLINGER, Runnels County. US 83, 87. Established as Hutchins City in 1886.

Ballinger Museum, 5th and Strong, has tools, Indian artifacts, other displays.

Cowboy and His Horse Statue, on courthouse lawn, US 83, 87, honors Charles Noyes, local cowboy killed in range accident, and all cowboys of the early West. Pompeo Coppini, the sculptor.

BALMORHEA, Reeves County. US 290.

Balmorhea State Park, at San Solomon Springs, 4 miles SW off US 290. This was once a popular watering place for Indians, pioneers and buffalo.

BANDERA, Bandera County. State 16. A cypress shingle camp in the 1850s, then a Mormon colony. Later Polish settlers arrived.

Frontier Times Museum, 506 13th St., has Texiana and frontier items, a western art gallery, an old bell collection and Buffalo Bill show posters.

St. Stanislaus Catholic Church, built in 1876, serves one of the oldest Polish parishes in the U.S. Consult Chamber of Commerce for information on the many scenic drives of the area, one of which goes to Camp Verde.

BARKSDALE, Edwards County. State 55. First called Dixie by the original settler of 1876, then named for Louis Barksdale, who located on a land grant ca. 1880. Settlers were wiped out by Indians up till 1880.

Camp Wood, 4 miles E. on county road. Marker at site and also on State 55 just N. of town. Established in 1857 on the Nueces River, the post was abandoned on March 15, 1861.

Mission San Lorenzo de la Santa Cruz, also known as El Canon, 4 miles SE but not easily reached. It was established in 1762 by Fray Diego Jiminez and others. Only ruins remain.

BASTROP, Bastrop County. State 95, 21. One of the 23 original counties of the Republic, named for Felipe Enrique Neri, Baron de Bastrop, who settled here in 1829. The town on the Old San Antonio Road was often raided by Indians and all but abandoned in the mid-1830s. The town has many historic homes and buildings. Geological formations in the area still yield interesting rocks. Bastrop Chamber of Commerce at Main and Paine Sts. has detailed information on sites.

Bastrop Advertiser, 1105 Main St., was established in 1853.

Bastrop Museum, 702 Main St. Restored 1850 house has frontier equipment, documents, furnishings.

E. Erhard & Sons Drug Store, 921 Main St. Oldest in Texas, it was established in 1847 and still owned by the same family. Among the products on display are: "Sweet Pea" perfume, "Mexican Mustang Liniment," "Cherokee Ointment" and "Bull's Sarsaparilla."

Lock's Drug, 1003 Main St. Another old drugstore with furnishings and equipment of an early doctor's office as well as drug items.

Memorial Medallion Trail is a marked route to many historic places in town, including antebellum homes. Map and interpretive folder from the Chamber of Commerce.

Wilbarger House, 1403 Main St., built on land settled by Joseph Pugh Wilbarger, who survived a scalping. Family furnishings.

Allen-Bell House, 1408 Church St., was built in 1855. A registered historic place.

BAY CITY, Matagorda County. State 60.

Matagorda County Museum, early maps, furnishings, paintings and frontier relics.

Hawley's Cemetery, on the banks of Tres Palacios Creek, has the grave of Abel Head "Shanghai" Pierce, cattle baron. In the days before fences, part of his enormous herd roamed to the coast and it was said that the Gulf of Mexico was Shanghai's drift fence. A statue of Pierce marks his burial site.

BEAUMONT, Jefferson County. State 124. Settled in the 1830s. French and Spanish fur traders established trade here.

Beaumont Art Museum, 1111 9th St. Archaeology exhibits, crafts, as well as art.

French Trading Post Museum, 2995 French Dr. Restored house used as trading post in the mid-19th century. J. J. French, merchant and tanner, came from New York in the 1830s. He operated a tannery and mills for corn and grain.

BELTON, Bell County. I–35, State 317. Established in 1850, first merchant used his wagon for a store; first saloon reportedly was a barrel of bourbon and a tin cup under a shade tree. A stop on the Chisholm Trail.

Old Sommers Mill, on Salado Creek,

ca. 6 miles S. of the I–35, State 317 interchange via FM 436 ca. 2 miles SE to junction with FM 1123, then 4 miles S. to mill, built in 1866, still in working order and has ground ca. 1 million bushels of corn.

BENJAMIN, Knox County. State 283.

Knox County Museum, in county courthouse, has barbed-wire collection and other frontier relics.

BIG BEND NATIONAL PARK, Brewster County. US 385. The Rio Grande makes a 90° bend S. of Marathon in the park. Headquarters at Panther Junction with exhibits in lobby. The park, which covers 708,-221 acres, is accessible from US 385, Texas 118, US 67 and FM 170. Park rangers present illustrated lectures, guided hikes and horseback trail rides. El Camino del Rio, scenic drive, is FM 170 which runs from W. edge of the park to Lajitas, Redford, Presidio and beyond and is a spectacular route, with mountains, canyons and the Rio Grande.

BIGFOOT, Frio County. FM 462.

Bigfoot Wallace Museum, Main St. Two-room log cabin and six-room school building house relics of early Texas; many items pertain to William Alexander "Bigfoot" Wallace. Wallace got his nickname because he had killed an Indian chief named Bigfoot. He had been captured in the Mexican War in the group which Gen. Santa Anna chose to execute by bean-selection. The prisoners drew beans from a jar; every tenth man must die. The one who got a black bean was thereby the tenth. Bigfoot drew twice and got a white bean each time. Yorkshireman Frank Collinson, who came to Texas in the 1870s to live a life in the saddle, met Bigfoot early in his adventures:

"Big-foot Wallace, who had a small horse ranch on Chacon Creek near the Atascosa County line, was usually on those big roundups, and the Dutch settlers said he made more noise than the balance of the roundup and scared the horses clear out of the country. When I met Big-Foot in 1873 he was wearing rawhide leggings made out of two calfskins, and was about sixty years of age. He lived alone in a picket shack and kept a Mexican helper who broke and branded horses. His mark was a seven on the left thigh. Big-Foot liked to talk, and he told the cowboys many of his experiences around the chuck wagon. I asked him if the things I had read about him in a book were true. He said most of the yarns were "just a pack of lies," especially the story about his having kicked a piano to pieces when visiting back in Virginia.

BOERNE, Kendall County. US 87.

Century Caverns, 11 miles NE off RM 474. From the Cretaceous geologic period more than 50 million years ago, large corridors and grottoes.

Cascade Caverns, 5 miles SE off US 87. Guided tours. A hermit once inhabited part of the caverns.

Old Kendall Inn, downtown plaza, stagecoach inn built in 1859, a recorded Texas landmark and a popular meeting place for frontiersmen.

Lee Headquarters, Main St. small native stone building once served as headquarters for Robert E. Lee.

BONHAM, Fannin County. US 82.

Sam Rayburn Library, W. Sam Rayburn Dr. (US 82), has Rayburn memorabilia and many historical items. The crystal chandelier in the library office hung in the White House from 1889 to 1907; fireplace and other furnishings are from Washington.

Bonham Statue, on courthouse lawn. Bronze of James Butler Bonham, messenger of the Alamo.

Old Fort Inglish Blockhouse, across from the Rayburn Library, built ca. 1836 for protection against the Indians.

Chamber of Commerce, 510 N. Main St., has information on local sites and happenings. John Wesley Hardin lived here as a boy. The Dalton gang were here and Quantrill is said to have shot up the courthouse. An old stage station is 8 miles away. Reed's old store and museum is 14 miles on St. 121. Brig. Gen. H. E. McCulloch was commanding officer of the Northern Military Sub-District of Texas during the Civil War with headquarters in Bonham. Whether or not he did any shooting in town, Quantrill did pass through in November 1863, after reporting to Lt. Gen. E. Kirby at Shreveport. When he stopped to see McCulloch, the general was in a hurry to get to dinner and Quantrill, reportedly, left town in a rage. Henry Eustace McCulloch was a brother of the more famous Ben who had been an Indian fighter and Texas Ranger and was killed at the Battle of Pea Ridge in March 1862.

Bailey Inglish Cemetery, E. 6th and Linn Sts., has interesting old headstones.

BORGER, Hutchinson County. State 136.

Alibates National Monument, in Lake Meredith Recreation Area, 9 miles W. and N. on State 136, FM 1319, then 1 mile N. of Sanford on FM 687. An area contains flint quarries used from 10,000 B.C. to 450 A.D. Bates Canyon Information Station is departure point for guided tours by park rangers daily in summer. The Texas Panhandle Pueblo Culture people who occupied the area ca. 1300 used limestone slabs for their buildings.

BRACKETVILLE, Kinney County. RM 674. Established as supply town for Fort Clark in 1852.

Fort Clark, established June 1852, on the right side of Moras Creek, was a part of the frontier defense system and helped guard the San Antonio–El Paso road. First called Fort Riley. The fort surrendered to the Confederate forces in March 1861. Regarrisoned after the war in 1866. Abandoned in 1946, now a housing development.

Alamo Village, 6 miles N. on RM 674. Set for John Wayne's film, *The Alamo,* it is one of the biggest and most authentic replicas in America. The Alamo was built by adobe craftsmen from Mexico; also a complete frontier village, used for movie-making in Texas. Stagecoach rides.

Seminole Indian Scout Cemetery, on county road ca. 3 miles S. of town. Scouts were descended from slaves stolen from Florida plantations by Seminoles.

Chamber of Commerce, Ann St. (RM 674) next to post office, has information on the many historic houses of the area. St. Mary Magdalene Catholic Church dates from 1878; Masonic Lodge, next to Courthouse, built ca. 1879, was the original courthouse.

BRADY, McCulloch County. US 87,-377. The town was settled in the mid-19th century on the Dodge Cattle Trail. The longest fenced cattle trail in the world once reached from a railhead here to Sonora. In Calf Creek,

14 miles SW, James and Rezin Bowie with a few others were besieged for eight days by more than 100 Tawakoni Indians. The Bowie brothers fought their way out of the trap, causing heavy losses to the Indians.

Camp San Saba Ruins, on San Saba River 11 miles S. off US 87, 377. Established on the river in 1862 for Frontier Regiment of the Texas Rangers, to protect settlers from Indians.

BRAZOSPORT, Brazoria County. State 36, 288. Freeport is now part of a composite which includes seven incorporated town and several villages, called Brazosport.

Brazosport Museum of Natural Science, 101 This Way in Lake Jackson. Fossils, minerals, archaeology and marine life exhibits.

BRENHAM,, Washington County. State 90.

Washington-on-the-Brazos State Park, 18 miles NE on State 90, then 1 mile E. on FM 1155. Site of the signing of the Texas Declaration of Independence in 71-acre park. *Independence Hall,* guided tours, slide show. *Anson Jones Home,* last president of the Republic of Texas lived here, original furnishings; doctor's office. *Star of the Republic of Texas Museum,* local historical exhibits, slide show. Observation deck. Extensive restorations have been made. A new star-shaped museum has excellent exhibits in special showcases. Pioneer homes, shops and stores along original streets will be an added attraction when the work is completed.

BROWNSVILLE, Cameron County, US 77,83.

Fort Brown, S. end of Elizabeth Street, downtown. Named for Maj. Jacob Brown, who was fatally wounded defending the post from the Mexicans. Established March 1846, by Col. Zachary Taylor, 6th U.S. Infantry just before the Mexican War. First called Fort Taylor. Brownsville Barracks established next to the fort in 1848. In February 1859, the garrison was transferred to Fort Duncan; but brought back when trouble flared up along the border. Union troops left in March 1861. Confederates left in November 1863, when the post was burned by order of Brig. Gen. Hamilton Bee, C.S.A. The town was occupied by Federal forces on November 7, 1863; retaken by the South on July 30, 1864 and held till war's end. After peace came the Union rebuilt the post. A college and community center use the buildings now. The site is a national historic landmark.

Resaca de la Palma, Parades Line Rd. N. end of town, site of battle in Mexican War on May 9, 1846. Gen. Zachary Taylor faced a superior Mexican force at Palo Alto and drove the Mexicans back in the first major encounter of the war on May 8; the following day in the Battle of Resaca de la Palma, a cavalry charged with infantry flank movements sent the Mexicans in a route across the river. Among the merchants and settlers to arrive in the vicinity of the fort were two steamboat captains, Mifflin Kenedy and Richard King, who formed the vast King Ranch ca. 1860. The battlefield is a national historic landmark. Palo Alto marker near intersection of FM 1847, 511, for battle of May 8. Palo Alto is also a national historical landmark, but on pastureland in use, not accessible to the public at present.

Stillman House Museum, 1305 Washington St., built ca. 1850, home of Charles Stillman, founder of Brownsville. Original furnishings, relics.

Palmito Hill Battlefield, 12 miles E. on State 4. Historical marker for the last land engagement of the Civil War. Col. John "Rip" Ford's command—he may not have heard the bad news of Lee's surrender (a point still disputed)—routed a Federal force in a running encounter on May 12, and May 13, 1865. The many reports of the last conflict varied even as to who was in command and how many were lost by each side. The Union men claimed they had word of the surrender more than a month earlier and had come upon the mainland expecting Confederate capitulation. Ford's men said the Federals had come looking for trouble and had found it.

BRYAN-COLLEGE STATION, Brazos County. State 6. In the area where Stephen Austin's colonists settled between 1821–31. El Camino Real passes just N. of town; laid out in 1691. Many fine old homes and plantation houses still standing.

The Ruth Heines Clark Memorial Museum, 102 S. Main St. Texas historical material.

Texas A&M University, at College Station, has campus tours. A large gun collection is on display.

BUFFALO GAP, Taylor County. FM 89. Located at a pass in the Callahan Divide through which buffalo traveled for centuries; a point on the Dodge (sometimes called Western) Cattle Trail.

Ernie Wilson Museum, in old Buffalo Gap jail and courthouse, is the oldest building in town, has a variety of artifacts, old branding irons, churns, etc.

BURKBURNETT, Wichita County. State 240. Once a community on 6666 Ranch property, called Nesterville by the cowboys. Theodore Roosevelt hunted here early in the 1900s.

The Gun Shop, State 240, Main St., has antique weapons and Indian relics with a large collection of arrowheads.

BURNET, Burnet County. State 29. US 281.

Fort Croghan, State 29 W., restored powder house, stone and log buildings, with relics of local frontier days. Moved from original site. The fort was established in March 1849, on the right bank of Hamilton Creek and formed part of the frontier defense system. Originally called "Post on Hamilton Creek," designated in 1850; abandoned in 1853.

Pioneer Museum, on US 281 near downtown, Indian and frontier relics. Mineral and geological displays.

Longhorn Cavern State Park, ca. 11 miles SW on US 281, PR 4. Third largest cavern in the world. Used by Confederates for making gunpowder secretly, then an outlaw hideout. Trails and museum.

CALDWELL, Burleson County. State 21, 36. Named for Mathew "Old Paint" Caldwell, Indian fighter and a signer of the Texas Declaration of Independence. In the 1880s a rendezvous point for emigrants headed west on the Old San Antonio Rd.

Burleson County Historical Museum, in courthouse, has pioneer items and exhibits pertaining to Fort Tenoxtitlan.

Fort Tenoxtitlan, established in the autumn of 1830, on the Brazos River near where the San Antonio–Nacogdoches road crossed. The post was to block illegal entry from the U.S. Plans have been made for restoration; historians are trying to locate the exact site near where the Damn (sic) Creek flows into the Brazos. Lt. Col. José Ruiz (also known as Francisco Ruiz) on orders from Gen. Manuel de Mier y Teran set up the post. An earlier Mexican government had given Sterling Robertson and his colonists a settlement contract; some of these settlers were at the fortsite. Ruiz wrote to Mexico City for instructions and was told to drive the Anglos out. By the time the message came, he had become friendly with the settlers and therefore he wrote back to headquarters that most had never arrived, and those who had arrived were scattered and his horses were in no shape to go searching for them. Ruiz and his troops went back to San Antonio where he later became aligned with the Anglos and was a signer of the Declaration of Independence. Inquire locally for directions.

CALVERT, Robertson County. State 6.

Hammond House, Burnet, Elm, China and Hanna Sts. Built ca. 1879 was built to be the courthouse but never used as such. In 1885 Banker Robert A. Brown converted this building and the adjacent jail into a home. Now a museum.

Cobb's Market, 517 Main St., built ca. 1868. Historic medallion at site.

Church of Epiphany, Gregg and Elm, in use since the early 1870s.

1st Presbyterian Church, 401 N. Barton Ave., built before the Civil War with materials from Calvert Plantation, except for the leaded-glass windows. Moved here in 1868.

Virginia Field Park was the site of a "prison" during the Reconstruction period. A jail was built atop a tall pole and held rebels. A large oldtime gazebo in park.

CAMP VERDE, Kerr County. County 689. The campsite was ca. 2 miles N. of town. One of the frontier chain, the post was established in 1856 and was headquarters for the famous camel corps experiment. Edward F. Beale, Superintendent of Indian Affairs, persuaded Secretary of War Jefferson Davis to test camels for desert transportation. Congress appropriated $30,000 in 1855 to try the animals. More than 70 arrived on Navy ships at Indianola, Texas, in 1856–57 and were herded here. In 1857 Beale led an expedition across the Southwest using about 25 camels. Lt. Col. Robert E. Lee was in charge of testing the animals here. Site is marked.

CANYON, Randall County. US 87.

Panhandle-Plains Historical Museum, 2401 4th Ave. on campus of West Texas State University. As the brochure states, the door "swings open into two hundred million years of the past." An excellent collection of cattle-industry relics, firearms, Texas artists, period rooms, etc.

Six-Gun Territory, 11 miles E. on State 217. Replica frontier town.

Palo Duro Canyon State Park, on the High Plains, covers 15,103 acres. Ca. 12 miles E. of town via State 217 and PR 5. Within park is a historical marker for the last great Indian battle in 1874 when troops of the 4th Cavalry under Col. Ranald S. Mackenzie surprised a Comanche camp. Mackenzie burned the village and slaughtered many of the horses. The surviving Comanches returned to Oklahoma. The part of the canyon formed by the Prairie Dog Town Fork of the Red River is in the park. The battlesite is down the canyon, accessible by foot only. A trail leads to an overlook on the S. rim at a point ca. 10 miles NW of Wayside. The trail used by Mackenzie leads from here into the canyon.

J A Ranch, Palo Duro Canyon, was developed by Charles Goodnight, pioneer cattleman of the Staked Plains. He was the first rancher in the Texas Panhandle and blazed several important trails. He managed the J A Ranch from 1879 to 1889; it grew to cover 700,000 acres of grassland. Some original buildings remain. A national historic landmark.

T-Anchor Ranch, on US 87, just N. of town. The second ranch in the Panhandle; established in 1877 by Leigh Dyer, brother-in-law of Charles Goodnight. Dyer used timber from Palo Duro Canyon for his log cabin, now maintained by the Panhandle–Plains Historical Society.

CARTHAGE, Panola County. US 59.

Frontier Jail Museum has original cell blocks and frontier items, firearms collection.

Chamber of Commerce, 316 W. Panola, has information on other local sites. The town was a stop on the Wells-Fargo line. Darnell's old sawmill is still standing and there are a number of scenic trails.

CASTROVILLE, Medina County, US 90.

Castroville Historic District: Count Henri de Castro brought Alsatian colonists in 1844 and it has the appearance of a Rhineland village. There are 96 buildings in the district, all constructed between 1844 and the 1880s. Castro, born in France, brought 27 boatloads of colonists to Texas. By 1847 there were 700 residents here.

Landmark Inn (Vance Hotel), US 90 and Florence St., once a stagecoach stop, a recorded Texas historic landmark, still has guests. Small museum.

St. Louis Catholic Church, called the "new church," was built in 1869 replacing chapel which is still on grounds. The chapel was the first community project of the pioneers.

Carle Store and Residence, Angelo and Madrid, was built ca. 1850.

CENTER, Shelby County. State 87.

Shelby County Museum, Shelbyville and Riggs Sts. Indian, farm, pioneer items. Period costumes, documents, coins, etc.

Shelby County Courthouse, Irish castle in style, was built in 1885. The Regulator–Moderator Feud of 1839–44 caused a small war in town with scores of victims. Many persons were hanged on the streets of nearby Shelbyville.

Chamber of Commerce, John C. Rogers Bldg., has information on local historic sites, scenic drives of area.

Sabine National Forest, nearest entrance 11 miles SE via State 87. On the Sabine River, the forest covers 183,840 acres. Headquarters in Lufkin.

CENTERVILLE, Leon County. US 75, State 7.

Leon County Courthouse was built in 1886–87 after the 1885 building had burned. It is one of the oldest in Texas; constructed of handmade slate bricks.

CHANNING, Hartley County. US 385.

XIT Ranch, in Hartley and Deaf Smith Counties; sites at Channing and Escarbada, the largest of the pioneer ranches in the Panhandle had headquarters here. The ranch consisted of seven divisions, ran 110,721 head of cattle. In 1887 the company owning it set up a branch in Montana. The headquarters has been greatly altered, now used as a private residence; the 1890s division headquarters at Escarbada still stands on the Reinaur Brothers Ranch. At one time the operation covered more than 3 million acres all fenced.

CHAPPELL HILL, Washington County. FM 1155.

Chappell Hill Historical Museum, site of former Female College, has pioneer utensils, furnishings and memorabilia. Many old homes in area, some restored. Restored Stagecoach Inn, just N. of business section.

Scher's Shoppe, Main St., is in the old Reinstein General Store with old fixtures and some original contents.

CHILDRESS, Childress County. US 287. Named for George Campbell Childress, author of the Texas Declaration of Independence.

Childress City Park. Historical marker for the Goodnight Cattle Trail. The town is on land once part of the OX Ranch. Jesse James was a visitor in outlaw days, legend says.

Schultz Hotel, corner of Ave. A and Commerce St., a longtime landmark and popular stopping place. An old rock building near the railroad station on Main St. was formerly the Ocean Wave Saloon.

CLARENDON, Donley County. State 70. Original townsite now covered by Greenbelt Lake was a temperance colony in 1878 founded by Lewis H. Carhart, a Methodist teetotaler. The cowboys called it "Saint's Roost." It was on the stageline to Dodge City, no saint's stopover. Old cemetery relocated on State 70, S. of new townsite, with graves of pioneers, old fencing and buildings. Stocking's Drug Store, established in 1885, claims to be the oldest in the Panhandle.

CLARKSVILLE, Red River County. US 82. Older than the Republic of Texas, founded in 1834 by Capt. James Clark, was the settlement first reached by emigrants coming into Texas at the Jonesboro Crossing. One of these was Sam Houston on December 2, 1832. Monument at site.

Red River County Courthouse, completed in 1885, had a clock tower with timepiece that ran without error from 1885 to 1961, when it was converted to electrical power. Then "Old Red" began striking—120 gongs until someone unplugged it. The tower flies the county's own flag.

Col. Charles DeMorse Home, 1 block N. of square, DeMorse was known as the "Father of Texas Journalism," founded *The Northern Standard* and took part in the Civil War.

Chamber of Commerce, 101 N. Locust, has up-to-date information on which of the several old homes may be visited. The McKenzie House is on the site of McKenzie College established in 1841. First Presbyterian Church was organized in 1833. There are many fine cotton plantations and ranches along the Red River.

CLEBURNE, Johnson County. US 67. Settled ca. 1854, the town was first known as Camp Henderson, renamed in 1867 to honor Confederate Gen. Pat Cleburne, called the "Stonewall Jackson of the West," killed at the Battle of Franklin, Tennessee, in November, 1864.

Cleburne State Park, 14 miles SW on US 67, has a wildlife refuge.

Layland's Museum, 201 N. Caddo,

Indian artifacts and regional relics.

Little Old House, 409 N. Buffalo, oldest house in town, restored, with period furnishings.

CLIFTON, Bosque County. FM 219, 182.

Basque Memorial Museum, South Ave. Q and W. 9th. Texas mineral and fossil collections, guns, coins, sailing ships, pioneer artifacts.

Norse Settlement, W. via FM 219 W. and FM 182 N. Pioneers came from Norway to this part of Texas in the 1850s. Cleng Peerson, early leader, is buried in the churchyard of Our Savior's Lutheran Church.

COLDSPRING, San Jacinto County. FM 2025. Called Coonskin in 1847, then Firemen's Hill.

Sam Houston National Forest, W. of town, covers 158,200 acres. Headquarters in Lufkin.

San Jacinto County Museum, in county courthouse, among relics are items from the family of Governor George T. Wood. Sam Houston met on nearby Council Hill to persuade his friends of the Alabama–Coushatta tribes to remain neutral during the Texas War of Independence. Museum has early documents of regional history.

COLEMAN, Coleman County. US 283.

Coleman City Park, on Hords Creek at US 283 N. Pioneer blacksmith shop, prairie-dog town, and County Museum, with pioneer relics. A horse statue brought to Coleman in 1884 to display saddles is larger than life.

COLORADO CITY, Mitchell County. US 80. In 1877 a Texas Ranger camp on present townsite was known as the Anglo-American settlement. It was soon a lively frontier supply town.

Colorado City Historical Museum, 3rd and Walnut Sts., off US 80. Relics include buffalo tracks from Seven Wells, frontier ranch house and equipment, horse-drawn hearse, many early photos.

COLUMBUS, Colorado County. US 90. State 71. Located on site of an Indian village called Montezuma, settled in 1823 by the Stephen F. Austin colonists.

Columbus Oak, Walnut and Travis Sts. The first court of the Third Judicial District of the Republic of Texas convened under this tree in 1837. Presiding Judge Robert McAlpon was known as "Three-Legged Willie." Tree is more than 2,000 years old.

Confederate Memorial Hall Museum, in old water tower built in 1883, has county histories and other historical relics. Attempts to demolish the 3-foot thick brick walls by dynamite luckily proved useless; they contain more than 400,000 bricks and thus far have been dynamite-resistant.

Koliba Home Museum, 1124 Front St. Period furnishings in century-old house, adjoining blacksmith shop and child's house.

Historic Homes: A Magnolia Homes tour is held each May for the several outstanding early structures which include the Stafford Opera House and Carriage House as well as private residences.

COMANCHE, Comanche County. State 36, 16. Established in 1858 but slow in growth because of many severe Indian raids.

Burks Museum, N. edge of town on State 16. Unusual variety of relics including outlaw memorabilia, Indian artifacts, county's first courthouse built in 1856 of hand-hewn logs.

COMFORT, Kendall County. US 87. German settlers coming from New Braunfels in 1854 were so pleased with the locale they named it Camp Comfort.

Comfort Historical Museum, 838 High St. Regional memorabilia.

Civil War Monument, on high school campus, is of unusual interest because it is in honor of Unionists, deep in the heart of Texas. The predominantly German residents were pro-Union. A group of Unionists led by Fritz Tegener planned to leave the area and go to Mexico. They were attacked by mounted Confederate soldiers on the W. bank of the Nueces River ca. 20 miles from Fort Clark. Nineteen settlers were killed and nine wounded. Confederates lost two. The nine wounded were executed shortly after the battle.

COMSTOCK, Val Verde County. State 163.

Camp Hudson, ca. 20 miles N. of town, on State 163. Established in 1857 in the wild Devil's River region of west Texas, the post guarded the lower San Antonio–El Paso Road. Its troops took part in the camel experiment by accompanying a caravan on a 75-day patrol in 1859. The Federals departed at the outbreak of the Civil War and were replaced by the Texas Mounted Rifles. The U.S. came back after the war. State marker and a small gravestone are the only memorials in a rocky field, at present. The lively and growing CAMP (Council on Abandoned Military Camps) has an interested membership which is preserving and restoring as many historic sites as can be managed. This may well be one of those to be saved with authentic locations and markings.

Seminole Canyon Archeological District, 7 miles W., S. of US 90. The canyon is a 6-mile tributary of the Rio Grande in the center of what is believed to be one of the richest pictograph areas in the world. Thousands of years of human habitation are represented by cave paintings and debris. Three of the most remarkable sites are Coontail Spin Site, Fate Bell Shelter and Panther Cave. Pre-Columbian deposits have been found. A registered historic place not open to the public at present.

COOPER, Delta County. State 24.

Delta County Library and Museum, 700 W. Dallas St. In restored Texas Midland Passenger Station, old furnishings, tools, etc.

CORPUS CHRISTI, Nueces County. State 44, 35. Bay was discovered in 1519 and named by Alonzo Alvarez de Pineda of Spain. Frontier trading post founded in 1838 by Col. Henry Lawrence Kinney.

Centennial House, 411 N. Broadway, built in 1849, restored, with period furnishings.

Corpus Christi Museum, 1919 N. Water St., Gulf Coast shells, artifacts, weapons and memorabilia. Hall of Man, Hall of Natural History, Hall of Earth Sciences.

Chamber of Commerce, 1201 N. Shoreline Blvd., information on industrial tours, other points of interest.

Padre Island National Seashore, John F. Kennedy Causeway, the 110-mile island is the longest in the U.S. National Park Service pavilion at N. end has a recreation building. Unspoiled seashores are exceedingly rare. Arrowheads are still found here.

CORSICANA, Navarro County. State 22, 31. The Kickapoo Indians massacred 17 surveyors here in 1836.

Pioneer Village, at City Park, Indian trading post, store, split rail fence, covered wagon, relics.

Methodist Church was the place where the First Texas legislature met free of carpetbagger rule in Reconstruction days.

Love Bridge, Pisgah Ridge Indian Trail, old stagecoach crossing.

Corsicana Sun Office, downtown, has old photograph display.

CRESSON, Hood County. US 377.

H. S. Smith Collection, outdoor museum of steam tractors and steam threshing machines, other farm relics.

Pate Museum of Transportation, 3.5 miles NE on US 377. Old railroad car, stagecoaches, wagons, saddles.

CROCKETT, Houston County. State 19, 21. On El Camino Real.

St. Francis of Assisi Catholic Church, formerly San Francisco de los Tejas, is a replica of the original permanent mission of this name established among the Tejas Indians in 1690.

Mission State Park, 20 miles E. of town, has a replica of the log cabin mission, founded 1690 by Spanish priests.

Davy Crockett Memorial Park, end of S. 5th St. Col. Crockett stopped here to camp on his way to the Alamo according to local legend.

Davy Crockett Spring, memorial plaque at water fountain, where Col. Crockett and men camped. W. Goliad at underpass, intersection of State 21, 7.

CROSBYTOWN, Crosby County. US 82.

Pioneer Memorial Museum, 101 W. Main, in a replica of Hank Smith Rock House, the first home in the county. Indian and pioneer artifacts. Early agricultural equipment in barn across the street.

CROWELL, Foard County. US 70.

Pease River Battlefield, a few miles past Margaret on FM 98. Historical marker at site where Cynthia Ann Parker was "rescued" after a skirmish between Rangers under Capt. L. S. Ross and a band of Comanches under Peta Nocona. Nocona was killed and his white wife, Cynthia Ann who had been captured in 1836 was returned to the white community with a daughter, Prairie Flower. Her son, Quanah became a war chief.

CUERO, De Witt County. US 87, 183.

De Witt County Historical Museum, 207 E. Main, Indian relics include scalps. Civil War exhibit has no Yankee scalps.

De Witt County Courthouse, N. Gonzales, E. Live Oak Sts. Built in 1896, a registered historic place.

St. Mark's Lutheran Church, built in Spanish mission-style. One of its three church bells once hung in a now vanished seaport of Indianola, Texas. The bell was stolen by Union soldiers, retrieved by Confederates and buried in the sands of Matagorda Bay for a quarter of a century.

DALHART, Dallam and Hartley Counties. US 54, 385. First called Twist.

XIT City Museum, 2 miles S. on Main Lake Rd. in Rita Blanca Lake Park. Wagons, ranch relics, etc.

XIT Ranch, site was given to a Chicago corporation (3,050,000 acres) for construction of the state capitol. (Also see Channing.)

DALLAS, Dallas County. I–30.

State Fair Park, 2 miles E. via I–30, I–20, or State 352. On grounds are:

Age of Steam Railroad Museum, steam railroad equipment.

Texas Hall of State, murals, dioramas, etc. Changing exhibits.

Dallas Museum of Fine Arts, pre-Columbian and American art among the many exhibits.

Dallas Museum of Natural History. Habitat groups of Southwestern animals, birds, plants, geological displays.

Dallas Heritage Center, Old City Park, Gano and St. Paul Sts. Early Dallas history with buildings, special exhibits, railroad depot, Millermore Museum and Log Cabin. Mansion from 1855; log cabin built in 1847.

Bryan Cabin, in Dallas County Historical Plaza, Main and Market, original home of John Neely Bryan, first settler, 1841.

DECATUR, Wise County. US 81, 287. First called Bishop, then Taylorsville. On the Butterfield Overland Mail route. Site of the trial and hanging of five Peace Party conspirators in 1862.

Wise County Courthouse, built in 1895 of pink limestone from Burnet.

Old Stone Prison, 103 E. Pecan St. Built by prison labor, now a museum with turn-of-the-century furnishings.

Administration Building, Decatur Baptist College, 1602 S. Trinity St. Built in 1892, a registered historic place.

DEL RIO, Val Verde County. US 90.

Whitehead Memorial Museum, 1308 S. Main St. Mementos of early days; replica of Judge Roy Bean's Jersey Lily Saloon. Judge Bean and his son are buried on museum grounds.

DENISON, Grayson County. US 69, 75. A stop on the Butterfield stage line.

Eisenhower Birthplace State Historic Site, 208 E. Day St. House restored to its appearance in 1890 when President Dwight Eisenhower was born here.

Hagerman National Wildlife Refuge, on upper end of Big Mineral Arm of Lake Texoma. 11,300 acres.

Thompson House Museum, E. Main St., just E. of city limits, earliest existing house in town. Restored and moved to this location.

State Tourist Bureau, 4 miles N. on US 75, 69. Maps, literature, free advice.

DENTON, Denton County. State 24.

North Texas State University, W. Mulberry and Avenue A., has the State Historical Collection on campus with displays of early firearms and other relics, archives, musical instruments.

Texas Woman's University, 1103 Bell Ave., has a D.A.R. museum with gowns of First Ladies and other displays. Also on campus at 1 Pioneer Woman's Circle is an art gallery with Indian wood carvings among displays.

DICKENS, Dickens County. US 82.

Dickens County Museum, in county courthouse, pictures, antiques, family histories.

EAGLE PASS, Maverick County. US 277.

Fort Duncan Park, entrance on Adams or Monroe Sts. Ten restored buildings of the 1849 fort. The post was located on the Rio Grande, evacuated by Union troops in March 1861, garrisoned for part of the Civil War by the Confederates. Reoccupied by the U.S. in 1868. Another post; known as Camp at Eagle Pass, was on the same site from 1886 to 1927.

EDINBURG, Hidalgo County. US 281.

Hidalgo County Museum, 121 E. McIntyre, pioneer relics, photos, etc. Housed in restored county jail.

EDNA, Jackson County. US 59. As commissary for Italian laborers on the New York, Texas, and Mexican Railway, the town was called Macaroni Station.

Texana Museum, in county courthouse, early life of the area in artifacts, documents, etc.

EGYPT, Wharton County. FM 102. Founded ca. 1830.

Northington-Heard Memorial Museum has weapons, furnishings, documents of early days in the area.

EL CAMPO, Wharton County. US 59. Called Prairie Switch in the 1880s.

El Campo Museum, Monsarette at Farenthold St. Pioneer toys, dolls, housewares, tools, displays changed quarterly.

EL PASO, El Paso County. I–10. Cabeza de Vaca was here in 1536. Juan de Onate named the settlement El Paso del Norte in 1598.

Chamber of Commerce, 820 N. Mesa St., is worth a visit for information on the many sites of interest on both sides of the border.

Sierra de Cristo Rey, the Mountain of Christ the King, has a 4-mile foot trail to the summit, begins near US 85.

Old Missions: The Lower Valley area is the site of several early missions; map at Chamber of Commerce. Among these are Nuestra Señora del Carmen, established as Corpus Christi de la Isleta, 1681, restored; Nuestra Señora de la Concepcion del Socorro; San Elizario Presidio Chapel.

Fort Bliss, E. of US 54, between Fred Wilson Rd. and Montana Ave. (US 62, 180). Established in 1849, the post occupied six separate locations. It was called Post of El Paso and Post at Smith's Ranch, at Smith's Ranch in 1849, 1851; Fort Bliss at Magoffinsville, 1854, 1868, including the time of the Confederate occupation in 1861, 1862; Camp Concordia and Fort Bliss, at Concordia Ranch, 1868, 1877; and Fort Bliss, at Hart's Mill and the present location. Fort Bliss is now an adobe replica of the Magonffinsville fort, donated by the El Paso Chamber of Commerce, which serves as a chapel and museum. The old brick mess hall has been remodeled. There are 14 sets of officers' quarters still in use and two original barracks buildings house offices. The four adobe museum buildings contain cavalry, infantry and artillery historical items.

Centennial Museum, on campus of University of Texas at El Paso, University Ave. and Wiggins Rd. Historical, geological and archaeological exhibits.

Cavalry Museum, 12901 Gateway Blvd., 10 miles SE off I–10. Exhibits from the time of the conquistadors to Pancho Villa.

Chamizal National Monument, entrance from Delta Dr., near Cordova Bridge. The 55-acre area commemorates the peaceful settlement of the 1860s boundary dispute. Museum.

El Paso Museum of Art, 1211 Montana Ave. Western, American and pre-Columbian art among exhibits.

El Paso County Historical Society, 515

N. Oregon St. in El Paso Library, has guided tours.

Ysleta, I–10 E., the oldest community within the present boundaries of Texas was established by refugees of Spanish settlers and loyal Indians who were fleeing from the Indian revolt of the late 17th century. Ysleta del Sur was founded in 1681. Museum in the Tigua Community Bldg., Ysleta Mission, 119 Old Pueblo Rd.

Aerial Tramway, N. on Alabama St., W. on McKinley Ave. Goes to Ranger Peak (5,620 ft.). Observation deck.

FAIRFIELD, Freestone County. US 75, 84.

Bradley House Museum, Coleman St., off N. Bateman Rd., antebellum house with period furnishings.

Freestone County Museum, 302 E. Main St., in old jail has period furniture, artifacts, historic documents. John Wesley Hardin said to have been imprisoned here.

Stewards Mill Country Store, 7 miles N., US 75 and FM 833, more than a century-old store and landmark, still operated by family of founder. Pioneer relics.

FALFURRIAS, Brooks County. US 281. The name is Spanish, meaning "Heart's Delight," a local wildflower.

Texas Ranger Museum, adjacent to Chamber of Commerce, has memorabilia of the Rangers and other pioneer artifacts.

FANNIN, Goliad County. US 59, 183.

Fannin Battleground State Historic Site, 1 mile S. on PR 27, where Col James W. Fannin, Jr. and his men surrendered to the Mexican Army after the Battle of Coleto Creek, March 20, 1836. Gen. Antonio López de Santa Anna ordered the Texans massacred at Goliad the next week.

FORT CHADBOURNE, Coke County. US 277. The fort is just off the highway, ca. 2½ miles N. of its junction with State 70, some 4 miles NE of the town of Fort Chadbourne. Established in October 1852, on the E. side of Oak Creek ca. 3 miles above its junction with the Colorado River, to protect the emigrant route from Fort Smith, Arkansas, to Santa Fe. named for 2nd Lt. Theodore Chadbourne, killed in May 1846, in the Battle of Resaca de la Palma. Surrendered to the Confederate troops in March 1861. Reoccupied by the U.S. in 1867 but abandoned before the year was out because of poor water supply. Now on private property. Historical marker indicates the ruins.

FORT DAVIS, Jeff Davis County. State 17.

Fort Davis National Historic Site, just outside of town. Established in October 1854, at the mouth of a canyon ca. ½ mile S. of Limpia Creek in the Limpia (Davis) Mountains, to protect the El Paso–San Antonio Rd. and to control Indians, particularly the Apaches and Comanches. The post was among the most active in the Indian wars, especially in the 1879–80 campaign against Victorio of the Apaches. It is considered the most extensive and impressive existing example of frontier forts. Museum in reconstructed barracks. Dioramas and films. Audio program of Retreat Parade.

Neill Museum, in Truehart House, 7 blocks W. of county courthouse, has early Texas toys and other exhibits.

FORT McKAVETT STATE HISTORIC SITE, Menard County. FM

1674. Established in 1852 on a bluff overlooking the San Saba River, part of the frontier system to guard the settlements and routes. A major restoration program is underway. First called Camp San Saba, then named for Capt. Henry McKavett, killed at the Battle of Monterrey in the Mexican War. Abandoned during the Civil War, reoccupied by Col. Ranald S. Mackenzie in 1868.

FORT STOCKTON, Pecos County. US 290. The town grew up around the military post established at Comanche Springs in 1859 at a site which long had been a watering place for travelers on the California Trail and the San Antonio–San Diego line.

Old Fort Stockton, 4 blocks off US 290 at Rooney St. between 2nd and 5th, State marker on the courthouse grounds borders James Rooney Park, surrounding Comanche Springs. The Chamber of Commerce has marked the fort buildings and a number of other historical buildings in town.

Old Fort Cemetery at the post has interesting headstones. Few graves are those of persons over 40.

Riggs Hotel, now a museum, was built in 1899.

Courthouse Square: courthouse was built in 1883, Catholic church, 1875, schoolhouse, 1883, Zero Stone laid by survey party in 1859. Nearby St. Stephens Church, 1872, First protestant church W. of the Pecos.

Dinosaur Park, adjacent to Highway Department rest, 22 miles NE on US 67,385. Historical marker. Preserved footprints of prehistoric animals.

Grey Mule Saloon, Callaghan and Main Sts., restored early day saloon.

Tunis Creek Stagecoach Stop, former way station on Butterfield line, moved to Texas Highway Department Roadside park, US 290, 20 miles E. Originally ca. 2 miles S.

FORT WORTH, Tarrant County. US 80, 377. The town grew from a military camp established by Gen. Winfield Scott at the close of the Mexican War, named for Gen. William Jenkins Worth, who was in the war. Fort Worth to Yuma stage line established in 1850.

Amon G. Carter Museum of Western Art, Camp Bowie Blvd. One of the finest collections in the world; permanent collections of Frederic Remington and Charles Russell.

Fort Worth Art Center, 1309 Montgomery, paintings and sculpture of the Southwest.

Fort Worth Museum of Science and History, 1501 Montgomery. Many historical exhibits designed especially for youth.

Fort Worth Nature Center and Refuge, 9 miles NW on State 199, 2 miles past Lake Worth bridge. Refuge of 3,300 acres with interpretive center, observation tower, self-guided trails. (Also called Greer Island Nature Center.)

Log Cabin Village, University Dr. and Colonial Pkwy. in Forest Park. Seven authentic pioneer homes from the 1850s, tools, furnishings, etc.

Santa Fe Railroad Station, 1601 Jones St., built in 1899, a registered historic place.

Tarrant County Courthouse, bounded by Houston, Elknap, Weatherford and Commerce, the third courthouse, of red Texas granite, built in 1895. A registered historic place.

Stockyards Area, along Exchange Ave. on city's N., has Western-style stores and restaurants and traditional boardwalks.

Natural History Museum, in campus of Texas Christian University, at 2900

S. University Dr. Texas reptiles and geological specimens, fossils, etc.

FRANKLIN, Robertson County. FM 2446.

Walter Williams Grave, in Mt. Pleasant, a rural church cemetery a few miles SE of town. Less than 4 miles on FM 2446. Confederate Walter Williams was the last veteran of the Civil War.

FREDERICKSBURG, Gillespie County. US 87. Settled on the Indian frontier in 1846 by German families from New Braunfels; in 1847 the Meusebach–Comanche Treaty made lasting peace.

Old Gillespie County Courthouse, built in 1882, restored, now library and community hall. Library has a German Room.

Pioneer Museum, 309 W. Main, settler relics, furnishings, tools, weapons. *Lange's Mill,* ca. 22 miles NW via US 87, RM 648.

Nimitz Hotel, Main St. at N. Washington, built in 1847 has had such guests as Rutherford B. Hayes, Robert E. Lee and Philip Sheridan. Now a naval museum honoring founder's grandson, Adm. Chester W. Nimitz.

Enchanted Rock, ca. 20 miles N. off RM 965, known in Indian legend for centuries and possible site of human sacrifices. Covers ca. 640 acres and is 500 feet high.

Vereins Kirche, W. Main St., octagonal first public building now houses Chamber of Commerce. Ask here about "Sunday houses"—small country houses of the area used by the first settlers. Marked with historic medallions.

FREEPORT, Brazoria County. State 288,332. Quintana, the oldest port in Texas, where Stephen Austin landed the first colonists in 1822, was on a tidal part of the Brazos River at edge of today's city. Velasco, an historic town, is within city limits. The treaty of peace between Texas and Mexico was signed in Velasco on May 14, 1836, after the Texan victory at the Battle of San Jacinto. Velasco was temporary capital of the republic. Chamber of Commerce, 420 Texas Highway 332 W. has details on old sites. The *Acadia,* wreck of a Confederate blockade runner is in shallow water off Surfside Beach, part of it may be seen at low tide. It ran aground on the night of February 6, 1865.

GAIL, Borden County. FM 669.

Borden County Historical Museum has pioneer relics, furniture, records, newspapers. The town and county are named for Gail Borden, Texas patriot and editor, who invented condensed milk and founded the Borden Company. The town was a ranch supply point in 1891 and is the only town in the county. The courthouse is the only large building on main street.

GAINESVILLE, Cooke County. I–35. Originally on the California trail, periodically raided by Indians.

Morton Museum of Cooke County, 210 S. Dixon, many exhibits covering pioneer life, Indians and geology of the area. In restored firehouse.

Texas Tourist Bureau, ca. 1 mile N. on I–35. Maps, literature, help.

Chamber of Commerce, Culbertson at California St., has information on the many historic homes in town; some of which may be open in season. Most are on Church, Denton and Lindsay Sts. Episcopal Church, 1884, First Methodist Church, 1892, and Catholic Church in Lindsay, 4 miles W. are historic buildings of interest.

GALVESTON, Galveston County. I–45.

Bishop's Palace, 1402 Broadway, one of the most photographed houses in America, was the residence of Bishop Byrne in the 20th century and therefore doesn't belong in an Old West roundup, but it looks as if it should have been a cattle baron's mansion. Built in 1886, completed in 1893. Guided tours.

Powhatan House, 3427 Ave. O at 35th St. Built in 1847, now headquarters for the Galveston Garden Club, open to public at changing times. Inquire locally.

Ashton Villa, 2328 Broadway at 24th St., built in 1859, restored, with period furnishings. Carriage house on grounds has visitors' information for the city.

Treasure Island Tour Train Inc., Seawall Blvd. at 27th St. An open-car tour of major points of interest, including the ruins of Fort Crockett, historic homes, waterfront and business district.

Chamber of Commerce, 315 Tremont, has more information on local sites.

Rosenberg Library, 823 Tremont, has Texas artifacts, with many original manuscripts, including letters of Jean Lafitte, Sam Houston, Stephen Austin, etc.

Williams-Tucker House, 3601 Avenue P, built in 1837–40, period furnishings.

Historic Churches: First Lutheran, 2415 G St., 1868; First Presbyterian, 18th and Church St., 1873; St. Mary's Cathedral, 2011 F St., 1848; Trinity Episcopal, 2216 H St., 1857.

Karankawa Indian Museum, ca. 20 miles from city, near W. end of island at Jamaica Beach, a small area of Indian burial site now glass-covered with skeletons and artifacts from excavations in area.

Texas Heroes Monument, intersection of Broadway and Rosenberg Ave.

GATESVILLE, Coryell County, FM 107, 182.

Fort Gates, on left bank of the Leon River, ca. 6 miles SE of town, was established in October 1849, as part of the frontier defense system. Abandoned in 1852. No remains.

Coryell County Courthouse, built in 1872; log jail, 1855, now a restored museum, in Raby Park.

Buckhorn Museum has frontier relics, restored to look like old barroom.

GEORGETOWN, Williamson County. I–35. On old Chisholm Trail. Southwestern University established in 1840.

Inner Space Caverns, 1 mile S. of town on I–35. Remains of mastodons, wolves and Ice Age animals.

Tinnen House, 1220 Austin St., built in 1880 is a registered historic place, not open to the public at present.

GLEN ROSE, Somervell County. US 67. A trading post in 1849.

Dinosaur Valley State Park, on Paluxy River, ca. 5 miles W. via US 67. The first sauropod tracks in the world were found here. There is a 1,204-acre park with nature trails.

Somervell County Historical Museum, Abernathy Bldg., on square, local history, fossils.

GOLIAD, Goliad County. US 183. In December 1835, the first Declaration of Texas Independence was issued from here. An Aranama Indian village was here when the first Spanish explorers arrived. Spain established a mission in 1749 and a presidio. In March 1836, after the fall of the Alamo, Col. James Fannin and 350 men surrendered, having been pro-

Presidio La Bahia at Goliad (rebuilt); here 343 Texas soldiers died during the Texas Revolution
(Texas Tourist Development Agency)

mised they would be treated as prisoners of war. They were massacred.

Presidio Nuestra Senora de Loreta de la Bahia, 1 mile S. of Goliad State Park on US 183. The presidio was moved from the Guadalupe River to its present site in 1749 to protect the early missions. During the Texan Revolution, it was headquarters for the troops under Col. James Fannin, executed in March 1836, by orders of President Santa Anna. A national historic landmark. Chapel in which Fannin and his men were kept has been restored. Officers' quarters now a museum.

Goliad State Historic Park, 1 mile S. on US 183. Replica of Mission Espiritu Santo Zuniga, museum in mission.

Fannin Plaza, City Park at S. Market and Franklin Sts. Texas Revolution cannon, memorial shaft and historical markers. Old Market Museum, Chamber of Commerce where more information is available, and the old hanging tree are all in the area.

Grave of Col. James W. Fannin Jr. and Men, 2 miles S. of Goliad off US 183, near Presidio La Bahia.

Ruins of Mission Rosario, 4 miles W. near San Antonio River. Mission was founded in 1754 for the Karankawa, Cujane and Coapite Indians.

GONZALES, Gonzales County. US 183. The first battle of the Texas Revolution was fought here in October 1835.

Gonzales Memorial Museum, E. St. Lawrence St. Monument to those who fought in the first battle and the 32 patriots who answered Travis's call for help from the Alamo. Replica of the cannon which caused the first trouble. The Mexican government had left a small cannon here for defense against the Indians. When American settlers opted for independence, they kept the cannon; the Mexicans wanted it back. The Texans said: "Come and take it!"

Kennard House, 621 St. Louis St., built in 1895, a registered historic place.

Braches House, 12 miles SE on US 90 Alt., was built by Bart McClure, first county judge. Later owned by Texas Congressman Charles Braches. A registered historic place.

Eggleston House, near Memorial Museum, built in 1848. Restored with antique furnishings representing typical pioneer life.

Confederate Square and Texas Heroes Square in downtown. Battle of Gonzales markers near community of Cost, State 97. Confederate earthworks, near US 90A and US 183 intersection.

GRAND PRAIRIE, Dallas County. Dallas–Fort Worth Turnpike. Established at close of Civil War as Deckman. Renamed in 1873.

Southwestern Historical Wax Museum, Turnpike at Belt Line Rd. Geronimo and Billy the Kid mingle in wax with Sam Houston, Judge Roy Bean and several U.S. Presidents. Old firearms, barbed wire, Indian artifacts.

GROESBECK, Limestone County. State 14.

Old Fort Parker State Historical Site, 6 miles N. on State 14, has a replica of the fort from which Cynthia Ann Parker was stolen by Comanche and Kiowa Indians in May 1836. (See Mexia.)

Fort Parker Memorial Cemetery, 2 miles N. of town on FM 1245. Large monument and settlers' graves from the 1836 massacre.

Old Springfield, 5 miles N. on State 14, once the county seat and only town in county. Historical marker on highway near entrance to Fort Parker State Park. Old cemetery on park entrance road.

HAMILTON, Hamilton County. US 281. Settled in 1858, early residents were often raided by Indians. Anne Whitney, frontier schoolteacher, was killed by Comanches while trying to defend her students. Memorial on courthouse lawn.

Hamilton County Museum, in courthouse, has artifacts, newspapers, etc.

HARLINGEN, Cameron County. US 77.

Six Shooter Junction, 2705 S. F. St. 1 mile S. on US 77. Replica frontier village with rides, etc. The town of Harlingen was known as Six Shooter Junction in the early days because Texas Rangers were stationed here.

Laguna Atascosa National Wildlife Refuge, 27 miles E. on FM 106, covers 44,580 acres. Walk-in and drive-in routes for visitors.

Lower Rio Grande Valley Museum, at Harlingen Industrial Air Park, historical and scientific displays.

HASKELL, Haskell County. State 24. Once a campsite for Comanche, Kiowa and Kickapoo Indians and watering place for buffalo hunters and pioneers, known as Willow Springs, then as Rice Springs; renamed in 1885.

Haskell Railroad Museum, S. Avenue C., in old railroad depot, railroadiana.

HELENA, Karnes County. State 80. An unusual ghost town, with a population of 39, was "killed" by one gunfight too many. The village was founded ca. 1854 near the Chihuahua Trail and the Indianola–San Antonio Rd., named county seat, and achieved a population of 3,000. It was one of the many rooting-shooting frontier towns but one night during a saloon shoot-out a stray bullet killed Emmett Butler, 20-year-old son of rancher Col. William Butler, who vowed to kill the whole town when he couldn't find which outlaw had struck down his son. He persuaded the new railroad to bypass the town by offering free land elsewhere. Helena lost its status as county seat and then most of its citizens. A deserted courthouse, an old church and a few other ruins remain.

HEREFORD, Deaf Smith County. US 60, 385. Deaf Smith was a commander of scouts under Sam Houston at the Battle of San Jacinto.

Deaf Smith County Historical Museum, 400 Sampson St. Pioneer ranch and farm implements, weapons, Indian artifacts. Chamber of Commerce offers free tours of farms and ranches daily except Sunday.

HILLSBORO, Hill County. State 22.

Confederate Research Center, Gun Museum, on campus of Hill Junior College. Dioramas and displays on the Civil War, particularly Hood's Texas Brigade. Gun Museum has Confederate-edged weapons and other relics, changing exhibits.

Hill County Courthouse, built 1889, has provoked comment if not compliments for years. A registered historic place.

HONDO, Medina County. FM 462.

Medina County Museum, 2200 block on 18th St., artifacts in restored 1897 Southern Pacific depot.

HONEY GROVE, Fannin County. US 82. Founded in 1842 in a grove of bee trees.

Museum of Arts and Sciences: historical documents, relics of the area and paintings. Also on square, oldtime general store.

HOUSTON, Harris County. I–45.

Museum of Fine Arts, 1001 Bissonet, has pre-Columbian artifacts among the many exhibits.

Houston Museum of Natural Science, 5800 Caroline St. Archaeological, geological, wildlife and prehistoric exhibits.

Harris County Heritage Society Tours, 1100 Bagby St., in Sam Houston Historical Park. Tours through any of four restored homes built in the period of 1824–68; a late 19th-century church and reconstructed street called "Long Row" connecting shops and library. Orientation film.

San Jacinto Battleground, 6½ miles SE on Gulf Freeway (I–45), then 12 miles E. on State 225, 4 miles N. on State 134. Stone shaft marks the site of the Battle of San Jacinto, April 21, 1836. Gen. Sam Houston routed the superior forces of Santa Anna, Mexican general, and took Santa Anna prisoner, ending the war and leading to the founding of Texas as a republic. Museum with interpretive exhibits. Elevator to top of monument.

Old Market Square; Allen's Landing, on Buffalo Bayou where the Allen Brothers arrived in 1836 became the nucleus of the future city. Many old shops restored to original look.

Bayou Bend Museum, No. 1 Westcott St., a branch of the Museum of Fine Arts, the former home of Ima Hogg, daughter of James Stephen Hogg, first native-born Texas governor. Ima Hogg served on the Civil War Centennial Commission and was active in many history-related community improvement affairs. The collection of American decorative arts from 1650 to 1850 is seen by reserved admission only; visitors must be 16 or older.

HUNTSVILLE, Walker County. I–45.

The Sam Houston Memorial Museum, opposite Sam Houston State University, has many Houston personal items and furnishings of his day; Gen. Santa Anna's saddle and bridle, and other relics of the revolution. Pioneer Room. The memorial includes the Houston Residence and the Steamboat House where Houston died. War and Peace House has weapons and pioneer artifacts.

Sam Houston's Grave, ca. 3 blocks N. of courthouse on side road, well marked. Andrew Jackson made the remark which was used for the inscription: "The world will take care of Houston's fame." In 1813 the young Houston had joined the Tennessee Regulars to fight the Creek insurrection with Andrew Jackson. In 1814 in the Battle of Horseshoe Bend Houston was struck by an arrow then by a musket volley and carried the injury all his life but by his bravery won the lasting friendship of Andrew Jackson.

Sam Houston National Forest, S and E. via US 75, I–45. 158,410 acres. Supervisor in Lufkin.

INDEPENDENCE, Washington County. FM 390.

Mrs. Sam Houston House, FM 390, 1 block E. of intersection of FM 50. Houston's widow and eight children lived here between 1863 and 1867. A registered historic place.

Houston Homesite, FM 390, Spur 390, granite marker at site near spring which served travelers in early days. "I bought the premises of Mr.

Hines on the Hill to the left as you go out of Independence," Houston wrote in September 1853. A biographer wrote of his family: "The residence made the fourth Houston home ready for immediate occupancy. Margaret and the 'flock' were as mobile as cavalry, moving in a great yellow coach at the General's slightest whim. Her mother also lived at Independence and helped sustain its Baptist Church."

Texas Baptist Historical Center, part of the old Baptist church, organized in 1839, where Sam Houston was baptized. Margaret Moffette Houston and her mother lie in the cemetery across the highway. Mrs. Houston died of yellow fever and was not buried beside her husband in Huntsville for fear by survivors of spreading the disease. Records and family memorabilia in Center.

Dr. Asa Hoxey House, 1 mile W. on FM 390, local road 1 mile N. A dog-run log cabin built in 1833, home of doctor friend of the Houstons.

Ruins of Old Baylor University; four pillars of the original building stand picturesquely on a hilltop overlooking the old town. Houston moved his family here in 1853 because he thought highly of the school. It then had a Male Department and a Female College with the buildings a mile apart. For a time Houston served on the Examining committee.

JACKSBORO, Jack County. US 281.

Fort Richardson State Park, SW edge of town, off US 281. The fort was established in November 1867, on the right bank of Lost Creek, as part of the frontier defense system, and was named for Maj. Gen. Israel B. Richardson, who died in November 1862, of wounds received in the Battle of Antietam. The post was sometimes called Fort Jacksboro. An 1871 massacre nearby and the punishment of the Indian leaders responsible caused an uproar which led to the Red River War of 1874. Several original stone buildings remain: the commissary, bakery, guardhouse, morgue, officers' quarters and hospital which now houses a museum. A national historic landmark.

JACKSONVILLE, Cherokee County. US 175.

Killough Monument, US 69 N. to Mount Selman, FM 855 W. to Larissa, site of an Indian massacre of October 5, 1838. Stone monument.

Vanishing Texana, in public library, regional historical items.

JASPER, Jasper County. State 64.

Angelina National Forest, nearest entrance 13 miles NW on State 63, with 154,000 acres; headquarters in Lufkin.

Chamber of Commerce, 244 N. Austin, has information on local sites. There are markers on 13 old homes and buildings of the area. The town was founded in 1838. Two Revolutionary War soldiers are buried in the town cemetery. Oldest Negro church in Texas, the Dixie Baptist, founded in the early 1850s and is still standing. Bevilport steamboat landing is on nearby Neches River.

Jasper County Museum, in courthouse, has Civil War records, other documents and mementoes.

Howard-Dickinson House, 2 blocks from square on S. Main St. The first brick house in county, built in 1855. Restored, authentic furnishings.

JEFFERSON, Marion County. State 134. The first river steamboat port in Texas, on Big Cypress Bend. Sidewheelers came up the Red River and the bayou. Many antebellum homes in the historic old city; tours of homes in early May.

Excelsior House, 211 W. Austin St. From the mid-19th century, in continuous operation. Authentically furnished in early period. Ulysses Grant, Rutherford B. Hayes and Oscar Wilde were among the many illustrious guests. Guided tours daily.

Atalanta, Jay Gould's private railroad car, in midtown opposite the Excelsior House, built in the 1890s.

Jefferson Historical Society and Museum, 223 W. Austin St. Artifacts of East Texas. Indian exhibits, gun collection, etc.

Jefferson Historic District, on the national register of historic places, takes in many streets and structures which remain much as they were in the 1880s. Two-story business buildings on Cypress Bayou saw many immigrants arrive by river to wait for wagons and oxen for inland trips. Wharves were built along the bayou to handle the traffic. Business thrived. After the Civil War another boom of westward migration took place. Steamboats were lined up at the wharves and wagon trains were made up in town. The railroad was not permitted to come through town. When the water level in the Red River above Shreveport became too low for steamboat traffic, the town settled down to quieter times.

Jefferson Playhouse, NW corner of Market and Henderson Sts. Originally St. Mary's Catholic School, ca. 1860, and Sinai Hebrew Synagogue, in 1876, minor alterations, a registered historic place.

The Magnolias, 209 E. Broadway, built by early settler Dan Alley in 1868. Registered historic place.

Historic homes also on the national register: Alley-Carlson House, 501 Walker, mid-19th century; Beard House, 212 N. Vale, 1860–70; Epperson-McNutt House, 409 S. Alley St., built by Benjamin Epperson (A Texas representative in the Supreme Court's case in which it was decided that the Federal Union could not be dissolved, thus the court declared the Civil War an act of rebellion on the part of the Confederate states); Capt. William Perry House, NW corner of Walnut and Clarksville Sts., ca. 1858 (he was a New Hampshire native in the river trade at Jefferson); Sedberry House, 211 N. Market; Capt. William E. Singleton House, 204 N. Soda St. (Singleton was a Missourian who had served in the Confederate Army before moving to Texas); Perry Woods House (Old Ligon Place), 502 Walker St.; Freeman Plantation House, just W. of town on State 49, ca. 1850; Presbyterian Manse, NE corner of Alley and Delta Sts., 1839, now houses the Garden Club.

Cypress Queen, replica paddle-wheeler with riverboat captain, trips down Big Cypress Bayou in summer months. Dock on Bayou and US 59.

JOHNSON CITY, Blanco County. US 290.

Lyndon B. Johnson National Historic Site, 1 block off Main St., pertains to the late President's boyhood home in the 20th century but also includes the restored ranch of his grandfather, Sam Ealy Johnson, from the mid-19th century. Johnson's birthplace, 13 miles W. via US 290, PR 49, is a reconstructed two-bedroom farmhouse typical of the late 1800s.

KARNACK, Harrison County. State 43.

Birthplace of Mrs. Lyndon B. Johnson, 2.7 miles SW on State 43, antebellum home contructed of slave-made bricks. The former First Lady was born Claudia Taylor, daughter of merchant T. J. Taylor.

Caddo Lake State Park, 2 miles N. off State 43, occupies an area once occupied by Caddo Indians. Nature trails and an interpretive center in 478-acre park.

KERMIT, Winkler County. State 18, 115.

Comanche Trails Museum and Zoo, 12 miles W. off State 302. Museum has contents of medicine man's grave and other Indian artifacts, a gun collection, early furniture.

Pioneer Park, 4 blocks N. of State 302 at E. city limits, has outdoor museum, oldest house and a "Nester's Shack."

KINGSVILLE, Kleberg County. State 141.

John E. Connor Museum, on campus of Texas A & I University, Santa Gertrudis and Armstrong Sts. Indian, early Spanish and Texas relics, weapons.

King Ranch, entrance to loop drive is just W. of town off State 141. The largest ranch in continental U.S. was established in 1853. Capt. Richard King bought 75,000 acres which had been Spanish land-grant territory called Santa Gertrudis. Ranch now covers 823,000 acres in Nueces, Kleberg, Kenedy and Willacy Counties. Lawyer Robert Kleberg married King's youngest daughter. Their descendants still control the enterprise. A 12-mile loop leads past headquarters, stables, etc.

LA GRANGE, Fayette County. US 77.

Monument Hill State Historic Site, 2 miles S. off US 77, on river bluff. Tomb of Texans massacred during the Mexican uprisings of 1842. Kreische Home Museum and ruins of an ancient brewery also on grounds.

Faison Home and Museum, 631 S. Jefferson. Restored with period furnishings. House dates from 1840; home of a massacre survivor.

LANGTRY, Val Verde County.

Judge Roy Bean Visitor Center, dioramas with special sound program in visitor center interpret the colorful life of Roy Bean, styled the "Law West of the Pecos" in the 1880s. Rustic saloon, courtroom and billiard hall maintained by the Texas State Highway Department. Bean had a lifetime crush on English actress Lillie Langtry.

Scenic Overlook, on US 90, ca. 18 miles E. of town. East rim of canyon affords a fine view of primitive land much as it was in pioneer days.

Mile Canyon (Eagle Canyon), NE of town off US 90, is a registered historic place from pre-Columbian times, not open to the public at present.

LAREDO, Webb County. US 81, 83.

Republic of the Rio Grande, 1000 Zaaragosa St., opposite San Agustin Plaza, now a museum with documents, weapons, period furniture. Over the building seven flags have flown from the time of the Republic in 1839–41.

San Agustin Church, on Plaza, oldest church in Laredo, was originally built in 1767.

Tourist Bureau, on I–35 N. of town.

Fort McIntosh, on banks of the Rio Grande at the foot of Washington St. Established in March 1849, originally called Camp Crawford, designated a fort in 1850 and named for Lt. Col. James McIntosh, who died of wounds received in the Battle of Molino del Rey. The fort was one of those established along the river at the close of the Mexican War to guard the frontier and block the movement of Indians from U.S. lands into Mexico. Abandoned and reoccupied in 1858 and 1860, it was evacuated in March 1861, and taken over by the Confederacy until the end of the Civil War. Reoccupied by the Union in 1865 and rebuilt in 1868–77. Laredo Junior College and Texas A & I occupy the grounds; some old buildings remain.

LIBERTY, Liberty County. US 90. Third oldest town in the state. A Spanish mission was established here in 1756. There is a marker at the site of Sam Houston's law office; others where Mexican town squares were laid out. Among the old homes are the Cleveland–Partlow House ca. 1869 and the Thomas Jefferson Chambers House. Chambers was not a friend but an enemy of Houston. His quaint house is circular, built around a central fireplace with six openings. Followers of Napoleon had tried to found a colony here in 1818.

Chamber of Commerce, 1915 Trinity, has information on houses and sites and on scenic drives into the Big Thicket area.

LIVINGSTON, Polk County. US 190. On the old Spanish Trail. Confederate markers on town square.

Alabama–Coushatta Indian Reservation, 17 miles E. on US 190, is the oldest reservation in Texas. Living Indian Village in area, woodland tours, train rides, Big Thicket tours and a museum.

Polk County Museum, 601 W. Church St. Indian handicrafts and relics, early American glassware, etc.

LLANO, Llano County. State 16. A wild frontier town with many Indian raids in the early days which began in 1855. There are legends of lost Spanish mines in the area.

Llano County Museum, N. end of Llano River bridge on State 16, has displays in restored old drugstore.

LOCKHART, Caldwell County. US 183. Originally Plum Creek, near site of an Indian battle of August 12, 1840, when Comanches plundered the Guadalupe Valley. Texas Rangers and a group of volunteers met the war party on its way home and defeated them.

Emanuel Episcopal Church, built in 1856, only minor alteration.

LONGVIEW, Gregg County. US 80.

Caddo Indian Museum, 701 Hardy St. Prehistoric and historic artifacts.

LUBBOCK, Lubbock County. State 116. Site of Singer's Store in City Park, one of the only two stores for years on the South Plains.

Museum of Texas Tech University, on N. boundary of the university, has a general store, Hall of Earth and Man and other displays, including a "Ranch Headquarters" from bunkhouses to windmills.

Mackenzie State Park, off I–27 within city limits, has a Prairie-Dog Town which is virtually irresistible. These animals once ran free and probably annoyed old westerners but are a fascination for spectators. A segment of Yellow House Canyon in the park was the site of the last fight in Lubbock county between buffalo hunters, white and Indian.

Lubbock Lake Site, N. of town near the intersection of Clovis Highway and Loop 289, a pre-Columbian registered historic place which offers evidence of a 12,000-year period of use by men.

LUFKIN, Angelina County. US 59.

Chamber of Commerce, 210 First St., should be a first stop for visitors. Complete details on sites in Angelina County. The town is headquarters for Angelina and Davy Crockett National Forests. A Forestry Museum, with relics of early logging days and firefighting, is at 1903 Atkinson Dr.

McALLEN, Hidalgo County. US 83.

McAllen International Museum, 2500 Quince, in Las Palmas Park, historical and scientific exhibits.

McCAMEY, Upton County. US 67.

Mendoza Trail Museum, US 67 E. In restored Adrian House, frontier relics, Indian artifacts, fossils.

Castle Gap Park, ca. 13 miles NW off US 385, old Comanche grounds. Wagon ruts from the 1860s Goodnight–Loving Trail in 232-acre park.

McKINNEY, Collin County. FM 1378. Settled in 1845, named for Collin McKinney, a signer of the Texas Declaration of Independence.

Heard Natural Science Museum and Wildlife Sanctuary, S. on FM 1378. Natural history displays, and nature trails through 256-acre sanctuary.

McLEAN, Gray County. US 66.

Alanreed–McLean Area Museum, 117 N. Main St. relics from Panhandle settlers, period rooms.

MADISONVILLE, Madison County. I–45.

Yesteryear, 12 miles N. on I–45 at Old San Antonion Rd. Replica frontier town with saloon, log cabin, museum, cobbler shop, etc.

MARATHON, Brewster County. US 385.

Camp Pena Colorado, also called Fort Pena Colorado, from midtown a road leads to a cattle gate of the Combs Ranch, 3 miles from town, R. through gate to old campsite near Pena Colorado Springs and Rainbow Cliffs. The post was established in 1879, under jurisdiction of Fort Davis, to control the Mescalero Apaches, who harassed the Chihuahua Trail. Ruins and a cemetery remain.

Black Gap Wildlife Management Area, ca. 55 miles S. on US 385, RM 2627. For the study and development of wildlife area management; 100,000 acres have been set aside; visitors are welcome, hunters are not, though fishing is permitted.

MARLIN, Falls County. FM 147. Town founded in the 1830s in area long used by Indians for the medicinal waters. Sites of many Indian conflicts are marked. Settlers were massacred at Fort Marlin, marker on highway.

Highlands Mansion, 1 mile NE on FM 147. Restored 19th-century mansion. Antique furnishings.

MARSHALL, Harrison County. US 80. Settled in 1839, city was one of the wealthiest in the state, producing saddles, harness, powder, ammunition for the Confederacy. After the fall of Vicksburg, the headquarters of the Trans-Mississippi postal department and the Confederate capitol of Missouri were here. Confederate monument on Courthouse lawn.

Site of Missouri Capitol, 402 S. Bolivar. Governor's mansion was at 109 E. Crockett. Confederate Governor Thomas C. Reynolds rented both the mansion and the capitol.

Confederate Hat Factory, 109 W. Grand Ave.

Harrison County Historical Society Mu-

seum, in old courthouse on Peter Whetstone Sq. Caddo Indian artifacts, pioneer and Civil War relics.

Old Cemeteries, in Marshall and in Scottsville, 8 miles away, have many pioneer and Civil War soldiers' graves.

Franks Museum, 211 W. Grand Ave. Thousands of historical items; old doll collection.

Ginocchio Hotel, Washington St. at T&P depot, was built in 1896 at the terminus of New Orleans section of the railroad. Actor Maurice Barrymore was shot and one of his troupe of players killed in front of the building in the 1880s. Period furnishings.

Chamber of Commerce, 301 E. Austin St., has maps, information on historic homes and trails.

MASON, Mason County. US 377.

Fort Mason, crest of Post Hill, ca. 5 blocks S. of courthouse. Established in July 1851, 2 miles W. of Comanche Creek, on the upper San Antonio–El Paso Road, to protect the German settlements of the area. Evacuated by Union troops in 1861, reoccupied after the war. It was primarily a cavalry post; Albert Sidney Johnston, John Bell Hood and Robert E. Lee were among those who served here. This was Lee's last command before the war.

Mason County Museum, 300 Moody St. Regional artifacts in old schoolhouse from the 1870s.

MATADOR, Motley County. US 62. Named for the ranch, whose headquarters ranch house is at the SW edge of town. The ranch was founded in 1879 when the original owners bought the range rights from a buffalo hunter. An old stone bunkhouse, icehouse, windmill ruins, milkhouse and wellhouse remain of early structures.

MENARD, Menard County. State 29. Town founded in 1858 near ruins of Spanish fort, Real Presidio de San Saba, abandoned more than a century earlier. A trading post and stop on cattle trails, the settlement used the old Spanish mission compound as a corral, sometimes having 3,000 cattle for overnight guests.

Ruins of Real Presidio de San Saba, now county park, 2 miles W. off State 29. In March 1759, a band of Comanches and other Indians attacked the mission nearby and murdered nearly all occupants, then burned the buildings. Three from the mission reached the presidio which managed to withstand attack. In years following, the presidio was under attack almost daily and was abandoned in 1769.

MEXIA, Limestone County. State 14.

Old Fort Parker State Historic Site, 8 miles SW on State 14. A private fort established in 1834 by the family of Elder John Parker to protect a small settlement. In 1836 Comanches attacked, killing five of the Parkers and carrying five into captivity, including Cynthia Ann Parker, probably the most famous white-girl-captured-by-Indians in American history; Olive Oatman, stolen by Yavapais of Arizona, next most famous; Lewis and Clark's interpreter, Sacajawea, with no runner-up, as the most famous Indian-girl-stolen-by-Indians. Cynthia, mother of Quanah Parker, was never happy when brought back to her white relatives and often tried to escape. She and her daughter, Prairie Flower, 2 years old when taken back to the white community, died within five years after they left the Comanches. The fort has been restored; pioneer relics.

Tehuacana Hills, 5 miles NW on State 171. In 1797 Philip Nolan and his trading expedition found Indians farming the land. Cherokees destroyed the Tehuacanas in the 1830s. Tehuacana Academy, organized in 1852, now occupied by Westminster Junior College and Bible Institute.

MIDLAND, Midland County. US 80.

Midland County Museum, 301 W. Missouri in city library, Indian and pioneer relics, Civil War items.

Museum of the Southwest, 1705 W. Missouri, documents, paintings and artifacts.

Permian Basin Petroleum Museum, 1500 I–20W. Diorama of the ocean floor, 200 million years ago, historical paintings and history of the oil industry.

Cole Park Zoo, E. on Cloverdale Rd., has West Texas animals, including Longhorns.

MISSION, Hidalgo County. US 83.

Chamber of Commerce has information on self-guiding Audubon tours. The town was laid out on La Lomita Ranch, owned by the Oblate Fathers. In 1824 a chapel was founded on the N. bank of the Rio Grande, as well as a pioneer citrus grove. At E. city limits leave US 83 for Bryan Road, 2 miles to home of William Jennings Bryan. S. from town on FM 1016, 6 miles to Anzalduas Dam and Bridge where a right turn leads to Capilla de La Lomita, 4.4 miles, the chapel built by the Oblate Fathers which still has the hand-hewn woodwork and much of the original adobe construction. It is on a hill overlooking the Rio Grande and the old Military Rd. in a rather lonely spot, relatively unspoiled by progress. (Also ¼ mile W. of Madero, which is on FM 1016.)

MOBEETIE, Wheeler County. State 152.

Fort Elliott, established in February 1875, on the Red River and known as Cantonment North Fork of the Red River. Relocated in June, N. of and near the headwaters of Sweetwater Creek, near the present town of Mobeetie. Gen. William Tecumseh Sherman, in ordering the establishment, planned a route for Texas cattle W. of the settlements into Kansas. The post also was intended to prevent the reentry of Indians into West Texas and to keep them on their reservation. As a subpost of Fort Sill, Oklahoma, it had various names. Designated Fort Elliott in 1876 for Maj. Joel Elliott, 7th U.S. Cavalry, who was killed in November 1868 in action on the Washita River, Indian Territory. (This was the controversial attack led by Custer on a peaceful Indian village.) The post was abandoned in 1890 and buildings were sold at auction later. (Singer's Store in Lubbock was for years one of the only two stores on the South Plains and stood where two important military trails crossed; one from Fort Concho to Fort Sumner, New Mexico, the other from Fort Elliott to Fort Stockton.) Inquire locally for exact site of fort.

MONAHANS, Ward County. State 18.

Monahans Sandhills State Park, I–20, US 80, 5 miles E. on Park Road 41. Sand dunes believed to be from the Trinity sandstone formation of the Permian sea. Self-guiding nature trails. Museum with historical and geological displays.

MORTON, Cochran County. FM 1169.

C. C. Slaughter Ranch Headquarters, 2 miles S. on State 214; 1 mile W. on

FM 1169. Adobe buildings still in use; visitors welcome. One of the famous ranches of the cattle baron times.

Cochran County Historical Museum, 206 SW. 1st St. Regional historical items.

MOUNTAIN HOME, Kerr County. State 31.

Y. O. Ranch, entrance 15 miles W. of town on State 41, headquarters 8 miles N. of entrance. Established in 1880. Several historic buildings have been preserved including an 1850s stagecoach stop. Wells-Fargo office moved here from Boerne area; pioneer cabin from near Fredericksburg and pioneer schoolhouse.

MULESHOE, Bailey County. State 214.

Muleshoe National Wildlife Refuge, ca. 20 miles S. on State 214. 5,809 acres.

National Mule Memorial, near intersection of US 70, 84 in downtown, honors the mules who pulled the pioneer freight.

NACOGDOCHES, Nacogdoches County. State 21. Founded by the Spanish in 1689. Mission established in 1716 to serve the Nacogdoches Indians. La Salle spent the winter of 1685 here.

Chamber of Commerce, Fredonia Hotel, has information on local sites.

Old Stone Fort Museum, on campus of Stephen F. Austin State University, North St. and College Ave. A Spanish trading post in 1779 and fort. Rebuilt, has artifacts including some of Houston's personal property. Jim Bowie and Davy Crockett were here before the Alamo.

Hoya Memorial Library and Museum, 211 S. Lanana St. in pioneer home of Adolphus Sterne, a friend of Houston, whose home was often a refuge in Indian raids. Sterne was alcalde when the town was under Mexican rule.

Old Nacogdoches University, on high school grounds, Fredonia St., founded in 1845 by the Republic of Texas; restored.

Oak Grove Cemetery, E. end of Hospital St., has the graves of four signers of the Texas Declaration of Independence.

Halfway House, at Chireno halfway to San Augustine on State 21, built in the 1830s. Period furnishings. Sam Houston often stopped here.

L. T. Barret Memorial and Oil Springs Marker, SE via State 21, S. on FM 226, ca. 10 miles to Oil Springs sign, turn left. Wellsite is restored. Memorial on Stephen F. Austin University campus honors the man who drilled the first oil well in Texas in September 1866.

La Calle del Norte may be the oldest public thoroughfare in the U.S. It once connected this Indian community with other Indian villages to the north.

NEW BRAUNFELS, Comal County. RM 32.

Founded in 1845 on Comal River, the town has many historic homes and buildings.

Sophieburg Memorial Museum, 401 W. Coll St. Pioneer relics.

Lindheimer Home, 491 Comal Ave. Restored home of Ferdinand Lindheimer, built ca. 1852.

Natural Bridge Caverns, ca. 17 miles W. via State 46, large underground maze recently discovered with vast rooms and many formations.

NEWCASTLE, Young County. State 251.

Fort Belknap, 3 miles S. off State 251, established in June 1851, on the Salt (Red) Fork of the Brazos River, to protect the emigrant route from Fort Smith, Arkansas, to Santa Fe. Occupied at times by Confederate forces during the Civil War; later maintained mostly as a picket post. Water was scarce and the fort was abandoned in 1867. Six original buildings have been restored. Two small museums. A national historic landmark.

ODESSA, Ector County. US 80.

Odessa College Museum, on campus, Andrews Highway at 25th St. Indian artifacts, pioneer relics from the Permian Basin area, Western items, including the curiosity, a transom from the ranch house where Billy the Kid once lived.

Odessa Meteor Crater, 5 miles W., 2 miles S. of US 80. Believed formed more than 20,000 years ago. Displays.

Jackrabbit Statute, 400 block of N. Lincoln St. 2 blocks W. of US 385. Jackrabbits were as common as bluebonnets but only in Texas are they ten feet tall.

Presidential Room, in Ector County Library, 622 N. Lee St., memorabilia of presidents of the Republic of Texas.

ORANGE, Orange County. I–10. Established in 1836. First known inhabitants were the Attacapa Indians in the early part of the 17th century. Tourist Bureau with maps and literature on I–10, ca. 3 miles NE of town.

OZONA, Crockett County. US 290.

Fort Lancaster State Historic Site, 33 miles W. on US 290. Fort was established in 1855 on Live Oak Creek above the junction with the Pecos River to guard the San Antonio–El Paso road. Evacuated at the beginning of the Civil War and not reoccupied. Restoration in progress. Visitor and Interpretive Center.

Crockett County Museum, 404 11th St. Frontier and Indian relics, artifacts from Fort Lancaster.

Davy Crockett Monument, in city park on town square.

PAINT ROCK, Concho County. FM 380. US 83.

Paint Rock Indian Pictograph Site, 1 mile NW off US 83. Pre-Columbian site, the most extensive pictograph area in central Texas; a registered historic place. Tours in summer months; inquire locally.

PALESTINE, Anderson County. US 287.

Bowers Mansion, (Watford Hall), 301 S. Magnolia St., built in 1878 in Victorian Steamboat Gothic style; period furnishings.

Howard House Museum, 1011 Perry St. There is an 1851 cottage with many relics from early days of settlement.

Pilgrim Church, 4 miles S. of Elkhart on FM 861, authentic reconstruction of 1833 church.

Fort Houston, between Palestine and Buffalo, has a marker at site. This was a military post of the Republic of Texas, not Fort Sam Houston, at San Antonio. It had an unusual double stockade and was erected ca. 1835 as a defense against hostile Indians.

PANHANDLE, Carson County. FM 293, State 207.

Square House Museum, Pioneer Park on State 207, many items of early days, Indian culture, cattle ranching, buffalo hunting, vehicles and a Santa Fe caboose.

Thomas Cree's Little Tree, S. edge of US 60, ca. 5 miles SW of town, first tree planted in the Panhandle (1888). State historical marker.

PARIS, Lamar County. US 271. Frank James in his later years worked in a dry goods store in town. Belle Starr was jailed here.

Maxey House, 812 S. Church St., was the home of Confederate Gen. Samuel Bell Maxey; many original furnishings. A registered historic place.

Lightfoot House, 746 Church, is a traditional ranch home.

Chamber of Commerce, 108 Lamar, will arrange tours of local sites on request.

PECOS, Reeves County. US 285.

West of the Pecos Museum, 1st St. and US 285, includes restored saloon with many early photographs, antiques, in early hotel, restored.

PINE SPRINGS, Culberson County. US 62, 180. Once a stop on the Butterfield Overland Mail Route; marker at ruins.

Guadalupe Mountains National Park, surrounds town. The park dedicated in 1972 contains 77,518 acres. Frijole Information Station near town. Check here first; many areas should be entered only by experienced hikers.

PLAINS, Yoakum County. US 380, 82.

Tsa Mo Ga Memorial Museum, 1109–B Ave. A. Pioneer ranch relics, Civil War items, in a homesteader's shack. The first land claim in Yoakum County was made by a family who lived in a dugout in the 1890s but had a piano.

PLAINVIEW, Hale County. US 70.

Mackenzie Statue, courthouse square, honors Col. Ranald S. Mackenzie, Indian fighter and the founder of the Mackenzie Trail in 1871. He smashed a Comanche camp in the Battle of Palo Duro Canyon, in September 1874.

Plainview Site, just W. of junction of US 70 and 87. Excavations found a spear point dating from ca. 7000 B.C. and an extinct species of bison associated with a hunting group of Indians. A national historic landmark.

PORT ARTHUR, Jefferson County. State 87. Settlement was called Aurora in 1840. Many historic homes and buildings are marked with plaques.

Port Arthur Historical Museum, 5th and Austin Sts. Relics from the Battle of Sabine Pass and other artifacts.

Chamber of Commerce, 530 Waco Ave., maps and information.

PORT ISABEL, Cameron County. State 100.

Port Isabel Lighthouse State Historic Site, W. on State 100. Fort Polk, a camp and depot during the Mexican War, commanded by Gen. Zachary Taylor, was established in March 1846, at the mouth of the Rio Grande near here. Abandoned in February 1850. The site overlooks Palmito Hill, last land battle area of the Civil War. Self-guiding tours.

PORT LAVACA, Calhoun County. State 238, 316. Founded by the Spanish in 1815; established as a community in 1840.

Calhoun County Museum, in old jail adjacent to courthouse. Artifacts from early days of the area.

Indianola County Historic Park, 13 miles SE via State 238,316. A ghost town on Matagorda and Lavaca bays. In the 1850s an army depot supplied Texas frontier forts from here, and here the two shiploads of Arabian camels arrived for Edward Beale's camel caravan experiment. The town was shelled, captured and recaptured in the Civil War, and survived yellow fever and storms until September 17, 1875, when an extremely severe storm wiped out most of the town and 900 of its inhabitants. Another storm 11 years later convinced residents that the town must be abandoned. A granite statue of Robert Cavelier, sieur de La Salle stands in the area where he stopped almost 300 years ago.

QUITMAN, Wood County. State 37.

Governor Hogg Shrine and State Park, 518 S. Main St. Buildings, museum and mementoes of the Hogg family. James Stephen Hogg was the first native-born governor of Texas. The Stinson house has been restored; this was the home of Ima Hogg's grandparents.

REFUGIO, Refugio County. (Seems to be pronounced Re-FURy-o locally, who knows why.) US 77.

Nuestra Señora del Refugio Mission was originally located in a swampy part of the county and was established by Franciscans. Reestablished in Refugio in 1795. Model of the old mission is exhibited in present church. National champion tree, an anaqua, is at site of present church. It was large when Gen. Urrea captured the mission in 1835; now measures 151 inches in circumference. Near the tree on January 17, 1836, Sam Houston begged the Texas soldiers not to advance upon Matamoros believing that the Mexicans would cooperate with them, but to regroup at Goliad. He was elected as a Refugio delegate to the people's convention at Washington-on-the-Brazos.

RIO GRANDE CITY, Starr County. US 83.

Fort Ringgold, off US 83 at E. city limits, was established in October 1848, on the left bank of the Rio Grande at David's Landing, as one of the system of frontier posts at the close of the Mexican War. First called "Post at David's Landing," then Camp Ringgold, and Ringgold Barracks, designated a fort in December 1878. Named for Capt. Samuel Ringgold, who died in 1846 of wounds received in the Battle of Palo Alto. The post was evacuated by Federal troops in 1861, reoccupied after the war and in 1869 rebuilt above the original site. It is one of the best preserved of early Texas posts. The Lee House was occupied by Robert E. Lee; the old hospital is still standing.

ROUND ROCK, Williamson County. I–35. The town gained its greatest fame when Sam Bass and his outlaws were ambushed here on the day before they planned to rob the old town bank. Bass and others were killed.

Round Rock Cemetery has the graves of Bass and Seaborn Barnes; Bass's monument has suffered from souvenir hunters as have those of other outlaws. The inscription reads: "Samuel Bass Born July 21, 1851/ Died July 21, 1878." That of his friend reads: "Seaborn Barnes Died July 19, 1878/ He was right bower to Sam Bass."

Historian Walter Prescott Webb, writing a history of the Texas Rangers, said:

> Sam Bass was a personable young man who rode fast horses, robbed banks, stage-coaches, and railway trains, outwitted detectives, whipped United States soldiers, and, for a time, outran

the Texas Rangers. Hired men and small boys sighed over his untimely end at the gun muzzles of the Texas Rangers, and consigned Sam's betrayer to the nethermost chunk of an orthodox hell. . . . Sam supped in every home, sat at every camp fire, and scattered the new minted gold of the Union Pacific robbery wherever he went. The only thing against him was that he came out of the North at a time when all southern children still believed that all Yankees wore hoofs and horns. But Sam overcame this stigma and was perhaps the first Yankee to gain popularity in Texas after the Civil War.

El Milagro Museum, rock farmhouse built in 1859, was the home of Washington Anderson, veteran of the Battle of San Jacinto. His personal effects are in museum.

Inn at Brushy Creek, off I–35 at US 79E, built ca. 1850 as the Cole House, now a restaurant. Restored, with antique furnishings.

ROUND TOP, Fayette County. State 237.

Winedale Inn, 4 miles E. via FM 1457, 2714, restored stagecoach inn of the 1830s, restored barns, etc.

Bethlehem Lutheran Church, 1 block W. of State 237, stone church of the 1860s.

Henkel Square, midtown, has 8 restored buildings of the 1840 settlement. Antiques, hand-crafted locally, furnishings.

Hackberry Hill, 1 mile S. on State 237, then 2 miles W. on gravel road, small farm and outbuildings from the late 1830s.

SABINE PASS, Jefferson County. State 87. The settlement was laid out in 1836 by Sam Houston and Philip Sublett as Sabine City. Name changed in 1839. Statue of Dick Dowling in Dowling Park honors hero of the Battle of Sabine Pass.

Battle of Sabine Pass took place on September 9, 1863, when Union forces tried to invade Texas; the Confederates successfully defended the fort and the pass and captured three gunboats. The dashing Confederate Admiral Raphael Semmes wrote a frank and entertaining account of his many wartime experiences in *Service Afloat and Ashore During the Mexican War* and *Memoirs of Service Afloat,* which dealt with the Civil War. Of Sabine Pass he writes about Gen. Nathaniel Prentiss Banks, who had succeeded Gen. Benjamin Butler in command of the Department of the Gulf late in the summer of 1863. (Neither general could have won a popularity contest in the South, nor in some areas of the North); "He [Banks] was here met by General Dick Taylor [it was Dick Dowling, in fact], who, with a much inferior force, demolished him, giving him such a scare that it was with difficulty Porter could stop him at Alexandria to assist him in the defence of his fleet until he could extricate it from the shallows of the river where it was aground. The hero of Boston Common had not had such a scare since Stonewall Jackson had chased him through Winchester, Virginia."

SAINT JO, Montague County. US 82. Known as Head of Elm when settled in 1856 on springs which were the headwaters of the Elm Fork of the Trinity River. Renamed for a teetotaler who opposed the sale of booze, Joe Howell. An important watering stop on the Chisholm Trail and the California Rd., with Indian raids keeping things lively until 1874.

Stonewall Saloon Museum, N. corner of square, restored barroom with cattle-drive relics and other historical items.

SALT FLAT, Hudspeth County. US 62, 180. The area was the scene of much fighting in the 1860s and 1870s, sometimes called the El Paso War, also called the Salt War. The dispute was over the salt deposits at the foot of the Guadalupe Mountains and led to murder, assassination and revenge killings, involving Mexican and American citizens, the Army and the Texas Rangers. The Salt Lakes were first noticed about 1862; in the following year Mexicans from El Paso opened a wagon road to the deposits. It was considered free for the taking and was taken by Mexicans on both sides of the border; then the Texans wanted to acquire legal rights to the land. Soon one company wanted a monopoly and trouble was underway. The Salt Ring and the Anti-Salt Ring clashed. After much bloodshed and reprehensible-to-outrageous acts on the part of both sides of the controversy the U.S. established a permanent military post at El Paso with a garrison of two hundred men, including 50 cavalrymen. The Salt War was over; Mexico was to punish its own citizens who had participated in the riots. Some of the salt deposits may still be seen from the highway.

SALADO, Bell County. I–35.

Central Texas Area Museum, Main and Forest, has regional relics and exhibits, pertaining to the colonization, Confederacy, cattle-empire period.

Historic Homes and Buildings, inquire at museum above for directions. Many structures from early pioneer days remain. Homes open at various times have authentic furnishings. Robertson House, classic frontier home with slave quarters and family cemetery. Ruins of early Salado College, founded in 1860, are on hill E. of FM 2268 at S. city limits. An annual pilgrimage to houses is held in April. Museum has details.

Stagecoach Inn, off I–35 just S. of Salado Creek, originally the Shady Villa Inn, had guests such as Robert E. Lee, Jesse James and Shanghai Pierce. Abel Head Pierce was a cattle king who was one of the first to bring Brahma cattle to Texas from India.

SAN ANGELO, Tom Green County. US 67, 277.

Fort Concho, 716 Burges St., established late in 1867 as Camp Concho, later known as Permanent Camp, on the middle branch of the Concho River, an outpost of Fort Chadbourne. The permanent post, part of the frontier defense system, and center of the line of forts from El Paso to the Red River, also had a variety of names: Camp Hatch, Camp Kelly and finally Fort Concho in 1868, for the stream on which it was located. The fort is well preserved with many original buildings in fine condition. Col. Ranald Mackenzie, noted Indian fighter, was one of the commanders. The museum has a diorama, military artifacts, wildlife and weapon displays. The Goodnight-Loving Cattle Trail and the California Trail, as well as the Chidester Stage Line, came here to avoid the Staked Plains to the N. and the desert to the S. Troops from here took part in the campaigns against the Kiowa and Comanche Indians in the early 1870s. A national historic landmark.

SAN ANTONIO, Bexar County. I–35.

Walking Tour starts at the Alamo, Alamo Plaza: The original mission, founded by Fray Antonio de San Buenaventura Oliveras in May 1718, has been restored. Museum.

Menger Hotel, S. of the Alamo, had many famous guests, including Robert E. Lee.

HemisFair Plaza, on Market St. Buildings from the 1868 fair are the Tower of the Americas, Lone Star Hall of Texas History, Institute of Texas Cultures, and Museum of Transportation.

Some wax museums are not worth the candle, so to say, but the Hall of Texas Wax Museum is excellent. Western history buffs can linger in the wax presence of many long-famous names. Álvar Núñez Cabaza de Vaca, survivor of a shipwreck on Galveston Island in 1528, here encounters another survivor in 1534; René Robert Cavelier, sieur de La Salle, who was shipwrecked on Matagorda Bay in 1685, plants the French flag on Texas soil; Pirate Jean Lafitte stands aboard his ship; Stephen F. Austin consults with the Baron de Bastrop, who is issuing land titles; Jim Bowie, Sam Houston, William Travis, Robert E. Lee and even Teddy Roosevelt are all in this great wax roundup.

Old San Antonio Museum, in Bolivar Hall, has life-size dioramas with authentic costumes and accessories. The museum is part of:

La Villita, reconstructed 250-year-old Spanish-speaking settlement.

Cos House, also part of La Villita, is the site where Gen. Perfecto de Cos signed the Articles of Capitulation on December 10, 1835.

Spanish Governor's Palace, 105 Military Plaza, was erected ca. 1749.

José Antonio Navarro House, 228–232 S. Laredo, is a complex of three 19th-century buildings with period furnishings and other historical displays.

Steves Homestead, 509 King St., built in 1876 on the river bank. Period furnishings and landscaped grounds.

Buckhorn Hall of Horns, 600 Lone Star Blvd. A collection of horns and mounted animals from the old Buckhorn Saloon, once located in the heart of town. Hall of Fins, and a firearm collection and the house in which O. Henry lived are all on display at the Lone Star Brewery.

Witte Memorial Museum, 3801 Broadway, has a stagecoach, early houses, a furnished log cabin and many other displays. The museum is in Brackenridge Park, which also has gardens, a zoo and a miniature railroad.

Fort Sam Houston is a modern military base; there are four others in the area which are open to the public at varying times; check by phone before visiting. The fort was established in 1879 as a quartermaster depot. In 1885 barracks, officers' quarters and other buildings were added for housing 12 cavalry companies, at what was then called Post of San Antonio. The fort was designated in September 1890. Museum has military artifacts.

Missions: Nuestra Señora de la Purisma Concepcion, 807 Mission Rd., established in 1731, well preserved; *San Jose Mission y San Miguel de Aguayo and National Historic Site,* on Mission Trail, well marked, the church, Indian quarters, granary and mill have been restored; *San Francisco de la Espada,* Espada Rd., was built in 1731, church still in use, friary and chapel restored; *San Juan Capistrano,* Graf Rd., still in use. "El Dia de las Misiones" (The Day of the Missions) is an annual salute to these 18th-century structures, on August 6.

SAN AUGUSTINE, San Augustine County. State 147, 21. Known as "The Cradle of Texas," on the historic road, Camino Real, now State 21. Tour of 32 Medallion Homes and Historical Places first weekend in June.

Bodine Place, 4 miles N. on State 147, then 2 miles W. built in 1886, third Bodine house on the site. The original builder served with Comdr. Perry and one son in each succeeding generation has been tagged Oliver Hazard Perry Bodine.

Ezekiel W. Cullen Home, Congress and Market Sts. The 1839 home of Judge Cullen is now a community house and museum. Headquarters for historic house tour. A registered historic place.

Garrett House, 11 miles W. on State 21. Pre-Republic house, oldest in the county, built in 1830s.

Old Town Well, in Stripling's downtown drugstore, was dug by slave labor in 1860 and served travelers on El Camino Real as well as locals. (But probably not its diggers.) Historical information available here.

Matthew Cartwright House, 912 E. Main St., built in 1830, is a registered historic place.

SAN FELIPE, Austin County. I–10. San Felipe de Austin, "Birthplace of Anglo-American settlement in Texas," was named for Stephen F. Austin, who brought his colonists in 1823. *The Gazette,* the first newspaper in Texas, began in 1829. San Felipe Post Office has historical information, literature.

Stephen F. Austin State Park, PR 38, just N. of town, covers 664 acres, includes dog-run cabin, many monuments, restored store, nature trails.

SEGUIN, Guadalupe County. US 90. Founded as Walnut Springs by Mathew Caldwell's Gonzales Rangers, named for Juan Seguin, Mexican-Texan of Houston's Army, in 1839.

Chamber of Commerce, 704 W. Court St., has information on the many historic homes and buildings of the area, including a Texas Ranger station built in 1823, Magnolia Hotel, 1824, restored post office, Zorn Home, 1850s, Erskine House, 1855, and others. Historical markers on all of these. Erskine House, 902 N. Austin, and Zorn House, NE corner of W. Court and N. Erkel, are registered historic places.

Los Nogales Museum, E. Live Oak and S. River Sts. Museum in old post office has historical documents, pictures and early furniture.

SHAFTER, Presidio County. US 67. 1880s silver mining town, now a ghost village. Old Cemetery is worth a visit. Fort Cibolo was located a few miles W. of town, named for the creek, often occupied by troops moving from Fort Davis to Fort Leaton, a trading post near Presidio on the Rio Grande.

SIERRA BLANCA, Hudspeth County. US 62,180.

Dogie Wright Collection, in courthouse (the only adobe courthouse in Texas), Texas Ranger and other artifacts.

Fort Quitman Replica, 18 miles W. on I–10 at FM 34. The post was established in September 1858, on the Rio Grande, to protect the stage line and emigrant route. Occupied by Confederate troops in 1861, reoccupied by Federals in August 1862, under the command of Capt. John Cremony, 2nd California Cavalry, but these men were withdrawn in 1863 and the post was not used again until 1868. Museum has artifacts.

Tinaja de las Palmas Battle Site, ca. 15 miles SE of town. Col. Benjamin Grierson's black troops defeated Victorio and his Warm Springs Apaches here in 1880. Site on private ranch. Remains of stone barricades. Marker at courthouse in Van Horn. Ruts of San Antonio–El Paso Road visible across the valley.

SINTON, San Patricio County. US 77.

The Welder Wildlife Refuge, 7 miles NE on US 77, is the largest privately endowed wildlife refuge in the world. Ranch was established on a Spanish land grant. Tours arranged by the Sinton Chamber of Commerce; also tours each Thursday at 3 P.M.

SNYDER, Scurry County. State 350.

Western Heritage Museum, on campus of Western Texas College.

White Buffalo Statue, on courthouse square. Other historical markers on square.

SONORA, Sutton County. US 290. Once a trading post on the San Antonio–El Paso Rd.

Caverns of Sonora, 8 miles W. on I-10 then 6½ miles S. on RM 1989. Spectacular formations have been called the most indescribably beautiful in the world.

Miers Home Museum, Oak St. across from jail, built in 1888, period furnishings. Miers came to town in a covered wagon.

Will's Museum, 105 7th St. pioneer blacksmith shop, barn and many relics.

Fort Terrett, ca. 1 mile N. of US 290, ca. 32 miles SE of Sonora, was established in 1852 and lasted two years, guarding settlements on the San Antonio Rd. from Comanche attacks. Site is marked but is on a private ranch. Some buildings remain.

STAMFORD, Jones County. US 277.

Buie's Store Exhibit, 114 N. McHarg, large collection of pioneer farm equipment and weapons, other relics.

Mackenzie Trail Monument, intersection of US 277 and 380 N.

STINNETT, Hutchinson County. State 136.

Battle of Adobe Walls, on unimproved road ca. 17 miles NE of town, make local inquiry. Site is marked. Two Indian battles were fought here. William Bent had an adobe trading post in the 1840s but gave it up because of Indian hostility. Col. Kit Carson fought the Kiowas and Comanches here in 1864 and was nearly defeated. Carson luckily for his side had two howitzers. The second battle took place in June 1874 when the Kiowas and Comanches tried to get rid of white buffalo hunters in the Panhandle. (The hunters not the buffalo were white.)

Isaac McCormick's Pioneer Cottage, on town square. Restored home of first settler.

SWEETWATER, Nolan County. US 80.

Nolan County Historical Museum, 304 Locust St. Indian and pioneer artifacts. The town began as a store in a dugout.

TASCOSA, Oldham County. State 385. Ghost town, now a Boys Ranch area, was once one of the toughest towns in the Panhandle. A blacksmith shop and a general store opened in

1876, then a saloon for the riders of the cattle and freight trail that crossed the Canadian River at Tascosa Ford. Pat Garrett and his future victim, Billy the Kid, Charlie Siringo, Frank James and Bat Masterson were among those who came and went. Those who came and stayed are in Boot Hill, on US 385, maintained by Boys Ranch.

Julian Bivins Museum, in old courthouse on Boys Ranch, has Indian and pioneer and ranch artifacts.

TEXARKANA, Bowie County US 82, 59. Tourist Bureau with maps and literature on I–30 W. of US 59.

Texarkana Historical Museum, 4 blocks S. of US 71, 59, 67, has a variety of historical relics.

TYLER, Smith County. US 271.

Camp Ford Site, US 271, 2 miles NE. Descriptive marker, in rest area, for Confederate prison camp which housed some 6,000 Union troops in the spring of 1864.

Goodman-LeGrand House, 624 N. Broadway, built in 1859 by wealthy young bachelor Gallatin Smith, who became a Confederate officer. Many fine antiques. Antebellum and Civil War items.

UVALDE, Uvalde County. US 83. Settled in 1853 as Encina. Home of John Nance Garner, Vice-President under Franklin Roosevelt. Also the onetime home of sheriff and outlaw, J. K. "King" Fisher. City park has historical marker for Fisher and for graves of early settlers killed by Indians. Fisher was killed in March 1884, with another gun slinger, Ben Thompson, in San Antonio on what had begun as a business trip. Contemporary reports indicate that paid killers were out to kill Thompson and got King also. Thompson had been a marshal in Austin. (His homesite on the SE corner of 21st St. and University Ave. in Austin, ironically, is now occupied by the Texas Bible Chair.) Fisher was buried in a tear-shaped coffin in a cemetery since removed to what is now Frontier Cemetery, Uvalde. When his corpse was brought back to town, all of Uvalde went to the depot to pay respects.

VERNON, Wilbarger County. US 287. First called Eagle Flats because of nearby eagle nests. Headquarters for the vast W. T. Waggoner Ranch.

R. L. More St. Bird Egg Collection, 1905 W. Wilbarger, 10,000 eggs and a taxidermy exhibit.

Red River Valley Museum, 2100 Yamparika, archaeological exhibits and Indian artifacts.

VICTORIA, Victoria County. US 59. Anglo-Americans were here before 1824 when Don Martin de Leon brought 41 colonists and named the area for Gen. Guadalupe Victoria, who became first president of Mexico. Victoria was one of the first three towns incorporated by the Republic of Texas.

Victoria Memorial Square, E. Commercial and De Leon Sts. Old gristmill, locomotive, etc. Mass burial ground for yellow fever victims of 1846.

McNamara–O'Connor Historical and Fine Arts Museum, 502 N. Liberty, has a wide variety of relics.

Evergreen Cemetery, Red River and Vine Sts. has the grave of De Leon and other early settlers.

WACO, McLennon County. State 6. Once Hueco Indian land.

Texas Collection, on campus of Baylor University, 5th and Speight Sts. in

Carroll Library Bldg. Historical exhibits.

Strecker Museum, on campus in Sid Richardson Science Bldg. with archaeology, geology, anthropology and other scientific displays.

Historical Homes: Earle-Napier-Kinnard House, 814 S. 4th St., 1860s; East Terrace, 100 Mill St., 1872; Fort House, 503 S. 4th St., 1868, Earle–Harrison House, 1901 N. 5th St., 1858. Restored, with period furnishings.

Fort Fisher Park, I–35 and University Dr. at Brazos River. Headquarters for a company of Texas Rangers and Waco Tourist Information Center. Homer Garrison Memorial Museum on grounds has Texas Ranger relics; replica of a Texas Ranger fort established in 1837.

WASKOM, Harrison County. Tourist Bureau at state line on I–20.

WEATHERFORD, Parker County. US 80.

Texas Railroad Museum, 3 blocks E. of courthouse on US 80. In old Santa Fe depot. Vintage steam engine, private presidential car from the Texas & Pacific line, and many other items.

Parker County Courthouse, 1884–86, a registered historic place.

WECHES, Houston County. State 21.

Mission San Francisco de Los Tejas State Historic Park, SW of town off State 21 to PR 44. Replica of the first Spanish mission in East Texas is in 118-acre park. A large Tejas Indian village was nearby in 1690 when the mission was established.

WICHITA FALLS, Wichita County. Tourist Bureau on US 277, 281, 287.

Museum and Art Center, No. 2 Eureka Circle, historical displays. Science exhibits.

WIMBERLEY, Hays County. FM 12.

Pioneer Town, 1 mile S. on River Rd. replica of Texas frontier village with some log cabins from the 1860s. Steam train.

UTAH

About a mile below Nebo the road enters the Indian Reservation, and six miles onward is Indianola, around which cluster the adobe houses and tepees of a branch of the great Ute tribe, whence Utah has its name. They do a little farming and stock-raising, and a good deal of hunting and fishing, and, all things considered, are generally doing well. Whirling on through twenty miles of pastures and farms, past Hilltop and Milburn, at Fairview a glorious view of the San Pete Valley, "the granary of Utah," burst upon the enchanted eye. Only two miles more, and the train sweeps into Mount Pleasant, nestled in peach and apricot, apple, pear and plum trees, all bowed down with their loads of fruit. . . . A new depot, new hotel and many other new buildings tell the story of prosperity. A dash of six miles onward, and Manti is reached, with 2,300 people, and hardly a poor man among them.

Stanley Wood, *Over the Range; to the Golden Gate,* 1896

Oh, sad was the life of a Mormon to lead,
Yet Brigham adhered all his life to his creed.
He said 'twas such fun, and true, without doubt,
To see the young wives knock the old ones about.

Put's *Golden West Songster,* 1857

Young, Brigham, high priest of the Mormons, b. Whittington, Vt., 1 June, 1801. In 1832 he joined the Mormons at Kirtland, O.; soon became influential by his shrewdness and energy; was one of the 12 apostics sent out to make converts in 1835; and on the death of Joe Smith in June, 1844, was chosen pres. and prophet. With most of the sect, he abandoned Nauvoo early in 1846;

persuaded his followers that the Salt-Lake Valley was the Promised Land, and founded there, in July, 1847, Salt Lake City. In the spring of 1849, having greatly increased by emigration, they organized a State they called Deseret; but Congress organized it as the Terr. of Utah, of which Young was U.S. gov. in 1850–4. The Mormons having defied the Federal govt., Pres. Buchanan in 1857 sent a force of 2,500 men to enforce its authority; and in 1858 a compromise ended the imbroglio. Brigham has 12 actual wives, besides many who have been "sealed to him" as his spiritual wives.

Francis S. Drake,
Dictionary of American Biography, 1876

UTAH FACTS: Utah entered the Union January 4, 1896, as the 45th state. Capital: Salt Lake City. Nickname: Beehive State.

There are five national parks: Arches, Bryce Canyon, Canyonlands, Capitol Reef, and Zion; six national monuments: Cedar Breaks, Dinosaur, Natural Bridges, Rainbow Bridge, Timpanogos Cave and Hovenweep. The Golden Spike National Historic Site marks the spot where the first transcontinental railroad was completed in 1869. Nine national forests are wholly or partly within the state. A part of Glen Canyon National Recreation Area and Flaming Gorge Dam and National Recreation Area are in Utah.

ALTA, Salt Lake County. (6,105 ft.) US 163. It was once a busy mining camp after soldiers found silver in Little Cottonwood Canyon. The Emma Mine was established in 1869; its ore traveled in ox-drawn wagons to Ogden where it went by railroad to San Francisco, then was shipped to Wales for smelting. Avalanches destroyed much of the town in the 1880s, but it survived to become a ski resort.

ARCHES NATIONAL PARK, Grand County. US 163. The 53-square mile area provides an outdoor museum and a wildlife sanctuary. Visitor Center at entrance should be visited first.

ASHLEY NATIONAL FOREST, Uintah County. Red Canyon Visitor Center is 40 miles N. of Vernal via State 44 and has a museum. The forest covers ca. 1,399,000 acres, with five peaks over 13,000 feet high. The Red Canyon of the Green River, the Flaming Gorge Dam and National Recreation Area are within the area. State 44 follows a route called, "The Drive Through the Ages," in which a billion years of earth's history lies ex-

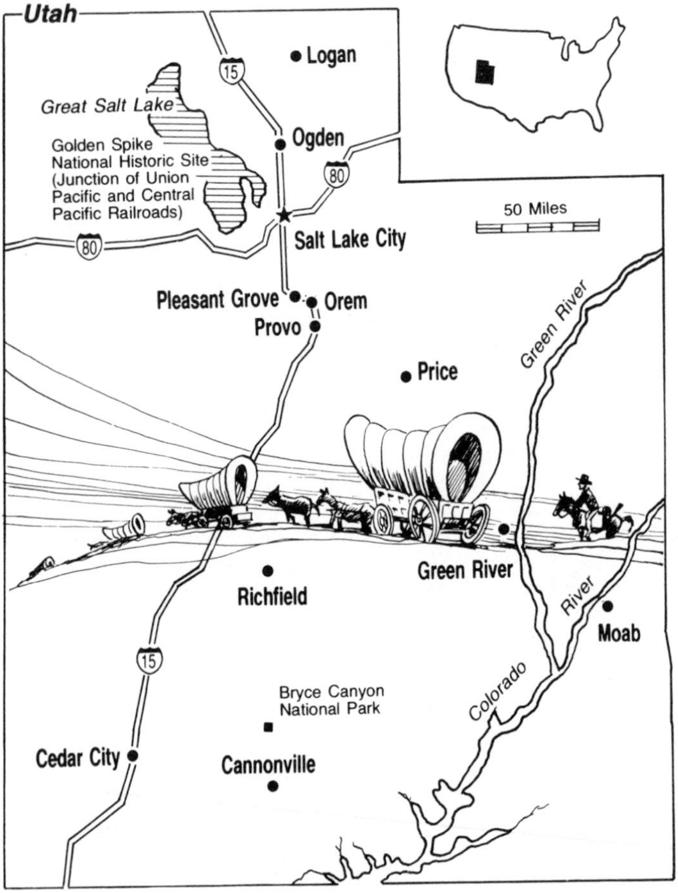
Utah
Logan
Great Salt Lake
Golden Spike
National Historic Site
(Junction of Union
Pacific and Central
Pacific Railroads)
15
Ogden
80
50 Miles
Salt Lake City
80
Pleasant Grove
Orem
Provo
Green River
Price
Green River
River
Moab
Richfield
15
Colorado
Bryce Canyon
National Park
Cedar City
Cannonville

posed, from Vernal to the Daggett County–Uintah County line.

BEAVER, Beaver County. (5,970 feet). US 91.

Old Cove Fort, via US 91, ca. 20 miles N. State 4. Erected in 1867, after the outbreak of the Ute Black Hawk War (not to be confused with the Black Hawk War of 1823 which was waged in Illinois and Wisconsin). The fort was built of volcanic rock on land bought by Brigham Young. A large bell hung in the entrance to warn of Indian approach. One of the 12 rooms was fitted up as a telegraph station for the new Deseret Telegraph Line. Now a state monument, with museum.

Fort Cameron, on the right side of the Beaver River, two miles E. of town, was set up to protect the newly opened mining district in the southern part of the area. Called Camp Beaver, it was formally designated a fort on June 30, 1874, for Col. James Cameron, 79th New York Infantry, who was killed on July 21, 1861, at Bull Run. Abandoned in July, 1885.

Beaver County Courthouse, 90 E. Center St., was constructed slowly from 1876 to 1882 because of Indian troubles. A fire soon after its completion partially destroyed the building. Rebuilt, it has been in use ever since and is a registered historic place.

BINGHAM CANYON, Salt Lake County. State 48. Mormons discovered gold and silver deposits here in 1848 but church officials kept the rumors down to avoid a rush. When Col. Patrick Connor, Army commander of the District of Utah, learned of the deposits in 1862, word was broadcast and prospectors came on the run. A railroad reached the canyon by the time gold had played out, making the operations for silver and lead profitable so that the area continued to be worked. The Utah Copper Co., organized in 1903, still uses open-pit mining methods here. There is an observation platform available daily from daylight till dusk.

BLANDING, San Juan County. (6,105 feet). US 163. The Edge of Cedars Pueblo here dates from 750, an Anasazi agricultural village which had a population of several hundred. A museum is being developed with an orientation program for the Trail of the Ancients.

Arch Canyon Indian Ruin, ca. 15 miles SW off State 95, Anasazi houses may be seen by a less than half a mile hike along the bottom of Comb Wash. The Bureau of Land Management at Monticello administers the site and has information on the ruins.

Natural Bridges National Monument, 4 miles S. on US 163, then 40 miles W. on State 95. Visitor Center for the 7,600-acre monument which contains three natural bridges and many unusual eroded formations. There is an 8-mile loop drive in the area, but the road to the monument is not paved all the way at this time and is treacherous-to-impassable in bad weather.

Hovenweep National Monument, SE via US 163 and State 262, is also in Colorado. Two of the six prehistoric towers are in Utah. All ruins date from the Great Pueblo Period of 1100–1300.

BLUFF, San Juan County. US 163. The first permanent town in southeastern Utah was settled in 1880 by what were called the Hole-in-the-Rock pioneers after what was known as an "impossible" journey in winter from Panguitch. It is an oasis with artesian wells. The Navajo Indian Reservation is S.; many Indians trade rugs and silver works in town. Inquire locally for land and river tours. Some are available year-round, depending on weather and water conditions.

BOULDER, Garfield County. State 12.

Anasazi Indian Village State Historical Monument, S. of town, Visitor Center at site of village (ca. 1050 to 1200) excavated by University of Utah archaeologists.

Calf Creek Recreation Site, State midway between Boulder and Escalante, has Indian ruins.

BRIGHAM CITY, Box Elder County. US 15.

Box Elder Tabernacle, 2 South and Main Sts., was begun in 1876. Guided tours.

Bear River Migratory Bird Refuge, 15 miles W., covers 64,895 acres. During fall months, whistling swans stop here as they may have in Brigham Young's day.

Inspiration Point, E. on US 89, 91, near summit of Willard Peak (Mount Baldy), offers a fine view of the Salt Lake Valley, but is reached by a narrow mountain road from Mantua.

BRYCE CANYON NATIONAL PARK, Garfield and Kane Counties, 26 miles SE of Panguitch on US 89, State 12. The 56-square mile, or 36,010-acre, park has a Visitor Center at entrance station with orientation program, detailed maps and geological displays. Ranger talks on history and geology of the park in summer months. The famous Pink Cliffs stretch for some 30 miles along the E. edge of the 8,000-foot Paunsaugunt Plateau.

CANYONLANDS NATIONAL PARK, Wayne, Garfield and San Juan Counties, via unnumbered road from US 163, 10 miles N. of Moab. The Needles section is reached by a road from US 163 at Church Rock, 15 miles N. of Monticello. Throughout the park which covers 337,258 acres, there are small ruins of dwellings and kivas of the Anasazi built between 900 and 1250, as well as many pictographs and petroglyphs. Information on tours and roads, many of which are safe only by four-wheel drive, available at park headquarters in Moab.

CAPITOL REEF NATIONAL PARK, several counties in S. central part of state, State 24. A 1,000-foot red sandstone cliff, 65 miles long, is part of a 3,000-square mile area where the Fremont Basketmaker Indians lived in caves along the Fremont River from 800 to 1,100. A Visitor Center is located on State 24 ca. 6 miles from the W. boundary and 12 miles from the E. Guided walks. John C. Frémont, who saw the area in 1854, named the site. Maj. John Powell explored the region in 1869.

CEDAR BREAKS NATIONAL MONUMENT, Iron County, off State 14, 21 miles E. of Cedar City. Exhibits at Visitor Center, Park Headquarters, pertain to the massive natural amphitheater carved from rock. Mormon pioneers mistook the mountain juniper for cedar in naming the site. The area which comprises ca. 10 square miles is in the Markagunt Plateau and is surrounded by the Dixie National Forest. It is open only in summer months.

CEDAR CITY, Iron County. US 15, I–15.

Palmer Memorial Museum, 75 N. 300 West, has pioneer and Indian displays.

Museum of Southern Utah, on campus of Southern Utah State College, 351 W. Center St.

First Log Cabin, in City Park, was built in 1851.

Old Iron Town, SW off State 56, ruins of pioneer iron plants. An old iron mine is just above State 56 in the same area.

Kanarraville, S. via I–15, founded in 1861, was named for Chief Kanarra, leader of a Piute Indian band. It was the center for old mining camps and towns, now ghost sites. It is still a division point for the Union Pacific.

CIRCLEVILLE, Piute County. (6,061 feet). US 89. The square-jawed leader of the Wild Bunch, who kept a personal promise to the governor of Wyoming not to molest *that* state, was born in 1867 on a ranch, S. of town. His name was George Leroy Parker and he was the oldest of seven. It has been said that horse thieves and cattle rustlers used the ranch because it was near the wilderness now a part of Bryce Canyon National Park. One of the cowhands was Mike Cassidy who knew a lot about livestock thievery and taught the boy who took his name how to ride and shoot. The youthful George Leroy used to help Cassidy drive stolen cattle to Robbers Roost, a popular rustlers' hangout. The Parker home, on US 89, 2 miles S. is now open to the public.

CORINNE, Box Elder County. State 83, 84.

Railroad Village Museum, railroadiana and an old railroad station.

DESERET, Millard County. State 257.

Fort Deseret, ca. 1 mile S. of town on highway, was built by the Mormons to protect settlers in 1866. Remains are in a state park.

Gunnison Massacre Site, on unimproved road, ca. 9 miles SW. Ute Indians massacred Capt. John W. Gunnison and his survey party who were sponsored by the War Department's Corps of Topographical Engineers. They were surveying for the Pacific Railroad when the Walker War broke out between the Utes and the Mormons in October 1853. Searchers found the bodies of the eight men who had been killed and buried them at the site. A monument marks the area. Surveying activities were suspended after this tragedy until more peaceful times the next year.

DINOSAUR NATIONAL MONUMENT, Uinta County. State 149.

Dinosaur Quarry Visitor Center, 7 miles N. of Jensen on State 149, has exhibits. The Monument Headquarters and Information Center is at park entrance in Colorado. About one-third of the 325-square-mile monument is in Utah.

FAIRFIELD, Utah County. State 73.

Camp Floyd State Historical Park, W. on State 73, has the Stagecoach Inn, the commissary building and the Johnston Army Cemetery, with 84 soldier graves from the period of 1858–59 when Col. Albert Sidney Johnston was based here. Johnston later served as a Confederate general whose death at Shiloh was a major loss to the South. The post, established during the hostilities, sometimes called the Utah War, was designated Fort Crittenden on February 6, 1861, after Secretary of War John B. Floyd for whom it had been named went with the Confederacy. Col. Patrick Connor and members of the 3rd California Infantry were here in October 1862.

Carson House, Main St., a two-story adobe, was built ca. 1858. Albert Johnston lived here while commander at Camp Floyd. Pioneer furnishings. The town was an important stop on the Pony Express. The Inn, which has been restored, was used by passengers. The Rush Valley Station, 12 miles W. of town, is marked by a stone and plaque. Farther west, Callao and Ibapah were stops. The old stone station at Callao still stands. Deep Creek was the last station before crossing into Nevada; one of the buildings used by the Express is now a store. At Lookout Pass Station, near Rush Valley, is a small cemetery, but the once well-marked route has been preyed upon by 20th-century vandals who have defaced the plaques and stolen the medallions.

FILLMORE, Millard County. I–15.

Territorial Statehouse State Historic Monument, 50 W. Capitol Ave, was built of red sandstone in the 1850s. Now a museum.

FORT DUCHESNE, Uintah County. State 44.

Headquarters for the Ute Indian Reservation. The post was established in August 1886, on a site chosen by Brig. Gen. George Crook, the "Gray Fox" of Indian War fame, on the Du Chesne River, to control the Uncompahgre and White River Utes.

GOLDEN SPIKE NATIONAL HISTORIC SITE, Box Elder County. Off State 83. The national park service area covers 1,542 acres and includes the site where the last spike was driven on May 10, 1869, to complete the first transcontinental railroad. To form a junction of the Union Pacific from the east and the Central Pacific from the west 1800 miles of railway had been laid in about 6½ years. Visitor Center open in summer months. Leland Stanford, President of the Central Pacific Railroad, was given the honor of driving the last spike, but he missed on his first swing.

GUNLOCK, Washington County. Off State 18. The town was founded by William Hamblin, brother of Jacob Hamblin, known as Gunlock Bill for his use of the rifle and knowledge of how to repair it. Indian writings will be found on rocks of the area. Shivwits Indian Reservation is S. on road running W. of State 18. The *Jacob Hamlin Home State Historic Monument* is SE (See Santa Clara).

HEBER CITY, Wasatch County. (5,-595 feet). US 189.

Wasatch Mountain Railway, 6 West and Center Sts. A 3½-hour ride on the "Heber Creeper" through the valley, Provo Canyon, to Bridal Veil Falls, behind a steam locomotive, in summer months.

KANAB, Kane County. US 89. A former fort site (in the 1860s), the area has been used often as background in Western films for motion pictures and television. Zane Grey wrote *Riders of the Purple Sage* when he lived here. Tours to Indian ruins, caves, movie sets and sandhills available in town.

LOGAN, Cache County. US 89.

Mormon Tabernacle, Main and Center Sts., was built in 1878. Guided tours.

Mormon Temple, 175 N. 3 East St., stands on a site selected by Brigham Young, who broke ground for it in

1877. Guided tours of grounds only.

Man and His Bread Museum and Historical Farm, 5 miles S. on US 89, 91, has exhibits of agricultural development in Utah.

Daughters of the Utah Pioneers Museum, 52 W. 2 North St., in Chamber of Commerce Bldg., has historical exhibits, featuring Mormon pioneer relics.

MEXICAN HAT, San Juan County. US 163.

Great Goosenecks of the San Juan State Reserve, 6 miles N. via US 163, State 261, then 4 miles SW. The last 4 miles are something like a washerboard. Below the park at 1,500 feet the river cuts a series of gorges through a convoluted area that must be seen to be believed. The river flows N., S., N. and again S., 6 miles above the state park road turnoff, another unpaved road leads from State 261 to Muley Point Overlook, which is ca. 1,000 feet higher than the park lookout. The river travels ca. 8 miles zigzag in order to go 1 mile ahead.

MOAB, Grand County. US 163.

Moab Museum, 118 E. Center, historical, archaeological, geological exhibits, collections of gems and minerals.

Dead Horse Point State Park, 12 miles N. on US 163, then 18 miles SW. A panorama of the Colorado River Canyons from the point. Visitor Center and museum.

MONTICELLO, San Juan County. US 163.

Newspaper Rock State Historical Monument, 15 miles N., then 12 miles W., off US 163, at Indian Creek Canyon. Indian petroglyphs.

Alkali Ridge, 25 miles SE on secondary road, 10 miles E. of Recapture Creek on State 47. Excavations lead to the theory that the Anasazi ceremonial kiva developed in this area which represents a culture of ca. 900–1100. A national historic landmark, not accessible to the public at present.

MOUNTAIN MEADOW, Washington County. Just W. of State 18. (Also known as Mountain Meadows.) In the fall of 1857, California-bound emigrants were killed in this lonely site; only 18 children were spared of the group of 120 persons. It was reported as an Indian massacre with a few white men present; only John D. Lee was named as being on the scene, and he was executed for his part in the crime much later. Many stories have been told about what took place on that sad day, but the affair seems to have stemmed from the fact that Capt. Charles Fancher, who led the wagon train had tried to get provisions at several points in Utah and had been overheard making remarks about what he would like to do with the Mormons, or would do when he had finished with the wagon train and could organize his own army. Hostility and rumor grew. The party camped in Mountain Meadows on September 5; the next morning Indians attacked, leaving about 20 dead and taking livestock. Fancher appealed to the Mormons for aid. John D. Lee, a Mormon elder, accompanied by some militia and Indians, agreed to escort the wagon train to Cedar City. On September 7, as the train was just getting underway, they were set upon by their escort with many not only killed but mutilated. The smallest children were spared on the grounds that they were too small to be witnesses. Years later John D. Lee was tried, found guilty and ex-

When they drove the Golden Spike at Promontory Point, Utah, May 10, 1896
(Utah Travel Council)

ecuted at the site of the massacre, March 23, 1877. Marker at site. Many believed that Brigham Young condoned the actions of the militia at the time, but he later excluded Lee from the Church. Mormons maintained silence on the matter over the years which delayed the apprehending of Lee, who was hiding in a hog pen at his ferry in Arizona when he was taken into custody on July 12, 1875. At his execution he said: "I studied to make Brigham Young's will my pleasure for thirty years. See now what I have come to this day." He took off his coat and muffler to spare them for his coffin and requested that his executioners shoot straight for his heart, not to mangle his body, a nicety he seems not to have had in mind on that September day 20 years earlier.

NEW HARMONY, Iron County. On secondary road, 5 miles W. of I–15, ca. 18 miles S. of Cedar City.

Fort Harmony was established at the base of the Pine Mountains and was the first settlement in the area in 1852. The fort was built by John D. Lee, who was later executed for his part in the Mountain Meadows Massacre. Indian troubles brought abandonment of the settlement. A few years later the town was settled.

OGDEN, Weber County. I–15.

John M. Browning Gun Collection, 450 E. 5100 S. at Washington Blvd., 4 miles S. on US 89.

Jedediah Smith Monument, in City Hall Park, Washington Ave. between 25th and 26th. The mountain man who led the Southwest Expedition of 1826–29 is one of the most interesting of early adventurers and merits more fame than he has received to date. Biographer Alson J. Smith in *Men Against the Mountains,* published in 1965, traced Smith's route to the Pacific. For the Utah part, Smith went west from Hyrum, in the Cache Valley, on what is now State 242; at Wellsville the route follows US 91 S. to Levan, following State 28 to US 89 at Gunnison. This parallels Smith's Sevier River route. At Cove, the route leaves the river and follows State 13 along the Clear Creek Narrows to Cove Fort. From here it follows US 91 to Las Vegas, Nevada.

Daughters of Utah Pioneer Relic Hall, 2148 Grant Ave., in Tabernacle Sq. Costumes and household relics. The Miles Goodyear Cabin here is the oldest pioneer dwelling in Utah. Goodyear came west in 1836 and settled on the banks of the Weber River building Fort Buenaventura, the first fort W. of the Wasatch Range. His home became a stopping place for California-bound emigrants. He met the first Mormons to arrive in July 1847. They bought Goodyear's cabin and stockade for $2,000. The building is a registered historic place.

Bertha Eccles Community Art Center, 2580 Jefferson Ave., was built in 1893, for James C. Armstrong, who sold it to David Eccles in 1896. Mrs. Eccles was a social leader in early Ogden. A registered historic place.

OPHIR, Tooele County. On spur off State 73 running 3 miles NE. in the Oquirrh Canyon. A ghost town where Indians mined silver and gold. Col. Patrick Connor's men, ever alert for gold news, heard of this spot, moved in and staked the St. Louis Lode claim in 1865, naming the town for King Solomon's mines. Within five years a boom was on. The ghost town of Mercur is SE off State 73. Ophir, before its day was over, produced one of the largest silver nuggets found in the

U.S. It was displayed at the St. Louis World's Fair in 1904.

PANGUITCH, Garfield County. (6,560 feet). US 89.

Panguitch Cemetery has the grave of John D. Lee, of the Mountain Meadows massacre. The inscription on his tall headstone merely reads: "In Memory of John D. Lee Sept. 6, 1812 Mar. 23, 1877."

Panguitch–Escalante–Boulder Scenic Drive runs for more than 120 miles with panoramic views of wilderness areas, canyons, cliffs and Indian pictographs as well as petrified wood. The Hell's Backbone area crosses the S. rim of the Aquarius Plateau along a narrow ridge that fits the name.

PARK CITY, Summit County. (6,980 feet). State 248. Silver, lead and gold deposits were found in 1869. The Flagstaff Mine was opened in 1870 and tents followed. At the bottom of Provo Canyon, tents and shacks became the grandly named Park City. The Ontario Mine in 1872 paid well. Fires failed to hold back the population growth which had reached 6,000 people by the silver crash of 1893. Park City is still a mining town, despite reverses and has produced more than $250 million worth of gold, silver, lead, copper and zinc.

"Historical" saloons, melodrama theaters, emporiums, etc., in the town now.

PAROWAN, Iron County. (6,000 feet). I–15. Known as the "Mother of the South" because it served as the base for the colonization of southern Utah. The town was founded in 1851, the oldest permanent settlement in the area. Old Rock Church, in town. Ancient Indian hieroglyphics on scenic drives.

PAYSON, Utah County. Off I–15.

Mount Nebo Scenic Loop, S. on Nebo Loop Rd., a 45-mile trip rather like natural roller coaster and Loop-the-loop with spectacular scenery goes around the E. shoulder of the mountain. The road which passes through Payson and Santaquin canyons climbs to 9,000 feet, with a view of Devil's Kitchen. S. on forest road to State 132, W. to Nephi, then US 91 back to Payson.

PLEASANT GROVE, Utah County. State 146. A small, wayward battle took place here in April 1863 between Ute Indians and a company of California volunteers. Historian Ray Colton classically describes the attack:

> . . . The cannon was hidden in an adobe house. At 6:00 A.M. on April 12, a band of about one hundred belligerent Utes approached the soldiers' camp. The concealed howitzer went into action. The first shell of grapeshot missed the Indians and killed five government mules. The second cracked the walls of the house. No more artillery shots were attempted. The Indians, firing from behind an adobe fence, kept up the siege until 8:00 P.M., when they withdrew, taking the soldiers' provisions and seven surviving mules.

PRICE, Carbon County. (5,566 feet). State 10. US 6.

Prehistoric Museum, in Municipal Building, Main St., has a mounted dinosaur skeleton from a nearby quarry; other prehistoric relics, rocks and minerals. Directions for tour of dinosaur quarry and Indian petroglyphs are available here.

Chamber of Commerce has maps

for several tours of desert, canyon and wilderness areas. Outlaws of Utah didn't need maps to find Price, which was a stopping place popular with the Wild Bunch and with the gangs that frequented Brown's Hole. Cassidy and his mob favored Robbers Roost. At one time word spread that he had been killed by a posse in the San Rafael Swell, south of town. Cassidy himself was one who came to view the corpse, according to local legend. He traveled in a covered wagon past the place where he presumably was lying in state. The corpse proved to be that of Jim Herron, a less legendary outlaw. Matt Warner of the Robbers Roost gang lived in Price, after he had raided much of the country even as far as Oregon, served time in the penitentiary, then took up ranching here and was twice in office as city marshal, then served a term as justice of the peace at Carbonville.

Cassidy and his gang took the mine payroll at Castle Gate in 1897 and skirted the city of Price in his escape. The Sundance Kid, Big Nose George Curry, Deaf Charlie Hanks and Kid Curry were other outlaws who used the canyons of the area to hide out and cool off after holdups.

PROVO, Utah County. US 91.

Pioneer Museum, 5th W. and 5th N. Varied collection of Utah pioneer historical exhibits and replica of a pioneer cabin.

Brigham Young University, was founded by Brigham Young. Guided tours arranged at Smoot Administration Bldg.; on campus, Geological Collection, Eyring Science Center; Botanical Collections, Grant Bldg.; Museum of Archaeology and Ethnology, Maeser Bldg.; Harris Fine Arts Center; Zoological, Entomological Collections, Brimhall, Grant Bldgs.; Summerhays Planetarium, Eyring Science Center.

Uinta National Forest, E. ege of town, comprises 797,579 acres.

Fort Rawlins, on N. bank of the Timpanogos River, 2 miles from town, near the base of the Wasatch Mountains, was established in July 1870. Two companies of the 13th U.S. Infantry were sent to the post but no buildings were erected and the troops were housed in tents in Provo. Abandoned in July 1871.

RAINBOW BRIDGE NATIONAL MONUMENT, on Navajo Indian Reservation, just S. of Glen Canyon area. Horses and guides available at Navajo Trading Post, at Utah-Arizona border, N. from a junction 6 miles E. of Tonalea on unnumbered road. The Navajos called it *nonnezoshi,* meaning "rainbow turned to stone." It is the largest natural bridge in the world, 278 feet long, 309 feet high.

ST. GEORGE, Washington County. State 15, 18. I–15.

Temple, 401 S. 300 East. Visitor Center, guided tour of grounds. The first Mormon Temple in Utah.

Tabernacle, Main and Tabernacle Sts. Visiting by appointment, inquire at Temple Visitor Center.

Brigham Young Winter Home, 2 North and 1 West, built in 1874, has period furnishings.

Daughters of Utah Pioneers Collection, McQuarrie Memorial Bldg., 145 N. 100 East.

SANTA CLARA, Washington County. 3 miles W. of St. George, off US 91.

Jacob Hamblin Home was built in 1863. The Mormon missionary was a peace-maker with the Indians. Furnishings are from the 1880s. A state historical site.

Joshua Tree Forest, SW, near Arizona border on unnumbered road.

SALT LAKE CITY, Salt Lake County. US 89, 40.

State Capitol, State St. A skyscape with huge seagulls is painted on the dome ceiling. The gull is Utah's favorite bird because a group of them once devoured a horde of crickets which endangered settlers' crops. Pioneer scenes and statuary are in the Rotunda. On the grounds is a statue of Massasoit, the Indian of Massachusetts history, which is a copy of the Dallin original at Plymouth Bay. The sculptor was born in Utah. The Mormon Battalion Monument on the capitol grounds commemorates the troops which marched 2,000 miles from Iowa to California in the Mexican War of 1846.

Council Hall, Old City Hall, State St. and 2 North. The original building of 1864–66 was dismantled and reassembled here in 1962. It was the meeting place of the territorial legislature. Now houses museum and travel Council offices.

Pioneer Memorial Museum, 300 N. Main, pioneer relics, documents; carriage house with Brigham Young's wagon, pony express items, and other early vehicles.

Utah State Historical Society, 603 E. South Temple St. is housed in a 32-room mansion with some original furnishings.

Marriott Library, on campus of University of Utah, 2 South St., has a collection of Western Americana. Also on campus, the Museum of Fine Arts and the Museum of Natural History.

Grave of Brigham Young, 1 Ave. between A and N. State.

Temple Square, Main and S. Temple, has a Visitor Center. Guided tours for the Tabernacle, Temple, Assembly Hall, Seagull Monument and the Osmun Deuel log cabin built in 1847. A national historic landmark.

Brigham Young Monument, Main and S. Temple.

Lion House and Beehive House, 67 E. South Temple, were Young family dwellings, also served as offices. Lion House closed to the public. Beehive House, also served as first governor's mansion, has been restored to its appearance in Young's day and is open for tours. Built in 1854 it was the first residence of Young and 19 wives, 56 children.

Pioneer Village Museum, 2998 S. Connor St., has 37 buildings restored to 19th-century appearance. Mormon meeting house, narrow-gauge engine and car at depot. Main museum has a gun collection. Buffalo roam, to a certain extent, and there are oxen rides.

"This Is the Place" Monument, Sunnyside Ave. E. edge of town, State 65, at entrance to Emigration Canyon. Here Brigham Young allegedly said the famous one-liner. Visitor Center at site; a national historic landmark.

Isaac Chase Mill, Liberty Park, 6th St. East, is believed to be the only gristmill built by Utah pioneers still standing on original site. In 1854 Brigham Young bought into the property owned by Isaac Chase and owned it outright by 1860. Much original machinery remains. A registered historic place.

Deveraux House, 334 West South Temple St., built in 1857 is a registered historic place.

Fort Douglas, on Fort Douglas Military Reservation, US alt. 40, NE edge of town, was established October 26, 1862, on a bench N. of Red Butte Creek. It was intended to protect the Overland Mail and telegraph and to keep a watchful eye on the Mormons. Col. Patrick Connor and the 3rd California Infantry were based here. There is a monument of Connor and his Volunteers in the post cemetery.

Mormon Irrigation Sites, along City Creek in downtown area, have been obliterated but a monument commemorates the achievement. The Mormons were the first non-Indians to irrigate extensively in the West. After their arrival in the Great Salt Lake basin, they found the soil too dry and built a dam at one of two creeks which flowed from the Wasatch Mountains, diverting the water to irrigate their fields.

Wasatch National Forest, E. of town, via US 40, includes the High Uintas Primitive Area in its 885,559 acres.

Liberty Park, 10 South and 6 East Sts., includes the Chase mill. Other pioneer mementoes are also on view in the 100 acres.

Great Salt Lake, 17 miles W. on US 40, I–80.

Lockerby Collection, on campus of Westminster College, S. 13 St., in Science Hall, has Utah rock and mineral displays.

Forest Farm House, 732 Ashton Ave., was built in 1861–63 on the site of an experimental farm founded by Brigham Young. The house has been restored and furnished.

Wire House, 668 S. Third St., was built in 1887 and is the place where Lester Farnsworth Wire invented the traffic light in 1912. Now a museum with some original furnishings. Traffic lights were one nuisance the pioneers were not plagued with.

St. Mark's Episcopal Cathedral, 231 E. First South St. The oldest non-Mormon cathedral in Utah was built in 1871. A registered historic building.

SILVER REEF, Washington County. Ca. 1½ miles off US 91. 4 miles S. of New Harmony. A ghost town, with a well-preserved Wells-Fargo Express office, was once a bustling mining camp in the 1870s and 1880s. Prospector John Kemple filed the first claims in 1866 but didn't come back until 1870. Others were skeptical about anyone finding silver in sandstone; bankers would not invest in the mines, but newspaper stories kept the rumors alive. Hyrum Jacobs set up a tent, then a store, and named the town in the 1870s. Some adobe and stone wall ruins remain.

SPRINGVILLE, Utah County. US 89.

Daughters of Utah Pioneers Museum, 175 S. Main. Pioneer relics.

TIMPANOGOS CAVE NATIONAL MONUMENT, Salt Lake County. 26 miles S. of Salt Lake City on I–15, then 10 miles E. on State 80. Visitor Center has museum. Headquarters are on State 80, 8 miles E. of American Fork. The monument is made up of three underground chambers. Guided tours.

VERNAL, Uintah County. State 17, US 40. Headquarters for the Ashley National Forest (which see) are here. The only major East-West mountain range in the U.S. is within the forest.

Utah Field House of Natural History, Natural History State Park, 235 E. Main St. Museum has a variety of of fossils, archaeological, geological and mineral displays.

Thorne's Photo Studio, 18 W. Main St., museum with artifacts of prehistoric people.

Uintah County Park, 7 miles NW. Petroglyphs in Dry Fork Canyon.

Pioneer Museum, 178 S. 5th West,

has settlers' relics, in house built of hand-quarried native rock, the first Mormon tithing office. Moved from original site.

Flaming Gorge National Recreation Area, 40 miles N. on State 44, 260. Two Visitor Centers, one at dam, one at Red Canyon on secondary road off State 44, W. of junction with State 260. At the dam site center is a relief map which will orient the visitor to present-day conditions; photographs and murals recall how it was in the days of William Sublette, Jim Bridger, William Ashley and other adventurers.

ZION NATIONAL PARK, chiefly in Washington County. State 15. Nearly all of outdoor Utah is spectacular and this is not the least of its wonders. The park covers 147,094 acres. Visitor Center near S. entrance has maps, weather and road information; lectures in summer. Guided tours are available.

WASHINGTON

I've wandered all over this country
Prospecting and digging for gold;
I've tunnel'd, hydraulicked and cradled,
And I nearly froze in the cold. . . .

I rolled up my grub in my blanket,
I left all my tools on the ground,
I started one morning to shank it
For the country they call Puget Sound. . . .

No longer the slave of ambition,
I laugh at the world and its shams,
And think of my happy condition
Surrounded by acres of clams.

(Anonymous)

I got in sight of the City of Walla Walla—it was a lively little place of about two or three thousand inhabitants, mostly transient miners, teamsters, packers and land-seekers. There were two or three hotels and a lot of boarding houses, some four or five restaurants, eight or ten saloons, three or four bakeries, three drug stores, four or five butcher shops, three or four barbers; at least 8 or 10 general stores, dry goods and groceries, boots and shoes, doctors, lawyers, two breweries, one nice theatre, and several churches (not very costly buildings) and some five or six livery, feed, and sale stables, some nice billiard rooms, and several large gambling saloons with all kinds of games and gaming tables where they had music and singing every night free, and one or two dance houses of evil repute, and one or two hurdy-gurdy dance houses of fair repute—taken altogether Walla Walla was a fast place, and a great outfitting place for the mines all over. . . .

The Golden Frontier; the Recollections of Herman Francis Reinhart 1851–1869 (Austin, 1962)

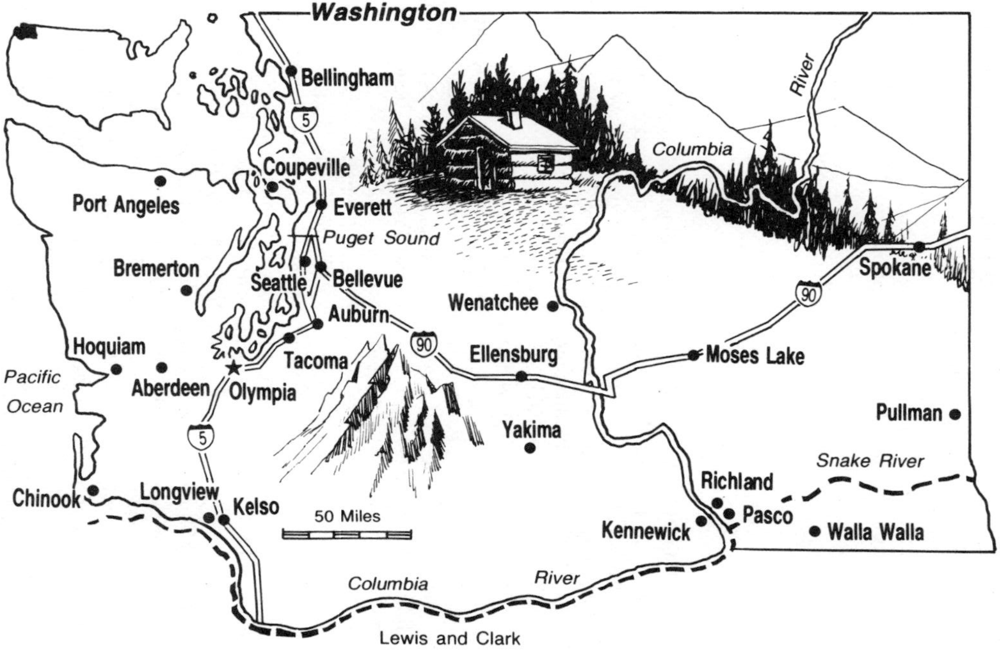
Washington
Bellingham
5
Coupeville
Port Angeles
Everett
Puget Sound
Bremerton
Seattle
Bellevue
Auburn
Wenatchee
Hoquiam
Tacoma
90
Ellensburg
Moses Lake
Spokane
90
Columbia
River
Pacific
Ocean
Aberdeen
Olympia
Pullman
Yakima
5
Snake River
Richland
Chinook
Longview
Kelso
Pasco
50 Miles
Kennewick
Walla Walla
Columbia
River
Lewis and Clark

WASHINGTON FACTS: Many early explorers came by sea. Capt. Robert Gray arrived at the entrance to the Strait of Juan de Fuca in April 1792. Lewis and Clark came overland in 1805–6. Washington Territory was established in 1853, and the state was admitted to the Union on November 11, 1889, the 42nd state. Washington has three national parks, three national recreation areas, and six national forests. Capital: Olympia. Nickname: Evergreen State.

Chief Tribes Chehalis, Cowlitz, Spokane, Walla Walla, Yakima, Nisqually, Squamish, Quinault, Makah, Klikitat, Chinook and Tillamook.

Early Trails Lewis and Clark Trail, Telegraph Road, Caribou Trail, Columbia River, Northern Pacific Railway.

ABERDEEN–HOQUIAM, Grays Harbor County. US 101, 12. The twin cities share the harbor.

Samuel Benn Home, 4th St. between G and F, the 1887 house of pioneer settler Benn. Samuel Benn Park, N. 1st St., was part of the original estate.

Hoquiam's Castle, 515 Chenault Ave., was the 1897 home of Robert Lytle, lumber baron. Restored 20-room, turreted mansion, with period furnishings.

Port of Grays Harbor, foot of Myrtle St., is named for Capt. Robert Gray, who sailed his ship, *The Columbia,* to port here in 1792.

AINSWORTH, Franklin County. US 410. Early railroad town near the junction of the Snake and the Columbia rivers was founded in 1879. Marker on US 410, SE of Pasco, near entrance to Sacajawea State Park. The state marker for Sacajawea begins conversationally: "Let us pause at this point along the Lewis and Clark trail of 1805 and pay tribute to the memory of the most dramatic figure in the history of the Northwest —Sacajawea, the Bird Woman." Dedicated history hunters will find many places along the trail to pause and pay tribute at a marker or monument for the Bird Woman, from the prairies of North Dakota to this Pacific Coast. At a guess, this unlettered Indian young woman may have more statues and bronze markers to her credit than any other female in U.S. history. She earned them all. Sacajawea had been stolen from the Shoshone Tribe when she was a little girl. She had married Toussant Charbonneau, a French half-blood guide, and was living in the land of the Dacotahs when Lewis and Clark arrived at the Mandan village above the site of present-day Bismarck, North Dakota. She gave birth to a son in February 1805, but agreed to go on the expedition when it was ready to leave in April, with her baby strapped Indian cradle-style on her back. They traveled in canoes made of willow poles and buffalo hides, and Sacajawea proved invaluable in her knowledge of the Missouri Valley Indians and their leaders. Her brother, Cameahwait, was a Shoshone chief.

ALPOWA, Garfield County. N. of US 410 above Snake River. Chief Timothy is buried on Alpowa Creek and the nearby bridge is named for him. He was helpful to Col. E. J. Steptoe in his campaign against the Palouse and their allies in May 1858. Lewis and Clark camped near here in 1805 and established good relations with the Nez Perce. Chief Red Wolf planted the first orchard in the valley with seeds given to him by missionary-explorer H. H. Spalding. John Silcott, for whom the present town is named, was married to Chief Timothy's daughter and ran a ferry across the Snake which was called Silcott's Landing until it was platted in 1882 and named Alpowa. Silcott is on US 410, S. of the Snake.

ALTOONA, Wahkiakum County. State 403, on the Columbia River. Whoever said "half the fun is getting there" could have been looking for ghost towns. Altoona is a picturesque old fishing village (which is like saying the Grand Canyon is big—but the weatherbeaten old houses and wharves of Washington's "Ghost Coast" are almost foolproof for photographers). Pillar Rock is 4 miles away. Megler and Knappton are on State 401. Skamowkawa on US 830 was once a riverboat stop on Steamboat Slough; Cathlamet, on US 830, is the county seat and has a museum. Lewis and Clark spelled it "Cathlamah" in their records for 1805–6.

AUBURN, King County. State 167, 18.

The 1941 WPA-sponsored state guide has an amusing paragraph to explain the name:

> In this pleasant valley, in 1887, Dr. Levi W. Ballard, one of the first settlers, platted the town of Slaughter to honor Lt. W. A. Slaughter, who was killed near the townsite during the Indian wars. It became a settlement, with one or two stores, a shingle mill and scattered hop farms. With the coming of the Northern Pacific Railway, the town boomed, and Slaughter's citizens became name-conscious. It was embarrassing to have the hotel runner board the trains and cry: "This way to the Slaughter House." By special act of the legislature in 1893, the name was changed to Auburn, from Oliver Goldsmith's opening line in "The Deserted Village": "Sweet Auburn, loveliest village of the plain."

Highway marker is less than 2 miles N. at site where Lt. Slaughter and two enlisted men were killed by Indians on December 4, 1855. There is also a descriptive marker on highway for the White River massacre of October 1855.

BELLINGHAM, Whatcom County. I–5.

Pickett Memorial Bridge, Dupont at Prospect, across Whatcom Creek. A memorial tablet is at N. end for Pickett who built the town's first bridge in 1856.

Pickett House, 910 Bancroft St., the home of George Pickett, later to make the famous Pickett's Charge at the Battle of Gettysburg, lived here with his Indian wife and son in 1856 when he was stationed at Fort Bellingham; it is maintained by the state historical society, with many relics among the furnishings. The fort was a small blockhouse in 1855, later a temporary post under Capt. Pickett, abandoned in 1860.

Whatcom Museum of History and Art, 121 Prospect Ave., is housed in what was once the City Hall, a late Victorian building which is a nationally registered historic place. Regional and historic displays.

Old Telegraph Road, N. of town at N. side of Guide–Meridian Road, ca. two blocks from the Lyndon exit, I–5. Marker denotes site of wilderness road where a telegraph line was partially built in 1865–67 to connect New York with London via a Bering Strait cable and a line across Russia. The project was dropped by Western Union in 1867 when trans-Atlantic cable service was in operation. The cooperation established between Russian and American workers in building the line aided negotiations for the purchase of Alaska in 1867.

BOSSBURG, Stevens County. State 25. A ghost town now, this was once a lead-silver mining settlement called Young America. (There was also a Young American lode in Wyoming.) In 1892 the town, on the banks of the Columbia, had a boom population of 800; a leading citizen was C. S. Boss. Other interesting old towns in the onetime area of mining camps are China Bend, Marble and Northport, N. on State 25. Evans and Marcus, S. on State 25, toward Kettle Falls, and Echo, SW on county road toward Colville. Ruins of the old brick smelter are still standing at Northport. A frame building that served as the town brothel stands next to the old meat market.

BOTHELL, King County. State 527, 522.

W. A. Hannan House, 10222 Main St. A pioneer residence built by the postmaster William Hannan for his bride has been restored as a house museum with period furnishings.

BREMERTON, Kitsap County. US 101.

Kitsap County Historical Museum, 837 4th St. Local history.

Naval Shipyard Museum, Ferry Terminal Building, has displays featuring Navy and shipping history. Models, weapons and other exhibits.

BREWSTER, Okanogan County. US 97.

Fort Okanogan State Park, 5 miles E. on US 97, comprises 46 acres at the confluence of the Okanogan and Columbia rivers. The fort was established in 1811 by John Jacob Astor's Pacific Fur Co. The British North West Co. took over in the War of 1812. From 1821 to 1860 the Hudson's Bay Co. owned the fort. It was moved nearer the Columbia in the 1830s; a flagpole marks the site. Museum has interpretive displays telling the history of fur trading in the Northwest by exhibits and dioramas. Indian artifacts.

BRUCEVILLE—BRUCEPORT, Pacific County. US 101. Marker on N. side of highway overlooking Willapa Bay describes the deserted site of a pioneer village where the crew of an oyster schooner settled in December 1851, after the vessel burned. The settlement was first Bruceville, changed to Bruceport in 1854. From the 1850s to the 1880s there was a brisk oyster trade; Indians gathered large quantities of native oysters for San Francisco-bound schooners.

CASHMERE, Chelan County. US 2.

Willis Carey Historical Museum, E. edge of town, has Indian displays, a Columbia River archaeology exhibit and a restored pioneer village, which includes a replica mission building, blacksmith shop and other relics. Father Urban Grassi, Jesuit priest, visited the Simpesquensi Indians near here in the summer of 1872 and baptized many of them. In 1873 he erected the original mission, St. Francis Xavier, and taught the Indians something about irrigation by diverting Mission Creek over a garden patch.

Wenatchee National Forest NW of town, comprises 1,614,420 acres. Headquarters in Wenatchee.

Arrasta, on Swauk Pass Highway, 11 miles S. of the junction of US 2 and 97, was built by gold miners in 1861 and used until 1880 when it was replaced by a stamp mill. Another *arrasta* is ca. 10 miles S. near Liberty and was used until 1932. Marker on highway S. of Leavenworth and due W. of Wenatchee. An *arrasta* was a water-powered, ore-grinding machine popular in the West before the 1840s.

CENTRALIA, Lewis County. I–5. The town was founded by a former slave, George Washington, who came to the West with his master from Missouri. He was made a free man and was, by some accounts, adopted by his former master as a son. Another story is that the master, who arrived here in 1850, filed a donation land claim and later sold it to his servant for $6,000. In any case, Washington prospered. Washington Park, Main and Pearl St., named for him, is on land he donated to the city.

Borst Blockhouse, in Borst Park, off US 99, S. of Harrison Ave., was built as a fortification at the confluence of the Shookumchuck and Chehalis rivers, and was moved here after the original site was flooded. Capt. Francis Goff and Oregon Volunteers established the fort on property belonging to Joseph Borst, who operated a stopover house on the ferry crossing.

CHEHALIS, Lewis County. State 6.

Claquato Church, 3 miles W. on State 6, is the oldest church remaining in state but is no longer in use. The bronze bell in the belfry was cast in Boston in 1857, sent via Cape Horn. The pews and pulpit are handmade; much of the work was done by John Duff Clinger—planks were cut on a jigsaw mill and the nails were forged by A. F. Gordon, a local blacksmith. Lewis Davis, who founded the town and donated the material for church, is buried in the small cemetery up the hill. Claquato was once a stop on the Military Rd. from the Columbia River to the Olympia area.

John R. Jackson House State Park, 10 miles S. on I–5, then E. on State 14. The first house built N. of the Columbia River was used as a courthouse in 1850. Jackson came to the area via the Oregon Trail.

CHENEY, Spokane County. Off I–90, State 904.

Turnbull National Wildlife Refuge, 4 miles S. on Cheney Plaza Highway, then 2 miles E. on Pacific Flyway.

CHINOOK, Pacific County. US 101.

Fort Columbia State Park, 1 mile E. Marker at park entrance. Capt. Robert Gray dropped anchor nearby after his discovery of the Columbia River in May 1792. In 1805 Lewis and Clark camped here. In 1843 Captain Scarborough became the first settler N. of the river who stayed on. Throughout fur-trading days the area was of major importance. Chief Comcomly of the Chinooks had only one eye but contemporaries said he never missed anything. The Chinooks who fished with as many as 30 persons squatting in a canoe were usually short, bowlegged with large flat feet; they lived mainly on fish and by fishing. Fort

Columbia was established late in the century to guard the mouth of the river. The Commanding Officer's House is now a museum with period furnishings. A national historic landmark.

CLARKSTON, Asotin County. US 410, State 129.

Lewis and Clark Route, marker 1 mile W. on US 410 near the Snake River.

Umatilla National Forest, 34 miles S. on State 129.

Early Indian Rock Writings, on cliffs of Snake River near Buffalo Eddy, can be seen from the highway (State 129).

CLE ELUM, Kittitas County. Off I–90.

Cle Elum Historical Museum, 223 E. 1st St. Displays feature the history of the area: The first settler, Thomas L. Gambel, a prospector, arrived in 1870. The town grew rapidly when coal was discovered in 1884. The railroad reached Cle Elum two years later. A forest fire devastated the area in 1889 but more coal veins were discovered, and the town was back in business by the time a new railroad linked the community with the Puget Sound region.

Liberty, NE via US 97, is a ghost town with many old buildings still on Main Street, which were erected when gold mining had a boom in the Blewett Pass area. Some say there is still gold in the gravel of Swauk Creek.

Ronald and *Roslyn,* ghost towns NW of Cle Elum via State 903. At Ronald are old stone buildings and mine ruins. Coal from here supplied trains crossing the Cascades.

COLFAX, Whitman County. US 195.

Steptoe Butte State Park, 14 miles N. The butte is more than 3,600 feet high and affords a fine view of the Palouse country. Toward the end of the last century pioneer settler James Davis, known as Cash-up because he never gave credit at his store, built a resort on the butte with an observatory and a telescope, but after his death in 1895, the hotel deteriorated and finally burned. The sheriff sold the whole butte in 1902, reportedly for $2,000.

COLVILLE, Stevens County. State 155.

Colville Indian Reservation, SW of town. Headquarters are at Inchelium at Franklin D. Roosevelt Lake.

Colville National Forest comprises 943,741 acres. Grand Coulee Dam is in the area. Tour Center at Dam. Dry Falls on State 17 is one of the world's wonders. It indicates a prehistoric cataract 40 times mightier than Niagara.

Fort Colville, on Mill Creek, 3 miles NE of town, was founded in 1859. It was established to control the Indians who were hostile in that period and to provide a base for the northwest boundary commission. First called Harney Depot, later took the name of the earlier post established by the Hudson's Bay Company, in 1826, near Marcus. Fort Spokane, established in October 1880, near the junction of the Spokane and Columbia rivers, replaced Fort Colville, but most Indian troubles were over by the time it came into existence. The garrison was withdrawn at the outbreak of the Spanish-American War and the post was abandoned in 1899. The military reservation was transferred to the Department of the Interior for use as an Indian school.

St. Paul Mission, on Lake Roosevelt, was founded by Father De Smet in 1854. It was closed from 1859 to

1865, and finally abandoned. Enemies of early missions were weather conditions as well as raids and white settlers bringing rowdiness, or wanting to take over the land. Poor attendance also was a factor in closing many early establishments. When St. Paul was abandoned, Chief Michael wrote a letter to the "Blackrobe head chief" at Rome apologizing for the poor showing the Kettle Indians had made as Christian converts, and blaming the gold miners for setting bad examples. ". . . Before the coming of the whites we were good, and happy."

COUPEVILLE, Island County. State 20, 525.

Fort Casey State Park, 3 miles S. on Puget Sound, includes 137 acres. Old fortifications and museum.

Alexander's Blockhouse, Alexander and Coveland Sts. is one of four blockhouses built on Whidbey Island to protect settlers during the White River Massacre and its aftermath. The Chamber of Commerce on Front Street has additional information.

Crockett Blockhouse, State 525 and 113, ½ mile from entrance to Fort Casey, was not named for the famous Davy of Alamo fame but for Col. John Crockett of Virginia who came west in 1838, and had a rough time on the Oregon Trail from Indian attacks. The Alexanders from Penn Cove helped in the building. After one blockhouse was completed, the Crocketts quickly raised another one on the other side of their farm. They then assisted the Alexanders in building their fortifications.

Davis Blockhouse, also called Cook Blockhouse, was one of the largest on Whidbey Island. It is located in Sunnyside Cemetery, where many grave markers are in Gaelic. Ebey Blockhouse is in a privately owned pasture farther along Sherman Road past the cemetery ca. 1½ miles.

Island County Historical Museum, Alexander St., has Indian and pioneer artifacts.

CURLEW, Ferry County. State 21. On the "Hot Air Railroad line." The town began in the 1880s with a few trappers' log cabins, then came farmers and fencing. Occasionally there were rumors of gold strikes, but these did not materialize nor did anything develop from the longtime rumor that the Spokane and British Columbia Railroad was coming to town with a line to connect Republic, Kettle Falls, Curlew and Grand Forks. A station was built for a train that never came until long after Curlew was past its prime.

DAVENPORT, Lincoln County. US 2.

Lincoln County Historical Museum, 7th and Park Sts., pioneer artifacts include clothing, furnishings, tools and photographs. Indian displays. Old farm machinery.

DAYTON, Columbia County. US 12. Once a stagecoach stop and center for miners.

Lewis and Clark Trail State Park, 5 miles SW on highway.

Kendall Skyline Drive, S., runs through the Blue Mountains and Umatilla National Forest, not open in bad weather. Check locally.

DECEPTION PASS, Island County. State 525. Marker near the S. end of the bridge on W. side of highway. Fidalgo Island N. of passage was named for the Spanish explorer, Lt. Salvador Fidalgo. Whidbey Island, S., is the second largest insular area in continental U.S. Capt. George Vancouver, exploring in 1792, thought it to be a peninsula; when he discovered his mistake, he gave the confusing landscape the name of Deception. The island was named for his officer, Joseph Whidbey, though it may sound like someone with hay fever trying to say Whitney.

DESTRUCTION ISLAND, off Jefferson County. US 101. Marker 1 mile S. of Ruby Beach on W. side of highway. At anchor in the lee of the island in 1775 Bodega Y Quadra, commanding the schooner *Sondra* sent seven men ashore for supplies; all were killed by Indians. Quadra named the island Isla De Dolores. In 1787 Capt. Barkley at anchor here landed six men who met the same fate at the mouth of the river which then was named Destruction. The island has been renamed Destruction and the river has the Indian name of Hoh. Hoh Indian Reservation is here. Olympic National Forest is to the E.

DISCOVERY BAY, Kitsap County. US 101. Marker is 4 miles N. of the town on E. side of highway. Capt. George Vancouver in May 1792, searching for a northwest passage, sailed his sloop *Discovery* and an armed tender *Chatham* down the Strait of Juan De Fuca into this harbor. In exploring the area he found the harbor of Port Townsend, naming it for the Marquis of Townsend.

ELLENSBURG, Kittitas County. I–90.

Ginkgo Petrified Forest State Park, 28 miles E. on I–90 in Vantage, includes 7,184 acres. Museum, Indian petroglyphs and Interpretive Center on grounds.

Olmstead Place State Park, 4 miles E. near the Kittitas Highway. Samuel Olmstead raised beef cattle here until 1892. His homesteading cabin, built in 1875, is an outstanding example of squared-timber construction, made of cottonwood logs from the Yakima River Canyon. Other historic buildings are on the site which is a national historic registered place, under the management of the Washington State Parks and Recreation Commission.

Wanapum Dam Tour Center, 29 miles E. on I–90, then 3 miles S. on State 243. Self-guiding tour of plant, fish-viewing room and Indian exhibits.

ENUMCLAW, King County. State 410.

Federation Forest State Park, 17 miles E. on State 410. There are 639 acres, interpretive trails, one of which follows the old Naches Trail, an early pioneer route between Puget Sound and the eastern sections of the territory.

Wilkeson, S. ca. 4 miles on State 10 to Buckley, then 5 miles S. on State 5, is an old coal-mining town now a ghost village with many remaining buildings. If coal comes back, so, hopefully, will Wilkeson.

EPHRATA, Grant County. State 17.

Grant County Museum, 742 Basin St. NW. Indian displays and pioneer history, with an old country store and period rooms.

EVERETT, Snohomish County. US 97.

Site of Vancouver's Landing, in Grand Avenue Park, 16th St. Capt. George Vancouver arrived at Possession Sound on June 4, 1792, and took possession of the area for Britain. White men did not populate the region until the 1860s, however, when a trading post was established at Elliott Point.

Marker for landing site on bluff overlooking Port Gardner Bay.

Totem Pole, 44th St. and Rucker Ave., was carved by Chief William Shelton of the Tulalip Indian Reservation to commemorate Chief Patkanim of the Salish Indians. In the 1850s, Patkanim signed the Mukilteo Treaty, as did three other chiefs; the document ceded to the U.S. lands from Elliott Bay to the Canadian border. The chief died in 1858 and is buried in the cemetery at Tulalip.

FORD, Stevens County. State 231.

Tshimakain Mission, ca. 7 miles NE, was established in the spring of 1839 by missionaries from the group who had joined Dr. Marcus Whitman and Rev. Henry H. Spalding in the Oregon country. After the massacre at the Whitman Mission in the autumn of 1847, the missionaries fled from this mission to Fort Colville. The mission was permanently abandoned. Marker on E. side of State 231 is at the site. No remains exist but the valley looks unchanged.

FORT CANBY, Pacific County. US 101. The fortsite is now within a state park; the post was begun in July 1863, garrisoned the following April. The site on Cape Disappointment, on the Columbia River, was chosen by Col. Réné de Russy, in charge of Pacific Coast defenses, and was originally called Fort Cape Disappointment. In 1875 the name was changed to honor Brig. Gen. Edward R. S. Canby, who was killed by the Modocs in April 1873. The Cape had been named in 1788 by British captain John Meares who had not recognized the mouth of the river.

FORT CASCADES, Skamania County. N. of US 830 on Rock Creek. Established in 1855 on the right bank of the Columbia River at the foot of the Cascades, near the present Bonneville Dam, to protect the travelers and supply wagons along the river route.

FORT CHEHALIS, Grays Harbor County. State 105. The fort was established near the mouth of the Chehalis River in February 1860, when the Chehalis Indians were threatening the settlers of the area.

FORT RAINS, Skamania County. On Sheridan's Point, N. side of Columbia River, E. of North Bonneville (US 830). The fort was established in 1856 and consisted of a blockhouse built by Maj. Gabriel Rains of the 4th U.S. Infantry, who was Brig. Gen. of Oregon Volunteers during the Indian Wars of the mid-1850s. The post disappeared in a flood in 1876.

FORT SIMCOE, Yakima County. State 220. US 97, 30 miles W. of Toppenish, in Fort Simcoe State Historic Park. It was established in August 1856 as a base of operations in the Yakima War. Much later the buildings were used as headquarters for the Yakima Indian Agency. Officers' quarters, the commandant's house and a blockhouse remain. There is a museum with Indian relics.

FORT STEILACOOM, Pierce County. Steilacoom Blvd., ca. 3 miles E. of town. The post was established in August 1849, near the head of Puget Sound, to protect settlers. The land was the property of Hudson's Bay Co., who were in charge of Fort Nisqually. In 1874 part of the area was given to the territory of Washington which established the Western State Hospital for the Insane. Military Road marker is on the S. side of highway near the hospital. Congress appropriated $20,000 to build a military road from here to Walla Walla. Capt. George McClellan was in charge of the road work. O. O. Howard and George Pickett, who both became leaders in the Civil War but in opposing armies, were stationed at Steilacoom after the post was attacked and nearly captured in 1855. Howard, the Union general, later was the founder of Howard University for Negroes, and took part in the Indian wars.

GOLDENDALE, Klickitat County. US 97.

Maryhill Museum of Fine Arts, 11 miles S. on US 97, then 2 miles W. on State 14 in Maryhill, has Northwest Indian exhibits and antique guns.

Klickitat County Historical Museum, 127 W. Broadway. A 20-room restored mansion has period furnishings.

KAMIAK BUTTE, Whitman County. State 27. Descriptive marker on highway near Kamiak Butte State Park 3 miles SW from Palouse. The butte was named for the Yakima Chieftain Ka-mi-akin.

KELSO, Cowlitz County. I–5.

Cowlitz County Museum, in courthouse annex, 4th and Church Sts. A homesteader's cabin was dismantled from its original site 10 miles E. of Castle Rock and reassembled here with authentic pioneer furnishings from the homesteading period of the 19th century. Replicas of post office, country store, kitchen, barbershop, livery stable and other exhibits, including Indian artifacts.

LA PUSH, Clallam County. Off US 101. An old Indian village on the Olympic Peninsula has many interesting old buildings including a Shaker church which is on the Quillayute Indian Reservation.

LONGVIEW, Cowlitz County. I–5.

Monticello Convention Site, Olympia Way and Maple St. Marker commemorates the 1852 meeting when residents of Washington met to petition the government to separate Washington Territory from Oregon.

LYONS FERRY, Franklin County. Palouse River.

Marmes Rockshelter, 1 mile N. of Lyons Ferry on W. side of river, is rated as the most outstanding archaeological site discovered in the Northwest to date. Eight geological strata have been excavated. A national historic landmark.

MONTE CRISTO, Snohomish County. SE of Silverton on unmarked road. There are a number of ruins from gold mining days. The Monte Cristo Museum has been housed in the old mess hall and may or may not be open. Scenic Glacier Falls is nearby.

MOSES LAKE, Grant County. State 171.

Adam East Museum, 5th and Balsam Sts., has prehistoric exhibits, artifacts of early human and animal life.

MOUNT BAKER NATIONAL FOREST, Whatcom County. State 542 and others. Marker for Mount Baker on highway between Glacier and Maple Falls. The peak rises to 10,750 feet. Lt. Joseph Baker, one of Vancouver's officers, sighted the snowy top from the sea on April 30, 1792. Beyond Heather Meadow from here is Mount Shukson, 9,038 feet high. The forest comprises 1,282,962 acres and spreads S. from the Canadian border ca. 60 miles along the W. slope of the cascades. Glacier Peak in the SE is 10,528, overlooking the Glacier Peak Wilderness.

MOUNT RAINIER NATIONAL PARK, Pierce County. US 410.

Visitor Centers and Information Stations, at Paradise and Longmire are open all year. At Sunrise and Ohanapecosh, in summer. Exhibits and information on trails available. Mountain climbing is at hand for experts. Wonderland Trail is a 90-mile all-day hike; there are many shorter ones. The park includes 378 square miles. Mount Rainier reaches 14,410 feet above sea level, 8,000 feet above the Cascade Range of central Washington and is one of the largest extinct volcanoes in the U.S. The Paradise Glacier Trail is well marked, 6 miles round trip and begins at the Paradise Visitor Center. Paradise Ice Cave is one of the many natural beauties of the park.

MUKILTEO, Snohomish County. State 525.

Site of Point Elliott Treaty, at lighthouse. On January 22, 1855, Indian chiefs signed a treaty which ceded much of their land to the whites. Mukilteo, ironically, is the Indian word for "good camping ground." They gave it all up in the warlike face of so-called progress, even here, with their backs against the Pacific Ocean.

MULLAN ROAD, Adams County. State 26. Marker on highway 4 miles E. of Washtucna at a point where it intersects the historic 624-mile road between Walla Walla and Fort Benton, Montana, which was then the navigable terminal of the Missouri River. From 1855 to 1862 Capt. John Mullan was in charge of soldiers and civilians building the 25-foot-wide road for immigrants who then came by thousands over this route. In 1866, 10,000 pack mules traveled back and forth between the Walla Walla and the Montana mining camps.

NEAH BAY, Clallam County. State 112. The settlement was begun by Lt. Salvador Fidalgo, May 29, 1791. The area is now headquarters for the Makah Indian Reservation. The Makahs are expert mask-makers. Cape Flattery historical marker and trail are due W. on the very tip of land. Tatoosh Island is ½ mile off the coast at the entrance to the Strait. The lighthouse was built in 1857, on the island named by Capt. John Meares in 1788.

NESPELEM, Okanogan County. State 155.

Grave of Chief Joseph, overlooking Little Nespelem River. The eloquent Nez Perce chief is probably quoted more than any other American of his period, and he had no speech writers. He spoke simply, directly and meaningfully for men in any age as is indicated by the frequent application of his words to today's problems. He preached forbearance, but this did him little good. "Better to live in peace than to begin a war and lie dead" was a philosophy that sustained him even in defeat. His tribe, driven off their lands, tried to flee to Canada, fighting off the pursuing cavalry. When they were hopelessly cut off, Chief Joseph surrendered. Most or perhaps all of his best young leaders were dead. He was a military genius, but the odds were insurmountable. He worked for peace after capture and won a return to the Northwest for his surviving people in

1885, but they were confined to the Colville Reservation.

NISQUALLY TREATY SITE, Thurston County. I–5. Just W. of the Nisqually River Bridge is an interpretive marker for the site where the Medicine Creek Treaty was signed under a fir tree. (The creek is also known as McAllister.) Isaac I. Stevens, first territorial governor, met with Chief Leschi and other chiefs of the lower Puget Sound tribes, including the Nisquallys, Puyallups and Squaxons, in December 1854. The treaty purchased land for white settlers. The Interstate highway included the site on its right-of-way.

NORTH BEND, King County. I–90.

Puget Sound Railroad and Museum, 5 miles NW on State 202 to Snoqualmie Falls, then E., offers a ride on an antique steam train through a forest to the museum which has many old vehicles, from streetcars to locomotives.

NORTH CASCADES NATIONAL PARK, in North Central Washington, is one of the newest national parks, established in 1968. Access from State 20, N. Cascade Highway, and from State 542. Visitor Center open all year. The Cascades are known as the American Alps; within the 1,053-square mile park are more than 315 active glaciers, the Ross Lake National Recreation Area and the Lake Chelan National Recreation Area.

OKANOGAN NATIONAL FOREST, Okanogan County. US 97, State 4, 16. Part of the North Cascade Primitive Area is in the 1,520,340-acre forest, as are a number of ghost or near-ghost towns which were once mining settlements. Oroville and Old Toroda are near the Canadian border on US 97. A number of little towns down the pike (US 97) have weathered relics of buildings. Riverside, 8 miles N. of Omak, was a river port. From Okanogan on US 97 take road N. to Conconully, once Salmon City, now a fishing resort with a state park, then to Ruby, a ghost town. The Caribou Trail of 1859–68, which runs across the state from old Fort Walla Walla on the Columbia River at the Oregon line to Canada, runs just E. of US 97 from a point where it crosses the highway ca. 12 miles N. of Fort Okanogan to a few miles above the little village of Cordell, where it recrosses to the W.

OLYMPIA, Thurston County. I–5.

Capitol Group, on Capitol Way between 11th and 14th Aves. From the dome of the Legislative Building, on a clear day, Mt. Baker, Mt. Rainier, Mt. St. Helens and Mt. Adams can be seen. From lower portico, the Olympic Mountains are visible. On the bronze doors of the main entrance are replicas of the first Capitol and an early homestead cabin. A frame building, more recently the Gold Bar Restaurant near Capitol Way and 2nd Ave., was the site of the first meeting of the Territorial Legislature on February 27, 1854. Marker on Capitol Way. The Olympic Masonic Hall was used for meetings in 1854 and 1855. Library Building houses murals as well as rare books on Western history. Marker on capitol grounds where first capitol was erected in 1855–56.

State Capitol Museum, 211 W. 21st St. History rooms and Indian exhibits pertaining to the Northwest housed in historic mansion.

Olympic National Forest, NW of city, via US 101, covers 650,940 acres.

OYSTERVILLE, Pacific County. State 103. One of the oldest communities in western Washington has some buildings of the 1860s. The old Baptist church has been carefully renovated in recent years.

PACKWOOD, Lewis County. US 12.

Goat Rocks Wilderness, E. and S. of town, in Gifford Pinchot National Forest, covers 82,680 acres. Ann and Myron Sutton in their *Wilderness Areas of North America* (Funk and Wagnalls, 1974) wrote, without understatement, of Washington and neighboring British Columbia turf:

> The earth as a greenhouse of rich and abundant vegetation is nowhere more (superb). . . . The Amazon jungles scarcely compare with it in sheer luxuriance, and only a few places, such as the montane oak and orchid forests of central Costa Rica, the mountain vegetation of Ecuador, or the Canary Island cloud forests of Tenerife, are comparably dense.

POINT ROBERTS, Whatcom County. I–5 to Canada then S. on Canadian 17 to boundary marker, a granite obelisk, which is one of a series along the 49th parallel, marking the border from the Strait of Georgia to the summit of the Rocky Mountains. The official survey began here in 1857, a joint enterprise by British and American commissions; it was completed in 1862.

If you want to mail a letter, try the next town

PORT ANGELES, Clallam County. US 101. Headquarters for Olympic National Forest are here, at Park Ave. and Race St. Lincoln declared the town was the second "National City," in 1863.

Juan De Fuca Strait, marker on US 101 ca. 5 miles W. of town near Laird's Corner. The state marker committee has made a fine effort to clear up the confusion about Juan de Fuca. Among early mapmakers the area was usually called the Strait of Anian, which was supposed—or believed—to stretch from the Atlantic to the Pacific (and would have been handy). But a later writer said that a Greek sailor, De Fuca, had found the strait when on a voyage with some Spaniards in the 16th century. The state marker says succinctly:

> In Venice, an old Greek mariner, Apostolos Valericanos, told of the trip that he had taken up the Pacific Coast on a Mexican expedition in 1592 under the name of Juan De Fuca and of his discovery of a passageway leading to an inland sea, his description of which fitted closely that of Puget Sound, lending credence to his story. Mapmakers of Europe marked this unknown inlet with his name, and while the career of the old Greek mariner ends in historical darkness, in 1788 Captain John Meares, on discovery of this inlet, named it the Strait of Juan De Fuca.

And very handsome of Meares it was, in view of the usual practice of naming everything possible for yourself or someone you owed a favor.

PORT GAMBLE HISTORIC DISTRICT, Kitsap County. State 21. Many 19th-century buildings are still in excellent condition. In 1926 the sawmill and docks were rebuilt to match the earlier period. A company town. The old cemetery dates from territorial days. The area is a national historic landmark.

PORT MADISON, Agate Point, Kitsap County. On Puget Sound. Chief Sealth (also written as See-yat and Seattle) is buried in Suquamish Memorial Cemetery. He was born in 1786 and died in 1866. His friendship for the new settlers was proved by his help during the Indian troubles of 1855. In gratitude for his support, the city of Seattle was named for him. Old Man House, his home, was variously reported to be anywhere from 500 to more than 1,000 feet long and only 60 feet wide. It was made of cedar logs and once housed eight great chiefs and their people. The Washington State Parks and Recreation Commission has reconstructed a segment which is used as a display shelter, ½ mile SW of Suquamish at the N. end of Agate Pass across from Bainbridge Island. A marker at Point No Point on Bainbridge Island commemorates the Indian Treaty of January 26, 1855. Port Madison has a number of old homes; W. on the main highway is an Old British Cemetery, with headstones dating back to 1854, containing the graves of British sailors.

PORT TOWNSEND, Jefferson County. State 20. Many buildings in town are registered historical places; among these are:

City Hall, Water and Madison Sts., built in 1891. Home of the Jefferson County Historical Museum.

Captain Enoch Fowler House, corner of Polk and Washington. Fowler came to the Northwest from Lubec, Maine, in 1852. His home was built before

1865 and is believed to be the oldest in town.

Francis Wilcox James House, corner of Washington and Harrison Sts., was built in 1889.

Leader (or Fowler) Building, 226 Adams St., dates from 1874. Enoch Fowler was a sea captain, see above, who opened a store when he settled in Port Townsend. This is considered the oldest standing, two-story, all-stone structure in Washington. It served as the county courthouse during territorial days. Later the Port Townsend *Leader* offices were here. They still occupy the first floor.

Manresa Hall (also known as Eisenbeis Castle), Sheridan St. Built in 1892 as a home for Charles Eisenbeis, first mayor of the town. A second part of the building was added by the Jesuits in 1928.

Old German Consulate (Olson-Hastings House), 313 Walker, was built in 1890 and was used by a German vice-consul early in the 20th century.

Point Wilson Lighthouse, on point of land between Juan de Fuca Strait and Admiralty Inlet, was built in 1879.

Rothschild House, Taylor and Franklin. David C. H. Rothschild came to California from Bavaria, then settled in Port Townsend where he opened a store and built this residence in 1868. Restored period furnishings.

St. Paul's Episcopal Church, corner of Jefferson and Tyler Sts., was erected in 1865.

Starrett House, 744 Clay St., was built for George E. Starrett, another native of Maine who settled here, in 1855 and became a builder. (End of registered sites.)

Old Fort Townsend State Park, 3 miles S. Site of the fort which was established in October 1856, on the W. side of the Bay at the entrance to Puget Sound, to protect settlers from hostile Indians in the area.

Chamber of Commerce, 2139 Sims Way, has a Sea Gull Tour Guide for the many historic sites in the area.

PROSSER, Benton County. US 12.

Benton County Historical Museum, 7th St. in City Park. Has a diorama and Western relics, furnished homestead cabin and Indian artifacts.

PUYALLUP, Pierce County. I–5.

Ezra Meeker Mansion, 321 E. Pioneer, is the 17-room Victorian manse built in 1890 where the pioneer founder of the town lived in his later years. Born in Huntsville, Ohio, he emigrated from Indiana in 1851. His log cabin home was located where Pioneer Park now stands, S. Meridian and 4th Ave. A statue of Meeker is in the park. He became famous for his conscientious efforts to mark the old Oregon Trail, made two trips by ox-team and one by plane when he was 95.

Frontier Museum, 2301 23rd Ave. SE., has logging, Indian, and pioneer displays.

Mount Rainier Marker, 5 miles S. on the E. side of State 162. Descriptive text for the impressive peak which has been called the "Great Pyramid" and the "Monarch of the Cascade Range," and may be seen from this vantage point.

RUBY, Pend Oreille County, on Pend Oreille River. State 31. (Not to be confused with the ghost town of Ruby in Okanogan County, off US 97.)

David Thompson Marker, 1 mile N. of town on State 31. Thompson, a partner in the North West Company, was the first to travel the Columbia River from its source to its mouth. He also was the first to map the Pend Oreille, Snake and other rivers in the Columbia Basin.

SAN JUAN ISLANDS, San Juan County. The land behind the "Fifty-four forty or fight" slogan of 1845.

San Juan Island National Historical Park, Friday Harbor vicinity. The park area is made up of 1,751.99 acres. Displays and markers interpret the American and British camps which were involved in the boundary dispute known as the Pig War. The treaty of 1846 was so vague both countries claimed the islands and tried to settle upon them. The bloodless conflict began when an American farmer shot a pig that happened to belong to one of the Hudson's Bay Co. men. British settlers demanded that the pig killer be tried in Victoria. The U.S. argued that the pig had been uprooting an American not a British garden. England sent warships to the island and the U.S. sent Capt. George Pickett with a detachment of troops to the defense of Americans involved in the argument. Emperor William I of Germany volunteered to be an arbiter and awarded the archipelago to the United States. The British camp, 8 miles NW of Friday Harbor on Garrison Bay, has a blockhouse, commissary and barracks, as well as foundations of other structures which were put up during the occupation. The American Camp, SE of the harbor, has several foundations and part of a defense work. The area is under development. Rangers are on duty in summer through October.

SEATTLE, King County. I–5. Although it has little to do with the Old West, the Space Needle is a fine place to see the countryside and the harbor. (In 1975, at least, restaurant prices soared even higher than the structure. A fruit salad turned out to be six strawberries costing about 60 cents each. A Seattle native pointed out: "But they grew them on top of the Needle. . . .")

Museum of History and Industry, 2161 E. Hamlin St., S. of Montlake Bridge, in McCurdy Park. The story of the city's first 100 years is told in displays and memorabilia. The fire of 1889 is the subject of a mural. In the transportation section are many old modes of travel from canoes to cable cars and fire-fighting equipment. Natural and marine history of the Pacific Northwest are also featured.

Pioneer Square, Skid Road Historic District 1st Ave., James St. and Yesler Way, is where the city was founded in 1852; restored buildings house shops and galleries, etc. Guided tours are available, also for the underground area, beginning on S. Jackson. After the fire of 1889, the street level was raised 10 feet, leaving many stores intact. While Seattle has many tours on land and water, all excellent, it is also a fascinating city to walk in. A number of historical markers will be found in this area.

Pike Place Market, 1431 1st Ave., a registered historic place, sells everything edible from Bolivian shrimp to Greek cheese, as well as curios, crafts and books.) Skid Road got its name when logs were skidded along it to the waterfront.

Washington State Fire Museum, at Seattle Center, 5th Ave. N. between Denny Way and Mercer St. Antique fire-fighting equipment and relics.

Seattle Harbor Tour, from Pier 56, foot of Seneca St., is a one-hour circle trip.

Washington State Museum, on campus of University of Washington, Vis-

"Pig War" took place here, Blockhouse at English Camp, San Jauñ Island
(State of Washington, Dept. of Commerce & Economic Development)

itor Information Center at University Way NE and NE Campus Parkway. Main entrance is at 17th Ave. NE and NE. 45th St. The University was founded in 1861, developing from classes held by Asa Mercer in a small frame building which stood on land cleared by townspeople. The site on Seneca St. between 4th and 5th Aves. is marked by a historical plaque. Professor Mercer offered young men a chance to split wood for $1.50 a cord against their tuition. In the beginning only one student managed to qualify above high school level.

Eliza Ferry Leary House, 1551 10th Ave., E., was built just after the turn of the century by John and Eliza Leary, active civic and church leaders. Now Episcopal diocese headquarters.

Wawona, Seattle Police Harbor Patrol Dock, at foot of Densmore St. The three-masted schooner was built in Fairhaven, California, and was made of wood; powered by sail only. A registered historic place.

Marymoor Prehistoric Indian Site, 6046 W. Lake Sammamish Parkway, NE. The pre-Columbian site is a registered historic place.

Blake Island Marine State Park, 4 miles W., includes 475 acres with the

Tillicum Village where Indian arts and crafts are displayed.

Fort Lawton, on Magnolia Bluff, overlooking Puget Sound, was established in 1897, too late for the Indian wars but with a fine view of the Sound and mountains from the parade grounds. A road winds to the beach where West Point Lighthouse was built in 1881, and once warned shipping with fish-or whale-oil-burning lamps.

Volunteer Park, E. Prospect to E. Galer between 11th and 15th S. Aves. N. has an observatory. The Seward Statue nearby commemorates the purchase of Alaska which was once called "Seward's Folly." William Henry Seward was Secretary of State under Lincoln and in 1867 when the purchase was made. In Lakeview Cemetery, N. end of park, is the grave of Princess Angeline, daughter of Chief Sealth (Seattle) for whom the city is named. A number of Confederate veterans are also buried here. A monument honors them.

Alki Point, on the beach front, at Alki Ave. and 59th Ave. Site of the first Seattle Settlement. Descriptive marker.

SEDRO WOOLLEY, Skagit County. State 20.

North Cascades National Park (which see) is 50 miles E. on State 20, but portions of the road may be closed in winter. Check locally.

Lake Whatcom Railway, 11 miles N. on State 9 in Wickersham, offers a 1½-hour ride on a steam train in old Northern Pacific passengers cars.

SNOQUALMIE, King County. State 202.

Puget Sound and Snoqualmie Valley Railroad, off State 202, a railroad museum with a 1½-mile round trip between Kimball Creek and Big Swamp. Much old equipment and many types of railroad cars, as well as other vehicles.

SPOKANE, Spokane County. US 2, 395.

Eastern Washington State Historical Society, W. 2316 1st Ave. Excellent collections of Indian arts, crafts; pioneer relics, natural history dioramas and various changing exhibits.

Pacific Northwest Indian Center, E. 500 Cataldo Ave. Museum in a five-story tower has a vast collection of Indian artifacts and art.

Indian Painted Rocks, near the Rutter Parkway Bridge which spans the Little Spokane River. Marker nearby.

Spokane Plain Battlefield, marker on US 2, ca. 10 miles W. of town. The last engagement fought by Col. George Wright's forces in the 1858 campaign in eastern Washington against the Spokans, Palouses, and Coeur d'Alenes, who had triumphed over Maj. Edward J. Steptoe in May at a fight which took place in what is now Whitman County, ca. 1 mile SE of Rosalia. (Granite shaft in memorial park at site). A large stone pyramid marks the battle here on September 5, 1858. An associated site is at the town of Four Lakes where a clash took place on September 1, and was the beginning of the running engagement that culminated here. Arrow-shaped pyramid in Four Lakes marks the site.

Spokane House, 9 miles NW in Riverside State Park. Interpretive Center at the confluence of the Little Spokane and Spokane rivers for the trading post which was established in 1810 by the North West Co. In 1812 John Jacob Astor's Pacific Fur Co. established a post nearby which was purchased by the Canadian company in

1813. After 1821 Hudson's Bay Co. administered Spokane House until it was abandoned in 1826 and moved to a new site, Fort Colville, on the Columbia River.

STEILACOOM, Thurston County. I–5.

First Jail, corner of Main and Starling Sts., was the first in Washington Territory, built in 1858.

First Protestant Church, Commercial and Wilkes Sts. Marker commemorates the first Protestant church building N. of the Columbia, built in 1853.

Byrd's Mill Road, marker at junction of Byrds Mill and Union Ave. for the route of escape from the Puyallup Valley to Fort Steilacoom during the Indian War of 1855–56. In 1864 the telegraph line constructed by joint efforts of Americans and Russians went along this route.

Fort Steilacoom (which see) became the Western State Hospital for the Insane.

SUNNYSIDE, Yakima County. I–82.

Sunnyside Museum, 4th St. and Grand Ave. Indian and pioneer artifacts.

TACOMA, Pierce County. I–5.

Totem Pole, 9th and A Sts., is one of the tallest in the U.S.

State Historical Society Museum, 315 N. Stadium Way. Illuminated photo murals present the state's history; Indian, pioneer and military exhibits.

Point Defiance Park, 6 miles N. Entrance at N. end of Pearl St. Covers 637 acres. Among features of the park are the *Job Carr House,* which served as the first post office and was the first home built in 1865. *Old Fort Nisqually,* a reconstruction of the 1833 Hudson's Bay outpost, purchased by the U.S. in 1867. The granary which was built in 1843 is the oldest existing structure in the state. A national historic landmark. Museum at fort.

Camp Six—Western Washington Forest Industries Museum, replica of early logging camp, with original bunkhouses and other relics.

St. Peter's Chapel-at-Ease, 2909 N. Starr St. at N. 29th, is the oldest church in the city, built in 1873. The organ came around Cape Horn in 1874 as did the half-ton bell in the tower, constructed from a cedar tree, beside the church.

Kla How Ya Trail, means welcome in Chinook, is a marked route to 22 points of interest in the area, which begins at the Totem Pole.

TORODA, Ferry County. State 21.

Grave of Ranald MacDonald, in Indian cemetery. MacDonald was the son of a Scottish fur trader and factor for the Hudson's Bay Co. and was born in 1824 at Fort Vancouver. He went to Japan before outsiders were welcome and is credited with helping to open Japan to the rest of the world.

TUMWATER, Thurston County. I–5. The first American settlement on Puget Sound was established in 1846. Marker at the S. end of the Deschutes River Bridge on Capitol Blvd. describes the river and the end of the Oregon Trail.

Captain Nathaniel Crosby House overlooks the sound. A Victorian-style cottage, built in 1858–60 by pioneer Capt. Crosby, grandfather of singer-actor Bing Crosby. Restored with some original furnishings.

VANCOUVER, Clark County. US 830.

Covington House, 4304 Main St., was

moved from its original site five miles E. of Vancouver, where it was built in 1846 by Richard Covington, near present town of Orchards.

First Sawmill, six miles E. has marker on highway. Built by the Hudson's Bay Co. in 1827.

First Apple Tree, E. 7th and T Sts., was planted by Dr. John McLoughlin in 1826.

Fort Vancouver National Historic Site, ½ mile E. on E. Evergreen Blvd. takes in 162 acres. Excavations have located original stockade walls and other foundations. The blockhouse and bakery have been reconstructed. Visitor Center with museum. The fort was established by the Hudson's Bay Co. in 1824–25.

Ulysses S. Grant Museum, 1106 E. Evergreen Blvd. Grant's office in 1852–53. Military and Indian displays. Some original furniture which belonged to Grant.

Clark County Historical Museum, 1511 Main St., has many items of local history, including Indian relics, and reproductions of a pioneer doctor's office and country store.

Providence Academy, E. Evergreen Blvd., is the state's oldest school building, designed and built by Mother Joseph in 1873.

WALLA WALLA, Walla Walla County. US 12.

Whitman Mission National Historic Site, 7 miles W. on US 12, then less than a mile S. A memorial shaft overlooks the site of the Waiilatpu mission established by Dr. Marcus and Narcissa Whitman in 1836. Mrs. Whitman and the wife of missionary H. H. Spalding were the first-known white women to cross the Rockies. In 1847 the Whitmans and 11 others were killed by Cayuse Indians and are buried here in a common grave. Self-guiding trail to grave and other parts of the memorial. Visitor Center with museum.

Fort Walla Walla Park and Pioneer Village Museum, Dalles Military Rd., 1 mile W. of State 125 on W. edge of town. Original and replica buildings include schoolhouse, log cabins, railroad depot, blacksmith shop and farm relics.

Fort Walla Walla, established in September 1856, was intended to control the hostile Indians of the area and to protect travel routes. Now occupied by a Veterans Administration Hospital. Another Fort Walla Walla was a trading post built at the junction of the Walla Walla and Columbia rivers in 1818, abandoned by the Hudson's Bay Co. at the start of the Indian War of 1855. Marker on US 410 near Wallula.

WENATCHEE, Chelan County. US 97.

North Central Washington Museum, 2 S. Chelan Ave. at Douglas St. Indian, pioneer and local history displays.

Lincoln Rock, US 2, 8 miles N. of East Wenatchee on E. side of highway. A natural rock formation which looks like Abraham Lincoln. Marker on highway.

Earthquake Point, 22½ miles N. on US 97. Marker on highway at site of Ribbon Cliff, called Broken Mountain, by the Indians where an earthquake occurred in December 1872.

Wenatchee National Forest extends from the Cascade summit to the Columbia River Basin and occupies nearly 2 million acres. US 2, over Stevens Pass, I–90 over Snoqualmie Pass and US 97 over Swauk Pass are the main roads. The Cascades Crest Trail follows the W. boundary. The old stage road crossed via Colockum Pass in the 1880s.

WINTHROP, Okanogan County. State 20.

Guy Waring Log Cabin, now the Shafer Museum, has pioneer vehicles, tools, furniture on display. There are many old buildings in the onetime mining town.

YAKIMA, Yakima County. I–82.

Yakima Valley Museum and Historical Association, 2105 Tieton Drive in Franklin Park, has a variety of relics from Indian to minerals, to pioneer household and costumes.

Painted Rocks, 7 miles NW on US 12, has Yakima Indian pictographs.

Union Gap and Pioneer Cemetery, 3 miles SW on US 97. Monuments mark the sites of battles between settlers and Yakima Indians. The Battle of Two Buttes took place on July 4, 1856.

Ahtanum Mission, 9 miles SW on unmarked roads, was founded in 1852, destroyed in the Indian War and rebuilt in 1867.

Satus Highway (US 97) follows a prehistoric route and crosses the Yakima Indian Reservation, then the Simcoe Mountains.

WYOMING

It is possible to stand on a ridge in the Rabbit Ears Range of Northwestern Colorado not far south of the Wyoming line and, from this vantage point, throw a stone into a creek whose waters eventually empty into the Pacific Ocean. Turn around and throw a stone in the opposite direction, and it will splash into water destined to reach the Atlantic via a stream which flows almost due north through Colorado's North Park and combines with similar small streams to enter Wyoming as the *North Platte River.*

No other watercourse in America has more difficulty deciding which direction it wants to go than does the North Platte. For the first hundred miles it flows north. Joined by the Sweetwater, it then dog-legs off to the Northeast. It runs almost due east from Casper to Douglas where, bending around the latter city, it continues in a southeasterly direction until it leaves the State. . . .

John Rolfe Burroughs,
Guardian of the Grasslands,
(Cheyenne: 1971)

Life is like a mountain railroad, with an engineer that's brave;
We must make the run successful, from the cradle
to the grave;
Watch the curves, the fills, the tunnels; never falter;
never quail;
Keep your hand upon the throttle, and your eye
upon the rail.

Old hymn, sung by the
Irwin brothers at the foot
of the scaffold in
Cheyenne when Tom
Horn was hanged

The Green River Valley was at this time the scene of one of those general gatherings of traders, trappers, and Indians. . . . About four miles from the rendezvous of Captain Bonneville was that of the American Fur Company, hard by which, was that also of the Rocky Mountain Fur Company. . . . Never did rival lawyers, after a wrangle at the bar, meet with more social good humor at a circuit dinner. The hunting season over, all past tricks and manoeuvres are forgotten, all feuds and bickerings buried in oblivion. . . . Here the free trappers were in all their glory; they considered themselves the "cocks of the walk," and always carried the highest crests. Now and then familiarity was pushed too far, and would effervesce into a brawl, and a "rough and tumble" fight; but it all ended in cordial reconciliation and maudlin endearment.

The presence of the Shoshonie tribe contributed occasionally to cause temporary jealousies and feuds. The Shoshonie beauties became objects of rivalry among some of the amorous mountaineers. Happy was the trapper who could muster up a red blanket, a string of gay beads, or a paper of precious vermilion, with which to win the smiles of a Shoshonie fair one.

Washington Irving, *The Adventures of Captain Bonneville,* 1837

WYOMING FACTS: Carved from sections of Dakota, Utah and Idaho Territories, Wyoming Territory was created on July 25, 1868. The territory was visited by nearly all the great travelers to the American West of the 18th and 19th centuries. On July 10, 1890, Wyoming entered the Union as the 44th state.

Wyoming has Yellowstone, the first national park, and Grand Teton; five national forests: Bridger-Teton, Bighorn, Medicine Bow, Black Hills, Shoshone, and portions of Targhee, Caribou and Wasatch National Forests. Big Horn Canyon and Flaming Gorge National Recreation Areas. Devils Tower and Fossil Butte National Monuments. There are three national refuges and the Wind River Indian Reservation.

Capital: Cheyenne. Nickname: Equality State.

Wyoming comes from two Delaware Indian words *Mecheweami-ing,* meaning "at the big flats."

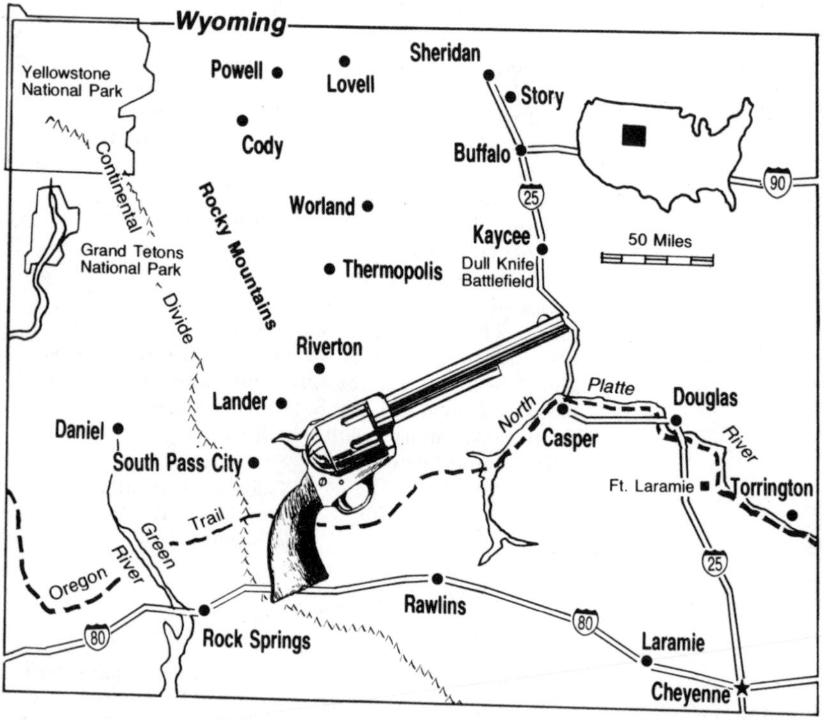
Wyoming
Yellowstone National Park
Powell
Lovell
Sheridan
Story
Cody
Buffalo
Continental Divide
Rocky Mountains
Worland
90
25
Grand Tetons National Park
Kaycee
50 Miles
Thermopolis
Dull Knife Battlefield
Riverton
Lander
North Platte River
Douglas
Daniel
Casper
South Pass City
Ft. Laramie
Torrington
Trail
Green River
Oregon
Rawlins
80
Rock Springs
Laramie
Cheyenne

Major Indian Tribes Arapaho, Arikara, Bannock, Blackfeet, Cheyenne, Crow, Gros Ventre, Kiowa, Nez Perce, Sheep Eater, Sioux, Shoshone, and Ute.

Major Trails Pony Express, Bridger, Mormon, Oregon, Overland, Bozeman, Union Pacific.

AFTON, Lincoln County. (6,134 feet). US 89. In 1896 Mormon immigrants reportedly surveyed the townsite using only the North Star, the noon sun, a carpenter's square, a rope and an almanac. The notorious McCarthy gang holed up here in the 1880s at a time when Butch Cassidy was a novice horse thief.

Pioneer Museum has early tools, including medical equipment.

ATLANTIC CITY, Fremont County. (7,665 feet). Off State 28. The town was settled in 1868 when miners from South Pass City found gold in the Atlantic ledge.

Site of Fort Stambaugh (also Camp Stambaugh), 3½ miles SE named for Lt. Charles S. Stambaugh, who was killed on patrol from Fort Bridger in 1870. This post at Smith Gulch was set up to protect miners from the Indians. Now part of the South Pass Historic Mining Area.

Site of St. Mary's Stage Station, E. of Beaver Creek on the old Oregon Trail, a telegraph and stage post, also known as Rocky Ridge, attacked by Indians in May 1865.

"Willie's Company" Campsite, SE of Fort Stambaugh, marker for the area on a bend of the Rock Creek, where Mormons perished in the late fall storms of 1856. A group of colonists, mostly European, led by Capt. James G. Willie were caught by winter at this point in their journey toward Utah. A memoir by a colonist named Chislett, who was in Willie's company, published in a history of the Mormons in 1873, told of the problems:

> For several years previous to 1856, the poorer portion of the Mormon emigrants from Europe to Utah made the overland journey from "the Frontier" to Salt Lake City by ox-teams, under the management of Church agents. . . . All the emigrants who were obliged to travel in this way were, if able, expected to walk all the way, or at least the greater part of the way. The teams were used for hauling provisions, and 100 lbs. of luggage were allowed to each emigrant. Old people, feeble women and children, generally could ride when they wished. The overland portion of the journey occupied from ten to twelve weeks. . . . The question was, how to transfer to Utah those who could not raise the necessary 10 pounds sterling. . . .

It was decided by Brigham Young and his leaders to try handcarts for the masses of emigrants recruited in Europe.

Hundreds arrived in Iowa to find no carts, and no shelter; this happened to Chislett. When his group reached the Iowa frontier town they found nowhere to sleep but under the sky and the carts not ready and so were delayed dangerously until past the 4th of July. Three hand-cart companies had already departed, in time to reach Utah before winter. Chislett found the carts, when ready, were wretchedly constructed and each person was limited to 17 pounds, not 100 as formerly agreed upon. Even so the carts were difficult; many were pulled by young girls.

> As we travelled along, we presented a singular, and sometimes an affecting appearance. The young and strong went along gaily with their carts, but the old people and little children were to be seen straggling a long distance in the rear. Sometimes, when the little folks had walked as far as they could, their fathers would take them on their carts, and thus increase the load that was already becoming too heavy as the day advanced.

As for food: "I do not know who settled the amount of our rations, but whoever it was, I should like him, or them, to drag a hand-cart through the State of Iowa, in the month of July on exactly the same amount and quality of fare we had." Many of the 500 in the company died in the snows of Rock Creek.

BAGGS, Carbon County. (6,245 feet) State 789. The town was named for settlers George and Maggie Baggs and was a popular rendezvous point for gunmen of the 1880s and 1890s. Reportedly, Tom Horn and Bob Meldrum, livestock detectives, looked for thieves here regularly. Meldrum is said to have killed his last man at Baggs when Chick Bowan, a cowpuncher, resisted arrest. Horn had been a government scout and interpreter for Gens. Wilcox, Crook, and Miles in the Apache wars, then a Pinkerton detective and finally a cattle detective. In his autobiography, published a year after he was hanged in Cheyenne for the murder of a 14-year-old boy (some say mistakenly), he polishes off his last career with few words:

> While Pinkerton's is one of the greatest institutions of the kind in existence, I never did like the work, so I left them in 1894. I then came to Wyoming and went to work for the Swan Land and Cattle Company, since which time everybody else has been more familiar with my life and business than I have been myself. And I think that since my coming here the yellow journal reporters are better equipped to write my history than am I, myself! Respectfully, TOM HORN.

Local stories are that the Powder Springs gang, led by Butch Cassidy, came here to celebrate successful thievery elsewhere. The citizens were always well paid for damages that occurred during celebrations.

Site of Jim Baker's Cabin, ca. 7 miles E. Baker was a foremost scout, trapper and guide, a contemporary of Jim Bridger and James Beckwourth. The cabin was on the Snake River in 1873. For years it has been in Frontier Park, Cheyenne.

Battle Lake, NE of town, is the place where Thomas A. Edison, as a member of the Henry Draper Eclipse Expedition in 1878, aided by the frayed ends of his bamboo fishing rod had the idea for a nonconducting enduring carbon filament which resulted in the later perfection of his incandescent electric lamp.

BAIROIL, Sweetwater County. (6,860 feet). W. of US 287.

Whiskey Gap, 5 miles E. then ca. 10 miles N., was named for the sad occasion in 1862 when a wagonload of illegal booze was destroyed in the first recorded enforcement of prohibition in Wyoming. Curiously enough it was an officer with the good Irish name of O'Farrell, commanding Co. "A" 11th Ohio Cavalry, who gave the command. The liquid was poured on the ground above what is now Whiskey Spring. Soldiers, teamsters, guides, and roustabouts hastened for spring water with cups, canteens, buckets, kettles and even plates. O'Farrell is said to have thanked heaven parenthetically in his evening report that no Indians chose that occasion for attack.

BIGHORN, Sheridan County. US 87.

Bradford Brinton Memorial, Quarter Circle A Ranch, museum has pioneer and Indian relics. The ranch was built by two Scotsmen, William and Malcolm Moncreiffe, in 1892. It was bought by Illinoisan Brinton in 1923 and enlarged for his fine collection of Western art, Indian handicrafts and historic documents. A stagecoach owned by Buffalo Bill is among the vehicle collection.

Bighorn National Forest, US 14, 14A, 16. There are 1,113,769 acres in the Bighorn Mountains of north central Wyoming, E. of the Continental Divide. The Cloud Peak Primitive Area is in the forest's southern half. Cloud Peak is 13,165 feet. The lowest elevation in the wilderness is the Main Fork of Paintrock Creek at 8,500 feet. US 14 crosses Granite Pass at 9,033 feet. US 14A passes by Medicine Mountain, which is 9,956 feet. Medicine Wheel on the mountain is a prehistoric structure, constructed of stones laid side by side, 70 feet in diameter. A national historic landmark. A forest road to the site is open in summer from US 14A. US 16 at S. edge of forest goes through the Powder River Pass at 9,666 feet and through Tensleep Canyon.

Bighorn Canyon National Recreation Area, also in Montana, US 14A. The old Bozeman Trail runs through the area. In the summer of 1867 the Sioux and Cheyenne tried to wipe out Fort Phil Kearny and Fort C. F. Smith in Montana but were divided by disagreement among themselves and the effort failed.

BRIDGER-TETON NATIONAL FOREST, US 89, 189, covers ca. 3,439,435 acres, borders both the Grand Teton and Yellowstone National parks and contains the Bridger and Teton Wilderness areas. Jim Bridger was a mountain man, trapper, explorer and partner in the Rocky Mountain Fur Co. The Lander cutoff of the Oregon Trail goes through the forest, starting at South Pass and continuing to Fort Hall, Idaho. Bronze plaques mark the route. Graves have been marked and identified wherever possible.

BUFFALO, Johnson County. US 87.

Johnson County-Jim Gatchell Memorial Museum, 10 Fort St. Dioramas of the Johnson County Cattle War, Indian and pioneer relics. Prehistoric artifacts from a nearby Buffalo jump. Gatchell spent years among the Blackfeet and Sioux and spoke their languages. His store was a favorite rendezvous for oldtimers.

Site of TA Ranch, 13 miles S., where the war ended. Buffalo had been settled by cattlemen, nesters, miners and freighters. The cattlemen and the farmers were natural enemies with life styles that clashed. Many of the big cattlemen were absentee owners, living at Cheyenne, and all were members of the Wyoming Stock Growers' Association. In the hard winter of 1887 some of the settlers probably turned to light rustling to keep alive. Some cowboys became settlers by assembling maverick herds. The town sheriff was solidly on the side of the homesteaders and Buffalo became known as the rustlers' capital. The cattlemen of the Growers' Association raised a fighting fund of $100,000 and hired gunmen from Texas and other Western states, putting an ex-Army officer in charge. The privately hired Union Pacific train carrying this war party reached Cheyenne in April where it was joined by a physician and two news reporters; wires to Buffalo were cut at Casper where wagons were waiting. The so-called Regulators heard of two wanted men at the K C ranch, 50 miles S. of Buffalo, and took time to kill these two before marching North. Word of mouth reached Buffalo, where the settlers and small ranchers quickly organized. The showdown was at the TA Ranch, but it was stopped by the arrival of cavalry from Fort McKinney. The war was over. The army commander escorted the gunfighters back to Cheyenne—not wanting to have more than 50 hangings on his conscience as would be the case if he turned them over to Buffalo authorities.

Occidental Hotel, 10 N. Main St., was made forever memorable by Owen Wister's novel, *The Virginian.* It is still in use.

Rangeland Tours, for ranches and historical sites, in your car with guide, may be arranged during summer months at the Chamber of Commerce, 55 N. Main; because of the terrain it is advisable to check here on road conditions.

Fort Phil Kearny Site, 13 miles N. off US 87. (which see).

Crazy Woman Creek & Invasion Gulch, ca. 13 miles S. on US 87. Several stories account for the name of the creek: one is that a demented squaw was buried on the banks of the stream, another that a trader was scalped here and his mate went crazy at the sight. The creek and the gulch are associated with the Johnson County War. The dry bed of the latter sheltered the settlers in the conflict. The Middle Fork of Crazy Woman Creek is about 9 miles farther S. and is supposed to have lost treasure hidden in its upper canyons. Swedish prospectors chased by Indians are said to have hidden some $7,000 in gold in a baking-powder can. Many searches have failed to uncover it. The "Lost Cabin Mine" supposedly yielded the $7,000 in placer gold in three days of digging.

Fort McKinney, 3 miles W. on US 16, now a Wyoming Soldiers and Sailors Home, S. side of highway. A stable, barracks and hospital building remain from the original fort, which was the second garrison with this name. The first was at Cantonment Reno, ca. 50 miles away on the Powder River. The second Fort McKinney was established in the summer of 1878. Troops from here stopped the Johnson County War.

CAMP WALBACH, Laramie County. On local road which runs NW from junction of US 85, 87, N. of Cheyenne. The campsite is on the N. side of Lodgepole Creek, W. of paved road, at Cheyenne Pass. In the mid-1850s the government found a shortcut to the goldfields from Fort Leavenworth, Kansas, across the plains to Bridger's Pass. The Lodgepole Creek Route crossed the Laramie Range through Cheyenne Pass, where a small garrison was set up in the summer of 1858. After a long hard winter the camp was abandoned. Low mounds mark the site.

CASPER, Natrona County. US 87.

Old Fort Caspar Museum, 3 miles W. on W. 13th St. and Ft. Casper Rd., in restored fort, interprets the history of the site. The post was set up where the Platte Bridge Station had been located in 1858 to guard the crossing of the river and an emigrant campground, for travelers, freighters, mail stages and supply lines of the Mormon expedition. A ferry nearby was operated by Mormons in 1847–50, then by a private company. The station was abandoned by troops in 1859 when the toll bridge was completed. With increased Indian troubles during the Civil War the post was reoccupied to guard the telegraph. In July 1865 Lt. Caspar (sic) Collins and four of his men were killed in ambush by the Sioux and Cheyenne. The fort and town were named for him, with an accidental incorrect spelling of his given name in the latter case.

Natrona County Pioneer Museum, W. of town on fairgrounds. The first church of Casper houses settlers' articles.

Central Wyoming Museum of Art, 104 Rancho Rd. has Western art among changing and permanent exhibits.

Fort Caspar, familiar to travelers in the mid-19th century, also restored
(Wyoming Travel Commission)

Goss Rock Museum, 25 miles SW on State 220 in Alcova, has many fossils and mineral specimens of the Wyoming area. Topographical maps.

Bessemer Bend, ca. 19 miles SW on State 220, is the site of the first cabin built by a white man in Wyoming and a campsite for the Robert Stuart party returning from Astoria in November 1812.

CHEYENNE, Laramie County. (6,060 feet). US 85, 30.

State Capitol, head of Capitol Ave., was completed in 1888 shortly before the state entered the Union. Guided tours. Eighteen oil paintings of frontiersmen are in the rotunda.

State Museum and Art Gallery, State Office Building, Central Ave. and 3rd. Historical exhibits and some prehistoric relics, mineral and gem collections. A Deadwood-to-Cheyenne stagecoach is a popular feature.

Site of Territorial Legislature, SE corner of Carey Ave. and 17th St. Tablet on wall of Bank Bldg.

Site of First Public School in Wyoming, SW corner of Carey and 19th, has a bronze tablet to mark the area.

Fort D. A. Russell, now Warren Air Force Base, W. end of Randall Ave. Museum traces history of the base. The fort and a quartermaster depot known as Camp Carlin were founded in 1867 to protect crews working on the Union Pacific Railroad. The city of Cheyenne developed from the railroad division point slightly to the SE.

Frontier Park, Frontier Ave. between Hynds and Reed Sts. has the cabin of Jim Baker, early scout, moved from its original site.

Holliday Park, end of E. 18th St., displays a locomotive.

Site of Tom Horn Trial, NW corner of Carey and 19th Sts. Horn had been a lawman of sorts for much of his life but toward the end of it, after serving in the Battle of San Juan Hill and getting a Cuban fever ailment, he turned into a hired gun for cattle barons. About a dozen men had been killed before Willie Nickell, 14-year-old son of an Iron Mountain rancher, was found dead and this was Horn's undoing. Under the influence of drinking, Horn is said to have boasted about the killing. He still had supporters who believed him innocent and there was some effort to blast him out of jail, but he was hanged and is buried in the cemetery here. Like Quantrill, John Wilkes Booth, Dillinger and others, he was "seen" in various places long after his official demise.

Chamber of Commerce Visitor Center, 500 N. Center, has brochures on other local sites.

Ames Monument, Lincoln Monument, 30 miles W. at the Vedauwoo exit on I–80 is the monolithic pyramid which is a memorial to Oakes and Oliver Ames, who were instrumental in the construction and completion of the first transcontinental railroad, the Union Pacific. In a highway rest area nearby at the "Summit" of I–80 is a memorial to Abraham Lincoln.

CODY, Park County. US 14, 16, 20.

Buffalo Bill Historical Center, Sheridan Ave. and 8th St., includes the Buffalo Bill Museum, the Plains Indian Museum and the Whitney Gallery of Western Art, one of the finest galleries in America, with paintings and sculpture by Frederic Remington, Charles M. Russell, Edgar S. Paxson, Albert Bierstadt and many others.

Buffalo Bill Village & Western Exhibits, Sheridan Ave. between 16th and 18th Sts., is partly a replica town with plenty of gimcracks, but it also contains restored or reconstructed historic buildings of old Cody.

Buffalo Bill Statue, at the head of Sheridan Ave., is an equestrian pose of young Bill, by Gertrude Vanderbilt Whitney.

Horner Site, 4 miles NE of town on US 20, is a national historic landmark. Excavations revealed prehistoric flint tools of early hunter origin, ca. 5000 B.C.

Wapiti Ranger Station, in Shoshone National Forest, is also a national historic landmark. It was the first to be erected at federal expense and is located within the area of the first national forest reserve, the Yellowstone Timberland, established by President Benjamin Harrison in 1891. The station dates from 1903. The forest extends N.W. and S. of town, and covers 2,431,948 acres.

Chamber of Commerce Information Center, 836 Sheridan Ave., maps and tour information.

DANIEL, Sublette County. (7,192 feet). US 187, 189.

Father De Smet's Prairie Mass Site, 1 mile E. of town, monument at site where Father Pierre-Jean De Smet celebrated the first recorded mass in the northern Rockies. The prairie mass was held at a fur traders' rendezvous on the Upper Green River.

Upper Green River Rendezvous Site, on river above and below town. This popular area was selected by Gen. William Ashley, who began the custom of an annual trading fair in the spring of 1824 to which trappers, traders and Indians came; some supply caravans made the journey all the way from St. Louis with goods to trade for furs. Kit Carson, Jedediah Smith and Jim Bridger were among the now historic figures who attended. The site which is virtually unchanged is a national historic landmark. These springtime affairs which have been called the "movable supermarkets of the mountains" lasted until 1840. An annual pageant is now staged by the citizens of Sublette County who manage to look amazingly like the frontier men and women they portray. Blondes are darkened to appear as Shoshoni squaws or papooses. Dr. Marcus Whitman and his wife, who were massacred in 1847, are very much alive during the rendezvous days as are Bridger, Frémont, Carson, Bill Sublette, Capt. Bonneville, Jed Smith and even Alfred Jacob Miller the Baltimore artist who went west with the Scottish nobleman Sir William Drummond Stewart. A museum is to be built with proceeds from the rendezvous.

Fort Bonneville, W. of town, was built in 1832.

DEVILS TOWER NATIONAL MONUMENT, Crook County. State 24. The first national monument was set aside by President Theodore Roosevelt in 1906. The volcano cone rises 1,280 feet above the Belle Fourche River and is as spectacular today as it was to the many early travelers who came upon it.

DOUGLAS, Converse County. US 26, 20. The town had its wild young days; the first church services were held in a saloon.

Wyoming Pioneer Museum, State Fairgrounds, W. end of Center St. Pioneer and Indian displays.

Ayres Natural Bridge Park, 12 miles W. on I–25, then 5 miles S. The great arch of red sandstone was eroded by La Prele Creek.

Fort Fetterman State Historic Site, 11 miles NW on I–25, Orpha exit. The fort is being restored; a museum is open in the officer's quarters. The old ordnance building is still standing. The post was established in 1867 on the North Platte River near the crossing of the Bozeman Trail and the Oregon Trail to protect settlers and travelers against hostile Indians and to guard supply trains. It served as a base of operations for Gen. Crook's 1876 Yellowstone Expedition and Col. Ranald Mackenzie's campaign against Dull Knife and the Cheyennes; and it was named for Capt. William J. Fetterman, who was killed in a fight with Indians near Fort Phil Kearny, December 21, 1866.

Thunder Basin National Grasslands, N. on State 59. The Bozeman and Texas Trails cross part of the grasslands. The national area comprises 572,315 acres.

Douglas Park Cemetery. 8 lines of verse adorned the gravestone of George W. Pike, an oldtime gambler.

Underneath this stone in eternal rest
Sleeps the wildest one of the wayward west.
He was gambler and sport and cowboy, too,
And he led the pace in an outlaw crew.
He was sure on the trigger and staid to the end
But was never known to quit on a friend.
In the relations of death all mankind's alike
But in life there was only one George W. Pike.

DUBOIS, Fremont County. (6,917 feet). US 287. On the Wind River in the Shoshone National Forest.

Togwotee Pass, 30 miles W. on US 26, crosses the Continental Divide at 9,658 feet. Historic *Union Pass,* SW of Dubois, 9,210 feet, is at a point where the mountain range forms a divide between the waters of the Mississippi, Columbia and Colorado rivers. There are many old Indian trails in the Union Pass area; John Colter, fur trapper, was here as were Capt. Bonneville, Capt. Reynolds, Jim Bridger, the Hayden surveying expedition and many anonymous prospectors, hunters, settlers.

Wildlife Exhibit, W. on US 26, 287, could more aptly be called a stuffed nonlife exhibit. More than 100 varieties of North American animals are mounted and displayed. For those who prefer to see moving and breathing wildlife the Audubon Society of Wyoming conducts a bird workshop in the Torrey Valley 12 miles SW of town. Field trips with experienced naturalists. Information at Trail Lake Ranch, Dubois.

ENCAMPMENT, Carbon County. (7,323 feet). State 130.

Doc Culleton Museum and Ghost Town has an interpretive center for the Grand Encampment Mining District. Fine pelts first attracted outsiders to the area. After the trappers came, other expeditions of hunters, then cattle barons, homesteaders, and miners when copper was found in 1897. After the copper boom was over the mining towns of Rudefeha, Dillon, Copperton, Rambler, Battle and Elwood became ghost towns. Riverside, nearby, and Encampment survived. A 16-mile aerial tramway was built across the Continental Divide at the height of the mining to ship ore to the smelter here. Some mine ruins may still be seen. Relics at museum. In the assembled ghost town here are the Lake Creek Stage

Station, a ranch house and transportation barn, the Saratoga cabin which was built before 1890 by John Cluff and located on the railroad right-of-way N. of the Sarasota and Encampment Valley railroad bridge. The old town of Battle is SW of Encampment on graded highway. The post built by Henry Fraeb and Jim Bridger in 1837–38 is also SW, past Battle. Both are in the Medicine Bow National Forest. Fraeb was killed at this fort in August 1841 while whites, including Jim Baker, battled a band of Cheyenne and Sioux. The road which runs near this site eventually reaches Baggs, after passing Savery and Dixon, part paved, part gravel, part take-your-chances.

EVANSTON, Uinta County. (6,748 feet). I–80. Pragmatic Harvey Booth, arrived in November 1868, put up a tent, then opened an eatery, a saloon and hotel and was ready for the Union Pacific which arrived in December with 600 would-be settlers. When the U.P. decided to switch headquarters to nearby Wasatch, Utah, the town was drained of all but two persons. Luckily for Evanston, the railroad switched back. A roundhouse and machine shop were established. When the mines opened in Almy, 6 miles away, many miners and Chinese came to town. Chief Washakie of the Shoshones was often in town. The treaty by which the Shoshone Reservation was established is in the courthouse.

EVANSVILLE, Natrona County. US 26, 20, E. of Casper.

Richard's Bridge was established by John Richard, with his partner Joseph Bissonette and others, in 1853. The timber bridge was adjoined by a trading post and blacksmith shop around which a small community grew. In October 1855 a detachment of troops moved in to guard the post which was called Fort Clay, then Camp Davis, then Camp at Platte Bridge. Richard's post continued to be important in Indian and emigrant trading. And of military use with the arrival of the Utah Expedition in 1857. It was regarrisoned in 1858 about the same time as Camp Walbach was established. Diggings have located the old cemetery and building sites. The town proposes a state historical park development.

FARSON, Sweetwater County. (6,580 feet). US 187, State 28.

Site of "Big Sandy" Stage Station, just W. of town.

Little Sandy Emigrant Camp; historic crossing of the Little Sandy River was a short distance NE above State 28. Farther NE, toward South Pass (7550 feet), is the Whitman Monument, which commemorates the stopping place of the Dr. Marcus Whitman party in July 1836, enroute to Oregon. Mrs. Whitman and Eliza Hart were the first white women to cross South Pass. (also see South Pass).

Sublette's Spring and Flat, NW off US 187 to the left, were campsites related to the travels of the famous early scout William L. Sublette.

FORT BRIDGER STATE HISTORIC SITE, Uinta County. Off I–80. US 30S. The fort was established in 1843 on the Black Fork of the Green River by Bridger, for whom it is named. It was a trading post for mountain men and Indians seasonally for some years before Bridger and his partner Louis Vasquez set up the permanent establishment. The area was still Mexican territory, and the partners claimed a land grant but did not file a proper title which led to much conflict over the land. The Mormons, in competition with the post, sent a militia to arrest the traders in 1853 on the grounds that they were harming the Indians by selling them whiskey. Much of the fort was destroyed in this disagreement and the Mormons established Camp Supply, 12 miles away. In 1858 the fort became a U.S. Army post. During the 1860s it served as a Pony Express, overland telegraph and overland stage station. It was not abandoned until 1890. Several buildings have been restored and furnished. A museum has a variety of artifacts pertaining to the history of this important frontier post. Also in the area are kilns which were used to process charcoal for use in mining smelters. At Piedmont, a station on the Union Pacific in 1868, three of the five kilns remain SW of the fort on secondary road, though the town has disappeared. The kilns were built by Moses Byrne in 1869.

FORT HALLECK, Carbon County. S. of US 30, E. of State 130. The fort, established July 20, 1862, was W. of the Medicine Bow River at the N. base of Elk Mountain. It protected the Overland Trail, the Denver–Salt Lake stage route and the telegraph line. Named for Maj. Gen. Henry Halleck. A registered historic place, the site is now a private ranch. One old fort building is used as a storage shed.

FORT LARAMIE NATIONAL HISTORIC SITE, Goshen County. State 160. Established as a trading center with the northern plains Indians in 1834 on the Laramie River crossing of the California–Oregon Trail. The army bought the post in 1849 to use as a base for guarding the trails and controlling Indians of the area. A Pony Express station was here in 1860–61. It was one of the most important of Western military garrisons. In the early days the log post here was called Fort William, having been established by William Sublette and his partner Robert Campbell. Later it was replaced by the larger adobe, Fort John, owned by the American Fur Co., then Pierre Choteau, Jr., and Co. acquired it. Much of the old post has been restored and its ruins stabilized. The National Park Service area includes more than 562 acres. In the summer Park Service personnel in period costume demonstrate old weapons and post life. Officers' quarters were famous among the military as "Old Bedlam"; it was a popular spot for off-duty hell-raising, as well as offices at times, and is the oldest standing military structure in Wyoming.

Hog Ranch, from fort road S. of hospital site, dirt road runs W. ca. 3 miles. Here soldiers found relaxation with liquor and ladies. Having started as a trading post, but with poor business, the ranch became busy when it imported women from Kansas City and Omaha. Rumors have Calamity Jane here in the 1870s.

FORT PHIL KEARNY, Johnson County. W. of I–90, between Buffalo and Sheridan, on secondary road W. of US 87. In this area the Sioux fought successfully to prevent invasion of their hunting grounds by prospectors and wagon trains headed for the gold fields of Montana. The Red Cloud War of 1866–68 laid siege to this post and the white men were forced to give up the Bozeman Trail which from the start had violated the Indians' rights; Pioneered by John Bozeman in 1863 as a shortcut to

Fort Laramie (earlier known as Fort William, then Fort John) was Built 1834, now largely restored
(Wyoming Travel Commission)

Montana gold it crossed the treaty-guaranteed Sioux hunting grounds. Historian Robert A. Murray, writing of early military posts in Wyoming, aptly described the establishment of the fort:

> Colonel Henry B. Carrington's column of infantrymen, with their great train of supplies and equipment, their swarm of civilian employees, the civilian construction contractors, and their own traders and assorted camp followers, arrived on Piney Creek in July of 1866. Here Carrington selected a site straight out of Sir Walter Scott for his citadel in the wilderness. Here he constructed a massive log-stockaded, bastioned post that would have been more in keeping with the colonial Indian experience of over a century before.

The area is now a national historic landmark, along with associated sites: The Wagon Box Fight, of 1867, W. of Story off US 87, in which Capt. James Powell and 31 men stood off nearly 1,000 Indians for three hours until a rescue party arrived; the Fetterman Massacre, N. of Story US 87, where in 1866 Red Cloud and his Sioux ambushed and killed the entire force of 82 under Bvt. Lt. Col. W. J. Fetterman.

FORT RENO, Johnson County. On secondary road NE of Sussex. Fort Reno was established in August 1865, as Fort Connor, on the left bank of the Powder River to protect the Bozeman Trail, part of which was an illegal crossing of the Sioux treaty-guaranteed hunting grounds. It ran along the E. base of the Big Horn Mountains. Named for Gen. Jesse L. Reno in 1865, the post was abandoned in 1868. A registered historic place; monument at site of Fort Reno, which is sometimes flooded by the Powder River. Cantonment Reno (Fort McKinney No. 1) was a temporary base built by Gen. George Crook's troops ca. 3 miles N. during the 1876 activities following Custer's defeat at Little Bighorn. Cantonment Reno site is not marked at present.

FORT STEELE, Carbon County. Off I–80, on the North Platte River between Walcott Junction and Sinclair. The post (also called Fort Fred Steele) protected workers on the Union Pacific. Established June 30, 1868, named for Col. Frederick Steele, U.S. 20th Infantry, a veteran of the Mexican and Civil wars who died of apoplexy, January 12, 1868. Soldiers from this post responded to the appeal of Indian Agent Nathan C. Meeker for aid when Indians at the White River Agency in Colorado went on the warpath, but were beaten in the Battle of Milk Creek, Colorado. Their commanding officer Maj. T. T. Thornburg was killed. A cemetery here has civilian burials from 1868. Soldier graves have been relocated though markers remain on a hill overlooking the fortsite.

FORT WASHAKIE, Fremont County. US 287. Established January 1871. On the Wind River Indian Reservation, near the confluence of the Little Wind River and the North Fork of the Wind, the post was on the edge of the Big Horn Basin, and was an important supply base. Originally called Camp Brown, which in turn stemmed from the unofficial Fort Augur, it was officially named in honor of Chief Washakie, a Shoshoni, whose grave is on the reservation in the post cemetery as is that of Sacajawea, the much traveled young Shoshoni woman of the Lewis and Clark expedition. Historic buildings of the old post are used as headquarters for the reservation. St. Michael's Mission, E. of the fort, was established in 1887 by Rev. John Roberts for the Episcopalians. The mission houses many valuable Arapaho artifacts and other cultural materials. A registered historic place. *Crow Heart Butte,* N. of US 26,287, gets its name from the legend that Chief Washakie displayed on a lance the heart of a Crow Indian he had beaten in battle in 1866.

GILLETTE, Campbell County. (7,-194 feet). US 14.

Weltner Wonder Museum, 1 mile S. on State 59, has a large gun collection, frontier and Indian artifacts.

GLENDO, Platte County. US 26, 87.

Site of Old Horse Shoe Stage Station, SW of town. The post was not large but was the first telegraph station W. of Fort Laramie. After the Fetterman Massacre near Fort Phil Kearney, prospectors Daniel Dixon and John "Portugee" Phillips carried the news here to be sent to Gen. Philip St. George Cooke at Omaha. Phillips went on to carry the message to Col. I. N. Palmer at Fort Laramie, interrupting a Christmas night dancing party with the bad news. From here orders were sent to Fort Reno to relieve Fort Phil Kearny. Civilian Phillips became a Wyoming hero for his long ride. There is a monument to him near Fort Phil Kearny.

Glendo Museum has pioneer relics.

Bridger's Ferry Marker, N. of town on highway. The historic crossing was 1½ miles S. of Orin, W. of the now Chicago, Burlington and Quincy Railroad tracks.

Site of Historic Burnt Wagon Train, NW of Glendo, on Elkhorn Creek.

GLENROCK, Converse County. US 20, 26.

Site of Deer Creek Stage Station, just W. of town. The Ohio Volunteers for a number of years were posted at garrisons along the old emigrant route which the telegraph line followed. They often occupied and improved upon earlier stations. Deer Creek was one of these. Joseph Bissonette had established it in 1849. With his partners he ran a ferry service a short distance up the Platte from the post. A bridge built by John Richard in the spring of 1851 was washed away the following year. Other stations which were later garrisoned were Sweetwater, Three Crossings, St. Mary's, the Upper Crossing of Sweetwater and South Pass, as well as Horseshoe Station (which see). Some of the men here and elsewhere in the Wyoming territory were the so-called Galvanized Yankees, recruited from Rock Island Federal Prison in the last days of the Civil War.

Glenrock Buffalo Jump, ca. 2 miles W. on I–25, dates from the Late Prehistoric Period. Buffalo herds were driven over the cliff and butchered at the base. A registered historic site.

Magill Grave, W. of Deer Creek Station, N. of highway. Ada Magill was buried in 1864 on a lonely part of the trail; she was an immigrant child who died of dysentery—a wagon box was used to make her coffin and she was buried in her best calico dress. A crude marker was put on the grave and the wagon train went on toward Oregon.

GRAND TETON NATIONAL PARK, US 89, 287, covers 485 square miles. John Colter was one of the first white men to see the imposing area. Two Visitor Centers have interpretive displays, one at Moose with a fur trade museum and at Colter Bay with an Indian museum. It is possible these days to Dial-a-Park, 733–2220 for last-minute road and weather conditions and travel data.

Menor's Ferry, across the Snake River just above park headquarters, was established by homesteader Bill Menor in 1892.

GRANGER, Sweetwater County. (6,240 feet). US 30W.

Granger Stage Station, edge of town, one original building remains. The stop was also known as Ham's Fork Station and South Bend Station; it was located on both the Oregon and Overland Trails and served the Overland Stage and the Pony Express. A major crossing was on Black's Fork near here. The Union Pacific laid tracks nearby in 1868. A registered historic place.

GREEN RIVER, Sweetwater County. (6,100 feet). US 30, State 530.

Sweetwater County Historical Museum, in courthouse, 50 W. Flaming Gorge Way. Indian, Chinese, pioneer artifacts.

Flaming Gorge National Recreation Area, S on State 530. Extends into Utah.

Powell-Colorado River Expedition Historic Landmark, on Expedition Island Park, marker where Maj. Wesley Powell and his party began their exploration of the Green and Colorado rivers in May 1869. They reached the mouth of the Grand Canyon on August 29, 1869. They again camped on the island and took off from here on May 22, 1871, for the second expedition. National historic landmark.

GREYBULL, Big Horn County. US 14.

Greybull Museum, 3 blocks E. of junction of US 14, 20. Western, Indian, prehistoric, mineral collections.

GUERNSEY, Platte County. US 26.

Oregon Trail Ruts State Historical Park, 1 mile S. on US 26. Some of the ruts are worn in rock to the depth of 6 feet; a national historic landmark.

Register Cliff State Historic Site, 1½ miles S. on US 26, is where early travelers on the Oregon Trail left their names in limestone since 1849.

Grave of Lucindy Rollins, across the river S. of town, ½ mile up the first road to the right. Plaque for grave of an emigrant to Oregon who didn't make it all the way.

Guernsey State Museum features life on the Oregon Trail.

Frederick Museum, 3 miles W. on US 26, has over 3,000 relics.

HARTVILLE, Platte County. Off US 26. The oldest incorporated city in the state (1884), the area was a mining center and a trading place for cattle and sheep ranchers. As a roaring frontier town it developed a Boot Hill and false-front stores some of which remain. Emigrant Hill on the Mormon Trail is NW of town on the N. side of the Platte. Eureka Canyon was a home of the Western Plains Indians when they followed great bison herds. The red dust of the canyon region was used for war paint. S. of Hartville and US 26 are the historic "Warm Springs," which provided a natural bath for emigrants, and a laundry tub.

HELL'S HALF ACRE, Natrona County. US 20, 26. Often called the Baby Grand Canyon, the depression was used as a buffalo trap by the Indians. Many fossils and Indian artifacts have been found in the area.

INDEPENDENCE ROCK, Natrona County. On the Oregon Trail near the Sweetwater River this 193-foot tall rock, covering 27 acres, was named the "Register of the Desert," by Father Jean-Pierre De Smet in 1840. It was a favorite campsite and many travelers left their names on it.

Devil's Gate, just N. of State 220, or 6 trail miles up the Sweetwater, was another landmark noted in early journals. One 18-year-old girl slipped over the edge in the 1860s. Her graveboard was inscribed with a quatrain:

Here lies the body of Caroline Todd
Whose soul has lately gone to God;
Ere redemption was too late,
She was redeemed at Devil's Gate.

Luckily for the versifier she had a one-syllable surname.

Tom Sun Ranch, 6 miles W. of the Rock, in the Sweetwater Valley, was established in 1872 by a French-Canadian frontiersman who became a much respected cattleman of the area. The site is a national historic landmark not accessible to the public at present.

JACKSON, Teton County. (6,209 feet). US 26, 187.

Jackson Hole Historical Museum, 101 N. Glenwood. Western relics. Trophy room. Jackson Hole in the Grand Tetons was named for the early explorer, David Jackson.

National Elk Refuge, E. edge of town, comprises 23,500 acres.

Bridger-Teton National Forest surrounds the town. There are 3,399,-651 acres.

Wax Museum of Old Wyoming, 50 S. Cash St. Famous and infamous life-size figures in wax.

KAYCEE, Johnson County. US 87. Ca. 23 miles W. of town is the site of the Dull Knife Battlefield where on the Red Fork of the Powder River in the winter of 1875 the U.S. Army finally defeated Dull Knife and his Cheyennes, who had helped to create Custer's defeat the previous year. Stone monument at site.

Site of the Hole-in-the-Wall Hideout, on Buffalo Creek, SW of town, not easily reached. Before Paul Newman and Robert Redford made Butch Cassidy and the Sundance Kid look handsome and light-hearted, only Western buffs remembered the Hole-in-the-Wall gang. On a dirt road across the Red Fork of Powder River in Red Canyon is the Hole-in-the-Wall, a natural gap made by the river. The area is old Indian hunting ground, crossed with creeks that have such meaningful names as Otter, Trout, Beartrap and Buffalo. Some local stories say that the James gang used this hide-out long before Butch Cassidy and his "Wild Bunch" were heard of in the East. It seems unlikely that the James boys holed up so far from home, but the natural hiding place was very popular with cattle rustlers of the area, and there were many. Cassidy was jailed for a time in Wyoming, found guilty of horse stealing at a trial in Lander and sent the penitentiary at Laramie City for two years. Historian James D. Horan says Cassidy was 27 when he entered the penitentiary as No. 187 on July 15, 1894. The Logans and other outlaws kept Hole-in-the-Wall busy while he was away. When Cassidy was asking for a pardon, the governor, who was a former president of the Wyoming Stock Growers' Association, asked if the outlaw would give his word to go straight. Cassidy said he couldn't do that, but he would promise never to molest the state of Wyoming again. So far as is known he never personally took part in any more raids within the state borders, although his associates did. It is said that years later the governor of Utah, when he heard the story, said: "I certainly wish you had gotten him to extend his amnesty to the state of Utah."

KEMMERER, Lincoln County. (6,908 feet). US 30N, 189.

Kemmerer City Museum has pioneer and nature exhibits, including a mineral collection.

Fossil Butte National Monument, 10 miles W. on US 30N.

LA BARGE, Lincoln County. (6,600 feet). US 189.

Names Hill, 5 miles S. just W. of highway, is one of three places where emigrants liked to leave their names. The earliest here dates from 1822. Even Jim Bridger in 1844 took time out to inscribe his name.

LANDER, Fremont County. (5,563 feet). US 287.

Fremont County Pioneer Museum, 1 block N. of highway at 6th and Lincoln, has Indian and pioneer artifacts and a large rock collection.

Sinks Canyon State Park, 10 miles SW on State 131. Middle Fork of Popo Agie River disappears into a cavern and rises again a short distance below. Nature trails, Visitor Center. Several early journals and letters mentioned this quirky river.

LARAMIE, Albany County. (7,165 feet). US 287,30. Named for early trapper Jacques La Ramie.

Laramie Plains Museum, 603 Ivinson Ave. Victorian house has a variety of furnishings and relics. Also oldtime carriagehouse. Home of a Laramie founder, Edward Ivinson.

Geological Museum, in geology building on campus of University of Wyoming, 15th St., 1 block N. of US 30. Regional fossils, minerals, rocks and a brontosaurus skeleton.

Western Historical Collection and University Archives, in university library at 13th St. and Ivinson Ave. just off US 30.

Medicine Bow National Forest, in any direction but straight south, covers 1,039,139 acres. Headquarters are here.

Fort Sanders (Fort John Buford), S. of town, was established by troops from Fort Halleck, named for Brig. Gen. W. P. Sanders, who died in the Battle of Campbell's Station, Tennessee, November 1863. In 1868 a conference with Union Pacific officials was attended by Gens. Grant, Sherman, Harney and Sheridan. Little remains of the fortsite; hopefully it will be reclaimed from the growing city. One of the most interesting after-the-war photographs of the above generals was taken at the meeting here. The ladies and even the children who were present stood still but the dog who couldn't keep from twitching his ears, apparently, is headless.

Rock Creek is a picturesque ghost town to the N.

Fremont's Campsite, W. of town. With Kit Carson as guide Frémont's party camped here in August 1843.

LINGLE, Goshen County. US 26.

Grattan Fight Site, ca. 3 miles W. of town, between the North Platte River and an unimproved road. A stone monument marks the area where enlisted men are buried who died in a curious affair which began when John Grattan, a young lieutenant, tried to arrest a Sioux for a trivial offense. By sundown all the troops except one were dead. The Indians had been relatively peaceful before this but intermittent warfare followed. Grattan was 24-years-old, fresh out of West Point, and made a fatal mistake in trying to settle a minor matter by ordering his men to fire a volley, chiefly to make a show of strength. Unfortunately, Conquering Bear of the Sioux fell mortally wounded and the war was on.

LUSK, Niobrara County. US 85, 20.

Stagecoach Museum, 342 S. Main. Pioneer, Indian relics. An original Cheyenne-Deadwood Concord stagecoach is in the collection; its running mate is in the Smithsonian in Washington, D.C.

Rawhide Buttes Station, on the Cheyenne-Deadwood stage line, from 1876 to 1887, stands ca. 12 miles S. of town just W. of US 85. The Running Water Station on the same route is marked by stone ruins.

MONETA, Fremont County. Ca. 28 miles S. on US 20, 26 is the Castle Garden Petroglyph Site with pre-Columbian incisions. The rock formation resembles a medieval castle. A registered historic place.

NEWCASTLE, Weston County. US 16.

Accidental Oil Company, 4 miles E. on highway, has guided tours to the bottom of the only known hand-dug oil well in the U.S. Museum with early equipment.

Jenney Stockade, on courthouse lawn, was a way station on the historic Cheyenne–Deadwood stage line.

Anna Miller Museum, in East Newcastle, has pioneer items, fossils, minerals, Indian articles and wildlife exhibits.

RANCHESTER, Sheridan County. US 87.

Connor Battlefield, S. of town, on river bottomland; The Battle of Tongue River was part of the Powder River campaign of 1865. Brig. Gen. Patrick E. Connor and 330 troops surprised an Arapaho village, killed 63 persons and destroyed 250 lodges before departing with more than 1,000 horses.

RAWLINS, Carbon County. (6,755 feet). I–80.

Wildlife Museum, 1 mile E. on US 287. Stuffed stuff.

Bridger's Pass, SW of town, on the Continental Divide. Bridger's crossing of the divide helped to publicize the route for overland travel. A registered historic place.

Carbon County Museum, in courthouse, has regional history displays.

RIVERTON, Fremont County. US 26. In the Wind River Reservation.

Riverton Museum, 7th and Park Sts., has Shoshone and Arapaho displays; a general store and a homesteader's cabin.

SHERIDAN, Sheridan County. US 14.

Sheridan Inn National Historic Landmark, Broadway and 5th St. from 1894 to 1896, the Inn was operated by Buffalo Bill Cody. It was built by the Chicago, Burlington and Quincy Railroad and used to cater to bigtime hunters.

Trail End Historical Home and Museum, 400 Clarendon, was the home of U.S. Senator John B. Kendrick.

SOUTH PASS CITY, Fremont County. (7,800 feet). Off State 28. Gold was found here in 1842 but the Indians were too wild for a boom to follow the rumors at first. In 1865 prospectors began to pay attention to the Sweetwater which had showed "color" long before. The old town is being restored, as a state historic site.

South Pass National Historic Landmark, 10 miles SW on State 28. The 7,550-foot-high pass was first used by Robert Stuart and his Astoria expedition in 1812 on their return trip. Jedediah Smith and Thomas Fitzpatrick led a party through the pass in 1824 and it became a popular route across the Rockies.

THERMOPOLIS, Hot Springs County. US 20.

Hot Springs County Pioneer Museum, 235 Springview Ave. Antique guns in the pioneer and Indian collections; trapper and stock-grower exhibits.

Woodruff Cabin Site, 26 miles NW on County Route 0900 from the intersection with State 120, was built in 1871, the first-recorded white man's home in the Big Horn basin. Rock marker at site. A registered historic place.

WORLAND, Washakie County. US 20.

Washakie County Museum, 110 S. 11th St. Indian displays, pioneer utensils.

YELLOWSTONE NATIONAL PARK is America's first (1872) and largest national park. It covers 3,472 square miles. The Mammoth Hot Springs Visitor Center, on US 89, from N. entrance, Grand Loop Rd. inside park, is the headquarters, with museum and orientation. Most park roads are open from May 1 to October 31.

ALICE CROMIE has written fiction and nonfiction for most major magazines. She is also the author of *A Tour Guide to the Civil War* and is a member of the Western Writers of America, the Society of American Travel Writers, Western Historical Association, Council on Abandoned Military Camps, and the National Trust for Historical Preservation. Born in Iowa, she now lives in Illinois and Italy.